LIBERTY, JUSTICE, and MORALS

Contemporary Value Conflicts

Fall, 1973

LIBERTY, JUSTICE, and MORALS

Contemporary Value Conflicts

Burton M. Leiser

THE MACMILLAN COMPANY, NEW YORK
COLLIER-MACMILLAN PUBLISHERS, LONDON

Copyright © 1973, Burton M. Leiser

Printed in the United States of America

All rights reserved. No part of this book may be reproduced or transmitted in any form or by any means, electronic or mechanical, including photocopying, recording, or any information storage and retrieval system, without permission in writing from the Publisher.

The Macmillan Company
866 Third Avenue, New York, New York 10022

Collier-Macmillan Canada, Ltd., Toronto, Ontario

Library of Congress catalog card number: 72–81073

Printing: 1 2 3 4 5 6 7 8   Year: 3 4 5 6 7 8 9

To
Leah Newman
and in Memory of
P. H. Newman and Harry and Rose Leiser

Preface

The idea for this book originated in "Controversy," a unique experimental course that I taught while I was a member of the Department of Philosophy at the State University of New York College at Buffalo. Without the constant encouragement of Professor Nicholas Fotion, who was then chairman of the department, and the liberal policies of President E. K. Fretwell, who shielded us against our critics during periods when the course itself became the most controversial issue on campus, neither the course nor the book to which it has given rise would have seen the light of day. I record with gratitude the moral support and solid advice that Mrs. Elsie Kaye offered, much of it indispensable to the success of the course.

Professor Vincent Tomas, Dr. Norman Halpern, Professor Perry Meyer, Mr. Morton Bessner, Mr. Nathan Leiser, Mr. Herman Hurowitz, and Mr. Maurice Tabor have contributed to this book—some of them without being aware of it—through their perceptive criticisms of arguments that I tested on them as I wrote chapters in their fields of interest.

I am deeply indebted to Professor Thomas T. Love, who read the first draft of the manuscript with great care and offered hundreds of detailed criticisms and suggestions that were most helpful, both in terms of content and in matters of style.

Among my students, so many of whom have taught me so much, I must single out for special mention Miss Sharon Lee Smith and Messrs. Allan Becker, Mark Leiffer, Lyall Nelson, Harry Newsome, Howard Shain, and George Wright, who made a number of important suggestions after they had read the manuscript; Mr. Kenneth MacQueen, who devoted many hours to the preparation of the bibliography; and Miss Eleanor Ryan, who assisted in the compilation of the index.

During the writing of this book I was most fortunate in having had the opportunity to work with Mr. Charles E. Smith and Mr. Kenneth Scott, two able editors whose encouragement and advice were invaluable.

To six fellow students of moral issues I owe a special debt of gratitude for their many stimulating conversations and their incisive thoughts on some of the topics covered here, as well as for their assistance in compiling the index: Ellen, Shoshana, David, Susan, Illana, and Phillip.

There is one person whose assistance took so many forms that nothing I can say would do justice to her. I shall therefore confine myself merely to recording her name, with gratitude: Bobbie.

B. M. L.

Contents

Chapter 16. War Crimes and Crimes Against Humanity—Cont.

Introduction

The law is often thought of as being the guardian of our liberties, and rightly so. When it imposes a duty upon my neighbor to refrain from taking my life, it enables me to live in relative security, free from the fear that I may be murdered. When it imposes a duty upon me to refrain from interfering with my neighbor's business, or to refrain from discharging my employees because of their hair styles, my neighbor and my employees are assured of a degree of freedom that otherwise they might not have.

But law and liberty are opposites, in a sense, for where the law governs a given kind of behavior, people are no longer free to decide for themselves whether or not to engage in that form of behavior.

Nevertheless, imposing duties upon some men, and restricting their liberties, is the only way to guarantee the freedoms of others. So long as Lester Maddox was permitted to give axe handles to his customers to prevent blacks from entering his restaurant, black citizens were denied the liberty of eating at Lester Maddox's restaurant. If all the restaurant owners along the highway enjoyed the same liberty and exercised it as Lester Maddox did, all black citizens would have been denied the right to eat anywhere along the highway. Liberty for the restaurant owners was incompatible with liberty for black travelers. The latter could acquire the liberty to eat along the highway in Georgia only if Lester Maddox and other restaurant owners were deprived of their liberty to refuse to serve them. Indeed, without the sanction of law, even the liberties of some restaurant owners might not have been assured; for if a restaurant owner had wanted to serve black customers, he might have been unable to do so, prior to the enactment of the Civil Rights Act, because informal community pressures might have been

1

exerted to prevent him from deviating from the norm. Passing a law that obliges everyone to adhere to a given standard may enable some who were anxious to adhere to the standard but were unable to do so to act according to their will and be relieved of an undesirable restriction. For example, a manufacturer of paper may want to clean up his operation so as to reduce the pollution of the streams in the neighborhood, but be unable to do so because of the economic advantage his competitors would derive if they were less concerned about the purity of the streams. By imposing the same standards upon all, the conservation-minded manufacturer acquires the freedom to do what he wants to do, though the others are deprived of the freedom they previously enjoyed to pollute the rivers without hindrance.

From these examples, it is evident that justice may require restrictions upon the liberties of some persons, or of all persons, whereas extensions of liberty may entail a certain degree of injustice. It is not always clear, though, what injustice is. It is sometimes said that injustice consists of treating persons unequally, but what constitutes unequal treatment? Among all the applicants for a position as captain of an airliner, the employer ought to distinguish between those who know how to fly and those who do not, be-tween those who are mentally stable and sober and those who give evidence of being unstable or alcoholic. Such positions certainly ought not to be handed out to applicants by drawing lots or by some other method that would give each applicant an "equal" status with every other. But justice may require that certain benefits be made available to all citizens, the only "qualification" being the fact that the individual is a human being.

It is sometimes thought that injustice is any act that deprives any person of his personal liberty, his property, or any other thing to which he is legally entitled. But as the case of Maddox's restaurant illustrates, the law may entitle one man to the right to deprive another of something that is very important to him, and that deprivation, though sanctioned by law, may nevertheless be unjust. It follows, therefore, that some lawful acts may be unjust, and that some forms of just behavior may be unlawful. Law, it seems, is not the final determinant of justice, though law and justice are clearly bound up with one another. When a law is unjust, we say that it violates human rights, or moral rights, the rights that we believe ought to be guaranteed to all persons, though in practice, they often are not.

Some laws prescribe sanctions—usually punishments—for forms of be-havior of which the lawmakers disapprove. When a person is judged to have committed some wrong, or to have violated some duty or obligation, that judgment is often expressed as a desire or a wish that he be punished for his wrongful behavior. If his behavior is thought to be particularly repre-hensible, but is not legally punishable, people will often say, "There ought to be a law," meaning that they wish that it would be possible to punish him for behaving in such a manner. Duty is a thing that can be, or that people think ought to be, exacted from the members of society. When there is a law, the duty it imposes usually can be exacted by bringing the power of the state to bear upon the law violator. Where there is no law and people believe that a person is violating his moral duties or obligations, then they say that those duties or obligations ought to be enforceable, that men ought to be compelled to behave in one way rather than in the other, and that they should not be free to behave wrongfully.

On the other hand, those who believe that society's business should be to secure as much liberty for all as is possible, consistent with a reasonable degree of order and security, argue that the law should be limited in its scope, and that the state should not be permitted to interfere in the private affairs of its citizens. They contend that morals are a private matter, and are no affair of the state, that state interference in private affairs is in itself unjust, and that any laws that attempt to impose moral standards upon all citizens ought to be abolished so as to increase the scope of each citizen's personal liberties. They sometimes appeal to the old cliché that one cannot or should not legislate morality. But one may entertain reasonable doubts about the truth of that old proverb. Most, if not all, of our legislation is based upon ancient moral principles. The laws prohibiting murder, rape, fraud, theft, and robbery are clearly based upon ancient moral codes and religious beliefs, as are the rules providing for compensation for victims of accidental, negligent, or deliberate acts that result in damage to themselves or to their property. The laws governing marriage, divorce, and other family matters are obviously bound up with moral conceptions. Such elementary business transactions as the making of a contract, the honest weighing of a commodity, and the timely payment of a laborer for his services were all embodied in the moral and religious codes of the Bible and of the peoples of the ancient Middle East thousands of years ago, before the distinction between law and morals had been drawn. If morality cannot be legislated, nothing can.

But the saying is not completely without foundation. Recently the distinction between crimes in which one person harms another and crimes without victims has been a subject of considerable discussion. Homosexual relations, prostitution, gambling, and the smoking of pot may be said to be victimless crimes, because everyone concerned with them voluntarily consents to participate in the activity. By way of contrast, the victims of murder, rape, and fraud do not consent to be murdered, raped, or defrauded. This analysis may not be completely satisfactory, for there may be indirect victims of so-called victimless crimes, such as the children of the pathological gambler who are deprived of the amenities of life because their father gambles away his paycheck, or the taxpayers of a community who must support the family with welfare assistance. But if such subtleties are laid aside, at least provisionally, the distinction is an important one. In general, victimless crimes are not thought to be evil because of the harm they do to others, but because of the harm they do to their perpetrators or because they are thought to be intrinsically evil or vicious. The state becomes an agent in the enforcement of morals, pure and simple. It goes beyond its *function of guarding the physical safety of its citizens and seeing that justice is done, and assumes in addition the paternalistic role of guardian of its citizens' moral and spiritual well-being. Those who advocate or support this role for the state sometimes argue by analogy: If we grant the state the power to control the food we eat in order to protect our physical health, we should give it the power to protect our moral or spiritual health, which is (so they say) far more important than mere physical well-being. If a state is founded upon certain moral principles, it may claim the right to prevent persons who do not accept those principles from destroying the moral qualities of the state through the expression of their own preferences and the development of a life style that is inconsistent with the state's principles. In denying to its citizens the right to develop new life styles, or to carry out ideas or fulfill desires that are new or different, the state may render itself incapable of carrying out its other functions. In its zeal to suppress immorality, the state and its agents may perpetrate grave injustices. When moral principles come into conflict with the principles of justice, all the elements of tragedy are present. The suppression of individual freedom goes hand in hand with the denial of equal rights and equal protection of the laws to all citizens. Some classes of citizens are singled out for special treatment. They are either accorded special favors or are subjected to harsher restrictions than others. From a zeal for morality arises a restriction of liberties, and such restrictions bring injustices in their train. The disappointment of what the oppressed consider to be their legitimate expectations through the enforcement of moral principles that are not universally accepted leads to resentment, anger, defiance, and in the end, to rebellion and revolution.*

Considering the practical consequences of the enforcement of morals and the punishment of those who commit victimless crimes, one may conclude that the evil effects of the laws outweigh the good that they are supposed to do. But other considerations may be sufficient to justify maintaining penal sanctions against those who violate moral rules that are considered to be fundamental. Where is the proper balance? Under what conditions is a state justified in interfering with its citizens' freedom of choice and of life style in order to maintain certain moral standards? This is the problem posed in Part I of this book—the problem of the enforcement of morals, the wisdom of passing laws whose chief goal is the maintenance of the community's moral standards, at the expense of individual freedom, when violation of the norm itself causes no demonstrable harm to others.

If the enforcement of morals is problematic, it might be supposed that the enforcement of laws designed to protect citizens against harm that might be done to them by others would not be problematic at all. But this is not so. Some persons argue that punishment is an outmoded concept and that criminal penalties ought to be abolished in favor of some other form of treatment. Some writers have suggested that those who violate the law are unable to do otherwise and that to punish them is barbarous. Others are inclined to place the responsibility upon society as a whole. Because of its manifest injustices, they say, men and women who might otherwise be completely law-abiding are driven to criminal behavior and, because the fault is not theirs but society's, they should not bear the entire burden of responsibility by being punished for their acts. On the other hand, if justice is dependent upon the existence of sanctions, it is difficult to see how a just society can exist without some form of social control embodying rewards or penalties. Even if enforcement of the criminal law by the imposition of penalties is accepted, the practical problem of the kind of penalty to be exacted of those who violate the law remains. From the harsh penalties of earlier days, many of which involved maiming or mutilating the convicted criminal, to modern prisons and such devices as parole, the indefinite sentence, and probation, it seems that no completely satisfactory treatment for those who are guilty of antisocial, destructive, or dangerous behavior has been found. Most difficult of all perhaps are the problems posed by the death penalty, which is unique in its severity and which many people feel should be maintained or reinstated because of its supposed deterrent effect, and those presented by the special case of the juvenile offender, who is thought to deserve some special considerations and methods of treatment. Part II is devoted to the general question of criminal punishment. In addition to chapters giving special attention to the death penalty and juvenile offenders, the reader will find an extended discussion of the utility and the morality of the penitentiary as a form of punishment.

The conflict between liberty and law, and between liberty and morals, goes beyond the criminal law. It extends into many other areas of our personal and communal lives and affects us in ways that go beyond the reach of the criminal law. Men and women hurt one another in many ways, not all of them amenable to rectification by legal means. One such area is illustrated in Part III, which is devoted to the morality of telling the truth. Immanuel Kant's absolutist approach to the question of lying is analyzed in some detail, and then a number of situations in which persons have lied, or are inclined to lie, are studied with a view to determining what their moral implications might be. The adman's freedom to distort the truth often results in a loss to the consumer when he or she buys the product. The physician's freedom to exercise his judgment as to whether to tell a dying patient the truth about his malady may deprive the latter of his right to die in dignity. But rigid adherence to the doctrine that the physician must always tell the truth might result in the untimely death of sensitive patients and unnecessary suffering for them and for their families. Should good or noble intentions excuse or justify distortions of the truth?

That deliberate distortions of truth raise legal and moral questions is not surprising, but that telling the truth can do so is sometimes overlooked. Yet it seems that there are occasions when it is wrong to tell the truth, or what one believes to be the truth, and that there are others when it is wrong to speak at all. Freedom of speech may be misinterpreted to mean freedom to say whatever one pleases whenever and wherever one wishes to do so; but we will see that considerations of justice and equality require the enforcement of restrictions even on that fundamental liberty.

The search for truth is intimately bound up with the quest for justice, for justice cannot be done where the truth cannot be determined with some degree of certainty. Therefore, we will see that although people may sometimes be required to remain silent, they may, on other occasions, be compelled to speak in the interests of justice; and special procedures must be devised to determine the truth for the sake of assigning responsibility and seeing that justice is done.

Finally, there exist some areas that have not yet been touched by the institutional machinery of organized society, though they are very much concerned with the fundamental questions that law has always attempted to resolve. What is to be done when the law is evil, or seems to be so, or when the state commands its citizens to commit immoral or barbarous acts? The personal consequences of disobedience can be disastrous, but morality is not always predicated only upon the consequences to oneself. In Part IV the troublesome issues raised by those who advocate civil disobedience and by those who would outlaw certain practices in time of war—or perhaps even war itself—are discussed. If personal autonomy can be carried so far as to permit individuals to disobey the laws laid down by the representatives of the people, what justification can there be for punishing criminals for their allegedly antisocial behavior? And if the state is to be the final authority for determining the rightness and wrongness of its citizens' behavior, then what is to prevent national leaders from committing the gravest atrocities under the cloak of sovereignty, while those who assist them enjoy an immunity conferred upon them by the fact that they were acting in strict accordance with the laws of their own states, and that they should not be held liable by any other standard? Under what conditions, if ever, may a person properly violate the dictates of law? And under what conditions, if ever, should some higher law be invoked to punish those who have obeyed the laws of their own nations but have nevertheless violated fundamental moral precepts of mankind?

The principles of liberty and law have always been in conflict, for, as we observed earlier, whenever one is permitted to expand, the other must necessarily contract. The fundamental dilemmas in our time are to be found in the search for means of accommodating the demand of freedom-loving people for greater liberties without at the same time dissolving the protections that law gives to all of us; of maintaining decent standards of morality without at the same time working grave injustices—for morality and justice are not always identical. In this book some of the major areas of conflict in the contemporary world are examined in an attempt to determine how they might be resolved while preserving personal liberties, without giving up our society's moral standards, and without abandoning either our legal system or the principles of justice upon which it is founded.

I have not hesitated to express my opinions about the questions and issues discussed in this book. Where I have done so it has always been with a good deal of trepidation and with the expectation that the reader will formulate his own judgments in accordance with his assessment of such facts as may be available to him, as well as his assessment of the arguments that I have set forth in support of my views. In a dynamic world such as the one we inhabit, Heraclitus's aphorism that no one can ever step into the same river twice, for the river is changing at every moment with new waters flowing in and old flowing out, seems singularly appropriate. Not only the rivers and the world change every moment, but so do we. The attitude of those philosophers of the Middle Ages and the eighteenth and nineteenth centuries who supposed that they had possession of the last word in science, or philosophy, or morals seems today to be born of arrogance. Perhaps there are some eternal verities, but in this time of rapid change, of revolutions in politics, in cultures, and in moral attitudes, it is at least the better part of prudence, if not of humility, to offer such a book as this to the reading public as a contribution to a continuing discussion rather than as the last word. Many will no doubt disagree with much of what I have had to say. Most will disagree with at least some of what I have had to say. If Heraclitus is correct, I will probably change my mind about some, at least, of the things that I have said here. I trust, however, that my exposition of the issues themselves and the arguments I have offered in support of my own views will make some contribution to the reader's thinking about them and will stimulate him to respond in some way—at least to inquire further about those issues about whose solution he entertains some continuing doubts. It was, after all, because of their abiding faith in men's capacity to arrive at reasonable and just solutions to such issues as these that our ancestors fought for the liberties we now enjoy.

Part One

The Enforcement
of Morals

1

Lord Devlin and the Enforcement of Morals

It has long been taken for granted that law was the servant of morals, that law was designed, among other things, to protect and enhance the moral tone of society. Recently this theory has fallen out of favor, at least in some circles. But it is still held by many influential thinkers, and has been ably defended by some. One of the most widely discussed statements of the theory that the law not only may but ought to enforce morals was made in 1959 by Sir Patrick Devlin, who served for many years as a judge of the Queen's Bench and was made a Lord of Appeal in 1961.

Lord Devlin had been asked to testify before the Wolfenden Committee, which recommended, in 1957, that England's laws on homosexuality should be liberalized, so that homosexuality between consenting adults would no longer be a crime. The committee based its recommendation upon its members' conclusion that there is a realm of private morality that is none of the law's business, and that there is a significant distinction between crime and sin that must be maintained. As the authors of the report put it, the function of the law is "to preserve public order and decency, to protect the citizen from what is offensive or injurious, and to provide sufficient safeguards against exploitation and corruption of others, particularly those who are specially vulnerable because they are young, weak in body or mind, inexperienced, or in a state of special physical, official or economic dependence." [1] They went on to say that they did not consider it the function of the law "to intervene in the private lives of citizens, or to seek to enforce any particular pattern of behaviour, further than is necessary to carry out the purposes we have outlined." [2] They added that they did not intend, in saying that, to encourage private immorality. [3]

There had already been some precedent for their action, taken by a committee that had looked into the question of the law on prostitution. That committee had defined private immorality as immorality that is not offensive or injurious to the public [4] and had concluded that such conduct should not be considered criminal unless it was accompanied by indecency, corruption, or exploitation. "It is not the duty of the law to concern itself with immorality as such," the committee on prostitution said. The Wolfenden Committee concurred, saying: "It should confine itself to those activities which offend against public order and decency or expose the ordinary citizen to what is offensive or injurious." [5]

In considering these assumptions, Devlin recalled that the criminal law never permits the consent of the victim to be used as a defense.* For example, consent of the victim is no defense against the charge of murder or assault. Further, the victim of assault or any similar crime may not forgive the offender and demand that the state cease to prosecute. This principle, which is followed quite consistently throughout the criminal law, is inconsistent with the Wolfenden Committee's assumption; for if the law were designed solely for the protection of the individual, there would be no reason why the individual should not forego such protection if he did not want it. From the fact that the law does not permit the victim to forego such protection, it would seem to follow that the law is *not* designed solely for his protection, but that some other purpose must be involved. That purpose, Devlin says, is the protection of society. Murder, assault, and other crimes for which consent is no defense are crimes against society, and it is for that reason that society neither permits the defense of consent nor the withdrawal of charges if the victim so desires. Devlin points out that where such offenses are concerned, it matters not whether anyone has been shocked, corrupted, or exploited, or whether the offenses have been committed in public or in private. He adds that they are not punished on the pragmatic ground that the punishment of violent men will protect other members of society, for a murderer who acts only at the consent or request of his victims is no menace to others who may not desire his services. Persons who commit such offenses are punished, in Devlin's view, because they "threaten one of the great moral principles upon which society is based, that is, the sanctity of human life." There are certain standards of behavior or moral principles, he observes, that society insists upon, and their violation is an offence against society as a whole as well as against the injured person.[6]

A number of examples may be offered of acts that can be done in private without giving offense to anyone and that do not involve the corruption or exploitation of other persons: euthanasia, the killing of another at his request, suicide, dueling, abortion, incest—all of these are of such a nature. Although some advocate reform of the law on some of these matters, Devlin observes, no one has advocated the abolition of all restraints on all of them. But if they adhered faithfully to the principle that the law should not inter-

---

* Rape is not an exception, because consent changes the nature of the offense.

fere in matters of private morality, they should be prepared to accept the lifting of all legal sanctions against all such behavior.

Devlin presents a number of arguments in support of his view that morals are not merely a matter of private judgment, that society has the right to enforce moral standards and that there are ways of distinguishing those moral standards that society should enforce from those that it may refrain from enforcing.

1. There is a difference between private morality and private behavior in matters of morals. Society, he says, is a community of ideas. It has, as part of its basic structure, a moral foundation, which determines, to a large degree, the manner in which its members are supposed to conduct their lives. The institution of marriage is an important example of an area in which morals and law intersect. The institution is itself based upon certain fundamental conceptions, which all societies have enforced in one way or another. Adultery is not merely a private matter, according to Devlin; it is a public matter, because the institution of marriage itself—which is a fundamental social institution—depends for its survival upon the observance of certain norms with regard to marital chastity. People in so-called Christian nations consider monogamy to be "something that is good in itself and offering a good way of life." For that reason, Devlin says, our society has adopted it as a norm for marriage. Although two people may commit adultery in private, the question of the morality of adulterous relationships is not a matter of private morality, for society has a deep and abiding interest in the preservation of that form of marriage which it has sanctioned; adultery, therefore, is a matter of public morality. Similarly, even though three people decide to enter into a polygamous relationship, they may not do so if they choose to remain in England, Canada, the United States, or any other Christian nation (or in any nation whose laws are derived from Christian norms), for such relations threaten the institution of marriage as it exists in those nations. "Without shared ideas on politics, morals, and ethics," Devlin says, "no society can exist. . . . Society is not something that is kept together physically; it is held by the invisible bonds of common thought. If the bonds were too far relaxed the members would drift apart. A common morality is part of the bondage. The bondage is part of the price of society; and mankind, which needs society, must pay its price." [7]

2. Once it is established that society has the right to preserve itself through the enforcement of those moral standards that are so important a part of its basic structure, the question of the extent to which society should use the law to enforce those standards is answered relatively easily. Society is entitled to protect itself from any dangers, whether those dangers threaten its existence from without or from within. Societies disintegrate more often from internal causes—particularly from "the loosening of moral bonds," according to Devlin—than from outside attack. Because this is the case, he concludes, "the suppression of vice is as much the law's business as the suppression of subversive activities; it is no more possible to define a sphere of private

morality than it is to define one of private subversive activity." [8] Consequently, there are no theoretical limits to the extent to which the law may move against immorality. If a man chooses to get drunk every night in the privacy of his living room, this *is* society's business, and not merely his own; for society would not long survive if large numbers of people got drunk every night in the privacy of their homes.

criterion

3. The measure of society's morals is, according to Devlin, the standards of "the reasonable man, . . . the man on the street," who may also be characterized as "the right-minded man" or "the man in the jury box." "Immorality," according to Devlin, "is what every right-minded person is presumed to consider immoral." [9]

4. Nevertheless, the individual cannot be expected to give up to society all rights to freedom of action. There are private interests as well as public ones, and the former must be given due consideration, together with the latter. Devlin supports the principle that individual freedom should be tolerated as far as possible, so long as it is consistent with the integrity of society.[10] The measure of the limit of tolerance, he says, is the ordinary man's feelings about a given practice. If the ordinary man has a "real feeling of reprobation," a deeply felt sense of disgust, then this is a pretty good indication that we have reached the outer bounds of toleration.[11] Reasoning alone is not sufficient, because it is possible, on logical grounds, to come to more than one conclusion with regard to a given matter on the basis of evidence and arguments that may be presented. This sense of disgust, indignation, and reprobation must, according to Devlin, be very strong indeed to justify invoking the sanctions of the law. Strong disapproval of a practice is not sufficient, in itself, to justify the invocation of such sanctions.[12] In addition, even where there is a general feeling of indignation and disgust, there must be a "deliberate judgment that the practice is injurious to society." [13]

Devlin recognizes the fact that there are shifts in the levels of tolerance and departures from the moral standards of one generation by the generations that follow. But he believes that in all such matters, the law should be slow to act, for if it acts too hastily, it may undermine very important principles or institutions that will be sorely missed later on, once the passionate cry for reform has passed.[14]

5. To be sure, privacy must be respected. But if one person has injured another, he has forfeited some of the rights that he might otherwise have enjoyed against any intrusions by the state's agents upon his privacy. By the same token, Devlin argues, where consenting adults have engaged in acts that society deems to be damaging to itself, they may also forfeit some of their right of privacy. Still, the detection of such crimes, committed in private between consenting adults, is likely to be rather haphazard, and the law must balance its own interests against those of individuals whose right to privacy should, in general, be respected. Where the enforcement of a moral prohibition would intrude too greatly upon the right of privacy, which must also be respected, the law must be moderated.[15]

6. The law is not completely consistent in its application of moral standards. Some very harmful kinds of behavior, such as adultery of the sort that tends to break up marriages, have been left outside the criminal law in England because, according to Devlin, it would be too hard to enforce a legal prohibition against it. It is too generally regarded, he says, as a human weakness of such a nature that punishment would not serve to deter those who are tempted to engage in it. "There is no logic to be found in this," he declares, but from the fact that adultery, fornication, and other immoral acts are not punished by the law, it does not follow that homosexuality should not be so punished.

7. The logical inconsistencies and the strange operations of legal reasoning become particularly evident when one considers the abortion laws. Abortionists are subject to severe punishment because their crime is considered a particularly harmful one. Their ministrations lead too often to serious injury or death. But the reason that abortion is so dangerous is that legislators have outlawed abortions, for if abortion were legalized, skilled practitioners would be performing them and there would be no need for anyone to turn to an unskilled amateur. The law is punishing those who do what they do only because the law has left no other outlet for those who want or need such services. The law has itself been at least partially responsible for the creation of the dangerous situation in which girls seeking abortions find themselves. This anomolous situation illustrates Devlin's contention that law and sin are not identical and cannot be made so by legislation. The community must be imbued with a sense of sin in other ways—principally by education. If the law is unassisted by the educational organs of the state, and those other instrumentalities that are in a position to influence human thought and conduct, it cannot bear the burden alone and is bound to be warped, as it has in the case of abortion and in other cases. Without the help of strong moral training, Devlin concludes, the law is bound to fail.

LORD DEVLIN'S CRITICS

H. L. A. HART

Devlin's theory has been the subject of intense discussion and widespread criticism since its publication. One of the most important critiques of Devlin and of others who hold similar views was published by H. L. A. Hart in a little book entitled *Law, Liberty, and Morality*.[16] Hart noted that the Wolfenden Committee's report was based upon John Stuart Mill's principle, enunciated in his essay *On Liberty,* that "the only purpose for which power can rightfully be exercised over any member of a civilized community against his will is to prevent harm to others.[17] Mill went on to specify that the law must not interfere with an individual's behavior for his own good, whether that be physical or moral. "He cannot rightfully be compelled to do or forbear because it will be better for him to do so, because it will make him happier, because in the opinions of others, to do so would be wise or even right." [18]

Hart proceeds under the assumption, with which one may suppose Devlin would agree, that one needs some special justification for depriving individuals of the liberties that may be taken from them if they are punished by the law. Secondly, he assumes that when there is a law forbidding a certain form of conduct, the existence of that law itself coerces people into conformance, and restricts the freedom they might otherwise enjoy to experiment in those areas of conduct; but freedom of choice is itself a valuable thing, and any interference with it requires some rather strong justification. Finally, he assumes that laws designed to enforce sexual morality, to the extent that they interfere with certain forms of sexual expression and restrict the sexual outlets that may be available, impose an acute form of suffering upon those who are thus deprived of the only outlets that may be available to them. Such laws, and the coercive measures that may be used to enforce them, "may create misery of a quite special degree," according to Hart.[19] All these restrictions, then, must be justified by rather strong reasons. The principal reason offered by Devlin is the danger to the fabric of society posed by moral breakdown and degeneracy. We shall see how Hart replies to this.

First, he argues that Devlin's appeal to the laws that exist is not convincing. By appealing to the existence of such laws as those forbidding incest, homosexuality, euthanasia, and the like, as supporting evidence for his argument that morals may be enforced, Devlin merely invokes "the innocuous conservative principle that there is a presumption that common and long established institutions are likely to have merits not apparent to the rationalist philosopher." [20] We might add that in doing so, Devlin argues from what *is* to what *ought to be*. But the whole point of those who support Mill's principle is that laws that presently restrict the freedom of the individual because such restrictions are supposed, by those in positions of authority, to be in his best interests ought to be changed. Their present existence, and their long history, prove nothing to the point.

Secondly, he points out that Devlin's assertion that the function of the criminal law is only to enforce moral principles is not completely true. The appeal to laws that allow of no defense on the ground that the victim consented does not prove, of itself, that the sole purpose of such laws is the enforcement of morals. Hart points out that there may be an element of paternalism, designed to protect people against themselves. Pure food and drug laws, which are designed to protect the consumer against his own ignorance, and the law that certain drugs may be sold only on prescription are clearly paternalistic. "It would seem very dogmatic," Hart says, "to say of the law creating this offence that there is only one explanation, namely, that the law was concerned not with the protection of the would-be purchasers against themselves, but only with the punishment of the seller for his immorality." [21] Devlin's assumption that laws were either designed to protect people from one another or to punish moral wickedness turns out to be insufficient, for there may be, and in fact there are, laws that endeavor to reduce suffering—not only human suffering, but even (as in the cases of laws against cruelty to animals) the suffering of animals.

The bigamy example is used by Devlin to show how the law is used to enforce morals. But Hart points out that the law will not interfere if a man lives with one woman, or even with several women, in adulterous relationships. He may even go through all the ceremony associated with weddings to celebrate the union, so long as he does not in fact marry her. When he marries, the law intervenes, not only to nullify the bigamous marriage but also to punish the offender. This is a strange way for the law to treat offenses against morality—or at least, an inconsistent way for it to treat them. Hart cites a number of attempts to justify the law's severe sanctions against bigamy and its hands-off attitude toward adultery. Some people say that bigamy is punished because it may lead to confusion of public records or to attempts to misrepresent illegitimate children as legitimate. Others say that it is "a public affront and provocation to the first spouse," and because cohabitation under color of matrimony is especially likely to lead to desertion, nonsupport, and divorce.[22] Still others have argued that a bigamous marriage ceremony performed in a country where there is a strong religious and moral tradition of monogamy will offend people's feelings and be regarded by many as a publicly sanctioned desecration. Some of these attempts to reconcile the inconsistencies in the laws on this point are, according to Hart, "more ingenious than convincing." But the last, he suggests, would, if correct, support the view that the bigamist is punished, not because he is morally wicked but because he is, in some sense, a public nuisance. This is not the only case in which public behavior may be punished because it is deemed to be a nuisance. Some forms of behavior, legitimate in themselves, are punishable if they are committed in public. A husband may quite properly have sexual intercourse with his wife, but not on the public streets, where it is an affront to public decency. The distinction between prostitution as such and street-walking is based upon this concept; for, though prostitution may be immoral, it may be legalized without legalizing street-walking on the ground that the latter offends the sensibilities of those who may be unwillingly exposed to its manifestations. A case may be made for the view that people have a right not to be offended by sights that are imposed upon them in public places, just as they have a right not to be made an unwilling audience to loud noises emanating from bars, record shops, and transistor radios in public streets, parks, buses, and beaches.

Devlin's principal thesis, that society has the right to enforce morality because immorality may weaken it or lead to its collapse, has, as an unexpressed underlying assumption, the theory that "sexual morality together with the morality that forbids acts injurious to others such as killings, stealing, and dishonesty—forms a single seamless web, so that those who deviate from any part are likely or perhaps bound to deviate from the whole." [23] Though

Hart is prepared to admit that society would not long endure if it were not reinforced by a morality that proscribed conduct that was injurious to others, he is not convinced that those who deviate from the norms of sexual morality are a general threat to society. Hart goes on to say that to the extent that Devlin holds that every society depends upon some degree of shared morality, he may be correct; but when he moves from that position to one which holds that a society is virtually identical with its morality, he has moved to an absurd position. According to Hart, the adoption of the latter position would require us to assume that the slightest change in a society's moral or legal code would be tantamount to the disappearance of that society and its replacement by a new one.[24] This latter assumption, labeled "absurd" by Hart, underlies Devlin's comparison of immorality and treason. Conventional morality, according to Hart, could change without destroying or subverting a society. Such change, he suggests, could be more aptly compared to peaceful constitutional change in a society, and is consistent, as he puts it, "not only with the preservation of a society but with its advance." [25]

LADY WOOTTON

Lord Devlin's thesis was also subjected to systematic attack in a series of lectures by Lady Wootton, who observed that his definition of a crime as an act about which the good citizen would feel guilty is circular, because one would presumably be able to identify a "good citizen"—or as Devlin put it, the "right-minded man," or the "man in the jury box"—only by determining whether he would feel guilty about the commission of such acts.

Further, Lady Wootton notes that some acts, though bad in some contexts, are proper or even beneficial in others, and that as a result, one must conclude that no act is bad in itself. Cutting open a man's chest and slicing into his heart is clearly wrong and is illegal in some circumstances; but if such an act is performed by a surgeon attempting to save a man's life, it is neither morally nor legally wrong. The moral law changes because of new conditions, and the criminal law tends to adapt itself as well. The tendency to regard wrongs that were condemned by ancient authors as being somehow *more wrong* than those that were not condemned by them because they could not have foreseen them is a mistake. "The fact that there is nothing in the Ten Commandments about the iniquity of driving a motor vehicle under the influence of drink cannot be read as evidence that the ancient Israelites regarded this offence more leniently than the contemporary British." [26] Of course not, for they did not regard them at all! But there is a tendency to suppose that because there is no Mosaic prohibition against drunken driving, whereas there is one against homosexual relations, the former is somehow less evil than the latter, or the latter is more deserving of severe punishment than the former.

There is no logic in the criminal law, Lady Wootton says. "For administering a drug to a female with a view to carnal knowledge a maximum of two years is provided, but for damage to cattle you are liable to fourteen years' imprisonment. For using unlawful oaths the maximum is seven years, but for keeping a child in a brothel it is a mere six months." [27] How the "good citizen" feels about such matters is a matter of speculation, perhaps, but Lady Wootton is convinced that most people will find these facts "quite fantastic." The point is that the good citizen will feel rather different degrees of guilt over stabbing his wife, having homosexual relations, and parking overtime. All of these are crimes, but not all of them are sins. "Whether or not they are also sins is a purely theological matter," she asserts, "with which the law has no concern. If the function of the criminal law is to punish the wicked, then everything which the law forbids must in the circumstances in which it is forbidden be regarded as in its appropriate measure wicked." [28] But obviously, not everything in the criminal law does correspond to anyone's view of wickedness, and there are some kinds of "criminal" behavior that everyone would presumably agree are not morally wicked in themselves.

If moral wickedness is indeed involved, she argues, then the law's former insistence on *mens rea*—voluntariness and intent—makes sense. But the law's present tendency to assign strict liability to some kinds of offenses cannot be squared with the view that the criminal law's function is to punish wickedness; for under strict liability, one may be held liable for an act even when he can establish that he had no knowledge of its possible effects and no intention to cause the harm that he caused, and even when he can show that he exercised due care to avoid causing any harm to anyone and to avoid violating any legal prohibition. Lady Wootton suggests that the recent tendency to hold people strictly liable for certain kinds of offenses reveals that the law is being thought of, to an ever larger degree, as a means of *preventing* certain kinds of behavior, rather than as a means of *punishing* them. The gravity of an offense under strict liability, such as a traffic offense in which a pedestrian has been injured or killed, is measured more by the consequences of the offense than by the state of mind of the offender. Thus, a driver who had knocked down a pedestrian was booked on a charge of careless driving, but the charge was raised a month later—after the death of the injured party —to causing death by dangerous driving. Offenses of strict liability reveal, according to Lady Wootton, that "in the modern world in one way or another, as much and more damage is done by negligence, or by indifference to the welfare or safety of others, as by deliberate wickedness." [29] She recalls that there was a time when animals, and even inanimate objects, such as trees and stones, could be held legally responsible for harm that they did to people.[30] Now, she suggests, perhaps the time has come "for the concept of legal guilt to be dissolved into a wider concept of responsibility or at least accountability, in which there is room for negligence as well as purposeful wrongdoing; and for the significance of a conviction to be reinterpreted merely as evidence that a prohibited act has been committed, questions of motivation being relevant only insofar as they bear upon the probability of such acts being repeated." [31]

THE ROLE OF MORALS IN THE LAW

There can be no doubt that, historically at least, the law and morals were very closely related and that in many areas the law continues to look upon its function as the enforcement of morals, the reinforcement of moral standards in society, and the punishment of moral depravity. Moral principles are appealed to in determining not only what laws will or will not be enacted by legislators, but also what sentences will be imposed upon violators. In some areas of the law—and not only in the criminal law—moral standards are implicitly or explicitly made an inherent part of the criteria for making certain important judgments.

This is not to say that there is no distinction between law and morals. Clearly, important distinctions exist, not the least of which is the fact that in law there are formal sanctions and formal means for determining guilt or responsibility that are lacking in morals. Also, though the law is not always concerned with motives or with the subject's attitudes, morals—at least according to many moral theorists—always are. And finally, even the most fastidious legal moralist agrees that the scope of morals is far broader than that of law. Nevertheless, the two norms—legal and moral—often intersect, as the following examples will illustrate.

CASE 1. MORALS AS A TEST FOR CITIZENSHIP

On September 22, 1944, a Mr. Repouille applied for naturalization as a United States citizen. The naturalization law requires that any applicant, prior to being approved, must show himself to have been a person of "good moral character" for the five years preceding the filing of his petition. On October 12, 1939, Repouille had deliberately put his thirteen-year-old son to death. His reason for this tragic deed was that the child had suffered certain injuries at birth that rendered him an idiot and left all his limbs grotesquely malformed. He was blind, mute, and deformed; he had to be fed; he had no control over his bowels or his bladder; and he had spent his entire life in a small crib.

Repouille had four other children to whom he was a loving and dutiful father. He concluded that he would not be able to give them the support that they needed and were entitled to if the deformed child were permitted to live. He therefore used chloroform to dispatch him. Although he was indicted for manslaughter in the first degree, the jury brought in a verdict of manslaughter in the second degree with a recommendation of the "utmost clemency." The trial judge, moved by the circumstances and by the jury's recommendation, imposed a sentence of five to ten years, but suspended the sentence and put the defendant on probation. He was discharged from probation in December, 1945. Aside from this one illegal act and his conviction for it,

Repouille conducted himself in such a way that the court conceded that he demonstrated "good moral character," but because he had filed his petition September 22, three weeks short of the five-year period, his petition for naturalization was denied, and, on appeal, the denial of his application was upheld. Judge Hand, in his majority opinion, said:

> Very recently we had to pass upon the phrase "good moral character" in the Nationality Act, and we said that it set as a test, not those standards which we might ourselves approve, but whether "the moral feelings, now prevalent generally in this country" would "be outraged" by the conduct in question: that is, whether it conformed to "the generally accepted moral conventions current at the time." In the absence of some national inquisition, like a Gallup poll, that is indeed a difficult test to apply; often questions will arise to which the answer is not ascertainable, and where the petitioner must fail only because he has the affirmative. Indeed, in [this case], the answer is not wholly certain; for we all know that there are great numbers of people of the most unimpeachable virtue, who think it morally justifiable to put an end to a life so inexorably destined to be a burden to others,—and—so far as any possible interest of its own is concerned—condemned to a brutish existence, lower indeed than all but the lowest forms of sentient life. Nor is it inevitably an answer to say that it must be immoral to do this, until the law provides security against the abuses which would inevitably follow, unless the practice were regulated. Many people— probably most people—do not make it a final ethical test of conduct that it shall not violate law; few of us exact of ourselves or of others the unflinching obedience of a Socrates. . . . There have always been conscientious persons who feel no scruple in acting in defiance of a law which is repugnant to their personal convictions, and who even regard as martyrs those who suffer by doing so. . . . It is reasonably clear that the jury which tried Repouille did not feel any moral repulsion at his crime. Although it was inescapably murder in the first degree, not only did they bring in a verdict that was flatly in the face of the facts and utterly absurd—for manslaughter in the second degree presupposes that killing has not been deliberate—but they coupled even that with a recommendation which showed that in substance they wished to exculpate the offender. Moreover, it is also plain, from the sentence which he imposed, that the judge could not have seriously disagreed with their recommendation.
>
> One might be tempted to seize upon all this as a reliable measure of current morals, and no doubt it should have its place in the scale; but we should hesitate to accept it as decisive, when, for example, we compare it with the fate of a similar offender in Massachusetts, who, although he was not executed, was imprisoned for life. Left at large, as we are, without means of verifying our conclusion, and without authority to substitute our individual beliefs, the outcome must needs be tentative; and not much is gained by discussion. We can say no more than that, quite independently of what may be the current moral feeling as to legally administered euthanasia, we feel reasonably secure in

holding that only a minority of virtuous persons would deem the practice morally justifiable, while it remains in private hands, even when the provocation is as overwhelming as it was in this instance.[32]

Judge Hand went on to explain that he believed that the ultimate test of moral character would be the attitude of "our ethical leaders," but that because of precedents, he would have to rely upon the moral feelings of the public at large—a matter which it was impossible for him to determine. He therefore ordered the case sent back to the court from which it originated, with instructions to the judge to have both parties present evidence on "contemporary moral standards" in the matter at issue. In the meantime, Repouille was entitled to file a new petition for naturalization, for the five-year period had clearly elapsed.

The practical problem faced by Judge Hand and his colleagues in the United States District Court—that is, the problem of ascertaining the moral sense of the community—will be discussed later. Meanwhile, it is abundantly clear from this case that morals enters very intimately into the operation of the law, at least in this area. In fact, it is an integral part of the law itself, and the law stipulates that moral character is a condition for the enjoyment of certain fundamental rights and privileges, including (in this case) citizenship.

This is by no means the only law to contain such moral standards in so integral a fashion. The Constitution of the United States contains a number of provisions embodying moral judgments, including, among others, the Seventh Amendment's prohibition against "cruel and unusual punishments." A given punishment's being unusual may be a matter for scientific or statistical determination. Burning at the stake, crucifixion, and the rack are all unusual today, though they were all common at various times in history. One could make a case for the view that a punishment's being unusual is not, in itself, a moral objection to such a punishment's being employed, and for the view that the assertion that a given form of punishment is unusual is not a moral judgment. But to assert that a punishment is cruel is to pass moral judgment on it; it is to say that that punishment is "inhuman" or "barbarous" or "uncivilized," all emotionally charged, evaluative terms.[33] Justice Frankfurter held that the Fourteenth Amendment was intended "to withdraw from the States the right to act in ways that are offensive to a decent respect for the dignity of man, and heedless of his freedom," and he asserted that "taking human life by unnecessarily cruel means shocks the most fundamental instincts of civilized man." [34]

Similarly, the due process clause has been interpreted to bar the execution of an insane man, for, as Justice Frankfurter put it, that clause "embodies a system of rights based on moral principles so deeply embedded in the traditions and feelings of our people as to be deemed fundamental to a civilized society as conceived by our whole history. Due process is that which comports with the deepest notions of what is fair and right and just." [35]

When morals are not written into the law in so explicit a fashion, they are insinuated into it in other ways. Men are sentenced according to the gravity of their crimes, and that gravity is often determined by its moral offensiveness. Thus, in a 1952 case, Justice Bell of the Pennsylvania Supreme Court quoted, with approval, a decision concerning a murderer:

> In turning to the individual who committed this crime, we are concerned with his *depravity*. The facts of this murder convince us that he is an individual who is dangerous to society and undoubtedly of *savage nature*. There was no reason to mow this victim down in *cold blood*, no occasion to fire so precipitously except as a manifestation of a *savage and depraved nature*.
>
> . . . We have searched his history carefully for some justifiable explanation. We have found none, only *a depraved, cruel, ruthless and brutal individual*. There can be but one choice.
>
> The court therefore adjudges the defendant, Theodore Elliott, to be guilty of murder in the first degree and fixes the penalty at death.[36]

The words emphasized clearly reveal their moral character, and illustrate how the trial judge was influenced by his assessment of the moral character of the crime or of the criminal (or both) in fixing the penalty. The highest court in the state approved of this approach.

Justice Musmanno dissented, partly on the ground that the imposed penalty was "directed to the offense," which he conceded was a "terrible crime," and "not to the offender." As he put it, "There is no punishment in the scale of justice heavy enough to make atonement for what Theodore Elliott did, but for what Theodore Elliott is, a different scale, it seems to me, must be used. Punishment is to be applied according to the capacity of the individual, as well as the enormity of the delinquent act." Justice Musmanno dissented because in his opinion, Elliott was a mental defective who did not have a meaningful choice when he committed his crime. In Justice Musmanno's view, then, Elliott should not be executed, but, being a "dangerous creature, he must be restrained, as the tiger is restrained." According to this opinion, then, the controlling factor is not the destructiveness of the crime, but the moral capacities of the criminal. In Justice Musmanno's opinion, when the defendant was incapable of having the intentions that are necessary for the commission of an immoral act, he should not be "punished" in the conventional sense at all—any more than one would punish a bull that had gored a man or a tiger that had slashed a person with its claws. Rather, one should lock him up as a menace to society—as one might pen a bull or cage a dangerous tiger—not as punishment, and not as a consequence of an "immoral deed" (for one can hardly think of a bull's goring as immoral), but as a simple prudential measure of self-protection. But Justice Musmanno did not rule out, in his opinion, the possibility that another man, committing a similar offense, but not so mentally incapacitated as Elliott allegedly was, might properly be punished for the savagery of his act and for his own moral depravity.

THE COMMUNITY'S MORAL STANDARDS

That moral standards enter into the law, both intrinsically (as in morals offenses and in rules against cruel punishment) and extrinsically (as in cases where penalties or levels of compensation are determined, at least in part, by the moral opprobrium of the act or of the actor) is now well established. Where moral standards are involved, though, there is often some disagreement over the exact nature of the moral norm that ought to apply. Lord Devlin appealed, as lawyers often do, to the "man in the jury box" or the ordinary "reasonable" man for some judgment as to what constitutes moral behavior and what is immoral, and for an authoritative pronouncement on what is and what is not beyond the limits of toleration. There are some problems, though, about ascertaining just what the ordinary man thinks, or what the current "community attitude" might be on any given moral issue.

Not the least of the problems is the definition of *community*. If a man in a small town commits an act that offends the citizens of his town but is generally tolerated as a minor aberration by the citizens of nearby communities, or the state as a whole, should he be judged on the consensus in the small town in which he happened to commit his "offense," or should the "community" be given a broader base, and consist of the entire state in which he lives? Or should the "community" be considered to be the entire nation in which he lives—particularly today, when communications are so rapid, and the entire nation is exposed to the same radio and television programming, the same magazines, and the same press service releases?

Even supposing that one has resolved the question of the definition of *community*, there may be some problem in determining just what the "community's" standards are. Letters to the editor won't serve adequately as a test, for, in the first place, they are edited. It would be very difficult to determine the extent to which the editors themselves permit an expression of the "community's views"—whatever those might be—to be reproduced in their letter columns. Further, there is no evidence that the people who write letters to the editor are truly representative of the community as a whole, or even of those who are informed about the issues on which they choose to write. And in this connection, it must not be forgotten that a substantial proportion of the community may not be at all informed about a particular issue. Should the community be defined in such a way as to exclude those who do not read newspapers carefully, or to include only the best-informed citizens? This would be a long way from Lord Devlin's man in the jury box.

Questionnaires won't do, either—no matter how scientific they may be. For those who reply to questionnaires tend, on the whole, to be more interested in the subject matter, to have a higher socioeconomic status, and to be better educated than those who do not respond.[37]

Judge Frank, in discussing a proposed test for "cruel and unusual punishments"—that "it shocks the conscience and sense of justice of the people of the United States"—concluded that such a test was impossible of application, for it relies on "common conscience." But, he said, "such a standard—the community's attitude—is usually an unknowable. It resembles a slithery shadow, since one can seldom learn, at all accurately, what the community, or a majority, actually feels." Even a carefully taken "public opinion poll" would be inconclusive in a case like this.[38]

It has been suggested that large-scale scientific studies, patterned after those of Dr. Alfred C. Kinsey,[39] might provide some measure of contemporary community attitudes. But there may be a significant difference between what people *do* and what they think they and others *ought* to do; and proof that they behave, on the whole, in one way is no necessary indication that legal obstacles in the way of such behavior ought to be removed. Kinsey did suggest that sex laws should be repealed because, as his studies revealed, so many people violate them. One might argue, though, that such promiscuous violation of the law and of moral standards should encourage legislators to strengthen the laws, that police should enforce them more strictly, and that judges should impose stiffer sentences on those who violate them. The Kinsey reports themselves demonstrated that the very groups that engaged in forbidden practices most strongly disapproved of those practices.[40]

A scientific study of false swearing and perjury might reveal that vast numbers of citizens testified falsely in court and deliberately misrepresented themselves in such instruments as income tax returns. But this would hardly be treated as good reason for repealing the laws prohibiting perjury.[41] Though such widespread disobedience of the laws against perjury might lend some credence to the view that they were "unrealistic" and "barbarous" and inconsistent with "normal" human behavior, most people would go on believing that the laws should be retained, both because of the supposed utility of the threat of punishment in deterring at least some of this behavior and because of the damage that removal of the legal sanctions might do to the overall moral climate of the community.

Finally, the Kinsey reports themselves have been subjected to searching criticism. There is serious doubt in the scientific community, not only about the accuracy with which they reflect community attitudes at the time that the studies were conducted, but even whether they accurately report the facts about sexual conduct at the time. Doubts about sampling techniques, populations, and statistical analyses, among others, have all been raised— serious enough, in many scholars' opinion, to compromise the value of the reports for making policy decisions.[42] It would seem, then, that the Kinsey reports, or any other report of a similar nature, would not serve well as a basis for making either moral or legal judgments.

ETHICAL RELATIVISM

Another approach has been that of the ethical relativists. The cultural relativists (some of them, at least) point to the many differences between cultures on matters of morals, even on matters as far-reaching as the sanctity of life (abortion, parricide, and infanticide, for example) and the nature of the family (widely varied attitudes and practices with regard to monogamy, incest, and adultery). They suggest that these differences reveal that there is no "right" or "wrong" in any absolute sense, that "right" and "wrong" depend entirely upon the culture in which one happens to live. Because there is no objective way of determining what is right and what is wrong, they say, it follows that moral judgments are neither scientific nor objective and that any rational person ought, therefore, to assume a neutral stance on all such matters. A rational legal system would recognize the relativity of morals, and, taking that relativity into account, it would permit a wide diversity of practices to flourish, refraining from pronouncing judgment upon any given set of moral values.

Notice how the argument has proceeded from a statement of objectively verifiable fact (that moral norms differ from one culture to another) to a normative judgment (that every "rational" person should remain neutral on moral issues, that every "rational" legal system ought to be liberal enough to permit a wide variety of practices to flourish, and so on). This jump, from fact to normative judgment, is anything but a logical jump. No rule of logic permits one to infer, from a statement of fact without some additional normative premise, that any particular normative judgment is true. For example, from the fact that most men shave, it does not follow either that men ought to shave or that they ought not to shave. Some additional premise is needed— a premise such as "Whatever is true of most people ought to be true of all of them," or "Whatever is true of most people is right (or wrong)." In the relativists' argument, there seems to be an underlying supposition that requires some independent proof. That supposition would have to run along these lines: "Wherever people in one culture have a moral standard that differs from that of some other culture, people ought not to act on the assumption that *either* form of behavior is right or that *either* form of behavior is wrong." Or, to put it somewhat differently, "Whenever a given practice is permitted in one culture and forbidden in another, it is right (or proper, or "rational," or "reasonable") to remove the legal bars to such behavior." Though these assumptions are absolutely necessary to establish the point that moral relativists want to make, they are accepted without argument. They are moral judgments themselves; and one would wonder whether they are not relative to a particular culture, too, or whether those who support them have some objective, scientific basis for maintaining them. Thus far, no scientific justification has been set forth for making such assumptions, and it seems unlikely that any such justification will be found.[43] Even the less sweeping assumption that there are no moral rules or standards that apply to every society, or its corollary that the only moral rule that ought to be applied to anyone is the rule adopted by his own society, is a moral or normative claim that does not follow from the observed fact that different societies have different value systems. One can concede that different societies have different value systems, and consistently ask whether they *ought* to do so. It is quite consistent for a missionary to say that he intends to bring his mission to the natives of New Guinea *just because* those natives have a moral system that differs from his own: because he believes that it is his duty to persuade them that cannibalism is wrong and that it would be right for them to stop eating their neighbors and his fellow missionaries and to adopt civilized standards of morality instead.

Margaret Mead, the noted anthropologist, once observed that people who wanted to break down a particular traditional value in our society sometimes compile a list of divergent practices, showing that various peoples in other places, or even our own people at other times in our history, had a different opinion on the moral propriety of that practice, and concluding from that that all moral practices are limited in time and place and have no ultimate validity. She went on to say that

> this mischievous and uninformed use of cultural material is often mistakenly called cultural relativity, but that is exactly what it is not, for cultural relativity demands that every item of cultural behavior be seen as relative to the culture of which it is a part, and in that systematic setting every item has positive or negative meaning and value. . . . The science of culture can insist . . . that when we consider contrasting types of behavior we shall attend always to the complete system, and that random, indiscriminate citations of cultural contrasts in detail be strictly recognized for what they are, iconoclastic polemic material, ammunition for agitators, but with no scientific validity.[44]

Dr. Mead recognized the difference, that is, between the science of anthropology, which is purely descriptive, and the use (or abuse) of anthropological data and materials in ethical argumentation about the norms of our own society.

If the ethical relativist is right in assuming that the only meaningful standards are those each social group maintains, then it would follow that any judgment that one civilization or society is better than another is meaningless, that no set of moral ideals can properly be judged to be "higher" than any other, and that moral progress is sheer nonsense. The culture of the most benighted savage cannot properly be deemed to be in any way inferior to that of the most civilized nation, and, because our own moral standard is no higher than that of any other people, it would make very little sense for anyone possessing that knowledge to put forth any great effort to live up to it. If any society or cultural group may lay equal claim to the value or worthiness of its set of values and practices as against those of any other society or cultural group, there would be little justification for anyone attempting to impose any moral standard upon any such group. The Mafia might well be tempted to consider itself such a society. It has its own set of values and practices and its own code of behavior. If the proper standard for judging each society is its own, then those who live up to the code of the Mafia must be deemed by all to be good men, and no one may properly condemn the murderers, the crooked gamblers, the pimps, and the whores who are associated with that organization for being morally depraved. On the contrary, the more successful a man is in fulfilling his "contracts," the worthier he must be deemed to be. As W. T. Stace has observed, the position of the ethical relativist, who maintains that cultural differences lead to the conclusion that rational and informed people should be tolerant of strange, foreign, and deviant moral beliefs and practices, leads, in the end, to the view that we ought to tolerate widow burning, human sacrifice, cannibalism, slavery, the infliction of physical torture, or "any other of the thousand and one abominations which are, or have been, from time to time approved by one moral code or another." [45]

Thus ethical relativism is seriously flawed. The facts that anthropologists have uncovered about other peoples are of interest to us, but they have no logical bearing upon our own moral judgments. We can recognize the differences between other peoples' value systems and our own without concluding that our own values are meaningless or invalid, and without condoning what those other people do. We may appreciate cultural differences fully and still be critical of other value systems, or, indeed, of our own. Prophets and moral reformers have never accepted the view that the prevailing value system of a given culture—however that may be defined— must be tolerated or sanctioned. They have exercised what they considered to be their duty to criticize those value systems, even when they had to do so alone and at the peril of their lives or their liberties. In our own day critics of our value system, from Martin Luther King to Bobby Seale, have not been deterred from doing so by their knowledge that others—perhaps the majority—did not share their views. They were arguing that the system under which most of us operate, or at least a part of that system, was *wrong*, and that it ought to be replaced by a *better* one. This kind of argument is forever barred to the cultural relativist, for his theory commits him to the view that *no* system can be considered better or worse than any other. If anyone wants to adopt this moral position as a matter of faith, he may be entitled to do so, but no anthropological facts or laws of science or logic constitute a justification for his doing so.

Ethical relativism is not the only moral theory to which opponents of the legal enforcement of morals have adhered, but it, or something very much like it, is more often behind their arguments than any other. The study of the meaning of moral statements (metaethics) is beyond the scope of the present volume. I must reluctantly forego the temptation to analyze the various

metaethical theories, both because such an analysis would consume an in-
ordinate amount of space in a volume devoted to normative ethics and
because many excellent books and articles on the subject are readily available. I have discussed ethical relativism at some length because it is so often
seen as a plausible theory and as a justification for the view that the moral
code of a given society ought not to be embodied in or enforced by that
society's legal code. I have attempted to show that the theory itself has grave
deficiencies and that it provides no justification for the toleration of moral
deviancy in a given society. This is not to say, however, that I am committed to moral absolutism—to the view that there is a single set of moral
principles that applies everywhere and at all times, and that those who know
those principles have the right or the duty to spread the word to those who
do not. As a matter of fact, I do not adhere to such a theory; and I do not
believe that Lord Devlin or any other supporter of the legal enforcement of
morals need adopt such a theory or anything at all like it. Devlin, in fact,
seems to accept the proposition that other nations might have moral codes
different from that of Great Britain, and he might well argue that they ought
to enforce their moral codes as Britain should hers, and for the same reasons:
to preserve their societies from internal decay and corruption.

A CRITIQUE OF DEVLIN'S THEORY

In the light of the preceding observations, it is possible now to consider
some additional criticisms of Lord Devlin's theory—criticisms that were not
advanced by either Professor Hart or Lady Wootton. These considerations
are important to any decisions that we might make on the particular issues
to be discussed later.

1. Devlin maintains that society is a community of ideas having a certain
moral foundation. This premise is fundamental to all that follows in his
argument, for his defense of society's right to enforce morals rests upon his
assumption that a breakdown in that moral foundation threatens the very
existence of society itself. But as we have seen, it is no easy matter to find the
"community of ideas" to which Lord Devlin refers, at least in such diverse
societies as the United States; and I would venture to guess that a "community of ideas" could not be identified in Great Britain or in any large
modern society. In any nation, composed of distinct and diverse racial, ethnic,
and religious groups, spread over vast territories and exposed to different
historical and geographical influences, cultural diversity is almost inevitable.
One might suppose that the "community of ideas" to which Lord Devlin
refers might have existed in earlier times, when life was simpler, when
people all had much the same education (or lack of education), and when
the swift and free flow of information and opinions did not exist and so could
not interfere with time-honored customs and ways of thinking. So one might

suppose. But I doubt whether such a "community of ideas" has ever existed in the pristine form that Lord Devlin seems to imagine it may be found even today. Societies have never been simple. They have always been subject to radical and revolutionary winds of doctrine. Populations have always been diverse, with exchanges taking place in times of war and as a result of commerce. It is quite possible, however, that they were more easily governed in earlier times, and that a "community of ideas" could readily be found among those who governed. For those who governed constituted a rather small class of people, and, so far as they found it desirable or convenient to do so, they imposed their ideas, their moral and even their religious beliefs and practices, upon the people who fell under their dominion. With the rise of democracy, that small group of rulers, who might well have held certain fundamental beliefs in common, was replaced by a vast number of rulers—an entire adult population—whose diverse backgrounds and interests would inevitably be reflected in a wide diversity of opinions on many matters, including questions of morality. Such a society could be called a community of ideas only in the loosest sense. More accurately, it should be considered a collectivity of ideas and attitudes, an assemblage or gathering of people who live together and work together and govern themselves collectively in spite of the great differences that divide them. Plato was right when he described a democracy, more than two millenia ago, as a regime in which "liberty and free speech are rife everywhere," where "every man will arrange his own manner of life to suit his pleasure," where there will be "a greater variety of individuals than under any other constitution," and where a man might rise to eminence even if he lacked the specialized education of the aristocratic elite.[46] Lacking the specialized education of the aristocratic elite, the rulers in a democracy—that is, every man—may not share the moral views of those who would, like Plato, impose their own moral standards upon everyone if they could. They may not approve of those standards, or of the standards of many of their compatriots. And in that respect they would not constitute a community of ideas. But Plato was wrong in supposing that democracy was doomed to failure because of its lack of central moral authority and its tolerance of moral diversity. The great experiments in democracy have demonstrated that such political systems can survive and flourish and that multitudes of men can be self-governing without imposing moral or religious uniformity upon one another in the process. Devlin's community of ideas does not exist, and I am not at all sure that it would be a good thing for it to exist if it could be brought about. To be sure, mankind needs some form of government, but "the price of society," as Devlin puts it, need *not* be the "bondage of a common morality."

2. Devlin is correct in saying that it is society's business if a man chooses to get drunk every night in the privacy of his home, but for the wrong reasons. And the sense in which he says that it is society's business is not totally acceptable. It is society's business, he says, because society would not long survive if large numbers of people got drunk every night in the privacy

of their homes. Of course not. But until society is in imminent danger because of such widespread private drunkenness, does it have the right to interfere with the private behavior of individual citizens? Because some activity might lead to disaster if it were carried out on a large scale, it does not follow that that activity ought to be outlawed if it is carried out on a small and relatively harmless scale. When vast numbers of people use detergents, there is danger of eutrophication of lakes, and such use can therefore properly be outlawed. But if only a few people had been using detergents, there would be no such danger and there would be no justification for the law's interfering with their washing habits. The rights of privacy and of freedom of action deserve to be protected, and should be interfered with only when private behavior ceases to be private and becomes a menace to the public or to some part of the public. I cannot play my electric guitar at top volume in the privacy of my home, because the sound reaches my neighbor, who would like to enjoy the privacy of his home undisturbed by my musical efforts. I must not dig up the soil in my backyard and truck it to my farm because such activity will undermine my neighbor's house, which is on the hill just above my property, and cause it to collapse. But I may get drunk in the privacy of my home because such private drunkenness constitutes no danger, in itself, to anyone. Still, society may consider such private drunkenness its business, *not* in the sense that society has the right to prevent me, forcibly or through the threat of punishment, from getting drunk privately, but in the sense that society may take an interest in my activity and try to persuade me, and others like me, to refrain from such potentially harmful behavior. It may tax the liquor I drink and thus make it more expensive for me to indulge my habit. It may conduct advertising and educational campaigns. It may offer medical advice and treatment. But so long as my activity constitutes no threat to society or to any of its members, I fail to see how it would be justified in applying criminal sanctions to me.

3. We have already seen how difficult it is to identify the "reasonable man" or the "ordinary man on the street" or the "right-minded man" upon whom Devlin pins his hopes for enlightenment on the moral standards of the community. We have seen how public opinion polls, surveys, and even scientific studies fail to give the kind of guidance Devlin looks for. But even if they did, even if it were possible to find out what the community's moral standards were, or what the majority of the citizens considered to be moral and immoral, it is not clear that such a judgment would constitute a justification for applying the sanctions of the criminal law against that minority of persons who believe otherwise, or those members of the majority who slip from time to time and fail to live up to the principles which they espouse when poll takers are in their living rooms.

4. Devlin's approach has a clear conservative bias, for, though the community's moral sense is to be the guide for legislation on morals, it turns out that the *present* community's moral sense is of less importance than is that of the *former* community. Why the community of bygone years should be permitted to govern the present community is not at all clear. If it is true, as

Devlin says, that hasty legislation may do away with institutions that will later be sorely missed, it is equally true that slow legislation will preserve institutions that are presently deeply resented.

5. Devlin notes that the law has long refused to sanction acts of certain sorts committed in private, even where the so-called victim gives his consent. Therefore, he argues, private homosexual acts between consenting adults may properly be forbidden by the criminal law. But those who adopt Mill's libertarian principle might well maintain that *all* acts of the same sort should be permitted, including not only homosexuality, adultery, and fornication, but suicide, euthanasia, abortion, and any others that Devlin might care to name. They are not impressed by Devlin's list of laws that are presently on the books forbidding consensual "immoral" acts done in private. They say that the list only shows how widely the law is abusing its powers. The issue, after all, is not what the law *does* forbid, for we are all more or less familiar with that, and there is no point arguing over it. Any dispute over what the law does or does not forbid may be settled by consulting a competent attorney. The issue is what the law *ought* to forbid, and no list of acts presently forbidden or permitted will suffice, in itself, to give us the answer to that question.

The criminal law, like law in general, is limited in its capacity to rectify all the wrongs that may be perpetrated in society. Any society, no matter how primitive or how advanced it might be, must rely upon the voluntary acquiescence and cooperation of its members in most areas of conduct in order for the business of the society to go on. Every society has developed an elaborate set of informal and unwritten rules that are learned at an early age and are generally accepted without question by its members. Through those rules, and the habits and manners which they engender, life proceeds in a relatively regular, dependable, and consistent way. Breach of those rules may be surprising, shocking, and highly provocative. Where the rules are deemed to be so important that their breach will likely provoke severe retaliatory measures, civilized societies have provided the formal procedures and remedies of the law as a substitute for the private retaliation that might otherwise ensue. No society, however, can successfully enforce every rule that governs the behavior of its members. There could not possibly be enough policemen, lawyers, and judges to handle such an enormous burden. Nor is it possible for every kind of complaint to be remedied by law; for the formal procedures of law require proof before a remedy can be granted, and some matters are simply not amenable to objective proof.* When the law tries to do too much it is likely to fail to do anything well. If the courts and

---

* How would one prove, for example, that he had suffered great emotional distress when there was no overt physical manifestation of such distress? A claim for damages for fright occasioned at the sight of a street action is rightly disallowed on the ground that it is too hard to prove that such a condition did occur as a result of the cause in question, and on the further ground that it is too easy to fake such claims to warrant permitting them and taking the risk.

other law enforcement officials are overburdened with trivial cases, or with the enforcement of rules that might be handled more effectively or more efficiently in some other way, they are likely to find themselves unable to perform their primary function of keeping the peace and protecting the persons, the liberties, and the property of the citizens who come under their jurisdiction. Swamped by great numbers of cases, they will be forced to delay consideration of each case and thus to risk denying justice to those who must wait to recover their money or their liberty, or to be relieved of the anxiety that inevitably accompanies an anticipated appearance in court. Denial of justice leads to contempt for the entire judicial process and for the law as a whole. Such contempt can lead more directly to the destruction of a social or political system than most, or any, of the allegedly moral offenses that we are about to consider. On pragmatic grounds, then—that is, on the same kinds of grounds appealed to by Lord Devlin when he compared moral offenses to subversion—one may maintain that private consensual moral offenses should not be legally prohibited because of the difficulty of enforcing such laws, the near impossibility of detecting most offenses without an unconscionable invasion of privacy, and the danger of flooding the courts with cases and imposing impossible burdens upon the police when they might spend their time more profitably solving crimes of violence, bringing those who have harmed others to book, and settling domestic and civil grievances.

Still, there are those who feel that some of these moral offenses involve such fundamental principles that they cannot be ignored by the criminal law. Let us turn to them, then, and see what conclusions we can draw.

2
Homosexuality

THE ROOTS OF THE PROBLEM

Severe condemnation of homosexual activity is not new. In the Hebrew Bible, copulation of one man with another is categorically condemned, and in one passage, the death penalty is prescribed for those who engage in such practices.[1] Temple prostitutes, both male and female, were common among the ancients, but were specifically forbidden in the Hebrew Bible.[2] According to one Jewish tradition, Sodom and Gomorrah were destroyed because of the "sodomy" that was committed within their borders. An ancient legend tells how Lot's house was surrounded by hordes of men demanding that his guests be produced so that they could engage in sexual relations with them, as was their right according to a law of their city.[3] The flood in Noah's time was also said to have been brought about, at least in part, because of the homosexuality and bestiality practiced by the people of that generation.[4] According to one tradition, the people of Israel were exiled because of their sins, one of which was sodomy.[5] But though homosexual activity was denounced, adultery, fornication, and other forms of sexual misbehavior were severely condemned with far greater frequency, and in later Jewish law, there is little evidence that the harsh penalties for homosexuality were actually enforced.

In the Epistle to the Romans, St. Paul wrote that the Gentiles were punished because their women engaged in lesbianism and men, "leaving the natural use of the women, burned in their lust one toward another; men with men working that which is unseemly." [6] Elsewhere, he warned that neither effeminate men nor those who "abuse themselves" with other men would inherit the kingdom of God.[7] St. Augustine, like most of the early Fathers of the Church, condemned homosexuality, remarking that such sins are "in all times and places to be detested and punished." He declared that even if all nations engaged in such conduct, they would still be held guilty by

33

God, and warned his readers that man's friendship with God is endangered when man pollutes his nature with "so perverted a lust." [8] When the Roman Empire became Christian, sodomists were ordered to be burned. Justinian offered an intriguing argument in justification of the application of harsh measures against homosexuals:

> Because some persons, instigated by the devil, abandon themselves to the most serious forms of lewdness, and commit crimes against nature, we enjoin them to fear God and his future judgment, and to abstain from these diabolical and illicit lewdnesses, so that their acts might not provoke the just wrath of God, nor serve as the occasion for the destruction of cities and their inhabitants. . . . Crimes against nature are responsible for famines, earthquakes, and plagues. To avert such evils, and to save men from losing their souls, we therefore want them not to give themselves up to such impieties.[9]

Sodomy and other forms of "unnatural" sexual behavior have been countenanced in some societies, encouraged in others, and subjected to the most severe penalties in still others. In ancient Greece, in Rome, and elsewhere, the ideals of masculine love were praised. Plato's famous dialogue on love is in fact an encomium to homosexual love.[10] The writings of Juvenal, Petronius, and Suetonius describe the debaucheries of the Roman rulers in great detail. It is said that Nero had his favorite male consort castrated and then went through a marriage ceremony with him. Julius Caesar was described by a senator of the time as being "every woman's man and every man's woman." Those who disapproved of such practices were amused by them or contemptuous of those who engaged in them, but there seems to have been no serious effort to deter people from engaging in them through criminal sanctions.

Nevertheless, some sexual practices were punished, and those that were punished carried severe penalties. A slave who had relations with a free-born youth was liable to be subjected to a public whipping. An Athenian citizen who became a male prostitute was liable to lose all his civil rights. And for pederasty (homosexual relations with a child) a man could be sentenced to death.[11]

A survey of anthropological literature reveals that in a rather high percentage of societies that have been the subject of anthropological research, some form of homosexuality is considered normal and acceptable, and in some it is actively encouraged. In some tribes, for example, all men and boys are expected to engage in homosexual sodomy, and if any man fails to have relations with both male and female partners, he is considered peculiar. In others, older men introduce young men to anal intercourse at puberty, and the latter are expected to do the same to their friends as they reach puberty and to continue to engage in such activities until they are sufficiently mature, in the eyes of their elders, to have relations with women. Some peoples have rigid rules against any form of heterosexual behavior up to a certain age, or hedge heterosexual relations around with a multitude of moral and legal restrictions; but they are completely indifferent to homosexual relations between men or between women.[12]

In our own society, however, homosexual relations, as well as certain other forms of sexual behavior that are considered to be "unnatural," "sinful," "abominable," or otherwise deplorable, have been subjected to severe restrictions for many centuries; and these restrictions are still reflected in our laws and in the attitude of public officials and private persons to those who engage in such behavior. In seventeenth-century England—a period often described as "the Age of Reason"—people were hanged for having homosexual relations. People were hanged and pilloried for the same offenses through the eighteenth and into the nineteenth centuries. Oscar Wilde was sent to prison after three sensational trials on homosexual charges.[13]

Though other times and other peoples have been tolerant of what we would call deviant sexual behavior, we are living in our time among our own people. It is instructive, of course, to be informed that other peoples have had attitudes different from those that are prevalent or dominant among us. But, as we have seen earlier, such information does not in itself provide a justification for supposing that our own values or practices are unimportant, foolish, backward, irrational, or unscientific; nor does such information provide a justification for the view that our own practices and attitudes are more advanced, more scientific, more rational, more sensible than those others. If there is some way of judging our practices, of determining whether they are right or wrong, just or unjust, it must be other than by comparing our system with others.

It is widely believed that married couples may legally practice any form of sexual gratification with one another in the privacy of their bedrooms. But this is not necessarily the case. In many states a number of forms of "unnatural" intercourse are legally prohibited even when they are performed by a married couple in private. In the state of Georgia, for example, sodomy is legally defined as "the carnal knowledge and connection against the order of nature, by man with man, or in the same unnatural manner with woman," and is punishable by life imprisonment. The law is similar in almost every other state in the Union. Such laws are not often enforced, but prosecution of cases under their provisions are not unknown; and so long as such laws exist, those who violate them are subject to prosecution and to heavy penalties.

In addition to statutes prohibiting "sex perversions" or unnatural sex acts, sex crimes are prosecuted under other acts, including "public indecency," "lewdness," "indecent exposure," "vagrancy," and "disorderly conduct." Such statutes are often construed very broadly by police, prosecutors, and judges, so that a multitude of sins or alleged sins may be covered by them.

Donald W. Cory has observed that the existence of such legal prohibitions on the statute books is not so harmless as one might suppose. These laws "transform the majority of our adult population into felons. We have become a nation . . . of law-abiding criminals. If our laws covering sex crimes were to be enforced, we should have to transform entire states into huge concentration camps, and there would hardly be enough people remaining free to act as jailors." [14] If more people were aware of the existence of laws condemning what they do in private, Cory says, the result would be either constant awareness that they have committed punishable felonies with the psychological toll that is likely to flow from such guilty awareness, or a growing contempt for a system of laws that brands as criminal what so many otherwise law-abiding citizens do.[15] Nevertheless, the laws remain on the statute books, unenforced for the most part, but available whenever prosecutors and police feel the need or the desire to bring them to bear against the citizens who fall within their jurisdiction.

It is impossible here to attempt to discuss thoroughly all the legislation that governs sexual relations, or even all the legislation that governs so-called unnatural sexual behavior. This chapter will concentrate, therefore, on homosexuality alone, under the assumption that many of the lessons to be learned from this paradigm may be applied to related areas as well.

REASONS FOR CONDEMNING HOMOSEXUAL BEHAVIOR

Many reasons have been advanced by those who favor the retention of legislation forbidding homosexual behavior. As we shall see, some of these reasons have considerable foundation in fact, whereas others do not.

1. Homosexual activity is offensive. It is a source of disgust to those who find themselves in a position where they must witness public displays of behavior that offend ordinary moral, religious, and even aesthetic feelings. Public lavatories, parks, and theaters become the gathering places of homosexuals who are looking for sexual contacts. The general public has a right to be spared such scenes. Not only children, but adults too, should be able to visit public facilities without being exposed to them. The impersonation of women by men, too, is unnatural, indecent, and offensive, and should be forbidden in public places, particularly where children may be exposed to it.

2. Homosexual activity is unnatural.

3. Homosexual activity is dangerous. Its practice by some people encourages others to do the same, and, if everyone or even if large numbers of persons were to become homosexuals, there would be no future for the human race. Furthermore, homosexuality may lead, as Lord Devlin pointed out, to a general moral breakdown and to the destruction of vital social institutions.

4. Homosexuals tend to molest children. Even the most liberal advocates of legal reform in this area agree that children and teenagers should not be fair game for homosexuals; but the effect of liberalized legislation would be to bring the homosexuals out into the open, to increase their numbers, and to encourage them to prey upon the young boys whom they find most attractive.

5. When homosexuals do seduce youngsters, they often initiate them irreversibly into their way of life. These young people are then prevented from having a normal sex life, and often end up, either unable or unwilling to be married and to make their contribution to society in a normal way; or, if they do marry, they find that they are irresistibly drawn back into the perverted forms of sexual activity that they learned when they were younger, thus causing irreparable harm to their wives and to any children that they may have had, and to society as a whole.

6. Homosexualty is a promiscuous way of life. Few homosexual relations are more than one-night stands, and fewer still have any semblance of permanence. Aside from the blatant immorality of such a life, it encourages the spread of veneral disease, and it leads to loneliness, misery, and unhappiness for those who become entangled in it. It is virtually impossible for homosexuals to enjoy warm and satisfactory personal relationships such as are often found in normal, heterosexual marriage.

7. Those who become entangled in the homosexual life are afflicted by serious psychological problems—by feelings of guilt, by insecurity, and by constant fear of disgrace and ruin.

8. Homosexuals are unreliable and are poor risks. They should not be given sensitive jobs, either in government or in industry, for they have proved themselves to be more likely than others to reveal secrets for sexual favors, or to submit to blackmail attempts that play upon their sexual weaknesses. And they should particularly be kept from jobs that may bring them into close contact with youngsters, such as teaching, camp counseling, and the like, because they are more likely than the normal person might be to use their positions to corrupt the morals of their young charges.

For all these reasons, then, homosexuality is condemned and legal sanctions against it are maintained. If the legal barriers are lowered, it is said, those who practice homosexuality will come out into the open, those who do not practice it may be encouraged to do so, and the evil consequences of a general lowering of moral standards, of family breakdown, of a spread of venereal disease, of psychological harm to those who are inducted into the homosexual life, and the rest, are sure to follow.

AN ANALYSIS OF THE ARGUMENTS

Now let us examine the facts, as far as they are known. We shall skip over certain objections initially, because they involve special problems of interpretation, and deal first with those that can be disposed of without extensive analysis.

Point 4, on the tendency of homosexuals to molest children, is based upon a confusion between homosexuality and pedophilia. The latter, a tendency on the part of an adult to find sexual satisfaction in relations with children, is not peculiar to homosexuals, for there are many heterosexuals who molest little girls; and homosexuals have no particular inclination, as a group, to seek out young boys—no more, at any rate, than their heterosexual counterparts.[16]

Most heterosexual men confine their sexual activities to women who are approximately their own age. As they (that is, the men) grow older, they tend to prefer sex partners of their own age and station in life, unless they are interested in a very temporary sort of affair. Even then, however, they will seldom consider entering into a sexual relationship with a girl who is under-age, either because of fear of the possible consequences—legal and social—that may follow upon such an encounter or because they find the contemplation of such a relationship distasteful. The attitudes of homosexual men seem to run along lines parallel to these. The scientific studies that have been made of homosexuals tend, almost universally, to reveal that homosexuals are no more prone to molest children than are heterosexuals. Scholars in the field now distinguish carefully between homosexuality and pedophilia, recognizing that there is no demonstrable connection between one and the other.[17] To be sure, liberalized legislation, doing away with criminal penalties for homosexual behavior between consenting adults in private, would "bring the homosexuals into the open"—or some of them, at least; but there is no convincing evidence that it would encourage homosexuals to engage in widespread pedophilia, and it would not reduce the penalties for pedophilia in any case.

Point 5, on the long-term results of pedophilia, thus becomes somewhat academic, for once a clear distinction is drawn between homosexuality and pedophilia, and between liberalization of the laws governing homosexual behavior on the one hand, and laws penalizing pedophilia on the other, it becomes clear that the one is not necessarily related to the other.

Point 6, that homosexuality is a promiscuous way of life, that it encourages the spread of venereal disease, and that it leads to loneliness and an absence of warm and permanent relationships, seems to be borne out by the available evidence. Few homosexual relationships last very long. On rare occasions they may last for many years. But they lack the stabilizing protections offered by the laws of marriage and the birth of children. They are easily dissolved; one partner merely packs his bags and moves out. There are no social sanctions—formal or informal—against the breakup of a homosexual union. On the contrary, the majority culture encourages such breakups. Most homosexual relationships are anonymous, lasting no more than a single night. Every description that I have been able to find of a "typical" homosexual's life reveals that very few homosexuals are able to establish lasting relationships with one another, and many of them are not interested in doing so. Many homosexual gathering places are specifically designed to encourage promiscuity. It is not uncommon for a given individual to have sexual relations with a number of individuals in a single night.[18] D. W. Cory, himself a homosexual, has written two highly regarded books on homosexuality under a pseudonym. In the first edition of his book *The Homosexual in*

America, Cory defended the life of the homosexual and mounted one of the most widely hailed defenses of the rights of the homosexual in recent decades. Ten years later, in the preface to the second edition of his book, he wrote regretfully about his failure to emphasize the abnormality, the sordidness, of many aspects of the homosexual's life. Reflecting on attempts of some defenders of the homosexual life to portray it as essentially normal but nonconformist, different from that of most people but every bit as healthy, Cory concluded that such attempts to defend the homosexual were misguided because the premises upon which they were founded were false. The homosexual's behavior, or his desire for homosexual behavior, he said, "is a symptom of an emotional maladjustment." He argued that the psychological disturbances of homosexuals should not be glossed over in order to win points in the fight for civil rights for them. "If I may be permitted a few analogies, the alcoholic is disturbed, but is not expelled from the society of man. The woman who engages in prostitution is likewise suffering from unhealthy motivations, as is the narcotic addict. To emphasize the disturbance of these individuals is not to betray them to some mortal enemy; in fact, when this is done by friends who would defend their rights, it could be the greatest aid they can be given." [19]

"The most serious problem for those who live in the gay world," according to Martin Hoffman, "is the great difficulty they have in establishing stable paired relationships with one another." [20] He reports this not as his own personal judgment, but as the opinion of homosexuals themselves. "In general," he says, "they are very unhappy about the grave difficulties which inhibit the formation of stable relationships. They are continually looking for more permanence in their socio-sexual lives and are all too often unable to find it." [21] Hoffman, in attempting to find the reasons for this, reduces them to the general male penchant for variety, one not shared by females, which leads, therefore, to a significant difference in the stability of lesbian relationships as opposed to those of male homosexuals. In his report on female sexual behavior, Kinsey noted that

> among all peoples, everywhere in the world, it is understood that the male is more likely than the female to desire sexual relations with a variety of partners. . . . The female has a greater capacity for being faithful to a single partner. . . . [She] is more likely to consider that she has a greater responsibility than the male has in maintaining the home and in caring for the offspring of any sexual relationship, and she is generally more inclined to consider the moral implications of her sexual behavior.[22]

Kinsey attributes this difference in behavior to the male's tendency to be more easily aroused than the female.

In addition to the lack of legal sanctions noted earlier, Hoffman notes how difficult it would be for a homosexual couple to live the kind of life that a heterosexual couple might lead. Homosexual couples are not likely to be invited to dinner parties, picnics, and family outings, for example. A business executive would ordinarily be ill advised to bring his male "wife" to the company's annual dinner dance at the country club. The social barriers, the legal barriers, the lack of legal sanction for a "gay marriage," the natural male propensity for sexual variety, if there is one, all contribute to the unstable nature of homosexual relations. In addition, there may be one further factor that could outweigh them all, though if it exists (as it clearly does in at least some cases), it may be conditioned by the existence of some of the others. This is the desire on the part of many homosexuals *not* to form lasting partnerships, but to keep their relations on a strictly temporary, anonymous, physical basis. Many homosexuals do not want a permanent relationship, possibly because of guilt feelings that make it undesirable, from their point of view, to attempt to develop the warm and intimate relationship that hetero-sexual couples strive to achieve and preserve, and that some lesbians seem to be able to maintain.

Point 7, on the psychological problems of homosexuals, and their fears of disgrace and ruin if they are found out, have already been touched on. Many of these problems are undoubtedly conditioned by the attitude taken by society toward homosexuals and toward homosexual relationships. There would be no fear of disgrace and ruin if society accepted homosexuality with equanimity; the strong likelihood of disgrace and ruin if a homosexual is found out constitutes excellent justification for his fears.

A detailed inquiry into the psychology of homosexuals is beyond the scope of this chapter. The results of those scientific studies that have been made are mixed. Some of them are rather startling, suggesting either that some-thing is wrong with the tests or that certain preconceptions about homosex-uals are not justified. For example, one test administered to a group of active homosexuals revealed that they were more "masculine," in terms defined by the test, than the average soldier.[23] According to some authorities, certain psychological tests will successfully distinguish homosexual males from heterosexual males three times out of four, but others maintain that at least some kinds of homosexuals cannot be identified by these tests.[24] In one test that has a reputation for a fairly high degree of accuracy in picking out persons suffering from mental illness, or liable to suffer from some form of neurotic breakdown, no substantial difference was noted between the scores of overt homosexuals and those of persons with a heterosexual bent. And in another investigation, based on a study of volunteers from American homosexual organizations, it was found that homosexuals were as well adjusted as their heterosexual counterparts. In fact, according to the experts who examined the tests, two thirds of those examined seemed to be average or above average insofar as psychological adjustment was concerned.[25]

There is room for some doubt as to the soundness of the arguments that have been offered in support of the view that homosexuality is a psychological disease, or that it is symptomatic of some form of mental illness. No doubt many homosexuals suffer from neurotic symptoms, as do many heterosexuals. Indeed, it would be surprising if they did not, in view of the persecution to which they may be subjected if they are found out and the anxiety to which such potential persecution is likely to give rise. Psychiatrists and psycho-analysts who generalize about the neuroses of homosexuals, based upon their experiences with their patients, tend too often to forget that their experiences are confined to those homosexuals who come to them for help. There may be many homosexuals who never bother to see a psychiatrist or a psychoanalyst because they feel quite secure, having made what they consider to be a satisfactory adjustment to their deviant mode of living. Of course, if the criterion for mental health is that the subject be living a "normal" or non-deviant life, then all homosexuals would be psychologically ill by definition; but such a conclusion would reveal less about homosexuals than it would about the predilections of those who had chosen to define their terms in that way. As Freud once wrote, "Inversion [i.e., homosexuality] is found in people who exhibit no other serious deviations from the normal. It is similarly found in people whose efficiency is unimpaired, and who are indeed distinguished by specially high intellectual development and ethical culture." [26] Many persons who engage in homosexual behavior seem to lead normal lives in every other respect. Whether they are more neurotic, on the whole, than those who prefer to engage in heterosexual behavior must remain, for the time being at least, an open question.

One point, however, should be made here. If it is true that homosexuals suffer from feelings of guilt and anxiety because of the social and legal sanctions that may be invoked against them if their sexual preferences are exposed, some of that guilt and anxiety might be relieved if the sanctions were removed. Many of the psychological problems that afflict homosexuals are a result of the combination of their homosexual propensities and society's attitude toward them, and not the former alone. Homosexuals may be compared, in this regard, to Jews, Negroes, and other members of minority groups that have been subjected to persecution and to social and legal disabilities. Jews, Negroes, and others may have suffered from feelings of anxiety, from inferiority complexes, and from a variety of other neuroses because of the persecution to which they were subjected. Their persecutors have on occasion attempted to justify their own behavior by pointing out how the members of these groups tend to "stick together," to be insecure, to have difficulty relating to people, and so on, assuming that these personality traits were a result of their personality makeup, when in fact they were a reaction to the persecutions and the disabilities to which they were exposed. Much the same thing may be true of those homosexuals who suffer from psychological problems. If the social barriers were eliminated, many homosexuals, freed of the stigma that presently attaches to them and of the fear of the consequences of exposure, might make an excellent adjustment.

Point 8, on the unreliability of homosexuals, their susceptibility to black-mail attempts, and the dangers of putting them into positions of trust with youngsters, is a mixed bag. From what has already been said on the distinction that must be drawn between homosexuality and pedophilia, it should be apparent that there is no justification for keeping homosexuals out of positions of trust where young boys are concerned. It would be as sensible to say that heterosexuals should not be permitted to serve as teachers or counselors where girls are concerned. In either case, the issue is not so much the homosexual or heterosexual propensities of the individual concerned as his proclivity to engage in sexual relations with underage persons. Certainly, if there is reasonable evidence that a given individual has such inclinations, whether he is homosexual or heterosexual, a responsible administrator will refrain from entrusting him with the care of youngsters. But there is considerable evidence that some homosexuals, who are not inclined to pedophilia, have made excellent teachers, counselors, and advisers to young people. Their talents should not be lost because of their personal sexual habits when the latter do not affect their conduct vis-à-vis their young charges.

On the problem of blackmail, there is general agreement among the authorities in the field that homosexuals are peculiarly susceptible to blackmail attempts. In a report submitted to the Committee on Expenditures in the Executive Departments (i.e., to the committee having to do with civil service employment policies) of the Eighty-first Congress, homosexuals were declared to be unsuitable for government employment because of their frequent victimization by blackmailers who threaten to expose their sexual deviations.

> Law enforcement officers have informed the subcommittee that there are gangs of blackmailers who make a regular practice of preying upon the homosexual. The modus operandi in these homosexual blackmail cases usually follow[s] the same general pattern. The victim, who is a homosexual, has managed to conceal his perverted activities and usually enjoys a good reputation in the community. The blackmailers, by one means or another, discover that the victim is addicted to homosexuality and under the threat of disclosure they extort money from him. These blackmailers often impersonate police officers in carrying out their blackmail schemes. Many cases have come to the attention of the police where highly respected individuals have paid out substantial sums of money to blackmailers over a long period of time rather than risk the disclosure of their homosexual activities. The police believe that this type of blackmail racket is much more extensive than is generally known, because they have found that most of the victims are very hesitant to bring the matter to the attention of the authorities.[27]

It should be remembered, though, that homosexuals are not unique in their vulnerability to blackmail and extortion. Heterosexuals, particularly those who are married, are at least as vulnerable as homosexuals are. More than one man has been ruined by a well-endowed prostitute working for an intelligence organization who has seduced him and then, after gathering incriminating evidence, threatened to expose him. The Profumo-Keeler-Davies scandal involved no homosexuality at all, but shook the government of Great Britain to its foundations.

It has been argued that if society were less stringent in its application of sanctions against homosexuals, the latter would be less likely to succumb to blackmail, and the risks in hiring them in any position would be minimal. But there is some reason to doubt whether this is entirely accurate. Italian psychiatrists have been quoted as saying that the threat of social exposure is often used quite effectively for purposes of blackmail in Italy, where homosexual practices are not subject to formal legal sanctions.[28] This would indicate that where there is considerable public repugnance to such behavior, even when it is not the subject of legal penalties, the opportunity for blackmail always exists. The law itself has recognized the vulnerability of the homosexual to blackmail in a number of ways, not all of them to the detriment of the homosexual. William Blackstone, who took a dim view of homosexuality, argued that it was "a crime which ought to be strictly and impartially proved, and then as strictly and impartially punished. But it is an offense of so dark a nature, so easily charged, and the negative so difficult to be proved, that the accusation should be clearly made out: for, if false, it deserves a punishment inferior only to that of the crime itself." [29] Modern courts have held that a threat to accuse a person of sodomy is "sufficiently equivalent to force and violence to constitute robbery if the threatened person parts with money because of the threat." American courts have held that the crime of sodomy is "so abominable, . . . and so destructive is even the accusation of it, of all social right and privilege, that the law considers that the accusation is a coercion which men cannot resist." Another court held that although the offense of solicitation for sodomy is a relatively minor one, where the law is concerned, rated less serious than reckless driving, "in the practical world of everyday living it is a major accusation." "It follows," the court said, "that threatened accusation of this offense is the easiest of blackmail methods. The horror of the ordinary citizen at the thought of such an accusation may impel him to comply with a demand for money under such a threat." [30] The court therefore concluded that the victims of such threats were entitled to special protections in order to prevent unwarranted irreparable destruction of their reputations.

The Wolfenden Commission concluded, on the question of blackmail, that there may be some truth to the charge that homosexuals are especially susceptible, though other persons with certain "weaknesses" are liable to be compromised to about the same degree—people who are prone to become drunk, for example, as well as gamblers and persons who may get into compromising heterosexual situations. "While it may be a valid ground for excluding from certain forms of employment men who indulge in homosexual behavior," the Commission concluded, "it does not, in our view, constitute a sufficient reason for making their private sexual behaviour an offence in itself."[31] This question, more fundamental than the question of the kinds of employment from which homosexuals might properly be excluded because of special problems that they might have to face, will be considered later.

Now that these points have been disposed of, it is possible to return to the first three points, which may require somewhat more extended discussion.

Point 1 concerns the offensiveness of homosexual conduct, and remarks that public displays of homosexual behavior, because they are disgusting and offensive to the ordinary man, should be outlawed, for the general public has a right to use public facilities without being assailed by such offensive scenes.

Most of those who advocate reform of the laws on homosexuality would agree with at least a part of these observations. Not only homosexual relations, but also heterosexual relations are offensive when they are acted out in public, at least to a sufficiently large number of people to justify some control over such public manifestations. A husband and wife have every right to engage in sexual intercourse with one another, but not in full view of the public on a beach, in a park, or in an airliner, as one couple is alleged to have done recently. The public has a right not to be assailed by offensive smells and noises, as the law has recognized for many centuries. Loud music emanating from transistor radios in public places is an outrageous interference with the rights of those who go to those places to enjoy their leisure in peace and quiet. The public has the right to zone certain areas in such a way as to keep factories, pig farms, and chicken coops, with their noise, their smells, and their filth, at a distance from places where people reside. By extension, it is not unreasonable to require those who would perform acts which may in themselves be harmless or even desirable but are offensive to substantial numbers of people when they are performed in public, to confine such behavior to the privacy of their homes, their private clubs, or such other private places as they may establish for such purposes. Whether the behavior is heterosexual, then, or homosexual, or even if it is neither (e.g., nudity), the public has a right not to be exposed to its manifestations if there is a general consensus that such manifestations are offensive. To be sure, there must be limitations on the public's right to prohibit public manifestations of what it finds "disgusting" or "offensive." The public may be offended by a demonstration for women's rights, for example, or for civil rights for black citizens; it may find beards disgusting; it may object to the display of a Star of David on the outside walls of a synagogue. Or—as in the Soviet Union or in some Moslem nations—the public may be offended by the display of a crucifix outside a church. Where does one draw the line between what the public may properly prohibit on the ground that it is offended by its display and what the public may not prohibit on such grounds?

The answer to this question depends, to a large extent, upon the extent of one's commitment to freedom of expression. Where freedom of expression comes into conflict with the public's sensibilities, a choice must be made between upholding the former and protecting the latter. In a free society the public must suffer more frequent ruffled feelings than it would in a more rigidly controlled society. Or it must learn to overlook some displays that it might otherwise consider offensive. In Nazi Germany those who were offended by the sight of a bearded Jew were able to demonstrate their disgust and to relieve it somewhat by pulling the beard that offended them, by slapping the face behind the beard, and, if they were sorely offended, they could kill the man who dared to display himself in public, and be congratulated for having rid the city of such an obscene person. Where the public is thoroughly committed to freedom of expression, it will learn to overlook displays of books that cater to the lowest and most sensation-seeking elements of the reading public; it will look the other way when girlie shows are advertised, concluding that such shows may be patronized by those who find their pleasures there and that their proprietors have as much right to advertise their existence as producers of Shakespeare have to advertise theirs for the benefit of those who find their pleasures in watching performances of *Hamlet* and *Macbeth*. It is dangerous to use the public sense of outrage and disgust as a measure of the propriety of a given public display, for nothing is more fickle than the public's standards of taste. Those who set themselves up as the guardians of public morality are always ready, if given the power, to outlaw what offends them rather than to give it an opportunity to win acceptance or rejection in the free market.

No easy criterion for distinguishing public displays that should be permitted from those that may properly be forbidden exists. Clearly, the fact that a given form of display disgusts some citizens, or even a majority of the citizens of a given community, is not enough, because, as we have just seen, such a criterion can lead to the banning of modes of personal behavior, ways of life, and expressions of religious, political, or other beliefs that should be permitted in a society of free men. It would be very neat if some general rule or principle that would apply to every case, enabling us to determine, in some logical fashion, what forms of behavior should be permitted and what should be forbidden, could be found. The infinite variety of conditions to which human beings are subject and their manifold desires, interests, and practices, as well as the constantly changing texture of human society make it impossible to arrive at such a rule. Nevertheless, reasonable restrictions on free expression may be necessary in some circumstances. Not only sexual freedom, but even so fundamental a liberty as freedom of religion may have to give way before other vital interests. If a religious cult conceives its divine mission in terms that threaten the very existence of the state, clearly the state has a right to interfere with the subversive activities of that cult. If a tenet of a religious sect obliges its members to engage in behavior that is harmful to other persons, then the state, as guardian of the welfare of its citizens, has a right to outlaw that practice. If a group of persons adopts a religious or moral principle that would run counter to the established laws and practices of the state, then they must either convince the legislators of that state to change the law, or they must refrain from putting their principle into practice—as the Mormons have, for example, with regard to the principle that polygamy is a religious duty, as Jews have when their religious laws of divorce come into conflict with those of the state in which they live, and as Jehovah's Witnesses do, albeit unwillingly, when one of their children is given a blood transfusion under court order even though such a transfusion is contrary to their religious beliefs. Still another alternative, although it is a harsh one, is open to the citizens of all free societies. If the members of a religious sect are unable to persuade the legislators to change the laws of their society to conform with their religious views, they may leave and settle elsewhere, presumably in a place more congenial to their religious practices. In closed societies, such as that of the Soviet Union, the option of emigration is unfortunately not available except at great risk and at great cost to those who wish to leave. Some abridgements of religious freedom then, and of freedom of expression, may not be inconsistent with the idea of a free and open society.

Now, if such fundamental freedoms as these are subject to abridgement under certain conditions, the freedom to engage in acts of public sexual activity, which has never been considered a liberty whose existence is fundamental to the existence of a democratic society, may be subject to reasonable restrictions. Even religious manifestations may properly be abridged, within limits, when they become abhorrent to the general public. A religious sect that erects a giant neon cross on top of a mountain overlooking a city may be prevailed upon to remove the structure—not because it represents a particular faith, but because it is unsightly and unaesthetic and because it detracts from the beauty of the city's skyline. Unaesthetic and unsightly public behavior on the part of individuals may be subject to similar reasonable restrictions, so long as such restrictions are not used to suppress the free flow of ideas and information. In the same way, public displays of sexuality may appropriately be forbidden without seriously compromising a government's commitment to freedom of expression. Most of those who have advocated the liberalization of laws dealing with homosexual behavior have confined their advocacy to a demand that prohibitions of *private* relations between consenting adults be relaxed. The Wolfenden Report was uncompromising in its attitude toward public manifestations of homosexuality, which it felt should continue to be forbidden, just as street solicitation by prostitutes for heterosexual relations would be forbidden even if prostitution were legalized.

A distinction should be drawn between overt homosexual activity—such as solicitation, mutual masturbation, or homosexual intercourse—and mannerisms or clothing styles that are supposed to be common to homosexuals. Most liberals seem to be in agreement that the former may properly be forbidden when they take place in public places. As for the latter, if there are persons who are so sensitive as to be offended by such displays, who find them unappealing or abhorrent, it would no doubt be best for them to look away. Where personal liberty comes into conflict with ultrasensitive aesthetic tastes, the balances should be weighted on the side of liberty.

Point 2, on the "unnaturalness" of homosexuality, raises the question of the meaning of *nature, natural,* and similar terms. Theologians and other moralists have said they violate the "natural law," and that they are therefore immoral and ought to be prohibited by the state.

The word *nature* has a built-in ambiguity that can lead to serious misunderstandings. When something is said to be "natural" or in confirmity with "natural law" or the "law of nature," this may mean either (1) that it is in conformity with the descriptive laws of nature, or (2) that it is not artificial, that man has not imposed his will or his devices upon events or conditions as they exist or would have existed without such interference.

1. *The descriptive laws of nature.* The laws of nature, as these are understood by the scientist, differ from the laws of man. The former are purely descriptive, whereas the latter are prescriptive. When a scientist says that water boils at 212° Fahrenheit or that the volume of a gas varies directly with the heat that is applied to it and inversely with the pressure, he means merely that as a matter of recorded and observable fact, pure water under standard conditions always boils at precisely 212° Fahrenheit and that as a matter of observed fact, the volume of a gas rises as it is heated and falls as pressure is applied to it. These "laws" merely *describe* the manner in which physical substances *actually behave.* They differ from municipal and federal laws in that they *do not prescribe behavior.* Unlike manmade laws, natural laws are not passed by any legislator or group of legislators; they are not proclaimed or announced; they impose no obligation upon anyone or anything; their "violation" entails no penalty, and there is no reward for "following" them or "abiding by" them. When a scientist says that the air in a tire "obeys" the laws of nature that "govern" gases, he does *not* mean that the air, having been informed that it *ought* to behave in a certain way, behaves appropriately under the right conditions. He means, rather, that as a matter of fact, the air in a tire *will* behave like all other gases. In saying that Boyle's law "governs" the behavior of gases, he means merely that gases do, as a matter of fact, behave in accordance with Boyle's law, and that Boyle's law enables one to predict accurately what will happen to a given quantity of a gas as its pressure is raised; he does *not* mean to suggest that some heavenly voice has proclaimed that all gases should henceforth behave in accordance with the terms of Boyle's law and that a ghostly policeman patrols the world, ready to mete out punishments to any gases that "violate" the heavenly decree. In fact, according to the scientist, it does not make sense to speak of a natural law being violated. For if there were a true exception to a so-called law of nature, the exception would require a change in the description of those phenomena, and the "law" would have been shown to be no law at all. The laws of nature are revised as scientists discover new phenomena that require new refinements in their descriptions of the way things actually happen. In this respect they differ fundamentally from human laws, which are revised periodically by legislators who are not so interested in *describing* human behavior as they are in *prescribing* what human behavior *should* be.

2. *The artificial as a form of the unnatural.* On occasion when we say that

something is not natural, we mean that it is a product of human artifice. My typewriter is not a natural object, in this sense, for the substances of which it is composed have been removed from their natural state—the state in which they existed before men came along—and have been transformed by a series of chemical and physical and mechanical processes into other substances. They have been rearranged into a whole that is quite different from anything found in nature. In short, my typewriter is an artificial object. In this sense, the clothing that I wear as I lecture before my students is not natural, for it has been transformed considerably from the state in which it was found in nature; and my wearing of clothing as I lecture before my students is also not natural, in this sense, for in my natural state, before the application of anything artificial, before any human interference with things as they are, I am quite naked. Human laws, being artificial conventions designed to exercise a degree of control over the natural inclinations and propensities of men, may in this sense be considered to be unnatural.

Now when theologians and moralists speak of homosexuality, contraception, abortion, and other forms of human behavior as being unnatural, and say that for that reason such behavior must be considered to be wrong, in what sense are they using the word *unnatural*? Are they saying that homosexual behavior and the use of contraceptives are contrary to the scientific laws of nature, are they saying that they are artificial forms of behavior, or are they using the terms *natural* and *unnatural* in some third sense?

They cannot mean that homosexual behavior (to stick to the subject presently under discussion) violates the laws of nature in the first sense, for, as we have pointed out, in *that* sense it is impossible to violate the laws of nature. Those laws, being merely descriptive of what actually does happen, would have to *include* homosexual behavior if such behavior does actually take place. Even if the defenders of the theological view that homosexuality is unnatural were to appeal to a statistical analysis by pointing out that such behavior is not normal from a statistical point of view, and therefore not what the laws of nature require, it would be open to their critics to reply that any descriptive law of nature must account for and incorporate all statistical deviations, and that the laws of nature, in this sense, do not *require* anything. These critics might also note that the best statistics available reveal that about half of all American males engage in homosexual activity at some time in their lives, and that a very large percentage of American males have exclusively homosexual relations for a fairly extensive period of time; from which it would follow that such behavior is natural, for them, at any rate, in this sense of the word *natural*.

If those who say that homosexual behavior is unnatural are using the term *unnatural* in the second sense, it is difficult to see why they should be fussing over it. Certainly nothing is intrinsically wrong with going against nature (if that is how it should be put) in this sense. That which is artificial is often far better than what is natural. Artificial homes seem, at any rate, to be more suited to human habitation and more conducive to longer life and better health than caves and other natural shelters. There are distinct advantages to the use of such unnatural (i.e. artificial) amenities as clothes, furniture, and books. Although we may dream of an idyllic return to nature in our more wistful moments, we would soon discover, as Thoreau did in his attempt to escape from the artificiality of civilization, that needles and thread, knives and matches, ploughs and nails, and countless other products of human artifice are essential to human life. We would discover, as Plato pointed out in the *Republic*, that no man can be truly self-sufficient. Some of the by-products of industry are less than desirable; but neither industry itself, nor the products of industry, are intrinsically evil, even though both are unnatural in this sense of the word.

Interference with nature is not evil in itself. Nature, as some writers have put it, must be tamed. In some respects man must look upon it as an enemy to be conquered. If nature were left to its own devices, without the intervention of human artifice, men would be consumed with disease, they would be plagued by insects, they would be chained to the places where they were born with no means of swift communication or transport, and they would suffer the discomforts and the torments of wind and weather and flood and fire with no practical means of combating any of them. Interfering with nature, doing battle with nature, using human will and reason and skill to thwart what might otherwise follow from the conditions that prevail in the world, is a peculiarly human enterprise, one that can hardly be condemned merely because it does what is not natural.

Homosexual behavior can hardly be considered to be unnatural in this sense. There is nothing "artificial" about such behavior. On the contrary, it is quite natural, in this sense, to those who engage in it. And even if it were not, even if it were quite artificial, this is not in itself a ground for condemning it.

It would seem, then, that those who condemn homosexuality as an unnatural form of behavior must mean something else by the word *unnatural*, something not covered by either of the preceding definitions. A third possibility is this:

3. *Anything uncommon or abnormal is unnatural.* If this is what is meant by those who condemn homosexuality on the ground that it is unnatural, it is quite obvious that their condemnation cannot be accepted without further argument. For the fact that a given form of behavior is uncommon provides no justification for condemning it. Playing viola in a string quartet is no doubt an uncommon form of human behavior. I do not know what percentage of the human race engages in such behavior, or what percentage of his life any given violist devotes to such behavior, but I suspect that the number of such people must be very small indeed, and that the total number of man-hours spent in such activity would justify our calling that form of activity uncommon, abnormal (in the sense that it is statistically not the kind of thing that people are ordinarily inclined to do), and therefore unnatural, in this sense of the word. Yet there is no reason to suppose that such uncommon,

abnormal behavior is, by virtue of its uncommonness, deserving of condemnation or ethically or morally wrong. On the contrary, many forms of behavior are praised precisely because they are so uncommon. Great artists, poets, musicians, and scientists are "abnormal" in this sense; but clearly the world is better off for having them, and it would be absurd to condemn them or their activities for their failure to be common and normal. If homosexual behavior is wrong, then, it must be for some reason other than its "unnaturalness" in this sense of the word.

4. *Any use of an organ or an instrument that is contrary to its principal purpose or function is unnatural.* Every organ and every instrument—perhaps even every creature—has a function to perform, one for which it is particularly designed. Any use of those instruments and organs that is consonant with their purposes is natural and proper, but any use that is inconsistent with their principal functions is unnatural and improper, and to that extent, evil or harmful. Human teeth, for example, are admirably designed for their principal functions—biting and chewing the kinds of food suitable for human consumption. But they are not particularly well suited for prying the caps from beer bottles. If they are used for the latter purpose, which is not natural to them, they are liable to crack or break under the strain. The abuse of one's teeth leads to their destruction and to a consequent deterioration in one's overall health. If they are used only for their proper function, however, they may continue to serve well for many years. Similarly, a given drug may have a proper function. If used in the furtherance of that end, it can preserve life and restore health. But if it is abused, and employed for purposes for which it was never intended, it may cause serious harm and even death. The natural uses of things are good and proper, but their unnatural uses are bad and harmful.

What we must do, then, is to find the proper use, or the true purpose, of each organ in our bodies. Once we have discovered that, we will know what constitutes the natural use of each organ, and what constitutes an unnatural, abusive, and potentially harmful employment of the various parts of our bodies. If we are rational, we will be careful to confine our behavior to our proper functions and to refrain from unnatural behavior. According to those philosophers who follow this line of reasoning, the way to discover the "proper" use of any organ is to determine what it is peculiarly suited to do. The eye is suited for seeing, the ear for hearing, the nerves for transmitting impulses from one part of the body to another, and so on.

What are the sex organs peculiarly suited to do? Obviously, they are peculiarly suited to enable men and women to reproduce their own kind. No other organ in the body is capable of fulfilling that function. It follows, according to those who follow the natural-law line, that the "proper" or "natural" function of the sex organs is reproduction, and that strictly speaking, any use of those organs for other purposes is unnatural, abusive, potentially harmful, and therefore wrong. The sex organs have been given to us in order to enable us to maintain the continued existence of mankind on this earth. All perversions—including masturbation, homosexual behavior, and heterosexual intercourse that deliberately frustrates the design of the sexual organs—are unnatural and bad. As Pope Pius XI once said, "Private individuals have no other power over the members of their bodies than that which pertains to their natural ends." [32]

But the problem is not so easily resolved. Is it true that every organ has one and only one proper function? A hammer may have been designed to pound nails, and it may perform that particular job best. But it is not sinful to employ a hammer to crack nuts if I have no other more suitable tool immediately available. The hammer, being a relatively versatile tool, may be employed in a number of ways. It has no one "proper" or "natural" function. A woman's eyes are well adapted to seeing, it is true. But they seem also to be well adapted to flirting. Is a woman's use of her eyes for the latter purpose sinful merely because she is not using them, at that moment, for their "primary" purpose of seeing? Our sexual organs are uniquely adapted for procreation, but that is obviously not the only function for which they are adapted. Human beings may—and do—use those organs for a great many other purposes, and it is difficult to see why any *one* use should be considered to be the only proper one. The sex organs, for one thing, seem to be particularly well adapted to give their owners and others intense sensations of pleasure. Unless one believes that pleasure itself is bad, there seems to be little reason to believe that the use of the sex organs for the production of pleasure in oneself or in others is evil. In view of the peculiar design of these organs, with their great concentration of nerve endings, it would seem that they were designed (if they *were* designed) with that very goal in mind, and that their use for such purposes would be no more unnatural than their use for the purpose of procreation.

Nor should we overlook the fact that human sex organs may be and are used to express, in the deepest and most intimate way open to man, the love of one person for another. Even the most ardent opponents of "unfruitful" intercourse admit that sex does serve this function. They have accordingly conceded that a man and his wife may have intercourse even though she is pregnant, or past the age of child bearing, or in the infertile period of her menstrual cycle.

Human beings are remarkably complex and adaptable creatures. Neither they nor their organs can properly be compared to hammers or to other tools. The analogy quickly breaks down. The generalization that a given organ or instrument has one and only one proper function does not hold up, even with regard to the simplest manufactured tools, for, as we have seen, a tool may be used for more than one purpose—less effectively than one especially designed for a given task, perhaps, but "properly" and certainly not *sinfully*. A woman may use her eyes not only to see and to flirt, but also to earn money —if she is, for example, an actress or a model. Though neither of the latter functions seems to have been a part of the original "design," if one may speak sensibly of *design* in this context, of the eye, it is difficult to see why such a use of the eyes of a woman should be considered sinful, perverse, or un-natural. Her sex organs have the unique capacity of producing ova and nur-turing human embryos, under the right conditions; but why should any other use of those organs, including their use to bring pleasure to their owner or to someone else, or to manifest love to another person, or even, perhaps, to earn money, be regarded as perverse, sinful, or unnatural? Similarly, a man's sexual organs possess the unique capacity of causing the generation of an-other human being, but if a man chooses to use them for pleasure, or for the expression of love, or for some other purpose—so long as he does not inter-fere with the rights of some other person—the fact that his sex organs do have their unique capabilities does not constitute a convincing justification for condemning their other uses as being perverse, sinful, unnatural, or criminal. If a man "perverts" himself by wiggling his ears for the entertain-ment of his neighbors instead of using them exclusively for their "natural" function of hearing, no one thinks of consigning him to prison. If he abuses his teeth by using them to pull staples from memos—a function for which teeth were clearly not designed—he is not accused of being immoral, de-graded, and degenerate. The fact that people *are* condemned for using their sex organs for their own pleasure or profit, or for that of others, may be more revealing about the prejudices and taboos of our society than it is about our perception of the true nature or purpose or "end" (whatever that might be) of our bodies.

To sum up, then, the proposition that any use of an organ that is contrary to its principal purpose or function is unnatural assumes that organs *have* a principal purpose or function, but this may be denied on the ground that the purpose or function of a given organ may vary according to the needs or desires of its owner. It may be denied on the ground that a given organ may have more than one principal purpose or function, and any attempt to call one use or another the only natural one seems to be arbitrary, if not question-begging. Also, the proposition suggests that what is unnatural is evil or depraved. This goes beyond the pure description of things, and enters into the problem of the evaluation of human behavior, which leads us to the fifth meaning of "natural."

5. *That which is natural is good, and whatever is unnatural is bad.* When one condemns homosexuality or masturbation or the use of contraceptives on the ground that it is unnatural, one implies that whatever is unnatural is bad, wrongful, or perverse. But as we have seen, in some senses of the word, the unnatural (i.e., the artificial) is often very good, whereas that which is natural (i.e., that which has not been subjected to human artifice or improve-ment) may be very bad indeed. Of course, interference with nature may be bad. Ecologists have made us more aware than we have ever been of the dangers of unplanned and uninformed interference with nature. But this is not to say that *all* interference with nature is bad. Every time a man cuts down a tree to make room for a home for himself, or catches a fish to feed himself or his family, he is interfering with nature. If men did not interfere

with nature, they would have no homes, they could eat no fish, and, in fact, they could not survive. What, then, can be meant by those who say that whatever is natural is good and whatever is unnatural is bad? Clearly, they cannot have intended merely to reduce the word *natural* to a synonym of *good, right,* and *proper,* and *unnatural* to a synonym of *evil, wrong, improper, corrupt,* and *depraved.* If that were all they had intended to do, there would be very little to discuss as to whether a given form of behavior might be proper even though it is not in strict conformity with someone's views of what is natural; for *good* and *natural* being synonyms, it would follow inevitably that whatever is good must be natural, and vice versa, by definition. This is certainly not what the opponents of homosexuality have been saying when they claim that homosexuality, being unnatural, is evil. For if it were, their claim would be quite empty. They would be saying merely that homosexuality, being evil, is evil—a redundancy that could as easily be reduced to the simpler assertion that homosexuality is evil. This assertion, however, is not an argument. Those who oppose homosexuality and other sexual "perversions" on the ground that they are "unnatural" are saying that there is some objectively identifiable quality in such behavior that is unnatural; and that that quality, once it has been identified by some kind of scientific observation, can be seen to be detrimental to those who engage in such behavior, or to those around them; and that *because* of the harm (physical, mental, moral, or spiritual) that results from engaging in any behavior possessing the attribute of unnaturalness, such behavior must be considered to be wrongful, and should be discouraged by society. "Unnaturalness" and "wrongfulness" are not synonyms, then, but different concepts. The problem with which we are wrestling is that we are unable to find a meaning for *unnatural* that enables us to arrive at the conclusion that homosexuality is unnatural or that if homosexuality is unnatural, it is therefore wrongful behavior. We have examined four common meanings of *natural* and *unnatural,* and have seen that none of them performs the task that it must perform if the advocates of this argument are to prevail. Without some more satisfactory explanation of the connection between the wrongfulness of homosexuality and its alleged unnaturalness, the argument of point 2 must be rejected.

Point 3, the last of the points in defense of legislation designed to punish homosexual behavior, is based upon the alleged social dangers of homosexuality. By permitting homosexuals to engage in their immoral behavior, it is said, others may be encouraged to do the same, leading to a general moral breakdown, to the destruction of the family—one of society's most fundamental institutions—and possibly to the destruction of the human race through a reduction in the number of fertile sexual unions.

In a time of overpopulation and a continuing population explosion, it would not be difficult to make a case in favor of *encouraging* sexual outlets that would not lead to an increase in population. Homosexuality might be one of them. It is unrealistic to suppose that homosexuality will become so popular, if it is permitted to flourish without molestation by the law, that the human species will be in danger of becoming extinct. At the moment, at any rate, it would seem that the world's governments should be less concerned with the control of homosexual behavior and more concerned with the control of heterosexual behavior. Even those countries that have made great efforts to educate their people in the techniques of birth control have thus far been unable to control their rising birth rates. The continuing rise in population, without a comparable rise in the production of food and other goods necessary for the maintenance of a decent standard of living, cannot but lead one to the conclusion that the suggestion that homosexuality could lead to extinction of the human species is, if not completely preposterous, at least so remote as to be unworthy of serious consideration for the remainder of this century. In some other age, perhaps, if human habits become quite different from what they are today, and if there is a serious shortage of manpower, the argument might have more plausibility.

Nevertheless, one may reasonably conclude that if homosexuality becomes more widely accepted, if the legal sanctions against it are abolished, and especially if the social consequences of homosexuality cease to be as serious as they are in most circles today, more people are likely to come out into the open as practicing homosexuals than there are at the present time. There can be no doubt that the risks associated with the so-called gay life make that life anything but attractive to most persons. The elimination of those risks may cause some persons who were deterred from sampling it, though they might have been curious enough to want to do so, to engage in some explorations that might lead some of them to adopt a way of life that most persons consider to be immoral or at least undesirable. The letters that authors of books and articles on homosexuality receive would indicate that many people who are homosexual, or are at least inclined to be homosexual, are deterred from following their inclinations by the obstacles placed in their way by society.[33] Removal of the obstacles would undoubtedly enable these people to come out into the open, to live as they choose without engaging in subterfuge, and to seek partners without fear of legal or social reprisals. This in turn could lead to the enticement into the homosexual life of many people who might otherwise have remained "straight." This effect, which may be regarded as undesirable from one point of view, may be seen as salutary from another. People who are now forced into hiding and ridden with feelings of guilt and persecution would be able to come out into the open, to admit to being what they are without shame and without fear. Surely this is a goal ardently to be desired in a society that prides itself on its tradition of freedom for all, including dissenters and members of minority groups.

As for the destruction of the family, the case seems to be very weak indeed. There is no evidence to support the suggestion that legitimation of homosexuality would lead to widespread breakdown in family life or to a failure on the part of many people to establish normal marriages and families. The argument itself is almost perverse, resting on the assumption, as it seems to do, that tens of thousands of people are eagerly awaiting the passage of legislation that would enable them to break away from the shackles of their heterosexuality so that they could do what they *really* want to do, namely, enter into relations with other men. I doubt whether a substantial number of men would be seriously interested in giving up their relations with women for the gay life, even if all the laws on sodomy were repealed and all the social stigma disappeared. Nevertheless, there is a certain plausibility in the argument that *some* families might be hurt by a legalization of homosexuality. Some men whose strongest inclinations are toward homosexual relations have married because of social or business pressures, but might be prepared to give up their families for a male lover if the sanctions against doing so were lifted. Here one must weigh the harm that is being done to many homosexuals because of the existence of these sanctions against the hurt that might come to some people as a result of their elimination. Not enough is known about the number of homosexually inclined persons who are married to enable us to make informed estimates of the number of families that could potentially be affected by such a problem; but because other factors would undoubtedly enter into any person's decision to break up his family and because some of these marriages are probably very unhappy anyway, the potential damage should not be exaggerated.

The problem of the possibility of a general moral breakdown has been dealt with in the earlier chapters of this section. It may be appropriate to observe here that Lord Devlin, the most articulate modern spokesman for the theory that society has the right to impose criminal sanctions upon those whose practices lead to moral breakdown, signed a joint letter to the editor of the London *Times* in 1965 in which he conceded that homosexuality does not constitute a threat to the moral foundations of the community, and argued in favor of the proposals of the Wolfenden Committee.[34] The problem of moral breakdown has more than one facet, as we shall see when we consider the methods employed by the police in tracking down homosexuals and effecting their arrest. These methods are so demoralizing and so corrupting that one could well argue that the legalization of homosexuality would be a boon to the community, for it would remove from the shoulders of the police department one of its most sordid and oppressive burdens and would eliminate one pretext for the use of corrupt practices by the police against the citizens of their communities.

The argument against the legalization of homosexuality on the ground of its danger to the community, then, is not convincing, for there is no evidence that open homosexuality would lead to a general breakdown in family life or even that it would seriously disrupt any large number of families presently existing; the chances of open homosexuality causing a general corruption in the morals of the community seem not to be very great; and the benefits that the community would reap from the new freedoms given to homosexuals, both in terms of the homosexuals' own relief from oppressive sanctions and in terms of the removal of a particularly sordid job from the shoulders of the police, would probably outweigh any harm that might ensue through the enlistment of new recruits into the gay life.

THE CASE AGAINST CRIMINAL SANCTIONS

We have seen how weak the case for criminal sanctions is. Wherever there is considerable doubt about the propriety of employing criminal sanctions against a given form of behavior, the most prudent path is the most conservative one—that is, the one that refrains from imposing sanctions or using the ponderous machinery of the criminal law and opts in favor of freedom of action. Where freedom is limited in doubtful cases, there is good reason to believe that the decision is not a good one and that society would be better off in the long run if the opposite course had been adopted. It goes without saying that those who find themselves hounded by the law for forms of behavior that harm neither society as a whole nor any of their neighbors feel that they are the victims of the gravest form of injustice. But society itself, far from being protected or improved by such legislation, may actually suffer because of it.

Consider the following case.

Case 3. The Down-and-Out Sailor

A few years ago Officer Arscott, of the District of Columbia police force, made a telephone call to a gentleman named Rittenour at the latter's home. Arscott represented himself to Rittenour as being "down and out," claimed that he did not have much money, and asked Rittenour if he could stay at the latter's home until he "could catch a bus out of town." On receiving Rittenour's permission to come to his home, Arscott and his companion, Officer Fochett, went to Rittenour's home, arriving there at about 9:30 in the evening. Fochett stationed himself outside the door and Arscott was admitted inside by Rittenour.

Arscott told Rittenour that he had just been discharged from the Navy and that he was "down and out." Rittenour asked Arscott where he had learned of his "place of business," and Arscott explained that he had heard about it from someone he had met at the bus station. Later in the conversation, Rittenour touched Arscott's genitals and made what Arscott considered to be a suggestion that they have homosexual relations together. Arscott called Fochett, who joined him in arresting Rittenour, and Rittenour then admitted that he had had homosexual relations with some of the men who came to his home.

In the penal code of the District of Columbia, there is a provision making it unlawful for any person "to make any obscene or indecent exposure of his or her person, or to make any lewd, obscene, or indecent sexual proposal, or to commit any other lewd, obscene, or indecent act in the District of Columbia, under penalty of not more than $300.00 fine or imprisonment of not more than ninety days, or both, for each and every such offense." [35] The court refused to convict Rittenour under this statute on a number of grounds: (1) The common-law conception of a lewd, obscene, or indecent act referred only to behavior that was open or public, but not to behavior that was done privately or in the presence of only one other person who solicited or consented to the act. (2) Officer Arscott led Rittenour to believe that he would consent, or at least not object, to the latter's homosexual advances. (3) Arscott's description of his own behavior—particularly his telephone call to Rittenour and his subsequent conversation with him while in his home—reveals clearly that Arscott suspected that Rittenour was a homosexual and embarked upon an investigation designed to confirm his suspicions. But that investigation involved entrapment, a procedure whereby Arscott trapped Rittenour into making a homosexual proposal so that Arscott could then arrest him. The court suggested that such entrapment invalidates an arrest. (4) Finally, the court held that Rittenour was arrested, tried, and convicted on a charge of being a homosexual, although homosexuality as such is not a crime. The court here distinguished carefully between homosexual behavior (especially homosexual behavior that is public and open) and homosexuality—that is, the tendency or inclination to engage in homosexual behavior. While homosexual behavior is a crime, the inclination to engage in such behavior is not.[36]

Because homosexuality almost invariably involves consent on the part of the persons involved, there is seldom a complainant against a homosexual. The exceptions are in cases where force has been used—very rare indeed with homosexuals—or where there has been an indecent assault on a non-homosexual, or where someone has been offended by a public display. Ordinarily, though, the police find it very difficult to enforce the laws against homosexual behavior, because they receive so few complaints from the general public. They are therefore forced, by the pressure of public opinion, which sometimes noisily demands that "something be done about the fags and the fairies," to resort to such tactics as those employed by Officer Arscott and his partner. In large cities, where the haunts of homosexuals are known to the police, patrols are regularly assigned to those places. Ordinarily, members of the vice squad, dressed in plain clothes, are assigned to such tasks. They sometimes dress in such a manner as to attract the attention of homosexuals who are cruising around, looking for a contact. They may also behave in a provocative manner. A British police expert has said, concerning such practices:

The term *agents provocateurs* is a justly pejorative name for young police decoys, whose squalid hunting ground is the public urinal. . . . I should have thought it apparent that the time had now come to discontinue this miserable stratagem in importuning cases, rather than go on denying that it exists. If the importuning is as difficult to detect as all that, it can't matter much to "public decency." [37]

A typical example of such entrapment procedures is illustrated by the Kelly case, which has served as one of the leading cases in the development of the legal doctrine on entrapment in the United States.

CASE 4. THE FRIENDLY STRANGER

Officer Manthos, a member of the vice squad, was in Franklin Park, dressed in plain clothes, for the purpose of making arrests of homosexuals. He was accompanied by Officer Winemiller, who stationed himself on a bench not far from the bench on which Officer Manthos seated himself. Shortly after midnight, Kelly walked through the park, and seated himself on an unoccupied bench between the benches occupied by the two officers. A conversation developed between Kelly and Manthos, about the time, the weather, their mutual interest in plastics; about Atlanta, Georgia, where both of them had lived; and about other matters. At the end of the conversation, which will be related shortly, the two men walked to Kelly's car. Manthos then placed Kelly under arrest and called to his partner, who had heard none of the preceding conversation.

According to Manthos, at the culmination of their conversation, Kelly proposed that they go to his (Kelly's) apartment for an act of perversion. Kelly, however, claimed that Manthos had suggested that they get a drink, and that Kelly then invited Manthos to his apartment, where he said that he had a bottle which they could share.

A number of facts are relevant here. First, Kelly shared his apartment with a roommate, and he knew that his roommate was at home at that time. Further, Manthos claimed that he could not recall how many such arrests he had made that night, but Winemiller informed the court that he had made six. Ten character witnesses, most of them fellow workers in the Public Health Service, testified in Kelly's behalf. And Kelly had had a date with a young lady before the incident in the park. Kelly was convicted and sentenced to a prison term.

The appeal court held that the uncorroborated testimony of a single witness could not support a conviction. The nature of the alleged offense is such, the judge said, that it must be proved beyond dispute. As he put it:

The public has a peculiar interest in the problem before us. The alleged offense, consisting of a few spoken words, may be alleged to have occurred in any public place, where any citizen is likely to be. They may be alleged to have been whispered, or to have occurred in the course of a most casual conversation. Any citizen who answers a stranger's inquiry as to direction, or time, or a request for a dime or a match is liable to be threatened with an accusation of this sort. There is virtually no protection, except one's reputation and appearance of credibility, against an uncorroborated charge of this sort. At the same time, the results of the accusation itself are devastating to the accused.

The threatened accusation of this offense is the easiest of blackmail methods. . . . The public has a great interest in the prevention of any such criminal operation.

So, as in all acute conflicts between public and private interests, the law must be exceedingly careful in its processes. While enforcement of this particular statute must seek the prevention of the offense, it must also seek to prevent unwarranted irreparable destruction of reputations, and it must seek to prevent the equally criminal offense of blackmail; it must not foster conditions or practices which make easy and encourage that offense.

As a result of these considerations, the court counselled the lower courts to receive the testimony of a single witness to a verbal invitation to sodomy only with great caution, and issued a number of other cautions as well. Kelly's conviction was reversed.[38]

The Kelly case illustrates the dangers inherent in entrapment procedures, but it offers only one part of the rationale behind the courts' refusal to admit evidence gained through such procedures. In a later case,[39] the court noted that when flirtation between one man and another is encouraged and mutual, and leads to an overt act that is neither discouraged nor repelled, such an act may not be considered to be a criminal assault. The court observed that "an officer of the law . . . has the duty of preventing, not encouraging crime. . . . An officer should not be permitted to 'torment and tease weak men beyond their power to resist' and then attempt to make out a case of assault."

Entrapment is one of the chief means of enforcing laws regarding morals offenses. When such techniques are employed, they prey upon the weaknesses of those who are so entrapped, they create crime where none might otherwise exist, and they constitute in themselves an unlawful and, I dare say, an immoral abuse of governmental authority and power. If the enforcement of such laws can be carried out only through the use of such means, then society might be better off if it were to tolerate the moral evil (if it is that) of homosexual behavior rather than to subject its citizens to such abuses at the hands of the police or run the risk of the public becoming contemptuous of the law and its enforcers.

More than once Socrates is reported to have observed that although it is bad to be the victim of injustice, it is even worse to be the perpetrator of injustice; for the victim of an injustice suffers physical harm, or loss of liberty, or loss of property, but he is not made a worse person for his experience. Morally, at least, he maintains his personal integrity. But the perpetrator of an injustice loses his personal integrity; he becomes a dishonest man, a corrupt and perverse personality. In Socrates's view, no man could suffer a greater loss than this. We may have some reservations about this doctrine, but there is good reason to believe that sordid, immoral, and unjust behavior tends to make a man sordid, immoral, and unjust. When a police officer works on the vice squad, his own character may suffer, to some extent, from his contacts. When his work involves the use of such techniques as those described, he may lose something himself in the process.* Society, too, if it permits its own agents to behave lawlessly, suffers from spiritual and moral impoverishment as a result.

Besides the corruption entailed in such practices as entrapment, the policeman who is assigned to the vice detail may be subjected to the temptation of giving in to bribery. In some cities it has been established that no gay bar operates for very long without the police becoming aware of its existence. It is only a matter of time, then, before the police are in a position to close it down, relying on liquor laws, public nuisance statutes, or other legal devices to justify their actions. In most large cities, however, the police tend to have a relatively tolerant attitude toward such operations. In many instances, their tolerance is rewarded by small favors that pass from the proprietors of the bars to the law enforcement officers. Many reporters have testified that they have seen police stop at gay bars nightly for a drink. Some bars are equipped with special lights or bells that are activated whenever a policeman enters, warning the men inside to keep their distance from one another until after the danger is past. Others, however, continue to operate normally when the police are present, secure in the knowledge that the police have been paid off. However, whenever the city administration is about to change, or when the public outcry against corruption grows too loud, a few bars must be raided and closed down. They spring up again, in another location, with the same bartender, the same clientele, and often the same cop raking in his payoff.

Police corruption is not the same as the exercise of police discretion, though the results may be similar. Officially, the police are seldom empowered to exercise any discretion in determining whether a particular offender should or should not be arrested. The statutes usually require the police officer to arrest "all" violators or "all persons committing an offense in his presence," or impose a duty to enforce "all" the criminal laws.[41] Nevertheless, studies

---

* David Senak, a Detroit policeman whose work was concentrated primarily in the morals squad, illustrates this point. In an interview with John Hersey after the Algiers Motel incident, in which Senak was involved, he explained that he had arrested close to two hundred girls and had succeeded in getting convictions on them for prostitution. "I think not so much being a police officer," he said, "as doing vice duties has on the whole given me a bad outlook on women in general." He explained that since he had joined the police department, he had had trouble relating to the women he dated. When Hersey asked him whether his experiences on the vice squad had made him think of women as essentially evil, or more apt to be criminal than men, he responded by asking, "Who gave who the apple?" [40]

reveal that the police exercise a considerable degree of discretion in carrying out their duties. The problem must inevitably arise: How *fair* are the police in deciding who should be arrested for a given offense and who should not? Indeed, can a reasonable standard of fairness be developed for such situations, in which the policeman is, in a sense, acting not only in his own official capacity but also as judge and jury by deciding in advance that some offenders should not be punished, regardless of what the law requires? To what extent will the policeman's own prejudices and personal tastes be permitted to influence these decisions? Will he base his decisions on such variables as the attractiveness of a particular offender, or his or her personal offensiveness, as measured by the policeman's personal standards? If such criteria are in fact employed, there is some question whether justice is being done. The problem of unfair and unjust exercise of discretion, whether such discretion is authorized by the law or not, undoubtedly pervades every aspect of a policeman's work. But there may be a special danger where morals statutes are concerned, for the temptation to prey upon those who exhibit special weaknesses may be more than some officers are able to resist. If homosexuals are particularly liable to be subjected to special discretionary treatment by the police—and I would assume that they, along with other offenders against the morals statutes, are more likely to be subjected to such discretionary treatment than are other classes of offenders—this would be one more argument for repealing the present laws against homosexual behavior between consenting adults.

The problem of the efficacy of the criminal law as a means of deterring homosexuality inevitably arises. Although some people have suggested that the criminal law is not at all effective in this area, I am inclined to doubt that that is the case. On the contrary, much of the evidence points to its effectiveness in a great many cases. The stories of homosexuals who suffer lonely and unhappy lives because of their fear of entering into the only kind of love affair that they feel able to participate in illustrate as well as anything can the effectiveness of the legal and the social sanctions in reducing the incidence of homosexual behavior. This is not to say that the threat of criminal sanctions is totally effective. Obviously, it is not. The threat of criminal sanctions is not totally effective in *any* field, whether it be gambling, prostitution, embezzlement, robbery, or murder. Some persons are willing to take their chances, hoping that they will not be caught. Others, however, afraid of the possible consequences, choose to stay on the right side of the law, even though it means giving up a form of conduct in which they might otherwise have wanted to engage.

Some of the most consistent opponents of homosexuality have advocated repeal of laws whose effect is to punish homosexual behavior between consenting adults in private. A Roman Catholic Advisory Committee formed to study the problems of homosexuality and prostitution in relation to the existing laws in England restated the Church's opposition to "all directly voluntary sexual pleasure outside marriage" on the ground that such pleasure is sinful. The committee's report distinguished carefully between sin and crime, defining the latter as a social concept and not a moral one. "Sin," it said, "is not the concern of the State but affects the relations between the soul and God." The committee also upheld the traditional justifications for criminal punishment on grounds of deterrence and reform and suggested that retribution, too, might be a legitimate reason for punishing certain kinds of behavior. However, the committee maintained that "the State should not go beyond its proper limits in this connexion," that is, in its effort to restrain individuals from committing the "more detestable offences." "Attempts by the State to enlarge its authority and invade the individual conscience, however high-minded, always fail and frequently do positive harm. . . . It should accordingly be clearly stated that penal sanctions are not justified for the purpose of attempting to restrain sins against sexual morality committed in private by responsible adults." The committee then advocated the abolition of all criminal sanctions for such behavior on the grounds that:

    (a) they are ineffectual;
    (b) they are inequitable in their incidence;
    (c) they involve severities disproportionate to the offense committed;
    (d) they undoubtedly give scope for blackmail and other forms of corruption.[42]

The committee noted that existing criminal procedures resulted in the burden of penalties falling upon a small minority of actual offenders, and often upon those least deserving of punishment. It noted also that imprisonment was ineffectual in helping to reorient persons with homosexual tendencies, and stated that incarceration often had deleterious effects upon them. This was one factor in its decision.

At a time when the public is rightly concerned over rising crime rates— that is, with the rising rates of such serious crimes of violence as muggings, rapes, robberies, and murders—another argument commends itself for serious consideration. When police manpower is diverted from the prevention and detection of such crimes to the tracking down of homosexuals, one must wonder whether society's resources are being used in the most effective manner. Is the punishment of homosexuals so important as to deserve *any* attention from undermanned police forces in cities where there is only one arrest for every ten crimes of violence? Would the meager resources available in such cities not be exploited more wisely if first priority were given to the protection of life and property, with the pursuit of homosexuals and other "immoral" persons being relegated to the bottom of the list, or removed from the list entirely?

It is sometimes said that if the penalties against homosexual relations were removed, that action would be tantamount to society's putting its stamp of approval upon behavior that our long tradition and some of our most respected theologians and moralists consider to be immoral. On such grounds, much progress in the reform of the law is thwarted. But the argument is not convincing. If society declares that it will not punish persons for certain kinds of behavior, that declaration does not constitute, in itself, a stamp of approval for such behavior. Parents have been known to declare to their children that they do not approve of those with whom the latter associate, though they may not penalize them for continuing to associate with those persons. A wise parent knows that some forms of behavior, though they may not be such as he approves of, are nevertheless not so bad as to warrant the expenditure of energy and emotion that are involved in the infliction of punishment. He reserves punishment for those offenses that he considers to be most destructive to the good order and welfare of the family, or of society, or—most importantly, perhaps—of the child himself. He relies instead upon education and persuasion and reason as means of inducing his children to adopt the norms that he considers to be good and to reject those forms of behavior that he considers to be bad. A society is not essentially different in this respect. Its lawmakers and others who are in a position to set social policy may consider the expenditure of wealth and human resources required for the enforcement of rules on sexual conduct to be too great for the benefits that might accrue from such enforcement. They may wish to rely instead upon education and other means of persuasion to convince the public that such behavior is not desirable. Instead of enacting a multitude of laws to enforce every petty offense, they may find, in the long run, that there is considerable benefit in relying upon the good will and the common sense of the people. Following such a course, the police would be free to fight dangerous criminals and to maintain order in the community, the courts would be relieved of a part of their crushing burden, jails and prisons would be emptied of those whose offenses are basically petty and of no great or immediate social consequence, and, most important of all, a great many people would be relieved of the constant fear that they might be arrested for forms of behavior that they consider to be completely harmless—if not to themselves, at least to society at large. The abolition of penal sanctions could be accompanied by wide publicity, if the legislature felt so disposed, in which its collective disapproval of homosexual behavior could be expressed, with appropriate reasons. At the same time, it could explain why it had concluded that the forces of the law were not appropriate for the control of that particular moral problem. And it would naturally want to inform the public, carefully and clearly, about the restrictions that would continue to exist— restrictions on offensive public behavior, on homosexual relations with children, and the like.

THE PROBLEM OF TREATMENT

The laws in various countries, and in various states within the United States, vary considerably. Only one state, Illinois, presently has no statute providing for criminal punishment of homosexual acts committed in private by consenting adults. The Model Penal Code of the American Law Institute proposed that private sexual acts, whether heterosexual or homosexual, should be criminal only where minors are involved or some force or coercion was employed, but only Illinois has adopted the proposed reform. Other states have harsh penalties on the books, ranging from three months in prison or one year's probation in New York to life imprisonment in one state of every seven. In some states, the *minimum* punishment can be quite harsh, as in South Carolina, for example, where a man must be sent to prison for not less than five years for such an act.

In England, the latest legislation (1967) generally followed the recommendations of the Wolfenden Committee. For private acts committed by consenting adults there are no penalties; but an adult who commits any homosexual act with a youth between sixteen and twenty-one years of age can be sent to prison for five years; and if the boy is under sixteen, the adult may be imprisoned for life.

In Europe the picture is mixed. For consensual relations between adults, Denmark, Belgium, France, Holland, Italy, and Sweden impose no penalties. In Finland, Norway, and Germany both parties are punishable; and in Austria, both parties are punishable, even if the offense is lesbianism.

The reader may have wondered why this discussion of homosexuality has concentrated, thus far, exclusively on the male variety. The answer is that except for Austria, lesbians are seldom prosecuted, even where lesbianism is illegal; and in most places, including those that have strict penalties against male homosexuality, there are no laws forbidding lesbianism. More than a decade ago, Kinsey observed that although there had been tens of thousands of prosecutions and convictions for male homosexuality in New York during the period covered by his study, only three women had been arrested for lesbianism, and all three of those cases were dismissed. Even in social relations, lesbianism—as long as it is not too open or blatant—is more readily accepted than male homosexuality. Women may room together without occasioning any comment from their neighbors. They may walk arm in arm down the street. They may dance together. They may even kiss one another warmly when they meet. For reasons into which we need not enter here, such forms of behavior between women are accepted quite readily in the Western world, but are not acceptable when engaged in by men. Austria seems to be the only country in the world that actively enforces its laws against lesbianism.[43]

From such measures, we turn to the question of psychiatric care, which some people consider to be preferable to prison. In Part II of this book we will see that the proposition that "all criminals are sick" lacks cogency. Some authorities are strongly inclined to believe that in the area of homosexuality, if anywhere, we have a clear case of mental illness; for it is alleged that no person who is psychologically normal would seek such abnormal sexual outlets. We have already observed that repeated attempts have been made to determine whether homosexuals could be distinguished from heterosexuals in psychological tests. As often as such attempts have been made, they have failed. It is beyond the scope of the present book to attempt to evaluate the psychiatric and psychoanalytic literature on the subject. It is sufficient, for our purposes, to note that many homosexuals seem, at least, to be well-adjusted persons in every other respect. Many of them are not at all interested in the services that psychiatrists can offer them. This may be a mistake on their part, but one would suppose that in a free society, such choices should be left to the individual. However, some well-meaning persons, interested in the "liberalization" or "reform" of the penal system, have suggested that instead of imprisonment, homosexuals and other so-called sexual psychopaths should be subjected to compulsory psychiatric treatment. Such treatment, of course, involves a number of deprivations of liberty not ordinarily considered a part of any punishment. Not the least of those is the right of an individual to maintain his personality intact, not to have it interfered with by other persons, no matter how well-intentioned their efforts might be. Another, scarcely less important, perhaps, is the indeterminate nature of such a sentence. Instead of a judge or a jury setting a certain time for the offender to serve out his sentence, the ultimate judgment is placed in the hands of a psychiatrist or a group of medical men, who will decide, in accordance with their own criteria, when the so-called patient is ready to be released.

In a number of American states persons may be designated sexual psychopaths even if no crime has been shown to have been committed. In New Hampshire, for example, a sexual psychopath is "any person suffering from such conditions of emotional instability or impulsiveness of behavior, or lack of customary standards of good judgment, or failure to appreciate the consequences of his acts, or a combination of any such conditions as to render such person irresponsible with respect to sexual matters and thereby dangerous to himself or to other persons." [44] A person may be sent to a mental hospital under such a statute, even if he has committed no crime; or he may be committed for an indefinite term for a minor offense whose penalty might have been no more than a few months in jail. And worst of all, such a law places into the hands of certain medical practitioners the power to deprive men of their liberty in accordance with their own standards, whatever those may be, and to return to society men who may well be highly dangerous, in spite of the fact that the latter may have committed grave offenses for which they might otherwise have had to remain in prison. Recent reports from the Soviet Union reveal how pernicious the use of psychiatric wards and mental hospitals may be when they are converted into compulsory treatment centers for those who are accused of criminal behavior. The czars who sent political prisoners to Siberia were guilty of monstrous injustices. They condemned men to live miserable existences in the wastes of the Russian wilderness. But they did not mount direct attacks upon the minds of their victims. In the Soviet Union today, men and women who are accused of "anti-Soviet" activities, of publishing subversive literature, or of wanting to emigrate to Israel or to any other free society, are condemned to mental hospitals where they will presumably be purged of their mental diseases and return to normalcy—i.e., to the value systems of the regime under which they live. For the courts of a free society to send men or women to mental hospitals against their will in order to "cure" them of their sexual predilections is very nearly a contradiction in terms. If a man chooses to engage in what most persons in a given society consider to be immoral behavior—particularly if that behavior is such as to harm no one but himself and those who consent to participate with him in those activities—then *at most* the authorities of that society should be authorized to punish him; but they should not be permitted to use drugs, electric shock, insulin shock, or the other methods of modern psychiatric medicine to change his personality to conform to the value system of the society as a whole or of the doctors who will treat him. Society has a right to protect its members, but not at the expense of their minds and their personalities when they violate its norms. Without the offender's consent no one should be permitted to tamper with his personality. The homosexual who wants to be a homosexual, who chooses to remain a homosexual, and who is not at all interested in becoming a "normal" heterosexual may have chosen a way of life that is repugnant to many, or even to most of us; but his personality should remain inviolate. To turn him over to a psychiatrist for "therapy" when he has no desire to be altered is an invasion of a man's very soul, an invasion which only the most totalitarian regime could countenance.

Sending homosexuals to prison is scarcely likely to effect a cure, if that is what is desired. In order to cure a man of his desire for men, we send him to a place where women are never seen, where his only companions are other men who are deprived of every sexual outlet but masturbation and homosexuality, and where other homosexuals are to be found in great abundance. It would make more sense, I should think, to send him to a place where he was surrounded by dancing girls, specially trained in the art of arousing men who tend not to be particularly interested in women. But this is scarcely likely to commend itself to the authorities as a feasible or suitable penalty for homosexuality.

In any event, most efforts to "cure" homosexuals have ended in utter failure. A few homosexuals who undertake one form of therapy or another are effectively "cured," in that they become heterosexual. But a very high proportion of those who seek to become heterosexual, particularly when they have been homosexual for a very long period of time, do not succeed.[45]

CONCLUSION

If Justinian were right, and sodomy caused earthquakes, plagues, and famines, harsh penalties for sodomy would certainly be in order, for it would be a serious crime against society, and it would cause much needless suffering to many innocent persons. But all the available evidence indicates that

Justinian was wrong and that if homosexuality is harmful to anyone at all, it is harmful only to those who engage in it. At that, most of the harm that comes to homosexuals is the result of society's attitude toward their peculiar form of erotic behavior rather than a direct result of that behavior itself. If society would reduce its condemnation of homosexual behavior, at least by removing the penalties that it imposes upon those who are caught, the condition of homosexuals would be greatly ameliorated. The dire predictions that Lord Devlin made, about the moral decay of society if such proposals as those of the Wolfenden Committee were adopted, seem not to be realistic, and Lord Devlin himself finally came out in support of those proposals. Society has better things to do with its resources than to enforce private morality, particularly in a time of great social disruption such as the one in which we are presently living.

There is another aspect of the homosexual scene to which I have been unable to do justice here. I shall only mention it without attempting to deal with it in detail.

Certain societies of homosexuals and their sympathizers have expressed a desire not only for the removal of criminal penalties for their behavior, but also for the introduction of legislation that would enable them to enjoy many of the privileges and rights that have heretofore been enjoyed only by married heterosexual couples. They have complained, for example, about what they consider to be the unfair tax laws, which offer considerable advantages to married couples. Homosexual couples are deprived of those advantages and must file individual returns, even though they may have very stable relationships—relations that may be even more stable than those of some male–female marriages. Again, some homosexuals have asked why they should not be permitted to adopt children. Like many heterosexual couples, they find themselves unable to have children of their own; but they feel that they might be able to offer a child a warm and loving home with two parents. Because of the laws of most states and provinces (if not all of them), they are unable to do so. And finally (to conclude this necessarily short list of requests or demands that homosexuals are making), if they were permitted to marry, their relationships might be given a degree of stability that they lack today, without the safeguards and protections to family stability offered by the laws of marriage and divorce. By bringing homosexuals within those laws, they would not only receive the tax and inheritance advantages that heterosexual couples enjoy, but they would be able to achieve a degree of stability in their relationships with one another that has eluded most such couples in the past. If the homosexual marriage could be "sealed" with one or more children, as most heterosexual marriages are, it is hoped that they would become even more stable, and achieve a higher degree of permanence.

Our society is obviously a long way from accepting such proposals as these. The institution of marriage has such a long history and is encrusted with so many emotional and historical and literary associations, all of them heterosexual, that it is not likely that anything called homosexual *marriage*, in the true legal sense, will come into existence in our time. But I suppose it is not beyond the realm of possibility that some of these proposals might be given effect in some form that does not embody the concept of marriage. Homosexuals might be permitted to form partnerships, for example, and the laws might be rewritten to permit persons living in special kinds of partnerships to enjoy the tax benefits and the inheritance advantages that have heretofore been reserved to married couples.

One wonders, however, why homosexuals would want to introduce legislation to legalize marriage for themselves at a time when so many people are complaining about the archaism of heterosexual marriage laws, and are demanding the right to have trial marriages, or periodically renewable marriage, or divorce on demand. It would seem that homosexuals, who have easily dissoluble relationships with one another—just what so many advocates of reform of the marriage laws are asking for—would be content to push for the financial benefits of marriage without the legal restrictions that marriage inevitably (at least in our society) entails.

Recently there have been reports of homosexuals adopting one another, thus achieving some of the goals mentioned above. It is of course quite unusual for one grown man to adopt another, but it can be done. Where it is, the adoption is permanent—far more permanent even than a marriage might be—and the benefits that the adoptive son receives from his adoptive father cannot be taken from him by a later act of the adoptive father. In those states, for example, where a son is automatically entitled to a certain proportion of his father's estate, even if the latter has cut him out of his will, the adoptive father in such a relationship may find himself with an unwanted son of whom he is unable to rid himself, and he may be unable to dispose of his estate as he would like to do.

Whether one agrees with the legislative proposals of the Mattachine Society and other organizations of homosexuals or not, one may sympathize with the members of this persecuted minority who are struggling, for the first time in living memory, for the recognition of rights that are granted to other citizens as a matter of course: for equal treatment before the law; for freedom from police harassment; for the right to pursue their way of life without fear of arrest, imprisonment, or compulsory psychiatric treatment; and for the right to be judged in their professions or trades on the quality of their work rather than on their private conduct when they are not on the job.

3

Contraception and Abortion

THE PROBLEM

In most parts of the world contraceptives may now be legally sold, and physicians or other persons may offer advice to those who wish to plan their families or to limit the number of children they bring into the world by taking deliberate steps to avoid conception. Some countries are afflicted with massive overpopulation and with all that that entails—serious overcrowding, food shortages, desperate conditions of poverty, misery, squalor, and disease, and, with all that, a continuing increase in the population in geometrical proportions. The governments of some of these nations have organized campaigns designed to introduce family planning to their people and to provide them with the means to carry out the program. Some, such as India, Jamaica, and Japan, have spent vast sums of money to educate their people on the desirability of family planning and the use of contraceptives and have provided financial and other incentives for those who use government-supplied devices and services.

However, there are still places where the use or sale of contraceptive devices is illegal, and the offering of advice on their use, even by physicians, is prohibited. Substantial segments of some communities oppose the use of artificial means of birth control on moral or religious grounds. Where possible, they use their influence to prevent the liberalization of laws governing such matters; and where that is impracticable, some of them use their powers of moral suasion to convince their followers not to employ such means in their own lives.

The problem may be viewed on at least two levels: on the level of the individual's own personal practices and on the level of state or national policy. Because the population problem is global in extent and in its impact, it may also be considered as a problem of international morality. As George N. Shuster, vice president of Notre Dame University, has written,

It is obvious that a continuation of [the present] rate of increase [in the population] is wholly out of the question. . . . All demographers, whether they be Catholic or not, are agreed that mankind must henceforth limit its power to procreate. Even if we assume that the world's food supply can be vastly increased and that economic productivity will reach hitherto undreamed of levels, simple arithmetic plainly points to inevitable disaster if the growth rate from two billion to six billion in eighty years were to be maintained.[1]

At the Inter-American Conference on Population Studies in 1967, President Carlos Lleras Restreop of Colombia recalled his visits to the poorest slums of his own country, and observed:

What can we say of the frequent incest, of the primitive sexual experience, of the miserable treatment of children, of the terrible proliferation of prostitution of children of both sexes, of frequent abortion, of almost animal union because of alcoholic excesses? It is, in consequence, impossible for me to sit back and examine the morality or immorality of contraceptive practices without thinking at the same time of the immoral and frequently criminal conditions that the simple act of conception can produce in the course of time.[2]

On the community level, those who are opposed to the use or distribution of contraceptive devices on moral grounds are bound to use whatever influence they can bring to bear against such distribution by government agencies. In the city of Chicago, for example, the cost of Aid to Dependent Children programs was some $90 million in 1963, when a government-sponsored birth control program was introduced for welfare recipients. One response to that program was reduced to the following "argument" by some Catholic taxpayers: "Contraception is immoral; as taxpayers we do not wish to support it; as citizens we must oppose it." [3] As a result of this type of thinking, not only in the United States, but in many nations throughout the world, government-sponsored attempts to initiate birth control programs have failed, and attempts to liberalize the laws governing the distribution and use of contraceptives have been blocked. In the United States, only a few years ago, several states had restrictive laws governing the sale, distribution, advertisement, and use of contraceptives. In Massachusetts, for example, the sale of contraceptives for any purpose other than prophylaxis (that is, as protection against disease) was strictly forbidden. The courts of that state held, in fact, that a physician could not lawfully prescribe contraceptives for his patients, even if pregnancy would mean certain death for them; but he was permitted to prescribe a contraceptive to prevent disease for anyone who was engaging in illicit intercourse.[4] In both Massachusetts and Connecticut, birth control clinics were outlawed. In Connecticut, a law was on the books forbidding married men and women from using contraceptives in their relations with one another. An ancient federal law (the Comstock Law of 1873, section 211 of the Federal Penal Code) bans the mailing of information on contraception or contraceptive devices on the ground that such materials are "obscene, lewd . . . lascivious, and . . . filthy." Since the decision of the United States Supreme Court overturning the Connecticut law, these statutes and others like them have been generally acknowledged to be unconstitutional and are no longer enforced.[5] Nevertheless, such laws continue to exist in other places, and there are powerful movements attempting to have them reintroduced in those places where they have been eliminated.

On the state or national level, then, the problem is whether the law should permit the use of contraceptives and whether the government should be permitted to utilize its social agencies to encourage citizens to limit their families through artificial means of control. Whether the individual citizen who considers the use of contraceptives to be morally wrong is obliged to oppose measures designed to liberalize restrictive laws or to spread information about contraceptive measures among the population must also be considered.

On the individual level, the question concerns not only the individual's attitude toward the practices of others, or his views on the propriety of particular legal norms or institutional practices, but also his personal behavior and his attitude toward his own use of contraceptives. Here the individual is confronted with moral choices on a very deep personal level. He must consider the impact of his own behavior upon himself, his wife, and his children; but if he is morally sensitive, he must also consider the long-run effects of his restraint or his lack of restraint, of his use or his failure to use contraceptives, upon his country, his people, and ultimately, upon all mankind. Though one may argue that no individual's sexual practices alone can make a significant impact upon the destiny of mankind, nevertheless, the moral question may hinge not upon any particular act taken in isolation, but upon the consequences of everyone's adopting the same form of behavior for himself. As Kant suggested, we must consider whether a given form of behavior would be acceptable if everyone did it. *Contra* Kant, however, one may properly ask what the consequences of any such universalization of a given form of behavior would be, in order to assess its desirability.

The Roman Catholic Church is the major institutional opponent of the use of contraception. Through its official spokesmen, the Church has stood firmly against any mechanical or chemical means of controlling fertility, admitting only the rhythm method, *amplexus reservatus,* and total abstinence as morally legitimate means of limiting conception. The current debate on this issue can be understood only within the historical framework of the development of certain doctrines in Christianity, for only thus can the position of the Church in contemporary controversies be appreciated. Because the same basic principles apply to the abortion problem, they may be treated together. For the issues are very similar to one another. In the first place, abortion may of viable children as a result of sexual intercourse. Secondly, some contra- be used as a kind of contraceptive; that is, as a means of preventing birth ceptives act as abortifacients: instead of preventing the union of sperm and ovum, as some contraceptives do, they prevent the fertilized egg from being implanted into the uterine wall, causing it instead to be diverted past the uterus and then outside. Thirdly, many of the arguments against abortion are identical to arguments urged against the use of contraceptives.

Nevertheless, the issues are distinct in many respects and must be given separate treatment to some extent. If we concentrate on those forms of contraception that prevent sperm from uniting with ovum, for the moment, we can see that certain special problems arise in abortion that do not arise with respect to contraception. It is extremely difficult, for example, to uphold the thesis that the practice of contraception causes the death of a human being; but a plausible case can be made for the view that every abortion causes the death of a living human being—not, perhaps, a human being who has reached his fullest potential, and perhaps not one who has achieved fully human form, but a living human being nevertheless.

Abortion, too, can be considered to be both a social and a personal moral problem. The woman who has conceived an unwanted fetus must decide whether she will carry the fetus to term or seek an abortion. If she chooses to carry the baby to term, she must then decide whether to keep the baby or to put it up for adoption. If she decides to seek an abortion, she must determine whether it is possible for her to find a legal abortionist or, if that is not possible, whether she can bring herself to take the risks and assume the guilt and the responsibility inherent in undergoing an illegal abortion. Most women who seek abortions become involved with others who either help them or hinder them in their search for a solution to their problem: family, friends, clergy, nonmedical abortionists, physicians, hospitals, and—possibly —police, courts, and other legal personnel. At every step of the game, these people must make moral choices. For some, such choices can be agonizing, particularly where there is a conflict between one moral principle and another, as there would be, for example, where the person involved is morally committed to the principle that abortion is wrong, but is also concerned for the safety and well-being of the woman who is suffering through an unwanted pregnancy and may have to suffer through the torment of bringing an unwanted child into the world, or of giving birth to a grossly deformed child who will himself spend all his days in suffering.

More broadly, there is the problem of the government's role in providing or in deterring the practice. Should the government, as guardian of the people's morals and as the protector of the weak and the innocent, act to prevent abortions by outlawing them and imposing stringent penalties upon those who break the law? Should it, in its capacity of protector of public health and welfare, provide facilities for those who seek abortions? Should it exercise some measure of control, permitting abortions for some purposes but prohibiting them for others? Or should it maintain a *laissez-faire* attitude, leaving the ultimate decisions to the women most directly concerned and those who become directly or indirectly involved? And what of the hospitals, their boards, and the physicians who might be called upon to perform abortions? Do they have a right, as a matter of policy, to forbid the performance of an operation that might be necessary for the well-being of one of their patients? Some operations are performed merely for the sake of convenience or for cosmetic purposes—as, for example, plastic surgery often is—and there is no serious objection to such surgery on the part of any medical board or hospital. Yet where abortion is concerned, though its nonperformance might cause irreparable harm to the mother or to her baby, some hospitals or other medical bodies or personnel refuse categorically to participate in any way. Do medical institutions or personnel have a duty to the public that they are failing to fulfill by refusing to perform abortions?

An aspect of the problem that must not be overlooked is the problem of illegal abortions. There is ample evidence that where abortions may not be performed legally, very large numbers of women seek them anyway, and either find other persons who will perform or attempt to perform abortions upon them, according to their abilities, or attempt to abort themselves. Estimates of the numbers of illegal abortions abound in the literature. They range from a low of 200,000 per year to a high of 1 million per year in the United States alone. Deaths caused by illegal abortions may run between 500 and 5,000 per year. These enormous ranges are accounted for by the fact that no accurate records are kept (obviously) of the number of illegal abortions, and the cause of death is often listed on death certificates and in public records as something other than abortion, even though the death may in fact have resulted from an illegal abortion attempt. Surveys, clinical studies, and estimates must therefore be relied upon to furnish whatever information we have. Whether the lower figures are accepted or the higher ones, there can be no escaping the fact that we are dealing with a major national problem. Even 200,000 illegal abortions per year comes to over 500 every day, and 500 deaths per year amounts to three deaths every two days. This leaves entirely out of account the pain and suffering caused by back-alley surgeons, the infections and other diseases brought about by their ministrations, and the girls who are rendered permanently sterile because of the methods used by the amateurs who operate upon them and the lack of adequate aftercare. Even the lowest estimates, then, represent a serious national problem. But if the higher estimates are even nearly correct, it is nothing less than a national catastrophe. A million illegal abortions per year amount to about 2,700 such abortions *every day*, and if there are 5,000 deaths from such abortions each year, about fourteen girls die as a result of such illegal surgery every day of the year. These figures have been the subject of considerable criticism, but even the critics agree that the lowest plausible estimate is ample reason for grave concern.[6] As a matter of state and national policy, then, the question of the government's responsibility must be faced, for whatever it does or fails to do, millions of lives are touched by this problem. It would seem, from the preceding statistics, that few people, in the course of a lifetime, are likely to be completely untouched by it.

A number of questions, then, must be answered:

1. Is contraception immoral?
2. If it is, then
   a. Is there ever an excuse or a justification for anyone using contraceptives?
   b. Does the state have the right to interfere with those persons who choose to participate in this immoral behavior by cutting off the source of supply, for example, or by outlawing the dissemination of information concerning contraceptives?
3. Is abortion immoral?
4. If it is, then
   a. Is there ever an excuse or a justification for anyone obtaining an abortion? (That is, are *some* abortions *not* immoral?)
   b. Should the state interfere with those who wish to engage in this form of immoral behavior by penalizing abortionists or women who have abortions, and should others (such as hospital boards and physicians) refuse to engage in the practice of aborting pregnant females who come to them for assistance?

In order to answer these questions intelligently, it will be helpful first to review some of the most important facts affecting current attitudes concerning the issues involved.

A SHORT HISTORY OF RELIGIOUS AND MORAL THINKING ON CONTRACEPTION AND ABORTION

HELLENISM
In ancient Greece and Rome, contraception, abortion, and even infanticide were not at all uncommon. According to Plato's calculations, men and women passed their prime child-bearing and child-begetting years after the ages of fifty-five and forty, respectively. Once they had passed those ages, he said, they should be permitted to have relations freely, so long as they were not incestuous. But they would be warned that "no child, if any be conceived, shall be brought to light, or, if they cannot prevent its birth, [they are] to dispose of it on the understanding that no such child can be reared." [7] The citizens were to be encouraged, then, to take precautions against conception, and, if those precautions failed, they were either to secure an abortion or to commit infanticide, on eugenic grounds. Even defective children born to parents in their prime were to be "hidden away, in some appropriate manner that must be kept secret." [8] According to Aristotle, "if no restriction is imposed on the rate of reproduction, . . . poverty is the inevitable result; and poverty produces, in its turn, civic dissension and wrongdoing." In order to reduce the chances for civil strife, then, and to eliminate poverty, Aristotle

advocates a limitation on the population, and therefore, the imposition of limits on family size. Such limits, he suggests, should be fixed to allow for infant mortality and the amount of infertility among married couples.[9] Elsewhere, he takes up the question of infanticide and abortion:

> The question arises whether children should always be reared or may sometimes be exposed to die. There should certainly be a law to prevent the rearing of deformed children. On the other hand, there should also be a law, in all states where the system of social habits is opposed to unrestricted increase, to prevent the exposure of children to death *merely* in order to keep the population down. The proper thing to do is to limit the size of each family, and if children are then conceived in excess of the limit so fixed, to have miscarriage induced before sense and life have begun in the embryo.[10]

From these quotations, it is evident that far more is involved here than the code of Sparta, which gave every father the right to dispose of his children by slaying them, but imposed upon all parents the duty of bringing their children before state inspectors, who would examine them for physical or mental defects. Any children who were found to be defective were thrown from a cliff and smashed on the rocks below.[11] In the Hellenistic period, abortion was freely permitted throughout Greece and Macedonia. Wives who had abortions would be punished only if they had done so without the permission of their husbands. Families were kept small, either by abortion or by exposure of infants, particularly girls. Few wealthy Greek families in the third pre-Christian century had more than one or two children. As a result, the population of some important cities began to decline drastically. Philip V of Macedon brought about a 50 per cent increase in the population of his country by forbidding such methods of family planning, and Polybius, in the second pre-Christian century, complained of houses and of entire districts becoming desolate because of the refusal of luxury-loving men and women to burden themselves with children.[12] At about the time Christianity arose, the Romans were engaging in profligate and luxurious living. Women thought nothing of having numerous divorces and even more numerous extramarital affairs. They avoided the burdens of motherhood by emulating the practices of their Greek mentors, by resorting to abortions and to contraceptives. They sometimes sought abortions in order to avoid ruining their figures by carrying to term. Men found that children were a burden in the city, though they might have been an asset if they were still on the farm. And they found, also, that if they were childless, they were more attractive to young and beautiful women as they grew older, for the women would be interested in the prospect of inheriting an estate that they would not have to share with others. Therefore, the men, too, avoided marital entanglements, finding sexual outlets in other ways—by patronizing prostitutes or by living with concubines. It was because of this widespread moral decay and the steady decline in population that Augustus passed the laws mentioned previously, and others as well, designed to restore some of the older moral virtues about which he had read.[13] But his laws failed of their purpose.

Marriage came to be a loose contract, entered into merely for convenience. Some women married eunuchs in order to be spared the trouble of contraception and abortions, while others entered into marriage agreements that specified in advance that they were not to be required to bear children and that they could have relations with other men at will.[14]

It is small wonder that there was such a strong reaction against these practices by the early Christians, as there must have been among some non-Christian Romans. But the development of church doctrine included new elements that exerted a profound influence upon later attitudes, practices, and laws.

THE DEVELOPMENT OF CHURCH DOCTRINE

Biblical Sources. According to the Biblical tradition, after God created man, he blessed him, saying, "Be fruitful and multiply; fill up the earth and subdue it." The same blessing was repeated after most of mankind was destroyed by the flood in Noah's time, and other versions of the same thought appear elsewhere throughout the Bible.[15] There is a positive emphasis on the value of having children and, where possible, of having many of them. Being barren, unable to conceive, is considered a source of great sorrow. There is a clear implication that having children is more than a mere blessing. It assumes the force of a positive duty.

One of the key texts to the understanding of the Church's attitude toward contraception is Genesis 38:8–10. Judah's son, Er, married Tamar, but died an untimely death. Tamar was left childless. According to ancient Jewish law, whenever a man died without leaving children to carry on his name and his estate, his nearest relative was obliged to marry his widow—unless he deliberately refused to do so—and to treat the first child born of their union as if it were the child of the deceased. Er's brother, Onan, married Tamar in accordance with this rule. The narrative then goes on to relate what happened: "Onan knew that the child [that would be born of his union with Tamar] would not be [considered] his own. So when he had relations with his brother's wife, he let his seed be wasted on the ground rather than providing an heir for his brother. God disapproved of his action, and took his life as well."

It is possible to read this passage as a condemnation of contraception—specifically, of "wasting one's seed" or of permitting one's seed to be spilled upon the ground. In the narrowest terms, it might be seen as a condemnation of coitus interruptus, but the principle may be broadened to include any "wasting" of sperm by not permitting it to enter the female at the climax of sexual intercourse. As we shall see, such interpretations of this text were given considerable importance throughout the Middle Ages and have assumed enormous significance for the question of the legitimacy of contraception down to our own time.

The New Testament made a radical break with Old Testament teachings on sex and marriage in a number of important respects. The most important of these was probably the New Testament's emphasis on the value of virginity, exalting virginity above marriage to such a degree that abstinence from marriage is regarded as a virtue and as a means of bringing on the second coming. As Luke puts it, "The children of this world marry and are given in marriage. But those who shall be accounted worthy of that world and of the resurrection from the dead neither marry nor take wives. For neither shall they be able to die any more, for they are equal to the angels, and are sons of God, being sons of the resurrection." [16] In other passages, Jesus is represented as having urged his disciples to make themselves eunuchs,[17] and as assuring them that "at the resurrection, they will neither marry nor be given in marriage, but will be like the angels in heaven."[18] Paul compares the unmarried virgin, who dwells upon the Lord and is holy in body and spirit, to the married person, who concerns himself with the things of this world.[19] According to this view, the only marriage worth consummating is the marriage of the individual with God or with Jesus.

However, in the New Testament there are also passages commending marriage, particularly monogamous, nonadulterous, and permanent marriage.[20] But the emphasis remains that of Paul, who maintained that marriage was acceptable as an alternative for those who were "unable to control themselves," suggesting that it is "better to marry than to burn." [21] Marital intercourse is lawful and permitted, but, in contrast to the Hebrew Bible's stress on the positive value of such relationships, it is rather considered, in the New Testament, to be a concession to human weakness.

A further important innovation was the introduction of the concept of original sin. "Through one man sin entered into the world." [22]

We need not dwell on questions concerning the original intentions of the authors of these texts, because it was the later interpretations of theologians and religious scholars that affected our ancestors' attitudes toward the issues that concern us now.

One final observation must be made at this point. The New Testament attitude toward marriage reflects an attitude that was common in the Roman world of the time. As the Stoics and others were saying, sexual intercourse was never right unless it served a procreative purpose; if it was indulged in for pleasure alone, it was morally reprehensible.[23]

The Church Fathers Through the Middle Ages.   The early Church Fathers taught that the ideal of continence required a constant battle against desire. "Our ideal is not to experience desire at all," Clement declared in the second century; and in the following century, Origen said that the only proper justification for intercourse with one's wife was for the sake of children. They argued against intercourse with pregnant women on the ground that such intercourse could not be fruitful and served only to satisfy animal lusts. John T. Noonan, whose study of the history of doctrines on contraception is probably the most thorough of modern times, was able to find only one statement prior to the sixteenth century countenancing intercourse for pleasure's sake, and even that was equivocal.[24] The same source insisted, however, that the sex organs had only one "proper" purpose, and that was procreation. To others, contraception was so unnatural as to be worse than homicide.

Early Christians reacted strongly against the prevailing Roman indifference to infanticide. Around the beginning of the fourth century, a council at Elvira enjoined excommunication until death for any woman who had an abortion, and another, at Ancyra, provided ten years of penance for such women. Later councils followed suit. They thus extended the Roman law on parricide, which originally applied to any intentional, unlawful killing of a relative, to the destruction of a fetus, which had not been included before. But they went even further, calling homosexuals parricides, thus suggesting that the semen emitted by a man contains children within it, and that the intentional waste or destruction of the semen causes the death of those human beings. From this it is a very short step indeed to the assertion that anyone using contraceptives is committing homicide.

Throughout the Middle Ages these doctrines were repeated and expanded. Augustine, for example, declared that marital intercourse for the sake of pleasure was a venial sin, but only if "no evil prayer or evil deed" was employed to obstruct procreation. "Those who do this," he said, "although they are called husband and wife, are not; nor do they retain the marital state in reality. Instead, they cover their shameful deed with a respectable name." He went on to denounce oral contraceptives: "Sometimes this lustful cruelty, or cruel lust, comes to this: they even procure poisons of sterility, and if these do not work, they destroy the fetus in some way in the womb, . . . killing their baby before it is born." He condemned those who used such methods of contraception or feticide in the harshest terms, declaring that they were not joined in genuine matrimony, but in fornication. If husband and wife conspire to engage in sexual relations for pleasure while employing contraceptive measures, the wife must stand condemned, he said, as a harlot, and the husband is guilty of committing adultery with his own wife.[25]

A study of sanctions imposed for various sins during the Middle Ages reveals that anal and oral intercourse were generally regarded as more serious crimes than intentional homicide, and were universally considered to be more serious than the abortion of a fetus prior to the fortieth day of gestation. Drinking contraceptive potions was treated by some authorities as more serious than premeditated murder, whereas other experts disagreed, maintaining that each conception that was prevented was just another homicide, and should be punished accordingly. Thus, for example, the eighth-century Canons of Gregory prescribe seven penances for a layman who commits intentional homicide, fifteen for one who engages in anal intercourse. St. Hubert prescribes ten for homicide or for contraception.[26]

Throughout the centuries that followed, Augustine's words were repeated, with insistent emphasis on the sinfulness of sexual intercourse—including intercourse of married couples—"for delight, the satisfaction of lust" or as a result of "concupiscence." [27] In the later Middle Ages, sanctions for improper sexual behavior extended beyond the penances that were prescribed earlier. St. Thomas Aquinas ranked the "sin against nature" as the greatest of all sexual vices, even worse than fornication, seduction, rape, incest, or sacrilege.[28] Bernardine followed the same line, saying that it would be better for a woman to permit herself to have relations with her own father than it would be for her to engage in "unnatural" relations with her husband. The woman who consents to her husband's commission of onanism was condemned as a mortal sinner in the thirteenth century by Alexander of Hales, and in the following century, women were advised to permit themselves to be killed before submitting to such indecencies. Contraceptive behavior was discouraged by enforced separation of spouses who engaged in it. A priest who learned from his confessant that she was engaging in intercourse in such a way that conception was impossible was told to go immediately to his bishop, who would enforce a separation decree against the sinning couple.[29]

Toward the end of the sixteenth century, Pope Sixtus V decreed that any person offering contraceptive potions to women, or participating in abortions, or counseling women on matters of contraception or abortion, as well as the women themselves who resorted to such measures, were to be excommunicated and turned over to the secular authorities. They were to be treated in all respects like murderers. Abortion, contraception, murder, and adultery, among other crimes, became capital offenses. After his death, his successor, Gregory XIV, annulled the penalties for most of these crimes, but kept those for abortion of forty-day fetuses.

With the passage of time some authorities took a more relaxed approach to these problems. In 1816 the Penitentiary gave permission to a woman whose husband practiced coitus interruptus to continue to have relations with him if refusal would result in harm to her. However, less than forty years later, the Holy Office of the Inquisition ruled that women could not participate in intercourse if the man used a condom, since "it would be participation in what is intrinsically unlawful." [30] But the Penitentiary continued to be more lenient, suggesting that confessors remain silent about such matters unless asked.[31]

St. Thomas Aquinas departed from the strict condemnation that had been the rule by appealing to a distinction Aristotle drew between an act and the pleasure associated with the act. "The pleasure proper to a worthy activity," Aristotle had said, "is good, and that proper to an unworthy activity bad."[32] It would follow, then, that if intercourse performed within marriage is good, the pleasure the couple derives from such intercourse is not bad. Nevertheless, the act itself determines whether the pleasure that accompanies it is legitimate, and not the converse. Therefore, if the purpose of the act is the pleasure it brings, according to Thomas, the act must be sinful. In other words, pleasure is legitimate if it is derived from legitimate intercourse, that is, from intercourse whose purpose is procreative. But if the sex acts are indulged in for the sake of pleasure, the acts themselves are sinful, and so is the pleasure derived from them.[33] Marriage, in fact, is a state that requires an "excuse," and is not good for its own sake.[34]

In the fifteenth century, Martin Le Maistre, a Parisian divine, introduced a new approach. Marriage, he said, was originally permitted as a means of preventing fornication. (This is reminiscent of some current arguments on the drug problem: If you can't stop people from doing it, legalize it so that they're not violating the law.) He concludes, therefore, that if a man is going to visit a woman with whom he had been accustomed to commit fornication before his marriage, and he fears that his old desires will come upon him, "his priest or any wise man would counsel him" to extinguish his desires through prudently having relations with his wife before setting out for his visit. Further, he said, one may take pleasure, either for the love of the pleasure itself, or "to avoid tedium and the ache of melancholy caused by the lack of pleasure." In either case, he says, the pleasure-seeking is not sinful, because deprivation leads to melancholy, and that in turn leads to illness, which is not good, for "the healthy are more fit for generation." [35] He argued that the view that copulation for the sake of pleasure is a mortal sin was dangerous for human morals; for it would then be no more sinful to have relations with another woman, under the impulse, than it would be to have them with one's wife.

Thomas Sanchez, in the seventeenth century, conceded that married couples could have intercourse without sin, even though they knew that the relationship would not be a fertile one; but he maintained that intercourse for the purpose of pleasure alone was sinful. This seems to have been the normative position for many centuries. If a spouse had an "urgent cause" to "show and foster mutual love," he was permitted to do so, even if it would result in unintentional semination.[36] Thus, the doctrine was maintained; the pleasure derived by spouses from their sexual behavior is not good in itself, but is tolerated only as a necessary evil—or, at best, as an unavoidable, or nearly unavoidable, by-product.

This emphasis on the undesirability of pleasure associated with sex is closely tied in with the concept of original sin, which assumes particular importance in the abortion controversy. According to St. Augustine, procreation was accomplished, before the Fall, by a virtuous act of the will, without the slightest hint of lust. After their sin, however, Adam and Eve "knew they were naked," that is, they became aware of a new and uncontrollable lust (concupiscence). Their genitals were no longer obedient to their will, but acted, as it were, of their own accord. Their sexual impulses could be satisfied only by an orgasm, a "shameful state" that completely engulfs the rational faculties. Every child, then, was literally conceived in the shameful, sinful heat of his parents' lust, and thus was transmitted to each child the original sin of his primordial ancestors, Adam and Eve. Some later theologians held that original sin was merely transmitted from father to son through the act of begetting, not as a part of the sex act itself, but as a part of the heritage of all mankind, suffered because "we were all present in his [Adam's] loins" when he committed his great offense.[37] Origen thought that baptism was designed to cleanse the soul of the stain of original sin, and that anyone who had not been so cleansed was doomed to a terrible fate in the next world. St. Fulgentius, in the sixth century, expressed the theory well when he wrote, "Even little children who have begun to live in their mother's womb and have there died, or who, having just been born, have passed away from the world without the sacrament of holy baptism, must be punished by the eternal torture of undying fire." [38] This doctrine has left its impress on later practice. It explains, at least partially, why abortion would be regarded as worse than murder; for the fate awaiting the unbaptized child is far worse than that which awaits the baptized victim of murder. Catholic physicians are supposed to remove the fetus from a deceased mother's womb for emergency baptism. To take care of those cases in which the fetus seems unlikely to survive birth, a special syringe has been invented that enables the physician to baptize the fetus while the latter is still in its mother's womb —with sterile holy water that is kept on hand for such emergencies. If a diseased organ containing a living fetus is excised, canon law requires that "the fetus should be extracted and baptized before the excised organ is sent to the pathologist.[39]

Modern Developments. In the middle of the nineteenth century, the Inquisition under Pope Pius IX declared that onanism (by which they meant coitus interruptus or other means of avoiding conception that resulted in "wasting" semen) was "scandalous, erroneous, and contrary to the natural law of marriage." [40]

The birth control movement became formally organized in the 1860's. Books and pamphlets advocating birth control were banned, and their authors and publishers were tried in England and elsewhere. But the movement caught on and hundreds of thousands of copies of the banned books and pamphlets were sold. Organizations for the dissemination of birth control information were formed in England, Germany, Spain, Brazil, Switzerland, Sweden, Italy, and elsewhere, and in the early twentieth century, a number of international congresses were held. The diaphragm was developed in 1880, and hundreds of other devices followed. As the movement gained momentum, efforts to check its effects became better organized, too. In France, a law was passed in 1920 forbidding the dissemination of "contraceptive propaganda" under pain of six months imprisonment. In the following decade the French government resorted to the ancient system of providing an inducement through cash bonuses or allowances that were increased as the size of the family increased. In the United States, the Comstock laws imposed penalties of up to ten years' imprisonment for anyone importing contraceptives, advertising them through the mails, or manufacturing, selling, or possessing them in the District of Columbia or other federal territories. As the years passed, however, the courts and Congress, as well as some of the state legislatures, whittled the laws down.

Modern arguments against contraception, in addition to those employed in earlier times, have included the argument that society ultimately will be brought to ruin and destruction if men are permitted to enjoy the pleasures of sex without the consequent burden of feeding and educating children. They will avoid bringing children into the world in order to be free of the burden of raising them, and will have lost nothing, because they will not be deprived of fulfillment of their sexual desires. Father John A. Ryan of the Catholic University of America argued that marriage is "the divinely appointed plan for cooperating with the Creator in perpetuating the race," and that true idealism of the highest sort "accepts the responsibility of bringing children into the world," where they may prove to be "either a blessing or a curse to society at large." Selfishness, however, leads to "race suicide," and is a "detestable thing." Further, through children, "the bond of love is strengthened, fresh stimulus is given to thrift and industrious effort, and the very sacrifices which are called for become sources of blessing." [41]

The Anglicans, after condemning contraception at the Lambeth conferences of 1908 and 1920, declared, in 1930, that a "clearly felt moral obligation to limit or avoid parenthood" could lead to measures to do so, based upon "Christian principles," of which the primary ones were complete abstinence from intercourse and a life of discipline and self-control. While strongly condemning the use of alternative methods from motives of "selfishness, luxury, or mere convenience," the bishops declared that they might be used, "provided that this is done in the light of the same Christian principles." [42] In December of the same year, Pope Pius XI issued the encyclical *Casti connubii*, which remained the principal Roman Catholic document on birth control for the next forty years. The Pope upheld the Church's traditional teaching that "any use whatever of marriage, in the exercise of which the act by human effort is deprived of its natural power of procreating life, violates the law of God and nature, and those who do such a thing are stained by a grave and mortal flaw." [43] Some people have suggested that this encyclical was not authoritative, that it did not carry with it the claim of papal infallibility. But according to Noonan, "it had immense doctrinal authority as a solemn declaration by the Pope." [44]

> By the ordinary tests used by the theologians to determine whether a doctrine is infallibly proclaimed, it may be argued that the specific condemnation of contraceptive interruption of the procreative act is infallibly set out. The encyclical is addressed to the universal Church. The Pope speaks in fulfillment of his apostolic office. He speaks for the Church. He speaks on moral doctrine that he says "has been transmitted from the beginning." He "promulgates" the teaching. If the Pope did not mean to use the full authority to speak *ex cathedra* on morals, which Vatican I recognized as his, what further language could he have used? [45]

The encyclical, for all practical purposes, was accepted as authoritative by the Church's officialdom. It condemned coitus interruptus; the use of condoms, diaphragms, and other contraceptive devices; the use of postcoital douches; and any form of sterilization. The use of the sterile period (i.e., the "rhythm" method) received cautious approval, and was accepted without reservation by Pope Pius XII in 1951. The use of *amplexus reservatus* seems to have more theoretical than practical interest, but theoretically at least it is sanctioned as a legitimate form of contraception by the Church. The male partner may bring his wife to climax, withdraw, take a cold shower, and go about his business, all with the sanction of the Church, so long as he does nothing "unnatural" either during or after intercourse.

In addition to the older arguments, a number of novel approaches were developed during recent years to answer critics of the Catholic doctrine. It was held, for example, that children in small families grow up spoiled and selfish; that contraception was a factor leading to family breakdown and divorce, as evidenced by the high proportion of divorces in families with one or no children; that it led to extramarital relations; that it caused physical or psychological harm to one or the other of the spouses (e.g., pelvic disorders in women, or cancers of various sorts, as well as nervous disorders); that it led to a "loss of reverence" for the wife, who was treated like a harlot by her contraceptive-using husband; that the use of contraceptives was selfish, exploitative, and destructive of meaningful relationships between husband and wife; that children born to parents who used contraceptives would die prematurely; that by increasing the number of children, those singing God's praises, both on earth and in heaven, are multiplied; and, of course, that any use of contraceptives was against nature.[46]

After extensive discussion, both in its inner councils and in various public forums, the Roman Catholic Church, through Pope Paul VI's encyclical *Humanae Vitae*, issued in 1968, reaffirmed its long-standing opposition to all forms of birth control except those traditionally found acceptable: abstinence and the rhythm method. The encyclical recognized the crisis posed by the world population explosion and acknowledged the problems faced by individual families who were sometimes taxed beyond their means to support themselves. It also noted the problems of the developing countries, whose economic, political, and educational development was threatened by overwhelming population growth. And it conceded that due consideration must be given to the role of women in modern society and the value of sexual love in marriage.

However, the encyclical adhered to traditional doctrines by insisting that proper sexual relations must be "fecund," for, as the Pope put it, "marriage and conjugal love are by their nature ordained toward the begetting and educating of children."[47] It follows, therefore, that husband and wife "are not free to proceed completely at will," but that they "must conform their activity to the creative intention of God," which is "that each and every marriage act must remain open to the transmission of life." Any behavior inconsistent with this rule contradicts the nature, "both of man and of woman and of their most intimate relationship," and is therefore contrary to God's plan and to God's will.[48]

On abortion, the Pope declared that "the direct interruption of the generative process already begun, and above all, directly willed and procured abortion, *even if for therapeutic reasons,* are to be absolutely excluded as licit means of regulating birth."[49] Similarly, direct sterilization, whether temporary or permanent, is specifically prohibited—thus eliminating the use of the pill—as is every other action which is intended to render procreation impossible, whether such action precedes intercourse, accompanies it, or follows it.[50] This effectively eliminates every known method of contraception, except the rhythm method, which the Pope considers to be acceptable on the ground that the latter method "make[s] legitimate use of a natural disposition," while other methods "impede the development of natural processes." Any act of marital intercourse that violates these rules "is intrinsically dishonest."[51]

In addition to the traditional arguments against contraception, the encyclical contains several that we did not notice earlier. (1) Young men, who are particularly vulnerable and weak, need special encouragement to abide by the moral rules governing marriage. The availability of contraceptives constitutes an incentive to violate those rules. (2) A man who uses contraceptives in his relations with his wife may come to lose respect for her, finally coming to think of her, and to treat her, as "a mere instrument for selfish enjoyment, and no longer as his respected and beloved companion." (3) Immoral public authorities may impose upon their communities a duty to use contraceptives favored by the authorities for the solution of social problems. If the use of such methods is legitimate for married couples in the solution of family problems, they will argue, it would be legitimate for the solution of community problems. Thus, "the most personal and most reserved sector of conjugal intimacy" would be placed "at the mercy of the intervention of public Authorities."[52]

The reaction of the Roman Catholic community to this encyclical is well known. Throughout the world influential Catholics, both lay and clergy, protested the Pope's decision and his reasoning. Others, more conservative in their approach, hailed the decision as an important landmark in the Church's battle against a "materialistic, permissive, humanist society," and called for unwavering, loving obedience.[53] There was a spate of resignations from the Church by clergymen and by nuns who were disappointed by the failure of the leadership in Rome to take the opportunity to liberalize the law and to relieve the anguish of those who had wanted to remain loyal to the Church but were finding it increasingly difficult to live within the framework of its policy on contraception.[54] The emotional reaction, and the extent of the problem, can perhaps be gauged from the following extracts from letters. The first was written by a Catholic mother and published in the *Catholic Herald.*

> I would like to let you know my experience as an ordinary Catholic woman trying to follow the Church's teaching on birth control.
>
> After having two babies soon after each other my husband and I practiced the safe period carefully but unsuccessfully, and we continued to have more babies. Our sixth child was born when the eldest was only eight, and he was epileptic and severely mentally handicapped.
>
> We knew we really mustn't have any more babies and were even more careful with the safe period. I kept a record of all my relevant dates and when I became pregnant again I just couldn't believe it.
>
> I spent nine weary months caring for our handicapped child and the five other little ones. I was terrified that the new baby would also be mentally defective.
>
> Fortunately the seventh child was quite normal, but now my husband said this really must be the end of our family; it was no use putting any more faith in the safe period. He said he was going to use contraceptives in the future; that it was his decision, his sin, and I could go to Communion with a clear conscience.
>
> I agreed, imagining myself going to the altar rails like a martyr suffering contraception. But I found it wasn't the terrible deed I had thought. . . . I felt better than I had for years—the sword which had been hanging over my head had gone. I began to live instead of just exist.
>
> But now, instead of suffering it as I had imagined, I condoned it and I couldn't with conscience go to Holy Communion. I began to dread going to Church. I sat at the back with the other people not going to Communion. I felt like an outsider in my own Church and used to ask myself "what are you doing here?" . . .

The second was written by a prominent Catholic theologian:

> Sympathy or even loyalty to the Pope must not blind one's judgement to the theological barrenness of the encyclical, to its lack of reality, and its imprudence. To call upon public authorities in our contemporary pluralist society to place a ban on contraception shows a divorce from the facts of the contemporary world which is both incredible and alarming.
>
> In fact the encyclical is an attempt to turn the clock back. Brutally and blandly it brushes aside the whole development of Catholic thought on birth control which has taken place since the calling of the [Second Vatican] Council. It reaffirms as a fact a natural law position which has been rejected by many of the best minds in the Church and gives no justification for doing so. It ignores the fact that once freedom of discussion was gained within the Church the traditional position was exposed as riddled with contradictions and unproved assumptions. In an attempt to escape from the rigours of its own logic it suggests that Catholics can always have recourse to the confessional. Is it seriously suggested that Catholics using contraceptives should go to confession, be absolved and then immediately return to the use of contraceptives? Such a situation far from strengthening the respect for spiritual

authority would radically undermine it. Catholics today do not require compassion in the confessional . . . but freedom and responsibility.[55]

Despite the outcry and the uproar, the official position of the Church remains what it has been for centuries, with a few minor modifications.

The Church's only major departure from the medieval stand on abortion has been toward a stricter definition of the time when abortion becomes a criminal act. During the Middle Ages, it was widely assumed that "ensoulment"—that is, the moment when a fetus received its soul and thus became a human being in the true sense of the word—occurred on the fortieth day for males and on the eightieth day for females.[56] Therefore, the abortion of a fetus prior to the fortieth or the eightieth day would not be as serious as the abortion of a fetus that had passed those landmarks, because an earlier abortion would be an abortion of a *potential* human being, but not of an *actual* one. Because no soul had entered the fetus, no one would suffer an eternity of torment in hell for having died unbaptized and therefore tainted with original sin. In 1869 Pope Pius IX eliminated the distinction between an animated and an unanimated fetus, decreeing that all fetuses should be considered to be ensouled from conception. Thus, *any* abortion would now be considered equivalent to murder.[57] In the United States, abortion before quickening (i.e., before the mother could perceive fetal movements) was not punishable until about 1860, and even after that the distinction between a "quick" child and one that had not yet "quickened" remained in most states.[58]

In Mississippi, for example, destruction of a fetus that has not quickened is no crime, whereas in other states, it may be less severely punished than abortion after quickening. A judge in Wisconsin justified the distinction between "quick" fetuses and those that are not "quickened" as follows:

> In a strictly scientific and psychological sense there is life in an embryo from the time of conception, and in such sense there is also life in the male and female elements that unite to form the embryo. But law for obvious reasons cannot in its clasifications follow the latest or ultimate declarations of science. It must for purposes of practical efficiency proceed upon more everyday and popular conceptions, especially as to definitions of crimes that are *malum in se*. These must be of such a nature that the ordinary normal adult knows it is morally wrong to commit them. That it should be less of an offense to destroy an embryo in a stage where human life in its common acceptance has not yet begun than to destroy a quick child is a conclusion that commends itself to most men.[59]

"Quickening" is thus defined, here, in its "common acceptance" as the time when human life begins; that is, as the time when ordinary people would conceive of the fetus as something more than a mere cluster of cells or a relatively undifferentiated mass of human tissue. Exactly when one state is transformed to the other is not defined here, but is presumably dependent upon the possession by the embryo of such features as independent movement, an operative circulatory system, and more or less well-developed human facial and bodily characteristics. It would be difficult to pinpoint the moment at which such a transformation might occur, but the prescientific forty- and eighty-day criterion of Aristotle and the medievals need not be adopted; nor is it necessary to adhere rigidly to the rather indefinite and subjective criterion of the mother's feeling of fetal movements. If the court should wish to have some clear and definite criterion, it might have to be disappointed; but it would seem that in this area, as in so many others, the existence of borderline cases should be no hindrance to rendering decisions in those that evidently fall on one side or the other of the fuzzy area that lies between. However, the existence of the fuzzy area does place a great burden on women seeking an abortion and on others who may wish to help them, because it leaves them in a state of uncertainty about the legality or the illegality of their actions—or, if they are attempting to calculate the potential costs to themselves in terms of fines or jail sentences, it leaves that up in the air, too, because if they are caught, it will be up to the judge to determine whether their case comes under the "popular conception" of serious crime, or that of a minor offense.

THE DEVELOPMENT OF JEWISH DOCTRINE

Judaism knows nothing of the doctrine of original sin. Pious Jews recite a prayer each morning thanking God for having given them a soul that is pure, and throughout rabbinic literature, the emphasis is upon man's capacity to maintain himself in a state of "purity" through good works and the avoidance of sinful behavior. Sin is viewed not so much as a state, as a form of behavior. An ancient commentary on the Bible says, "Even as the soul is pure upon entering upon its earthly career, so let man return it pure to his Maker." [60] Sin, according to the ancient rabbis, was universal, but not because of a hereditary blemish. Rather, human weakness and the multitude of wrongful acts that one may perform, intentionally or unintentionally, cause damage or harm to persons or to the order of the state or the universe.[61]

The problem of interpretation posed by the Biblical story of Er and Onan is a difficult one, too complex to be discussed in detail here. In Jewish tradition there has been considerable disagreement over the true intent of the passage, and over its legal and moral implications. Some authorities have accepted an interpretation similar to that which was adopted by Christian commentators—that the sin for which Er and Onan were killed was coitus interruptus. They have accordingly concluded that any "wasting" of seed is sinful and is prohibited. But most of them, including Maimonides, ruled that because there is no explicit condemnation of the practice in the Bible, nothing more can be inferred than that it is undesirable and that it may be punished by divine wrath, but that it is beyond the jurisdiction of human courts.[62] From about the thirteenth century, after the publication of the Zohar, a mystical work that had enormous influence on some persons but was totally rejected by others, a tendency to be more severe, along the lines of Catholicism, developed, comparing the wasting of seed to homicide. But for the most part, the authorities clung to the older assumption that the story of Er and Onan offered no justification for judicial condemnation of coitus interruptus or of other contraceptive acts.[63]

Some Talmudic passages suggest that Er's sin consisted in selfishly preventing his wife from conceiving in order to preserve her physical charms, whereas later commentators thought that he didn't want to be burdened by the responsibilities of raising children. In either case, the sin consisted of a violation of the commandment (as it is interpreted by these commentators) given to Adam and to Noah—to be fruitful and multiply. But Onan's transgression, which is the only one actually mentioned in the Biblical text, was not understood by most rabbinical authorities as the Church understood it. The rabbis connected it with Onan's duty as a levirate; that is, his duty, as Tamar's deceased husband's closest relative, to bring a child into the world to carry on his late brother's name and estate. The death penalty inflicted by God may be understood if we recall that elsewhere in the Bible, a man is forbidden to marry his deceased brother's wife on pain of an untimely death; that is, early death through natural (or divine) causes.[64] Strictly speaking, then, Onan had no right to marry Tamar. But he had a duty to marry her as a consequence of his being the levirate after his brother's death. The prohibition against his having relations with Tamar was lifted so that he could fulfill his obligation under the duty of levirate marriage, namely, to provide an heir for his deceased brother. When he frustrated that purpose by using contraceptive methods—whatever those methods may have been— he violated the condition upon which the original prohibition was lifted. Therefore, the prohibition returned in full force, and he suffered the penalty for violating it.[65] The rabbis of the Talmud clearly understood the implications of these passages, for they declared that one might take a wife for beauty, for money, or for other qualities, but "he who has relations with his levirate wife because of her beauty or for similar reasons has engaged in illicit intercourse." [66] Because of the special circumstances in Onan's case, it is impossible to apply the rule to ordinary marital relations.

On the question of virginity as opposed to marriage, there was no equivocation among Jewish authorities. Of course virginity was desirable, but only up to the time of marriage. Marriage itself was not a state that was merely tolerated because of human weakness and lust, but rather a divine commandment. "It is not good for man to be alone," the Bible had said, and the rabbis of the Talmud and of later generations reaffirmed the principle by urging their followers to marry early and to fulfill the sacred task of bringing children into the world. But a wife was more than a mere breeding machine; she was a "helpmate for him." "He who has no wife," said one authority, "lives without good, or help, or joy, or blessing, or atonement." And another added, "He is not really a complete man; he diminishes the image of God." [67] Still another said, "If a man marries a goodly wife, it is as though he had fulfilled the whole Torah from beginning to end," that is, he has fulfilled every divine commandment.[68] Although men were encouraged to marry young in order to avoid falling into evil behavior through temptation, marriage itself was not considered an escape valve for persons having a disposition to sinful thoughts or behavior, but as a state that was desirable in itself.

The rabbis were not hedonists. They reserved some of their most vituperative remarks for "Epicureans," that is, materialists who denied the existence of spiritual beings and followed a hedonistic ethic. But being antihedonistic does not necessarily require the adoption of an ascetic ideal. Pleasure may not be the ultimate end of all action, but that is not to deny that it might be the legitimate end of some actions. Pleasure may not be the only good, but that does not entail the denial that pleasure is good at all. The rabbis of the Talmud and most of the rabbis of later generations could see nothing wrong with the pleasure that accompanied sexual intercourse. There was nothing wrong with pleasure, though the intercourse itself, and therefore the pleasure that accompanied it, might be illegitimate for any of a number of reasons, such as adultery, incest, and the like.

If sexual pleasure is not evil, then perhaps intercourse for the sake of pleasure alone, including intercourse that one knows cannot result in impregnation, is legitimate. In fact, the rabbis were remarkably liberal in their attitudes toward unions in which procreation was impossible. Because marriage was valuable in itself, regardless of its possible procreative outcome, they permitted men and women who were childless to remain together, even though it was evident that no children would ever result from their marriage. A fourteenth-century decision by Isaac ben Sheshet held that a childless couple who did not want a divorce were to be left undisturbed, for their marriage involved "nothing immoral or forbidden or even offensive to holiness." [69]

The rabbis of the Talmud found justification in a Biblical text for their view that marital intercourse is a duty, a positive obligation, regardless of its possible outcome.[70] In their view this entailed a number of consequences. One was the nullification of any premarital agreement entered into by husband and wife which relieved either of his or her duty .to give sexual satisfaction to the other. Another had to do with vows of abstinence. Pious men would occasionally vow to abstain from one kind of pleasure or another (such as drinking wine) as a form of penance or as a means of approaching a state of oneness with God. If anyone vowed to deny his wife the pleasure of marital intercourse, however, the Talmudists declared that his vow—even though it might have been made in accordance with all the religious forms— was null and void. And if he took a vow to deny such pleasure to *himself*, a time limit of one week was imposed upon him since, after all, his wife was involved too.[71] A woman was obliged to fulfill her husband's desire. Sex was considered a beautiful and a holy thing, as well as a pleasurable one. With such attitudes as these, "spiritual marriage," in which husband and wife live together as brother and sister in the name of sexual asceticism—a practice that was not uncommon in early Christianity and is still practiced from time to time—is virtually unthinkable.[72] When a man has relations with his wife, he is said, by rabbinic authorities in all ages, to be fulfilling the divine command of "giving his wife pleasure," recalling the Biblical draft law: If a man had been married recently, he was to be granted a year's deferment from military service so that he might "rejoice with the wife whom he had married."[73] In the thirteenth century, Maimonides summed up Judaism's attitude toward asceticism as follows.

> Some people suppose that since jealousy, lust, pride, and the like are considered to be vices, it would be best to avoid them by going to the opposite extreme, by not eating meat, or drinking wine, or marrying, or dwelling in a nice home, or wearing beautiful garments. . . . But this too is wrong, and one is forbidden to behave in such a way. One who lives an ascetic life is considered sinful. . . . Our sages have decreed that no man should deprive himself of anything unless it is specifically forbidden by law . . . for they asked, "Has the law not prohibited enough for you? Must you impose additional deprivations upon yourself?"[74]

Even the most pietistic sects among the Jews of the Middle Ages rejected asceticism, particularly sexual asceticism. Sexual abstinence was never considered an appropriate vehicle for penitence, and sexual asceticism was never considered to have any religious value.[75] One of the most important works of medieval Jewish piety assigned a prominent place to the establishment and maintenance of normal and reasonable sexual life within marriage.[76]

If pleasure is not only legitimate but desirable, then many restrictions, though certainly not all of them, may begin to fall away. The purpose of intercourse is not only procreation, but also pleasure. Again, Maimonides, who was by no means in favor of overindulgence in sex, either from a moral point of view or on medical grounds, expressed the traditional law, which was reiterated throughout the centuries:

> A man and his wife have the right to have relations with one another. Therefore, he may do what he wishes. He may have intercourse with her at any time [except during her menstrual period], he may kiss her wherever he pleases, and he may have relations with her either in the usual fashion or in some other way. . . .[77]

In the eighteenth century, Jacob Emden, in his commentary on the traditional prayer book, observed that the Sabbath was a particularly appropriate day for marital relations, since it was a day that was both sacred and joyous. Then he continued:

> To us the sexual act is worthy, good, and beneficial even to the soul. No other human activity compares with it; when performed with pure and clean intention it is certainly holy. There is nothing impure or defective about it, rather it is most exalted.[78]

Judaism is not monolithic. It has no central organization, comparable to the Roman hierarchy, empowered to pass final judgment on faith and morals for all Jews everywhere. Each community has its own spiritual leader, whose judgment sets the tone for that community. He will naturally consult other authorities, particularly if he respects them for their wisdom and their learning, and he will base his judgments, as far as practicable, upon precedents recorded in the literature. But because of the lack of central authority, considerable differences in practice may be observed from one community to another, and there is no lack of disagreement among the authorities on many issues. Nevertheless, certain trends are distinguishable, and in this area, the consensus seems to be that the first five foundations upon which the Catholic condemnation of contraception and abortion rests were not acceptable to traditional authorities from early times onward; they were even more explicitly rejected by the more liberal movements in modern Judaism. Original sin is unknown; the story of Er and Onan is interpreted in such a way as to deny that they were put to death for what has come to be known as onanism; marriage is not a concession to human weakness, but a positive divine commandment, a duty that every person is expected to fulfill; even the most ascetic sects, who were always a tiny minority, refused to deny the legitimacy of sexual pleasure; and most authorities, for the past 2,000 years at least, have maintained that marital intercourse *for pleasure alone* is not only legitimate, but may, in certain circumstances, be a positive obligation. *Pleasurable* sex, and not only procreative sex, is *natural.* It should not be surprising, therefore, if we find that contraception and abortion are not looked upon with the abhorrence that are so common within the Christian tradition. From Talmudic times, dating back at least to the second century, we find references to the use of contraceptive devices and practices; and most such references do not condemn the practice. Indeed, some references prior to the second century which remain authoritative to this day in traditional circles, impose an obligation upon women to use contraceptive tampons when pregnancy may cause physical harm to them or to their children, as it might, for example, if the woman were too young or too weak to bear children, or if she were still nursing and a pregnancy would cut off her baby's supply of milk.[79]

Although there was considerable disagreement over the use of mechanical devices to prevent conception, there was near unanimity, even in ancient times, over the use of oral contraceptives. The latter are mentioned as early as the Mishnah and the Tosephta (prior to about the second century), where women are explicitly granted permission to use them.[80] Though the authorities had some reservations about mechanical contraceptives, their only major concern about oral contraceptives had to do with the safety of the product. Even the most conservative authorities on the question of mechanical contraceptives agreed that oral contraceptives may be used, for "it is agreed, without dissent, that this is the best of all measures to take." [81] Early in the nineteenth century, the renowned and highly respected Hatam Sofer (Moses Schreiber Sofer of Pressburg) was confronted with a case in which a woman suffered unusual pain in childbirth. He ruled that she should use contraceptives, for, as he put it, "she need not build the world by destroying herself." He added that if her husband refused to grant her permission to use oral contraceptives, she could either obtain a divorce or refuse to engage in sexual relations with him. She had no duty to endure such pain for his sake.[82]

In recent years, as new methods of contraception have been developed, the literature has been full of opinions; and here, again, the most orthodox rabbis are surprisingly lenient. They welcomed the invention of the diaphragm because, as Hayyim Sofer, a disciple of the Hatam Sofer, wrote in the 1860's, it does nothing to impede contact, and thus does not diminish the natural gratifications of the sex act or the "full physical pleasure and . . . the flaming ardor of passion."[83] Spermicides were accepted quite readily, and intrauterine devices were received by some with mixed feelings only because of the possibility that some form of abortion might be involved. Thus far, however, there has not been much reaction, either to the IUD's or to the pill. The legitimacy of the pill seems to be taken for granted in the literature that has appeared so far, based upon analogies with oral contraceptives permitted through the centuries. The only major reservations have been based on medical grounds, on fears that some unforeseen harm may come to the mother as a result of resorting to these relatively new and untested methods. As for the so-called safe period, the consensus seems to be that although there are times when a woman may not conceive, it is too difficult to know just when those times may occur with any degree of accuracy. Abstinence is of course permitted, under proper conditions (namely, when neither the husband nor the wife is unreasonably deprived of marital rights); but when pregnancy must be avoided on medical grounds, it is deemed to be an inadequate safeguard.[84]

So far as contraception is concerned, then, the Jewish tradition, because of its rejection of the major principles upon which the Catholic rejection of artificial means of birth control is based, is quite lenient. With some exceptions, even the most orthodox authorities throughout the past two millennia have permitted some forms of birth control. Where a hazard to the woman's health is concerned, they are unanimous: she is not only permitted to resort to artificial methods of contraception; she may have a religious duty to do so.

We turn now to the question of abortion.

The principal issue here is whether feticide is a form of homicide. The answer was given in the Talmud in the early Middle Ages, during the course of a discussion of a passage in the Book of Exodus. "He who causes the death of a man must be put to death."[85] By comparing this passage with another, in the Book of Leviticus, which contains the same legal principle but an important variation in wording, the authorities arrived at an answer to the question of the status of abortion. In Leviticus, the text reads, "If a man causes the death of any living human being, he must be put to death." The qualification introduced by the word *living*, they said, indicates that the rule on homicide applies only to a human being who has already been born.[86] The Biblical text itself offers further support for this view, for in Exodus 21:22, a person who negligently causes a woman to miscarry is held liable for payment of damages, but there is no suggestion that he is guilty of homicide.[87] Until the moment of birth, then, there was no criminal liability for the destruction of a fetus; but from the moment of birth, the fetus assumed a status different from that which it had had the moment before, and it acquired rights—including the right of inheritance, for example—that it had not enjoyed while it was still in its mother's womb.[88] Because the fetus is considered to be merely a part of its mother's body, like her appendix, prior to its actual birth, there is no legal prohibition whatever against causing its death or destroying it, though one would not ordinarily encourage people to do so unless there were some special justification for such an action. But when there are special justifications, as when the mother's life is threatened, there is no question whatever in the rabbis' minds that the fetus may be destroyed. As they put it, if the mother's life is threatened, the fetus may be cut out limb by limb, if that is necessary to save her.[89]

The time of animation or ensoulment, it would appear, would not be particularly important if, as we have seen, a child may be sacrificed right up to the moment of its birth. (From that moment on, the rabbis are in unanimous agreement that it may not be destroyed, no matter what the reason.) This opinion is borne out in many sources, including one that dates back to the thirteenth century. Meir Abulafia concludes that the soul enters the fetus at the moment of conception, but that this has nothing whatever to do with the question of feticide, because the fetus is not a "living person" until it is born. Most of the Jewish religious and legal thinkers who considered the question seem to have concluded that the precise moment when a child becomes a person in a sufficiently "complete" sense to warrant admission to heaven is one of the secrets of God which no amount of speculation will ever reveal.[90] Because they were untroubled by the doctrine of original sin, they had no need to concern themselves over the possibility of an eternity of torment for the soul, or even a period in limbo, if the fetus died without baptism.

Therapeutic abortion is accepted in most of the sources. But what of abortion for other causes? As we have seen, the prevailing view is that if any person causes the death or destruction of a fetus prior to its birth, he is not criminally liable, though he may be liable for damages. However, though one may not be *liable* for causing a nontherapeutic abortion, in that no penalty attaches to such an act in Jewish law, it seems clear that one may have a *prima facie* duty not to participate in such an abortion, unless there is some justification for doing so. The question remains, then, as to what other justifications there might be.

Among the justifications that Jewish legal thinkers have found for abortion —both in previous generations and in recent and contemporary literature on the subject—are the following:

1. Where the woman's continuing pregnancy or her giving birth to the fetus will result in her death or constitute a serious threat to her physical well-being.
2. Where the pregnancy poses a danger of extreme mental anguish to the mother. The most conservative authorities limit this to cases where the mother shows suicidal tendencies, but others maintain that a risk to mental health is as serious as a risk to physical health and that abortion is indicated even when the woman shows no suicidal tendencies.
3. Where the pregnancy poses a danger to the health of an existing child, as in a situation where the infant depends upon its mother's milk and cannot be put on a formula, and the new pregnancy threatens to shut off the flow of milk.[91]
4. Where the woman has become pregnant as a result of rape. As Yeruham Perilman put it in 1891, though a woman may be a vehicle for reproduction, she must not be compared to Mother Earth, for she need not nurture seed implanted within her against her will. On the contrary, he said, she has the right to uproot seed that was sown illegally.[92]
5. Where carrying the child or bearing it will cause serious mental suffering to the mother—even though such suffering may be short of mental illness. Included under this rule would be thalidomide babies, fetuses whose mothers have been exposed to German measles (rubella), and even illegitimate babies whose birth would cause great anguish to their mothers.[93]

All the authorities cited in this discussion are extremely conservative. In modern terms they would all be considered orthodox. No authority from the more liberal branches of modern Judaism has been discussed here. Many of the latter advocate abortion on demand and would eliminate all legal sanctions against abortions performed for any purpose. The authors whose views have been discussed here, representing some of the most respected thinkers in Jewish jurisprudence and religious thought of the past 2,000 years, do not go that far. With a few notable exceptions, they would not allow abortion on demand. But they would clearly not favor criminal prosecution of persons who had participated in abortions, and they recognized most, if not all, of the grounds for abortion that are being advocated today by those who would reform our laws. Clearly, they were able to develop positions such as these because they were unfettered by the ideological presuppositions that have done so much to determine the Catholic Church's stand on this issue.

Recently in Great Britain and in a number of American states the abortion laws have been revised to enable many women, under certain circumstances, to obtain therapeutic abortions. In a few states, such as New York, all restrictions on abortion have been removed. Now, not only women who fear for their lives if they carry to term, who have been exposed to rubella or to other diseases or drugs that might cause grave deformities in the fetuses they carry in their wombs, or who have become pregnant because of rape or incest, but even girls who have become pregnant as a result of an indiscretion may arrange legally for medical experts to remove the unwanted fetuses from their wombs in the sterile conditions of modern hospitals and clinics.

We are not concerned here with history as such, and we are therefore not concerned with the historical developments that gave rise to these legal innovations. We are concerned, rather, with questions of morality. Are these developments good or are they bad? Should those responsible for the legalization of abortion, for the distribution of contraceptive devices, and for the popularization of such practices be considered immoral? Have they contributed to a general breakdown in the moral fabric of our society? Are those who use such devices or resort to abortion—legal or illegal—guilty of moral crimes? These are the questions to which we must direct our attention.

A CRITIQUE OF RESTRICTIVE LAWS

CASE 6. THE THALIDOMIDE TRAGEDY

In 1962 Mrs. Sherri Finkbine learned about the terrible effects a supposedly harmless sleeping pill was having upon children born to mothers who had been using it. An extremely large number of children had been born in Europe, where the drug was being sold over the counter, with the most grotesque deformities. Mrs. Finkbine, a mother of four healthy children, had innocently taken a pill that her husband had brought home from a trip to Europe. After reading the article, she checked with her doctor, who wired the pharmacy that had filled her husband's prescription in England. Upon receiving the response, he told her, "Sherri, if you were my own wife I'd tell you the exact same thing. The odds for a normal baby are so against you that I am recommending termination of pregnancy." He assured her that it was a very simple matter, that a number of abortions were performed every year in Phoenix, and that she merely had to write a note to a three-doctor medical board explaining her reasons for wanting the operation.

After all the arrangements had been made, she began to think of all the other women who might have taken thalidomide and remained unaware of the tragedy that might be awaiting them. Out of concern for them, she called the local newspaper and suggested to the editor that a suitable warning should be published. Of course, she asked the editor not to use her name. He kept his word, but the next day's paper bore a sensational front-page article, bordered in black, with the headline, "Baby-Deforming Drug May Cost Woman Her Child Here." The wire services picked up the story, and, because of the national publicity the case had received, the doctors canceled her operation. Concerned over the possibility that someone might bring a court challenge to their right to perform the abortion, in view of the state's rather vague law, which permitted abortion only to save the life of the mother, they sought a declaratory judgment in court, but were turned down by an unsympathetic judge.

The official Vatican newspaper did pronounce judgment, however, and condemned Mrs. Finkbine and her husband as murderers. She received thousands of letters, many of them sympathetic, but some of them seething with religious hatred: "I hope someone takes the other four and strangles them, because it is all the same thing," one said, and another expressed the hope that God would punish her for her "murderous sin." Many letters were written by well-meaning persons who put themselves in the position of Mrs. Finkbine's unborn child: "Mommy, please dear Mommy, let me live. Please, please, I want to live. Let me love you, let me see the light of day, let me smell a rose, let me sing a song, let me look into your face, let me say Mommy." And there were many, many more.

Unable to obtain a legal abortion anywhere in the United States, she decided to go overseas. Japan, which had a lenient abortion law, refused to issue a visa out of fear of anti-American demonstrations. Finally, she went to Sweden, and, after going through the rigorous Swedish screening process, she was given the medical board's approval for an abortion. After the abortion, she asked her doctor whether the baby was a boy or a girl. He replied that it was not a baby, but an abnormal growth that would never have been a normal child.[94]

CASE 7. CHILD OF VIOLENCE

In 1955 a twenty-seven-year-old mother returned to her home after visiting her husband at the hospital. A 220-pound guard from a nearby Air Force base forced his way into her home, gagged her, tied her hands, and attacked her. In spite of medical treatment that she received, both at a hospital and from her own physician, she became pregnant as a result of the episode. No hospital in her state was willing to permit her to have a therapeutic abortion, although that state's law was at that time one of the most liberal in the nation.

She and her husband could not afford to travel abroad for a legal abortion. They were accordingly left with two alternatives: a clandestine, illegal abortion or bringing the baby to term. Because they were deeply religious people, and deeply committed to respect for the law, they chose the latter alternative. She carried the fetus in her womb, hating it—as she said many times—every minute, waiting for the moment when she would at last be rid of it. Thus the child, conceived in violence and born in hatred, came into the world.

These cases are only two of many possible combinations of events that lead women to seek abortions. At Johns Hopkins hospital some years ago, the Children's Aid Society was unable to procure an abortion for a fourteen-year-old girl who had become pregnant as a result of an attack upon her by her drunken father.[95] The potential damage to this young child, both physically and psychologically, was judged by the state's legal authorities to be insufficient to warrant an abortion.

Women who suffer from serious diseases, such as heart disease, tuberculosis, and leukemia, receive sympathetic understanding, though usually they can expect very little more from those to whom they turn for help. But women who have become pregnant by accident and feel that they are past the child-raising stage of life, having sent all their children through school; and women who believe that a pregnancy will destroy their careers or possibly even their marriages; and women who conceive out of wedlock—all of these women receive little sympathy or understanding for their problems in many hospitals and doctors' offices, and even less in their state capitols.

Part of the moral problem is a function of sympathy for women in such circumstances as these, of compassion for them and their families, and of concern for the children who may be born as a result of such unions or to women who are unable or unwilling—often for very good reasons—to care for them. But the problem is aggravated by other factors, not the least of which is the grave risk that every woman who seeks an illegal abortion takes and the danger to her life and her health. Because there are no accurate figures on the number of illegal abortions performed each year in any given area, it is impossible to determine what percentage of such abortions leads to serious injury to the patient. But the cases that come to the attention of the police are sufficiently numerous and sufficiently shocking to give reason for serious concern. One case, authoritatively reported, concerned a quack doctor who displayed a counterfeit diploma in his office. He had no medical training, but "practiced" for a number of years in Harlem's black ghetto. Among other gimmicks, he used a machine that he designed himself. This machine, the "electrohelomat," consisted of a large cabinet with numerous switches and flashing lights. During the treatment the patient was instructed to press certain switches. Meanwhile, the so-called doctor operated an impressive array of buzzers, relays, and sparking devices. He was arrested following the death of one of his patients, a young waitress. The autopsy revealed "that the defendant had punctured the uterus in five places with a sharp loop-type currette and had also pulled down sixteen inches of intestine before he became panic stricken and deposited the dying girl in Central Park." According to the autopsy report, he also managed to rupture the girl's bladder.[96] Not only quacks who know nothing of medicine or female anatomy, but even some licensed physicians have been known to treat their desperate victims brutally and sadistically. More than one woman has discovered that part of the price of her abortion consisted of satisfying the sexual appetites of her abortionist, with or without her consent. The literature abounds in well-documented horror stories which we need not dwell upon here.

Another kind of horror story concerns the woman who attempts to induce an abortion on herself. Most such attempts, it seems, are simply unsuccessful. Desperate women employ every device imaginable, from hat pins, clothes hangers, and knitting needles, to injections of soap solutions, lye, and other poisons. Some attempt to abort themselves by jumping from high places, by falling down stairs, or by resorting to other means of bringing on physical trauma. When an abortion follows such attempts, it is not necessarily a result of the woman's efforts to induce it, for it might have occurred spontaneously anyway. In the meantime she has exposed herself to serious danger of permanent injury or death. When women have injured themselves through such efforts, their stories make excellent material for advocates of abortion law reforms.

Opponents of such reforms have their own chamber of horrors. They are sometimes given to projecting slides showing fetuses at a fairly mature stage of development to their audiences, or to relating tales of aborted infants crying for twenty minutes or more after the operation before expiring in the pans or trays or cans into which they had been consigned. Occasionally they produce real human fetuses in jars or bottles, which may be examined by those who are sufficiently curious in order to produce in them an appropriate sense of revulsion. The president of the Catholic Physicians Guild of Colorado brought four such pickled fetuses to a hearing that the State Senate was holding prior to passage of that state's liberalized abortion law. After he was gaveled down, he told a reporter, "I got mad. They said a fetus wasn't a human being. I wanted to show them they were dealing with babies, not blobs of protoplasm." [97]

Such emotion-packed stories and displays are not entirely inappropriate in discussions of this issue, though they are surely not conducive to dispassionate consideration of the arguments on either side. The issue is, after all, at least partly an emotional one. Strong feelings are evident on all sides. The existence of such feelings must not be overlooked, for it is indicative of the depth of the moral concerns involved. Nevertheless, because stories and displays prove very little, though they may be highly provocative, we shall concentrate here upon the arguments themselves.

For similar reasons, we shall not consider the evidence that has become available through the efforts of various opinion research organizations. Such research reveals, quite consistently, that public opinion has swung strongly to the side of the reformers, particularly where an abortion is sought for medical, as opposed to social or economic, reasons. Among physicians, a poll of some 40,000 doctors revealed that nearly 90 per cent approved of liberalization, and that nearly half of those were of the Catholic faith. But such findings, though of interest, prove only that public opinion is changing and that the chances for further liberalization of the laws in some states may be greater than they were some years ago. But they provide no measure of the depth of moral thinking that is going on in the country, and they do nothing to answer the moral questions that have been posed by philosophers and theologians and others who are concerned to determine whether there ought to be changes in these laws and practices, regardless of what public opinion at one particular time in history may be. Having mentioned the fact that public opinion seems to be swinging, we may now ignore it and proceed to other questions.

Some questions are beyond the scope of this book, though they have a profound bearing upon some of these issues for some people. This is not the place to undertake a critique of the dogmas of any particular religious faith. I doubt whether any rational criticism of such dogmas would make any difference to those who believe in them, because many persons accept them for what they are—dogmas, whose acceptance depends not upon rational argument and justification, but upon religious faith and authority. Those who believe in original sin or in the ascetic ideal are not likely to be changed in their thinking on those subjects by any arguments that I may offer here, though they may be offended by them. Similarly, those who do *not* believe in such dogmas are not likely to be persuaded that they are true by any arguments that I might adduce through scriptural citations or quotations from other holy books. We shall therefore direct our attention to questions upon which some agreement might be sought among all rational men, whatever their religious persuasion.

Judaism and Christianity in all their manifestations are in complete agreement about the principle of the sanctity of human life. In spite of many differences in detail, these religious traditions have undoubtedly made a great contribution to the advancement of civilization through their propagation of the doctrine that all human life is sacred and inviolate. They also agree, with certain notable exceptions, that mercy and compassion are great human virtues and that needless suffering is abhorrent to the human conscience. Though one may disagree with the Catholic doctrine of original sin and with the Church's firm opposition to every attempt to liberalize abortion laws, it would be unfair for anyone discussing this issue not to acknowledge the deep moral concern that lies behind that position; for if the dogma of original sin were true, if it were true that every fetus possesses an immortal soul, and if it were true that unbaptized souls would be condemned to spend all eternity in limbo, then compassion for the innocent would move any man of conscience to adopt the same position. The thought of innumerable small children being consigned to limbo and deprived of the beatific vision of God that they might otherwise have enjoyed might be enough to persuade him to abandon any efforts he might be making to provide a mere temporary relief in this world to those who might suffer physically or psychologically because of an unwanted pregnancy. If the state's function is to protect the innocent from harm, then the state might—if these dogmas were true—have a duty to use every means at its command to prevent the abortion of one single fetus.

But many persons do not accept these dogmas. Many Protestants, all Jews, and those of other faiths and of no faith reject the dogma of original sin. Many persons doubt whether the doctrine of the soul is at all meaningful, and they have marshalled powerful arguments against the traditional position.[98] Others, who either have taken no position on the soul–body problem or have accepted one or another version of the theory that there is a soul, nevertheless reject the theory that the fetus is "ensouled" at conception. Still others believe that even if a fetus has a soul or acquires one at some time prior to its birth, it is still not fully "human" until after it is born; for they believe that there are other characteristics that must be present before an organism can qualify as human. And finally, some people who accept *both* of the preceding might be dubious over the proposition that God, who is represented as a loving and merciful father, would permit children innocent of any deliberate sin to be deprived eternally of God's blessings because of the sins of some ancestors at the beginning of time.

To say that each ovum that is fertilized by a sperm becomes a human being at that moment is clearly arbitrary. Such a fertilized ovum is *potentially* a human being, capable of *developing* into a human being, but, one may assert with some plausibility, it is *not* a human being. If a squirrel eats an acorn, it consumes what might have developed into an oak tree, but it would be a gross error to suggest that the squirrel had swallowed an oak tree. If a woman has a miscarriage at the end of her first month of pregnancy, what she aborts does not resemble a child in physical appearance, it has only a rudimentary nervous system, it certainly possesses no memory, no feelings, no capacity to reason, and no personality. If some, at least, of these characteristics are necessary for humanness, as some philosophers have held, then the early fetus, and even the later fetus and perhaps even the newborn infant, do not qualify as fully human. "Human," in the context of the abortion issue, clearly possesses evaluative or normative force. It is wrong to cause the death of a human; but if an organism is less than human, subhuman, or not human, most persons have less repugnance over its being killed or being permitted to die. Sherri Finkbine's Swedish doctor did well to tell her that he had removed an abnormal growth and not a baby, for he recognized the distinction between the emotive force generated by the one term and that generated by the other. No one becomes depressed over the removal of inflamed adenoids, nor does anyone go into mourning over the excision and death of a cancerous growth. An abnormal growth is one which by definition does not belong where it is. We react negatively to its presence, and we accept its removal without regret. But people do become depressed over any harm that befalls a baby, and they react emotionally, even to the point of going into mourning, over a baby's death, whether from natural or from other causes. Emotionally, we react positively to babies. They are "cuddly," "adorable," "cute," "soft," "helpless," and so on. The destruction of a baby is abhorrent to us. By accepting her physician's description of her ordeal as the surgical removal of an abnormal growth, Mrs. Finkbine was able to avoid at least some of the emotional impact of the thought of destroying a cuddly, adorable, helpless baby. What was removed from her womb was whatever it was, no matter what it might be called. But her reaction to that episode, and ours, depends to a large degree upon what we choose to call it. If it was a growth, one's reaction may be neutral or even favorable. If it was a baby, any sensitive person hearing of it is bound to experience some negative reaction. The question of definition, then, becomes tangled in questions of morals and public policy. Anyone who insists upon calling a fetus a "baby" or a "human being," whatever the stage of its development and whatever the circumstances, has already committed himself, in some sense, to the proposition that abortion is always wrong. On the other hand, those who are prepared to call unborn fetuses, at some stages in the development, at least, "tissues" or "growths" or even "fetuses," without insisting that they are also "babies" or "human beings," indicates by his choice of words that he is prepared to grant that in some circumstances, if not all, abortion may be permitted.

Our choice of language, then, is determined, to some extent, by our position on the moral issues; and our moral stand will determine, to some degree, the kind of language that we choose to employ in discussing the issues. Words that are emotively charged tend to sway the discussion in one direction or the other (e.g., *abnormal growth* and *baby*), whereas neutral terms (such as *fetus* and *tissue*) leave more room for discussion without prejudice.

The law determines the extent to which rights are conferred upon persons in any society; it also defines what the word *person* is to denote, insofar as that word designates the bearers of rights. There is no metaphysical definition of *person* or *human* or *baby* that is correct for all times and all circumstances, and is in some sense "superior" to the law so that the latter must take cognizance of it. Those who write the laws will determine who will be considered legal persons and who will not; who will bear legal rights and who will not; and which persons will bear which rights. No law is so sacred that it is not amenable to change. At one time considerations of public policy may require the withholding of certain rights from persons who have not yet attained the age of twenty-one, but circumstances may arise that will require a lowering of that age to some other. For some purposes it is evident that there are advantages, both to society as a whole and to juveniles themselves, for children not to have certain rights, because they lack the maturity and the judgment to exercise their rights wisely and without harm to themselves and others. The law has made many distinctions, more or less arbitrary, between persons of various ages and at various identifiable points in their lives. A child under the age of seven, for example, is conclusively presumed, in most common-law jurisdictions, to be incapable of committing a crime, but once he passes his seventh birthday, the presumption is not so strong, and is rebuttable. Nothing happens to the child during the night prior to his birthday that makes him more capable of committing a crime, but the law makes the rule on the assumption that most children under seven certainly lack capacities that some children over seven may possess. The law fixes certain times in a person's life as ages of consent for one thing or another. It defines the moment of death, for its purposes, in one way, though for other purposes (such as medical and scientific ones) death may be defined more usefully in some other way. The law decides who may inherit and who may not; in most places a fetus in its mother's womb may not inherit any of its father's estate if its father dies before it is born. For purposes of inheritance, therefore, a fetus is not a person.

Why, then, should the law not deny a fetus the status of *person* until after it has emerged into the light of day through natural birth or Caesarean section? There is no reason, a priori, why the state may not do so. There is also no reason, a priori, why it may not confer upon the fetus the status of *person* at some time prior to birth—either at the moment of conception, as the Catholic Church insists it should, or at some other point in the fetus's development. Any decision on this matter must be made in the light of considerations of public policy, including the probable long-term effects of the law upon the state itself, and upon all those whom the law touches, as well as the morality of abortion in various circumstances.

We turn now to some of the principal arguments raised against any liberalization of abortion laws.

The Right to Life. *"It is a basic principle . . . that every man possesses his right to life from God—not from man or society. . . . There is thus no man, no human authority, no science, no indication (whether medical, eugenic, social, economic, or moral) that can justify deliberate and direct destruction of innocent human life. The life of an innocent human being is simply inviolable, altogether immune from direct acts of suppression."* [99] The author of this statement, Father Richard A. McCormick, notes that it contains an important qualification: *innocent* human life; for capital punishment and defense against unjust aggression constitute exceptions to the rule. A further qualification is the word *direct*, which is meant to exclude acts that result in death of the fetus but are not intended to do so—such as removal of a cancerous uterus when the uterus contains a fetus. Aside from these points the principle is unqualified: there is no price on human life.

However, one may accept this principle without accepting the conclusion that all (or any) abortions are wrong; for one may insist that the life of a fetus is not the life of a human being, because a fetus is a potential, and not an actual, human being. Certainly there can be no objection to the destruction of human cells and tissues; such destruction takes place every day in the operating rooms of hospitals, and no one thinks that it is immoral. Under proper conditions, and with sufficient technical advances, it is now believed that *any* cell taken from any part of a person's body can be developed into a human being, complete and sound in every respect, and identical in its genetic makeup with the person from whom the first cell was taken.[100] One could carry the antiabortionist argument to absurd lengths and argue that *any* cell, being a potential human being, deserves the protection of the law and ought not to be destroyed. Certainly any sperm should fall under the ban. (Is this where the ban on onanism comes from?) If a line can be drawn at one point, it can as easily be drawn at another—say, birth, or the fifth month of pregnancy.

The rejoinder is this:

> The presence of a rational soul is attributable to a creative act of God. Since it is a creative act, the time of its occurrence ultimately escapes the tools of direct human inquiry. . . . And secondly, the spiritual and material interests of the child are not sufficiently protected if we are allowed to act on non-conclusive estimates (by embryologists and physiologists) of the time of animation. If there is a human being, in the fullest sense, present from the moment of conception, directly destructive actions based on an opposite assumption will be in violation of his inviolable rights. The practical conclusion, therefore, is that there *is* a human being—because no other conclusion protects sufficiently the most voiceless, voteless, helpless, unorganized minority imaginable.[101]

We shall leave aside the obvious emotionalism of the last sentence in order to examine the argument. First, it assumes that there is a rational soul—a dubious assumption that we shall not attempt to challenge here. Second, it assumes that the soul enters the embryo through a creative (miraculous) act of God. If not for the miraculous intervention of God, the fetus would develop into something nonhuman. The mere biological process with which we are all familiar is not sufficient to produce human beings. But these assumptions are not merely assumptions; they are articles of faith, unprovable by any empirical test, as Father McCormick himself concedes. Without evidence, those who are untouched by the faith have the right—both the moral right and the intellectual right—to reject these assumptions. If the assumptions are not granted, the rest of the argument falls to the ground. Many embryologists and physiologists are not at all interested in the moment of animation, for they do not believe that such a moment exists. They are quite satisfied that they can, at least in principle, explain all the phenomena of human life without such an otiose assumption. Applying Occam's Razor, they slice off the "rational soul," and with it the "moment of animation," and work with what is empirically observable.

But there is more. "Sufficient" protection of the right to life turns out to be an absolute ban on abortion, right from the moment of conception, because of our lack of certainty about the moment of animation. Even though we do not *know* when the fetus is animated, we must *act as if* it were animated at conception in order to protect what *we will assume* is human life, though we cannot be sure that it is. How does this compare to those cases in which the mother's life is in danger? About the mother's life there is no doubt. We *know* that she is a human being, and there is no dispute over the fact that to kill her would be morally wrong. Yet Father McCormick maintains that if the choice is between the life of the mother and the life of the fetus, the mother must lose. Even if the choice were between aborting the fetus and losing both mother *and* fetus, he opts for the latter; for as he puts it, "the choice was never between one death and two deaths, but rather between two unavoidable deaths and one murder." [102] He fails to see that the abortion is murder only if the fetus is a human being, only if it *is in fact animated* (to use his own terminology). Because he does not know when animation takes place, it would be reasonable to assume that the fetus is only a *possible* human being, whereas the mother is *certainly* a human being. Permitting the mother and the fetus to die by doing nothing may not be murder, technically speaking, but for the mother and her family the end result is the same. The refusal to save the life of a living human being, who is loved and needed by others, on such technical grounds, strikes me as being indefensible.

The argument is sometimes extended in other ways. If abortion is allowed on medical, social, economic, psychiatric, or eugenic grounds, it is said, then why not permit the deliberate elimination of adolescents, the elderly, and others who become a burden upon others? Because we know that it would be wrong to kill an adolescent or an old man for the sake of some other person's health or economic well-being, it must therefore be equally wrong to take the life of a fetus. [103] The answer is that the analogy simply does not hold. A fetus is not comparable to an adolescent or an old man. It has established no relations with other persons, it has no personality, it has contributed nothing to anyone; it has not participated in the life of its family or of the community in any way. Though it has done no wrong to anyone, it need not be regarded as entitled to the absolute protection of its right to life, because it may be regarded as a nonperson, as a being that lacks the protection of the law.

The proponent of abortion reform may not be saying that the fetus has *no* right to life. He may merely be saying that that right should not carry with it the sanctions that the law brings to bear against those who wrongfully cause the death of an adolescent or of an old man, or of a day-old baby. My right to speak freely may be violated by someone; if it is, the wrongdoer will not be sent to prison for life, and he will not be prevented from practicing his profession. Though we might say that he *ought* to respect my right to express myself, we do not ordinarily think it appropriate to bring the penal force of the law into play to protect that right. The proponent of abortion law reform is not altogether denying that the fetus has a right to live. He says, merely, that that right should not carry with it the penal sanctions that most states presently enforce.

Legal Abortion Leads to Increased Promiscuity. *It is said that if abortions become readily available, a general moral breakdown will follow, with widespread promiscuity becoming the rule, because the fear of becoming pregnant is one of the most important deterrents to promiscuity.*

There is no statistical evidence to support this assertion. No significant rise in rates of premarital or extramarital coitus has been verified in those countries and states that have had experience with legalized abortion, though, as one might expect, there has been a great increase in the number of legal abortions.

If the argument were valid, it would follow, by the same reasoning, that contraceptives should be banned. Some people *do* use this argument. If a woman insists on having her pleasure, they say, let her—and, one must assume, her baby—suffer. The same reasoning would lead to the conclusion that if a girl contracts venereal disease, she should be denied treatment for it. If people can avoid the evil consequences of sex (pregnancy, carrying a fetus to term, or venereal disease), they will become promiscuous. Therefore, to prevent promiscuity, keep the evil consequences.

So goes the argument, when broken down to its essentials. It completely ignores the evils of bringing motherless children into the world, the scandal and shame of an illegitimate birth, and the harm that may result to young women who are forced to go through pregnancy against their will. All these evils, it is assumed, are as nought when compared to the evil of illegitimate sex. However, without advocating indulgence in illicit sex, one can quite properly argue that some of its possible consequences may be still worse, and that failure to remedy the latter when remedies are available is no cure for the former. Besides, most women who seek abortions—more than 80 per cent, according to some statistics—are married mothers of two or more children and have not become pregnant because of illicit intercourse.

The "Tacit Promise" Argument. *"Whenever a woman willingly engages in coitus," it has been said, "she, in so doing, makes an implicit promise that in the event of conception she will bear and give life to the fruit of her act. This promise exists even in the case of the woman who responsibly uses contraception in an attempt to avoid pregnancy."* [104]

Every promise entails the existence of at least two persons—one who makes the promise and one to whom the promise is made. Also, genuine promises exist only when the person who promises knows that he is promising and intends to promise. But when a woman has intercourse, she may have no intention to promise; her intention may be only to have sexual relations. If contraceptives are employed, it would seem that there is a deliberate withholding of any commitment. And further, to whom is the promise made? To the child who might be born of the union, in spite of all precautions that are taken? What a strange promise! "I promise you, whoever you may be, that, although you do not now exist, *if* you ever do come into existence. . . ." A promise to a nonexistent but possible person. This is stretching the meaning of the word *promise* beyond all recognizable limits.[105]

Legalization Doesn't Work. *A number of countries have tried legalization of abortion in the hope that it would reduce the rate of illegal abortions, but such plans have not worked, it is said. The Soviet Union outlawed abortion*

*after permitting it for many years. In the Scandinavian countries illegal
abortions are still quite common, in spite of liberal laws.*

In fact, the opposite is true. Where abortions have become more readily
available, the rate of legal abortions has increased dramatically, and in most
such places the rate of illegal abortions has declined—in some instances, very
rapidly. The Soviet Union has reversed itself several times. One reversal was
due to fear of war, during Hitler's day. Stalin felt that an increase in population was necessary, and, as it turned out, he was tragically correct. Most
Eastern European countries today have liberal laws. The Scandinavian countries are not as liberal as some people imagine. In fact, Sweden—to take only
one example—has a very rigid law, which requires the approval of a ten-
member medical board. Such approval is not readily given and is limited to
very few clinical indications. It is not always easy to get an abortion in Scandinavia under the law, and the process is so lengthy that some women must
wait until they are well along in their pregnancies before they find out
whether they have been approved for an abortion or not. Therefore, many of
them, desperate for an abortion, go to illegal abortionists, as they do in the
United States and Canada and other countries that have restrictive laws.

*Legalization Will Lead to Governmental Abuses. As we noted earlier,
Aristotle alluded to the possibility of the state's compelling certain persons
to undergo abortions or to permit their children to be slaughtered on eugenic
or other grounds. Humanae Vitae makes the same point, in a slightly different
way, by alleging that loosening the restrictions on abortion laws and on laws
restricting the sale and use of contraceptives could lead to a loss of respect
for human life and could give the officers of a state an excuse for instituting
compulsory abortions or infanticide.*

This objection is unsound because of its failure to deal with political
realities. Any government that is so tyrannical as to want to order the
institution of such laws, as Hitler did, does not need to base its policy upon
such humanitarian measures as liberalized abortion laws. It *might* do so
as a public relations gimmick, but certainly the liberal abortion law would
not have *led* to the repressive measures. There is a world of difference
between a law that gives women the freedom to determine how their
bodies shall be used (such as a liberal abortion law) and one that takes that
freedom away from them. Notice that both *restrictive* abortion laws, which
do not permit *any* abortion or which permit the state to interfere with a
woman's right to determine whether she shall have a child or not, and
compulsory abortion laws have in common a very important feature: state
interference in the use of a woman's body and in the determination of
whether she *must* or *must not* have a baby. A tyrant could well seize upon the
Church's advocacy of such interference as justification for his own, if he
were interested in offering rationalizations for his repressive legislation.

The arguments in favor of liberalization may briefly be summarized as
follows:

Present Laws Assume That Women Are Chattel. Women are treated as if they were property, the property of the state, perhaps—as if the control of their bodies did not belong to them but belonged to someone else—the legislature, the courts, the doctors, or whoever presumes to make the decisions for them. This is a demeaning and degrading state of affairs, hardly consistent with the professed goal of freedom in a democratic society. A woman should be the master of her own body, and should not be forced, against her will, to serve as the soil for the growth of seed that she does not want to be there. As Baroness Summerskill said, in the debate on the British bill,

> Today, literate people of the space age . . . are not prepared to accept taboos unquestioning, and in the matter of abortion the human rights of the individual mother . . . with her own fully developed personality and her responsibilities to her family, must take precedence over the survival of a few weeks old foetus without sense or sensibility. . . . A girl who has been the victim of rape . . . [has had] her human rights . . . totally disregarded, and when pregnancy results it violates her maternal functions. Can it be argued that it is socially desirable and reconcilable with human rights that she should be compelled to bear and rear a child criminally begotten? [106]

Concern for the Fetus. Where abortion is illegal, women are driven to seek illegal abortions in abominable conditions, and sometimes to attempt to abort themselves. Aside from the terrible danger that they are in when they resort to such measures, they endanger the well-being of the fetuses they bear within them, if the attempt should fail and no subsequent abortion attempt succeeds. Many children have been born to women who had attempted to induce an abortion; the children have been seriously malformed in a significant number of cases as a result of trauma to them or to the womb. It would be better to permit the fetus to be aborted in sanitary conditions by an expert than to risk its being born with defects that could destroy its chances for a happy life. Even if the fetus is brought to term and is normal in every way, if its mother was desperate enough to try to destroy it while it was in her womb, its chances for a happy childhood and a normal upbringing would seem to be considerably reduced. The social cost, as well as the cost to the child and its family, is incalculable. The problem is compounded when the child is given up by its natural parents, and is made still worse if the child is a victim of its mother's German measles or some other deforming disease or drug.

Psychological Effects May Be Beneficial. Opponents of abortion reform sometimes argue that women who have abortions are more likely than others to suffer from acute anxiety and from severe guilt feelings. However, no convincing statistics on this matter are available. In addition, three further possibilities must be considered. First, some women who have had abortions seem to have a positive sense of relief, a feeling that they are rid of an unendurable burden. Sherri Finkbine seems to have been one such person.

Second, the psychological trauma of bringing an unwanted child into the world, or of bearing a child whom one knows is bound to be severely handicapped, must be enormous. It is difficult to see how the continuing suffering—lifelong, perhaps, particularly in the latter case—can be compared to any postpartum depression that the mother might suffer from an abortion. And finally, some thought should be given to the remote causes of such depressions and guilt feelings as do occur. If theologians would change their attitudes and their preachings, perhaps some women who now feel guilty over what they have done out of an instinct for self-preservation would instead rejoice over their good fortune in having averted a nearly certain tragedy.

The Drop in Maternal Death Rates. In both England and New York a significant decline in the maternal death rate was observed almost immediately after the enactment of abortion reform legislation. In New York only five deaths attributable to criminal abortions occurred in the first eight months of 1971, as opposed to fifteen in the first few months of the new law's operation. The maternal death rate dropped to two for every 10,000 births, the lowest in the city's history, a decline of more than half the prevailing rate prior to the enactment of the liberalized legislation. In Great Britain, there were only twenty-nine maternal deaths during 1970, as opposed to an average of more than fifty in the years preceding the new law.[107] A further dividend, of a somewhat different order, was noted in New York, where there was a decline in the number of illegitimate births after the abortion law was passed.

Discrimination Against the Poor and the Black. Under the present system, in most places, those who are moderately well-to-do can get a safe abortion, either by traveling to one of the abortion havens or by paying a private physician to get the job done. But the poor are shut out, because they are unable to travel and they do not have access to private physicians. Virtually no therapeutic abortions are performed on ward patients, but a significant number of private patients in the same hospitals have them done. Ward doctors are unwilling to take the risks that private doctors take for their patients, for there is no financial incentive to do so. In New York, after passage of the liberalized law, 53 per cent of the abortions were performed on black and Puerto Rican patients, indicating that for the first time legal abortions were available to the poor and to the members of minority groups, and they were taking advantage of the law's protection.

In 1962 the American Law Institute published a draft abortion bill in its Model Penal Code which many persons thought would eliminate the major problems, but which seems today to be inadequate. It would legalize abortion if a physician believes that there is a substantial risk to the health of the mother, or if there is a substantial risk that the child would be born with grave mental or physical defects, or if the pregnancy resulted from forcible rape or incest. In practice this means either that most women and their doctors must lie and connive in order to have an abortion authorized or that at least 80 per cent of the women who seek abortions must be turned away, because a very small percentage of abortion cases falls within these rules.

This proposal, which has served as the model for a number of reforms, has the further defect of placing upon the physician the burden of deciding when a particular case falls within the permitted area and when it does not. The risk remains that he may be wrong, or at least that he may be hauled into court, with all the unfavorable publicity that that entails, to defend himself against a charge of having committed an illegal abortion. To protect themselves, doctors have caused provisions for panels or boards which must pass on every request for an abortion to be written into the laws of their states or to be incorporated into the rules of their hospitals. The tendency of such boards has been, on the whole, to take a very conservative approach to all requests. As a result, many hospitals today have fewer abortion cases than they had before liberalized legislation was brought into effect. As one physician has explained, "Many of the doctors who are supposed to present the cases of the women are afraid of these boards. They know the boards very often have a policy of discouraging abortions and they're afraid to be tagged as pro-abortionist." [108] Some hospitals have no boards at all, and therefore have no abortions. One large hospital ruled that where psychiatric grounds were alleged, the patient would have to have been a psychiatric patient before she became pregnant and that her psychiatrist had to be on the staff of the hospital. These rules excluded women who might have had psychiatric problems prior to their pregnancies, but were either unaware of them or too poor to go to a psychiatrist. They also assumed, wrongly, that a physician's hospital affiliation has something to do with his ability to diagnose his patient's problem and with his patient's need for help. It goes without saying that where the hospital is under Catholic control, the board will seldom, if ever, find an indication justifying abortion, no matter how liberal the law might be.

A particularly difficult problem arises with regard to the Catholic physician, nurse, and hospital. In many localities Catholic medical and para-medical personnel have taken the position that they will not participate in any abortion, and in some, where they are heavily represented on hospital staffs, they have threatened to go out on strike if abortions were performed. We shall not discuss such coercive measures here, except insofar as our comments in the next section may apply. But a serious question arises when a patient applies to a Catholic physician, for example, for medical treatment. Suppose that the physician feels that in good conscience, he cannot recommend an abortion, though he has diagnosed a situation that would be considered by many physicians, and by the law, to be an indication for the performance of an abortion. Is he obliged to violate the dictates of his conscience and perform the abortion if his patient requests it? Does he have the right to withhold information upon which the patient might act? Is he obliged to refer her to another doctor, who might have a more liberal attitude? Consider the hospital: Should a Catholic hospital be used for purposes that go against Catholic doctrine? Some writers have suggested that Catholic physicians and hospitals should not refer patients to non-Catholic colleagues who might treat the patient in a manner forbidden by Catholic moral opinion. It may be argued that this constitutes an unconscionable subordination of the patient's interests to the religious beliefs of the physician or the hospital staff.[109]

To conclude this discussion of abortion, it may be desirable to reiterate what should have been obvious all along: The liberalization of abortion laws gives no one the right or the authority to force another to undergo an abortion against her will. All such laws, whether they abolish all restrictions or some only, merely extend the rights of the individual over her own fate and her own destiny. They take from the state some of the rights that it has heretofore exercised over the bodies of women, and places those rights in the custody of the women themselves. Anyone who believes that women are incapable of using those rights wisely must have a very low opinion of modern women. Whatever he may think of them, however, the fundamental question must be this: Can anyone rightly force another to "build the world by destroying herself," or to serve as an unwilling ground for the growth of unwanted tissue? My own opinion is that the answer must be negative. Although no one questions the right of any religious group to condemn abortion or any other practice that it considers immoral, one may rightly question the propriety of any group attempting to impose its beliefs or practices upon others who happen to believe otherwise. To give only one example:

Tay-Sachs disease is a hereditary disease peculiar to Jews whose ancestors came from Eastern Europe. It is transmitted by a recessive gene, and, though many people may be carriers, it manifests itself in only one of every 3,600 births. Recently-discovered techniques enable doctors to determine which couples are liable to transmit the disease to their children, and a relatively simple test can single out those fetuses that actually have the disease. Tay-Sachs disease is always fatal. It produces dreadful symptoms which culminate in a wasting away that ends in death at a very young age.

Now, suppose a young Jewish couple, having had several children (though that is not really relevant), discover that the fetus that was recently conceived by them has this terrible disease. Suppose further that they want to have this fetus aborted in order to spare themselves, their families, and the child that would otherwise be born the anguish, the pain, and the suffering that will certainly follow its birth. They are prepared to have the abortion performed by a physician, who agrees that it is highly desirable. None of the persons involved accepts the premises upon which the antiabortion argument is founded. But because of a law that was written 100 years ago they must either have the baby or seek an illegal abortion. If they do the latter, they and those who conspire with them may be sent to prison. Such an imposition of the beliefs and practices of one group of people on the members of another group is simply unconscionable, particularly where it imposes hardship and suffering upon them. For the reader will recall that at the beginning of this discussion we mentioned a great moral and religious principle that has not yet been brought explicitly into our treatment of this subject, though it has not been far from our minds at any time—namely, the principle of mercy, compassion, and love of fellow men, which would surely forbid anyone to cause another to suffer needlessly.

Finally, let us recall the important principle we discussed earlier in this section. The law is not designed to cope with every human situation. It has its limits. When those limits are overstepped, it quickly loses its usefulness, and those the law is intended to protect suffer the most because of the contempt in which it comes to be held and the resentment that it fosters. Even if abortion is immoral—which I am not prepared to grant except for the sake of argument—it does not follow that the instruments of the law are appropriate to enforce this particular moral rule. The violations of the rule are so widespread and are causing so much anguish and pain and loss of life that one must question whether the values being preserved by the rule, whatever they may be, are not superseded by the evil being done by it. As Glanville Williams has said,

> A realistic humanitarianism—or a true Christianity—might say that it is impossible to judge others, because one cannot live their lives and experience their inner drives and compulsions; and particularly is this true in matters of sex, marriage, and parenthood. But at least we may say this, that if moral rules are to be externalized and enforced by law, they should so far as possible be those that human beings in the mass are able to comply with, without excessive repression and frustration and without overmuch need for the actual working of the legal machine. It is evident that this cannot be said of the present law of abortion.[110]

APPENDIX ON CONTRACEPTION

The principles employed in my arguments on the abortion problem apply equally to the problem of contraception, and should be sufficient, in themselves, to dispose of any attempt to justify use of the state's power to prevent men and women from regulating the size of their families and determining for themselves when to bring children into the world. I append here a few comments on some of the more popular arguments used by opponents of birth control.

Many of them are based on no scientific evidence whatever, or on false generalizations.

Children in small families grow up spoiled and selfish. This generalization is based on no scientific data, so far as I have been able to discover. Even if it were true, it ignores other factors that may be present in small families and operate to the advantage of the children in them.

Contraceptive use is a factor leading to family breakdown and divorce, as demonstrated by the high proportion of divorces in families with one or two children. It is true that small families have more divorces than large ones, but it does not follow that the use of contraceptives is a factor in such divorces. Divorce occurs most often in young families, and the rate of divorce decreases as the marriage and the partners grow older. Many factors are relevant, including finances, personal maturity, and personality clashes that may be intolerable in the early years of marriage, though the couple may adjust to them if they stay together long enough. When a marriage is unstable, failure to use contraceptives and the consequent birth of unwanted children may drive the couple apart. The use of babies as a means of keeping warring couples together is dying out, as it should, for it is a risky business at best. We should note, incidentally, that either of these arguments would count against the rhythm method as well as against any other form of contraception.

Children born to parents who use contraceptives die prematurely. Scare tactics. Completely unfounded.

The use of contraceptives leads to extramarital relations, loss of reverence for the wife, and physical or psychological damage to her. No doubt extramarital relations are safer nowadays than they used to be, because those who engage in them can be relatively certain that children will not follow. But there is no solid evidence that the rate at which people are engaging in such relations is significantly higher than it has been at other periods in history prior to the development of modern birth control methods. To judge from the volume of literature on the subject and the vehemence with which adultery has been condemned in all ages, it must have been a pretty common problem in the old days. If some people will submit to temptation anyway, as seems likely if past history is any indication, it would surely be better for them not to involve innocent children in the matter.

Why anyone would suppose that the use of contraceptives would lead a husband to have less reverence for his wife (is *reverence* the right word to use, by the way?) is beyond me. If the employment of birth control precautions enables them to enjoy their love with one another without the fear of unwanted and possibly harmful consequences, I should think that that would lead to a more relaxed, healthy, happy, and loving relationship rather than the reverse.

As for physical or psychological harm, I know of no documented case (except those relatively rare ones in which the particular contraceptive device has undesirable side effects) in which the use of contraceptive devices *in itself* caused such harm. If one method turns out to be unacceptable, others usually work without any trouble at all. If a rare person develops symptoms of some psychological disorder after engaging in intercourse with contraceptives, I would be careful about arguing *post hoc ergo propter hoc.* The cause might be something altogether different. Among other possibilities it might be a bad conscience developed as a result of listening too consistently to such bad arguments as those we are now considering.

Anything but the rhythm method is unnatural. In an earlier discussion of the meaning of *nature,* we noted that it is an ambiguous word whose use proves nothing so far as moral issues are concerned. The present statement assumes that any "unnatural" method is bad or wrong. It is based upon the assumption that the only proper use of sex is procreation. Aspirins are no more unnatural than contraceptive pills, yet they may be used for the relief of headaches. How, then, does one distinguish between those "unnatural" acts that are permitted and those that are not, if not by the question-begging device of restricting the rule to cases where sex is involved. It is certainly not true that the only "natural" use of sex is procreation, for, if we may judge by the behavior of animals as well as that of people, it is evident that pleasure is one of the most common reasons for indulgence in sexual behavior, even when such behavior cannot possibly be fecund.

Some people have advocated the imposition of strict limitations upon the number of births any woman would be permitted during her lifetime.[111] I would not go so far. But clearly no solution to the problems posed by the world population explosion exists but rational and deliberate limitations on individual fertility. Such limitations may take the form of abstinence for those who wish to follow that path. Others may prefer to use contraceptives. And still others may prefer the certainty and the freedom that follow from sterilization. When personal suffering, national catastrophe, or worldwide starvation are likely to follow from uncontrolled human fertility, then the use of contraceptives is not immoral. Rather, a person who deliberately limits his own reproduction, in full consciousness of the long-range effects of his act and in a spirit of self-sacrifice, has made a genuinely moral decision.

4

Divorce

SOME STRANGE FEATURES OF DIVORCE LAW

Because of the strong emphasis by Church leaders on the principle of strict monogamy, divorce in Christian countries has generally been exceedingly difficult. In some countries dominated by the Catholic Church, it is still illegal to procure a divorce, and even in those countries that have liberalized their divorce laws, there are often very long waits between the petition for a divorce and its finalization, and there are other obstacles in the path of the couple seeking to dissolve their marriage.

Generally, the laws of divorce are founded upon the principle that marriage, unlike any other contract, ought never to be dissolved, and in particular that it *may not* be dissolved with the consent of the parties to it.

When the parties to any other contract find that it is in their best interests for the contract to be dissolved—whether it is a business partnership, an employer–employee relationship, or a purchase agreement—a few relatively simple steps are sufficient to bring the matter to an end. If there is some dispute as to the terms of the final settlement, it may be resolved by arbitration or adjudication. Once a decision is rendered, a definite sum of money is ordered to be paid to one party or the other, or one party is ordered to perform certain services or to deliver certain goods to the other, and the relationship between them is terminated. There is no burden of guilt or "fault" on either of them. In perfectly rational fashion, the law permits them to sever their relationship when they agree that it is best for them to do so.

However, when a man and his wife agree that the dissolution of their marriage would be in their own best interests and in the best interests of their children, if they have any, they *are not permitted* to be divorced in most states. If it can be shown in court that they have entered into an agreement to divorce, they can legally be prevented from doing so. One of the parties must be shown to have been guilty of an "offense" against the marriage. The

114

divorce is then "granted" or "awarded" to the "injured" party against the one who is supposedly at fault. In some states, if both parties can be shown to be at fault, the divorce is awarded to *neither* of them, and they are sentenced to a lifetime of misery together. One judge, in Michigan, unable to grant a divorce petition because it had been proved that both parties had been extraordinarily cruel to one another, remarked in' sheer frustration, "These parties should not only be separated but should be compelled to live in different states. But that doesn't make any difference. My opinion doesn't count for anything in this situation."

Another anomaly of the present system is the rule of condonation. Under this rule, if Mary discovers that her husband, John, has been paying regular nocturnal visits to her best friend, Sally, Mary may sue John for divorce and, if she has sufficient evidence, she may win the case. But if Mary permits John to return home after she has listened to his entreaties for forgiveness, she may no longer use the evidence she had gathered prior to his return home in any subsequent divorce action that she might bring. In other words, the present law works against reconciliation in some instances, because an all-out attempt at reconciliation may be regarded as condonation, and thus invalidate the grounds on which the case for a divorce had been built. Suppose John had deserted Mary for two years and then returned just as she was about to file for a divorce under their state's two-year desertion clause. Suppose Mary, anxious to preserve her marriage if she can, decides to take him back. If John takes off again the next day, Mary must wait another two years before she can file again for a divorce on the ground of desertion. Many moralists have declaimed against trial marriage for single persons. But here we have a rule that makes it difficult for persons who are *married to one another* to have a "trial marriage" for a time before moving on to the absolute dissolution of their relationship.

GROUNDS FOR DIVORCE

Each state recognizes a different set of "offenses" as grounds for divorce. Until 1970 every state recognized adultery as being such a ground, and until 1967 one state (New York) recognized no ground but adultery. Most states recognize desertion or separation as a ground for divorce, but the time that must elapse between the separation and the divorce is as little as one year in some states and as much as ten years in others. In some states insanity is a ground for divorce, and in others it is not; and even where it is, the condition must last for eighteen months in some before a divorce may be granted, and for five years in others, whereas in still others, if one of the parties is insane, *no* divorce will be granted to the other party on *any* ground. Thus, if a woman is unfortunate enough to be living in one of the latter states, and her husband becomes incurably insane, she may be forever barred from remarriage, and her children will have to remain in a single-parent home, even though she might have had opportunities to remarry. In most states mental or physical cruelty or incompatibility may be grounds for divorce, but in a number of states such grounds are not recognized.

Some states continue to have a punitive attitude toward divorced persons, maintaining laws that prohibit the remarriage of the guilty party for a period of time. In South Carolina a person who is divorced on grounds of adultery is forbidden to remarry except to the innocent spouse so long as the innocent spouse is still living. Other states permit their judges to impose similar restrictions.

When the defendant in a divorce case is accused of adultery, a divorce may be granted to the plaintiff if he (or she) can prove that one lone incident has taken place. More than one marriage has been dissolved because of the unforgiving stance of the aggrieved partner toward a single, misguided affair entered into by the other. A single adulterous act is sufficient, in the eyes of the law, to justify the termination of the marriage, even though the wayward spouse may be genuinely repentant and sincerely committed to playing a constructive role in the life of the family. A husband or wife who deserts the family, however, may not be divorced until the desertion has been established as a continuing fact over a period of years, though it may be quite evident that the deserter has no intention of contributing to the family or taking part in its affairs or concerns. Similarly, a person who becomes a menace to the other members of the family as a result of severe mental disease may not be divorced for a number of years, though his or her presence may constitute a danger to the physical or mental well-being of all concerned and a continuing drain on the family's emotional and financial resources. If the adulterer may be divorced forthwith and torn from his children, though he constitutes no threat to them, is willing to support them, and is sincerely committed to mending his ways, then it is difficult to see why the deserter's crime should be defined as one that must take place over so long a period of time. If the indignant spouse of the adulterer may win a divorce based upon proof that a single act of adultery has taken place, why should the deserter's spouse, or the spouse of the seriously ill mental patient, have to wait for years before being able to rebuild his or her shattered life? One might argue that moral reprobation is at issue: that the mentally ill patient is deserving of special consideration because he has done nothing to deserve the reprobation of society, whereas the adulterer has engaged in a morally reprehensible form of behavior, and therefore deserves to be cut off at the will of the woman whom he has betrayed. But this will not do, for the deserter's behavior is at least as reprehensible as that of the adulterer, and possibly a good deal more so, because he has deliberately abandoned his wife and children and has forsaken his obligations toward them. It would seem that the difference is based upon the extreme repugnance with which adultery was viewed by both Christian and Jewish authorities from very ancient times. In the Bible, it will be recalled, adultery was punishable by death, but there was no comparable penalty for desertion or abandonment. Later, adulterers were branded and humiliated and subjected to many forms of severe punishment. Present divorce laws in most jurisdictions seem to derive their differential treatment of adultery from such ancient practices and attitudes.

In this connection one ought to consider whether divorce is, or ought to be, a penalty for the wicked and a reward for the righteous, or a means to enable persons who have erred in their choice of mates, or have discovered (for whatever reason) that their marriages are no longer viable, to rebuild their lives in a different way or with different partners.

A few states have adopted a relatively new concept in their divorce laws. California went further than any state in the Union when it adopted a law that reduced the grounds for divorce to two: irreconcilable differences that have caused the irremediable breakdown of the marriage and incurable insanity. Under the first of these grounds there is no plaintiff and no defendant. It permits, for the first time in American jurisprudence, an open and immediate claim on the part of both parties to a divorce based upon the fact that their marriage has broken down, rather than upon the guilt of one party or the other. Thus it recognizes the right of divorce by consent. A few other states have recognized the same right, but have hedged it around by setting up a number of restrictions and technicalities. In New York, for example, it is possible to enter into a separation agreement, which may be converted, after two years, into a divorce. In the meantime, however, the parties must submit to a complex conciliation apparatus that attempts to effect a reconciliation and can block the granting of a divorce until the conciliator is satisfied that the marriage is not salvageable.

COMPULSORY CONCILIATION

Two questions may be asked about compulsory conciliation attempts: (1) Do they do any good? (2) Even if they do, does the state have a moral right to force men and women to submit to them?

At this time no reliable figures are available on compulsory conciliation; but some significant statistics are available from Wayne County (Detroit), Michigan, which has made available a free voluntary conciliation service for a number of years. In a typical year (1965) 11,000 couples filed for divorce. Of these, 401 accepted the services of the counseling agency. Of those, fewer than 100 were actually reconciled. And, because there was no follow-up on these "reconciled" couples, it is impossible to say how many of them have since separated again or been divorced. From these figures, and similar ones that could be produced from other localities that offer such services, it is evident that most couples who reach the divorce courts have made up their minds and are firmly resolved to bring their marriage to an end. There are many places along the road where efforts are usually made to halt the escalation that finally leads to a divorce: the days and weeks of doubt and soul searching; of discussion and consultation with clergy, friends, and relatives; and, in many cases, of renewed efforts made by their attorneys to bring the estranged couple together for a reconciliation. (Though some lawyers accept divorce cases without question, and devote themselves merely to winning the case and getting the best possible deal for their clients, there are many who try, as a matter of personal policy, to persuade their clients to make one more attempt to reconcile before pushing on toward a divorce.) In addition, many persons who end up in the divorce courts have spent periods of time ranging from a few weeks to several years in some kind of personal or family counseling, and have seen psychiatrists, psychologists, or social workers in an effort to get to the root of their problems. Where these have failed, it is not likely that last-ditch court-ordered counseling will save the foundering marriage.

On what ground does the state claim to have the right to impose compulsory conciliation upon couples who are involved in a divorce action? Legally, of course, the state is on firm ground, because it has traditionally had the power to set the conditions under which couples residing within its jurisdiction could be divorced or to deny them the right to divorce entirely. The question here must be confined to the moral issue, or to the problem of public policy, and it may be extended to the larger question of the extent to which the state may properly impose severe restrictions upon couples seeking divorce; for once that question is answered, the problem of compulsory conciliation will fall into place.

This problem, in turn, is largely dependent upon the answer to the prior question of the extent to which the state ought (morally) to interfere in the private, consensual relations of its adult citizens when those relations have no direct or measurable harmful effect upon other persons. Does the state have the right to compel its citizens to behave "morally" or to prevent them from behaving "immorally" (even if we assume—what is problematic in its own right—that divorce is inherently immoral, and that it is possible for a person to be compelled to behave morally)? However that question may be answered,* other questions remain. (1) Is divorce inherently immoral? (2) What considerations, other than the alleged "immorality" of divorce and remarriage, are relevant to the question of public policy on divorce legislation?

THE "IMMORALITY" OF DIVORCE

The doctrine that divorce is always immoral has been repudiated by most Christian denominations. It was never accepted by Jews or Moslems, who have always believed that men and women should have the right to

---

* It has already been discussed in Chapter 1.

dissolve their marriages when they feel a desire or need to do so. In practice, this right was more often restricted to the husband; because of the inferior place of the woman in most ancient and medieval societies, women had to play a more passive role, both in marriage, where the man took the woman and the woman merely accepted the man, and in divorce, where the man divorced his wife or sent her away, whereas the woman was for the most part unable to take the initiative. In Jewish and Islamic law divorce has been hedged with very few restrictions. It was not necessary to provide the court with "grounds," and the court did not attempt to adjudicate between the parties to a divorce, to determine which of the two was responsible for the breakdown of the marriage. The court merely served as an instrument for the completion of a legal arrangement, as it might have done had two persons wanted to dissolve a business partnership. It also attempted, at least in Jewish law, to see that an equitable distribution of property was made between the husband and the wife. Elaborate rules defined precisely what the wife might expect in the division of property after the dissolution of the marriage. The court served as a kind of arbitration board in the event that any dispute arose over the equitable distribution of real estate, furniture, and other assets. But the court did not intervene at all when the parties had decided to bring their marriage to an end. The right of a husband to divorce his wife was absolute, and he needed no grounds for it. However, if his wife refused to accept the divorce, he continued to be bound by the obligations of marriage, including the obligation to support her. The court could intervene by forcing the recalcitrant woman, through threat of contempt proceedings, to accept the divorce document from her husband. Similarly, if a woman sought a divorce, and her husband refused to give it to her, the court could force him to do so by imposing legal sanctions upon him (for example, by jailing him) until he complied with its directives. It was a little more difficult for the woman than it was for the man, but in practice there seems to have been little difference. A woman needed grounds for demanding a divorce from her husband, but the grounds were so broad that it would have been exceedingly difficult not to grant the request of almost any woman who applied. Thus, in Jewish law, if a woman complained that her husband did not sleep with her often enough, or that she found him so loathsome that she could not bear to have sexual relations with him, this was sufficient to ensure the court's granting of her request. Physical or mental cruelty were always adequate grounds. And there was never any suggestion that it was sinful for a divorced person to remarry, or that remarriage was in any way equivalent to adultery. Divorce was absolute, both for the woman and for the man, and entitled each of them to seek another mate and to remarry at will.*

Initially, the divorce proceedings had to take place in a face-to-face en-

---

* The woman was sometimes required to wait for a reasonable period of time before remarrying, in order to be certain that she was not pregnant from her first marriage. This measure was designed merely to assure the second husband that he would not be required to carry the financial burden of supporting her first husband's child.

counter between the husband and his wife. However, the authorities were solicitous of women who had been deserted by their husbands and were thus doomed to live out their lives in loneliness. In order to lighten their burden they decreed that divorces could be arranged through proxies. If the husband could be located, he could hand the document to a messenger who would deliver it, in his place, to his wife; or, in particularly difficult cases, the court could appoint proxies who, through a kind of legal fiction, would fill the role of one party or the other and would thus perform the legally required actions to bring the marriage to an end.

Not only Judaism and Islam, but many other systems have recognized the right of divorce. Christianity, in fact, seems to be rather unique in its condemnation of divorce and remarriage on moral grounds. Moral issues cannot be resolved by an appeal to majority opinion. But it is evident that no consensus on this subject exists and that most of mankind does not share the moral intuition that some persons have claimed to have according to which divorce is by its very nature a sinful institution. The burden of proof would seem to be upon those who maintain that there is a justification for universal condemnation of divorce, or for laws that make it difficult or impossible to obtain a divorce.

If the claim that divorce is immoral is based upon the vows made at the time of the marriage ceremony, in which (in some rituals, at least) eternal fidelity "until death do we part" is promised, then perhaps the vows ought to be changed. Perhaps no man should sunder what God has united, but if the state of many marriages is any indication, either God has not united the couples involved or he has botched the job, and man ought to perform some much-needed repairs.

The "immorality" of divorces seems to be built upon the supposition that every marriage ought to be permanent and that strict monogamy requires complete fidelity to one's first mate as long as he or she lives. But one must ask whether such a strict version of monogamy—or perhaps even whether any form of monogamy—is or ought to be required by law or by a reasonable moral code. Vast numbers of persons, both in the West and in the East, have accepted both simultaneous polygamy (in which one has more than one wife at any given time) and serial polygamy (in which one has a number of wives, but only one wife at a time—a practice that has become very common in the United States). Many men, women, and children have grown up happily in such societies and in polygamous families. There is no evidence to support the view that polygamy leads to any evil other than that people in polygamous societies tend to be polygamous. Where the number of women in a given society exceeds the number of men, as it does in many countries throughout the world because of war or an unequal death rate, polygamy might be of positive benefit to many women who would otherwise have to live lonely and unhappy lives.

But leaving aside the question of polygamy, one must ask what reason anyone would have for supposing that divorce is an evil institution, or that marriage is or ought to be an indissoluble bond. There is no reason to suppose that civilizations depend for their survival upon the strict enforcement of such rules, for relatively small societies have survived for millennia, though they permitted easy divorce. Legal permission to obtain a divorce does not in itself lead to the breakdown of families or to the spread of personal immorality; rather, it is the breakdown of families and personal immorality that leads people to demand divorce. It is true that where divorce is easily obtainable, some people will be tempted to resolve their problems by fleeing from the marriage rather than facing up to them and trying to resolve them within the framework of the marriage. But the denial of relief to suffering persons is not effective, because they often find it in illegal channels or in other, legally permissible ways. The poor man's divorce—desertion—was extremely common in New York so long as only the rich could afford to go to Mexico or to Nevada for their divorces. Nor does it seem to be reasonable or moral to prevent people from rectifying the mistakes of their youth or to deny them the opportunity to escape from relationships that are abhorrent to them and to find new ones that might be meaningful to them and make their lives happier and more worthwhile.

What is moral about preventing a woman whose husband deserted her three years ago from marrying a man who might love her and care for her and her children? Why is it evil to permit a man whose wife is subject to periodic attacks of paranoid schizophrenia, in which she threatens his life and the lives of his children, to divorce her and attempt to find a wife who will provide a normal home for himself and his children? One might reply that the woman who bears her burden courageously is to be admired and that the man who lives with his sick wife, protecting his children against her when she has her delusionary spells and loving and caring for her in spite of all her attempts to destroy him, is to be praised for his love and dedication. But the state was not established in order to make saints and martyrs of its citizens. According to some political philosophers the citizen is the slave of the state, but according to others the state was founded for no other purpose than to serve its citizens, to provide them with the means to live longer and to have happier lives. If the denial of divorce serves no socially useful purpose, and if enabling men and women to terminate their marriages helps them to live happier and more productive lives and relieves the tensions in homes where children are growing, then it would seem that every state should permit divorce. And if restrictive divorce legislation tends to make it difficult or impossible for the poor citizens of a state to acquire a divorce; or if it encourages persons to engage in fraud, deceit, or blackmail; or if it results in long delays before the divorce becomes final; or if it causes men and women whose marriages have disintegrated to develop even greater animosities toward one another than they might otherwise have had, then the legislation should be liberalized to remove these effects and to permit easy and quick divorces on the simple ground that the marriage itself is no longer viable.

So much, then, for the argument that divorce is in principle an immoral institution or that easy divorce is fundamentally immoral. Consider now the consequences of such restrictive legislation and judicial practice as still remain, as compared to the relatively permissive rules introduced in California in 1970.

THE CONSEQUENCES OF PRESENT DIVORCE LAWS

Where traditional rules prevail, the couple desiring a divorce must enter into an adversary proceeding in which one person has to be accused by the other of a violation of one of the conditions of marriage—of adultery, physical cruelty, desertion, or some other act recognized by the law as a ground for divorce. If the divorce suit is uncontested, the defendant is branded "guilty," and the plaintiff is granted a divorce, after a hearing in which she (for the plaintiff is usually the wife) enumerates the instances in which her husband has perpetrated the offenses of which he is accused.

If this were merely a bit of play-acting, designed to go through the motions required by the law, it would be bad enough. But it is very often much more than that. During the months preceding the court hearing, each party devotes much time to plotting means of "getting the goods" on the other. Private detectives may be hired to trail wayward, or allegedly wayward, husbands, to identify their female contacts, to pinpoint the times and places where they consorted, and, if possible, to snap photographs of them in compromising situations. Meetings between the estranged husband and wife are necessarily strained because of the emotional impact of the situation itself, but they are rendered even more painful and damaging by the fact that they are pitted as adversaries against one another. Instead of encouraging them to settle their differences in a friendly way, the law forces them to see one another as enemies, as opponents in a legal battle. Instead of recognizing that the breakdown of a marriage is often the result of personality problems, incompatibility, or mutual failures of one sort or another, the law forces each of them to examine and re-examine one another's behavior in order to find as many incriminating facts as possible on the other side, and as many excuses or justifications as possible on his or her own. Instead of helping the distressed couple to bury their dead marriage with dignity, the law forces them to enter into combat with one another, sending their lawyers into the arena as if they were involved in a gladiatorial contest, and in full view of the public, opening wounds that might well have been left to heal in private.

Many advocates of restrictive divorce laws contend that they are concerned for the welfare of the children, claiming that the children of broken homes are more prone to become delinquents, to suffer severe psychological disorders, and to have family problems of their own later in life than are the children of stable families. There is some statistical justification for these claims, but there is some doubt as to whether the desired conclusion follows from the statistics. Is the higher rate of delinquency among the children of broken homes, for example, a result of the divorce of the parents of these children, or is it the result of some other cause? Both the delinquency and the broken home may have resulted from the same, more remote cause, such as poor psychological adjustment on the part of the parents or extreme poverty.* Have the studies broken down the samples to take special note of children of families where there is considerable strife and discord, but no divorce? Those studies that have been made of children who are being raised in such homes reveal that their chances of having serious personality disorders are much higher than those of children whose parents are divorced. Divorce, in other words, may offer welcome relief to children whose parents are unable to get along together. The trauma of a child whose parents are in constant or periodic strife is hard to measure, but must be considerable. Though the shock of divorce must leave its scars, it seems to be less deleterious, on the whole, than the continuing disturbance of living in a home that is constantly torn by strife and emotional tension.

There is no proof, at this time, that divorce is less harmful to children than no divorce would be. It is difficult even to determine what data would be relevant to such a "proof." In the meantime there can be no doubt that many children have benefited from the remarriage of the parents into whose custody they were given. They have been given the opportunity to enjoy a happy and healthy family life with two parents, rather than being compelled to remain in a single-parent home or a home that bristled with hatred and unhappiness.

For the most part, however, the issue is not whether there shall be divorce or no divorce, but how easy it should be to get a divorce, or what conditions ought to be placed upon divorce legislation. If the intent is to see that married couples having a temporary spat do not rush blindly into a situation that they may later regret, present divorce laws are guilty of overkill. Indeed, some critics have contended that once couples become entangled in the legal machinery with its built-in enforcement of accusatory postures, belligerence, anxiety, and guilt feelings, it becomes increasingly difficult to become disentangled, to view the situation objectively and dispassionately, and to give serious thought to reconciliation. As charges and countercharges are hurled back and forth, with the lawyers jockeying for position and advantage, suspicion and hostility almost inevitably grow, and such deep wounds may be inflicted that they may be more long-lasting than any that occurred during the course of the marriage itself. These critics have therefore urged legislatures and courts to consider revamping the rules to permit couples to divorce without the recrimination inherent in

---

* Contrary to popular belief, the rate of divorce among poor persons is far higher than the rate among persons in higher income brackets.

the adversary system. Instead of making it impossible for a couple to divorce by consent, they would grant them a divorce whenever they claimed that their marriage was "dead" or that it was torn by irreconcilable differences. Under this procedure the couple might come to court together, after having worked out their financial and custodial problems, and ask the court to dissolve their marriage. There would be no restriction on either party's future plans. Either of them would be permitted to remarry at any time in the future. There would be no need for either party to go to the trouble and expense of hiring a detective agency to spy on the other in order to acquire evidence that would stand up in court when the divorce action was heard.

As for the problem of the impetuous lovers who might run to the divorce court at the first sign of a minor difference in opinion, that problem, unfortunately, is well taken care of by the incredible delays imposed upon all parts of the American and Canadian legal systems by a shortage of judges and other court personnel. It is unlikely that any divorce proceeding would commence in less than two or three months' time—and by that time any minor differences would have been ironed out and the hearing would have been canceled. As we noted earlier, most people who have reached the divorce court are no longer interested in reconciliation. They are interested in divorce, and the courts should help them to perform the surgery as painlessly and quietly as they can. If they wish, they may always reconcile later and remarry.

One of the worst features of present divorce laws is the opportunity they provide for unscrupulous men and women to blackmail their spouses in exchange for cooperation in obtaining a divorce. When a divorce petition is contested, it becomes very costly because of the amount of time that both parties' attorneys must devote to it, and it may be delayed for months or even for years. When one of the parties is anxious for the divorce, whatever the reason, the other party may resort to a number of forms of blackmail. If the wife is anxious, her husband may coerce her into agreeing to accept a very small portion of their mutual assets or an inadequate amount of support for herself and her children. If the husband is anxious, his wife may coerce him into committing himself to pay extortionate alimony payments for many years to come and to sign over to her virtually everything they own. A divorce law that would permit either party to obtain a divorce without the consent of the other within a reasonable period of time would eliminate such abuses.

THE TIME TO SAVE A MARRIAGE

The concern of those who would preserve the family is not misplaced. But the manner in which they attempt to answer the problem often is. If one is interested in keeping houses from crumbling and crashing down on their inhabitants, one does not wait until beams have split, roofs have sagged, and walls have buckled; one introduces a stringent construction code which specifies what materials may be used in homes of a given architectural type, so that the inhabitants may know in advance that they have purchased a sound and secure structure. The laws of marriage and divorce put the remedy at the wrong end: They wait until the marriage has crumbled before bringing the instruments of the state to the scene in an attempt to salvage the wreckage. The remedy lies at the opposite end, prior to the marriage itself. Instead of making it possible for anyone with a clean Wasserman test and $2 to buy a marriage license, perhaps there should be more stringent rules governing the issuance of such licenses. If the state has a legitimate interest in the preservation of marriage, then it should have as much right to prevent marriages that are likely to lead to divorce as it has to impose conditions on the dissolution of marriages that have foundered. If, on the other hand, the right to marry is absolute, subject only to very limited restrictions (such as age, health, and only one marriage at a time), then it would seem that the right to divorce should be at least as unrestricted.

So long as the states insist on maintaining restrictive laws for divorce, would they be well-advised to impose new restrictions on the right to marry? Perhaps, as John Stuart Mill suggested, each couple applying for a marriage license should be required to produce evidence of financial responsibility. This might assure the marriage a certain probability of success, because most divorces are caused, at least in part, by financial problems. It might also assure any potential children of the marriage of at least a modicum of security.

The trouble with this—aside from the obvious problem of its being totally unacceptable to almost everybody—is the likelihood that it would simply lead to an increase in premarital or nonmarital relationships and illegitimate births. Men and women are not likely to defer their desires for sexual gratification and their need for the closeness and intimacy that are associated with a love relationship between a man and a woman until such time as they may have saved up a given sum of money or found the kinds of mates that might be permitted by a strict licensing law.

The romantic love ethic, as applied to marriage, was unknown for most of the world's history, and is still not accepted by most of the world's population. Outside the Western world, marriages have generally been arranged for reasons other than romantic love. Where professional matchmakers were involved, or where the marriage was arranged by concerned parents or relatives, the immediate feelings of the boy and the girl were of secondary importance, or of no importance at all. It was assumed that if the match was a good one, the young couple would very soon fall in love with one another and would be devoted to one another. This assumption seems to have been largely correct, and still seems to be correct in those communities where matchmaking continues to play a major role in arranging marriages. In contemporary America a new form of matchmaking has arisen that may provide some interesting studies in the future. Computer dating services, which match people according to a large number of personal characteristics, habits, backgrounds and interests, are doing much the same thing that professional matchmakers used to do with their little notebooks. Using these characteristics as criteria, they are attempting to match people who are likely to be compatible with one another.

The more typical American pattern has been more hit and miss, and may, for that reason, have been uniquely unsuccessful. Boy meets girl (at school, at a party, at the movies, at the amusement park, at the penny arcade, on the street), boy dates girl, boy and girl fall in love, get married, have children, find that they can't bear one another, and become divorced.

This is a caricature, of course, but with the highest divorce rate in the world, this "system" can scarcely be called an unqualified success. In 1969 there were approximately 2.146 million marriages in the United States and 660,000 divorces—or nearly one divorce for every three marriages. Only nine years before, the rate was one to four; in 1940 it was one to six; and in 1890 it was one to eighteen. A careful and complete analysis of the statistics would probably reveal that some of this increase in the divorce rate (from 0.5 per thousand population to 3.3 per thousand in 1969) can be traced to more liberal divorce laws and to the elimination of much of the stigma that used to attach to divorced persons, as well as to other factors. No doubt many unhappy people used to remain together because of the social, the financial, and the personal cost of separation. However, one cannot help but wonder whether the older ways of matching potential mates may not have been more effective in producing happy, lasting marriages than the present method, which leaves the decision entirely to a kind of random sampling (modified to some extent by neighborhood, choice of college, and other factors) and the judgment of the young people most immediately concerned, with the proverbial blindness that accompanies every love relationship, but most especially young love.

One of the most important assumptions made by many persons in North American society—an assumption made without question, as if it were a divine revelation—is that romantic love is the foundation upon which marriage is, or ought to be, based. As a corollary it is assumed that young men and women should be completely free to choose their own mates, with or without the guidance of other persons, if they so choose. This assumption, too, may be worth questioning—if not on strictly moral grounds, at least on prudential grounds. One question that ought to be asked, but seldom is, is whether this approach is more likely or less likely to result in longer and happier marriages in the long run. The answer offered by conventional North American wisdom is at least doubtful.

ALIMONY

In most states the man who is divorced must pay alimony to his ex-wife as long as she lives, unless she remarries. Although the amount of alimony is often settled by the parties themselves, in negotiations carried on through their attorneys, it may be fixed by the court. No general rule applies either to the amount of alimony a man will be required to pay or to the proportion of his income that he may be required to contribute to his ex-wife's support. Whatever the amount, the average middle-income wage earner is often hard-pressed to provide a decent income for his ex-wife, their children, and himself, living in separate households. Everyone involved usually suffers a substantial decline in his or her standard of living.

There is little dispute over the obligation of every father to support his children, whether they are living with him or his ex-wife. However, there is no such general recognition of the duty of the mother to contribute to the support of her children, even though they may not be living with her. This is undoubtedly a vestige of earlier days, when it was almost impossible for women to earn decent wages on their own. Today, when women are far more independent and are able, if they so choose, to enter business, the professions, and the labor market on terms roughly equivalent to, if not yet identical with, those of men, the rationale behind these laws seems to have lost much of its past justification. The mother generally participates in the act of procreation quite as actively as the father, and at least as deliberately. Her responsibilities, therefore, should be equal to his. If the father is given custody of the children after the divorce, parity of reasoning would require that the mother contribute not only to their support, but to the father's as well, if such supplemental support would make the difference between the children's having a competent nurse while he is at work and their being cared for by a less competent person during those hours. In fact, though, few women have ever had to contribute to the support of their children in such circumstances; and women who pay alimony to their ex-husbands are so rare that whenever one is ordered to do so, the case makes headlines.

Those who support the institution of alimony argue along the following lines:

1. A divorced woman has often given the best years of her life, her youth, to the man who has left her. She deserves to be compensated for the many services she has performed for him and for the opportunities she has lost while remaining faithful to him.

2. Few young men start out with the fortunes they have amassed during their married life. Nor do they often have the knowledge, the skills, the positions, or the earning power at the time of their marriage that they have at the time of its dissolution. Countless young women have helped their hus-

bands through college, through graduate or professional school, and through the rough spots that inevitably accompany the beginning of a career, only to be cast off just as the rewards begin to come in. As one attorney has put it, once they have contributed so much to the planting of the tree and its nurture, they should receive their fair share of its fruit.

3. In order to provide pleasant homes for their husbands and proper care for their children, many women interrupt their own schooling or their careers. After an extended absence it is not easy to pick up where they left off. They should be compensated for time lost from their careers, lost positions, and lost seniority, and they should not be left destitute at a time in life when it may be extremely difficult to return to a long-abandoned career or to start training for a new one.

Although these arguments possess a certain plausibility, they do not stand up to close analysis.

The first argument assumes that the contributions to the marriage have been in one direction only—from the wife to the husband—and that the many sacrifices made by the wife for her husband during their marriage ought to be paid for if the marriage is dissolved. In reality, of course, marriage is always a reciprocal relationship. It is rare indeed to find a marriage that has existed for any time at all in which *some* satisfaction has not been derived by the wife from the relationship. One would expect, in the typical case, that she has received at least some of her support from her husband and that if she had not received *some* emotional satisfaction from the marriage, she would have terminated it even sooner. Above all, one must remember that he has given the best years of his life to her—at least as much as she has given to him. For every "service" that the young bride and housewife performs for her husband, she receives one of equal value in return. The young man entering into marriage and raising a family assumes responsibilities and gives up opportunities quite as much as his wife does. If one must speak in these terms, one must conclude that the divorcee has received "compensation for services rendered" during her marriage and has no right to demand more when her marriage has come to an end.

If the second argument were valid, it should apply with equal force to parents. They have contributed immeasurably to the "planting and nurture of the tree," and should, on this reasoning, receive their fair share of its fruits. But the common law imposes no life-long obligation upon children to support their parents, and few parents would make such a demand. Even if the argument were valid, it would apply only to that portion of the husband's income that was directly attributable to his wife's assistance. No woman can claim full credit for her husband's earning power. After all, he must have had *some* abilities, skills, knowledge, status, resources, and experience before she came along, and he may have acquired some during their marriage without her help or *in spite of her interference.* But in setting alimony payments, courts seldom entertain such considerations. They consider the husband's *total ability to pay,* regardless of whether his income is derived from gifts, inheritance, or property he owned or skills he may have had prior to his marriage. Seldom is consideration given to the possibility that his present and future earning capacity may actually have been *reduced* as a result of his wife's behavior during their marriage. No woman has ever been ordered to compensate her ex-husband for losses he may have sustained as a result of her profligacy or her interference in his business or professional affairs.

The third argument has a great deal to commend it. Many women who might have had fine careers have given them up in order to raise their families. This is seldom, if ever, true of men. When a marriage is terminated, a woman who has become dependent upon her husband for support cannot be expected to find a means of supporting herself immediately after the divorce. Nor should the state have to assume the burden of providing for her. Clearly, then, her ex-husband must bear the responsibility of continuing to support her until she is prepared to support herself.

This does not mean, however, that she should be permitted to become what New York Supreme Court Justice Hofstadter has called an "alimony drone, neither toiling nor spinning," living parasitically on the monthly or weekly checks sent to her by her ex-husband. Because there are ample employment opportunities for women in the Western world today, there is no justification for alimony laws that permit women to live perpetually on the earnings of their ex-husbands. Each woman should be given a reasonable period of time in which to rehabilitate herself—to finish her schooling or to learn a trade, and to find a job. This period of grace might be shorter or longer, depending upon her age, her background, and whether she will be caring for very young children. But in any case, once her children are all in school, she should receive support payments from her ex-husband for a few years at most. With the knowledge that her income from this source will gradually be reduced to nothing after five or six years, she will have some incentive to contribute to her own support and to the local and national economy.

CUSTODY

The law presumes that the children's best interests are served if they are given into the custody of their mother. Because the question has never been subjected to careful scientific study, no one knows whether there is any truth to this generalization. There are countries where the presumption is just the opposite—that the children will fare better if they are given into the custody of their father. The legal presumption in courts in the English-speaking world is so strong that when the parents disagree, they are not on an equal footing before the law. The burden of proof rests entirely upon the father. He must demonstrate to the court's satisfaction that the mother is unfit and that he is better equipped to care for them than she is. The latter alone is insufficient, and it is in practice almost impossible to prove the former. In contested cases, custody has been awarded to adulteresses, to prostitutes, and to women who were suffering from the most extreme forms of mental illness. A man can win custody of his children only if he is prepared to spend a great deal of money, if he is blessed with an extraordinarily competent and dedicated attorney, if his case is heard by an unusually progressive judge, and if his wife is utterly beyond redemption. If his children are very young, even this unusual combination of circumstances may not help.

In practice, the courts' actions, which are supposed to be founded upon concern for the welfare of the children, translate into a simple procedure of disposing of cases expeditiously, often to the detriment of the children and always at the cost of the father. The problem is so acute and so widespread that divorce lawyers generally urge their male clients not to fight for custody of their children because the costs are so high and the chances of winning so low.

Some states continue to tie custody to the punitive aspects of divorce. In such states the "guilty" party may not be awarded custody unless there are overwhelming reasons why he (or she) should be; other states grant preference to the party who is "not at fault." There is, of course, no necessary relationship between the "guilt" of a defendant in a divorce case and the likelihood that that person will be better able to provide a healthy, happy, and secure home for the children of the marriage than the "innocent" party.

Other states have held that communists and other persons with unpopular political beliefs are unfit to raise their own children, and have placed them instead in foster homes or in state institutions, where, presumably, they would not be exposed to the pernicious influences of foreign ideologies.

Some courts weigh the preferences of older children (particularly children who are more than twelve years of age), but other states do not consider the children's wishes at all. Where the children are or may be consulted, there is often a nasty battle on the part of the parents to indoctrinate their children with the "line" they want them to take in their court appearance. Such propaganda campaigns may last for weeks, for months, and even for years, shifting back and forth as the children move from the home of the custodial parent to that of their "visiting" parent and back again. In such cases each parent vies with the other in attempting to bribe the child into accepting his or her superiority to the other parent. Such contests can hardly have good effects on the children who are tossed back and forth in the middle of them, but they do go on incessantly. Because custody is never awarded on a permanent basis, but is always open to reconsideration, it is difficult to imagine how this problem can ever be resolved satisfactorily.

Current practice usually puts the man at a considerable disadvantage. Even though he may want to win the custody of his children, and be perfectly capable of giving them excellent care, his chances of winning the custody battle are quite minimal. Nevertheless, he must pay for the support of the children and usually for the support of his ex-wife as well. And to top it all off, he must also pay his own lawyer, his ex-wife's lawyer, and the fees of all of the expert witnesses who may have been called in the course of the divorce hearings, the custody hearings, and the support hearings. In a day when women are demanding equal rights and "liberation" from a male-dominated society, it is reasonable to hope that the presumption in favor of the mother will be abandoned; that women will be prepared to accept alimony payments for a limited period of time only; and that when their ex-husbands win custody of their children, they will gladly assume their fair share of the financial burden of caring for them, even though they may be granted very limited visitation rights.

SUMMARY AND CONCLUSION

With few exceptions, present divorce laws are based upon the premise that divorce is immoral and that if it is to be granted at all, it must be on the ground that one and only one party has committed an offense against the marriage. There is no general agreement about the nature of such offenses, however, except in the case of adultery, which is recognized as a sufficient ground for divorce everywhere in the English-speaking world (except Ireland, where divorce is not granted on any grounds whatever).

In a major break with tradition, a few legislatures have sanctioned divorce by consent, but in most places, if it can be shown that the parties are cooperating to obtain a divorce, the divorce may be denied to both of them.

Outside Christian nations, or nations with a Christian religious heritage, divorce has not been widely regarded as immoral. Where the law has taken an interest in the matter at all, it has been primarily devoted to protecting the wife and children and to assuring all parties who might be affected by the divorce that it was duly recorded and attested. Only in Christian nations has the state enacted severe restrictions designed to prevent many (or in some cases, *most* or even *all*) persons from dissolving their marriages when they wanted to do so. The effects of the prevailing attitudes and policies on divorce may discourage some people from seeking relief from their unhappy marriages; but they may encourage others to escape their responsibilities through desertion or abandonment, and they may perpetuate unhappy marriages that will adversely affect the health and stability of everyone concerned. Where divorce is possible, the adversary system so inflames the passions and emotions of husband and wife that it may become impossible for them ever to discuss their problems or their mutual concerns amicably again —though, if there are children, they must inevitably have many such discussions through the years.

Alimony laws are based for the most part upon the premise that the divorced woman cannot fend for herself, and presume that her ex-husband ought to support her for the rest of her life. The first assumption is no longer true, and the second is demeaning to women and exploitative of men. Though there are excellent reasons for providing temporary support for some women, in exceptional cases only would permanent alimony be justified. If genuine equality is to be achieved, men should, in some circumstances, be granted support from their ex-wives.

Custody laws and practices are stacked against men, who face nearly insurmountable obstacles if they wish to gain custody of their children. As a result, not only the fathers, but their children as well may suffer a loss that cannot be justified by any empirical evidence that the children are better off if they are in their mother's custody. Here again, equity requires that the laws be reformed to provide men an equal opportunity to win custody of tl eir children, when it is felt that the children's best interests will be served if they are entrusted to the care of their father rather than that of their mother. And when the father is awarded custody of the children, consideration should be given to the mother's responsibility to contribute to their support; for, though every father is required to contribute to the support of his children when they are given into his ex-wife's custody, a mere handful of women have ever been required to do so when the situation has been reversed.

The law on divorce is one of the most widely neglected areas of jurisprudence, though the chances are that at least a third of all Americans will at some time be directly involved in some way with divorce courts. It is time for a thorough reexamination of these laws, of the moral foundations upon which they were built, and of their effects upon all of those who are touched by them.

One last word may be appropriate here. Many people, in considering whether it is proper for another person to enter into a divorce action, and even in deliberating over whether they should themselves file for a divorce, are inclined to base their decision entirely upon their estimate of the consequences such an action might have upon the welfare of any children who might be involved. Of course, the welfare of the children must be given considerable weight, particularly since they are unable to take any action on their own behalf and are at the mercy of others. But adults have a right to happiness, too, and when calculating the effects of a possible divorce, their interests should not be ignored. If the law is designed to enable people to live fuller, happier, more meaningful lives, then it must give due consideration to the concerns of adults who may find that they have become involved in a marriage that is destructive to them or to their personalities, or that is stifling and oppressive, and it should allow them to escape without further damage to themselves or to others.

5

Marijuana

In 1970 a survey of students at five colleges in the Boston area revealed that 48 per cent had smoked marijuana during the previous year. Of those who had smoked pot, 60 per cent admitted to having smoked it occasionally or frequently. Another poll covering all of Massachusetts indicated that half the college students, 25 per cent of the employed persons, and about 20 per cent of the high school students admitted to having smoked marijuana at least once during the preceding year. The impressions of those who were interviewed revealed that they believed that marijuana use was even more widespread than they themselves admitted it to be. A conservative estimate of the California drug scene is that of all persons in that state between the ages of sixteen and twenty-nine, one third have used marijuana. As each year passes, the rate of such use increases significantly. For example, nationwide surveys of students who admitted using marijuana found that from 1968 to 1969 the number of freshman boys who had done so rose from 26.8 per cent to 34.9 per cent. Among the freshman girls the figures were only slightly lower: 22.9 per cent and 31.8 per cent. More significant, perhaps, is the revelation that by 1969 the same class (that is, the sophomores, who had been freshmen the previous year) had had considerably more experience with marijuana, for fully 41.7 per cent of that class had by that year experimented with the drug. Again, the girls were only a little behind, with 35.5 per cent, as opposed to 22.9 per cent who had used the drug the previous year.[1] At this rate it will not be long before at least half, and probably far more, of the young people in the United States will have committed the serious crime of using or possessing marijuana. Although such use seems to be more common around college and university campuses than in small towns far from such intellectual centers, and though the campuses that attract more intellectually inclined students (as opposed, say, to agricultural colleges, engineering schools, teacher colleges, and the like) have a higher rate of use, it seems evident that the phenomenon is widespread and touches

133

just about every segment of the population. In Canada, the Commission of Inquiry into the Nonmedical Use of Drugs estimated that 8 per cent of all high school students and 25 per cent of college and university students have used the drug, and this was taken as a conservative estimate.[2]

The general public and the governments of both Canada and the United States have expressed considerable concern about this phenomenon. There is widespread belief that consumption of drugs is closely related to the increasing crime rate, to violence both on and off campus, to a general deterioration in morals, and to terrible personal tragedies for many persons, young and old. The establishment of the Canadian commission and of the United States Task Force on Narcotics and Drug Abuse, as well as action on the state and provincial levels and in the private sectors is indicative of the deep concern of persons all across the North American continent over the use of drugs. Part of this concern naturally revolves around the legal aspects of drug use, for there are state, provincial, and federal laws in both nations regulating the sale, use, and possession of certain drugs, and in many cases setting heavy penalties for such activities. Within the past few years serious questions have arisen concerning the scope of such laws and the wisdom of the penalties attached to them. Indeed, some persons are advocating that, in the case of marijuana at least, all laws restricting sale, use, or possession should be repealed, and that the drug should be considered a relatively harmless social drug, less harmful, perhaps, than alcohol, and serving many of the same functions in the consumer's personal and social life. Others, however, insist that heavy penalties be maintained, as a deterrent to use of what they allege is a dangerous substance. They contend that the repeal of present laws would put society's stamp of approval upon a menace to the health of the nation, and would encourage use, both by those who have already become involved and by those who have not.

Early reports of the Federal Bureau of Narcotics described marijuana as a drug having powerful and dangerous effects. It was said to lead to violence frequently and to give rise to hallucinations and to wild and uncontrollable outbursts of emotion. Those who used the drug were said to lose moral control and will power, laying themselves open to any suggestion that might be made by any unscrupulous villain. Because of distortions of space and time and frequent "blackouts," the user was liable to function in strange ways and to have no recollection of his bizarre behavior afterward. Marijuana was said to be responsible for rape, murder, and kidnapping, and it was thought to lead to promiscuity and to the commission of sex crimes because of its powerful aphrodisiac effects. If used in large quantities or over a long period of time, it could lead to insanity or to organic brain damage, as well as to a general deterioration in the user's moral character. Marijuana was thought to be merely a stage in the process which ultimately culminated in the addict's graduation to the hard drugs, such as the opiates—morphine, opium, and heroin—with the dreadful results that that entailed. A typical summation of the evils of marijuana use is contained in the following statement by Judge G. Joseph Tauro of the Massachusetts Superior Court,

> There are certain important areas on which there is no substantial controversy among reputable and informed authorities.
>
> First, marijuana is universally recognized as a mind-altering drug which in varying degrees and with unpredictable effect produces a state of intoxication sometimes referred to as "euphoric."
>
> Second, in the United States marijuana is customarily used for the explicit purpose of inducing this state of intoxication.
>
> Third, in varying degrees this state of intoxication can cause a lessening of psychomotor coordination and distortion of the ability to perceive time, distance, and space. However, there is usually no interrelated diminution of muscular strength.
>
> Fourth, the *habitual* use of marijuana is particularly prevalent among individuals with marginal personalities exhibiting feelings of inadequacy, anxiety, disaffiliation, alienation, and frustration or suffering from neuroses, psychoses, or other mental disorders. Such persons constitute a significant percent of our population, and it is precisely among this type of individual that marijuana may cause psychological dependence.
>
> Fifth, marijuana may have a disinhibiting effect upon the user which tends to aggravate his pre-existing mental state or disposition. Thus its effects can vary with individuals and can vary during different occasions of use by the same individual.
>
> Sixth, marijuana has no accepted medical use in modern medicine and serves no useful purpose in any other way.
>
> Seventh, the use of marijuana is not part of the dogma of any recognized Western religion.
>
> Eighth, marijuana has had a growing attraction for the young and the adolescent.
>
> Last, but probably most significant, no one can guarantee with any degree of certainty that continued use of marijuana will not eventually cause permanent physical injury.[3]

On the basis of these points, Judge Tauro concluded that marijuana is a dangerous drug, "possessing a potential of harm both to the user and to society," and that the current penal laws against the use or possession of marijuana are therefore justified. "No foreign enemy poses a greater danger to our nation than a self-imposed danger of permitting drug use to become part of our culture," he concluded, "and no outside force would be more destructive."

The American Medical Association, too, concluded that cannabis (the generic term for the marijuana plant, which includes other forms of the product, such as hashish, as well) is "a dangerous drug and as such is a public health concern."[4] This conclusion is based in part upon the fact that such severe reactions can follow from the use of potent forms of cannabis. The AMA argues against those who say that marijuana is less toxic than alcohol by stating that the comparisons drawn are not legitimate:

[Advocates of the legalization of marijuana] are actually comparing the relatively insignificant effects of marijuana at the lower end of the dose-response curve with the effects of alcohol at the toxicity end of the curve— i.e., the "spree" use of marijuana vs. acute or chronic "poisoning" with alcohol. If they compared both drugs at the upper end of the curve, they would see that the effects on the individual and society are highly deleterious in both cases.[5]

According to Harry J. Anslinger, former commissioner of the Federal Bureau of Narcotics, marijuana leads to heroin addiction. At one time he insisted that marijuana was a direct cause of much violent crime; however, he has recently conceded that it is not a "controlling factor" in the commission of crimes.[6] Other critics have noted what they consider to be the general moral deterioration of those who use marijuana and other drugs. Such use, it is said, is a "shortcut to happiness or tranquility" which should be achieved only after many years of hard work and self-discipline. Drugs lead to self-indulgence, dependence, and promiscuity, which are antithetical to such values as self-restraint, independence, and sexual propriety, to say nothing of the important virtue of sobriety. Those who lean upon drugs, it is said, have an aversion to work and tend to become lazy, slovenly, and dirty, to have no sense of ethics or even of simple human decency.[7]

It is also suggested that the international drug traffic is under the management of organized crime and that the conspiracy to seduce young Americans into the use of hard narcotics by way of marijuana is led by the leaders of the major crime syndicates who stand to make major profits from the long-term market that is thus produced. Another version of this doctrine, not necessarily inconsistent with the first one, holds that Communist China is behind the penetration of American markets, both through the sale of inexpensive drugs to American servicemen in Southeast Asia and through sales to the domestic market for consumption in the continental United States. The ultimate purpose of this scheme was to cause such demoralization among American troops that they would have to be removed from the sphere of Chinese influence, and eventually, to weaken the fabric of American society so that it might more easily be penetrated by those who would bring about the enslavement of the American people.

This view may be contrasted with that of certain liberals, who proclaim that marijuana is never harmful. It is argued that marijuana is a new social drug, one facet of the new life style that includes such other elements as certain types of clothing, beards, long hair, music, freedom from social restraint, sexual license, and nonviolence. It is said that marijuana fills the same function in the lives of young people as alcohol in the lives of their elders, that in some circles anyone who totally abstains from any form of consumption of marijuana is considered to be as much a misfit as a tee-totaler is in others. In a society whose past traditions have become meaningless to many of its young people, whose institutions seem unresponsive to their needs and their demands for social justice, and whose future is frightening to contemplate, many students and others in the adolescent and post-adolescent years may have given up all thought of the irrelevant past and the ominous future in favor of exclusive concentration upon the present. In their own immediate experience they are able to find a world that is both meaningful and important. Thus, they turn to transcendental meditation, new forms of religion, sex, and the inner world that is revealed by drugs.[8] Such respected scholars as Margaret Mead have commented upon the hypocrisy of those who stand with a cocktail in one hand and a cigarette in the other, telling their children that they must not try marijuana, though the latter is believed by many to be less harmful than either alcohol or tobacco.[9] For some it may be a means of escaping from a crowded world that is so littered and cluttered and so aesthetically unappealing that the inner world provides solace and relief, if only for a time. People have always sought a brief respite from the burdens of the real world. Some have been satisfied with such innocent amusements as are provided by various games; others turn to fiction, dance, the theater, art, or music; still others have tried religion. Some, not satisfied with any of these, have attempted to provide for themselves a bit of heaven on earth, as Norman Taylor put it.[10] "In spite of occasional danger," he says, "men have always sought for some flight from reality and always will. Next to the instinct of survival it has dominated more people than any religion, costs more than any food, and it yields in this country more than three billion dollars' yearly revenue to the United States Treasury." In addition to the legitimate escapes provided through the consumption of alcohol, tobacco, tea, coffee, and other more harmless entertainments, it is now suggested that marijuana should be legalized so that the social drug of the new generation may gain its rightful place in modern society.

This chapter is dedicated to the resolution of this problem. Should the use and sale of marijuana be legalized? I shall not attempt here to resolve the much more difficult question, whether such other drugs as the opiates, LSD, and the amphetamines (speed) should be legalized, for they present special problems that would require extensive technical discussion. However, some suggestions for possible solutions to those problems may emerge from our discussion of the marijuana issue.

MARIJUANA'S EFFECTS

There is considerable controversy about the effects of marijuana upon those who use it. Some of the effects are now well established as a result of careful research under controlled conditions; others remain doubtful; and still others, as we shall see, depend very much upon the definition of certain crucial terms, rather than upon any observable facts. Most careful students of the subject are in agreement that further scientific studies must be done before firm conclusions can be reached about the long-term effects of the drug. But the present state of our knowledge enables us to reach certain conclusions that may have some effect upon attitudes toward legislation in the field.

PHYSICAL EFFECTS

Smoking of marijuana results in an increased heart rate, no significant change in respiration, no change in the size of the pupil of the eye (contrary to a widely held belief that it causes dilation of the pupil, probably because of the fact that marijuana is usually smoked in dark rooms), significant reddening of the conjunctivae around the eyes resulting from dilation of the blood vessels, and no significant change in blood sugar level. Such changes as do take place disappear relatively soon after consumption of the drug ceases.[11]

PSYCHOLOGICAL EFFECTS

Under laboratory conditions some decrease in functional abilities is observed, including memory, coordination, and time sense. Normal doses of the drug have no noticeable effects on balance, perception, or the performance of relatively simple mental tasks. Some persons become dizzy, but it is not clear whether this is an effect of the drug itself or of the deep breathing that persons smoking marijuana cigarettes employ to get the full effect of the drug.[12] However, there is a substantial impairment of the ability to perform complex tasks, probably as a result of the effect upon near-term memory. The subject rapidly forgets what has just happened, though he can remember, with fair accuracy, events that have occurred in the more distant past.[13]

More subjective experiences include a feeling of happiness, increased conviviality, free play of the imagination, unusual capacities to notice aspects of the environment of which one is not normally aware, vivid visual imagery, changes in perceived sense relations, enhancement of sense experiences, lessening of inhibitions, and, as some users put it, greater religious or philosophical or other insight and understanding. Under higher doses users claim to have greater creative abilities. Though there is no evidence to support the claim that marijuana has aphrodisiac qualities, it does enhance sexual pleasure. Some persons also experience headache, backache, feelings of fear and anxiety, depression, irritability, nausea, dizziness, a dulling of attention, convulsions, a sense of heaviness and weakness. A few persons have also become disoriented and suffered from delusions, suspiciousness, paranoia, panic, and loss of control culminating in psychotic states.[14]

No description of the psychological effects of marijuana use seems to be adequate to convey the users' subjective experiences to those who have never shared them. A few excerpts from firsthand accounts of such experiences should give the reader some appreciation for the attraction the drug has for those who have tried it.

Allen Ginsberg, who has since given up the use of drugs, once wrote of an experience he had after smoking a considerable quantity of marijuana and then going to the New York Museum of Modern Art, where he looked at some Cézanne water colors:

> I suddenly got a strange shuddering impression looking at his canvases, partly the effect when someone pulls a Venetian blind, reverses the Venetian—there's a sudden shift, a flashing that you see in Cézanne canvases. Partly it's when the canvas opens up into three dimensions and looks like wooden objects, like solid-space objects, in three dimensions rather than flat. Partly it's the enormous spaces that open up in Cézanne's landscapes. And it's partly that mysterious quality around his figures. . . . They look like great huge 3-D wooden dolls, sometimes. Very *uncanny* thing, like a very mysterious thing—in other words, there's a strange sensation that one gets, looking at his canvases, which I began to associate with the extraordinary sensation—cosmic sensation, in fact—that I had experienced catalyzed by Blake's "Sun-flower" and "Sick Rose" and a few other poems. . . . He produced a solid two-dimensional surface which when you looked *into* it, maybe from a slight distance with your eyes either unfocused or your eyelids lowered slightly, you could see a great three-dimensional opening, mysterious, stereoscopic, like going into a stereopticon. . . .[15]

Similar results have taken place when persons under the influence of cannabis have listened to music. They find that their appreciation for the music is vastly enhanced, and that their ability to hear the separate parts of the harmony and the richness of the counterpoint is increased.

The sense of euphoria is sometimes accompanied by a feeling of lightness, sometimes described as a sense of becoming "hollowed out," or being inflated, of floating weightlessly through the atmosphere and of passing effortlessly through solid objects. Such sensations may alternate with feelings of physical density, solidity, and dead weight. Occasionally the user feels that his body is slowly disintegrating, that his fingers, his hands, his arms, and other parts of his body are floating off in all directions, and that he himself has become detached from his body. Regardless of such sensations of lightness or heaviness, there is often a feeling of great hilarity. The subject may be seized by fits of uncontrollable laughter which may last for quite some time. Many persons experience what they call a "joyous state," a feeling of complete freedom, "bliss," "rapture," "expansive good-will," and sometimes, an age regression, a return to childhood or to the relatively secure world of childhood that enables them to throw off the cares of their adult lives and enjoy the pleasures of the moment without inhibition.

Sometimes there is a sense of being a dual personality, of doing things with one "part" of oneself that one "observed" and possibly disapproved of with another.

A very common phenomenon is loss of proximate memory and a distortion of time perception. Events flow into one another without apparent connection, and the subject experiences an inability to recall what has happened or what he has said only a moment before. As a result his speech tends to be disconnected and incoherent, though the subject himself thinks that he is being extremely witty and that he is thinking more rapidly and more effectively than usual. In fact, he jumps in almost random fashion from one topic of conversation to another, often stopping in the middle of a sentence because he has forgotten what he was talking about. Time perception is quite distorted, with minutes seeming to be hours, and seconds expanding into minutes.

Synesthesia, the perception of one kind of sensation as another, is one of the most important pleasure-producing components of the marijuana experience. Sounds may be seen as vivid colors, and numbers may be heard as musical tones or harmonies. These perceptions are said to be very beautiful. Hallucinations in the form of flashes of light and constantly changing forms of vivid color, which transmute themselves from geometrical shapes into human faces, parts of bodies, and pictures of great complexity and detail, are said to add to the pleasure of the experience. Some experts maintain that true hallucinations do not actually occur, but that the effects are more in the nature of illusions, or "variable seeings" of things that are actually present in the environment. However, the description of "technicolor movies" that appear in viewers' heads or on the inside of their eyelids seems very much to be of a kind of hallucination. Many of these phenomena occur only with extremely large doses of the drug, particularly when it is taken orally (as hashish), and not when it is smoked in the relatively mild doses available in marijuana cigarettes sold in North America.[16]

Other sensations, including those of taste, smell, and hearing, are said to be heightened and enhanced.

According to the American Medical Association, marijuana smoking results in "impaired judgment and memory, irritability and confusion." Other studies confirm this finding, and add that faulty perception is accompanied by heightened suggestibility and an exaggerated notion of clear thinking, profundity, and creativity. They suggest that the feeling of wit, clarity, and brilliance is purely subjective, with no correspondence to objective fact. The sense of elation is said to be more responsible for the feeling of brilliance than any genuine capacity to do creative or useful work. On the other hand, some studies indicate that there is strong evidence in favor of the theory that marijuana does have some capacity to be of some use to the creative artist. Many jazz players are known to have used marijuana, contending that it enhanced their musical abilities. Allen Ginsberg and William Burroughs have testified to the benefits they believe they have received from use of the drug. Concerning this aspect of the drug's effects, one scientist who has used marijuana wrote:

There is a myth about such highs [as those experienced by the marijuana user]: the user has an illusion of great insight, but it does not survive scrutiny in the morning. I am convinced that this is an error, and that the devastating insights achieved when high are real insights; the main problem is putting these insights in a form acceptable to the quite different self that we are when we're down the next day. Some of the hardest work I've ever done has been to put such insights down on tape or in writing. The problem is that ten even more interesting ideas or images have to be lost in the effort of recording one. It is easy to understand why someone might think it's a waste of effort going to all that trouble to set the thought down, a kind of intrusion of the Protestant Ethic. But since I live almost all my life down I've made the effort—successfully, I think. . . .

I find that most of the insights I achieve when high are into social issues, an area of creative scholarship very different from the one I am generally known for. I can remember one occasion, taking a shower with my wife while high, in which I had an idea on the origins and invalidities of racism in terms of gaussian distribution curves. It was a point obvious in a way, but rarely talked about. I drew the curves in soap on the shower wall, and went to write the idea down. One idea led to another, and at the end of about an hour of extremely hard work I found I had written eleven short essays on a wide range of social, political, philosophical, and human biological topics. . . . From all external signs, such as public reactions and expert commentary, they seem to contain valid insights. I have used them in university commencement addresses, public lectures, and in my books.

. . . I am convinced that there are genuine and valid levels of perception available with cannabis (and probably with other drugs) which are, through the defects of our society and our educational system, unavailable to us without such drugs. Such a remark applies not only to self-awareness and to intellectual pursuits, but also to perceptions of real people, a vastly enhanced sensitivity to facial expressions, intonations, and choice of words which sometimes yields a rapport so close it's as if two people are reading each other's minds.[17]

Some people have terrifying experiences, some of which lead to suicide attempts, or at least to the desire to commit suicide in order to escape from the terror of the experience. They imagine that they are surrounded by hideous beasts, that they are being pursued by demons, that they are falling into a maelstrom or into a bottomless chasm. One person on a hashish trip imagined that he had been transformed into the clapper of a gigantic cathedral bell. When the bell tolled, he imagined that he was smashed to pieces, and was surprised to find that he was still alive some time later. Others have felt their heads exploding, and have sensed blood streaming from their ears and their eyes. The heavenly visions that produce such raptures for some people are paralleled by hellish visions for others.

One of the most thorough studies of cannabis was undertaken by the Indian Hemp Drugs Commission in India during the 1890's. The commission consulted more than a thousand witnesses and 300 physicians. In 1968 T. H.

Mikuriya wrote that the commission's report was "by far the most complete and systematic study of marijuana undertaken to date." [18] The commission concluded that:

a. "It has been clearly established that the occasional use of hemp in moderate doses may be beneficial."
b. Moderate use of the drugs causes no harmful physical effects.
c. Excessive use causes weakness and may result in any of a number of physical ailments.
d. "Moderate use of hemp drugs produces no injurious effects on the mind."
e. "It appears that the excessive use of hemp drugs may . . . induce insanity. It has been shown that the effect of hemp drugs in this respect has hitherto been greatly exaggerated, but that they do sometimes produce insanity seems beyond question."
f. Moderate use of the drugs produces no moral deterioration whatever.
g. Excessive use intensifies "moral depravity," but "even the excessive consumer of hemp drugs is ordinarily inoffensive. . . . For all practical purposes it may be laid down that there is little or no connection between the use of hemp drugs and crime."
h. "The injury done by the excessive user is . . . confined almost exclusively to the consumer himself; the effect on society is rarely appreciable." [19]

Other major studies, including the famous La Guardia Report,[20] have arrived at the same general conclusions. A sophisticated study published in 1969 found that driving performance was unimpaired in simulated circumstances under fairly high doses of marijuana.[21]

The 1967 Report of the Task Force on Narcotics and Drug Abuse of the President's Commission on Law Enforcement and Administration of Justice concluded, on the basis of its studies of all the information available, that marijuana produces no physical dependence and that no withdrawal symptoms are associated with it. It noted that psychic dependence could be associated with marijuana, but that the same was true of any substance that alters the state of consciousness. It classified marijuana as a "mild hallucinogen," following a study by the Medical Society of the County of New York, in which it was observed that it was less likely to produce impairment of judgment and memory; to cause anxiety, confusion, or disorientation; or to induce psychotic episodes in persons who had a disposition to such illnesses, than peyote, mescalin, hashish, or LSD. It agreed also with the Society's finding that "there is no evidence that marijuana use is associated with crimes of violence in this country." [22] It also concluded that marijuana does not necessarily lead to heroin use. "There are too many marijuana users who do not graduate to heroin, and too many heroin addicts with no known prior marijuana use, to support such a theory. Moreover, there is no scientific basis for such a theory. The basic text on pharmacology . . . states quite explicitly that *marijuana habituation does not lead to the use of heroin.*" [23]

In surveys conducted by the Canadian Commission of Inquiry into the Nonmedical Use of Drugs, no significant difference was found to exist between the grades of university students who used cannabis and those of nonusers. Two American surveys have revealed that light or infrequent users had better academic records than either nonusers or heavy users. Other surveys and tests seem to justify the conclusion that marijuana use leads to no chronic changes in intellectual functions. The best scientific evidence available indicates that the danger of acute intoxication is quite minimal.

Numerous studies have revealed that virtually no effects of marijuana consumption were serious enough to require hospitalization.* After an exhaustive study of mental hospital admissions, the Canadian Commission concluded that "no significant clear cases of 'cannabis psychosis' were identified, although it appeared that in some instances the chronic use of cannabis may have contributed significantly to the condition which resulted in hospitalization." The commission also concluded that there is "little evidence at this time that cannabis causes a significant degree of pathology in the general population of users studied in North America," although many users have experienced at least one unpleasant "high" from the drug. Although cannabis has been blamed for or associated with some psychotic reactions, the commission noted that the causal relationships are not at all clear, and that it is possible that persons who are already suffering from one form or another of psychopathology may be more disposed than others to use cannabis or to use it heavily than persons who are psychologically sound. Alternatively, other factors, such as social alienation, family relations, or socioeconomic conditions may influence both psychopathology and cannabis use. Noting that cannabis is used as a tranquilizer in many cultures, the commission suggested that the use of cannabis might actually reduce the overt symptoms that some mentally ill persons might otherwise have, leading to a lower incidence of manifest psychopathology among some cannabis-using groups than in the population at large.

The American National Commission on Marihuana and Drug Abuse made similar findings, concluding that experimental and intermittent users developed little or no psychological dependence on the drug and that no organ injury was demonstrable, whereas heavy users tended to become strongly dependent upon it and did develop some organ damage, particularly in the

---

* The Boston University Student Health Service, which services a student population of 20,000, saw only five to seven anxiety reactions per year that were associated with marijuana use. At UCLA, where at least one fourth of all undergraduates are estimated to have been using marijuana two or more times a week for more than two years, no acute psychiatric reaction was observed during the course of an entire year. Over a two-year period, the University of British Columbia infirmary saw only six cases of acute cannabis intoxication out of a total student population of 25,000, of whom one half have probably used marijuana or hashish. See *Cannabis: A Report of the Commission of Inquiry into the Non-Medical Use of Drugs* (Ottawa: Department of National Health and Welfare, 1972), pp. 80 ff., and the reports and surveys cited there.

pulmonary system. The commission concluded that "experimental or intermittent use of this drug carries minimal risk to the public health, and should
not be given overzealous attention in terms of a public health response." *

SOCIAL EFFECTS

We have already seen that earlier studies concluded that marijuana, used
in moderation, did not lead to criminality or to the use of hard drugs. The
official line of the Federal Bureau of Narcotics has been that marijuana
does conduce both to overt criminal behavior and to experimentation with
and ultimate dependence upon such hard drugs as heroin. There seems to
be no scientific basis for such conclusions. The "evidence" that marijuana
leads to heroin addiction is based upon the verifiable fact that many heroin
addicts used marijuana prior to their experimentation with heroin. This does
not prove that the marijuana was a *cause* of their later addiction to heroin,
because many persons who use heroin have had no prior experience with
marijuana; a great many people who use marijuana do not "graduate" to
heroin; in other countries where marijuana is widely used, there is little or
no incidence of "graduation" from marijuana to other drugs; and there is
no evidence of a physiological connection between the use of marijuana and
the use of other drugs, as there is between the use of one opiate and another.
(When a person is addicted to one of the opiate narcotics, he can escape
withdrawal symptoms and achieve much the same pleasurable effects by
using another. This is not true as between marijuana—which produces no
withdrawal symptoms in any case—and other drugs.) If mere temporal
priority were sufficient to establish causal relationships, it would be possible
to show that tobacco and alcohol both lead to heroin addiction, because most
heroin addicts have had prior experience with those drugs. Because most
heroin addicts have had prior experience with milk and baked beans, one
might seek a connection there, as well.

Those who make the unsubstantiated claim that marijuana use leads to
heroin addiction tend to disregard the evidence that other causal factors are
at work. Available evidence indicates that with a few exceptions, the heroin
addict of today is about the same as the heroin addict of twenty years ago:
he is usually a product of a slum environment, a dependent, inadequate individual, unable to cope with problems of everyday life. College students and
others from middle-class backgrounds tend to avoid heroin and the other
addictive drugs, because they realize the dangers of becoming "hooked."[24]

---

* In this connection, it may be worthwhile to note that the common opinion that
marijuana is responsible for a number of deaths is pure myth. The American commission
made an exhaustive search of the literature and consulted health officials all across the
country without being able to find a single human fatality that could be traced solely
to the ingestion of marijuana. See the National Commission's official report, *Marihuana:
A Signal of Misunderstanding* (New York: New American Library, 1972), p. 104.

From a study of statistics kept by the state of California on marijuana and opiate drug violations, J. Mandel has reached the following conclusions:

> Dangerous drugs (amphetamines, barbiturates, etc.) are more often "starters" toward opiates than is marijuana.
>
> . . . Opiate use *without* a past history of marijuana is seven times likelier than opiate use *with* a past record of pot smoking.
>
> . . . On the average, over 60 times as many Californians are arrested for marijuana without having a history of "hard drugs" than appear to "graduate" from marijuana to heroin.[25]

Other studies reach similar conclusions. For example, a study of 100 heroin users in the Chicago area in 1952 found that only eleven had any history of marijuana use, and the Federal Bureau of Narcotics found that only 7 per cent of persons who had been convicted of opiate charges had started on marijuana. In short, the evidence of the alleged connection between heroin addiction and marijuana use is not convincing. The conclusion that there is such a connection tends to rest upon inadequate analysis of the samples; upon a failure to consider alternative factors; upon a failure to give due consideration to the possibility that where both marijuana use and heroin addiction are present, the cause for both may be some more remote condition or event; and upon the unwarranted assumption that if A follows B, B must be the cause of A.[26]

As noted, some studies have concluded that users of marijuana have no noticeable increase in inclination to commit offenses against the law. The President's Task Force on Drug Abuse arrived at the same conclusion, as have studies in Brazil, Nigeria, and India, as well as a number of studies in American cities.[27] Heavy cannabis use, in fact, has been held to be a deterrent to crime, because it produces a stupor that is hardly appropriate to effective criminal behavior. Where the use of marijuana has been linked with criminal behavior, *no causal relationship has been established.* Confidential interviews with law enforcement officers by the La Guardia Commission revealed that "they unhesitatingly stated that there is no proof that major crimes are associated with the practice of smoking marijuana. They did state that many marijuana smokers are guilty of petty crimes, but that the criminal career usually existed prior to the time the individual smoked his first marijuana cigarette." These officers added that they believe that professional criminals would not associate with marijuana smokers on the ground that the latter were "inferior and unreliable." The commission concluded that "marijuana is not the determining factor in the commission of major crimes," and that "juvenile delinquency is not associated with the practice of smoking marijuana." [28]

However, one form of criminal behavior is engaged in by all marijuana users: the use and possession of marijuana. Every time a marijuana user purchases a "bag" of pot for his own use, he commits a federal offense as well as one or more state offenses, and puts himself into a position where he may be arrested and convicted of a felony. It would follow, then, that repeal of the laws against the use or possession of marijuana would instantly do away with the major source of criminal behavior and criminal convictions in this area. One might argue that it is not so much the smoking of pot that leads to criminal behavior as the law prohibiting the smoking of pot that creates the crime associated with marijuana.

We may now comment on Judge Tauro's nine points. First, it should be observed that Judge Tauro nowhere makes it clear who the "reputable and informed authorities" are among whom there is "no substantial controversy" on those points. There is no denying the first and second points. Marijuana is a "mind-altering drug," like alcohol, tea, coffee, tobacco, and many drugs that are sold with doctors' prescriptions; and, like those drugs, it is consumed precisely *because* of its "mind-altering" effects. One should be cautious, however, about the use of the term *mind-altering*. It does *not* mean, as one might suppose on first reading, that consumption of the drug induces some permanent change in the mind of the consumer. *Mind-altering* in this context means no more than is meant by such innocuous terms as *stimulant* and *depressant*. If *mind-altering* means "pleasure-producing," then chicken soup would have to be classed as a mind-altering substance as well.

Tauro's third point does not tell the whole story, as we have seen, for the extent to which marijuana affects psychomotor coordination is still under study. It is true that there is a distortion of temporal and spatial senses, and it *may* be true that the user suffers no diminution of muscular strength; but Judge Tauro fails to mention the important point that there is a tendency to become passive and that persons who use marijuana are not disposed to commit violent crimes because of their use of the drug.

The fourth point may have been true at one time, but it is no longer so easy to accept it without further inquiry. Nor is it easy to tell what a "significant per cent" of the population would be. Unless the percentage of "disaffiliated, alienated, frustrated, neurotic, and psychotic" persons in our society is catastrophically high, we must conclude that many normal, well-adjusted, creative, and productive citizens must be using marijuana today; and, as we shall see, there is some question about the scientific usefulness of the concept of psychological dependence.

There is no evidence of a dangerous disinhibiting effect, or of marijuana's "aggravating" (note the loaded term!) its users' mental states.

Although no medical use for marijuana has yet been discovered, it is not quite fair to say that it "serves no useful purpose in any other way." Those who use it are convinced that it *is* useful, for it seems to serve *their* purposes very well indeed. Unless one is prepared to deny that those purposes have any claim to be respected in our society—a kind of natural-law claim, it would seem—one must concede that the drug has *one* useful purpose, at least. If nothing else, it provides pleasure to those who use it, and serves as a social drug, making parties more pleasant than they might otherwise be. The truth of the eighth point would seem to bear this out.

It is not clear that distinctions should be drawn to the advantage of users of dangerous drugs, such as alcohol, that have been sanctified by traditional religions, as Judge Tauro suggests.

Judge Tauro's final point is true. No one can guarantee that continued use of marijuana will not cause permanent physical injury. No one can guarantee that continued use of alcohol will not cause permanent physical injury, either. Indeed, one can guarantee, with a reasonably high degree of probability, that such use of tobacco *will* result in permanent injury or death; but so far, no one has seriously suggested that tobacco smokers should be sent to jail for as much as ten years for mere possession of a single cigarette. The continued use of potatoes, of bread, or of seafood from Judge Tauro's home state can result in physical injury under certain conditions; but this does not seem to be sufficient reason for outlawing *all* consumption of any of these products. Excessive consumption of ordinary table salt can lead to serious physical disturbances, but the state would be guilty of a gross violation of the rights of its citizens if it were to deprive them of the pleasures that they derive from salting their foods on the ground that some people might injure themselves by consuming more salt than they should.

This is not an answer to the basic question that we wish to answer here. But the beginnings of a pattern may have begun to emerge. We must still consider the social effects of marijuana, particularly the question of the extent to which its use leads to criminal behavior, and the problem of the drug's influence upon perceptions of reality, before turning to the question of the justice of the criminal sanctions that are imposed upon those who are caught with the drug.

SOME LINGUISTIC PROBLEMS

Many of the terms used in discussions of drugs are emotionally charged. A choice of words can make a considerable difference to the outcome of a given discussion, unless the participants are highly sophisticated, for though two words may refer to the same objective set of circumstances, one may carry strongly negative connotations, whereas the other may carry equally strong positive or commendatory connotations. An analysis of some of these terms may be useful for those who read the literature, for it is well to be on guard against emotional appeals that may be hidden behind seemingly objective and scientific terminology.

Drug use and *drug abuse* are two terms that are obviously emotionally charged. *Use* of a drug is morally, socially, and usually medically permissible, but *abuse* of a drug is wrong. However, it is difficult to decide precisely what constitutes the difference between use and abuse in objective terms. *Abuse* may be used in any of a number of ways: (1) to signify disapproval of what the speaker considers to be an excessive *amount* of the drug being taken; (2) to signify disapproval *of the drug itself,* regardless of the amount (e.g., to some persons, *any* use of heroin, marijuana, or even alcohol, constitutes *abuse*); (3) to signify disapproval of the *setting* in which the drug is taken (e.g., an adolescent drinking wine with his gang rather than at the family dinner table); (4) to signify apprehension over the possible *behavioral outcome* or *physical or psychological effects* of taking the drug (e.g., crime, dependence, accidents, suicide, and so on).[29] When physicians use the term *abuse*, they lend it a kind of clinical objectivity that it does not have. The AMA, for example, has defined drug abuse as "taking drugs without professional advice or direction."[30] Taken literally, this would mean that any person administering aspirin to himself or his children is guilty of drug abuse, as is any person drinking a cup of coffee at breakfast or providing an antacid for a guest who suffers from that great American malady, acid indigestion. Aside from the patent absurdity of such a proposition, it loads the dice on the *moral* issues, issues which physicians are no more qualified to judge than ordinary laymen. When a physician is consulted, he may offer advice on means of avoiding certain maladies and of curing others, based upon his expert knowledge; or he may advise his patient as to the best means of achieving certain ends with regard to his physical or mental state; but when he attempts to decide what is morally best for his patient, or for everyone in society, he has stepped outside his role as physician and has entered the realm of politics. His special expertise in medicine does not qualify him to make such political or moral decisions, though interested persons may want to know what scientific data bear upon the decisions that must be made. To prejudge the issue by calling any use of a drug that is not sanctioned by the medical profession an "abuse" is itself an abuse of medical prerogatives. No scientific data can, of themselves, justify the moral or political condemnation of the use of any drug, regardless of the nature of the drug, its effects, the setting in which it is administered, or the amount of the drug that is consumed. It is one thing to recite the facts and to predict, on the basis of those facts, what will result from the use of any given drug under given circumstances; it is something else to *condemn* such use as "abusive." It is important to maintain a careful distinction between scientific predictions and moral judgments; though physicians have a right to engage in the latter, both they and those who consult them should be aware of the fact that their professional expertise does not extend to the latter kind of judgment. Whether society as a whole, or any particular individual, should be permitted to use any given drug without the benefit of medical advice is a matter of public policy that involves value judgments upon which persons other than medical experts may have opinions and in which broad segments of the public may have a right to participate. More particularly, if a drug, taken in its ordinary dosages, is not biologically harmful, then it is difficult to understand how any such use can constitute "abuse" from a purely medical standpoint. There is no evidence that marijuana, in the doses commonly available in North America, is a source of biological harm. Therefore, to say that anyone who uses it is guilty of drug abuse is to make a judgment that is not warranted by the facts presently available.

Another value-loaded term is *adverse reaction*. An adverse reaction is, by definition, a bad reaction. But what, more specifically, is meant by *adverse* or *bad*? A survey of nearly 3,000 medical professionals in Los Angeles County produced the startling sum of 1,887 cases of adverse marijuana reactions; but no one seems to have taken the trouble to describe, in detail, what would constitute an adverse reaction, so that it could be distinguished from reactions that were benign, harmless, or perhaps even beneficial. Without some careful demarcation of the limits, each professional is left to his own subjective determination of the meaning of the term, and the study becomes meaningless. Would drowsiness constitute an adverse reaction? Would red, itchy eyes constitute an adverse reaction? How about a distorted time sense and colorful illusions? In certain circumstances, and for some persons, some of these would be considered *excellent* reactions, whereas the temporary discomfort from inflamed conjunctivae would be a small price to pay for the pleasure obtained during the drowsy, euphoric, illusion-filled state.

We have already commented upon the implications of the charge that marijuana is a mind-altering drug. It may be appropriate here to add that when the user is interested precisely in the mind-altering properties of the drug, and uses it because of its capacity to produce certain changes in mood or (as he conceives it) cognition and perception, there is an irreducible conflict between his values and those of the opponent of drug use. Both the user and his critic may agree about the effects of the drug; their dispute is a matter of attitude only, the one approving of and seeking those effects, the other disapproving of them and avoiding them. It is difficult to see how any scientific evidence might resolve such a conflict.*

The claim that marijuana use is a manifestation of medical *pathology* is related to the claims that those who smoke marijuana are drug abusers. As experts on pathology, physicians can claim that those who use marijuana are suffering from one form or another of psychological disturbance, that their experiences with marijuana are nothing but temporary psychotic episodes, and that such manifestations of illness require treatment. This is very much like the approach taken by many psychiatrically oriented

---

* This is not to say that scientific evidence might not resolve the issue on *other* grounds. If science could show, for example, that marijuana caused irreversible sterility, or chromosome damage, this would no doubt lead to a reassessment of the risks involved in the use of the drug; but it would not have contributed to the solution of the question of the value of the drug's mind-altering properties.

physicians who treat homosexuality as a kind of disease that calls for treatment, regardless of the homosexual's own feelings about it. A marijuana user may feel completely comfortable about his use of the drug. He may be a useful and productive member of society. He may have no trouble whatever with his family or his friends, and he may not feel at all inadequate professionally or personally. Yet there are some who insist that he must be sick! His behavior is not *normal* (there's another loaded term!), it is *deviant* (and another!), and it therefore *requires an explanation* (still another, for who ever asks for an explanation for "normal" behavior?). No explanation is ever demanded of those who do *not* use drugs, because their behavior is "normal," "nondeviant." One is reminded of H. G. Wells's story, "City of the Blind," in which a stranger stumbles into a city inhabited by men who have been congenitally blind for so many generations that they have never heard of vision. When they discover that the stranger has strange "growths" in his head and that these "growths" cause him to speak abnormally about such nonexistent qualities as colors, they order surgery to remove the growths in the hope that he might thus be cured of his delusions. Our own physicians, who order treatment to rid people of their desire for homosexual affairs, or for the pleasures that are derived from marijuana, may be compared to the surgeons in the City of the Blind, particularly when they would order such treatment for those who are causing no harm to other members of society but seek only to find their own pleasures in their own way. Like "nature," these terms— *normal, pathological,* and *deviant*—have both descriptive and normative uses. *Normal,* when used descriptively, may refer to a characteristic that is found in a very high proportion of a given population. Used in this way, there is no implication of approval or disapproval, of good or evil. Similarly, *deviant* may have such a descriptive use, referring to any characteristic or form of behavior that is rare in a particular population, without judging its rightness or wrongness. Thus, in a given community, homosexuality during adolescence may be *normal,* and any person who refrains completely from homosexual relations during his adolescence would be *deviant.* Using the terms descriptively, the most rigid moralist could make this statement without the slightest inconsistency. In their *normative* senses, however, the same terms would have very different meanings. The moralist would say that in *those* senses, those adolescents who engaged in homosexual practices were *deviant,* even though they were in the majority, and even though they were conforming to the patterns of behavior that were expected of them in their society; on the other hand, those who refused to engage in such relations were *normal,* even though they deviated considerably from what was expected of them in their community; for the former did what was morally wrong, whereas the latter did what was morally proper. The medicine man in that community might have been tempted to effect some kind of cure on those whose sexual behavior exhibited "pathological" deviations in that they were unable or unwilling to consummate proper homosexual unions. He might even have sought an explanation for such pathological behavior through an appropriate theory of demonic possession, which would have raised in incurable victims of heterosexuality a terrible feeling of shame, guilt, and frustration. Parallel examples can be drawn for those who do—or do not—indulge in the use of mind-altering drugs.

Psychological dependence is another of those strange terms that has entered the drug vocabulary. It is contrasted with physical dependence, which is characterized by an overpowering compulsion to continue to use the drug and to obtain it by any means, by a tendency to increase the dose, and by withdrawal symptoms. Drug habituation was defined thus by the World Health Organization:

(1) A desire (but not a compulsion) to continue taking the drug for the sense of improved well-being which it engenders;
(2) little or no tendency to increase the dose;
(3) some degree of psychic dependence on the effect of the drug, but absence of physical dependence and hence of an abstinence syndrome;
(4) detrimental effects, if any, primarily on the individual.[31]

Professor Leslie Wilkins has said that he experienced precisely the same symptoms when he was deprived of his automobile. More than one person, including the present author, has a strong desire to read the *New York Times* for the sense of improved well-being that it engenders. Such persons have no tendency to read the *Times* more than once a day, and they have some degree of psychic dependence upon it. My wife informs me that the detrimental effects of my habit extend to her and our children, so this may not be a good example. However, it should be sufficient to demonstrate that the WHO definition is so broad as to include a great many habits that are not seriously harmful, and certainly ought not to be the subject of repressive legislation.[32]

Those who oppose the use of marijuana have no monopoly upon the use of emotion-packed, value-laden, question-begging words. Where "Establishment" critics call the marijuana experience psychotomimetic (imitating a psychosis), those who advocate legalization speak of it as being psychedelic (implying that the mind works best under the influence of the drug). While the critics inveigh against hallucinogens, which produce hallucinations (an extremely negative word in our culture), the advocates tell us that the same drugs give users a "clearer vision of reality" (hooray for reality!), that they "increase or deepen one's insights" (everyone favors deeper insights), and that they make for a better state of "spiritual health" (though we may be a little suspicious of the spiritual, everyone is in favor of health).

Everyone, no matter what side of the controversy he may be on, seems to suppose that he is on the side of reality. I suppose everyone always *is* on the side of reality. The problem is to determine precisely what is real and what is not, and that is not so easy, particularly when we live in a world that is so full of the illusory. In the present case, the opponents of drug use maintain that reality is whatever is perceived during one's waking moments, through the use of the five senses, whereas the advocates of drug use insist that there is another dimension to reality, a dimension that may be visited by some persons without the aid of drugs but that is available to all through the "mind-expanding" (there's another one!) powers of marijuana and the other psychedelic drugs. Whereas the opponents say that those who use drugs are trying to escape from reality, some drug users assert that they are gaining insights into a reality that others have barely glimpsed in their dreams and have hidden from their conscious minds because of the conventions of our "hung-up" society. I cannot resolve this dispute, for it goes far beyond the scope of this book. However, it will be worth our while to examine it further before turning to the legal issues.

THE TWO REALITIES

In one of the most remarkable passages in all of philosophical literature, Plato once described two concepts of reality in the most vivid terms. Imagine a race of people confined to a cave for many generations, he said. Bound securely to one place, they could see nothing but the shadows of images projected against the wall of the cave as they passed along a ledge between the wall and a fire. To them, reality consisted of the shadows, for that was all they had ever seen. They built their scientific theories around the passing shadows, learning to predict when a given shadow would reappear, eagerly anticipating the verification of the latest refinements in the theory.

One day, a young man was released from his bonds. He made his way to the mouth of the cave, but was driven back by the dazzling sunlight. At night, however, he ventured forth into the outside world—the first of his race ever to have done so. Even the light of the moon and the stars was too brilliant for his eyes, in their weakened condition, but he found that he could look at their reflections in the pools of water that he discovered. As time went on and his vision improved, he learned more and more of the remarkable world that he had been privileged to visit. At last he emerged into the full light of day, and beheld the splendor of the earth in springtime, resplendent in all its colors, with all its forms and shapes and textures. The display was so startling that he felt that he must be mad, but he realized that this was the real world, a world from which he and all his people had been hidden for so many centuries, and that the shadows in the cave were in fact nothing but shadows, pale and colorless and empty shades of reality, scarcely worth the time and effort that his compatriots spent upon them when they could instead be contemplating the magnificent world outside the cave.

It was hard for him to consider leaving this beautiful world, even for a short time, but he resolved that he owed it to his friends in the cave to bring them the news of his discovery. So he made his way back. Now his eyes were unaccustomed to the darkness. He had lost his capacity to see in the dim recesses of the great cavern. The shadows had become meaningless to him, and he was unable to make much of them. When he told his fellow prisoners about the wonders of the world outside, they laughed at him, and mocked him, and thought him mad. When they perceived how little he was able to see of the shadows that were so important to them, they concluded that the world outside had caused him to lose his sight, and they vowed to punish anyone who would remove another of their members from the security of the *real* world of the cave for that false and spurious world of illusion outside.[33]

Although the allegory of the cave was written by Plato for the purpose of introducing his theory of knowledge and the concept of the eternal Forms, the parallel between it and the experiences of many mystics—both religious and nonreligious—is too remarkable to pass unnoticed. They too claim to have had an insight into a far more perfect and magnificent world than the ordinary world of daily experience, which may be compared to the cave of Plato's allegory. The experience is blinding and dazzling for those who are not accustomed to it, and it is hard for them to return to the drabness of earthly existence once they have gazed upon the wonders of that other world that is opened to them by drugs or by the techniques of mystical communion. When they do return, they, like the man who returned to the cave, find it difficult to adjust to the darkness. They may not see the shadows as well as they once did because their minds are diverted to visions of the world outside the cave and their eyes have grown accustomed to the light of the sun. Those who inhabit the cave become incensed at what they consider to be the damage that has been done to their compatriot, and they demand punishment for those who are responsible for the harm that they believe has been done to him. The protests of the mystic himself, that he has *not* been harmed, but that his life has been enriched and enhanced by the experience he has undergone, are considered by them to be of no value, for they believe that *they* are better able to judge what is in his interests—by their well-established standards—than *he* is by his "distorted" ones.

The Talmud relates a story of four great religious thinkers who entered Paradise. In modern terms, they went on a trip. Upon their return, one died, one went mad, and a third lost his former sense of values to such a degree that he became a social and religious outcast. Of the four who went, only one returned unharmed, and rose to become one of the greatest leaders in Israel's history.[34] The point of the tale would seem to be that the risks of taking such a trip are enormous; but the authors of the tale do not deny that it is possible to take such a trip or that what is seen at the other end is in some sense a part of reality.

Students of mysticism have noted time and again how intensely those who have had mystical experiences cling to their conviction that what they have experienced is *real*, and that they have acquired a kind of firsthand knowledge that they did not have before. This conviction runs very deep and is quite tenacious. Most persons who have had the experience are reluctant to let it go. Another feature of the mystical experience is the difficulty the subject has in expressing or communicating to others the essence of what he has learned. It has the peculiar quality of ineffability, of being beyond expression in mere words. Those who have tried to communicate something of their experiences to others who have not taken the trip themselves are forced to resort to metaphors, because they cannot find language capable of expressing directly what they wish to say.

William James, who made an extensive study of mysticism, concluded that "as a matter of psychological fact, mystical states of a well-pronounced and emphatic sort *are* usually authoritative over those who have them. They have been 'there,' and know. . . . If the mystical truth that comes to a man proves to be a force that he can live by, what mandate have we of the majority to order him to live in another way?" James conceded that we can, of course, throw the mystic into prison or into the mental hospital, but that will scarcely change the confirmed mystic's mind. "The mystic," he said, "is invulnerable."

However, James added an important condition to his acceptance of the mystic's right to adhere to his creed: "Mystics have no right to claim that we ought to accept the deliverance of their peculiar experiences." Non-mystics are under no obligation to accept the authority of the mystic when the latter makes a claim to superior knowledge in any realm. The pronouncements of mystics are so confused, so contradictory, so open to varying interpretations, that no one mystic can claim all the truth for his own and demand that others recognize that claim. Because the mystic's experience is not open to public inspection, as the ordinary experiences of nonmystics in the waking world are, and because any truth claims he may make are not open to verification, the nonmystic is and ought to be free to reject any such claim for himself.

The mystic, then, is to be granted the freedom to believe whatever his experience impels him to believe, and the nonmystic is to be free to reject, for himself, any claims the mystic may have made. But according to James, the latter qualification is not a denial of the mystic's claim to have an insight into an aspect of reality that is not open to the rest of us. "The existence of mystical states," he wrote, "absolutely overthrows the pretension of non-mystical states to be the sole and ultimate dictators of what we may believe." "It must always remain an open question," he went on, "whether mystical states may not possibly be such superior points of view, windows through which the mind looks out upon a more extensive and inclusive world." [35]

These conclusions are not completely acceptable. The mystic's having been "there" does not necessarily mean that he *knows*. States resembling those of the mystic have been observed not only by persons who have been in a state of religious excitation or under the influence of drugs or the practice of yoga, but also by persons who have been suffering from mental disease, epilepsy, and other disorders of the nervous system. The alcoholic who has gone through the agonies of delirium tremens has "been there," too, but there is no reason to accede to his claim to have seen and felt rats and bugs crawling around his room and over his body. To be sure, he has experienced something; but his subjective experience simply does *not* correspond to any objective reality. No matter how vehemently he may claim to have seen and felt them, the bugs and the rodents simply did not exist. Upon his recovery from his illness, it would scarcely be a favor for those who were there to permit him to believe that such creatures were actually crawling about. It would be better to explain that persons who are suffering from delirium tremens frequently have such unpleasant hallucinations, that when they occur, they have great verisimilitude, but that like nightmares, they are not real. To be sure, if he insists on believing that he has lived through such a nightmarish experience, no one can or should attempt to *compel* him to believe otherwise; but his having had the experience is not in itself sufficient reason to give up all attempts to demonstrate to him that his experience was purely subjective and bore no resemblance to reality.

Nevertheless, James's point is well taken. Unless the mystic or the madman, if that is what he is, attempts to force his doctrines upon those who choose to maintain a skeptical attitude, or gives evidence of engaging in acts that are likely to cause harm to others, he should be given the freedom to believe whatever he pleases, and to win converts to his faith in any lawful manner. For as James observed, the mystic is invulnerable. Unless society chooses to employ the cruelest methods of brainwashing, it has no way of piercing his mental armor. He and his doctrines may be tolerated, thus preserving freedom of religion and of the human intellect; or such freedom may be sacrificed in order to achieve a degree of religious, doctrinal, or social conformity. If a society is truly dedicated to freedom of speech and freedom of religion, it cannot choose the latter course.* Yet there seems to be such a tendency in our society—a tendency to compel a degree of conformity among those people who wish to express themselves in highly unusual, but harmless, ways, or to follow religious or social practices that differ radically from accepted norms. Those who follow the paths of mysticism, either with the aid of drugs or in some other way,

---

* For a more extensive discussion of the questions raised by the principle of free speech, see Chapter 14.

are sometimes hounded out of society or are subjected to precisely those sanctions that James warned would never work: prison or the insane asylum. Socrates, too, had his strange visions, as Plato reported them, and he was found to constitute so great a danger to the youth of Athens that the Athenian court condemned him to death. His visions did not conform to those of the received religion, and his political and religious theories seem not to have been acceptable to the respectable Athenians of his day. By their persecution of Socrates, the Athenians succeeded both in depriving him of the opportunity to teach and in depriving themselves of the opportunity to hear what he had to say. No one had an obligation to accept his views or to concur in them, as no one is obliged today to adopt the life style of any given class of persons, or to accept the visions of drug-inspired mystics as veritable representations of reality. When mystics are driven out of society, others are deprived of the opportunity to hear them and to learn from them. Perhaps mystics have nothing worthwhile to say. But we shall never know that that is so unless we are prepared to give those who wish to hear them the chance to do so. I am not convinced that a world exists beyond the threshold of perception, but if there is one, I would like to know about it. Though I have not yet been convinced by the claims of the mystics whose writings I have read, I have nevertheless been inspired by them and thrilled by their adventures. The world would be spiritually impoverished, I think, if all its "deviants" had been forcibly set upon the path of "normalcy" as that term is interpreted by some contemporary psychiatrists and lawmakers. Those who wish to function in the everyday world and find that the supernatural world is intruding into their affairs should be given all possible aid to find their way; but those who prefer to dwell in the metaphysical realm should be permitted to do so without hindrance from those of us who know not what they see and are unable to share their experiences with them.

MARIJUANA AND THE REVOLUTION
IN MANNERS AND MORALS

The public reaction against the entire drug scene, of which marijuana is only a part, is a complex phenomenon that should not be oversimplified. It is in part a reaction against the youth rebellion, which has manifested itself in many ways: in the use of drugs, in sex, in radical politics, in new styles of dress, in a rejection of the manners and mores of the older generation, in a positive effort (on the part of some members of the rebellion, at least) to tear down the social, political, and educational institutions that symbolize the so-called Establishment. One of the most arresting phenomena in this rebellion has been the open and unabashed proclamation by some of its members that they will no longer accept the prevailing

Protestant work ethic, with all that that implies. They have "dropped out" of college as an act of defiance against a system that imposes upon them a prolonged adolescence while dangling before them the rewards of a materialistic society that they refuse to consider worthy of the effort. Such rewards are not important to people who are content to live in slums, doing menial tasks, and therefore they provide no incentive to stay in the rat-race. When community moral standards are flouted as some young people have done, especially when they are flouted by young people who have been given such opportunities as are associated with "nice homes," a good education, and the other amenities that presumably go with the North American middle class, and when they engage, in addition, in such unlawful and possibly dangerous behavior as the consumption and distribution of drugs, it is scarcely surprising that the community reacts, as it has, in a repressive and sometimes even violent fashion. The rebellion is fueled, in turn, by what the rebels consider to be the hypocrisy of the older generation and the Establishment, as illustrated by the latter's participation in and support of war while mouthing slogans of peace; its failure to provide conditions of true equality and genuine democracy for all citizens, including the members of the more conspicuous and the most poverty-stricken minorities; and the repressive and punitive laws on marijuana in spite of all the talk about freedom of expression and in spite of the enormous consumption of tobacco and alcohol—drugs which the rebels and others consider to be far more harmful than marijuana. They believe, along with Justice Brandeis, that part of the democratic ideal consists in the *right to be let alone;* [36] that this right includes the right to one's own sensations and enjoyments and pleasures without interference by any outside agency, including the police; and that the methods used by the police in enforcing the laws against use and possession of marijuana are more suited to a police state than to a democracy, and are therefore one more reason to rebel against the system and to bring it down so that it may be rebuilt on genuinely democratic lines.

Whether one agrees or disagrees with the views, the aims, or the methods of the youth rebellion that has swept this continent and a major part of the rest of the world in the last two decades, it is necessary to understand the rationale behind some of the actions and the reactions that they have provoked. It is not difficult to see why many young people are disappointed. Their impatience is understandable. Their methods have not always been well suited to the achievement of their aims, and their goals have not always been well articulated. But it is impossible for any thoughtful observer of the North American scene to deny that the youth rebellion has had a major impact upon political, military, social, and educational institutions during the past decade, and that important changes in public policy must be attributed to the influence of young people who insistently and impolitely and forcefully kept certain matters at the forefront of public attention when others would have preferred to have seen the issues fade into the oblivion of forgotten causes. One of these issues, and by no means the most important, is the question of the legalization of marijuana, which has become a matter of public concern because of the persistent use of the drug, rather than because of any organized campaign to legalize it.

Pot is part of the general youth scene. One may argue that if there had not been a general decline in the respect accorded national and state institutions and the laws of the land, marijuana would not have become as popular as it did. However that may be, the fact is that the laws against marijuana possession and use are probably as widely violated as any laws on the books today, and this may be partly *because* such violations constitute a means of expressing discontent with the system as a whole.

THE MARIJUANA LAWS

The late Senator Thomas Dodd of Connecticut once told a White House Conference on Narcotic and Drug Abuse about a war veteran who had been sentenced to five years in the penitentiary without parole by a reluctant federal judge. This is what the judge had said:

CASE 8. THE MARINE VETERAN AND THE JUDGE
The mandatory sentence can work extreme injustice. I was compelled to impose a five-year sentence on a Marine veteran of the Korean campaign who was found with three or four marijuana cigarettes. He had been drinking in Tijuana and was arrested at the border. Obviously, three or four cigarettes did not make him a peddler and these were not commercial amounts. He had a spotless civilian record and an excellent military career. He had received a Purple Heart and had been wounded in action and had a wife and children. I held up sentencing 60 days with the defendant's consent, to attempt to get the U.S. attorney to file a tax consent on a smuggling charge which would not have carried at least a 5 years sentence. I was unsuccessful. I sentenced the man to 5 years in the penitentiary without parole.[37]

Public Law 91-513, which became law on October 27, 1970, did away with such harsh mandatory sentences for mere possession. Simple possession of marijuana under this law is punishable by a fine of not more than $5,000 and a prison term of not more than one year, and the court may give a first offender probation rather than a jail sentence. Subsequent offenses are punished more severely, and sellers of the drug may be sentenced to prison for as much as ten years on a second conviction, whereas those who are engaged in a "continuing criminal enterprise" of selling drugs may be sent to prison for life. The practical effect of these reduced penalties is hard to predict, though, because state laws define cannabis as a narcotic and carry penalties that exceed those attached to such offenses as larceny, arson, kidnapping, or, in California, second-degree murder.[38]

In view of the fact that marijuana is not a dangerous drug, or at least that it has not been demonstrated to be a dangerous drug, it is strange that mere possession should be punished at all—let alone that it should be punished so severely. It is stranger still when one recalls that neither the sale nor the possession of firearms is outlawed, though there is no doubt at all about the danger such weapons pose to life and limb. The number of lives lost through both accidental and deliberate discharge of firearms in the United States is hard to estimate because of the lack of accurate statistics; but in 1969, 2,600 persons died from the accidental discharge of firearms alone, and it is probably safe to assume that most of the 11,000 homicides reported during that year were committed with the aid of guns.[39] Though there is no evidence that *anyone* died because of marijuana, those who possess it risk years of imprisonment, whereas those who derive pleasure from guns run no legal risk at all.

The enforcement problems here are as great as, if not greater than, those that we noted in our discussion of homosexual behavior. There we saw that because there is no victim and therefore no complainant, the police are forced to engage in entrapment and in various forms of trickery. Much the same is true here. Police must rely upon informers, spies, wiretaps, or eavesdroppers. Their job is extremely difficult because most of the population in those areas where use is heavy are unsympathetic to them. They therefore appeal to the courts and to the legislatures for such antilibertarian special powers as the power to "stop and frisk" and to break into private premises without knocking. When such tactics are resorted to in attempting to enforce laws designed to deter the use of marijuana, they are as great a threat to liberty and justice as we found them to be in the earlier chapter on homosexuality. The use of "blank warrants," which violate both the spirit and the letter of the Sixth Amendment to the American Constitution, which guarantees the right to be confronted with the witnesses who testify against a defendant, and the Fourth, which guarantees against search or seizure without a warrant, is not unknown in drug cases. Cases have been documented in which the police "planted" marijuana on the person or premises of an individual whom they wanted to frame.[40] Such incidents do little to increase the respect of the public for those who have sworn to protect them and to uphold the Constitution and the laws of the land, and they are damaging to the police themselves, who are corrupted by the public demand that they arrest marijuana users while they find it almost impossible to do so without violating the Constitutional guarantees that they are sworn to uphold.

Not only the moral cost, but the financial cost of the enforcement of antimarijuana laws is enormous. It is estimated that California alone spent some $75 million in processing marijuana violations during 1968.

The squandering of such resources on an enterprise that the Los Angeles Deputy District Attorney conceded was nearly hopeless, because "for every arrest that takes place there are 1,000 or 2,000 other people that are using marijuana," is criminal in itself, in view of the important work that police could be doing in solving crimes of violence and preventing such crimes from occurring.

More important, perhaps, than any of these considerations is the incalculable cost to society that results from the criminalization of hundreds of thousands of young and not-so-young citizens. The long-run effects of the contempt that they are developing for our laws and our institutions cannot even be estimated, but it ought to be taken into account in any formulation of public policy. When injustice is seen to be done, as it is here, respect for the system that permits it to be perpetuated must inevitably be diminished. And injustice *is* done, for substances that are demonstrably harmful and dangerous, both to those who use them and to others, may be advertised and sold and purchased openly and consumed *ad libitum*, because (it seems) they are accepted by the older and more powerful generation; on the other hand, substances that have not been shown to be harmful must be purchased furtively, and those who do purchase them lay themselves open to totally unreasonable penalties. The drugs of the older generation are advertised and consumed in enormous quantities, in spite of the harm that some of them are known to do and despite the addictive properties of some of them, whereas those of the younger generation are forbidden on pain of ruin to one's life and career. The sheer stupidity of the government, in its treatment of the marijuana problem, as well as its cruelty and its lack of respect for elementary liberties, is evident for all to see and cannot help but contribute to the alienation of many young people from society and its institutions. Consider the following passages from the Task Force Report, which deal with heroin addiction, rather than with marijuana, as an example:

> There are persuasive reasons to believe that enforcement of these laws has caused a significant reduction in the flow of these drugs. The best evidence is the high price, low quality, and limited availability of heroin today as contrasted with the former easy availability of cheap and potent heroin. . . . [Page 8.]
> The nondrug offenses in which the heroin addict typically becomes involved are the fund-raising variety. Assaultive or violent acts, contrary to popular belief, are the exception rather than the rule for the heroin addict, whose drug has a calming and depressant effect. . . . [The price] is never low enough to permit the typical addict to obtain it by lawful means. So he turns to crime, most commonly to the theft of property. . . . Addicts would be responsible each year for the theft of property valued at many millions of dollars in New York City alone. . . . [Page 10.]

In two pages the Task Force has congratulated the law enforcement agencies on the excellent work they have done in raising the price of heroin on the retail market, and then gone on to explain that the high price of heroin on the retail market is the *only factor* responsible for the millions of dollars of thefts committed by heroin addicts in New York City. Because of the distance between page 8 and page 10, the authors apparently were unable to perceive the causal connection: the millions of dollars lost by the residents and businessmen of New York City could have been saved if the government's forces had been less efficient in reducing the flow of heroin into the New York market; for if the drug had been less expensive, the addicts would not have been stealing so much. Once this connection is seen, it is a simple step to the next inference: If the government would supply heroin addicts with all the drugs they needed, the latter would be responsible for no crime at all, based upon the government's own assessment of their propensity to commit criminal acts. This has in fact been the policy in Great Britain for a number of years. Addicts there register with the Home Office and are then certified to receive a maintenance dose of the drug to which they are addicted for as long as they wish. They may receive their doses each day at the offices of their National Health Service physicians, and are then free to go about their business. There is a drug problem in Great Britain, but it is not at all of the same magnitude as it is in the United States or Canada, which have taken a much more punitive approach. Though there are addicts, drug-related crimes are quite minimal, because there is no illegal market for drugs and because each addict may obtain his supply either free of charge or at a very minimal cost.

The legalization of marijuana would eliminate all, or virtually all of the crime associated with that drug. The Canadian Commission appeared to be headed in that direction, for it recommended, in its Interim Report, that "the Narcotic Control Act and the Food and Drugs Act be amended to make the offence of simple possession under these acts punishable upon summary conviction by a fine not exceeding a reasonable amount. The Commission suggests a maximum fine of $100." The commission went further by recommending that in respect of offenses of simple possession of psychotropic drugs, the fines should be collected through the civil courts, in order to avoid the possibility of the defendant's being imprisoned because of inability to pay, and urged police, prosecutors, and courts to exercise discretion in order to minimize the impact of the criminal law upon those who merely possessed such drugs.[41] The commission made these recommendations after concluding, provisionally, that the cost of enforcement of laws regarding cannabis was "out of all proportion to the relative effectiveness of the law" and that the cost in individual and social terms was far too great to justify the harsh penalties that had previously been in effect for simple possession. However, in its final report, issued in 1972 under the title *Cannabis,* the commission's five members were sharply divided and submitted three reports. Three members felt that although there was no clear statistical correlation between the use of cannabis and the use of such obviously harmful drugs as LSD, the use of the former "probably reduces inhibitions" about the use of the latter, and they felt that a small proportion of cannabis users might become disposed to try more dangerous drugs. This hypothesis, together with the "probably harmful effect of cannabis on the maturing process in adolescents," the likelihood of impairment of driving ability among persons who are intoxicated by the drug, and the possibility that long-term use of cannabis might lead to significant mental deterioration and disorder, led the commission's majority to conclude that it would be prudent to discourage use of the drug. However, they continued to be troubled by the social costs of laws that made the use, sale, or possession of cannabis a major criminal offense, particularly in view of the fact that the *known* dangers of the drug did not seem to justify such harsh measures, and in view of the grave consequences for the small minority of users who were ever confronted with the possibility of a drug conviction. They therefore recommended repeal of the prohibition against simple possession of cannabis, but they recommended that cultivation of the plant or trafficking in marijuana be punishable by a maximum prison sentence of five years.

The only woman on the Canadian Commission expressed her conviction that prohibition was expensive and ineffective. She reasoned that cannabis could not properly be classed as a dangerous drug, that the allegedly detrimental effects of marijuana upon maturing adolescents had not been demonstrated to exist, and that the arguments against total legalization were not convincing. She therefore recommended that cannabis be removed from the *Narcotics Control Act,* thus effectively lifting the prohibitions against sale, possession, and use of the drug. She recommended further that both federal and provincial governments place the sale and use of cannabis under controls similar to those governing the sale and use of alcohol, including legal prohibition of unauthorized distribution and analogous age restrictions. Government-distributed cannabis could be marketed at a quality and price that would make it impractical to sell the drug on the black market, she said. She also recommended that the government look into the possibility of producing synthetic preparations, as well as a standard form of natural marijuana, and that it initiate epidemiological research to monitor and evaluate changes in the extent and patterns of the use of cannabis and other drugs and to explore possible consequences to health and to personal and social behavior brought about as a result of the implementation of her recommendations.

The fifth member of the commission was altogether opposed to repeal of the prohibition against simple possession of cannabis. He argued that such an action would likely have the effect of increasing the frequency of use of many who have already used cannabis as well as removing whatever deterrent the prohibition might have exercised upon those who had never tried the drug. He was concerned that such an act by the government might be misinterpreted by many persons as a stamp of approval or as a sign of acceptance of the drug by society. It is an "unassailable proposition," he said, "that the majority may properly prohibit through the law conduct that is manifestly offensive or disturbing to them whether or not that conduct inflicts an injury on any particular person beyond the actor." Taking this "unassailable proposition" in conjunction with the proposition that public use of cannabis is offensive and disturbing to the vast majority of Canadians, he concluded that it was "not inappropriate that such behaviour should be forbidden by law." As for private use, he saw in the use of cannabis a "clear and potent danger" both to the individual and to society, and therefore— arguing along lines similar to those employed by Lord Devlin—he concluded that the prohibition should stand. However, he was prepared to reduce the penalties for possession of cannabis to a fine of $25 for the first offense and $100 for subsequent offenses, with similar penalties for cultivation of the drug for purposes other than trafficking. Late in 1972 the Canadian government acted upon the recommendations of the commission by removing cannabis from the *Narcotics Control Act,* thus distinguishing it from such substances as heroin and morphine. However, it stopped short of legalizing marijuana, proposing instead to reduce the penalties for private use and possession.

The American commission concluded that the criminal law was "too harsh a tool" to apply to personal possession, because it implied an "overwhelming indictment of the behavior which we believe is not appropriate," namely, consumption of marijuana. "The actual and potential harm of use of the drug is not great enough," the commission said, "to justify intrusion by the criminal law into private behavior." In addition to such philosophical considerations, the commission found that from a practical point of view, prohibition had little actual effect upon the amount of marijuana being consumed in the nation, and that it carried a heavy social cost, including a rising disrespect for the law among younger citizens. Further, the commission felt that the nation's law enforcement resources would be better spent in enforcing the laws on hazardous drugs and in decreasing the number of violent crimes. The commission therefore recommended that the law be changed to permit possession of marijuana for personal use and to remove the legal restrictions on distribution of small amounts of the drug for no remuneration. However, it recommended that "cultivation, sale or distribution for profit and possession with intent to sell" should remain felonies, and that possession in public of no more than one ounce of marijuana, distribution in public of small amounts of marijuana for no profit, and public use of marijuana should be punishable by a fine of $100, with much stiffer penalties for disorderly conduct associated with public use of or intoxication by marijuana (a misdemeanor punishable by up to sixty days in jail, a fine of $100, or both) and operating a vehicle or dangerous instrument while under the influence of marijuana (a misdemeanor punishable by up to one year in jail, a fine of up to $1,000, or both, and suspension of permits or licenses for up to 180 days).

In effect, the American commission urged the adoption of laws that would *permit the private consumption* of marijuana, but would make it *illegal to grow or sell* the substance. Although the commission attempted to rationalize its proposals, they do not seem to be justified by the commission's own findings; for if the government is not justified in bringing the weight of the criminal law to bear against those persons who smoke marijuana in private, then it is difficult to see why it would be proper for it to make it impossible for them legally to acquire any. A policy that prohibits the production or sale of a substance which the government finds to constitute no significant danger to those who would consume it or to others is inconsistent and self-defeating.

It is evident, then, that a number of alternative policies on marijuana have been suggested, including the possibility of doing nothing at all. This is the least acceptable of all the alternatives, because the present system is both inequitable and antilibertarian. Outright abolition of all controls is not likely to be acceptable to enough legislators to make it a viable alternative. Marijuana consumption might be treated as a vice, similar to prostitution, in which the consumer is not held liable by the law, although the seller is. There are serious difficulties with this, not the least of which is the likelihood that organized crime would become deeply involved, as it has in other forms of vice. The most appealing alternative seems to be along the lines of legislation that regulates the sales of liquor. If producers and distributors were licensed and regulated, the potency of the product could be standardized, law enforcement officials and agencies would be relieved of the burden under which they now labor, and governments could realize a substantial income from the taxes that could be imposed upon sale and manufacture of the drug. Although some persons would see in such a licensing program evidence of state condonation of use of the drug, it could be made clear, through advertising and educational programs, that the state is no more favorably disposed to the smoking of marijuana cigarettes than it is to the smoking of tobacco or the imbibing of alcohol, though it licenses both, and in some cases operates outlets for the sale of the latter. By operating such a system, where marijuana could easily be purchased by all except minors, dangerously misleading comparisons between marijuana and the more dangerous drugs, such as the barbiturates, the amphetamines, and the opiates, might be brought to an end; for at the present time, with both marijuana and heroin being treated by the law as if they were equally bad, some people assume that heroin is no more dangerous than marijuana, and are inclined to try it. If the law made a clear and sharp distinction between the drugs, some persons might be saved from a lifetime of addiction to heroin or other narcotics. No doubt some who have thus far refrained from trying pot would do so once its use was legalized. Because there is no solid evidence that marijuana has evil effects, this result is not necessarily a bad thing. Some of those who try it will undoubtedly find that it is not to their liking and will quickly give it up. Others may enjoy it and smoke it from time to time, or on some more or less regular basis. If such use brings people pleasure with no harmful side effects, while at the same time doing away with the evident evils of the present system, it would seem that on balance, positive benefits would result.

Men seldom learn from history, it seems. When tobacco was first introduced to Europe and the Arab world, it was widely condemned on grounds of health, religion, and the fear that it would lead to criminal behavior. The Arabs resisted the introduction of coffee in the seventeenth century with the imposition of stiff penalties, including the death penalty. Such draconian measures did not work then, they did not work during the American experiment with Prohibition, and it is becoming increasingly obvious that they are not now working with the prohibition of marijuana.[42]

Some three hundred years ago, Spinoza wrote:

> Vices . . . cannot be forbidden by law, [particularly] such as those into which men fall from excess of leisure, and from which the ruin of a dominion not uncommonly follows. For men in time of peace lay aside fear, and gradually from being fierce savages become civilized or humane, and from being humane become soft and sluggish, and seek to excel one another not in virtue, but in ostentation and luxury. . . .
>
> To avoid these evils many have tried to establish sumptuary laws; but in vain. For all laws which can be broken without any injury to another, are counted but a laughing-stock, and are so far from bridling the desires and lusts of men, that on the contrary they stimulate them. For "we are ever eager for forbidden fruit, and desire what is denied." Nor do idle men ever lack ability to elude the laws which are instituted about things, which cannot be absolutely forbidden.[43]

This phenomenon, remarked upon so long ago, is one that we cannot afford to ignore. Even if we do not go so far as John Stuart Mill did in his essay *On Liberty* in denying to the state the right to exercise any control over the private lives of its citizens, we may still arrive at the same result in practice, if we find that the machinery of government is not suited to enforce morals or to compel citizens to do what is for their own private good. Where the state is incapable of enforcing compliance without the expenditure of enormous resources that might otherwise be put to more constructive use, practical and political wisdom may dictate a liberal policy that leaves each citizen to find his own way to heaven, so long as he does not harm others should he be making his way toward the other place. It has been said, with some reason, that the laws on marijuana have contributed substantially to an erosion of respect for the law among those who will soon inherit the reins of political power. The revolution that we have been witnessing may not be irreversible, but the attack upon some of our most fundamental and vital institutions by significant numbers of our young people may be diverted into constructive action if those who presently rule come to grips with the inconsistencies and the injustices within the system and act immediately to rectify them. An early change in the drug laws would constitute a step in the right direction.

6

Obscenity and Pornography

The Congress of the United States, in establishing a National Commission on Obscenity and Pornography, whose members were to be appointed by the president, declared that the traffic in obscene and pornographic materials was "a matter of national concern." Estimates of the trade in such materials in the United States alone range from $500 million to $2.5 billion per year. At the most conservative estimate, then, there is considerable demand for pornographic magazines, books, photographs, films, sound recordings, slides, and other devices. Because the Supreme Court has been involved in so many controversial cases involving pornography and has had to pass on the constitutionality of so many state and local statutes designed to limit the sale and distribution of erotic materials, as well as upon administrative actions (such as actions by the Post Office and by Customs officials in seizing or destroying these books and magazines) that were directed against allegedly obscene matter, the questions that the commission was directed to answer are clearly of wide concern. One of the fundamental liberties guaranteed by the Bill of Rights—the First Amendment right of free expression, both in speech and in the press—is involved in these disputes. Some defenders of the right of purveyors of allegedly pornographic materials to publish, display, distribute, and sell their wares maintain that the right of free expression is itself under attack whenever any attempt is made to interfere with the traffic in obscene materials. They compare antipornography statutes to the proverbial camel, who managed to get his nose into the Arab's tent, only to take over the tent and destroy it. Allow the censor to get his nose in the door, they say, by permitting him to put the ban on the most offensive books, films, and magazines, and he will soon be passing judgment on serious works of art, political tracts, and treatises that he considers to be damaging to the public welfare, and social documents that he (or those whose opinions he respects) deems to be dangerous or offensive. There is ample evidence from the past, these libertarians say, that works of art and literature that are today considered to be great classics were once banned by censors: works by Chaucer, Montaigne, Shakespeare, Ovid, Boccaccio, Aristophanes, Fielding, Balzac, Jonathan Swift, and Mark Twain, to mention only a few. So have the ideas of great iconoclasts, inventors, innovators, and dissenters from the predominant views on science, religion, and politics been condemned, including those of Galileo, Giordano Bruno, Maimonides, Spinoza, Socrates, and Jesus of Nazareth. More recently, works by William Faulkner, Ernest Hemingway, James Joyce, Erskine Caldwell, James T. Farrell, and Theodore Dreiser have fallen under the ban.[1] It is one thing to prohibit what virtually everyone may concede to be worthless trash; it is quite another to deprive the reading public of important works of literature.

How far do censors go, and on what do they base their opinions? A few instances of film censorship may give some indication of the answer to this question:

- In some cities Walt Disney's nature film *The Vanishing Prairie* was censored. The officials deleted a sequence showing the birth of a buffalo.
- Before World War II, the Chicago censor denied licenses to a number of films portraying and criticizing life in Nazi Germany, including the *March of Time* documentary *Inside Nazi Germany* and Charlie Chaplin's satire on Hitler, *The Great Dictator*. This censorship was apparently out of deference to Chicago's large German population.
- In 1959 the Chicago censor refused to license *Anatomy of a Murder* because the words *rape* and *contraceptive*, which were essential to the story, were objectionable.
- In Memphis, censors banned *The Southerner*, which dealt with poverty among tenant farmers, "because it reflects on the South," and *Curley* because it contained scenes of white and Negro children in school together.
- In 1950 Atlanta's censors banned *Lost Boundaries*, a film that told the story of a Negro physician and his family who "passed" for white, on the ground that it "will adversely affect the peace, morals, and good order" of the city.
- A Russian film, *Professor Mamlock*, portraying the persecution of Jews by the Nazis, was banned by the Ohio censors on the ground that it was "harmful" and would tend to "stir up hatred and ill will and gain nothing." The police in Providence, Rhode Island, did not permit it to be shown because it was, in their opinion, "Communist propaganda."
- Ohio and Kansas banned newsreels considered pro labor; and Kansas ordered a speech by Senator Wheeler opposing the bill for enlarging the Supreme Court (during Roosevelt's second term) to be cut from the *March of Time* because it was "partisan and biased."

- *Carmen* was rejected by censors in a number of states: in one, because cigarette-girls smoked cigarettes in public; in another, because a kiss lasted too long.
- In New York, censors forbade the discussion in films of pregnancy, venereal disease, eugenics, birth control, abortion, illegitimacy, prostitution, miscegenation, and divorce.
- The police sergeant in charge of censorship for the city of Chicago was quoted by the Chicago *Tribune* as saying, "Children should be allowed to see any movie that plays in Chicago. If a picture is objectionable for a child, it is objectionable period." [2]
- In an important censorship case in New Jersey, a psychiatrist called as an expert witness by the state testified that portrayal of any sex abnormality or perversion was necessarily obscene. She also testified that if sex is used for excitement and as an end in itself, it becomes obscene. "When sex isn't just for the propagation of the race and of the species," she said, "or the intent isn't, then it is abnormal or perverted." [3]

It is evident not only that censorship can go to extreme lengths, but that it has done so, and that important social documents, artistic productions, and even news items have been suppressed by zealous censors who felt impelled to impose upon the entire community their own views of what the community could or should be permitted to consume. Their criteria range from political opinions to social theories, concern for preservation of the peace, and theories about sexual morality that may or may not be widely held in the community at large.

Aside from its obvious capacity to prevent the public from seeing or reading what has already been produced, censorship possesses the power to inhibit artistic expression. The great Russian novelist Leo Tolstoy once wrote: "You would not believe how, from the very commencement of my activity, that horrible Censor question has tormented me! I wanted to write what I felt; but at the same time it occurred to me that what I wrote would not be permitted, and involuntarily I had to abandon the work. I abandoned, and went on abandoning, and meanwhile the years passed away." [4] Who knows how many creations of artistic genius have been lost because of the artists' conviction that they would be banned by the censors.

It will not do, though, to accept the "camel in the tent" argument without more careful examination. There is evidence enough that in the past, censors have been overzealous in fulfilling their assignments; that they have not always been well chosen for their tasks; that they have been unable or unwilling to distinguish between pornographic trash and serious works of high literary or artistic merit or social importance which have sex or violence as their themes or contain erotic or violent passages. But this does not do away with the charge that pornography is having a deleterious effect upon the country; that it is contributing to a general moral breakdown among both youth and adults; and that it is encouraging experimentation with and even addiction to perverse forms of sexual behavior that are not and should not be acceptable in a civilized society. Nor does it help to answer those who maintain that pornography is not literature at all by noting that when the founding fathers wrote the First Amendment into the Constitution they did not intend it to cover the rank sewage that is sold in the porno shops, and that such materials have no redeeming social importance and do not deserve the protection of the laws. And most importantly, it does not answer those critics who say that pornography is sometimes the trigger that sets off the reaction in some people that leads them to commit acts of violence against others. These critics point to the unstable young man who raped a young girl after he had been aroused by the lurid scenes in an obscene comic book and to other incidents in which persons guilty of sadistic crimes have been found to have allegedly obscene publications in their possession. If good literature can have desirable effects upon those who read it, they say, then it is reasonable to assume that bad literature may have undesirable effects upon them.

In other words the issue may not be reduced so readily to a simple choice of no censorship at all or unreasonable and all-pervasive censorship. As in so many other areas, it is possible to restrict certain kinds of harmful behavior without going to the extreme of tyranny, repression, and the denial of fundamental rights.

The principal issues which must occupy us here are the following: Can meaningful definitions of the key words *obscenity* and *pornography* be offered, and if so, what are they? What evidence is there that erotic works or works that dwell upon the vivid depiction of violence, sadism, and death have harmful effects upon those who read them or are otherwise exposed to them? What public policies have been advocated to deal with the conflict between liberty and the spread of pornography, what may be said on their behalf, and what would the consequences of each be if it were enacted and carried out?

THE PROBLEM OF DEFINING OBSCENITY

The word *obscene* is said, by most experts, to be derived from the Latin *obscenum*, which they claim to be related to *caenum*—"dirt," or "filth." Others have suggested that it may refer to that which is "out of the scene," that which ought not to be depicted on stage because of its lewd or lascivious character.

Whatever the derivation of the word may be, it is evident that in ordinary English usage, it has a pejorative effect: anything that is said to be obscene is disapproved of by the speaker. In calling any word, book, or picture obscene, one expresses one's disgust with it or one's revulsion at it. Obscenity is not a property or quality like weight or magnitude. It is the propensity of certain kinds of things to induce in people belonging to a particular culture feelings of disgust, revulsion, shock, horror, and outrage. Naturally, people differ from place to place, and even from one time to another in the same place, in the extent to which they will react to given forms of human display (for example) with feelings of disgust or outrage. Some years ago any woman's neighbors would have been scandalized if she had walked down the street with her skirts above her ankles. Today very few people are scandalized by a considerable exposure of female flesh. A significant, though still relatively small, proportion of younger people is not at all scandalized by complete nudity in public. At some of the rock festivals and at other large gatherings of youth in recent years, some participants have disrobed without provoking any noticeable feelings of outrage on the part of other participants. But in the wider community, there are still limits to what will be tolerated.

Because of the constant changes in public attitudes, some authorities have concluded that it is impossible to assign an operationally meaningful definition to such terms as *obscenity* and *pornography*, and have accordingly inferred that any legislation in which such terms are used must be unconstitutionally vague.

Judge Bok of Pennsylvania put the problem as well as anyone has in his classic decision in *Commonwealth* v. *Gordon*. Commenting on the modern rule that obscenity "is measured by the erotic allurement of a book upon the average modern reader," he said:

> Current standards of what is obscene can swing to extremes if the entire question is left open. . . . What is pure dirt to some may be another's sincere effort to make clear a point. . . .
>
> I can find no universally valid restriction on free expression to be drawn from the behavior of "l'homme moyen sensuel," who is the average modern reader. It is impossible to say just what his reactions to a book actually are. Moyen means, generally, average, and average means a median between extremes. If he reads an obscene book when his sensuality is low, he will yawn over it or find that its suggestibility leads him off on quite different paths. If he reads the Mechanics' Lien Act while his sensuality is high, things will stand between him and the page that have no business there. How can anyone say that he will infallibly be affected one way or another by one book or another? When, where, how, and why are questions that cannot be answered clearly in this field. The professional answer that is suggested is the one general compromise—that the appetite of sex is old, universal, and unpredictable, and that the best we can do to keep it within reasonable bounds is to be our brother's keeper and censor, because we never know when his sensuality may be high. This does not satisfy me, for in a field where even reasonable precision is utterly impossible, I trust people more than I do the law.

In reference to the definition of *obscenity* as "sexual impurity" and its allegedly dangerous qualities, so dangerous as to constitute a "clear and present danger," Judge Bok observed:

A book, however sexually impure and pornographic, . . . cannot be a present danger unless its reader closes it, lays it aside, and transmutes its erotic allurement into overt action. That such action must inevitably follow as a direct consequence of reading the book does not bear analysis, nor is it borne out by general human experience; too much can intervene and too many diversions take place. . . . [The law] only proscribes what *is* obscene, and that term is meaningless unless activated by precise dangers within legal limits. [But] the law provides no standard. . . .

The public does not read a book and simultaneously rush by the hundreds into the streets to engage in orgiastic riots. . . . How can it be said that there is a "clear and present danger"—granted that anyone can say what it is—when there is both time and means for ample discussion? . . .

Who can define the clear and present danger to the community that arises from reading a book? If we say it is that the reader is young and inexperienced and incapable of resisting the sexual temptations that the book may present to him, we put the entire reading public at the mercy of the adolescent mind and of those adolescents who do not have the expected advantages of home influence, school training, or religious teaching. . . . If the argument be applied to the general public, the situation becomes absurd, for then no publication is safe. How is it possible to say that reading a certain book is bound to make people behave in a way that is socially undesirable? And beyond a reasonable doubt, since we are dealing with a penal statute?

We might remember the words of Macaulay:

"We find it difficult to believe that in a world so full of temptations as this, any gentleman, whose life would have been virtuous if he had not read Aristophanes and Juvenal, will be made vicious by reading them." [5]

Hugo Black, late Associate Justice of the United States Supreme Court, in a dissenting opinion in the case of *Ginzburg* v. *United States* (1966), argued along similar lines—as he did consistently through many years on the Supreme Court—that obscenity is indefinable. Wise and good governments, he said, hedge the great power given to them by confining it within "easily identifiable boundaries." Written laws came into being in order to enable men to know in advance what areas of conduct were proscribed and what kinds of conduct were likely to bring the power of the criminal sanction to bear. In contrast, he noted, evil governments have written no laws at all, or have written them in unknown tongues, or have made it so difficult for the public to get access to them that no one could know what conduct might later be considered criminal by the government. He concluded that the criteria employed by the Court in upholding the conviction of Ginzburg for publishing or circulating obscene materials were "so vague and meaningless that they practically leave the fate of a person charged with violating censorship statutes to the unbridled discretion, whim and caprice of the judge or jury which tries him." He went on, then, to discuss these criteria in detail:

(a) The first element considered necessary for determining obscenity is that the dominant theme of the material taken as a whole must appeal to the prurient interest in sex. It seems quite apparent to me that human beings, serving either as judges or jurors, could not be expected to give any sort of decision on this element which would even remotely promise any kind of uniformity in the enforcement of this law. What conclusion an individual, be he judge or juror, would reach about whether the material appeals to "prurient interest in sex" would depend largely in the long run not upon testimony of witnesses such as can be given in ordinary criminal cases where conduct is under scrutiny, but would depend to a large extent upon the judge's or juror's personality, habits, inclinations, attitudes and other individual characteristics. In one community or in one courthouse a matter would be condemned as obscene under this so-called criterion but in another community, maybe only a few miles away, or in another courthouse in the same community, the material could be given a clean bill of health. In the final analysis the submission of such an issue as this to a judge or jury amounts to practically nothing more than a request for the judge or juror to assert his own personal beliefs about whether the matter should be allowed to be legally distributed. Upon this subjective determination the law becomes certain for the first and last time.

(b) The second element for determining obscenity . . . is [supposedly] that the material must be "patently offensive because it affronts contemporary community standards relating to the description or representation of sexual matters. . . ." Nothing . . . that has been said . . . leaves me with any kind of certainty as to whether the "community standards" referred to are world-wide, nation-wide, section-wide, state-wide, country-wide, precinct-wide, or township-wide. But even if some definite areas were mentioned, who is capable of assessing "community standards" on such a subject? Could one expect the same application of standards by jurors in Mississippi as in New York City, in Vermont as in California? So here again the guilt or innocence of a defendant charged with obscenity must depend in the final analysis upon the personal judgment and attitude of particular individuals and the place where the trial is held. . . .

(c) A third element which [is supposedly] required to establish obscenity is that the material must be "utterly without redeeming social value." This element seems to me to be as uncertain, if not even more uncertain, than is the unknown substance of the Milky Way. If we are to have a free society as contemplated by the Bill of Rights, then I can find little defense for leaving the liberty of American individuals subject to the judgment of a judge or jury as to whether material that provokes thought or stimulates desire is "utterly without redeeming social value. . . ." Whether a particular treatment of a particular subject is with or without social value in this evolving, dynamic society of ours is a question upon which no uniform agreement could possibly be reached among politicians, statesmen, professors, philosophers, scientists, religious groups or any other type of group. A case-by-case assessment of social values by individual judges and jurors is, I think, a dangerous technique for government to utilize in determining whether a man stays in or out of the penitentiary.

My conclusion is that . . . no person, not even the most learned judge, much less a layman, is capable of knowing in advance of an ultimate decision in his particular case by this Court whether certain material comes within the area of "obscenity" as that term is confused by the Court today." [6]

Note that Justice Black, consistently with his long-held view that "obscenity" is indefinable, stated that the Court had *confused* the term, not that it had *defined* it.

According to Justice Black and Judge Bok, then, no meaningful definition of *obscene* is possible because: (1) Each man will tend to look upon the offensiveness of a given book or photograph or film from his own individual viewpoint, and even that, as Judge Bok pointed out, may differ from time to time with the same individual. (2) There are no objective criteria by which to judge the effects that a given book will have upon the public, for the effects that any book may have upon any particular individual depend very much upon many variables that are completely unpredictable. (3) There is no "average" man to whom the question can be addressed. (4) Any attempt to ban a book by the effects it allegedly has upon adolescents restricts the reading matter of mature adults to what will presumably be acceptable for consumption by adolescents. (5) It is impossible to define the "community" by whose standards publications are supposed to be judged. And (6) there is no way to determine objectively whether any particular work has "redeeming social value" or not.

Many eminent authorities, including the majority of Justice Black's colleagues on the Supreme Court, do not agree with this point of view.

For about 100 years the standard legal definition of *obscene,* known as the Hicklin definition, was that "the test of obscenity is this, whether the tendency of the matter charged as obscenity is to deprave and corrupt those whose minds are open to such immoral influences, and into whose hands a publication of this sort may fall." As long ago as 1913, Judge Learned Hand objected to this definition on the ground that instead of leaving the test of obscenity to the normal, average adult, it fettered it to the lowest and least capable, "those whose minds are open to such immoral influences." He questioned the wisdom of reducing the permissible treatment of sex in literature to the standard of a child's library in the interest of a salacious few. The word *obscene,* he suggested, being incapable of exact abstract definition, should not be tied to the standards of a bygone age, but should be allowed to indicate "the present critical point in the compromise between candor and shame at which the community may have arrived here and now." Others attacked the Hicklin definition on the ground that it permitted undue concentration on parts of the work without giving sufficient attention to the effects or purposes of the work as a whole. Thus, in an appeal against an order of postal and customs officials that imported copies of James Joyce's *Ulysses* be destroyed on the ground that they were obscene, Judge Augustus N. Hand held that even if some passages in the book might be objectionable, the book, taken as a whole, did not tend to promote lust. "We believe," he wrote, "that the proper test of whether a given book is obscene is its dominant effect." But Judge Manton, in a vigorous dissent, enumerated the pages on which objectionable passages appeared, and said, "Who can doubt the obscenity of this book after a reading of the pages referred to, which are too indecent to add as a footnote to this opinion?" He quoted with approval the charge of the judge in an earlier obscenity case: "The test of obscenity is whether the tendency of the matter is to deprave and corrupt the morals of those whose minds are open to such influence, and into whose hands a publication of this sort may fall. . . . Would it suggest or convey lewd thoughts and lascivious thoughts to the young and inexperienced?" But another judge observed that under the Hicklin test, the Bible could be banned, for it contains numerous passages that could lead immature minds to lascivious thoughts. The story of Lot's daughters, who conspired to put their father into an alcoholic stupor, after which they both had incestuous relations with him, is one of the milder examples.

The Hicklin definition, then, did not fare well, and was replaced, for a time, by another, alluded to above, in connection with the attempt to burn *Ulysses*. Judge Learned Hand, in his opinion in the case, wrote:

> That numerous long passages in Ulysses contain matter that is obscene under any fair definition of the word cannot be gainsaid; yet they are relevant to the purpose of depicting the thoughts of the characters and are introduced to give meaning to the whole, rather than to promote lust or portray filth for its own sake. . . . The book as a whole is not pornographic, and, while in not a few spots it is coarse, blasphemous, and obscene, it does not, in our opinion, tend to promote lust. The erotic passages are submerged in the book as a whole and have little resultant effect.[7]

The new rule, then, rested upon the *dominant effect* of the book, rather than upon the effect that any given passages, taken in isolation, might have. Other decisions broadened the base of the public upon whose morals the book might be judged from the weakest among them to the average. In the late 1950's the American Law Institute drafted a model penal code, in which the following definition of "obscenity" was enunciated:

> A thing is obscene if, considered as a whole, its predominant appeal is to prurient interest, i.e., a shameful or morbid interest in nudity, sex or excretion, and if it goes substantially beyond customary limits of candor in description or representation of such matters.[8]

There is some problem about the meaning of "prurient interest." Some people say that it refers to physical sexual arousal. Others maintain that it may refer to curiosity alone. Compare, for example, Justice Brennan's definition of prurience as material having a tendency to incite lustful thoughts, or to arouse in them morbid or lascivious longings, with that of Justice Harlan, who says that "appeal to prurient interest" refers to "the capacity to attract individuals eager for a forbidden look." [9]

In his history-making opinion in *Roth* v. *United States*, Justice Brennan contended that obscenity, unlike even the most hateful ideas, is "utterly without redeeming social importance," for obscene utterances "are no essential part of any exposition of ideas." He concluded, therefore, that obscenity does not fall within the constitutional protections afforded to speech or press, which are offered because of the social value of permitting untrammeled expression of *ideas*. Obscenity may be distinguished from discussions about sex, then, by determining whether ideas or opinions are being expressed. If the material deals with sex in a manner appealing to prurient interest—i.e., in such a way as to excite lustful thoughts—then it is obscene, and if not, then it is not obscene. It should be noted, however, that though this seems, on the surface, to be a definition of *obscenity*, it does not really tell us what obscenity is. Relying upon the ill-defined term *prurient*, it tells us what obscene material presumably *does* to the reader or viewer.

Justice Harlan added yet another element: Regardless of its effect on the beholder, he said, obscene works must consist of "debasing portrayals of sex" and be patently offensive. Without such an additional criterion, he maintained, the public might be denied access to many worthwhile works of art and literature; for many such works might tend, on the whole, to appeal to the prurient interest but nevertheless not be "patently offensive." What it is to be "patently offensive" is never defined. But perhaps Justice Stewart's answer to the question, "What is hard-core pornography?" will provide a clue: "I shall not today attempt further to define the kinds of material I understand to be embraced within that short-hand definition; and perhaps I could never succeed in intelligibly doing so. But I know it when I see it." [10] As one critic has observed, this approach is no help whatever to book publishers and distributors, theater managers, and trial judges who do not "know it when they see it" or who "see it" differently from Justice Stewart. This definition, if it can be called that, is subjective, and if adopted in law, would be subject to Justice Black's criticism of any society that does not offer its citizens clear and well-defined rules for their conduct.

It may be well to leave the courts with their problems, and to see how others have fared in their attempts to define this term whose meaning is assumed to be so clear that one thoughtful writer doubted whether there is anyone who does not know what it means.

Harold Gardiner, S.J., says that an obscene work is one that "must, of its nature, be such as actually to arouse or [be] calculated to arouse in the viewer or reader such venereal pleasure." Venereal pleasure is sexual passion, or, more concretely, "the motions of the genital apparatus which are preparatory to the complete act of sexual union." Any voluntary stimulation of the sex organs outside of marital sex is sinful and any literary work that provides such stimulation is obscene. This definition is precise enough, but is so broad as to be unacceptable to any large percentage of the general public outside the Catholic Church, and even, perhaps, to many of the members of that Church. It goes much farther than Justice Brennan went in the Roth decision, for it brands as obscene anything whatever that arouses sexual interest, and not merely those that lead to "lustful desires" or "prurience." [11]

Eberhard and Phyllis Kronhausen, who have devoted much of their career as psychologists to the study of pornography and obscenity, assert that "the main purpose [of hard-core pornography] is to *stimulate erotic response* in the reader. And that is all." They contrast this to writing that may be classed as "erotic realism." The latter, they say, is a *truthful description* of the basic realities of life, as the individual experiences it," and may move the reader, through humor or revulsion, to decidedly antierotic responses; or it may move him to erotic responses, just as the sensitive reader may respond to a sad scene by crying, or to a humorous one by laughing.[12] The distinguishing features of pornographic works include a succession of increasingly stimulating scenes; heavy emphasis on the physiological sexual responses of the participants, and on deviant forms of sexuality; extremely sadistic scenes in which the victims respond passively or with positive enjoyment to the pain inflicted upon them (sadomasochism); gross exaggeration of the sexual powers and desires of the participants; and complete lack of realism in the portrayal of the characters.

This elaborate definition may be useful to psychologists, but is unlikely to be helpful to anyone concerned with the formulation of public policy or the enforcement of laws designed to prevent the spread of pornographic literature. To distinguish pornography from erotic realism on the basis of the "truthfulness" of the latter, for example, is to suppose that judges have a special insight into the truth and that in such matters as sex, there is a meaningful criterion by means of which truth can be distinguished from fantasy. In any case, much literature does not clearly fall into either of these categories, but lies somewhere in between.

Another psychologist, George Elliott, says that pornography "offends the sense of separateness, of individuality, of privacy; it intrudes upon the rights of others." [13] Certain barriers that people have around themselves are broken down by pornographic works. Such barriers serve an important function, and intruding upon them may not be in the interest of those who are affected. Beyond being an intrusion upon one's privacy, obscenity degrades and debases the subjects of which it treats and those who partake of it.

In one of the most thoughtful analyses of recent years, Harry M. Clor observes that "art is not primarily concerned with making us *want* something; it is primarily concerned with making us *see* something." He goes on to say that if a work promotes lust or disgust to a high degree, then it is not a work of art; for "art teaches by promoting an experience of some aspect of life and presenting that experience for contemplation and interpretation. The predominance of lust or disgust is incompatible with that detachment which is a prerequisite for the interpretation of experience. Therefore good literature cannot literally invade man's private affairs and it does not promote an obscene experience of life." Obscene literature, then, is "that literature which presents, graphically and in detail, a degrading picture of human life and invites the reader or viewer, not to contemplate that picture, but to wallow in it. . . . Obscenity is a depreciating view of intimate or physical things which is accompanied by desire or loathing." The difference between a scientific study of sadomasochism and an obscene novel that centers around sadomasochism consists in the fact that the readers of the latter would not be invited "to reflect upon the nature of degrading human experiences, but, simply, to have such experiences." It does not maintain the intellectual or artistic "distance" that is necessary to enable the reader to maintain his identity, to keep himself separate from the action of the novel.

"Art" is here being used in an evaluative sense. Clor does not analyze the difference between "contemplative" art and graphic and detailed pictures that lead to "wallowing" rather than to contemplation. There are experiences that may be provoked by the plastic arts or by literature that may "invade one's private affairs" and lead to a kind of "wallowing" rather than to "contemplation," but which no one would call obscene. Consider a deeply moving description of a mystical religious experience, one that describes the experience in great detail, and is so powerful and magnetic in its effect that it closes the gap between the reader and itself, engulfing him in the experience portrayed in the book, transporting him outside himself, and conveying a feeling of contempt or loathing for physical things. Such a work would not invite the reader to reflect upon the nature of mystical religious experiences, but would induce such experiences in him.

Yet I doubt whether it would be called obscene on that account, and it is not clear that such a work would for these reasons alone be classed as nonart. Some of the best art (or works that are widely regarded as superb art) was originally designed for just such purposes: to induce certain feelings and passions in those who were exposed to them, and not necessarily to lead them to contemplation.

Clor concedes that his definition is "not wholly free of vagueness or ambiguity," and that it is incapable of serving alone as a means of distinguishing works of art that deal with the obscene from obscene works. But its most distinguishing feature is its emphasis upon the *dehumanization,* the *depersonalization* that takes place in the obscene work. Pornography is "sexual obscenity in which the debasement of the human element is heavily accentuated, is depicted in great physiological detail, and is carried very far toward its utmost logical conclusion." [14]

Clor claims that his definition does a great deal to clarify what previous definitions had left unclear. Where earlier definitions relied upon "prurient interest," which might be anything from mild curiosity to overwhelming sexual arousal, Clor's definition makes it clear that the obscene is that which is characterized by "sexual passion in the absence of love or affection, . . . *depersonalized* sexual desire." This, he says, is what the ordinary man means when he speaks of prurience or lust—not sexual relations in marriage, or in a relationship that can be broadly defined as love, or in a situation in which the participants are concerned with one another as human beings. What the law denounces (or should denounce), he says, is not mere sexual arousal or desire as such, but "impersonal lust," in which human qualities are "stripped away and a person becomes an instrument existing solely for the pleasure of manipulation of others." [15]

Further, he claims that earlier definitions, such as that of the American

Law Institute, have confined their attention to "a shameful or morbid interest in nudity, sex, or excretion." But there are other kinds of obscenity as well, including a morbid interest in brutality, death, and the human body. A more elaborate definition, then, is the following:

> An obscene book, story, magazine, motion picture, or play is one which tends predominantly to:
>
> 1. Arouse lust or appeal to prurient interest.
> 2. Arouse sexual passion in connection with scenes of extreme violence, cruelty, or brutality.
> 3. Visually portray in detail, or graphically describe in lurid detail, the violent physical destruction, torture, or dismemberment of a human being, provided this is done to exploit morbid or shameful interest in these matters and not for genuine scientific, educational, or artistic purposes.
> 4. Visually portray, or graphically describe, in lurid physical detail, the death or the dead body of a human being, provided this is done to exploit morbid or shameful interest in these matters and not for genuine scientific, educational, or artistic purposes.[16]

Though this is one of the clearest definitions of obscenity to have been produced thus far, it suffers from a number of serious difficulties. How, for example, is one to determine whether a given book, story, or other article tends to do any of these things *predominantly?* Is a work to be judged by the subject matter of most of its pages? By two thirds, or three quarters of them? Or is it to be judged by the effect it has in society as a whole? Does *predominant* refer to the book or to the people who read it? If it is the latter, how is one to make such a judgment in a particular case?

How is one to distinguish those works that are designed to exploit persons who have a morbid and shameful interest in sex, violence, death, and the human body from those who have a "genuine" scientific, educational, or artistic purpose? Who shall judge whether a given work's purpose is genuinely artistic? Shall the judges be drawn from the art community, from among those who are presumably conversant with the deeper purposes of artists and writers? Will rival schools of art be represented on the jury, including the school of the defendant himself (assuming he belongs to one)? Or shall the judges be drawn from the general community, a community that may have little or no knowledge or appreciation of the kind of work on which judgment is to be rendered? Scientists would presumably be in a better position to determine whether a given work had "genuine" scientific interest or not, because a certain degree of expertise might be helpful in making such a determination. By the same token, artists, critics, and perhaps collectors and students of art might be in a better position than the ordinary layman to judge whether a work has "genuine artistic purpose." But there is always the danger that by submitting works to a jury, whether the jury be chosen from laymen or from professionals, one may perpetuate established and conventional values and techniques and stifle daring innovativeness. For a group of scientists might well conclude that a work that proceeds along radically novel lines has no genuine scientific interest. The word *genuine* is the villain here. Before Clor's definition becomes embodied in the law, some clear and precise guidelines on the manner in which *genuine* scientific, educational, and artistic works are to be distinguished from those that are *not* genuine must be developed.

Finally, how can one distinguish those works that are predominantly devoted to "impersonal" or "degrading" or "dehumanizing" lust from those that are not? Even if such a distinction can be made, on what ground does society presume to prevent those who get their thrills from reading such materials from doing so? It is said that works that fall within this definition of obscene have evil consequences, either for the individual who reads them or for society as a whole. But this is at least in part a statement of fact that must be proved by scientific means before it may be used to restrict the right of parts of the public to have access to works from which they derive much pleasure.

Some people maintain that everyone should have only the best pleasures. But the best pleasures turn out to be those pleasures that the people with the best taste enjoy. And to most people, those who have the best taste always turn out to be those who agree with *them*. But it is not clear why any one person or any one group in society should impose his or its preferences upon any other group. Some people like scotch, and others prefer beer. Some people like Mickey Spillane and others prefer Jane Austen. It is not clear that there is any principle, moral or otherwise, that would give the lovers of one beverage or one kind of literature the right to deprive lovers of the other of that which they enjoy. If fans of Mickey Spillane were to write treatises on the merits of various types of literature, they could undoubtedly come up with some excellent reasons for banning Jane Austen!

THE EFFECTS OF OBSCENITY

If no satisfactory definition of *obscenity* has thus far been developed, it cannot be for lack of effort. When the nine justices on a single court cannot arrive at a single definition that they can work with, but consistently come up with as many as seven or eight separate views on the meaning of the term in a given case, it is obvious that the problem is not only a difficult one, but that it has serious practical consequences. For the student who is interested in studying the effects of obscene materials, such a state of affairs must be most disconcerting; for if no definition of the key term can be found, then it is impossible to inquire meaningfully into the effects of obscene materials, because there is no way to distinguish such materials from those that are not obscene.

Until quite recently no sustained scientific research had been done in this area. But the Commission on Obscenity and Pornography, armed with a

$2 million appropriation from Congress, was able to initiate a number of studies that have started to provide some answers to some of the most troublesome questions.

Instead of attempting to define *obscenity,* the commission chose to discuss "erotic materials," without passing moral or legal judgment on them. The problem, then, was to determine what effects erotic materials of various sorts have upon people in a variety of contexts.

Some of the research findings can be dismissed as trivial. Surveys, for example, revealed that at least half the population believes that explicit sexual materials provide information about sex, and that more than half of all police chiefs believe that obscene materials contribute to juvenile delinquency. They have also found that erotic materials cause sexual arousal in many males and females and that females are not as aroused by material designed to arouse male homosexuals as they are by material depicting heterosexual conduct.

Other findings, however, are more important for our purposes. The commission's studies concluded that a significant number of persons increased their masturbatory activity after exposure to erotic materials. Persons who reported increased rates of intercourse were generally those who were already experienced and had established sexual partners. In general, the commission concluded, any such increase in sexual activity tended to be temporary and was not significantly different from the kind of sexual behavior in which the individual had engaged prior to his or her exposure to the erotic materials. Erotic dreams, sexual fantasies, and conversation about sexual matters all tended to increase after exposure to such materials. Some married couples reported more agreeable relations and greater willingness to discuss sexual matters after such exposure than before.

One might have expected delinquent youth to have more and earlier exposure to erotic materials than nondelinquent youth. Both of these expectations turn out to be ill founded, according to the commission. Both delinquent and nondelinquent youth have wide exposure to such materials.

According to the commission's report, there is no statistical correlation between sex crimes and exposure to erotic materials. Although the United States has experienced a significant increase in arrests for rape during the past decade of relaxed restrictions on erotic material, arrests for juvenile sex crimes decreased during the same period. In Denmark there was a notable decrease in sex crimes after Danish law was changed to permit virtually unrestricted access to erotic materials.

The commission's overall conclusion was that "empirical research designed to clarify the question has found no evidence to date that exposure to explicit sexual materials plays a significant role in the causation of delinquent or criminal behavior among youth or adults. The commission cannot conclude that exposure to erotic materials is a factor in the causation of sex crime or sex delinquency." [17]

Other authorities had earlier come to much the same conclusion, but without the benefit of the extensive studies sponsored by the commission.

This is not the place for a detailed summary or evaluation of the commission's report or the data on which it based its findings. It is appropriate to note, however, that several members of the commission protested its findings, and wrote a minority report that contained the following major disagreements with it: A number of studies available to the commission were ignored or underrated by it in its final report. Thus, one research team found that there was a definite correlation between juvenile exposure to pornography and precocious heterosexual and deviant sexual behavior. Another study found that there was a direct relation between the frequency with which adolescents saw movies depicting sexual intercourse and the extent to which the adolescents themselves engaged in premarital sexual intercourse. In a third study it was found that "the rapists were the group reporting the highest 'excitation to masturbation' rates by pornography both in the adult (80%) as well as teen (90%) years." The dissenters add, "Considering the crime they were imprisoned for, this suggests that pornography (with accompanying masturbation) did not serve adequately as a catharsis [as some researchers have suggested it might], prevent a sex crime, or 'keep them off the streets.'" The same study reported that 80 per cent of prisoners who had had experience with erotica reported that they "wished to try the act" they had witnessed in the erotic films they had seen, and when asked whether they *had* followed through, between 30 and 38 per cent replied that they had. In still another study, 39 per cent of sex offenders reported that "pornography had something to do with their committing the offense" of which they were convicted.[18]

In addition, the minority accused the majority of being biased, of suppressing evidence, of misinterpreting statistics and conclusions of researchers, and of misrepresentation.

No attempt will be made here to analyze these findings. However, a number of venerable fallacies may have been perpetrated in them. One, known by its Latin description, *post hoc ergo propter hoc*, consists of supposing that because one phenomenon follows another, the later phenomenon must be caused by the earlier one. But this is not necessarily the case. I know a man who begins to eat his lunch every day promptly after the whistle at the steel mill blows; but the blowing of the whistle is not the cause of his eating, or even of his eating at that particular time. He eats at that time because that happens to be the beginning of his lunch hour. Nor, contrary to David Hume's opinion, is the fact that one phenomenon regularly accompanies another evidence that the one is necessarily the cause of, or caused by, the other. They may both be caused by some unknown third factor. Thus, in the cases before us, both the delinquent behavior and the reading of erotica may have been caused by some other factors in the lives of the adolescents who were surveyed; there is no way, with the information presently available, to show that the erotic material caused the delinquent behavior. Nor is the fact that some sex criminals report that they read pornographic books or saw pornographic films prior to the commission of their crimes an unequivocal indication that the pornography contributed to their criminal behavior. For one thing, they may have been seeking some excuse for their behavior or a scapegoat on whom to fasten the guilt. It would be useful if a rapist could claim that he is really not to blame for his crime. The man who should be in jail, he might claim, is the one who published the obscene book he read just before he raped his victim, or the governor who signed the liberalized censorship law, or the Supreme Court Justice who removed the ban on it. But this will not do at all, because so many persons read the same pornographic works and do not commit sex crimes.

This is not to say that there is *no* causal connection between erotic literature and sexual behavior. It is to suggest merely that the answers are not in yet, and that even such research as is presently available must be approached with considerable caution.

Thus far, one must conclude that available evidence does not support the thesis that erotic materials have socially undesirable effects upon the people who are exposed to them, but it does not support the thesis that such materials do *not* have such effects either.

SOLUTIONS TO THE PROBLEM

Proposed solutions to the problem of obscenity and pornography are many and varied. Some groups, particularly some Church groups, favor strict censorship laws. Some of these groups advocate the removal of all "obscene" books from bookstores, drugstores, and all other places where they might be sold; from libraries; and in some instances even from private collections. They urge legislatures to impose harsh penalties upon the publishers and purveyors of what they consider to be obscene materials. When they have the power to do so, they drive men out of business in order to demonstrate the wickedness of pandering to the public taste for the sensational and to show how risky it can be for a businessman not to accept *their* guidelines and *their* judgment in determining what he may sell or exhibit. A theater owner in upper New York State exhibited a film, during the summer resort season, of which some townspeople disapproved. He refused to bow to a local clergyman's insistence that he stop displaying the offending film, because there was great box office demand for it and because he was in principle opposed to permitting any group to become unofficial censors for his community. When the summer season was over, the protectors of public morals organized a boycott of the theater (though it was then displaying innocuous films) and eventually forced its owner to close its doors and to move out of town.

Justices Douglas and Black, on the other hand, have consistently opposed *any* interference with the right of free speech or free press. Justice Black has put his position succinctly as follows:

> Certainly the First Amendment's language leaves no room for inference that abridgements of speech and press can be made just because they are slight. That Amendment provides, in simple words, that "Congress shall make no law . . . abridging the freedom of speech, or of the press." I read "no law . . . abridging" to mean *no law abridging.* The First Amendment, which is the supreme law of the land, has thus fixed its own value on freedom of speech and press by putting these freedoms wholly "beyond the reach" of *federal* power to abridge.[19]

He goes on to explain that under the court's interpretation of the Fourteenth Amendment, the protections of the First Amendment extend to the states as well, so that *no* governmental power in the United States may abridge the rights to free speech and free press in any way whatever—except, presumably, where there is a "clear and present danger," as when a person shouts "Fire" in a crowded theater.

Between these extremes, we have already seen how various authorities attempt to justify some kind of censorship. The United States Supreme Court has tended to ever greater liberalism in its treatment of obscenity cases. The one setback that has occurred in recent years, from the libertarian point of view, was the Ginzburg decision. In that decision, the Court held that Ginzburg, publisher of *Eros* and other erotic magazines, had been properly convicted under an obscenity statute, not because the materials he had sold were more obscene or more pornographic than those sold or produced by other defendants whose convictions had been overturned by the Court, but because they were obscene under the *Roth* definition and because he had been engaged in "pandering." That is, he had not only published and distributed erotic materials; he had "purveyed textual or graphic matter openly advertised to appeal to the erotic interest" of his customers. For example, Ginzburg went to some lengths to find a town whose name was suggestive from which to mail his publications. One such town was Intercourse, Pennsylvania, but its post office was too small to handle the volume of mail. He finally settled in Middlesex, New Jersey. An advertisement for *Eros* claimed, "*Eros* is a child of its times. . . . [It] is the result of recent court decisions that have realistically interpreted America's obscenity laws and that have given to this country a new breath of freedom of expression. . . . *Eros* takes full advantage of this new freedom of expression. It is *the* magazine of sexual candor." Direct mail advertising for *Eros* and other Ginzburg publications contained a slip labeled "GUARANTEE: Documentary Books, Inc., unconditionally guarantees full refund on the price of . . . if it fails to reach you because of U.S. Post Office censorship interference." One of the publications at issue, incidentally, was entitled *The Housewife's Handbook on Selective Promiscuity.*

Ginzburg went to prison, but since the Ginzburg decision, most obscenity convictions that have reached the Supreme Court have been overturned. Some commentators have concluded from this that some members of the Court were stung by Ginzburg's open exploitation of the Court's earlier decisions in his advertising. This is pure conjecture. But the main tendency, toward extremely liberal construction of the First Amendment's guarantees, seems to be holding, even in the more conservative Burger Court.

THE CASE FOR CENSORSHIP

Harry M. Clor contends that no society can be so libertarian as to blind itself to its avowed enemies when confronted by them. He contends also that it is a mistake to suppose that anything any person who calls himself an author or an artist does must necessarily benefit society. Some so-called authors and artists, he says, are actually enemies of civilized society and their works can do a great deal of harm. He concludes that society has the right to censor their works in order to protect itself against their pernicious influences.

What kind of harm does he envision as flowing from obscene works? He concedes that there is no conclusive scientific evidence that obscene works in themselves are the cause of criminal or immoral behavior but English and American law has always recognized the right of the state to preserve the moral welfare of the state. In 1890 the Supreme Court upheld laws against the teaching of polygamy as "legislation for the punishment of acts inimical to the peace, good order and morals of society." [20] And in an earlier case, the Court said, "The foundation of a republic is the virtue of its citizens. They are at once sovereigns and subjects. As the foundation is undermined the structure is weakened. When it is destroyed the fabric must fall. Such is the voice of universal history." [21] Aristotle held that the aim of legislation was to make citizens good by training them in habits of right action. Men come together in political communities not merely for mutual protection against aggression that might lead to the destruction of their lives or their liberties or the deprivation of their property, but for the cultivation of those qualities in man that are distinctively human, as distinguished from those that he shares with the brute creation. Law performs a civilizing and humanizing function, he said, and is *not* (contrary to Mill's view) intended merely to protect the citizen against physical harms that his neighbor might be tempted to inflict upon him.

Thus, under this view of society and the law, censorship may serve a very important function: it may protect the citizen against those influences that would tend to dehumanize or brutalize men and the societies in which they live.

As Lord Devlin wrote:

> A sense of right and wrong is necessary for the life of a community. It is not necessary that their appreciation of right and wrong, tested in the light of one set or another of those abstract propositions about which men forever

dispute, should be correct. . . . What the lawmaker has to ascertain is not the true belief but the common belief.[22]

Government, then, has the right to search out those common values that all men in a given society cherish, and to reinforce them through legislation. It need not remain indifferent to the moral standards of its citizens. And it may utilize censorship to restrict "such forms of sensualism as are contrary to our deepest values."

Finally, those who favor this view maintain that the government may have the duty to prevent those vices that are incompatible with the well-being of society and the security of the government. If a man fails to observe reasonable standards of health and morality, he does less than his share toward the welfare of all. Society is harmed when its members are weakened by sickness, by poverty, or by vice. This is not paternalism, for paternalism is concerned to benefit the individual, even against his will. This is not so much concern for the well-being of the individual as for the well-being of society, which may be damaged by the corruption or sickness of the individual.

Men and women who become overly concerned with the gratification of their own desires, whatever they may be, cannot make their full contribution to society. Certain vices cannot be tolerated, even in the most liberal society, according to the advocates of censorship, for their spread can lead to the destruction of that society itself, or to the deterioration of the very conditions under which liberty can thrive. Thus, even a liberal society may have to suppress certain kinds of publications on the ground that their distribution tends to undermine the moral foundations of that society itself.

Every society exercises control over "standards of decency," particularly with respect to sex, because of the powerful nature of sexual passions. Men need guidance, either from the law or from the more informal sanctions of custom, as to the manner in which these emotions may be expressed. The law, in a civilized society, provides such guidance. It sets the tone for the moral community; it maintains the standards of the civilization when temporary fads and fashions may veer off in other directions. As Clor puts it, "there is a more stable and more continuous 'underlying' public opinion" that has, among its more important sources, the tradition and customs that are supported by the laws of the country. The home, the church, and the school do a great deal to maintain public morality; but they are incapable of doing the job alone, because they are molded by the law themselves, and the law provides the context and the framework in which they must operate.

Censorship, then, can serve to support and promote public morality—that morality upon which a good society depends—in two ways: "(1) by preventing or reducing some of the most corrupt influences and (2) by holding up an authoritative standard for the guidance of opinions and judgment." [23]

Clor advocates censorship "primarily" of the "most vicious materials." Among the more significant effects of such censorship, he says, would be the deterrent effect: "Publishers are deterred from publishing, and authors from writing, materials which cannot legally be circulated. Thus the results of legal censorship consist not in the confiscation of the relatively few obscene publications which the censor catches, but in the general reduction in the circulation of materials of that kind." [24]

Even more important, however, is the educative effect of legal censorship of obscene publications. Censorship laws "announce a moral decision of the community. . . . They assert, in effect, that the organized community draws a line between the decent and the indecent, the permissible and the impermissible. . . . Individuals . . . are made aware that the community is committed to a distinction between what is right and what is not. In the long run this awareness must have an effect upon the moral attitudes and values of most people." The community, by taking a stand, shows to one and all that it is serious about morality.

THE CASE AGAINST CENSORSHIP

Many Americans have an innate distrust of government. Since the Revolution, they have hedged government about with manifold restrictions, with "checks and balances," that restrain its power and jealously guard the liberties of the people. In this respect, it has been said, they differ from Canadians and British subjects, who generally trust and respect their governments and who are not as particular as Americans about securing written guarantees against governmental interference in their affairs. The long experience of mankind with censorship has convinced many people of the danger of permitting government agents to sit in judgment over what the people may or may not be permitted to read. Though Clor's comments on the social importance of certain moral standards, and on the vital need of every society to protect itself against the moral depravity into which its people may fall, are true, censorship may not be the best way of assuring a society of the maintenance of high moral standards. The libertarians have proceeded under the generally optimistic assumption that most men are fairly sensible, and given the choice, will usually choose what is best for them in the long run. They have also proceeded under the generally pessimistic assumption that given sufficient power, most governments will misuse it to perpetuate themselves and to constrict the liberties available to the citizenry. As Lord Acton said, "Power corrupts, and absolute power corrupts absolutely." It may be more desirable, therefore, to rely upon the educational instruments of government and upon positive measures to inform the public with a sense of responsibility, rather than upon the police power of the state.

Clor's prediction that censorship will have inhibiting effects upon publishers and writers is borne out by Tolstoy's complaint, quoted previously; but there is a notable difference in emphasis. Clor looks upon this inhibiting effect as a positive contribution to public morality. Tolstoy felt it as an oppressive force that stopped up his energies and wasted away his most creative years. What is no loss at all to one man is an irretrievable loss of something that might have been of great value to another.

Nor is it any help to permit the legislatures or the courts to pronounce on the "moral decision of the community," for even if they can assess what that vague and ill-defined decision might be, there is some reason to wonder whether it ought to be imposed upon *all* members of the community, whether they share the community's standards or not. No tyranny is more oppressive than that of the majority upon the minority. It was recognition of that fact, and of the right of the minority to live by its lights, that impelled the framers of the U.S. Constitution to incorporate the Bill of Rights into it, and to write the First Amendment in the categorical and absolute terms emphasized by Justice Black.

When Clor pronounces his readiness to permit "classics" and "recognized" works of art and literature to be exempt from the general censorship regulations that he advocates, he forgets that there is seldom any unanimity, even in the academic community, as to whether a given work is a "classic" or not. The censor would thus be burdened not only with weighing the proportions of obscene and redeeming materials in a given work, but also with determining whether it is a classic or not. Because many new works are not recognized as "classics" until some years after their publication, Clor's censor would be obliged to predict which works might be considered classics in the future—an impossible task—in order to avoid depriving the world of them.

THE RECOMMENDATIONS OF THE COMMISSION ON OBSCENITY

The Commission on Obscenity and Pornography made the following recommendations:

1. *All statutes prohibiting the sale, exhibition, or distribution of erotic materials to consenting adults should be repealed.* This recommendation was based upon the commission's conviction that there is no evidence that exposure to such materials plays a significant role in the causation of social or individual harms; that they are a source of entertainment for many adults; that they sometimes have a salutary effect on married couples; that key terms (*obscenity, salacious, prurient, community standards, patently offensive*) are indefinable; that laws against erotic materials are largely unenforceable and are not consistent with the spirit or the letter of the Constitution's prohibition on interference with free speech and free press; that the trade in such materials is relatively small in any event; that there is no evidence to support the view that such literature has a deleterious effect upon the moral climate of the nation as a whole or upon the morality of individual citizens.

2. *The commercial distribution of explicit sexual material to young persons*

should be regulated by law. This includes the sale, lease, commercial exhibition, or display of such materials in places to which young persons have access. Prohibited materials are defined as those which are "made up in whole or in dominant part of depictions of human sexual intercourse, masturbation, sodomy . . . [etc.]; provided, however, that works of art or of anthropological significance shall not be deemed to be within the foregoing definition."

The commission justified this recommendation on the following grounds: There is even less information available on the effects of erotic materials upon children than there is on their effects upon adults, for there are strong ethical reasons for not subjecting children to experimentation in these areas. Further, there is widespread agreement that children should not be exposed to such materials, and the commission felt that parents should be free to make their own conclusions regarding the propriety of exposing their children to them. In drawing up its recommendations, the commission defined the forbidden materials as explicitly as possible. But the commission concluded that such definition is impossible insofar as textual materials are concerned. The commission therefore confined its recommendations to pictorial representations only, for without a clear definition, there was some concern that booksellers and others would be put in needless jeopardy and that the distribution of books and magazines would be endangered.

3. *State and local legislation prohibiting public displays of sexually explicit pictorial materials should be enacted, and the post office should be authorized to compile and keep lists of persons who do not wish to receive certain materials and to prohibit mailers of unsolicited advertisements of such materials from sending their advertisements to persons on those lists.* Persons who do not wish to be subjected to such displays and who do not want to receive through the mails unsolicited materials that they consider to be offensive should be protected against them. The right of free speech and free press does not include the right to subject unwilling persons to such utterances, displays, or publications.[25]

These proposals (not accepted by a dissenting minority of the commission) recognize some of the problems that have troubled us throughout this discussion: the problem of defining obscenity, the conflict between the alleged right of the individual to set his own moral and literary standards and the supposed right of the government to regulate public morals; the important difference between the mature adult and the immature child or adolescent, so far as the law is concerned (i.e., the law's duty—or right, if you will—to protect the parent's control over his child's environment and his moral, intellectual, and social development); and the right of the public to be protected from offensive public displays and from the intrusion of what they may consider to be offensive materials into the privacy of their homes.

In keeping with their commitment to make recommendations on the basis of scientific findings, they proposed what seem to many observers to be excessively permissive legislation. Because, in the commission's view, there is no convincing evidence that erotic materials harm either individuals or society, there is no justification for restricting their distribution, except to minors, about whom there is greater doubt. The reader will recall, however, that in the minority report referred to earlier, there was a claim that the evidence is not as inconclusive as the commission claimed it to be.

When the report was presented to President Nixon, he flatly rejected it, stating that it was completely unsatisfactory. He remarked on the fact that there is a general consensus that good literature has good effects upon people. He could not see, therefore, why bad literature would not have bad effects.

Since the release of the report there has been little movement to implement its recommendations. The controversy continues, and is likely to continue for many years to come. The facts, whatever they may be, are unclear. Research in this field has been minimal, and such research as has been done is not easily assessed, because of the difficulty of constructing adequate experimental procedures, because of the large number of variables that inevitably intrude into any research into human behavior, because of the inherent difficulty in discovering the causes of complex events, because of the welter of definitional problems, and because of the emotions surrounding all aspects of this issue.

The tension that has developed between those who have adopted a libertarian stance on this issue and those who favor the imposition of more rigid regulation of erotic or violent materials is not likely to slacken in the near future, for even when there is agreement on the facts, there remains a persistent disagreement in attitude. Such attitudinal disagreements are not ordinarily dispelled by any amount of research or by any scientific findings, no matter how thorough they may be.

Perhaps the most accurate assessment of the situation was made by C. P. Magrath, in an article he wrote on the obscenity cases which he subtitled "The Grapes of Roth." Commenting on the plethora of cases and opinions, and on Justice Black's objection to the Supreme Court's becoming a Supreme Board of Censors, he said, "On the question of obscenity and the law a more appropriate imagery would liken the Court to the Tower of Babel."[26] On the question of obscenity, not only the Court, but the entire world may be likened to the Tower of Babel.[27]

In Chapter 14 we shall return to this problem and see whether a more definitive judgment can be rendered on the question of censorship of pornography.

Part Two

Criminal Punishment

In Part One society's attitudes toward those whose behavior is not socially acceptable, but does not demonstrably result in harm to anyone but the person or persons who participate in such activities, were examined. The thrust of the argument was that where such behavior is concerned, it is reasonable to expect the law to maintain a hands-off attitude. For a great many reasons criminal sanctions are out of place. In some instances, as in the area of divorce and such related questions as alimony and custody, the law applies a kind of civil penalty and maintains a punitive approach that is both archaic and incompatible with the ideas of a free and democratic society. In general, the conclusion was that in the area of private morality, the machinery of the state ought not to be permitted to interfere.

To suppose that the same conclusion would follow from application of the principles discussed in Part One to criminal behavior that is demonstrably harmful to others would be fallacious. Nothing in the preceding chapters would justify the conclusion that in a free society all things must be permitted. Nor has there been the slightest hint of any principle that would warrant the conclusion that the punishment of criminals, as such, is wrong, or evil, or repressive, or that it is somehow inconsistent with the ideals of democracy and freedom. When the law condemns a form of behavior just because many people consider it to be evil, such legal condemnation and the penalties that follow upon it constitute an unnecessary and improper invasion of the liberties of the citizen who chooses to deviate from the norm. Punishing such persons is unjust because the law ought not to interfere with the citizen's right to choose whether to behave in a manner that is considered respectable, proper, or moral by the community as a whole, or

191

*to follow his own "unrespectable," "improper," or "immoral" desires. But
if an individual's behavior is both immoral by community standards and
harmful to others, the question as to whether he ought to be subjected to
criminal sanctions is on an altogether different footing. We turn now to the
question of whether penalties ought to be exacted of such persons, and, if
the answer to that question is affirmative, to the problem of deciding what
penalties are appropriate and ought to be enforced.*

7

The Concept of Punishment

When a man is brought into court and is accused of having committed a
grave offense against society, all the machinery of the state is set into motion
to bring him to justice. The public prosecutor or the district attorney often
has a veritable army of men at his disposal, all trained to ferret out information that may be relevant to the crime, all paid by the state to spend their
working hours questioning witnesses, examining evidence, and building a
case that will presumably lead to conviction of the accused. The latter, on
the other hand, usually has very limited means at his disposal. More often
than not, he must count himself fortunate if he has enough assets to pay the
fees of his attorney. Few men can hire teams of private investigators who can
devote their time, skills, and resources exclusively to the search for evidence
and the building of a defense. No private citizen can match the modern
state when the latter brings all its forces into play after he has been accused
of having violated the law.

It is because of the inherent inequality of the contest that common-law
countries have built into their laws special protections for the citizen who is
accused of a criminal offense. He is legally presumed to be innocent, placing
the entire burden of proof upon his accusers. To overcome this presumption
of innocence, it is not sufficient that the prosecution provide a preponderance
of evidence that the accused is guilty. The prosecution must prove "beyond

a reasonable doubt" that he is guilty. Nor is it sufficient if a majority of the jurors are convinced of his guilt. Nothing less than unanimity will do. If even one juror is not convinced of the guilt of the defendant, the court is obliged to continue to presume that he is innocent.*

As a further protection for the accused against the power of the state, the agents of the government are forbidden to extort confessions from him. Some countries have moved a long way from the days when the most fiendish tortures were employed to extract confessions from men and women who were suspected of wrongdoing. There is little doubt that virtually any man can be forced, through ceaseless physical and mental torture, to confess to almost anything if he is promised relief from his agonies. Unfortunately, there is ample evidence that some totalitarian regimes, including those of most of the nations of the Communist world, nearly all of the Arab states, Greece, and several Latin American regimes, are still resorting to this barbaric means of getting their opponents out of the way. Interested in convictions rather than truth or justice, they use any device that will further their aims. By contrast, in the United States, the Supreme Court has in recent years extended the Fifth Amendment's protection against self-incrimination to many areas where it had traditionally been considered to be nonoperative. In the controversial case of *Escobedo* v. *Illinois* (1964), the Court broke new ground in this area and in the Fourth Amendment's guarantee of the right to counsel. The latter had originally been construed as an absolute right only in the federal courts. It was later extended to state courts, but only in capital cases. Finally, in 1963 the distinction between capital and noncapital cases was abandoned. Again, at first the right applied only to the trial. It was later extended to the arraignment and then to the preliminary hearing. At last, in *Escobedo,* it was carried to the very beginning of the police interrogation of a suspect, for, as Justice Goldberg pointed out, if confessions could be wrung from suspects at an early stage in the investigation, the formal trial would be a "very hollow thing." Quoting an earlier decision, he added, "One can imagine a cynical prosecutor saying: 'Let them have the most illustrious counsel, now. They can't escape the noose. There is nothing that counsel can do for them at trial.' " †

Thus, although the defendant in a criminal trial faces severe disabilities because of the great machinery the state may bring to bear in carrying out its investigation and prosecution, the balances are tipped in the defendant's favor by the guarantees and protections that are built into the system under which we live.

Some people are prepared to argue that for the sake of individual security

---

* A recent decision by the U.S. Supreme Court permits convictions by less than unanimous decisions in state courts. A similar rule has prevailed in Great Britain for some years. This trend marks an important departure from common-law tradition.

† Another landmark decision was that in the *Miranda* case, dealing with illegal searches. These decisions of the Warren court provoked a great public outcry and are now being modified by the Burger court.

and "law and order," citizens must be prepared to sacrifice certain liberties that they had previously taken for granted. So long as you obey the law, they say, you have nothing to fear. These so-called guarantees are merely guarantees for the criminal; they protect the lawless elements in society and leave law-abiding citizens open to victimization by them.

Some of the world's most orderly societies and some of its safest streets and parks are to be found in precisely those totalitarian countries where guarantees of individual liberties are the weakest. Safety in the streets and security at home can be bought, for a time, by a citizenry that is prepared to forfeit certain rights and liberties that were considered to be fundamental during the development of the Western democracies. That price, however, is too high. The insidious process by which governments take unto themselves the liberties of their people on the ground that only thus can the security of the population be assured ultimately leads to tyranny, whose absolute power is far more fearsome than the evils that engender it. Such regimes are seldom replaced by less oppressive ones without great social upheavals and much death and destruction. In the meantime, the innocent have been deprived of their liberties because of the behavior of the guilty. In case of emergency, it is not inappropriate for government to ask the citizens of a state to give up some of their liberties. But a state of affairs that lasts for many years is not an emergency, and a people that gives up its liberties to fight crime ceases to be a free people.

Crime can be combatted in other ways. Where its causes are known and are curable, their elimination will result in a diminution of the crime rate. And when it is possible to apprehend and convict the lawbreaker, punishing him may help to reduce the dangers that criminal behavior poses to the society that brings him to justice.

Although the theories propounded here have some applicability in any society, we are concerned principally with the existing social order in the United States, Great Britain, Canada, and other liberal democratic societies where it is not only possible, but in fact highly probable that any person accused of criminal activity will receive a fair trial. In spite of certain self-proclaimed experts' insistence that it is virtually impossible for members of certain groups to get a fair trial—particularly in the United States and most especially in the Southern states—there is very little evidence to support this assertion. To be sure, in certain notorious cases, judges and juries have acted upon irrational fears and prejudices and have therefore brought about serious miscarriages of justice. But the generalizations indulged in, particularly by some critics of American culture, to the effect that there is no justice in the criminal courts for black, Chicano, and Indian defendants, are without substantial foundation. In most cases all parties concerned make an honest and conscientious effort to see that justice is done, to convict the guilty and to acquit the innocent.

Let it be assumed that in each of the following cases, the person convicted of a crime has been found guilty by a fair and conscientious jury, that the judge has been scrupulous in his insistence that the rights of the accused be respected, and that the attorneys for both the prosecution and the defense are competent, ethical men who have put forth their best efforts. (No one, after all, wants to argue for the punishment of innocent men.)

Even under these conditions, certain problems inevitably arise:

1. What is the nature of punishment, and how does it differ from other kinds of events that may happen to people, and from other kinds of things that people can do to one another?
2. What are the aims, goals, purposes, or ends of punishment?
3. What justifications can be offered for a private person, or an agent of society, deliberately inflicting harm upon another person?
4. If a man has violated one of the rules of society whose infringement ordinarily calls for punishment, what conditions, if any, ought to serve to excuse his behavior and so to free him from the odium of being punished?
5. Are there any conditions so general that they supply every person accused of a criminal violation with an excuse, the recognition of which would require of society that it abandon all programs of punishment in favor of some other form of treatment for such offenders? For example, would the theory of determinism, if it were true, be such a universal excuse for antisocial behavior? Are there grounds for saying that every person who deliberately violates a criminal statute does so because of some illness, so that he cannot be held responsible for his acts?
6. How can modern penal institutions—particularly prisons or penitentiaries —be evaluated, and how do they stand up under critical scrutiny as a means of punishing persons convicted of violating the criminal law?
7. What are the arguments in favor of the abolition of the death penalty, and what may be said against its abolition? How do these arguments stand up under critical examination?
8. Is the treatment of juvenile offenders unique, or is it merely a subclass of the punishment of offenders in general? Are there any special problems connected with the treatment presently accorded to juvenile offenders?

THE NATURE OF PUNISHMENT

Every punishment may be analyzed into the following elements:

1. There are at least two persons, one who inflicts the punishment and one who is punished.
2. The person who inflicts the punishment causes a certain harm, or unwanted treatment, to occur to the person who is being punished.

3. The person who inflicts the punishment has a right to harm the person who is punished in the particular way in which he does harm him.
4. The person who is being punished has been judged to have done what he is forbidden to do or to have failed to do what he is required to do.
5. The harm that is inflicted upon the person who is being punished is *for* the act or omission mentioned in item 4 above.

This analysis may be better understood if it is illustrated by an example, which may serve also to demonstrate how the analysis may be used to distinguish punishments from other kinds of undesirable events that may take place in a person's life.

Suppose that Burger takes $1,000 from Deckelbaum. The loss of $1,000 is a harm, or an unwanted event, in the life of Deckelbaum. Deckelbaum himself undoubtedly would agree that he would have preferred to have kept the money in his own account.

Burger's taking this money from Deckelbaum is not a *punishment* unless all the other conditions are met. If condition 3, for example, were not met, then Burger would be guilty of a crime. If Burger were a holdup man, a con man, or an extortionist, he might relieve Deckelbaum of his money but this loss would not be a punishment for Deckelbaum. But meeting condition 3 alone is not sufficient. Burger might have a perfect right to take Deckelbaum's money from him, and still not be punishing him. Burger might be a tax collector, for example. If the harm inflicted upon Deckelbaum is to count as punishment, conditions 4 and 5 must also be met. If Burger had had the right to confine Deckelbaum but Deckelbaum had not violated a rule, Burger's action against Deckelbaum would not count as punishment. Consider quarantine, for example.

Condition 4 requires that Deckelbaum be judged to have violated a rule, and 5 stipulates that the harm he suffers be *for* that violation. Neither of these alone is sufficient. If Deckelbaum is "punished" for a crime of which he has not been convicted, he is clearly not being *punished* at all. The state may decide to use him as an example to potential violators of a given regulation by pretending that he has been convicted of violating it; but this is not punishment. It is rather a form of brutality. One cannot properly *punish* a man for a crime unless one has first determined that he has in fact committed the crime for which he is being punished.

Though this is essentially a legal definition of punishment, it may be usefully applied to other forms of punishment as well. When a mother spanks her child, she ordinarily does so because she believes that he has violated some rule of the household. She first satisfies herself that he has violated the rule, and then applies the penalty she deems appropriate to the violation. Being his mother, she has a right to spank him—a right that the neighbors do not have.* If she spanks the child merely to vent her

---

* The mother's right is legal, moral, and customary. The neighbors lack the right, in all of these senses, to punish another person's child.

anger or to assuage her personal frustrations, then her behavior is not properly punishment at all. In its most extreme forms it becomes transformed into an all too common form of aggression and brutality.

A subtle distinction must be drawn between the infliction of a harm and the withholding of a benefit. Withholding a benefit or a privilege is not a punishment, though the two bear remarkable resemblances to one another. The hurt of a boy who is not accepted on his school's football team because he is not as well qualified as others who have applied is very real, but his rejection is not a penalty for his failure to have the physical prowess of his classmates. To harm a man is to take away what he has or to deprive him of what he otherwise has a right to have or to do or to enjoy. A fine involves depriving a man of money that he would otherwise have every right to keep. Imprisonment involves depriving him of liberties that he would otherwise have the right to expect to enjoy. In short, failing to qualify for a benefit is not to be confused with breaking a rule and depriving a person of a benefit to which he does not have a pre-existing right is not to be confused with punishment.

When a professor or a teacher records an F for a student, one might be tempted to suppose that this is a kind of punishment—for the student's failure to study, perhaps, or for his failure to provide enough correct answers to the questions on the final exam. This, too, is a false comparison, but for significantly different reasons. To say that a professor "gives" a student his grade is misleading. It would be more correct to say that a professor *records* the grade that the student has earned. The student who fails to do passing work in a course and finds an F on his record is not being punished any more than the worker who fails to show up at his job for a week and discovers that his pay envelope is empty.

To sum up: *A punishment is a harm inflicted by a person in a position of authority upon another person who is judged to have violated a rule or a law.*

THE AIMS OF PUNISHMENT

Some philosophers have confused the aims of punishment with its nature, or have defined punishment at least partially in terms of its supposed aims. This can be misleading, for by packing into its definition those aims of which one approves, one can refuse to allow any behavior that has some other aim to be called punishment, even though such behavior is quite generally considered to be a form of punishment. Such question-begging techniques and attempts at "persuasive definition" do not resolve questions. They merely add to the confusion that already exists. It is best, therefore, to consider the aims of punishment separately from its nature.

The aims or goals of punishment have traditionally fallen into the following categories:

1. Protection of society from the depredations of dangerous persons.
2. Reform of the offender, or deterring the offender from future violations.
3. Deterring persons other than the offender.
4. Vengeance, retribution, or "righting the scales of justice."

PROTECTION OF SOCIETY

In addition to all of the preceding motives, one of the most important is that of affording the innocent members of society protection from the depredations of dangerous persons. One of the major purposes of establishing and maintaining governments is the need of all persons to band together to protect one another from all forms of danger. The skin of man is soft and easily pierced. Whether the danger is from tooth or claw, or from the knives or bullets of members of his own species, man is susceptible to attack. He lacks the instincts and the built-in capacities of some of the lower animals that provide them with protection against the predators that would feed upon them. Men have therefore had to learn to work together with other members of their own kind for mutual protection.

The enjoyment of the earth's bounties is impossible, then, to men who live in a state of anarchy, where all men are in perpetual terror that their lives may be brought to a sudden end. In such a state, there is no true freedom, for there is no security. As Hobbes said long ago, in a state of anarchy

> there is no place for industry, because the fruit thereof is uncertain: and consequently no culture of the earth; no navigation nor use of the commodities that may be imported by sea; no commodious building; no instruments of moving and removing such things as require much force; no knowledge of the face of the earth; no account of time; no arts, no letters; no society; and, which is worst of all, continual fear and danger of violent death; and the life of man solitary, poor, nasty, brutish, and short.[1]

Our ancestors, then, in ages far more remote than historical records go, must have organized themselves into bands or troops or tribes, at least partly because of their instinctive drive for self-preservation. And this same instinctual drive undoubtedly brought them to the conclusion that when a man became a threat to the community or to the individuals within it, the community or its members had the right to use all means necessary to protect themselves from him, including banishment or death, where other means failed. For by violating the primary purposes for which the group had constituted itself, he literally made himself an outlaw—that is, one who is outside the law. By repudiating the discipline of the group, either through his words or through his actions, he placed himself outside the group, and thus lost the immunities that membership in the group conferred upon him, including immunity from physical harm by other members of the group.

REFORM

It is easiest to secure general agreement on the use of punishment to secure reform of the offender. If the infliction of a certain degree of harm will induce a person to conform to standards of behavior that he has previously tended to ignore or to violate, and if his violation of those standards is harmful (or perhaps even annoying) to others, then it might be reasonable to inflict that harm upon him. Presumably from the painful experience of being punished, he will emerge a "better" man than he was before, less likely to engage in unacceptable behavior. Having been punished once, the fear of another penalty—even more severe than the first, perhaps—may suffice to deter him from future offenses.

Reform by punishment often goes hand in hand with efforts at rehabilitation, but the two should not be confused. Out of humane considerations, and a desire to offer the convict the opportunity to find a useful place in society once he has "paid his debt to society," modern penal institutions commonly provide educational and vocational services, as well as facilities for religious services, recreation, and so on. But, though these services may serve the same long-term goal as the penalty that is inflicted upon him, and though they may be administered by the same persons who administer the "penal" institution of which they are a part, they are not part of the penalty itself. If a prisoner had been sentenced to forty lashes, and if, after the penalty was inflicted, the authorities provided him with bandages and soothing ointments, no one would suppose that the bandages and ointments were any part of his punishment. The recreational and educational programs of penal institutions should not be considered a part of the punishment of their inmates (as indeed they are not), but a separate enterprise that may be intended to achieve the same overall results.

DETERRENCE

People learn from the experiences of others as well as from their own. Reading reports of one or two tragic automobile accidents that have resulted from heavy drinking is sufficient to persuade some people not to drive after they have been drinking, or not to drink if they intend to be driving. It is not necessary for them to go through such a tragic experience themselves. Similarly, reading a few reports of the penalties inflicted upon persons who have broken the law is enough to persuade many people not to risk incurring similar penalties for themselves.

As a general rule, as the penalty becomes more severe, people become less likely to engage in the proscribed conduct. If the fine for overtime parking is $1, many people will feel that it is worth the risk, because in the long run, it may turn out to be less expensive than utilizing private parking lots. If the fine is raised to $5, fewer people are likely to take the risk. If it is raised to $15, violators will be fewer still. As the fines go up, the propensity to risk having to pay them goes down. And as other penalties, such as jail terms, corporal punishment, and death are imposed, one may assume that people will become even more reluctant to subject themselves to the suffering and deprivation that they entail. Punishments, then, may serve not only to reform those who have violated the rules, but also to deter those who might otherwise be tempted to violate them.

VENGEANCE OR RETRIBUTION

There is a widespread feeling that justice requires that no man should be allowed the advantage that accrues to him from his misdeeds; that any man who has committed a crime should somehow "pay his debt to society," regardless of whether he is reformed by having to do so and regardless of the deterrent effects such "payment" may have upon others. By his wrongful act, it is said, the offender has "tipped the scales of justice out of balance," and it is necessary to rectify the imbalance by taking from him what he has taken from others.

Some thinkers have said that when an injustice has been committed in the world, there is a stain that must somehow be washed away. The Hebrew Bible and the tragedies of ancient Greece are full of incidents that seem designed to illustrate this concept. Once Oedipus has violated the moral law by committing patricide and incest, misfortune comes to his kingdom and remains until his guilt has been expiated. In the Hebrew Bible many passages clearly presume that the earth itself is stained by the guilt of the murderer, and that nothing can cleanse it of this stain but punishment of the guilty or some form of expiation. Thus, after Cain has murdered his brother, Abel, God says to him, "What have you done? The blood of your brother is crying out to me from the ground! Now you are cursed by the earth that has opened its mouth to swallow the blood of your brother that you have spilled." [2] And again, in connection with the need to punish the murderer, God commands the children of Israel by saying, "You must not defile the land in which you reside, but blood defiles the earth; and there is no way to cleanse the earth of the blood that has been spilled upon it but by the blood of him who has spilled it." [3]

In modern times, the popular demand for retribution is often expressed when the public, informed of a particularly brutal crime, demands revenge, feeling that justice is served only when the guilty party has been punished. Many of those who advocate the return of the death penalty argue that murderers should be put to death "because they deserve to die for their crimes." The popular demand for punishment is often unaccompanied by any thought of reform or deterrence; rather, it seems to be activated by the thought that the criminal ought to "get what is coming to him" or "get what he deserves." There is little evidence of any popular feeling that the earth has been defiled by spilt blood. But some expressions, such as, "The victim of this crime will not rest easy until her killer has been caught and justice has been done," reveal an underlying sentiment that derives from the same source. There seems to be a feeling, too, that one who commits a crime owes a "debt" that he must pay, and that so long as that debt remains unpaid, there is an imbalance in the community or in the universe, a kind of state of being—injustice—that can be rectified only with the punishment of the wrongdoer.

One of the most respected moral thinkers of modern times, Immanuel Kant, maintained that from a moral point of view, punishment is primarily retributive. In discussing the problem he went so far as to say that if the world were about to come to an end, and it was therefore evident that no one would benefit from the punishment of prisoners who have been sentenced to death, those prisoners should be executed nevertheless, in the interest of righting the balance of justice.[4]

Thus far, we have discussed the various aims of punishment without attempting to evaluate them. It is necessary now to turn to that task.

First, it should be noted that each of the justifications or aims discussed above has in fact been considered by respectable philosophers and moralists to be a proper goal for particular penalties or for punishment in general. Furthermore, each of them has a certain plausibility of its own. Whether one considers criminal punishment or the kinds of penalties that parents impose upon their children or that referees assess against ballplayers, the same kinds of rationale seem to be involved. Consider a game for a moment, and see how penalties are exacted and the reasons that might be given for them.

In hockey, a player can be sent to the penalty box for high-sticking. By sitting in that box for a certain period of time, he is, in a sense, subjected to a kind of humiliation that may help to deter him from breaking the rules of the game as he has done. Because his penalty is also a penalty against his team, he has an even greater incentive to reform, for a player who consistently sits in the penalty box is less valuable to his team than one who is out on the ice scoring goals. When one man is excluded from playing, the entire team is weakened, so that the other players have a stronger reason than usual for refraining from engaging in behavior that might be construed by the referees to be rule infractions. Thus, there is both a reformative effect and a deterrent effect in the imposition of penalties upon hockey players.

In addition, there is a clear sense in which the penalty constitutes a "righting" of the unbalanced scales of justice. When members of one team engage in high-sticking, or when they play off-side, they gain an advantage over the other team that ought to be rectified. They should be deprived of their unfair gain, and the other team should be compensated, somehow, for the loss that it incurred (or might have incurred) as a result of the unfair playing of their opponents. Thus, in basketball, the victimized team gets a free throw, in football the offending team loses yardage, and so on.

Players who commit grave offenses may be assessed heavy fines, in professional play, and if their offenses are so serious as to warrant even more serious action, they may be suspended from the league or the association, or be forbidden to play altogether. Thus, the association of players "outlaws" the offender, removing him entirely from the society of participants in that game, on the ground that to permit him to continue to play constitutes a danger, either to the personal safety of other participants or to the respectability of their sport as a whole.

Some people have insisted that some of these justifications for punishment are really no justification at all. The one that has come under the strongest and most consistent attack is the third one, retribution. Some philosophers, particularly those associated with the utilitarian tradition, maintain that only forward-looking penalties (that is, penalties that are principally intended to have some effect upon the future well-being of mankind) ought to be imposed, and that any sanction that is imposed primarily to settle a score for something that has already taken place is unworthy of a civilized society. If no good can reasonably be expected to result from the imposition of the penalty, they say, it is barbarous to impose it. Some (like Hobbes) have gone so far as to say that any penalty that is not forward-looking is no punishment at all, but naked hostility or brutality.

Although these views have some plausibility, they are also subject to certain serious objections. Popular acceptance or rejection of a theory is not necessarily an indication of its correctness, but it is nevertheless a factor that may not be overlooked. As we have already noted, many people accept the view that punishment is at least partially retributive, though few would go so far as Kant went in his extreme formulation of the retributive theory of punishment. The popularity of the retributive view, in spite of powerful attacks upon it over a number of centuries, may be attributed, in part, to a strong feeling on the part of many people that justice is not done unless a criminal suffers for his crime. The sense of justice, or the sense of injustice, may not be overlooked. As Edmund Cahn once observed, "The evolutionary connectedness of human life and of man's relations is the root fact of law. . . . Justice, as many attempted definitions have rather clearly demonstrated, is unwilling to be captured in a formula. Nevertheless, it somehow remains a word of magic evocations. . . . Perhaps the human mind does contain self-evident truths concerning justice, from which legal norms less obvious in their nature may be deduced." [5] When a murderer is convicted of a murder he did not commit, or a gangster who cannot be convicted of any of the crimes that "everyone knows he did" is convicted of income tax evasion, there is little feeling that injustice has been done, because there is a feeling that somehow, they have gotten what they deserved. Such feelings cannot be overlooked by the philosopher.

Suppose that reform and deterrence are the only goals thought to be worth entertaining insofar as punishment is concerned, and that retribution is thought to be irrelevant or uncivilized. It then becomes possible to conceive of circumstances in which one might be able to justify the punishment of innocent persons; that is, of persons whose guilt has not been established in accordance with proper procedures in a court of law.* Suppose, for example, that there is a serious riot and that the entire fabric of society is threatened with destruction. Suppose further that the lives and property of thousands of innocent persons are at stake and that the authorities are unable to apprehend those responsible for the insurrection. Finally, suppose that the authorities have good reason to believe that if one or two of the insurrectionists are brought to justice, the others will be shocked into submission and that the insurrection will thus be brought to an end. In order to deter others from continuing with their unlawful activity, then, it becomes imperative that at least one person be hanged for his part in the insurrection. However, because the authorities do not know the identity of any of the insurrectionists, they have only one choice: to select someone at random, to stage a trial for him, to convict him of complicity in the insurrection, and to execute him in such a way that the loosely knit band of revolutionaries abandons its violent tactics, thus restoring relative tranquility to the state.

Because, according to the supporters of the utilitarian theory, the purpose of punishment is reform or deterrence, and because the "settling of old scores" or the "righting of the unbalanced scales of justice" has nothing to do with punishment, it is difficult to see why only the guilty should be punished. For deterrence, at least, it is quite obvious that the punishment of the innocent will work quite as well. And if "reform" is the aim, it might be argued that one who has been "punished" once, even for a crime that he has not committed, will be even less likely to commit it than he would have been had he never tasted the lash or known what it is to be deprived of his liberty, unless the punishment is hanging, in which case there is no point to any talk of reform, whether the punished party is innocent or guilty.

It would seem, then, that unless some considerations other than reform or deterrence are brought to bear, it is possible to justify the punishment of the innocent—a conclusion that is scarcely likely to commend itself to those who reject retribution on the ground that it is barbarous and uncivilized. On the contrary, it would seem that *some element of retribution* must be involved if we are to make sense of the theory that *only* the guilty ought ever to be punished.

Some people confuse the retributive theory of punishment with certain moral views of what are and what are not proper attitudes to hold toward those who have committed various kinds of wrongful acts. "It is proper," they say, "to be forgiving, and it is uncharitable to be vengeful. Retributive

---

* Such treatment would not qualify as *punishment*. Professor John Rawls has suggested that one might want to call it *telishment* instead. See his classic article, "Two Concepts of Rules," *Philosophical Review*, Vol. 64 (1955), pp. 3 ff. This article has been reprinted numerous times in anthologies and collections.

punishment is therefore morally wrong, though punishment inflicted for reform or deterrent purposes *might* be acceptable since it is more concerned with the future well-being of mankind than with the past misdeeds of a single individual."

This objection is open to several objections. First of all, one may claim that it confuses legal punishment with moral vindictiveness. There is a sense in which legal punishment may be bound up with moral vindictiveness, but it is necessary to sort out the various functions being served and the persons who are operating in the legal system in order to find out just where such vindictiveness may lie, if it exists at all. One might say, for example, that the judge who sentences the defendant is being vindictive; but clearly there is a difference between a judge carrying out the duty prescribed for him by the law—a duty that may be very unpleasant both for him and for the defendant who must suffer the penalty he pronounces— and the same person (i.e., the judge) in his private capacity, as a citizen seeking vengeance against someone who has wronged him. A person who, acting in an official capacity, performs an act that is required of him by the laws, rules, or regulations governing his performance in his job, may sometimes not be said to have the attributes that he would be said to have if he did the same thing as a private citizen. For example, a person who dispenses large sums of money to the poor may properly be described as generous and charitable. But if he is the director of a welfare agency, though he is distributing large sums of money to the poor, that fact alone is not sufficient to justify calling him either generous or charitable. It is not his money, after all, that he is distributing; it is his job to distribute it; and, though one might say that the *government* is generous in its welfare program, it would be incorrect to say that the agent who signs the checks is generous and charitable (though he *might* be both, of course, in his private life). In the same way, the judge who dispenses harsh sentences required by law may not be a harsh man at all. But feeling bound to do what he is required to do by the conditions imposed upon him by the position he holds in the structure of government, he regretfully hands down harsh sentences. It might be appropriate to say that the laws are harsh, or that the government that passed the laws is harsh; but it is not strictly correct to say that the judge who administers those laws is harsh.

Still, a plausible case can be made for the view that the welfare clerk and the judge are generous and vindictive men, respectively. One might point out that either man could find another job, and that both men probably took the jobs that they have because of the kinds of people they are. The judge swears to uphold the law so long as he remains on the bench; but it is always open to a judge to resign his position if he finds that he cannot stomach the laws he is asked to support. If the laws are harsh and vindictive, then, one may argue that a judge who rules in accordance with them, rather than stepping down or finding some loophole, is a harsh and vindictive man.

Still another might point out that more than one judge has ruled in accordance with a law or a precedent of which he strongly disapproved, but remained on the bench because he felt that his presence there enabled him to perform an important and valuable public service. Weighing all the factors and the alternatives, he might conclude that he would have a greater opportunity to make the administration of justice *less* harsh from his position in the judiciary, even though he might occasionally have to make rulings that went very much against his own convictions, than he would as a private citizen. Similarly, the welfare clerk might have taken his job precisely because he was a man of generous spirit, wanting to have a part in distributing money—even if it had to be other people's money— to those who were in need of it. The moral quality of the individual who acts in an official capacity is obviously not amenable to simple solution. We shall encounter it again in our discussion of war crimes and crimes against humanity.

A second objection against those who maintain that retributive punishment is wrong because it is proper to be forgiving and charitable rather than vengeful is based upon the fact that it is not at all clear what it would be like to be "forgiving" in the criminal law. Does it make any sense to speak of anyone forgiving the criminal but his victim? * The district attorney, the judge, the jailer, all of these have jobs to do. Their jobs require that they administer the law. If a person has committed a crime, it is the district attorney's job to prosecute him, the judge is supposed to preside over his trial, and, if he is convicted and sentenced to a prison term, it is the jailer's duty to attend to him for the duration of his stay in prison. None of these people, though, has been harmed by the offender; at least, none of them has been harmed more than any other citizen has. It makes no sense, then, to suggest that any of these officials or employees of the government might "forgive" him, for only those who have been injured by him can forgive him.

There is a sense in which he *might* be "forgiven" by the prosecuting attorney or the judge; that is, if the former decided to abandon the prosecution of his case, or if the latter decided to dismiss the case in spite of the evidence pointing to the defendant's delinquency. But strictly speaking, the state and its officials do not have the power to forgive, though they may *excuse* certain forms of wrongful behavior under appropriate circumstances.

A disposition to forgive is not to be confused with the virtues of mercy or compassion. Though no one but the victim may forgive the criminal who has harmed him, anyone—whether he is victim, judge, prosecuting attorney, or interested bystander—may have compassion for the man who

---

* I have heard well-meaning people upbraid their Jewish neighbors for their "refusal" to forgive the Nazis for their crimes. How *can* they? Only the victims of Nazi murderousness and brutality can forgive them, and most of those victims are no longer living.

has been found guilty in a criminal court. In a criminal case, no one but the judge may be merciful toward the defendant who has been found guilty, for none but the judge is in a position to dispense mercy by mitigating the sentence. Even the judge may be unable to be merciful toward the guilty party, despite any compassionate feelings he may have for him, because his discretionary powers are limited by the law that he is sworn to uphold.*

There is no reason to suppose that the world would be significantly improved if judges were allowed wider discretion than they are. One of the purposes of law is to take certain important matters of public interest out of the hands of individuals and to provide a certain regularity and uniformity of expectation for all the members of the society. This aim would be defeated if judges were given wide powers of discretion in individual cases.

Third, the effect that one man's punishment may have on others, by way of example, is not an adequate reason for punishing him. If it were, penalties could be adjusted by determining how severe they ought to be to deter potential offenders. But in fact, penalties are made more or less severe depending upon the seriousness of the crime that *has been committed*. And so it ought to be. No man should be deprived of his life, his liberty, or his property simply in order that others might be deterred from committing a crime some time in the future. The theory of deterrence says, in effect, that John should be punished in order to prevent Joe from committing a crime in the future, or in other words, that John should be punished for the crime that Joe might commit. This scarcely seems to be consonant with the sense of justice that enjoins against punishing one for the crime of another, and even more against punishing one man for the possible future crime of some other.

In actual practice, all of these motives enter into the treatment accorded to criminal offenders. In some parts of the criminal law there seems to be a greater concern for reform or deterrence, and in others for retribution. The legislator's quandary, when he considers changes in the penal code, rests upon the kinds of confusions we have discussed. Should the penalty be more or less severe? If it is less severe, will this be an invitation to more persons to engage in what is, in the minds of the legislators, a form of wrongful conduct? If it is more severe, will it be too harsh for the crime committed? Consider the drug problem as an example. Many legislators seem to feel, rightly or wrongly, that the use of certain drugs is a practice that ought to be discouraged by the law. The penalties for such use are

---

* Some legal theories hold that judges "make" law, and that they do not merely "follow" what the books say. There is some truth in this theory, but it is limited in its application, particularly where lower, trial courts are concerned. These courts must follow statute law and precedent, except where highly unusual questions arise (the so-called hard cases which Justice Holmes described as being in the "interstices" of the law). When they fail to do so, the chances are that they will be reversed on appeal.

severe, but they could be more severe or more lenient. There is a demand on the part of some people that penalties for drug use be made more lenient. If they are, the opponents argue, the drug problem will increase, for fewer people will be deterred. If they are not, say advocates of reform, our society is guilty of inflicting a harm upon certain persons far out of proportion to the gravity of the offense that they have committed. Notice that the one is arguing on deterrent grounds, the other on retributive. Notice too that retributivists can argue for *less severe* penalties on retributivist principles, in spite of their reputation for heartlessness and lack of compassion.

EXCUSING CONDITIONS

In law and in morals it is recognized that no person should be held responsible or be blamed for any act over which he has no control, as in the following case.

CASE 9. THE KNIFE-WIELDING MOTHER

A rare form of epilepsy causes its victims to repeat, automatically and blindly, certain forms of behavior that can result in great harm to others. In one case, a young mother was slicing a loaf of bread when she was suddenly stricken by an attack of this form of epilepsy. In a trance, completely unaware of what she was doing, she wandered about the kitchen, continuing to make the slicing motions that she had been making when the attack struck her. When she recovered, she was horrified to discover her baby's slashed and mutilated body.

There is no meaningful sense in which this unfortunate woman can be considered to be guilty of causing her baby's death. Where there is no intention to cause harm, and no negligence, there is no guilt or responsibility. Nevertheless, the state has the right to protect other persons against the harm that a person suffering from such a malady might unwittingly inflict upon them in similar circumstances. To be sure, the woman in Case 9 was sick and should not have been punished for the death of her infant. But the state may institutionalize her until it is quite certain that she is cured of her illness, or that her illness is so completely under control that she no longer poses a serious threat to anyone, just as it may quarantine a person with a dangerously infectious disease.

The law recognizes a number of "excusing conditions" that are sufficient to render a person immune to criminal punishment. All of them presuppose that the defendant could not have helped doing what he did or that he could not reasonably have been expected to foresee the consequences of his actions, and that he ought not, therefore, to be held responsible for the action or its consequences. They all entail the absence of *mens rea*, the intention that is necessary as a part of any criminal act. Generally, actions that are not preceded or accompanied by *mens rea* (criminal intention) are not criminal acts. Thus, it is possible to distinguish between murder that is committed by using an automobile as the weapon and an accident in which a pedestrian is killed by an automobile. In murder, there must have been an "intention" on the part of the driver to kill the pedestrian, whereas in an accident, he has no intention to kill the pedestrian.

These excusing conditions are known as *mistake, accident, provocation, duress,* and *insanity.* In addition, some persons, such as very small children, are presumed to be incapable of forming the intention to commit a criminal act.

Suppose a person is charged with manslaughter because he lit a match in a place whose atmosphere was permeated with gas fumes and thereby caused a violent explosion that took the lives of several persons. Suppose also that he lit the match with the intention of lighting a cigarette, completely unaware of the presence of the explosive fumes which had entered the atmosphere undetected from a leak in a gas main. It would be quite unreasonable for the law to hold him responsible for the deaths of the victims of the explosion, for he had no knowledge of the presence of the dangerous gas; he performed an act that was in itself completely innocent and without malice, and no reasonable person could have expected him to foresee the disastrous consequences of igniting a match in that place at that time. Because his action was not malicious, there are no evil inclinations (none that are revealed by his act of lighting the match, at any rate) that punishment might rid him of. Because neither he nor anyone else in similar circumstances could foresee the consequences of lighting a match, no punishment, no matter how severe, could deter others from similar acts in the future. It is hard to see in what sense he might be "guilty" of the deaths of the victims of this tragic accident.

One should not be misled into thinking that *mens rea* is narrowly construed in the law. It is not. For example, it is sometimes assumed that "malice aforethought" and "premeditation" exclude the possibility of a man's being convicted of murder if he fires a gun on a sudden impulse. This is not the case. A man may be convicted of first-degree murder in some jurisdictions even if his intention to fire his weapon was formulated only a split second before he fired it, or, as the law sometimes puts it, "if the time that separated the intention from the act was that that separates one thought from the next." Furthermore, for a conviction of first-degree murder, it is not necessary for the defendant to have intended to kill his victim. If he intended only to "wing" the person at whom he was shooting, and if, when the bullet struck the victim's arm, it shattered his bones in such a way that bone fragments pierced his chest, causing fatal wounds, the defendant may be guilty of first-degree murder in some states. In

New York State, for example, the Revised Penal Code of 1967 states that a person is guilty of murder when "under circumstances evincing a depraved indifference to human life, he recklessly engages in conduct which creates a grave risk of death to another person, and thereby causes the death of another person." In some cases a person may be guilty of murder even when he did not pull the trigger himself and never intended to participate in an action that would cause serious injury to another person. Thus, in the state of New York, a person may be found guilty of murder if he is engaged in an attempt to commit robbery, burglary, or any one of a number of other crimes and if, while engaged in that crime, "he, *or another participant,* if there be any, causes the death of a person other than one of the participants."

It is obvious, therefore, that in the criminal law, the concept of intention, or *mens rea,* is not identical with the common-sense definition of the term that one might encounter in daily, nontechnical conversation. Although the notion of criminal responsibility is closely related to common-sense conceptions of responsibility, it is not identical with them. In the course of its growth and development, the law has evolved special, technical uses of terms that are also employed in nontechnical ways by laymen. It can be dangerous for the layman to confuse the technical and the nontechnical uses of such terms.

STRICT DETERMINISM

Strict determinism is not so much a means of defining an excusing condition under which some persons may be absolved of criminal responsibility as a theory which, if accepted, would lead to the conclusion that all persons should be excused of whatever allegedly criminal misconduct they might have engaged in. It holds that no one is genuinely free, no one can choose his own actions, everyone's actions are determined by pre-existing conditions over which no one has control. It concludes, therefore, that no one ought to be punished or blamed or held responsible for any acts in which he might have participated.

If this theory were true, the conclusion that no one should ever be held responsible for anything would certainly follow. Because excellent treatments of the deterministic theory abound, the following points will suffice for our purposes.

1. If determinism were true, it would follow that no one should ever be rewarded for his "good" deeds, as well as that no one should ever be punished for his "evil" deeds. People should not be held responsible for their behavior, whether it is admirable or totally abominable.

2. If the advocates of determinism were consistent, they would have to admit that it is not appropriate to blame the judges and other officers of the state for punishing the "criminals" who come their way. For the actions of the judges and the jailers and the executioners are as much the

inevitable outcome of *their* genetic heritage and upbringing as the "criminal" behavior of their victims is of theirs. But determinists generally tend to condemn the behavior of judges and other officers of the state. If the criminal cannot help fulfilling his destiny, the jailer and the executioner cannot help fulfilling theirs. A fully consistent determinist would have to refrain from criticism of political leaders, even when the latter plunge their nations into "unjust" wars. But those who advocate merciful treatment of criminals on "deterministic" grounds are often merciless in their denunciations of presidents, secretaries of state, and secretaries of defense.

3. If determinism were true, the "statements" made by determinists would actually not be statements at all. If a "statement" is merely the automatic product of a long sequence of events, it is not an intelligent statement, but merely another event, a brute fact. If strict determinism were true, the "statements" made by determinists would be such brute facts and would have no more meaning than the exclamations of parrots and the grunts of hogs. Determinists, too, would merely be fulfilling their destiny by uttering their so-called theories (how can a series of noises emanating from an automoton be a *theory?*), and would no more be entitled to be heeded than would a parrot trained to utter the same sounds. Indeed, it would make no sense to speak of "heeding" the determinist, because, according to his own theory, everyone does what he is programmed to do anyway.

"ALL CRIMINALS ARE SICK"

One often hears that all criminals are sick and that instead of subjecting them to the brutal treatment that is entailed in punishment, whatever form that might take, a civilized society ought to provide some form of *treatment* for them as it does for all its sick and disabled members. The criminal, it is said, is unable to do other than he does. He is the unfortunate victim of the heredity with which he was endowed and the environment into which he was thrust. He chose neither. Yet both his heredity and his environment have made him what he is. If only he had been raised in other circumstances, he would not have become what he did in fact become. If only he had been born to parents other than his own, or if only the chromosomes that made up the germ plasm from which he came had had slightly different genetic coding, he would have been a very different kind of person from the one that he is today. He is as much the master of his own actions as the epileptic is of his when he thrashes about in a *grand mal* seizure. It makes as much sense to punish the murderer as it does to punish the epileptic or the insane; and, indeed, it was not so very long ago that the latter were treated much as the criminal is treated today. Samuel Butler, in his remarkable novel *Erehwon,* pictured a society where criminals were provided with special hospitals where they might be treated, but persons suffering from various forms of illness were hauled into court and subjected to increasingly severe penalties, according to the severity of their illnesses. Thus, for a common cold, a man might be required to pay only a moderate fine, but for pneumonia he might be sentenced to several years in prison. The burglar, the rapist, and the arsonist, however, were given the benefit of the latest medical advances, and once their treatments were completed they were sent on their way, because they were cured.

Butler's point is obvious. He is suggesting that there is no significant difference between the kinds of conditions that we call illness and the kinds that we call criminal behavior, and that the form of treatment accorded to each ought to be similar. He suggests that it is no more sensible to subject a burglar to fines or prison sentences than it would be to subject persons suffering from gout to such treatment. Thus, for example, John Hospers, after describing an incident in which a woman refused to do what was necessary to save the life of her child until it was too late, concludes:

> Was she responsible for her deed? In ordinary life, after making a mistake, we say, 'Chalk it up to experience.' Here we should say, 'Chalk it up to the neurosis.' *She* could not help it if her neurosis forced her to act this way—she didn't even know what was going on behind the scenes, her conscious self merely acted out its assigned part. This is far more true than is generally realized: criminal actions in general are not actions for which their agents are responsible; the agents are passive, not active—they are victims of a neurotic conflict. Their very hyperactivity is unconsciously determined.[6]

Hospers goes on to explain that this "is not to say that we should not punish criminals." He explains that "for our own protection, we must remove them for our midst so that they can no longer molest and endanger organized society." But such means of self-defense are not quite what is meant by punishment. They are a form of preventive detention. The "criminal" is not punished for his crime, under this scheme, but for the danger he poses to society. In this respect, his treatment does not differ at all from the detention enforced upon the epileptic in our earlier example, or from the victim of tuberculosis, who can legally be required to be hospitalized and quarantined until all danger of infection has been eliminated.

This theory, that all criminals are sick, sounds suspiciously as though it might be guilty of begging the question. What definition of *sickness* entitles one to claim that criminal behavior is necessarily symptomatic of some form of illness? Is it not possible that some criminals are actually quite in possession of all their faculties, but that, unlike most persons, they have chosen to achieve their ends by illegal means rather than by the conventional, legal means that most persons use?

CASE 10. THE MAN WHO BLEW UP HIS MOTHER

A young man once purchased a large insurance policy on his mother's life just before she boarded an airliner that was about to depart from Denver's airport. He had previously placed a bomb in one of her suitcases. The bomb exploded, causing the plane to crash, killing its entire crew and all its passengers, including the young man's mother. He collected the insurance money, but as a result of a careful investigation, he was finally apprehended. Many people are inclined to believe that no one who is in full possession of his faculties, and who is not seriously deranged, would be capable of such a monstrous crime. But the psychiatrist who was assigned to the case concluded that the defendant knew perfectly well what he was doing, that he planned and executed his scheme as carefully as any merchant might have done if he were embarked on a major business enterprise, and that it was impossible to diagnose any particular mental illness as being responsible for his bizarre behavior. The defendant was accordingly found guilty and was executed in Colorado's gas chamber.

Those who say that all criminals are sick often have in mind those offenders who have engaged in the most brutal forms of crime—rape, armed robbery, murder, and the like. There is little reason to doubt that some people who commit such crimes *are* sick. Some of them are subject to uncontrollable fits of rage and passion, others are known to be subject to delusions and hallucinations. Whether the usual procedures of the criminal law should be brought to bear upon such persons, and whether they should be subject to punishment in the usual sense, has been discussed previously. But the proponents of the theory now under discussion tend to forget another very important class of criminals—those who clearly do not act in fits of passion, but with due deliberation, carefully and methodically working out their plans of action, sometimes alone, but often in concert with others. Their motives are frequently the same as those of perfectly normal persons. They want the better things in life; they want the leisure to enjoy the benefits of their prosperity; they want to provide their families with nice homes, nice clothes, and the little amenities that our society provides and that most of us consider to be good and desirable. The manner in which they attempt to achieve those goals, however, is not legal. Ordinarily, those who engage in such illegal activities do so with the hope that they will not be caught. They are often quite clear-headed about the entire business. They seldom become involved because of paranoid delusions or schizophrenic flights from reality. And interestingly enough, they seldom receive the attention of the press or become the objects of campaigns of citizens demanding that they be considered the unfortunate victims of circumstances. Consider the embezzler, for example, and the businessman who is convicted of income tax evasion. Consider also the corporation executive who engages in illegal restraint of trade or monopolistic practices, and the food processor who allows his products to become contaminated. And finally, consider the logger who deliberately encroaches upon national park land, felling trees that will not be replaced for generations, if ever; and the operator of a steel mill who knows that his smokestacks and the sewer lines of his plant are pouring out effluents that are poisoning the atmosphere and the water supplies of the towns downriver. If these persons were called to account for their lawless behavior, for their callous disregard of the public welfare and their duties as citizens, and for their unjust encroachments upon the property of the state and their depredations against their fellow citizens, it is unlikely that those who argue so vehemently on behalf of the rights of murderers and rapists would form committees to secure lesser penalties for these businessmen; and it is even less likely that they would urge the public to think of these men as the victims of their genetic heritage and their environment, or that they would plead that they were unable to choose to do other than they did and that they should therefore be given medical treatment rather than the full penalties prescribed by law.

Those who urge that criminal punishment be abandoned in favor of some form of medical treatment tend to forget about such crimes as fraud, forgery, counterfeiting, perjury, bribery, graft, corruption of public officials, and contempt. It is difficult to see how a case can be made for the view that such crimes are exclusively the products of diseased minds or of persons who are incapable of behaving other than they do. The con artist who sets up an elaborate plot to persuade an old widow to hand over to him her life's savings acts with as much deliberation and foresight as the scientist who sets up a new experiment in his laboratory, the public official who plans a new election campaign, the sales manager of a large firm who sets up an elaborate advertising campaign, or the architect who draws up the blueprints for a new building.

INSANITY

The laws governing pleas of insanity are among the most seriously disputed of all. According to the M'Naghten Rules, which still govern many cases, insanity is defined as a state in which the perpetrator of an otherwise criminal act is unable to distinguish between right and wrong, or is under an insane delusion as to circumstances which, if true, would relieve him of responsibility, or is so deranged that the commission of his act is the natural consequence of his delusion. When any of these conditions is present, the perpetrator of the act is regarded as insane and is not criminally responsible. In some jurisdictions, the Durham Rule, which provides that the accused is "not criminally responsible if his unlawful act was the product of a mental disease or mental defect," has been adopted.

Under the older and more widely accepted M'Naghten Rules, the jury had the onerous task of determining whether the accused was capable of distinguishing right from wrong at the time he committed the act in question. Under the Durham Rule, the existence of a state of mental disease or mental defect at the time of the "crime" is treated as an objective fact upon which expert testimony can be given.

In spite of the liberalization of the rule governing the definition of insanity, relatively few cases end with a verdict of insanity. Not the least of the reasons is the confusion of the "experts" themselves. For every psychiatrist that the defense is able to produce, the prosecution is able to produce twenty who are prepared to testify that the defendant's mental state did not so interfere with his behavior that he was unable to control his actions. There is the ever-present suspicion that the defendant may be malingering, feigning mental illness. And finally, there is the utter absurdity of the views of some of the psychiatrists who are called upon to testify in criminal trials. For example, one noted psychiatrist, explaining why prostitutes steal money from their clients, offered the following explanation: "A prostitute is by the nature of her occupation a robber of men's strength. She steals their virility. Unconsciously, therefore, she seeks continuously to carry out this robbery of men, though in another form." He called this form of larceny a "castration complex." One critic wondered whether the explanation might be somewhat simpler. Perhaps, he said, prostitutes take money from the pockets of their clients because they like money!

In another case a psychiatrist was called to speak on behalf of a young man who pleaded guilty to a charge of indecent assault. He testified that the lad had "defective eyesight, and that this handicap was the cause of certain emotional disturbances which were the real cause of the man's behavior." The psychiatrist advised the court that what the prisoner really needed was not punishment for the crime of rape, but a new pair of eyeglasses!

Such ludicrous opinions scarcely serve the interests either of the defendants or of justice. They do serve to indicate how far the practitioners of psychiatry may really be from having any scientific justification for being given the last word on the dispensation of criminal justice. This is not intended to deny the importance of psychiatric testimony in some cases. It is merely to suggest that we are a very long way indeed from the day when we should be prepared uncritically to accept any psychiatrist's claim that all criminals are in need of his or his colleagues' services, and that we should maintain a healthy skepticism toward any psychiatrist's judgment that all criminals are so ill at the time when they commit their crimes as to deserve to be declared innocent by reason of insanity.

Nevertheless, there are cases in which the accused are clearly suffering from serious mental diseases which so impair their judgment or functioning as to render them totally incapable of making reasoned decisions or of behaving in any way other than in a violent and destructive one. Such persons should not be punished for their acts, for the latter are as little *their* acts as they would have been if they had occurred by accident or by mistake. The most serious problem is the difficulty of proof. How does one distinguish between a person who has suffered from an "irresistible impulse" and one who has simply not resisted the impulse that he had? There are cases where the evidence is so strong that it would be unreasonable to conclude that the defendant could have acted other than he did. From the existence of doubtful cases, one should not conclude that there are no meaningful criteria for distinguishing between situations where the defendant is lying or malingering and those where he is not.

Clearly, much work remains to be done in this area. It will not do, however, to conclude out of hand either that all persons who have committed criminal acts are criminally responsible or that none of them are.

8

Imprisonment

From the early Middle Ages until relatively modern times, punishment was as much for the salvation of the sinner's soul as it was for the protection of the innocent and the deterrence of crime. If nothing else would bring the sinner to cry out to his Lord for mercy, the lash, the rack, the gallows, or the flames could be counted upon to convince him to do so.

Some groups of Puritans concluded that a long stretch of absolute silence, combined with isolation, the stench of human excreta, vermin, and a starvation diet would encourage those who did the work of Satan to repent. Thus, for the greater glory of God, they built sanctuaries of penitence which were called, appropriately, penitentiaries.

In the late eighteenth century, and on into the nineteenth and twentieth centuries, movements for prison reform have been a constant feature of the social and political scene in England and in North America. The argument has generally centered upon the wisdom of "coddling" criminals by allowing them to live in quarters that had at least minimal standards of hygiene and comfort. At times, too, the debate has been devoted to the question of the kind of treatment that ought to be accorded prisoners in the penitentiaries. Should they be forced to engage in hard labor, labor that was basically useless, serving no function other than its supposed "softening" effect upon the criminals themselves? The inmates of some prisons have been forced to work at splitting rocks, forever having to start a new pile when the old one was depleted. Others have had to walk treadmills or turn cranks that merely plowed through piles of sand—backbreaking, degrading, dehumanizing labor.

In some prisons, inmates were confined in long rows of steel cages. They were cut off, not only from the rest of humanity, but even from the world of nature.

In some prisons the sanitation was so primitive that disease was rampant, sometimes spreading to the general community through delivery men, visitors, and released prisoners. The sanitation system consisted of buckets that were left in each cell. These were emptied by the prisoners once a day into open holes or trenches that carried the waste out, whenever they were not blocked.

"In prisons which are really meant to keep the multitude in order," an English divine wrote in 1816, "and to be a terror to evil-doers, there must be no sharing of profits—no visiting of friends—no education but religious education—no freedom of diet, no weavers' looms or carpenters' benches. There must be a great deal of solitude; coarse food; a dress of shame; hard, incessant, irksome, eternal labour; a planned and regulated and unrelenting exclusion of happiness and comfort."

Over the years, reformers have managed to overcome some of these "Christian" sentiments, and have brought some measure of humanity to the administration of a few prisons. The addition of medical treatment for the sick, wholesome (if unappetizing) food, opportunities for education, libraries, meaningful work, and counseling services have done much to alleviate the suffering of hundreds of thousands of men and women who are consigned to spend years in penal institutions.

Nevertheless, there remain many vestiges of the primitive and barbaric prisons of the eighteenth century. In the United States a third of all prisons in use were built in the last century, more than seventy years ago. Those that are in use sometimes house two, three, or even four times as many prisoners as they were built to accommodate. Small cells become crowded dormitories. Experiments have repeatedly demonstrated that rats forced to live in overcrowded conditions go mad, becoming vicious and destructive and exhibiting the symptoms of schizophrenia. The same thing happens to men, but the lesson seems to have made no difference in prison architecture or in the budgets allotted by state legislatures to the penal system. Nor has knowledge of this fact had much effect upon the thought of those who continue to believe that prison sentences are suitable penalties to inflict upon men who have committed crimes against society.

When a man is sent to prison, what is the penalty that is being imposed upon him? Clearly, it must be the deprivation of the liberties that he would otherwise have enjoyed. But consider the liberties that are taken away from him. He is taken away from his wife, from his parents, from his children. He is deprived of every opportunity to engage in useful work. He is unnaturally deprived of every possible normal outlet for his sexual impulses, and is thus left with no alternatives but homosexual relations and masturbation to relieve himself of the agony of sexual starvation. He cannot choose his own associates, but must live in close quarters with every manner of derelict. His conversation may be confined to talk about sex, crime, and money, for lack of anyone with whom to discuss other topics. He may be subjected to sexual assaults by fellow inmates, to physical assaults by inmates or guards, and to a constant psychological conditioning that renders him outwardly subservient and dependent while he rages inside. After several years of such torment, he is supposed to emerge from his cell a grateful member of the society which condemned him to it. It is hardly surprising that of every thousand persons in maximum security prisons in Canada, five either commit suicide or attempt to do so. This is nearly five times the rate for all Canadians.

When he comes out, his job is gone, his wife may be gone, his family life is destroyed. He must learn to be independent again, to find his own way, to make his own meals, to find gainful employment and to stay out of trouble. But his criminal record follows him everywhere, making it impossible in most instances to find a decent job. Try as he may, he may not be *able* to find an employer who is willing to hire an ex-con, to trust him with his goods or to give him access to his money. How, then, is it possible that people are surprised when they read the sorry statistics that reveal that more than half of all the men and women released from prison are back again within five years? These are the ex-prisoners who are caught and convicted! No one knows how many are not, though they too may have returned to a life of crime because nothing else was open to them.

In spite of the efforts of some foresighted penologists, too many institutions today are still too small, too crowded, and too backward in their treatment of the criminal offender. Though they claim to be principally interested in reform, they still function as if they were primarily interested in vengeance. Clearly, when a man is condemned to a prison sentence, his punishment is the deprivation of liberty itself. The prison is not a place which is supposed to add to this most fundamental deprivation by degrading him and dehumanizing him and taking away every vestige of human dignity that is left to him. To pile punishment upon punishment day after day is neither humane nor civilized. Many prisons are no better than the old slave ships, though if anyone were to propose that the latter be returned to service, an outraged howl of protest would immediately—and rightly—be raised.

No one who has ever read an account of a Siberian prison camp written by a former inmate would suppose that it is a civilized form of penal institution. It is cruel and inhuman. But in some respects, it is superior to the American prison. For one thing, convicts sent to Siberia are frequently allowed to bring their wives along, so that they are able to maintain some degree of sexual normalcy in their lives and are not completely separated from their families.

In a few parts of the United States, arrangements are made for prison inmates to spend some time alone with their wives. Parchman Prison in

Mississippi, for example, has cottages on the prison grounds that married men may occupy on weekends with their wives. In this way, the men are able to maintain some semblance of a normal sex life, and their wives are able to do so as well, without resorting to adultery or divorce. But such facilities are available to a very small percentage of all the prison inmates in the United States.

In a few institutions, weekend passes are available; in others, it is possible for inmates who are nearing the end of their terms to work on the outside, returning to the institution at night and on weekends. Thus, the men begin their rehabilitation before they leave their prison cells for good. Elsewhere, there are halfway houses or other rehabilitation centers that devote their efforts to making the transition from prison life to life outside the prison walls a little easier.

It must be pointed out once again that one ought not to confuse rehabilitation with punishment, at least from a purely philosophical point of view. Nevertheless, if one is concerned about the long-run results of the penal system and its moral justifications, then one must consider both the effects that imprisonment has upon the prison population and the extent to which prison conditions are degrading and dehumanizing to those persons who are subjected to them.

Vocational training, an important aspect of the rehabilitative work of any modern prison, is often handicapped by lack of skilled instructors and even more by opposition from unions and industries who object to competition from prison laborers. More than one farsighted project has been scuttled by just such opposition on the part of powerful forces within the community.

Mental health services, so obviously important to any meaningful rehabilitation of that very large proportion of prison inmates who are mentally ill, are quite minimal. It is not likely that they will be improved significantly, in view of the extreme shortage of trained personnel and the general unwillingness of lawmakers to allocate large sums of money to such programs.

Most of the personnel in these systems (some 80 per cent in the United States) are concerned solely with custodial duties. In short, they are the guards and maintenance personnel who supervise the prisoners while they are in custody. The remainder perform the many other tasks that make up the penal system, including the so-called rehabilitative tasks, parole supervision, and the like. Because there are so few of them, and because they must service such large numbers of prisoners or parolees, it is impossible for them to give meaningful attention to any of the convicts who come under their jurisdiction. When they are saddled with a myriad other tasks in addition, it becomes all but impossible for them to do more than give token attention to the rehabilitation of the men and women whom they are supposed to help.

The so-called rehabilitative function of the prison system is, for the most part, purely fictitious. Prisons breed contempt for the entire legal system in the minds of those who must serve time in them. When a man is sent to jail, he knows as well as anyone can that he is being sent there not because society is genuinely interested in making him a better man, in giving him a new opportunity to remake his life, but because society wants to punish him for a crime that he has been found guilty of having committed. He knows as well as anyone that his punishment is to consist of a multitude of deprivations. But no one can ever anticipate the genuine reality of prison life unless he has had to live through it himself. Far from being the "hotel" that so many conservative critics say it is, even the most modern prison facility is still a penitentiary—a place where men are supposed to repent but where instead (with few exceptions) they learn more about the techniques of crime as they are brutalized and degraded by the institution. If education consists at least partially of character building, then prisons must be considered antieducational institutions, because they serve so often to destroy character and to instil hatred, anger, and brutality in those who enter them.

Because no one is very clear about the real purpose of prison (is it penal, rehabilitative, or custodial?), there is no clear policy on the sentencing of offenders. A man convicted of a certain crime in a certain city may be fined $100. Another man, in the same city, convicted of the same crime, may be sentenced to five years in prison. One judge may think principally of rehabilitation, and thus sentence the offender who stands before him to a period of probation. The other may be more concerned with the protection of society or with the punitive aspects of criminal punishment, and will sentence the offender who stands before him to a long stretch in prison. Or, to make the entire business even more tragic, the same judge, with the same motives, may sometimes do the one and sometimes the other.

Some contemporary reformers argue in favor of the indeterminate sentence. By setting an upper limit ("Not more than ten years," for example), they believe that the judge is able to permit the introduction of a degree of flexibility into the penal system that ultimately will result in better administration of justice and better treatment of the offender; for the latter will be able to win his release much earlier by cooperation with the authorities. There is some reason to doubt, however, whether placing such power in the hands of prison officials or parole boards is necessarily beneficial. How is the system improved if the sentencing is done, in effect, by a prison official or a parole board, rather than by a judge? Will these officials possess a kind of wisdom that judges do not possess? Will they have meaningful information on the chances of a particular prisoner's returning to a life of crime that the judge does not possess? Are they more or less likely to be influenced in their decisions by such considerations as the administrative burden of maintaining an overcrowded prison facility, or by personal whims and prejudices? How meaningful can such a proposal be when one of the strongest advocates of the indeterminate sentence admits that the cunning of some prisoners is such that even the most skilled professional prison officials can be fooled by them? In the next breath he admits that "we know most prisoners who are released will commit more crimes."

The prison, as it exists in the modern democracies, is an archaic relic of an outmoded and cruel religious and social ethic. The thesis that life in prison is somehow a more desirable fate than death in the gas chamber is dubious at best. Most penal institutions are inhumane places where men are deprived, not only of their liberties, but even of such elementary rights as will enable them to preserve their human dignity. Prisoners may be stripped of their rights as citizens, including the right to return to the practice of their occupations, once they have "paid their debts to society." How, then, have they been helped along the way to "repentance" or "atonement"?

One common rejoinder is this: "No one is to blame but the criminal himself. He knew the price of his misbehavior before he misbehaved. It was his own mischief that brought this fate down upon him. Now let him suffer the consequences."

But this answer is too facile. It will not do under the reformative theory, under the rehabilitative theory, or for that matter, even under the deterrent theory. If the aim of punishment is reform or (as some people incorrectly suppose) rehabilitation, then clearly a form of treatment that demonstrably fails to perform either function can hardly be appropriate for such functions. As for deterrence, one would hope not only that other potential criminals would be deterred by a given convict's punishment, but that he would himself be deterred from further offenses. Any treatment that actually increases both the number and the "quality" of offenses (as the "school for criminals" manifestly does) can hardly serve as a model of deterrence. When even the men who have been to prison are not deterred by the fear of being returned there from committing further crimes, one may suspect that its deterrent effects on others may be quite minimal.

As for the retributive theory, there is nothing in the theory itself that would justify such cruel and unrelenting forms of punishment. A retributivist can quite properly advocate the death penalty, but insist that prison is too cruel and inhuman to be tolerated in a civilized society. He might add the observation that under his theory, if a man has been punished for his crime once, there is no justification for punishing him further. If a man has been deprived of all his liberties for a period of time, it is unjust to deprive him of anything, including any of the rights he might have enjoyed in society if he had never been convicted of a crime, once he has been punished. Having paid his debt, he should not be asked to continue to pay. The exaction of interest upon such a debt is the worst form of usury imaginable.

During the Middle Ages, men and women were sometimes "immured" as a form of punishment for the worst sorts of crimes. They were forced to stand in a given spot, and a brick wall was then built all around them. Once the last brick was laid in place, it was not long before they would die of suffocation—or, if the wall was not airtight, of thirst and starvation. Prisons, however, were unknown, except for certain relatively small institutions that were used for the incarceration of suspects and criminals prior to their trials and executions. In ancient times, prisons were used on occasion, as we can see in the Biblical story of Joseph, but those occasions seem to have been quite rare. Our ancestors generally executed criminals, mutilated them, or lashed them and sent them home. They sometimes sent them off to exile or enslaved them. According to the Talmud, in ancient Israel, when a man was convicted of a noncapital crime, he was fined or flogged if the law called for that kind of punishment. Otherwise, he was sold into slavery for a period not to exceed six years. During that six-year period, he was permitted to engage in any occupation that was suitable to his station in life prior to his conviction. If he were a physician, for example, he might continue to practice medicine. If he were a skilled laborer, he would continue to do the kind of work that he was trained to do, and all of his earnings would go to the family of the person who had been harmed by his violation of the law. No one, however, could ever be sent to prison, or stripped of his dignity as a human being. In some Scandinavian countries, men convicted of criminal offenses are permitted to return to their families and to their jobs, unless they are deemed to be so dangerous to themselves or to others that they *must* be institutionalized, but a portion of their earnings is turned over to the victims of their crimes. Thus, the offender is not required to "pay his debt to society" by being deprived of rights or liberties. Instead, he must literally pay the debt he owes to the person whose rights he violated. He must compensate him for the harm he has done. Compensation is not punishment, though the two bear some resemblances to one another. If one is prepared to give up punishment altogether, for some crimes, at least, then some form of enforced compensation would seem to be a reasonable substitute. It is certainly less damaging to the offender and his family, and thus to society, in the long run, than the prison system with all its manifest evils. And it has the further advantage that those who are hurt most by the criminal's behavior—his victims and their families—are compensated, to some extent, at least, for the losses they have suffered. The criminal whose life is wasted away in prison can contribute nothing to the alleviation of the suffering of his victims. Instead, suffering is added to suffering with no evident advantage to society, which not only loses a potentially productive member, but must provide for all his needs in an expensive custodial institution, and then suffer from his further offenses once he is released. It is difficult to conceive of a form of punishment that has more disadvantages—socially, economically, and morally—than the imprisonment of men who might otherwise be doing useful work.

9

The Death Penalty

Though the Ten Commandments are often quoted as saying, "Thou shalt not kill," that passage is more correctly translated, "Thou shalt not commit murder." It is all too easy to gloss over the important distinctions entailed by these words, but in life, the distinctions will remain, whether or not we choose to acknowledge them.

It is said that life is sacred, that no decision is more momentous than the decision to take a man's life. Some people insist that no man ever has the right to take any other man's life, no matter what the provocations or the circumstances. Others allege that there are occasions when homicide is justifiable.

Some say that no war is ever justified and that the taking of human life in war is always morally wrong. Others maintain that in a struggle for national survival, or even for national honor, it is permissible, and perhaps even noble, to take the lives of enemy combatants.

Some say that the police have a right, and perhaps even a duty, to take the life of a felon who is fleeing or resisting arrest, and that any citizen has the right to take the life of another who is threatening him with a deadly weapon; others deny that anyone ever has the right to take the life of another human being, even under such extreme circumstances.

Some say that there are some offenses for which the death penalty is appropriate. Others argue that for the state to take the life of any of its citizens, even those who have been convicted of the worst offenses against their fellow citizens and against society (such as rape, kidnapping, treason, and murder), is uncivilized and unjustifiable.

If *all* deliberate taking of human life is morally wrong, then no meaningful distinction may be drawn between killing and murder as those terms are applied to human beings.* If one is to be consistent and uphold the strong

* It may be possible for those who oppose all deliberate taking of human life to preserve the distinction between "manslaughter," "accidental homicide," and "murder,"

position, then it would seem that one would be obliged, not only to oppose capital punishment and war, but also killing in self-defense, abortion, and euthanasia.

In addition to the moral argument that all taking of human life is tantamount to murder (which seems highly suspect on the face of it), a number of arguments have been put forth by those who oppose capital punishment. The most important of them may be reduced to the following.

1. Capital punishment cannot be considered a reformative measure. Statistically, there is no evidence that it has a significant deterrent effect. Therefore, it must be a retributive measure, stemming from primitive and uncivilized impulses for revenge.

2. A glance at the figures on executions carried out shows quite clearly that the poor and the underprivileged are executed far more often than the rich and that black citizens suffer the death penalty far out of proportion to their numbers in the general population. It is apparent, therefore, that the death penalty is a form of repression used against the poor and the black by the rich and the powerful.

3. All too often have innocent men been sentenced to death. Human life is too sacred to be taken when there is even the slightest possibility that justice has not been done. If a man accused and convicted of a serious crime is subjected to any other form of punishment, the penalty is not irrevocable. He can be released from prison if an error is found, and compensated for the time he has lost. But there is no way to call a man back from the grave if he has been executed for a crime he has not committed.

4. The use of the death penalty diminishes the value that is placed upon human life. When the state itself takes the lives of its citizens, there is an inevitable pandering to the desire of some people for the sensational. The spectacle of the deliberate snuffing out of a human life, with all the bizarre ceremony that accompanies it, is hideous and revolting to anyone who possesses civilized sensibilities; it is degrading to the state itself; and it exercises a corrupting influence upon those who follow it through the detailed reports that inevitably follow. Far from exercising a salutary influence upon the population, capital punishment can be maleficent, arousing perverse and vicious dispositions in the hearts of men. Inmates of prisons where executions take place, knowing the men who sit in death row, are *more* likely, rather than less, to commit murder if they return to a life of crime upon their release; for, having seen the torment of the condemned, they are not likely to suffer arrest lightly. And those who are mentally unstable have been known to emulate the crimes of men who have become notorious because of their long trials and the wide publicity that is accorded them.

5. Juries and judges in both trial courts and appellate courts are likely to strain the evidence and the law to acquit those accused of capital offenses, so

---

as a means of apportioning blame, responsibility, guilt, or punishment to those who have been involved in the killing of a human being.

repugnant is capital punishment to the moral feelings of men today. Juries may acquit even in the face of clear evidence that the accused is guilty of a capital crime. Justice is thus perverted by the existence of the death penalty. And the years of delay during the long appeal process subject the victim to unconscionable torments.

These, then, are the principal arguments raised by those who favor abolition of capital punishment. There is much to commend them to any humane person who has genuine reverence for human life. But the arguments seem to be unsound.

1. It is true, of course, that capital punishment is not a reformative measure. It is not true, however, that anyone has demonstrated that it does not have a deterrent effect. There is no clear proof that it *does* have such an effect, but one must not confuse the lack of proof for the proposition that capital punishment *does* deter with proof of the proposition that it *does not*. Thus far, the evidence is completely inconclusive.

It is sometimes argued that the rates of murder committed in adjacent states, where one has and the other does not have the death penalty, are quite comparable, thus demonstrating that the death penalty makes no difference. Indeed, some states that still have the death penalty have significantly *higher* crime rates and *higher* incidence of murder than others that have abolished the death penalty. However, such statistics prove nothing. Even those who believe that the death penalty is a deterrent acknowledge that other factors enter into the crime rate, including economic, political, social, and psychological conditions. Furthermore, murderers are not always fully aware of the latest legal developments in the state in which they happen to commit their crimes. The long-term effects of many centuries of capital punishment very likely continue to influence the conduct of many persons. A believer in the deterrent effect of the death penalty need not suppose that there are hundreds of potential murderers who are straining at the bit, waiting for the death penalty to be abolished so that they can commit their crimes without fear of being executed.

Even after the death penalty has been abolished, the deterrent effect is likely to linger on for quite some time. It is impossible to determine when the fear of the death penalty ceases to be effective. If there is a significant decline in the homicide rate after the abolition of the death penalty, it does not necessarily follow that the abolition of the penalty was the cause of the decline in homicides. Consider, for example, the following facts: In England, the ten-year average murder rate fell from 4.1 to 3.3 per million from 1910 to 1939, a period during which England not only had the death penalty, but used it. Suppose the death penalty had been abolished in 1910, and suppose further that this had resulted in 100 more murders than were actually committed during that period. There would still have been a decline in the murder rate from 4.1 to 3.5 per million. This would have led critics of the death penalty to the erroneous conclusion that the abolition of capital punishment had been followed by a decrease in the murder rate, and would seem to have lent support to their contention that there is no connection between the death penalty and the crime rate.[1]

It is quite possible, therefore, to argue that the death penalty does act as a deterrent, or at least that no one has proved that it does not. Furthermore, as we have attempted to show, even if one accepts a retributive theory of punishment, it does not necessarily follow that one is brutal or uncivilized. On the contrary, one can make a very good case for the view that of all the justifications for punishment, retribution is the one that allows the greatest measure of human dignity to the criminal.

2. It is true that the poor and the black are executed far more often than their numbers in the population would warrant. From 1930 to the end of 1970, 2,066 Negroes and 1,751 white persons were executed in the United States, though in the total population, black citizens were outnumbered by white eight to one. It is well known that neither death nor any other severe penalty is often imposed upon those who are at the top of the economic ladder, even though they may have committed the same crimes as those who are at the bottom. But this is not an argument, either against the death penalty or against any other form of punishment. It is an argument against the unjust and inequitable distribution of penalties. If the trials of wealthy men are less likely to result in convictions than those of poor men, then something must be done to reform the procedures in criminal courts. If those who have money and standing in the community are less likely to be charged with serious offenses than their less affluent fellow citizens, then there should be a major overhaul of the entire system of criminal justice, from the district attorney's office on down. But the maldistribution of penalties is no argument against any particular form of penalty.

3. Very few men have been executed for crimes they have not committed, at least in modern times, in the United States, in Canada, or in Great Britain. Because of the sanctity that attaches to human life in these countries, judges and juries are exceptionally cautious in such cases, tending to give the defendants the benefit of the doubt as far as possible.

It must be admitted, however, that mistakes can occur, and sometimes have, and that innocent men have lost their lives through judicial error.

This too is inevitable in any aspect of any judicial system. No human institution is infallible. It is unreasonable to expect any legal system to be so. Any error that results in the loss of a human life is tragic and should be avoided if it is at all possible to do so. But there are risks to living in any society. There are risks that all men take, even possibly fatal risks, every time they step into an automobile or an airplane. It is our duty to minimize these risks as much as possible, but it seems unlikely that they will ever be completely eliminated from human life. If there are overriding reasons for the maintenance of the death penalty, then perhaps the risk of inflicting the death penalty (or the risk of suffering it) when it is not deserved is one that society and the persons who live within it will have to bear.

It is a mistake to suppose that the death penalty is the only one that is irrevocable. Time spent in prison can never be regained. The horror and tragedy that afflict a man and his family when he is sent away for a cruel and monstrous crime, whether he has committed it or not, can never be effaced. More than one man has been released from prison only to find that his wife had deserted him and gone to another man, that his children were no longer his in any meaningful sense of the word, that his job was gone, that his friends no longer welcomed him into their midst—in short, that his life had as truly been destroyed as if he had been executed, but that the suffering and anguish had been prolonged. The assumption that such penalties are "revocable" or are in any way preferable to the death penalty is dubious at best. Still, there is much truth in the view that the death penalty is irrevocable in a sense that does not apply to any other, for despite all that has been said above, society cannot repair the damage that has been done to a man who has been executed and cannot offer him an opportunity to restore his shattered life, whereas those who have suffered wrongful penalties of other kinds can be granted reparations and can attempt to rebuild their lives.

4. The deleterious effects of sensational publicity attending the trials and executions of notorious criminals cannot be gainsaid. But this is more an argument for a responsible press than for a revision of the criminal code. And it is an argument for a more responsible education of our people, one that will inculcate in them a sensitivity to human suffering and a feeling of repugnance toward the cheap, lurid voyeurism of the yellow press. But it is no more an argument for the abolition of the death penalty than the exploitation of sex by pornographers would be for the abolition of love.

There is no solid evidence that capital punishment itself leads persons who would otherwise have "gone straight" to lives of crime. The publicity attending the trials of notorious criminals and their executions *might* serve as a catalyst, setting off reactions in the minds of men who were already seriously unbalanced, stimulating them to commit crimes to which they were already disposed. Even this, however, is not a reason to interfere with the freedom of the press (which is not at issue here), for only through the publicity that a case receives can it have the deterrent effect that one hopes it will have.

5. Again, from the fact that judges and juries are not disposed to convict men of charges that carry the death penalty, it does not follow that the death penalty should be abolished. It follows that if the death penalty is retained, judges and juries must be prepared to render judgments in accordance with the law *as it is*, and not as they would like it to be. If any system of law is to work, it must be administered dispassionately and fairly, and those who are involved in decision making must proceed in accordance with the rules. If they attempt to let their consciences rather than the facts and the law be their guides—in spite of what some television detective and lawyer series would have us believe—they result not in justice, but in a perversion of justice.

One must concede that the long delay between judgment and execution must be a dreadful experience for those who must live through it. There is nothing in the nature of the death penalty itself that requires that there be such extremely long and agonizing delays, or so many stays of execution as there have been in the United States in recent years. In England there was never a delay of more than three months between the sentence and the execution. Because of the enormously complex system of government in the United States and the many opportunities its judicial system affords a condemned man to appeal his sentence, this period has sometimes stretched out to many years. But this is not an argument against the death penalty itself so much as an argument against certain aspects of the system, if it is even that. One finds it difficult to suppose that anyone would seriously want to have the execution proceed with greater speed, if that meant that a condemned man might have fewer avenues of appeal open to him or that his appeals might be given less than the fullest attention of those to whom they were directed.

So much, then, for the arguments of those who are opposed to the death penalty. What reasons can be adduced in its favor?

If part, at least, of the purpose of punishment is deterrence, then it is evident that certain major crimes cannot possibly be deterred by any other penalty. The revolutionary who contemplates blowing up a school bus as a means of terrorizing the population is not likely to be deterred by the threat of life imprisonment, for he believes that even if he is caught, he will be released and be given a hero's welcome by his fellow revolutionaries when the revolution succeeds. Similarly, the potential traitor in wartime will not be deterred from betraying his country by the fear of life imprisonment, for he believes that when his country is "liberated" by the enemy, his imprisonment will be brought to an end. The same must be true of criminals who are already serving life sentences in prison. The threat of yet another lengthy sentence is meaningless, and can therefore have no effect at all upon the lifer who contemplates doing in his cellmate or the guard on duty in his cell block. If anything at all will deter such men from the crimes they are contemplating, nothing less than the death penalty will do. Even in those jurisdictions where the death penalty has been abolished for most other crimes, these crimes often continue to be punishable by death.

One might argue that men bent on murder or revolution will not be deterred by any penalty, no matter how severe. But with the exception of those who are insane (who are not included in this discussion, because they are not punishable) and those fanatics who would welcome martyrdom, men generally tend to weigh costs or the risks of acts that they contemplate. When the costs or the risks are too high, they usually do not do them. As the costs go down, the temptation to perform the act is more often translated into action. Thus, where the penalty for speeding is $5, people are more likely to violate the law than they are if the penalty is $50. When potential speeders realize that they are more likely to be caught (e.g., when they fear that a policeman may be waiting around the corner), they are more likely to keep to the legal speed limit. It is next to impossible to reduce the pleasures or the imagined advantage that people might derive from performing acts that the law forbids. However, the law is able to increase both the cost of performing such acts and the risks entailed by them. By increasing the penalties attached to behavior that they are particularly anxious to deter, legislators can assure, to a higher degree, that fewer people will indulge in the forbidden behavior.

If human life is sacred, as opponents of the death penalty say, and if the threat of capital punishment will avert some murders or acts of treason, then capital punishment ought to be retained; for at the cost of some lives, many more may be saved—the lives of those who might otherwise have been the victims of capital crimes, and (what is sometimes overlooked) the lives, or at least the liberties, of those who would have committed such crimes if they had not been deterred by the threat of the death penalty. If one has genuine reverence for human life, one must be at least as concerned for the lives of those who are the innocent victims of murderous assaults as one is for those who are convicted of having committed murder. And this may entail taking the lives of those who have demonstrated their lack of control where other human lives are concerned. The assailant is often seen as an object of pity, as an innocent victim of circumstances beyond his control. But compassion for the assailant should not be permitted to misguide us into disregard for his victim. Such misplaced anxiety over the fate of the attacker has gone so far that in some schools, for example, the victims of assaults are blamed for their misfortunes. The president of one of the nation's largest teachers' unions has said:

> Victims of assaults (teachers and students) are reluctant to report assaults and to press charges because of the all-too-prevalent strategem of shifting blame from the assailant to the victim himself. A pupil-victim who has been mugged and had several dollars taken from him may be accused of having "invited" the attack by carrying too much money with him. Teacher victims may be accused of having "provoked" assault by demanding, for example, that a student return to his classroom rather than "cut" class and loiter in the cafeteria. The assailants soon learn that they can continue in their actions with virtual impunity because the innocent victims, instead of receiving official support, are themselves denounced when they ask for help.

Because the accused can call upon a host of legal experts to protect him from prosecution and punishment, whereas the victim is left to his own devices, "the assailant goes free. The teacher or student victim if he is lucky, can transfer to another school in order to be spared the anguish of being assaulted by the same person again." [2]

This grossly unjust situation in the public schools of one city (though it is certainly not confined to that school system or to that city) is merely a reflection, in microcosm, of attitudes that have come to dominate the thinking in our society as a whole. One of the fundamental purposes of the state is the protection of its citizens from bodily harm. If any legal or political system loses its capacity to protect its citizens from such harm, it has lost most of its reason for being, and any claim it may have upon the allegiance of its citizens becomes very tenuous. Ordinary men and women should not have to arm themselves against attacks by lawless persons who roam the streets. School-children and teachers should not have to go to school dressed in armor to protect themselves from brutal assaults that might be directed against them by undisciplined or vicious students who roam the halls. Pity and compassion for the assailant, and recognition of the miserable conditions in which he may (or may not) have been brought up, is no justification for permitting him to return to the streets or to the school to repeat his crimes and to injure other innocent persons. Neither the judges nor officers of the school administration can plead that *their* backgrounds make it impossible for them to treat offenders other than they do. If they are unable to carry out their mandate to protect the public, they should resign from their posts.

The imposition of penalties is one way society has of protecting its members from injury. Once a man, or even a boy, has placed himself outside the law, it is the duty of the guardians of the state to apply the sanctions of the law to him. According to Ramsey Clark, the criminal offender is the victim of circumstances. The society that allowed such circumstances to exist is, in his view, more guilty than the offender. If poverty causes crime (as it sometimes undoubtedly does), then on that ground as well as others, the government should do all it can to eliminate poverty. If sickness, despair, prejudice, and frustration cause crime, as Clark correctly says they do, then for this reason as well as strictly humanitarian ones, the government should do whatever it can to remove those evils from society. But when a particular individual has committed a crime, it will not do to say that he should be excused for his part in the injury he did to another because he was himself a victim of poverty, sickness, prejudice, despair, and frustration. If the government has a duty to remove the causes of crime, then clearly it has a duty to remove from society those persons who are the direct participants in criminal behavior and have demonstrated by their actions that they have criminal tendencies, whatever the more remote causes of those tendencies might be.

A government that fails to use its penal powers on the ground that it should concentrate instead on the prevention of crime by elimination of its more remote causes is like the physician who refused to treat sick patients on the ground that the proper business of medicine is the elimination of the causes of disease. Though one might agree that preventive medicine should be an important part of the concerns of the medical profession, one would not want to entrust either his own health or the health of his community to a group of physicians who refused to treat the sick because of their preoccupation with the eradication of the sources of infection.

Those who argue that every known method of execution is cruel and ghastly and sometimes inadequate (some men have had to be jolted by several shocks on the electric chair, others have had to be hanged more than once because of incorrect placement of the noose or because of ropes breaking, and so on) appeal to the feelings of horror that all normal men conceive at the thought of the deliberate taking of a human life; but the argument is not to the point. To the extent that any mode of execution is painful or frightening to the victim, it is to be deplored. Not all methods of execution are painful. There is reason to believe that some of them are very rapid, nearly foolproof, and quite painless. In ancient Israel, men who were about to be executed were anesthetized first. This strikes me as being an act of mercy, and one that might be emulated. Every man who is executed should be put to death quietly, painlessly, and regretfully. Executions have in the past been accompanied by sensational and lurid news stories. In the future an execution ought to be the occasion for sober reflection and for public examination, by respected intellectual, religious, and political leaders, of the crime for which the state was taking a human life, of the social and moral issues raised by the case, and of society's own responsibility for the tragedy that has occurred—the tragedy for the executed prisoner, for his victims, for their families, and for society as a whole.

The only real alternative to the death penalty is detention, either in prison or in a mental institution. The deficiencies of penal institutions have already been discussed. If one believes, as Socrates did, that not life itself, but only a good life is worth living, then life in one of those institutions can hardly be preferable to death. More important, however, is the possibility—indeed, the probability—that the convicted murderer will someday be released and returned to society. If prisons are indeed schools for crime, as most modern penologists agree they are, then the dangerous criminal who emerges from the system is likely to be even more dangerous when he emerges than he was when he was first committed. The exceedingly high rate of recidivism (repeaters, men and women who are convicted again after they have been released from prison) is the strongest argument possible against both the prison system and against the premature release of men who have been committed to prison for serious crimes. In one recent year two thirds of all the men sent to federal prisons in the United States had been in prison before. Year after year, in one study after another, it has been reported both in England and in the United States that more than half of the convicts released from prison are convicted of another crime, often within three years of their release. Of the remainder it is not known how many truly "go straight" and how many have committed crimes that were not reported or that lacked sufficient evidence to convict. No one has yet made a convincing case for the view that criminals should be released from prison when there is substantial reason to believe that upon their release, more innocent victims will fall prey to their unwillingness or inability to abide by the restraints imposed upon all members of society by the law.*

* The United States Supreme Court abolished the death penalty in a decision rendered on June 29, 1972. Each of the nine Justices wrote a separate opinion. Justices Douglas, Marshall, and Brennan, three members of the five-man majority, argued that the death penalty was a cruel and unusual punishment within the meaning of the

10

Juvenile Delinquency

In the early part of the twentieth century, many concerned citizens began to rethink the problem of the juvenile who was accused of having committed a crime. In the common law it had always been assumed that children under a certain age were incapable of forming the intention (the *mens rea*) necessary for criminal activity. Children under the age of seven are *conclusively presumed* to be incapable of forming a criminal intent, so that whatever they may do in fact, they cannot be convicted in a criminal court. Children between the ages of seven and fourteen are *presumed* to be incapable of forming a criminal intention; thus, the prosecution is faced with the burden of proving not only that the accused child had actually committed the act for which he was being tried, but also that he was capable of forming a criminal intention—the intention of committing an act that he knew was illegal and whose wrongness he was capable of understanding and appreciating. The child might be convicted of having committed the crime, but only after the prosecution had demonstrated that he was capable of forming criminal intentions. Once a person passes his fourteenth birthday, it is presumed that

---

Eighth Amendment to the Constitution, whereas Justices White and Stewart reasoned that the present system operates in a cruel and unusual fashion because it gives judges and juries the discretion to decree life or death and that they do so erratically, capriciously, and wantonly. Justice White also noted that the death penalty is so seldom invoked that it is no longer a credible threat and that its deterrent capacities were therefore weakened. The four dissenters (Chief Justice Burger and Justices Blackmun, Powell, and Rehnquist) suggested that the principal objections voiced by Justices White and Stewart might be overridden if legislatures would provide clear and unequivocal standards for juries and judges to follow in capital cases or if they would define such crimes more narrowly. "Real change would be brought about," they said, "if legislatures provide mandatory death sentences in such a way as to deny juries the opportunity to bring in a verdict on a lesser charge; under such a system, the death sentence could only be avoided by a verdict of acquittal." They also expressed their displeasure at what they considered to be the Court's intrusion into territory that they conceived to be more properly within the prerogatives of the legislatures.

231

he is capable of forming such intentions, and, if he claims that he was not (as he might if he contended that he was insane at the time of the crime, for example), then the burden of proof is upon him, and not upon the prosecution.

Even at a very early stage of its development, then, the common law made special provisions for the very young. But if a child was proved to be guilty of a crime, then the penalty for him was no different from the penalty for an adult who had committed the same act. As a result, it sometimes happened that young boys were sent to the gallows for murder or to prison for lengthy terms and that young girls were committed to prisons or other institutions for many years for crimes committed when they were barely into their teens.

This seemed to be so cruel and so grossly unjust that some persons began to think of possible new approaches to the problem of juvenile crime. What developed is the concept that has come to be known as juvenile delinquency.

Properly understood, juvenile delinquency is not a form of crime, the juvenile delinquent is not regarded as a criminal, and the treatment to which he is subjected is not a form of criminal punishment or, indeed, any form of punishment at all. The juvenile court movement was dedicated to removing the stigma of conviction for criminal behavior from youthful offenders and to emphasizing rehabilitation rather than punishment. It was thought that the courts, instead of treating boys and girls as defendants who were to be prosecuted for their offenses against society, should consider them to be under the protection of the court. Instead of thinking of a case concerning a juvenile as a case of the state *against* the child, the courts were urged to look upon them as being *on behalf* of the child. The court, instead of sitting in judgment on the youngster, acted in his behalf, and devoted its attention to protecting him and treating him rather than punishing him. Juvenile courts, then, were to be thought of as social agencies designed for the protection of youngsters who were in trouble, rather than as arms of the law designed to protect the rest of society against possibly dangerous criminals.

Because the court was acting on the child's behalf and not sitting in judgment over him, it was deemed desirable to do away with the adversary system as it functioned in the criminal court. There was to be no "trial" in the juvenile court, but a "hearing" in which the court would be advised, by various parties, as to the facts and the best manner for disposing of the case—i.e., for treating the young offender once it was determined that he was an offender in fact. The chief object of the hearing was always supposed to be the best interests of the youngster himself. Because the hearing was not to be a trial in the proper sense, because the child was not charged with a criminal offense, and because the state was not acting "against" him but "on his behalf," it naturally followed that there was no need to bring the procedural protections of the Constitution into play on behalf of the allegedly delinquent child. There was no guarantee of the right to be released on bail, for example, because he was not charged with a criminal offense and was being held not as a criminal suspect, but for his own protection. There was no right to a trial by jury, for there was no trial. Hearsay evidence was admissible, though in criminal prosecutions it was excluded. Finally, though in criminal prosecutions the guilt of the accused must be established "beyond a reasonable doubt," in a delinquency hearing a mere preponderance of the evidence is sufficient to establish the charge.

All of this was intended to minimize the terror of the highly formalized criminal proceedings, to avoid the stigma that a criminal record might leave upon a young offender for the rest of his life, and to provide more leeway for the court to deal with the case in a manner most consistent with the best interests of the youngster who was before it. It scarcely seemed reasonable to suppose that a child could benefit from the formal protections afforded criminal suspects in their trials; it seemed more reasonable to assume that he would benefit more from the benign protection of a court that was genuinely concerned with his welfare. It was better to give the court great freedom to proceed informally, so that *all* the evidence, including evidence that would have had to be excluded in a criminal trial (though it might be favorable to the accused), could be heard.

In theory, too, juvenile offenders were not to be punished or sent to the jails or prisons that were reserved for adult criminals. Instead they were to be committed to special institutions, "training schools" or "reformatories." These special institutions and custodial arrangements were supposed to assist the boy or girl who was assigned to them to grow up in a more healthful environment and to return to society, at a suitable age, rehabilitated and ready to assume a responsible place as a full citizen with all the rights that any citizen may enjoy. This was the idea, but unhappily, the reality bears only a faint resemblance to the dream.

In a few places juveniles are brought before judges who are truly concerned about their welfare and who are specially trained to deal with their problems with compassion and understanding. The judges in these juvenile courts are assisted in their tasks by large staffs of highly skilled social workers, probation officers, psychologists, and other professionals who are able to provide them with the best advice and guidance in the fulfillment of their difficult and complex task.

But in many instances the vision of special treatment for juvenile offenders has been transformed into a nightmare for the young people themselves, for their families, and for all those who truly care for the well-being of the nation's youth. The special procedures that were adopted by the courts on the ground that they were acting in behalf of the youth who came before them have in fact been turned against the youngsters whom they were supposed to have benefited. Denied bail, they are detained, as often as not, in facilities that are overcrowded and filthy; they are forced into close contact with budding experts in all aspects of the underworld who introduce them to operations and techniques, as well as personalities, that will enable them to leave petty amateur crime behind for the world of organized crime. In many communities, where no special facilities have been made available for the pretrial detention of juveniles, they are thrown into lockups or jails with hardened criminals who quickly introduce them to the brutal ways of the underworld. Even the judges in juvenile courts may not be competent. A recent study showed that half of them have no undergraduate degree, one fifth have not been to college, and one fifth are not members of the bar.[1]

Because of the informal procedures in juvenile court—those procedures that were supposed to have been introduced for the benefit of the children—they may be found "guilty" of "crimes" much more readily than they would have if they had been tried in regular criminal courts. It is far easier, for example, to establish in a juvenile court that a given child is delinquent because he committed a burglary than it would be to establish the guilt of that same child for the same action in a criminal court. Indeed, in cases where it would be *impossible* to establish guilt in a criminal court, the juvenile court can establish that a child has been delinquent and treat him accordingly. For the very safeguards that were erected to assure an accused adult of a fair trial have been torn down (with the best of intentions) in the juvenile courts, thus rendering it very easy for the authorities to remove so-called problem children from the streets.

The very definition of delinquent behavior is so broad as to include practically anything that a legislator or a judge may wish to bring within its confines. In addition to the usual crimes that one finds enumerated in criminal codes everywhere, a child may be found to be delinquent for "wandering in the streets at night," wandering about railroad yards or tracks; using vile, obscene, or vulgar language in a public place; refusing to obey a parent or guardian; smoking cigarettes around a public place; engaging in an occupation or being in a situation that is dangerous to himself or to others; or being "incorrigible." These, among many other "offenses," are so broad as to enable the police and the courts to label virtually *any* child delinquent if it suits their fancy. In some parts of the country, especially in some of the larger cities, boys may be found to be delinquent and committed to training school for doing what *all* boys in their neighborhoods do, even though their behavior is quite acceptable to those among whom they live and is in no way harmful to anyone.

Suppose now that a young boy is accused of stealing a small item from a variety store. If he were tried in the criminal court, it might be rather difficult to convict him, because of the procedural safeguards guaranteed to every criminal suspect by the Constitution. He might be released on bail. But because he is sent instead to the juvenile court, he may not be released on bail and his case is heard on the much more lenient rules that govern delinquency hearings. As a result he is found to be delinquent, whereas if he had been tried in criminal court he might well have been acquitted.

Now presumably the court will act in his interests by sending him to a training school or "reformatory." For how long? If he had been convicted in criminal court, the sentence in most states would be determinate and, for such a minor offense, very short. But for the delinquent the time he must spend in the training school is indeterminate and may be for as long as he remains a juvenile. Thus, if he is only ten years old, he may spend as many as eleven years in the training school to which the court, acting in his best interests, sends him.

If such training schools were actually designed to "rehabilitate" the youngsters who are sent to them, perhaps there would be less reason to complain. Perhaps it is desirable to remove young boys and girls from the environments in which they have committed their offenses and to place them in healthy environments where they stand a better chance of living a more normal life, getting a better education, and being better prepared for adulthood. But evidence that such beneficial effects actually flow from detention in such institutions is thus far sadly lacking. The number of boys and girls who leave state training schools only to enter the world of petty or even professional crime is astonishingly high.

Descriptions of such training schools abound in the literature. Many of the descriptions are shocking. Though one must concede that some of these institutions are making, or at least that they are attempting to make, a real contribution to the rehabilitation of juvenile offenders who might be salvaged, one must at the same time express astonishment at the incredible and shameful failure of some states to improve the grotesque conditions into which they thrust their children. Those who have political and economic power *may* be uninformed about the conditions in such institutions, but that seems unlikely. More likely, they are unconcerned because their own children, and the children of their friends and neighbors, never go to such institutions. Those juveniles whose parents have money, influence, or social standing seldom do. How else could one explain the fact that in literally hundreds of localities no juvenile detention center exists, so that children are incarcerated with hardened criminals? How can one explain that in some states reformatories are grossly overcrowded and understaffed and that those staff members who are there are undertrained and underpaid? What other explanation can there be for the fact that in most states more concern has been expressed about saving money in the construction and operation of such institutions than about their effectiveness, so that enormous "schools" housing 800 to 2,000 boys or girls are built in isolated areas, far from where they may be visited by their relatives—though experience in other countries has shown that smaller units are far more effective in reducing the rate of recidivism? How else can one explain that in many states laws have been passed that prevent delinquents from engaging in productive work (for their products might compete with those of unionized workers), so that boys and girls must spend long hours watching television—though studies abroad have revealed that an active training program, with useful, productive work, is an invaluable aid toward effective rehabilitation?

The most shameful fact of all is the clear proof that these so-called training schools are really schools of crime. Young boys enter these schools as petty thieves and leave as well-trained burglars. If proof be needed, let it be noted that between 60 and 80 per cent of all prison inmates are graduates of these "training schools," and that by the most conservative estimates, at least 50 per cent of all the alumni of such institutions go on to a life of crime and are eventually committed to other institutions.

In a sense this chapter is out of place in the present section, for it has not dealt with punishment as such. Delinquents are by definition people who are *not* punished. By definition! But the plain fact is that in great numbers of cases in the United States, juveniles are *not* rehabilitated. It is a monstrous deception to claim that a juvenile is being treated differently from the adult criminal when he may be sent to the very same jail and be forced to live in exactly the same corrupt and corrupting environment as the adult criminal, who is presumably being punished for his crime. It is difficult at times to perceive the difference—unless it is that the juvenile is deprived of fundamental protections that are accorded his adult counterpart, and is "committed," though not "sentenced," to even longer terms.

One may be able to make a case for a return to the old system, under which juveniles were punished for their crimes, if they could be convicted of having committed crimes, just as adults were. Some people apparently believe that society would be better protected if youngsters who engage in illegal or antisocial behavior were locked up and put out of the way. They might be able to make a case for the view that through punishment, these boys and girls might be reformed and others might be deterred from following in their footsteps. At the same time, the argument might run, society would be protected from their depredations.

In view of the total failure of the prison system, however, it is difficult to see how this program could possibly do anything more than keep these "undesirable" boys and girls out of sight for the time being. No one has yet given a satisfactory answer to the question of what they will feel when they are finally released and how they will behave once they have regained their freedom. No one, that is, except those who have pointed out how angry and frustrated former "delinquents" who have been through these "schools" have been and how often they have turned to crime—either out of bitterness and resentment at a society that could treat them so inhumanly or out of sheer frustration at their inability to get a decent job on the outside and to establish normal relations with the rest of the world. For in spite of the talk about the courts' desire to avoid the stigma of a criminal record for the youthful offender, the fact is that in too many cases the former delinquent's record somehow manages to follow him around for many, many years.

Much of the promise of the juvenile court system has been unfulfilled, and in too many states and localities the programs instituted by reformers earlier in this century on behalf of young offenders have resulted in dismal failure to achieve their goals. It was hoped that the delinquent would not be stigmatized with a criminal record, but the confidentiality of juvenile court records is often violated. It was hoped that hearings in juvenile courts would be held soon after the occasion for the hearing's being held had occurred, but many weeks sometimes intervene between the offense and the hearing. It was hoped that the hearing would be fair and easily understood and that the informality with which it was conducted would be to the advantage of the young offender; but hearings are often assembly-line formalities, hurried through as rapidly as possible in order to clear the deck for the next busload of delinquents—and, as stated earlier, they are often marked by a disregard for the juvenile's rights and work to his disadvantage, depriving him of the protections that the Constitution has guaranteed to the adult offender. The "training schools" have succeeded, in too many instances, in training more youngsters for a life of professional crime than they have in training them for useful lives as tradesmen, workmen, or professionals in their communities.

In 1967 the Supreme Court of the United States ruled, in a landmark decision, that such Constitutional safeguards as timely notice of charges, right to counsel, privilege against self-incrimination, and rights of confrontation and cross examination of accusers must be extended to juveniles. This was a belated recognition of the overall failure of the juvenile court system to treat juvenile offenders in accordance with the norms of justice and fairness. This decision has opened the door to a complete re-evaluation of the problem of the juvenile offender. Is he to be punished for his "crimes" or "treated" for his problems? If the former, then it would seem that he should be tried in criminal courts with all the protections that the Constitution guarantees to criminal suspects, and the penalty he receives should be no more severe than that which would have been meted out to an adult convicted of the same crime. If the latter, then the state and the federal governments should appropriate the funds necessary to provide proper institutions, manned by trained staffs, to give these troubled youngsters the rehabilitative therapy that they need.

Other possibilities suggest themselves. Certain old-fashioned forms of punishment, such as corporal punishment—not brutal, but harsh enough to make an impression—might succeed in changing the behavior of some of the children who are now subjected to years of institutionalization. Such treatment—swift, certain, and quickly brought to an end—might conceivably be at least as effective as the obviously ineffective and extremely costly nonsystem now in use. Though the imposition of corporal punishment is repugnant to contemporary conventional wisdom, our ancestors believed in it, perhaps not without reason. It might be interesting to try some controlled experiments on the relative efficacy of corporal punishment and other forms of punishment or "therapy."

Still other alternatives commend themselves, including some that have reportedly worked well in England and on the European continent, particularly in some of the Scandinavian countries. By treating boys with compassion and kindness, while at the same time being firm with them and insisting that they engage in useful and productive work, they have managed to rehabilitate many seemingly incorrigible boys and to reduce recidivism to a negligible factor.

Like most social programs, those designed to deal with juvenile delinquency are very costly. Thus far, few governments have been willing to allocate the funds necessary to do the job thoroughly. It is a complex problem, to be sure, made all the more complicated by such difficult social problems as poverty and all that goes with it, including poor housing, poor child care, poor nutrition, inadequate educational systems, less than adequate recreational facilities, and many more. Because of its complexity it requires a multidirectional approach and the expenditure of large sums of money for both research and the implementation of programs. Until now, such programs have been relegated to the bottom of the priority lists, for the children who ended up in juvenile courts were seldom the children of families who had money, influence, or position in the community. To a large extent, this is still true, but more and more, the middle class is having to confront problems that have long plagued the lower classes. If the epidemic of middle-class delinquency spreads, it is not unlikely that there will be a new focus on means of providing adequate protection and more effective treatment for those who become entangled in the system and are confronted with the prospect of being "heard" in juvenile courts and being "treated" in a "detention home," or "training school." Some radical changes, long overdue, may emerge.

Part Three

Truth, Fraud, and Deception

At the beginning of the Republic, *Cephalus, a wealthy old man, expressing a widely held opinion of the time, defined right conduct or justice as telling the truth, not deceiving anyone, and paying one's debts.* Socrates promptly demonstrated that this would not suffice as a definition of these difficult terms and that there were cases in which telling the truth, not engaging in deception, and paying one's debt would be the wrong thing to do.*

When the question of whether one ought to tell the truth or not arises, there are three possible answers: (1) one is obliged to tell the truth, (2) one may (i.e., one has the right to) tell the truth, and (3) one is obliged not to tell the truth.

Moral *rights* and *duties* must generally be distinguished from legal *rights and duties, though there is often a concurrence between what one is legally permitted or obligated to do and what one is morally permitted or obligated to do. However, there are cases in which the law remains silent on matters that some moral thinkers consider to be clear and evident. In still other cases the law seems to come into conflict with what morality requires. These latter cases are most difficult, sometimes providing the grounds for civil disobedience or even rebellion.*

It is not sufficient, either, to say merely that in a given case one is obliged to tell the truth; for among other things, there is a problem of quantity. *A salesman may speak nothing but the truth, but* fail to mention *certain important facts about his product. His silence may be enough to mislead his*

---

* Plato, *Republic*, Book I, Chapter 1.

client into believing what is in fact not true about the product. Similarly, certain statements, though true, may give rise to false inferences because of the context in which they are uttered. What principles might, or ought, to govern such situations?

Further, what is meant by an obligation not to tell the truth? Aside from the obvious moral puzzles inherent in such a statement, there are certain ambiguities that must not be overlooked. There is a world of difference, for example, between not telling the truth and lying. One may not tell the truth about a certain subject by evading the issue, by discussing something else, by making misleading (but not false) statements about it, or by remaining silent.

Finally, there are all kinds of false statements and a multitude of circumstances in which false statements may be made that have a great bearing on the propriety of making them. A mother relating the story of the three bears to her young child is uttering a number of statements that are not "true" in one very important sense of the word, but no one would seriously maintain that she had been lying to her child. An actor on a stage may do his best to deceive his audience into believing that a certain stage prop is the skull of Yorick, but few men are purist enough to suggest that such deception is immoral. Nearly everyone would concede that there is a significant difference between a "white lie" and a con artist's attempt to defraud a widow out of her life's savings. If a neighbor asks for directions to the parade route so that he can see the president, there is no reason not to tell him the truth; but if a madman asks for directions to the parade route so that he can assassinate the president, there is every reason to mislead him. The moral issues affecting a doctor's decision as to whether to tell his patient that she is suffering from an inoperable, malignant tumor are exceedingly complex. If the patient asks what the doctor has discovered in his examination, should he conceal the truth by evading the question? Suppose the patient asks directly whether everything is normal. Is the doctor under a moral obligation to tell her the truth? Are there circumstances that would justify his evading the question—thus arousing suspicions in the patient's mind—or would lying to his patient be justified under some circumstances? What, if anything, justifies the lies and deceptions practiced by spies in wartime? Aside from the purely moral issues involved in all these questions, what role, if any, should society play in regulating these practices? Under what circumstances should moral wrongs be transformed into legal wrongs? For example, on the basis of the ancient warning caveat emptor *("let the buyer beware"), many manufacturers, salesmen, and advertisers have made false and misleading statements about their products, in some cases causing serious harm to their customers, to say nothing of financial losses. Bankers and moneylenders have concealed the true rates of interest that they have charged for the loans they made to borrowers by a variety of devices. Is the state justified in forcing them to reveal the truth plainly, even though it may cause them to lose business and possibly even contribute to a serious slowdown in the economy?*

Truth may be a divine attribute, and the way to freedom, peace, and justice; it may be the sovereign good of human nature, as Bacon put it; and it may be greater and mightier than all things, as a Hebrew poet wrote some 2,000 years ago. But there are other values as well, and they sometimes come into conflict with those represented by the general principle that people ought only to speak the truth; these values may require that in the real world people sometimes have the right, and sometimes perhaps even the obligation, to refrain from speaking truthfully, or even to say what they know to be false. On the other hand, if speaking the truth is of such great value, perhaps it should be reinforced by legislation, in some areas, so that those who are occasionally led astray by the rewards that may be gathered by serving at some other god's altar may be encouraged to remain faithful and true.

11

The Ethics of Truth Telling

KANT ON TRUTH: THE ABSOLUTIST APPROACH

There are a number of possible general or theoretical approaches to the problems associated with truth telling. One of these is the absolutist approach that has come to be associated with the name of Immanuel Kant. Late in his life Kant was criticized for going "so far as to affirm that to tell a falsehood to a murderer who asked us whether our friend, of whom he was in pursuit, had not taken refuge in our house, would be a crime." Kant replied that even in such circumstances, one has no right to be dishonest. "The duty of veracity is an *unconditional duty* which holds *in all circumstances*." [1] "To be truthful in all declarations," he said, "is a sacred unconditional command of reason, and not to be limited to any expediency." [2]

Somewhat earlier in his career, Kant had written that "lying is the throwing away and, as it were, the obliteration of one's dignity as a human being. . . . In [lying,] he renounces his personality and, as a liar, manifests himself as a mere deceptive appearance of a man, not as a true man." Lying, Kant said, does not have to be harmful to others in order to be declared blameworthy. Whether one tells an untruth out of "mere levity," or "good nature," or even in order to achieve some good end, the untruth is still a lie, and as such, is "a crime of man against his own person and a baseness which must make a man contemptible in his own eyes." [3]

Kant conceded that there was a difference between telling an untruth and lying, and he admitted that under some circumstances, one might be permitted to tell an untruth. "I may make a false statement when my purpose is to hide from another what is in my mind and when the latter can assume that such is my purpose, his own purpose being to make a wrong use of the truth. Thus, for instance, if my enemy takes me by the throat and asks where I keep my money, I need not tell him the truth, because he will abuse it, and my untruth is not a lie because the thief knows full well that I will not, if I can help it, tell him the truth and that he has no right to demand it of me." But suppose the victim of this assault has told the assailant that he will tell him the truth? In that case, says Kant, he must follow through and tell the truth—not because he owes anything to the assailant, but because if he lies, his conduct "is an infringement of the rights of humanity," because, according to Kant, the act of lying sets him "in opposition to the condition and means through which any human society is possible." Even necessity is not an excuse, he said, for, in the first place, it can be used to justify stealing, cheating, and killing as well— so "the whole basis of morality goes by the board." And secondly, everyone will decide for himself what is necessity and what is not. The absence of any universal standard would make the application of moral rules indefinite and uncertain. [4]

Now what leads Kant to this extreme position? Even if we make the doubtful assumption that he was willing to concede that the victim of an assault might be permitted to lie to his assailant, [5] the fact remains that he thought of the uttering of the most innocent-seeming falsehood as a very grievous moral wrong, one that struck at the very foundations of human society. How did he arrive at this position?

According to Kant, the fundamental rule of all morality may be summed up as follows: "Act only on that maxim which you can at the same time will to be a universal law." [6] This rule, called by Kant the categorical imperative, means that when considering what to do in a given situation, one should act in accordance with a principle that could apply universally, to all people and (presumably) at all times. Suppose, for example, that I was confronted with a situation in which it might seem more advantageous for me to break a promise I had made than to keep it. Kant would have me inquire what the consequences might be if *everyone* adopted the principle that promises might be broken whenever it seemed advantageous to the promisor to do so. It does not require much thought to realize that the universal adoption of such a rule would result in the complete destruction of the institution of promising; for if everyone could break his promises when it seemed advantageous for him to do so, no one would rely upon anyone else to keep his word and promises would lose all meaning. The same is true of truth telling. People rely upon the statements of one another only because they find that statements made by their fellow men are usually truthful. However, if everyone adopted the rule that he would tell the truth only when it served his immediate ends and would lie whenever that was more to his advantage, no one would ever know whether anyone else was telling the truth in any particular situation and useful communication between persons would dry up. The only reason that the occasional promise breaker and the occasional liar can get away with what they do is because most people keep their promises and tell the truth most of the time. The honesty and the veracity of most people enables swindlers and deceivers to ply their trade. The ordinary man, who might be tempted to violate the rules only now and again, contributes, to that extent, to the breakdown of the important institutions of promise keeping and truth telling. It would seem that this is want Kant means when he says that the liar "infringes the rights of humanity," for men have the right to expect that their fellow men will act in accordance with those rules that they expect others to follow. In the long run, self-interest requires that every man keep his promises and tell the truth, for it is evident that if people could pick and choose the occasions when they would keep their promises and tell the truth, each man would sometimes be victimized by those who decided to break promises made to him and be misled by lies told to him. Kant is not concerned with self-interest, though, as a motive for moral behavior. His point is that we owe it to mankind and to our own dignity as free and independent human beings to observe the dictate of the categorical imperative, which requires strict adherence to the rule that the truth and only the truth be uttered by us. Human society would be impossible were it not for such institutions as promise keeping and truth telling. It is every man's duty to avoid doing what would tend to destroy these vital institutions. Therefore, every man must steadfastly observe the rule against lying.

Still, it is difficult to accept Kant's conclusions. First, because there are innumerable occasions when these seemingly universal maxims come into conflict with one another. To use the example that Kant himself rejected: When I am asked by a potential assassin for information that would render his mission of murder easier, my duty to tell him the truth comes into conflict with my duty of beneficence, which Kant defines as the duty "to be helpful to men in need," [7] and with the duty to have compassion for one's fellow men, illustrated by Kant's reference to the Stoic who said, "I wish I had a friend, not that he might give me help in poverty, sickness, captivity, and so on, but in order that I might stand by him and save a human being." [8]

Secondly, the categorical imperative itself has been the subject of heavy criticism. It is scarcely sufficient even as a formal requirement for moral rules, for it is easy to dream up rules that do not violate the categorical imperative's conditions but are nevertheless clearly immoral. One example that was offered in a recent essay that was basically sympathetic to Kant was the rule that the mothers of all babies weighing less than 6 pounds ought to do everything possible to bring about the death of their babies. There is nothing inconsistent about this "maxim," there is no contradiction inherent in it, and there is no reason to believe that human society would cease to exist were it universally adopted. Yet it is patently immoral.[9] Furthermore, the categorical imperative, being a purely formal rule, fails to provide any substance to the rules of morality unless it is somehow brought into contact with the real world of experience. But more important than any of these objections, perhaps, is the fact that Kant's stand on the problem of truth telling is not consistent with his own formulations of the categorical imperative. One of Kant's alternative formulations of the categorical imperative reads as follows: "Always treat all human beings, whether yourself or any other person, as ends, and never as means." [10] Now, if I truthfully answer the potential assassin's questions as to the whereabouts of his victim, I have failed to treat his victim as an end. I have used him as a means, sacrificing his life in order to adhere rigidly to a (supposedly) moral rule.

Kant had some important insights, and we can learn much from him. But his absolutist approach to the moral problem of telling the truth has fatal weaknesses. His rigid formalism makes it impossible for him to appreciate the subtle nuances of human experience that make it impossible for all situations, though they may be characterized as situations where "truth telling" is involved, to be subsumed under the same moral rule.

If Kant's approach will not do, some other must be found, for there must be some criteria that will enable us to distinguish those situations in which we are *justified* in uttering falsehoods from those in which we may be *excused* for having done so; to resolve the quandary that we may be in if we are asked whether a given form of truth telling should be required by law or be left to private discretion and the informal sanctions of social life; to decide whether some kinds of lying may properly be condoned by the law, and others encouraged by it.

One way of exploring such questions is to examine specific cases, illustrative of various kinds of problems that actually arise in daily life. Whether such an examination will lead to clear principles or rules or criteria for the resolution of moral and legal issues remains to be seen. But the consideration of such issues is instructive in itself and is worth pursuing for the light it may shed upon the workings of ethical principles and the problems of moral decision making in human society. Let us turn, then, to some of the problems associated with the telling of truth in our society.

FRAUD AND HUMAN SUFFERING

Men have not condemned lying and elevated the principle of telling the truth to such a high position among the moral virtues because of some abstract doctrine that is unrelated to the realities of human life. The case of Larry illustrates, as well as any case can, the terrible damage that men and women can do to one another through the simple expedient of lying.

Case 11. Larry

Larry, a thirty-year-old patient in a hospital for the retarded, was stoop-shouldered, had a dull, vacuous expression, and spoke very little. But he was not retarded. Though his record indicated that he had never been to school and had never been tutored, he had taught himself how to read by examining old picture magazines that were scattered around the hospital wards. But no one was aware of this.

Shortly after her graduation from high school, Larry's mother had become pregnant during a summer affair with a drifter, who disappeared as soon as he learned that he was about to become a father. She left home and became engaged to a junior executive in a bank where she had found a job. By this time she was five months pregnant. In order to conceal her condition from her fiance, she left town on the pretext of visiting her dying mother. While awaiting her baby's birth, she sent amorous letters to her future husband, informing him of the sad deterioration in her poor grandmother's health.

A physician she met agreed to deliver her baby and to care for it in a home for the retarded that he was opening until arrangements could be made for the baby's adoption—all for a fee, of course. The baby, Larry, was born; his mother wrote to her fiance that her grandmother had died, and she returned to work, marrying soon after.

The doctor informed Larry's mother that Larry was retarded and could not easily be placed for adoption. Through the years, she kept up the increasingly heavy payments for Larry's care in the doctor's home for the retarded. When her husband died and she became unable to meet the doctor's financial demands, Larry was transferred to a state institution, where a careful examination uncovered the fact that, aside from the obvious lack of development caused by his abnormal environment and upbringing, Larry was quite normal in every way.

Because of his mother's lies and the deceit of the physician who had helped to bring him into the world, Larry had lost more than thirty years of his life. He had been kept in an abnormal environment and been deprived of the opportunities for a normal life that he might otherwise have had.[11]

Throughout the recital of these events, one is struck by the extent to which the people involved have used one another, by the manner in which they have treated one another, in Kant's terminology, as means rather than as ends. We have no way of knowing just what the relationship between Larry's mother and his natural father was, but it is obvious that one of them, at least, was using the other as a means for the gratification of his own personal desires. He seems to have given little thought to the long-range consequences, either to the girl with whom he was sleeping or to the child who was to be born as a result of their union. We do not know what he said to her; whether deception played a part in the very beginning of the chain of events that led to Larry's long life in an institution for retarded youngsters must remain open to speculation. Later developments, however, are more obvious, and in them, it is possible to see how people may pervert the truth for their own ends at the expense of others, and—what Kant seems to ignore—how damaging deceit can be and how much useless suffering it can cause.

By promising to deliver her baby and to care for it until it was ready for adoption, an unscrupulous physician persuaded a desperate girl to entrust herself and her baby to his care. By lying to her after the child's birth and convincing her that the child was hopelessly retarded, he used her and the child to further his own interests. Whether she was *prepared to hear what he had to say* is an interesting question in itself. Whenever one person tells a lie, there must be another to hear it; if there is a responsibility on the part of the liar for what he has said, there may also be some responsibility on the part of his audience for having listened to what he said and for having accepted it without further investigation. Among the important questions that must be answered in any thorough analysis of this problem are these: What counts as adequate evidence for acquiescence in a statement that someone else has made, and how far should one investigate before accepting the statement of another on a matter that may, if accepted, have a major effect upon the future well-being of a third person?

What responsibility do people have to other persons who may be affected by their statements? What was Larry's mother's responsibility to her future husband when she led him to believe that she was off visiting her dying grandmother, when in fact she was off bearing another man's child? One can easily imagine how she must have rationalized her behavior during the fateful months preceding Larry's birth. Weighing her own right to happiness—and, as Kant pointed out, every person should treat *himself* as an end, too, and not as a means—and concluding that her future husband would not be harmed by the "white lie" that she was telling him, whereas the future happiness of both of them might be compromised if she were to tell him the truth, she concluded that it was best to tell him the grandmother story. But what of *his* rights in all this, including, perhaps, his right to know, through all those years, that some of his income was going toward the support of another man's child? And his right to know, if he cared, that his future wife bore another man's child during the time that he was courting her?

The Stoics observed long ago that people acquire certain rights, responsibilities, and obligations through the various roles they play in society, the offices they hold, and the special relationships that they have to other persons. A father has certain duties with respect to his children that he does not have with respect to other children, just because he is their father and they are his children. Similarly, a child has certain duties toward his own father and mother, by virtue of the fact that they are his parents, that he does not have toward other persons' fathers and mothers or to other persons in general. When a man accepts the position of teacher, judge, juror, police officer, mayor, or governor, he assumes certain responsibilities that he would not have if he did not occupy such an office. With the special powers that are vested in such offices go corresponding responsibilities.

Physicians hold a position of peculiar power over other persons. Because of their expert knowledge and the general public's lack of knowledge on many aspects of medicine, people tend to have a degree of confidence in them that they do not confer upon the members of many other professions. We entrust our bodies, our minds, and our very lives to them. Part of the reason for this is their knowledge and our ignorance, but part of it is justified by the relatively high standard of professional ethics that the medical profession has generally maintained and by the high percentage of cases that doctors are able to bring to a satisfactory conclusion. If physicians had a reputation for failing to cure their patients, for using their expert knowledge to exploit their patients for personal gain without regard to the harm that they might do to them, or for making false diagnoses —either through ignorance or because of venality—they would soon lose their effectiveness and people would cease to rely upon them. The harm that can be done to a person by a mendacious physician is immeasurable. It would seem, therefore, that there must be a peculiar obligation on the part of the physician to be truthful, for an untruthful physician can do considerable damage to his patients. Furthermore, much of the effectiveness of the medical profession depends upon the confidence reposed in its members by the general public. If that confidence is undermined by any significant amount of fraudulent treatment, the extent of the services that might be rendered to the public by doctors might be seriously compromised. Finally, because of the vital interests that are at stake when a person entrusts himself or his loved ones to the care of a physician, there is a special responsibility on the part of the latter to treat his patients honestly and not to take advantage of their vulnerability.

LIES OF HUMAN SYMPATHY

Some untruths are not fraudulent, of course. Some are uttered out of deep concern for those toward whom they are directed. Again, medicine provides an excellent example of the kind of moral dilemma that exists with regard to the telling of another kind of untruth.

CASE 12. THE POLIO VICTIMS

A few years ago, a study was made in a large hospital that offered specialized treatment to victims of polio. Patients who were brought into the hospital with paralytic polio were studied for the first three months or so to determine the extent of the damage that had been sustained by their nervous systems. During this period of "medical uncertainty," the parents of the victims naturally continued to believe, or hope, that their children would recover and be able to walk again. No parents were told the full truth until the end of the full three-month period, though by the end of the sixth week, members of the research team were able to predict quite confidently, to their colleagues, which patients would recover completely, which would need braces, and which would have to undergo bone-fusion operations.

Members of the staff explained their behavior by saying, "We try not to tell them too much. It's better if they find out for themselves in a natural sort of way." They argued that absolute certainty doesn't exist in medical matters, that it was always *possible* for a given patient to fool everyone by making a sudden recovery. Still other doctors insisted that it is contrary to the best interests of their patients to reveal too much, that it may be "psychologically harmful."

There is no general agreement among doctors as to the best policy to follow when confronted with such a situation, a situation exemplified by the polio victims, but most often encountered, in its most radical form, in the case of the person who is suffering from an incurable malignancy. Some physicians believe that it is necessary, in all cases, to be perfectly straightforward and to present their patients with the straight, unvarnished truth. Others believe that it is best, in the most difficult cases, to hedge, to avoid answering direct questions, to let their patients "hang on to hope," so as to avoid the possibility of contributing to latent suicidal tendencies, to possible mental breakdowns, or to such a complete surrender to the inevitable that death may actually be hastened. Physicians who have taken the "hard line" by telling their patients the plain truth that they had only a certain number of months to live, have reported that some of their patients have crumbled before their eyes. Others, who have concealed the truth from their patients, have watched them cling to false and illusory hope as they slowly withered away. There are those who try to steer a middle path, delicately probing their patients to see how much of the truth they can take and how much they want to hear. Many patients, they say, don't want to hear the truth. They want to be reassured rather than to be informed; and in some cases, they know the truth, or suspect it, anyway. If they were told the full story, it is said, their reactions might be more damaging to them, in the short run at least, than the illnesses from which they suffer. Though they might be able to lead productive, useful, and relatively happy lives for some time before the full impact of the illness strikes them down, a premature revelation of their true condition might be so crushing to them that they would become incapable of carrying on normally, even for the few months or years that they might otherwise enjoy. On the other hand, however, there are patients who must set their affairs in order, bringing their wills up to date, making necessary business transactions, arranging for the transfer of property, and taking care of the multitude of other things that a man or woman might want to do if there were advance warning of his or her impending death. And there are those who may have specific desires as to *how* and *where* they want to die. Some people feel that the slow and agonizing death that so often awaits the cancer victim in the hospital is costly, undignified, and unnecessary. They have grave doubts about the value of the artificial prolongation of a merely biological existence in a hospital bed after virtually all human attributes have been drained out of them. This is particularly evident in the case of those who are afflicted with cancer of the brain. They may linger on for many months, sustained by extremely costly medical procedures, long after they have ceased to function mentally or to communicate with their loved ones. While they are still able to make decisions on their own, perhaps they should be presented with the options that may lie before them. Some may choose to go the hospital route all the way. Others may prefer to die in bed at home, with their loved ones nearby, and without the medical paraphernalia that would prolong their earthly existence at great emotional and financial cost to their families. And still others may choose, at some point, to commit suicide, a solution that cannot be ruled out as immoral *a priori*, without further argument. Nor can one rule out the possibility that every person may have a right to make such choices for himself and that there may be a corresponding duty on the part of members of the medical profession to make informed choices possible by sharing such information as they may possess.

It goes without saying that when the patient does not press for an answer to questions he may harbor about his own fate, the physician may exercise a degree of discretion in deciding just how much he ought to reveal. But when the patient asks direct questions and clearly wants direct answers, there is grave reason to doubt whether the physician has a right to withhold information that is in his possession from the patient, or to lie to him.

It may be argued, and often is, that the ordinary layman cannot understand the technical details of a medical diagnosis and that it is impossible for a layman fully to appreciate the variables and probabilities inherent in any medical prognosis. The chances of misunderstanding and misinterpretation are so great, it is said, that the physician is justified in maintaining a discrete silence about many of his findings.

There is some room for doubt, however, about the soundness of this response. It lumps all laymen together, failing to discriminate between those who may be highly sophisticated and those who are not, between those who may be prepared to read some fairly technical material in order to get a more thorough understanding of their problems, if that should be necessary, and those who are unable to do so. It glosses over the fact that many important medical facts can be—and are—presented in layman's language, so that the ordinary man may be informed about the nature of various diseases, about symptoms to look for and procedures to follow, and about the kinds of assistance that may be available in the form of drugs, appliances, or other kinds of treatment, when he is afflicted with a specific illness. So much medical knowledge has been disseminated to the general public in layman's language that it is difficult to accept the proposition that a man may not be told about his own illness because he is not likely to have a full appreciation of all the facts. He may not have to have a full understanding of all the facts in order to appreciate what is happening to him.

No generalization will cover all the possible cases that a physician might encounter. As Socrates pointed out to Cephalus, there are occasions when other moral considerations overweigh the necessity to tell the truth. Where the truth may cause the loss of a human life, Socrates said, it may be best not to tell the truth. If the physician is convinced that by revealing the truth to his patient, the latter may suffer far more than he would if he were kept in ignorance about the facts of his case; or if he has adequate reason to conclude that his patient's life may be significantly shortened by telling him the truth, then he *might* have a case for withholding information from him. But there is still another consideration that must be weighed.

The great danger of a policy of lying to some people, even with the noblest intentions, is that it soon becomes known that such a policy exists. Once people know that some doctors sometimes lie to their patients about the nature of their illnesses, it becomes extremely difficult to know when a doctor may be trusted and when he may not. Communication between doctor and patient tends to break down, at least in those areas where lying is condoned or is practiced on a more or less regular basis. It is reasonable to assume that some persons who suspect that they have serious illnesses may not believe their physicians because they know of the extent to which dissimulation takes place when such problems arise. For every patient who *has* a terminal illness and is *helped* by not being told the full truth, there may be another who is suffering from a minor affliction that resembles, in his mind, some dreadful malady, and *cannot be convinced* by his doctor that his illness is minor because he knows how often they lie to spare their patients the anguish that sometimes results from knowledge of the truth. The harm that may be done by the practice of sometimes lying to victims of cancer may outweigh any benefits that may result from such a policy. Though Kant's absolutism may not be acceptable in general, there are strong reasons for believing that any policy that condones the telling of untruths may be self-defeating in the long run.

The physicians in Case 12 argued that it would be "psychologically harmful" to those concerned to know the truth. But it is not clear either that there is adequate evidence to justify such an assertion or that permitting them to learn the facts gradually and in piecemeal fashion is less harmful to them than a direct confrontation with the truth would be. One would want to know what evidence the doctors involved might have had to support their contention that all of the persons concerned might have been psychologically harmed by being given the facts before the end of the three-month observation period, and what remarkable change might have occurred that would have enabled all of those people to accept the facts at the end of the three-month period without undue risk of such harm.

The issues involved here, where information is withheld, are not quite the same as those involved where distorted information is offered. But in either case, patients, their relatives, or both are permitted to cling to illusory hopes. In either case, one vital question remains: Does a doctor have the *right* to withhold information that is available to him about a given patient, or, if he cannot avoid giving answers to questions about the matter, to give untrue or misleading answers to those concerned? Or, to put the question somewhat differently, *to whom does the information which a physician gathers about a given patient belong?*

An analogy suggests itself. For many years, IQ scores were kept secret from students and their parents. But the schools that administered those tests are the servants of the parents and the students who go to them, and it would seem that information extracted by the schools about the students should belong to them rather than to the schools, or at least that it should be made available to them if they ask for it. The schools maintained the confidentiality of such records on the ground that it was not in the best interests of the students to know what their scores were. Some parents argued that that was for *them* to decide, and not for the schools. After a lengthy court battle, initiated in New York, the schools were finally required to reveal the contents of those files. Physicians use a similar argument. They, too, argue that it would not be in the best interests of their patients to learn the contents of their files. But one may argue in response that that is not for the physicians to decide, but for their patients. If a patient wants to take the risk of learning what his doctor has written about him, then he should be permitted to do so. After all, it is *his* life and *his* health that are at stake. Whether a physician may assume the paternalistic prerogative of making such decisions for his patients, or of deciding what truths they may know and what they may not know, is highly questionable. Perhaps there is something in the doctor–patient relationship that justifies this attitude; but thus far, I have been unable to search it out.

12

Truth in the Marketplace: Advertisers, Salesmen, and Swindlers

The advertising industry and those that are allied with it, including general merchandising and salesmanship, have been subjected to severe criticism in recent decades because of widespread and flagrant abuses, most of them having to do with fraud and deception. So much advertising is offensive and obtrusive, so much of it is in poor taste, and so much publicity has been given to the "hidden persuaders," the "motivational researchers," and the Madison Avenue "men in the grey flannel suits" that it is easy to lose perspective and assume that the advertiser is a callous huckster concerned only with selling his product and earning his commissions, and not at all bothered with ordinary standards of taste, decency, or morality. Yet there can be no doubt that the advertiser sometimes performs a valuable service, not only for those who employ him, but for the general public as well.

CASE 13. AN ADMAN'S CONFESSION

One day when I was young in advertising I slipped a piece of paper into my typewriter and wrote an advertisement for a life insurance company. It was addressed to young husbands and fathers. One of the coupons received in reply came from a traveler in Rio de Janeiro, whose home was in New Jersey. He was thirty-eight years old, married, and the father of three children. He wanted information on a policy that, in case of his death, would guarantee his family an income of $3,000 a year.

On the man's return to New Jersey, the policy was written and the first payment made. A few days later he went to his dentist to have a wisdom tooth extracted. Somehow the cavity became infected, the infection spread and he died.

That incident made a deep impression on me. Many times in the intervening years I have been reminded that somewhere in New Jersey there are a mother and three children, now grown up, who, without the slightest suspicion of my existence, have had their whole lives changed by the fact that one day I put together some words that were printed in a magazine, and read in a faraway country by their husband and father, who was influenced to do what I suggested.*,1

In the United States in 1969 more than $19.5 billion were spent on all forms of advertising. This was nearly double the amount that had been spent just ten years before.[2] There can be no doubt about the tremendous impact that the advertising industry has upon the nation's economy and upon the way of life of its people. Those who are inclined to scoff at the effectiveness of advertising should ponder those figures for a moment and consider whether hardheaded businessmen would spend such enormous sums if they did not have solid evidence that their advertisements were effective, in spite of all the complaints that might be voiced about them by intellectuals, government officials, and the public at large. The business of advertising is persuasion. Most advertisements are placed in the interests of commerce, their business being to persuade potential customers to buy some product or service. But some advertising is used for other than commercial purposes: to gain votes for a political candidate, for example, or for a bond issue, or for some other political proposition. Some are directed toward persuading people to change their personal habits, not to engage in certain practices, or to lend their support to some charitable

---

* The importance of advertising to the economy and its contributions to the public welfare must not be overlooked in any balanced discussion of the subject. Whether the methods advertisers employ are ethical is another matter. The author of this "confession" advocates honesty in his profession, but admits that he frequently suppresses the truth. Are the benefits of advertising outweighed by the damage done by such unethical practices? See pages 278 ff.

cause. Examples would be advertising campaigns conducted by associations dedicated to discouraging smoking or drug abuse, and fund-raising campaigns of the Red Feather agencies.

Because the fundamental aim of advertising is persuasion, it is natural that all the devices and techniques of persuasion should be employed by advertisers to achieve their aim. Because of the tremendous financial stake that business has in advertising, it is not surprising that great efforts have gone into perfecting the art, to developing new techniques, and to finding out just what factors motivate people to do one thing or another, so that advertisers may exploit that knowledge in order to motivate persons to do what they want them to do. This has given rise to the charge that advertisers "manipulate" the public, that they wield an unconscionable amount of power over the general populace, and that they are capable of molding people to their will. Phrased in this way, these charges are grossly exaggerated. But advertisers themselves admit, and even boast about the fact, that they are able to create desires in people for products and services that they had never wanted before, and that they can motivate them to change their life styles, to some extent at least, to conform with the desires of their (the advertisers') clients. One may argue that this may be very good, that from the skills of the advertising profession much of America's prosperity has been derived. If people had not been motivated to purchase automobiles and vacuum cleaners, great industries would never have been born, and millions of people would not be employed as they are today. In the case of the automobile, to the extent that advertising has contributed to the growth of the industry, it has helped to make America and the rest of the world what they are today, and has done its part to change a whole way of life. Whether this is good or evil is not altogether clear, but its existence is indisputable. To the extent that advertisers have persuaded people to buy soap, it may be argued, they have contributed to the cleanliness of the American people, and therefore to their high standards of hygiene and health. Anyone who has visited the Middle East, where vast numbers of people have never been reached by the salesmen of Procter and Gamble and Lever Brothers, and where governments are spending vast sums of money to introduce habits of personal hygiene to the populace, can appreciate the positive achievements of both the advertising and the soap industries.

But one may argue, too, that these "benefits" are mitigated by serious disadvantages, and that in spite of the good that has derived from advertising, the evil that has resulted from it may be enough to make one have grave reservations about the practitioners of the art. Because of false, deceptive, and misleading advertising, millions of people have been bilked out of vast sums of money. They have been inveigled into enrolling in "plans" and "schools" that promised to give them great benefits, when in fact the "plans" were ineffective, the "schools" did not employ teachers, and the benefits were totally illusory. They have been persuaded, by false

promises of swift cures for the illnesses and ailments that afflicted them, ·
to buy nostrums and remedies that were ineffective and on occasion damaging or even deadly. They have been bilked into purchasing merchandise,
or land, or burial plots, or services, that were either worthless or nonexistent. They have been conned into paying outrageously inflated prices
for products that provided no benefit to anyone but their makers. We
will have more to say about false and deceptive advertising. But there
are other reasons to question the claims made by the supporters of the
advertising industry for the benefits that it has conferred upon the public.

THE SOPHISTS AND MODERN ADVERTISING

The art of persuasion was highly developed in ancient Greece by a
group of men who came to be known as Sophists. The Sophists' greatest
critic was Plato, who devoted many of his dialogues to excoriating them
for their verbal trickery and for their unscientific attitudes. The Sophists
claimed to be teachers, and some of them were in fact paid large sums
of money by wealthy Greeks who hired them to teach their sons the art
of persuasion, which they called rhetoric, on the theory that it was the
key to a successful career. The Sophists claimed—correctly, no doubt—
that their art gave men power over others that they could not readily
achieve in any other way. In one of Plato's dialogues, a supporter of
sophism argues that if he were pitted against a physician in a contest
over a public health measure that came before the senate, he would be
able to persuade the senators to vote in accordance with his views, whereas
the physician would be helpless.

Plato, in inquiring into the nature of this art of persuasion, has Gorgias,
a Sophist, explain to Socrates that rhetoric is the art of persuasion that is
used in law courts and at public gatherings, and deals with justice and
injustice. This is not very far from the claim that might be made by a
modern public relations firm that attempts to influence legislation on behalf of a major industry. Socrates points out that there is a difference
between belief and knowledge; for there can be no false knowledge,
whereas people can have false beliefs as well as true beliefs. With this
distinction in mind, he suggests that there must be two kinds of persuasion—one that produces belief (whether true or not) and the other that
produces knowledge. And Gorgias, the Sophist, concedes that rhetoric is
concerned only with producing beliefs in its subjects and is not concerned to give them scientific certainty or even reasoned arguments for
such beliefs as they may have. He concedes also that the rhetorician (or—
in modern terms—the advertising man or the public relations expert) is
interested only in producing the desired belief, but does not particularly
care whether the beliefs he propagates are true or false. To Socrates this

is tantamount to an admission that rhetoricians are not *teachers* or *instructors* of men in any true sense. Instead they are merely manipulators of men. Though they may deal with law courts and assemblies over matters in which right and wrong, justice and injustice are at stake, they are not teachers of what is right and what is wrong, or of what is just and what is unjust. They may attempt to influence men on questions of public policy having to do with medicine, architecture, commerce, and engineering, but their efforts—though they may be more persuasive, in one sense, because of their knowledge of the techniques of persuasion—cannot be compared to those of experts in those fields, who may be less accomplished as public speakers and who may not be familiar with the gimmicks of the public relations man but who are able to bring their expert knowledge on the *subject* to bear in the discussion. When the Sophist is more persuasive than the doctor in a question where public health is at stake, it is a case of the ignorant being more persuasive with the ignorant public than the expert is able to be. The Sophist does not have to know the facts that are relevant to the issue, for he has devices that enable him to convince the public (that is, those who do not have knowledge about the subject themselves) that he knows more about the subject than those who really *do* know the facts. He merely *seems* to know, even when he knows nothing.

Socrates came up with an intriguing analysis that is worth pondering before we move on to consider advertising in more detail. He distinguished between genuine arts and fraudulent ones.[3] A genuine art is a technique for achieving some genuine benefit to humanity, whereas a fraudulent art (which ought not, properly speaking, to be called an art at all) is a technique that masquerades in the form of an art, that makes a pretext of conferring a benefit upon those who apply to its practitioners, but that actually does them no good at all and may even cause considerable damage to them.

As examples of genuine arts, Socrates offers gymnastics and medicine, both of which are concerned with the health of the body. The gymnastics teacher prescribes a regimen of exercise, diet, work, and rest that is designed to preserve the body's health, and the medical doctor prescribes a similar regimen, in addition to such drugs and other treatments as he may deem necessary, to restore health to a person who has lost it. Both of these people are genuinely concerned for the health of the persons who consult them, and both of them base their prescriptions upon scientific knowledge that they have gained about the body itself and about what is necessary for good health.

As opposed to the gymnastic teacher and the medical doctor, there are the makeup artists and the confectioners. (In modern terms, the former would be called beauticians, cosmetic salesmen and manufacturers, girdle and brassiere manufacturers, and fashion designers, and the latter would be called gourmet chefs, convenience-food packers, bakers, candy makers, and so on.) These people are not interested in the true well-being of those who consult them or purchase their products. Their principal concern is that their customers should derive *pleasure* from their services and products, regardless of whether it is to their real benefit or not. The use of these means, Socrates says, is deceitful, for to the extent that they succeed, they merely cover up the truth and offer a false sense of security and well-being.

The Sophists of those days, like some of the image makers of today, imagined that they wielded much power, for, as they put it, they were able to cause men to be put to death, to be sent off into exile, and to lose their fortunes. They did these things without regard to the rightness or the justice of their actions.

Socrates asked whether it was worse to do injustice or to be the victim of injustice, and concluded, for his own part, that it was bad to be the victim of injustice, but that it was far worse to be the perpetrator of injustice. For in his view the unjust man was doomed to be wretched and unhappy. Injustice, as he saw it, was a psychological disease, a disorder of the mind that consisted of the individual's inability to control his emotions and desires. A rational person whose personality was not afflicted with the disease of injustice would know that the pleasures of the moment are detrimental to himself in the long run, and, though he might be sorely tempted to give in to his desires for them, he would control his impulses in order to maintain both his physical and his psychological health. Similarly, greed, avarice, and anger can lead a man to perform acts that will harm others; but from Socrates's point of view, the harm that the tyrant does to himself is far greater than any hurt that he can inflict upon his victims. For every time that he gives in to an impulse to hurt another man, he gives rein to an irrational part of his personality, he permits it to overcome his own instincts for self-preservation (like the man who becomes addicted to tobacco when he knows how damaging smoking may be to his health in the long run), and he brings himself ever closer to the time when those baser instincts will take complete control of him. When that time comes, Socrates said, they will destroy him as a human being as surely as anarchy and revolution will destroy a state. Real power, then, is not the power that one wields over other men—the power to expropriate their money, to send them off into exile, or to put them to death—but power over one's own desires, impulses, and emotions. Self-control is the sign of a well-ordered personality, of a healthy and sound man; and the self-controlled man does what is fitting and right to other men, and behaves toward them in accordance with the principles of justice. Such a person, Socrates maintained, is happy, whereas the person who lacks self-control and lets his irrational impulses rule his behavior toward others, prompting him to behave unjustly, is unhappy and wretched, however much outward appearances may deceive us into thinking otherwise. And the truly just man, he concluded, is not interested in persuading his fellow citizens to enjoy themselves at the expense of their physical or their psychological well-being. He tries, as far as possible, to fulfill the principal task of a citizen: to bend all his efforts toward persuading his fellow citizens to improve themselves, to become the masters of themselves, to behave rationally rather than impulsively, and to behave justly toward one another.[4]

The Sophist, then, and (one may suppose) his modern counterpart, the stereotype of the advertising man, may be characterized as one who attempts to wield power over other men for selfish ends; who devotes himself to the pseudoart, or the fraudulent art, of rhetoric, whereby he attempts to inculcate beliefs in other men without regard to the truth of those beliefs; and who furthers the ends of such other fraudulent arts as makeup and confectionary, playing upon the desires of other men rather than trying to improve them. To the extent that this characterization is true, it would follow, in Plato's scheme, that these men are unjust and that they are therefore not acting in their own best interests, though they may imagine that the financial profits that they earn are indicative of the extent to which they are acting in their own best interests. If he were here today Socrates might point to the high incidence of ulcers that is alleged to be endemic to advertising men as a symptom of the inner sickness to which he referred.

In spite of the strong arguments that Plato offers in support of his point of view, it cannot be accepted uncritically. Certain assumptions that Plato makes run counter to common sense and have not been satisfactorily established by other means.

His attempt to prove that the unjust man is worse off than the just man seems more a wish that one would like to see fulfilled than a true picture of reality. Too often one sees those who have lived by nefarious practices waxing rich, respected in their communities, and—to all appearances, at least—smug and happy with themselves and their families while honest and conscientious men and women groan under their burdens and live with a broken spirit and even with broken health. That the perpetrator of injustice *should* be more wretched than his victim is devoutly to be desired, perhaps, but it is not a fact of life.

Plato's "fraudulent arts" may not be the unmitigated evils that he paints them as being. There may be some virtue in pleasure seeking, in enjoying the pleasure of the moment and not thinking always of the long-range consequences of every action. The skills of the confectioner do give much pleasure to people, and the skills of the beautician, the corset maker, and the cosmetic manufacturers may be valuable *precisely because* they make the unshapely shapely, the unseemly seemly, and the ugly beautiful, if only for a time. Can it be said unequivocally that man ought never improve upon nature, especially when nature has not been overly generous? A woman who has lost her hair because of a childhood illness can hardly be blamed for wearing a wig, and the suggestion that the wigmaker is guilty of helping her to perpetrate a fraud is extraordinarily narrow and shortsighted. Perhaps changes in style and fashion are a conceit artificially nurtured by Sophists and their followers; but they do give a great deal of pleasure to many people, including not only the vain people who change with every breeze of fashion, but those who enjoy looking at them as well.

Finally, it is not always possible to explain all the reasons for every move to each individual who ought to make it. Time does not always permit all the facts and the reasons to be presented and digested, and not everyone is prepared to grapple with all of the arguments that might be presented on every side of every issue. There are excellent reasons for the use of soap, and some that may not be so excellent. There may also be good reasons for not using soap. Many arguments might be marshalled in favor of the use of one brand of soap as against the use of some other. But it scarcely seeems worth anyone's while to get all of those facts and arguments together and to weigh them in order to make a reasoned judgment on the matter. It is not so momentous as to justify much expenditure of time or energy, unless one happens to live in a place where large numbers of people are endangered because of lack of proper hygienic practices. On the other hand, if one has to decide whether to submit to an electroshock treatment, or whether a certain dam should be constructed, it might be worthwhile to get as much information as possible on the matter before doing so, in order to be sure that a proper judgment is being made.

The Sophist and his modern counterpart, the advertising man, may have their place, then. They take shortcuts, to be sure, on the way to getting people to make practical decisions, but there may be room for such shortcuts in a well-ordered society.

The art of persuasion, as opposed to the art of teaching, is not evil in itself. Only the perverse uses of that art are evil, those practices that make use of lies and deceptions in order to persuade people to do what the advertisers or their clients know in their hearts that they ought not to do! This is the aspect of advertising to which we now turn.

CAVEAT EMPTOR

The ancient maxim *Caveat emptor* ("Let the buyer beware") was coined, no doubt, because merchants in those days were known for their sharp practices. The meaning of the maxim might have been, "Buyer, be careful, for those from whom you make your purchases are not always truthful. They do not always represent their products as honestly as they might. They have a reputation for charging more than a product is worth. They sometimes sell you one thing and then, in the dark recesses of their stalls, wrap another for delivery to you. Be careful, then, lest you be cheated." This *might* have been the meaning of the maxim at one time. Later, though, it is evident that it acquired a wholly new meaning. It was raised from the status of a *warning* based on general knowledge of certain unsavory practices engaged in by some merchants to that of a *principle:* "In any commercial transaction, if there is a dispute between buyer and seller, the burden of proof shall be upon the buyer. If he has any complaints or reservations about his purchase, let him make them before he signs the sales agreement or takes delivery of the merchandise; for once the sale is consummated, the purchase is completed, and the officials of the state are obliged to enforce its provisions, whether the customer is satisfied or not."

In all the centuries that men have been selling things to one another, many devices have been perfected for making things appear to be what they are not, and for wording sales pitches and sales contracts so that they seem to say what they do not say—always to the advantage of the seller, for he is the one who writes the agreement or buys pads of printed forms that have been written by his attorneys to afford him the greatest possible protection against any action that might be brought against him by a disgruntled customer. The customer is presented with a printed form and is asked to sign it. He seldom reads it, and if he does read it he does not understand all of its implications, and he hardly ever takes it to his own attorney for advice. If he does and his attorney advises him not to sign it because of possible trouble later on, he is confronted with the choice of complying with the dealer's terms or not having the product that he clearly wants to buy. In almost all cases, then, customers make their purchases on the *seller's* terms, and not on those that would be in their own best interests. In addition, the law has been heavily weighted in the seller's favor; for until quite recently, the consumer had no advocate to argue for him before the legislatures, there was no organized consumer lobby, and very little publicity was given to any but the most flagrant abuses. Manufacturers and retail associations, on the other hand, sent well-paid lobbyists to work on their behalf at the legislative level, and assured themselves of legislative courtesies by contributing heavily to the election campaigns of those who were sympathetic to their goals.

CASE 14. THE TELEVISION SET

Mrs. Amanda Jones was a poor black woman who lived with her three children in a small rented house in a Midwestern town. She worked as a sorter in a cannery, standing on her feet for eight hours every day. For years she saved a portion of every week's earnings so that her boys could go to college some day.

One day, attracted by an ad in a local newspaper, she went to a discount store to purchase a color television set on very easy terms—$20 down and $20 per month. A few days later the set was delivered, and she and her children sat down to enjoy their new possession. Three weeks later, the set caught fire because of an overheated transformer. When Mrs. Jones called the store the following morning, she was given a long runaround. At last, the manager explained that the store was not responsible for any defect in the merchandise. It was covered by a warranty, he explained, and would be repaired by the manufacturer. The nearest authorized repair station was 300 miles away. Mrs. Jones paid a mover to pack her set and deliver it to the service outlet, and then to return it to her. The service outlet, after examining the set, concluded that it was not authorized to replace the set, but made the necessary repairs. It returned the set to Mrs. Jones at her expense, and enclosed a bill for $125 for the labor, because under the warranty, which Mrs. Jones had not read carefully, only defective parts were covered. By this time, Mrs. Jones had paid nearly $600 for her television set, though she had used it for less than three weeks.

When it was reinstalled, she noticed that human figures had a sickly green cast to them. No amount of dial-twisting and adjusting helped. The set was hopelessly out of adjustment. In anger and frustration, she complained again to the manager of the store from which she had purchased the set and threatened to make no further installment payments unless he repaired the set. (The interest on these installment payments, incidentally, added another $90 to the cost of her set, a fact that she did not fully appreciate because she had never sat down to figure it out.) The manager assured her that he had no responsibility for her problems, that that was for her and the manufacturer to work out, and that she was fully responsible for continued payment of her debt to his firm.

When Mrs. Jones tried her set once more, the green picture faded and the sound went out. She wrote an angry letter to the store and to the manufacturer, and tore up the next bill that came to remind her of the monthly installment that was due. After several reminders from the store, she received a letter from the attorney of a collection agency, informing her that her account had been turned over to him and that if she did not pay the full amount due, she would have to go to court.

Mrs. Jones was only too happy to learn that she would go to court for she felt that at last justice might be done. But to her sorrow, she found that the judge would not listen to her complaints about the set; the only question before him was whether she had failed to make payments in accordance with her contract. Because she admitted that she had failed to make the necessary payments, she was required, under terms of the contract, to make full payment of the entire amount due, plus a 10 per cent "service charge," plus court costs and the fees of the finance company's attorneys, as well as her own attorney's fee. Because she could not possibly pay this amount in one lump sum, the judge imposed a garnishment on her wages. Her employer, assuming she must be a "deadbeat," informed her that she was no longer needed. As a result of her continuing inability to pay the judgment, the court ordered the sheriff to seize everything she had that was of any value, except those items that she needed to exist, and to sell them at public auction. At last, the savings account in which she had deposited her sons' future tuition was attached, more than $1,000 was withdrawn from it to pay all the expenses she had incurred, and Mrs. Jones and her children were left with nothing.

Case 14 actually happened and illustrates only a few of the practices engaged in by businesses when the merchandise they sell is defective. Efforts to correct these abuses are often countered by new methods that effectively leave the consumer in the same vulnerable position he had been in prior to the enactment of the legal remedy.

An example of this is the "specious cash sale," a gimmick that was developed by New York merchandisers when the state legislature passed laws designed to protect people like Mrs. Jones from some of the abuses just described.

In the state of New York legislation was passed a few years ago placing some of the responsibility for defective merchandise on the retailer who sold it. In some cases the customer who purchased the item on the installment plan would be permitted to withhold payment until he was given satisfaction for any claims he may have had about defects in the merchandise he had purchased. In order to get around this, merchants assigned the debts to finance companies and banks, who would then collect, regardless of any claims that might be made against the original seller. In 1970 a new law gave the consumer the right to file claims against the bank or finance company in an installment transaction where the dealer failed to make good on any legitimate complaints that the purchaser might have. As a result, these financial institutions refused to deal with retailers who acquired a reputation for being unscrupulous.

The boycotted dealers had to find a way to continue their practices so that they could stay in business and at the same time protect themselves and the finance companies against their customers' complaints. The solution consisted of the "specious cash sale." The retailer, after making the sale, sent his customer to a finance company that lent him the money for the sale. The customer then returned to the merchant and made a "cash" purchase.

Now if the merchant cheated his customer, overcharged him, or refused to replace defective merchandise, the customer was without recourse. He had already paid the merchant for the merchandise and the finance company had lent him the money in a separate transaction. Both the dealer and the finance company were thus in the clear.

In 1971, because of pressure from a million-member consumer lobby and labor unions, the state legislature closed the loophole for some purchases, but not for all. Under the new legislation, where the finance-company personnel are related to the dealer, where the dealer and the finance company are under common control, or where the dealer prepares the forms for paying the loan, the buyer will have the right to redress against the finance company as well as against the dealer.

Four out of five states still adhere to the old doctrine, which gives the finance company or bank that buys an installment contract from a dealer complete immunity against any complaint that the purchaser may have against the dealer. In opposing proposed rulings by the Federal Trade Commission that would do away with these practices, the American Industrial Bankers Association asserted that their practices were "time honored and recognized" and "practiced in the marketplace for many, many years." Consumer groups, on the other hand, have alleged that many cases of consumer fraud would have been impossible were it not for the doctrine that permits such transfers of indebtedness to take place without a corresponding assumption of responsibility for the original sale.[5]

Because there are so many kinds of fraud and deception in business practices, it is impossible to discuss them all here. A few of the more common types, however, will serve to indicate how varied these practices are and how difficult the moral and legal issues involved may be. We shall concentrate on false claims of effectiveness, false claims of need, misleading statements or contexts, the use of illusions, the exploitation of ambiguities, and failure to reveal all relevant information.

It should be noted that not all of these fall under the category of truth telling. In some of the instances to be discussed, it may be argued that no falsehood has been uttered and that the moral issue of truth telling does not arise. If the moral issue of truth telling must be confined within the rigid limits set by the distinction between "stating what is true" and "stating what is false," the discussion that follows clearly goes beyond those limits. But the moral issues surrounding truth telling are actually more subtle than that distinction allows, for the two alternatives set forth—stating what is true and stating what is false—are not exhaustive. In real human discourse there are other possibilities, including telling the truth in a misleading way; not saying anything that is false, but not providing all the information that is needed to make an informed decision; and using various devices to make things seem to be what they are not, without saying anything in words at all. In short, "stating what is true" and "stating what is false" are contraries. "Telling the truth" and "not telling the truth" are contradictories, whose meaning is not exhausted by the contraries just mentioned. Part of the complexity of our problem is bound up with the extremely complicated meanings of these phrases.

FALSE CLAIMS OF EFFECTIVENESS

An ad in a magazine directed at the teen-age market carries a picture of a young girl whose tears are streaming down her cheeks. "Cry Baby!" the ad proclaims.

> That's right, cry if you like. Or giggle. You can even pout. Some things you can do just because you're a woman. And, also because you're a woman, you lose iron every month. The question is, are you putting that iron back? You

may be among the 2 out of 3 American women who don't get enough iron from the food they eat to meet their recommended iron intake. . . . But One-A-Day Brand Multiple Vitamins Plus Iron does. . . . One-A-Day Plus Iron. One of the things you should know about, because you're a woman.

Two claims, at least, are made or implied by this advertisement. The first is that most American women do not get enough iron in their diets to make up for the "deficiency" that results from menstruation. The second is that One-A-Day tablets will fill the gap. As for the first claim, the American Medical Association pointed out long ago that "the average diet of Americans is rich in iron." This statement was made during the AMA's campaign against Ironized Yeast, which also claimed to offer beneficial results from the Vitamin B that was included in its compound. The AMA showed that Vitamin B was found in sufficient quantities in the average American diet to require no special supplement.[6] Now, if there is no significant lack of iron in the average person's diet (and this includes the average woman), there is no deficiency for One-A-Day tablets to fill. To be sure, some Americans do suffer from a lack of certain vitamins and minerals because they do not have an adequate diet. But the answer to this is not for them to take One-A-Day pills, but to eat more nutritious food.

Prior to 1922, Listerine had been advertised as "the best antiseptic for both internal and external use." It was recommended for treating gonorrhea and for "filling the cavity, during ovariotomy." During the years that followed, it was also touted as a safe antiseptic that would ward off cold germs and sore throat, and guard its users against pneumonia. Mothers were urged to rinse their hands in Listerine before touching their babies, and, after prayers, to "send those youngsters of yours into the bathroom for a goodnight gargle with Listerine." During the Depression the promoters of Listerine warned those who had jobs to hold on to them. To do that it was necessary to "fight colds as never before. Use Listerine." [7] Gerald B. Lambert, a member of the family that manufactured the product, told how Listerine came to be advertised as a mouthwash. He was deeply in debt, and, needing some cash to bail himself out, he decided to move into the family business. In discussing the advertising of the mixture, his brother asked whether it might be good for bad breath. Lambert was shocked at the suggestion that "bad breath" be used in advertising a respectable product. In the discussion that followed, the word *halitosis*, which had been found in a clipping from the British medical journal *Lancet*, was used. The word was unfamiliar to everyone at the meeting, but immediately struck Lambert as a suitable term to use in a new advertising campaign. The campaign caught on, Lambert paid off his debt, and in eight years made $25 million for his company.[8]

Now, how effective is Listerine for the ailments it claimed to cure? The AMA pointed out that the manufacturers of these antiseptics exaggerated the germ-killing powers of their products, that they did not tell of the hazardous germs that were not affected by Listerine, and that they failed to mention that the ability of a compound to kill germs in a test tube or on a glass plate in the laboratory is no indication of its capability of killing them in the mouth, the teeth, the gums, or the throat, let alone in other parts of the body.[9]

A recent case that is merely an echo of similar cases that go back many years is that in which the Federal Trade Commission ordered the ITT Continental Baking Company to stop promoting Profile bread as being less fattening than ordinary bread because it had fewer calories per slice. The advertisers neglected to mention that Profile bread had fewer calories per slice because it was sliced thinner, and that the difference between Profile and other bread slices was 58 as opposed to 63 calories, a rather insignificant amount. In addition, it had been claimed that people could lose weight by eating two slices of Profile before every meal. This was so, the FTC held, only if the consumer ate a lighter meal; and Profile bread had no special virtue, in this respect, over any other brand of bread.[10]

A similar misrepresentation was discovered in ads sponsored by the General Foods Corporation, claiming that two Toast 'ems Pop-Ups contained at least as many nutrients as a breakfast of two eggs, two slices of bacon, and two slices of toast. In a commercial showing a child mulling over such a breakfast, a voice told parents whose children were unhappy at breakfast that "two hot Toast 'ems provide 100 per cent of the minimum daily requirements of vitamins and iron. . . . As long as you know that—let them think it's just a big cookie." General Foods signed a consent order prohibiting it from making false nutritional claims for Toast 'ems or any other consumer food product.[11]

I have mentioned only a few of the better-known nationally advertised products that do not do what they claim to do. The reader is no doubt familiar with the claims made by quacks and fakers of all kinds who promise relief from a multitude of ailments through the purchase and use of their nostrums, devices, and treatments. Many people who have not found relief through normal medical channels for such diseases as arthritis, rheumatism, and cancer are prone to take the attitude that they have nothing to lose if they try these cures, particularly when virtually every "doctor" who represents such a nostrum can produce a multitude of written and living testimonials to his success. Such "doctors," whose degrees are seldom medical degrees and are often purchased from mail-order houses or from unknown and unrecognized institutions, never mention their failures, and are unwilling to submit their patients or their treatments to scientifically controlled tests.

One of the most celebrated cases of medical quackery is that of Harry M. Hoxsey, who operated cancer "clinics" for more than a third of a century. He claimed to have received the secret formula for the cure of cancer from his father, but did not disclose the fact that both his parents had died of cancer. He managed to persuade the Taylorville, Illinois, Chamber of Commerce that his "practice" would be good for local business, and thus his advertising directed inquirers to write to the Taylorville Chamber of Commerce. Before long, patients began to come, and some of them died not long after Hoxsey applied his secret paste. One doctor examined such a patient two days before his death and found "necrosis of not only the soft tissue of his face, but a complete destruction of the malar bone. This man died of hemorrhage at the hospital." Analysis at the laboratories of the AMA revealed that the paste Hoxsey used was an escharotic, a corrosive chemical mixture, whose chief active ingredient was arsenic. It ate away the flesh without distinguishing between healthy and cancerous tissue, and sometimes destroyed the blood vessels, causing death through hemorrhage. Hoxsey also prescribed certain medicines that were to be taken internally—one of them consisting of water, potassium iodide (an expectorant), cascara sagrada (a laxative), sugar syrup, prickly ash, buckthorn, alfalfa, and red clover blossoms.

Throughout his long career Hoxsey was arrested and convicted on charges of practicing medicine without a license. He sued numerous people for libel. And he was under constant attack by the AMA and various organs of the government. Pharmacologists and members of the American College of Physicians testified at his various trials to the effect that there was no remedy for cancer among the ingredients that Hoxsey used. Despite countless setbacks in court after court, Hoxsey managed to come back. It is estimated that in 1954, he treated more than 8,000 patients and grossed more than $1.5 million. In 1956 the Food and Drug Administration issued a warning to the public, stating that his methods were worthless and that it was "imminently dangerous to rely on [his treatments] in neglect of competent and rational treatment." This warning was distributed to the press and was contained in a "Public Beware" poster that was sent to 46,000 post offices and postal substations throughout the nation. Finally, by late 1960 the Hoxsey treatment had disappeared. In 1966 the American Cancer Society issued a catalogue of *Unproven Methods of Cancer Treatment* available to the public, containing more than twenty-five major promotions available to Americans who feared they had the disease. After years of battling Hoxsey, the FDA succeeded, in spite of an expenditure of a quarter of a million dollars, in stopping only Hoxsey. Others took over where he left off.[12]

When a false claim of effectiveness is made, it is claimed that a product (treatment, remedy, or whatever) does X, when in fact that product does not do X. This is true of all false claims of effectiveness. But if a product does not do X, it does not follow that it does nothing else. Some products may do nothing; they may give the consumer no benefit, but at the same time do him no harm, other than the financial loss that he has suffered by buying the product. But some products may have *harmful* effects that are ignored in the promotional literature or advertisements that prompt people to buy them. Listerine may be harmless, though it will not prevent colds. Hoxsey's pastes and many other preparations were (and are) harmful. Clearly, though the promoters of both Listerine and Hoxsey's treatments are guilty of false and misleading advertising, there is a further element of guilt in Hoxsey's kind of operation.

Still, the abuses go on, by some of the most respected firms in the food and drug line. In one recent year, the Food and Drug Administration seized shipments of Peritrate SA, a drug prescribed for the massive chest pain of the heart condition known as angina pectoris (Warner-Chilcott Laboratories); Serax, a tranquillizer (Wyeth Laboratories); Lincocin, an antibiotic (Upjohn); Lasix, a diuretic (Hoechst Pharmaceuticals); and Indoklon, an alternative to electroshock in some cases of depression (Ohio Chemical and Surgical Equipment Company)—all for false and deceptive promotion directed to the medical profession. Ayerst Laboratories was required by the FDA to send a "corrective letter" to some 280,000 doctors, retracting a claim that Atromid-S had a "beneficial effect" on heart disease, and the FDA ruled that Searle, Mead-Johnson, and Syntex had sent literature to physicians that misleadingly minimized the hazards of their birth control pills (Ovulen-21, Oracon, Norquen, and Norinyl-1).[13]

Unfortunately, moral suasion is not enough. Many persons, whatever their line of work, are not sufficiently resistant to the temptation to profit at the expense of others, and they are not touched by the moral arguments that might be brought to bear against their practices. One of the state's principal functions is the protection of its citizens against harm that might be done to them by others, even when they are unwitting collaborators in doing harm to themselves. It is the government's duty to require all hazardous substances to be labeled as such, so that everyone can see for himself what dangers he might expose himself to by ingesting them. It is no infringement on the citizen's freedom for the government to require of manufacturers of poisons that they clearly label their products with a warning that everyone may recognize. And the government is not interfering unreasonably with drug manufacturers when it demands that they print only scientifically verifiable facts in the literature that they distribute to the physicians who may be prescribing those products for their patients' use. Nor is it an unconscionable denial of freedom for the government to prevent persons who claim to cure diseases from practicing upon others unless they can offer some proof that the "cures" they offer are efficacious. For the government's right to protect its citizens against physical assault has never been questioned, and the purveyors of false and misleading information about harmful substances are as surely guilty of assault (if not in the legal sense, then at least in the moral sense) as they would have been had they poured their poisons into their victims' morning coffee. To argue that because the consumer has a choice and does not have to buy the product or use it, he is responsible for whatever happens to him, is like arguing that the poison victim had the choice of not drinking his coffee, and that by lifting the cup to his lips, he absolved the poisoner of all responsibility. The law has long maintained that a person who harms another is responsible for the harm that he does, even if he did so at the victim's request and with his active assistance. When a man is seeking relief from pain or illness and in that search relies upon the statements and claims made by drug salesmen, he is certainly entitled to no less protection than is offered to one who is determined to commit suicide.

FALSE CLAIMS OF NEED

Part of the American scheme of things seems to be the creation of needs, the introduction of a conviction into the minds of people that they ought to have something that they had never needed before, often because it had never existed before. Not only Americans, but people the world over today feel that certain items that would have been regarded as luxuries by their grandparents—or even by themselves a few years ago—are necessities today. Yesterday's luxury has become today's necessity. Electric refrigerators, hair driers, canned foods, soup mixes, and instant potatoes are considered by many to be necessities, though the "need" for some of them has been created. The automobile is probably the most outstanding example of a product whose increasing use has in fact created a genuine need for itself by driving all the competition—including not only the horse, but passenger railroads and commuter bus services—out of business. Cosmetics of all kinds are generally regarded by American women as being quite necessary, though women in other countries, including some very advanced nations, feel no particular compulsion about using them, and some American women are now beginning to question the necessity of using them as well. The need for razor blades was created some years ago by clever advertising by the Gillette Company, which convinced men that they were "cleaner" and more attractive if they were "clean-shaven" than if they wore beards or long sideburns. Many members of a new generation have not only called these premises into question, but have acted upon the assumption that it is not necessary to shave in order to be attractive.

The creation of a need is best exemplified by a new line of products that is just emerging. The advertisers have been going all out to convince women of the need for vaginal deodorants. Full-page advertisements have appeared in women's magazines recently, and on television as well, designed to convince women of the need for these deodorants and of the effectiveness of particular brands. A typical ad says:

> Some sprays hide it. Some sprays mask it. But Vespré actually prevents intimate odor.
> *Made especially for the external vaginal area.* Unlike sprays that only hide odor, Vespré feminine hygiene deodorant stops odor-causing bacteria. Contains twice the active odor-fighter of other leading sprays.
> *Tested by gynecologists.* Vespré was tested in leading hospitals. It's so effective it works all day, every day of the month. . . .

Another product, Easy Day, is advertised as "the most effective feminine hygiene deodorant spray you can buy" because "it's the only one with an extra ingredient. . . . This particular combination of ingredients gives you superior protection against odors of the vaginal area. More protection . . . more confidence."

In a recent public discussion on these products and their advertising, one of the commentators, questioning a representative of the firm that produces Vespré, observed that because the pharmaceutical companies had exploited every other part of the body—the head for headache preparations, the eyes, the nose, the throat, the stomach for hyperacidity and a multitude of other ailments, the kidneys, the bowels, and all the rest, nothing was left but the vagina. "Conquer the vagina," she said, "and you conquer the world!"

Another woman on the panel objected to the ad campaigns that were being conducted on behalf of these deodorants on the ground that they were insulting to women. "What you are telling us," she said to the gentleman who represented the pharmaceutical firm, "is that we stink." She had strong doubts about the legitimacy of that claim.[14]

Many gynecologists are opposed to the use of douches because they tend to remove certain bacteria from the vagina that produce a mild acid that protects it against inflammation and infection. Women who douche, it has been observed, have a higher incidence of vaginal infection than women who do not.

The natural odor of vaginal secretions is not widely regarded as offensive, and is considered by some experts on sex to be highly attractive.[15] Offensive odors originate, for the most part, only where disease is present or where foreign matter (including stale perspiration) has been allowed to accumulate. Any artificial attempt to cover natural odors may cause unnecessary delay in consulting a physician in the event of disease that would first be noticed by an abnormal odor. And, where the offensive odor is caused by perspiration, frequent bathing or the application of talcum powder is a good remedy. One of the dangers associated with deodorant sprays is the possibility of sensitive reactions which can be quite troublesome.

Vespré, Easy Day, and similar preparations are totally unnecessary and may be harmful. But a demand is being created for them by extensive advertising campaigns designed to market products that would never have been missed if they had not been produced. In this respect they do not differ at all from many products that we now use regularly without ever wondering whether we really need them, or ought to use them, at all.

We may suppose that nothing false has been stated in these advertisements. But lying behind each of them there is a suppressed premise—one that the reader is expected to supply for herself—namely, the assumption that women need vaginal deodorants. But this suppressed premise is false. To be sure, every woman can consult her physician to find out whether she really needs these products, but few will ever do so. Many, worried about their attractiveness, and insecure, perhaps, over a fear that they may have an unappealing odor that they themselves cannot perceive, will accept the suppressed premise uncritically and, in the process, make the marketers of Vespré and Easy Day and similar products rich.

That is precisely what these advertisers want. The executive vice president of the American Advertising Federation, Jonah Gitlitz, objected to legislation that would require warning signs on poisonous products on the ground that such warnings are "opposed to the whole concept of advertising." "We are opposed to the whole concept of warnings in advertising," he said, "because our primary purpose is to sell. If we do inform, it is only in order to sell." [16]

The principle that the merchant should inform his customer only when it will help him to sell his product, and its corollary—that the customer should not be informed of anything that might deter him from making a purchase, even when such information may be vitally important to him—are just a step from the swindler's principle—that the customer may be told anything, whether it is true or false, so long as he is persuaded to buy.

The swindler's principle operates in much the same way as that of the respectable advertising man. He too is interested in persuading his customer that the latter has a need for a product or service that the swindler is prepared to sell him, even though he knows that the customer does *not* need it, even when he knows that the customers' well-being may be seriously compromised by his purchase. But the principle that the sale must be made, whatever moral principles must be bent, prevails. A few examples may be instructive.

In the 1930's complaints began to pour in to Better Business Bureaus and the Federal Trade Commission about the Holland Furnace Company, a firm that had some 500 offices throughout the United States and employed more than 5,000 persons. Salesmen, misrepresenting themselves as "furnace engineers" and "safety inspectors," gained entry to their victims' homes, dismantled their furnaces, and condemned them as hazardous. They then refused to reassemble them, on the ground that they did not want to be "accessories to murder." Using scare tactics, claiming that the furnaces they "inspected" were emitting carbon monoxide and other dangerous gases, they created, in the homeowners' minds, a need for a new furnace—and proceeded to sell their own product at a handsome profit. They were so ruthless that they sold one elderly woman nine new furnaces in six years for a total of $18,000. The FTC finally forced the company to close in 1965, but in the meantime, it had done some $30 million worth of business per year for many years.

Similar frauds have been perpetrated by home repair men who climb onto the roof, knock some bricks from the chimney, and persuade the homeowner that he must replace his chimney—at highly inflated prices—or suffer serious consequences. And some automobile repair shops, such as some Aamco Transmission dealers, have been accused in a number of states of declaring that perfectly good transmissions were "burned up" or "shot" and needed replacement or rebuilding at enormous cost.[17] Again, the gimmick is to create a "need" for something when in fact there is no need at all. That is, to persuade the consumer that he ought to buy something that he really ought *not* to buy; to persuade him that it is in his best interests to pay a large sum of money for a given product or service when in fact it is highly detrimental for him to do so, and he gains no benefit whatever from his purchase.

The difference between the cosmetic manufacturer who is trying to persuade women that they need vaginal deodorants and the exterminator who brings his own termites to display to customers whose homes he has inspected, claiming that he found them in the foundation of the home, is one of degree only. To be sure, the advertiser does not victimize any one person to the same degree. He gets rich by extracting a little money from multitudes of women, rather than by taking a lot from a few very gullible people. He has not pulled bricks from his victim's home or dismantled her furnace. But he has produced a pocketful of termites that weren't there when he arrived on the scene.

MISLEADING STATEMENTS OR CONTEXTS

Campbell's Soups concocted a television commercial that showed a thick, creamy mixture that the announcer suggested was Campbell's vegetable soup. Federal investigators, intrigued by the fact that the soup shown in the commercial was much thicker than any Campbell's vegetable soup they had ever seen, discovered that the bowl shown in the commercial had been filled with marbles to make it appear to be thicker than it really was and to make it seem to contain more vegetables than it did. Max Factor promoted a wave-setting lotion, Natural Wave, by showing how a drinking straw soaked in the lotion curled up. The FTC pointed out, however, that it did not logically follow that human hair would react as drinking straws did. The implication left in the viewer's mind, therefore, was false, because, in fact, straight hair did not curl after being soaked in Natural Wave.

Such visual trickery is quite common in television commercials, in newspaper and magazine advertisements, in direct mail advertisements, and on package labels. The bowful of plump, luscious-looking golden peaches pictured on the label often turns out to be a half-bowl full of sickly looking, stringy brown peaches and a pint of syrup.

Misleading statements are also very common. A number of so-called management companies have been advertising for talented men and women, and especially for children, who would be given an "excellent chance" of being put to work doing television commercials "at no fee." As it turned out, the agencies seldom placed anyone, and, though they charged no fees, they sent their clients to photographers who charge them substantial fees for taking their publicity pictures, or referred them to a firm that took "screen tests," also for lots of money. As it happens, the photographers were always closely allied with the "management" agencies, and the latter always shared a very healthy proportion of the fees charged by the former.[18]

In none of these cases could one say that false statements were made. Strictly speaking, these advertisers are not guilty of lying to the public, if *lying* is defined as the deliberate utterance of an untrue statement. For, taken literally, none of the statements made in these advertisements is untrue. But the messages of the ads are misleading. Because of the pictorial matter in them, the reader or viewer makes inferences that are false; and the advertiser juxtaposes those pictures with the narrative in such a way that false inferences *will* be made. It is through those false inferences that he expects to earn enough money to pay for the ad and to have something left over for himself.

The land promoter who sends a glossy pamphlet advertising his "retirement city" in Arizona may not make a single false statement in the entire pamphlet. But by filling it with beautiful color photographs of swimming pools, golf links, and lush vegetation, none of which exist within 100 miles of the land he is selling, he leads his prospects to believe that certain features exist within that area which do *not* exist. Thus, without uttering or printing a single false statement, he is able to lead his prospects to believe what he knows is not true.

Such deceptions are fraudulent in the moral sense of the word; but unfortunately, in the legal sense of the word, they are very often not considered to be fraudulent. For fraud, legally, is a criminal offense. In order to prove that a man has committed any criminal offense, one must first prove that he did what he did maliciously and with intent to cause injury (financial, mental, physical, or other) to another person. In such cases as these it is almost impossible to prove that such an intent existed, for it is impossible to creep into a man's mind to determine what his intentions or motives really are. It is sometimes possible to gather sufficient evidence to establish, beyond a reasonable doubt, that the accused had the state of mind necessary for a criminal conviction. But in cases of fraud, it is generally impossible to find enough evidence to establish such a proposition satisfactorily. The man accused of fraudulently advertising, promoting, or selling any product whatever can claim that he did not intend to harm anyone through his actions, that he honestly believed in his product, and that he had no idea people would make such false inferences on the basis of the evidence he presented to them. Because it is usually impossible to refute such a stand, very few people are ever convicted of fraud, no matter how much harm they may have done to others as they made themselves rich.

The FTC in the United States has broad powers to deal with perpetrators of fraud when their activity crosses state lines, and the post office has been granted some power to put an end to some of the mail frauds that have been perpetrated upon the public; but these powers are civil rather than criminal in nature, and they consist primarily in the power to stop mail services, to order persons to "cease and desist" from certain practices, and to impose civil fines upon them if they violate such orders. But few states have given their own authorities even that much power, and the federal government is handicapped by a lack of personnel and funds, and is thus unable to handle all the cases that fall within its jurisdiction. As a result, the government is able to exercise very little control over those who publish or write misleading advertisements, and millions of persons are bilked out of billions of dollars every year because of them.[19]

THE EXPLOITATION OF ILLUSIONS

Closely related to misleading pictures and statements is the use made by manufacturers and advertisers of illusions in selling their goods. This is best illustrated by the use merchandisers make of certain optical illusions in their choice of packaging. Cereal boxes would be much more stable, less apt to spill over, if they were short and squat. But the packaging experts at Kellogg's, General Foods, and General Mills know that if housewives are given the choice between two boxes of cereal, one short and squat and the other tall and narrow, they will almost invariably choose the tall and narrow box, *even if it contains less cereal and costs more.* Most housewives judge by the outward appearance of the box and do not look for the net weight and attempt to calculate the price per ounce (a project that is virtually impossible anyway, unless one is equipped with a slide rule). Two lines of equal length, one horizontal and the other vertical, do not *appear* to be of equal length. The vertical line always appears to be longer. Tall boxes appear to be larger than short ones, and the housewife doing her shopping thinks she is getting more in the tall box than she would be getting if she were to purchase the short box.

Bottles follow the same principle. Shampoos, for example, are packaged in tall, narrow bottles—often with the waist pinched to make them even taller—to give the illusion of quantity. Some jars and bottles are manufactured with inner compartments, or double glass walls, so that the actual quantity of goods in the container is much less than it appears to be. Fruit and other goods are canned in large quantities of syrup, and cookies, nuts, and other dry foods are packed in tins or cartons that are stuffed with cardboard—allegedly to prevent breakage, but more realistically to reduce the quantity of goods in the package while giving the customer the illusion that he is purchasing more than is actually to be found in the package.

Manufacturers argue that these stuffings are necessary to prevent breakage, that there is a certain amount of "settling" in some products that results in their packages being a third empty when they reach the consumer, and that their machines have been designed in any case to fill the packages by weight so that the customer always receives an honest measure, regardless of the size or shape of the package. But these explanations do not explain the hiss of air that escapes from my toothpaste tube when I open it (the tube seemed full and firm until then, but turns out to have been full of air); and it does not explain the manufacturers' aversion to standardized weights and their vigorous battle against requirements that the net weight be printed boldly and prominently on the front of the package. Until recent legislation was passed, the net weight of many products was printed in obscure corners of the packages, in microscopic type, and in a color that was just two shades lighter than the background color of the package (e.g., red against a dark red background) so that it was almost impossible for the normal shopper to find out how much merchandise was contained in the package.

However, the producer and the manufacturer may have legitimate excuses for some of these practices. A relatively small macaroni company, for example, may produce a number of different products, in different shapes and with a variety of densities. By standardizing all of its packages by *dimensions* rather than by *weight*, it is able to purchase packages and cases in great quantities and to save considerable money both for itself and, one would hope, for its customers. If it were required to standardize its packages by *weight*, it would have to invest a considerable amount of money in new plant and equipment, and the time during which its plant and equipment were standing idle would be increased significantly, thus raising its costs and, eventually, the cost to the consumer.[20] If standardized packaging were suddenly legislated into existence, it is conceivable that a number of smaller firms would be forced out of business because of their inability to absorb the added costs, and that the giant corporations would be bequeathed an even larger share of the total market than they now have. Still, none of these considerations should apply to a requirement that all packages bear, in clear and unmistakable type, a true and unambiguous statement of the nature of their contents and their weight.

CONCEALMENT OF THE TRUTH

Merchants and producers have many ways of concealing truth from the customers—not by lying to them, but simply by not telling them facts that are relevant to the question of whether they ought to purchase a particular product or whether they are receiving full value for their money. A particularly good example of this is the great ham scandal that broke into the open a few years ago. Major packers, including Swift, Armour, and others, were selling ham that was advertised as being particularly juicy. The consumer was not told, however, that the hams were specially salted and that hypodermic syringes were used to inject large quantities of water into them. The "juice" was nothing but water that evaporated away during cooking, leaving a ham some 40 per cent smaller than the one that had been put into the oven. The housewife purchasing such a ham had no advance warning that she was purchasing water for the price of ham, unless she knew that the words *artificial ham* that were printed in small letters on the seal of the package meant that that was the case. Even that small warning, if it can be called such, was added only because of pressure brought to bear against the packers by the FTC. And there was no publicity to arouse the consumer to the special meaning of that odd term, *artificial ham*.[21]

Probably the most common deception of this sort is price deception, the technique some high-pressure salesmen use to sell their goods by grossly inflating their prices to two, three, and even four times their real worth. Again, there may be no "untruth" in what they say; but they conceal the important fact that the same product, or one nearly identical to it, can be purchased for far less at a department or appliance store. It is not the business of salesmen and businessmen to send their clients to their competitors, but it is certainly unethical for them to fail to tell their customers that they are not getting full value for their money.

Perhaps it may be put as follows: A burglar or a thief may be heavily fined or sent to jail for many months for stealing a relatively small amount of money or valuables from a single person. But a salesman who cheats hundreds of people out of equal sums of money that total, in the aggregate, hundreds of thousands of dollars, is immune to prosecution, and may, in fact, be one of the community's most respected citizens. If Armour and Swift and other large corporations can bilk their customers out of enormous sums of money and do it with impunity, why, one might ask, should the petty thief be subjected to such severe penalties for his activities? He may plead that he desperately needs the money he derives from his dishonest activities, but that excuse would hardly be credible if it was uttered by corporate executives.

OUR DECEPTIVE LANGUAGE

Equivocation was recognized by Aristotle as one of the most deceptive of all logical tricks. The ambiguity of language makes man's most valuable instrument subject to distortion so that it may be used to take advantage of unsuspecting persons who are not familiar with the ways in which seemingly precise terms can actually be used to make considerable profit for those who know how to use them to mean what they want them to mean.

One might suppose that mathematical terms would be the most precise and unambiguous of all, and that "8 per cent of $1,200" would mean the same thing everywhere and at all times. But it is easy to show that this seemingly innocent expression, "8 per cent of $1,200," can have a number of meanings and that the precise meaning conferred upon that expression can make a considerable difference to the person who borrows $1,200 for one year at what is said to be 8 per cent interest.

Though there are many variations, the following three will serve to illustrate the point.

CASE 15. THE 8 PER CENT LOAN

Suppose you go to a bank or a finance company and ask for a loan of $1,200. After all the necessary formalities have been completed, you are told that your credit is good, and that the loan will be made "at 8 per cent interest." This might mean any of the following things:

1. You are given $1,200 by the banker, and, at the end of each month or whenever you make your payments, you pay interest on the outstanding balance at the rate of 8 per cent per year, or .08/12 per month. You will then pay a total of $1,252 and have the use of an average of $650 of the bank's money through the twelve-month period during which you are paying it back, for a true interest rate of 8.05 per cent.

2. Eight per cent of the total amount of your loan is deducted from the amount given to you when you make the loan. That is, you pay your interest in advance, and then repay the loan in monthly installments. Suppose that you intend to make the loan for one year. Ninety-six dollars will be deducted from the sum given to you, and you then pay the bank $1,200 in monthly installments. Under these circumstances, because you start off with only $1,104 and repay a part of it each month, you would have the use of an average of $554 of the bank's money throughout the loan period. The interest of $96 constitutes 17.3 per cent of this amount.

3. Your interest is added to the total amount of the loan you make, and then you pay that amount to the bank in equal installments. Thus, your loan is for the amount of $1,296, but you receive $1,200 cash, and repay the loan in monthly installments of $1,296/12, or $108 per month. Because the average amount of the bank's money in use by the borrower is only $530, he pays a true interest rate of 18.1 per cent on his loan.

When the bank or finance company adds "service charges" and insurance charges, the rate can climb considerably higher still. Your friendly neighborhood banker, despite his reputation for honesty in financial affairs, is not above using such verbal trickery to make you believe that you're receiving the prime rate on your loan, when in reality, you're paying two or three times as much for your loan as a wealthy businessman pays for his. A true 8 per cent loan on $1,200 would permit the borrower to take $1,200 and keep it for the time agreed—say, one year. At the end of that time, he would return the principal ($1,200) and pay the interest ($96). He would have had the use of the full amount for the full time. When you pay the interest in advance, or have it added to or deducted from the amount of money you receive or the face amount of the loan, you pay considerably more for your use of the money, for you start returning the money to the lender at the end of one month and continue to return it to him throughout the period of the loan, though you have paid interest on it as if you had been able to keep it throughout the period of the loan. The money you have had in your hands during the full period of the loan is not the $1,200 you borrowed, but about half as much—for you must average it out over the number of months that you have been returning it. Thus, in real terms, the money you hold is half as much as you think, and your interest rate is doubled or trebled. Such practices have become more difficult since the United States government passed its truth-in-lending law, but many consumers still don't know how to tell a good loan from a bad one.

A FINAL WORD ON ADVERTISING

Advertising has an important and constructive role to play in the life of the nation. It is not true that all advertising men are unscrupulous or that all businessmen are concerned only with selling, no matter what the cost to their customers. Nor is it true that advertisements are necessarily misleading or fraudulent.

David Ogilvy, one of the most successful advertising executives in the United States, is the creator of such successful advertising images as Schweppes's Commander Whitehead and Hathaway Shirt's man with the eye patch.[22] In his discussion of techniques for building a successful advertising campaign, he says,

> *Give the Facts.* Very few advertisements contain enough factual information to sell the product. There is a ludicrous tradition among copywriters that consumers aren't interested in facts. Nothing could be farther from the truth. Study the copy in the Sears, Roebuck catalogue; it sells a billion dollars' worth of merchandise every year by giving *facts*. In my Rolls-Royce advertisements I gave nothing but facts. No adjectives, no "gracious living."
>
> The consumer isn't a moron; she is your wife. You insult her intelligence if you assume that a mere slogan and a few vapid adjectives will persuade her to buy anything. She wants all the information you can give her.[23]

And he adds the following bit of advice that bears directly on our subject:

> You wouldn't tell lies to your own wife. Don't tell them to mine. Do as you would be done by.
>
> If you tell lies about a product, you will be found out—either by the Government, which will prosecute you, or by the consumer, who will punish you by not buying your product a second time.
>
> Good products can be sold by *honest* advertising. If you don't think the product is good, you have no business to be advertising it. If you tell lies, or weasel, you do your client a disservice, you increase your load of guilt, and you fan the flames of public resentment against the whole business of advertising.[24]

In short, Ogilvy believes that aside from any ethical reasons that might be advanced for factual, informative, and truthful advertising, it is in the best interests of both the advertising man and his client—from a purely practical point of view—to adhere to these principles, for they keep the attorney general and the FTC away from the door, and in the long run, they are more successful in the marketplace. He claims that the "combative-persuasive" type of advertising that so many people have condemned for its lack of taste is not nearly as profitable as informative advertising.

He argues also that advertising is a force for sustaining standards of quality and service. The advertisement contains a promise that must be fulfilled if the customer is to be satisfied. The public will eventually turn against any advertiser who fails to keep the promises he has made in his public pronouncements. Ogilvy tells of firms that have warned their employees to maintain the standards of service that have been described in their advertising, and of others that have warned that they would move their accounts to other agencies if their commercials were ever cited by government agencies for dishonesty. The fear of exposure by government agencies and consumer groups in the public press, and the adverse publicity that would result, is enough to deter some firms from engaging in deceptive advertising.

As for the charge that advertisers create needs or desires for things that people might well do without, this is what Ogilvy has to say:

> Does advertising make people want to buy products they don't need? If you don't think people need deodorants, you are at liberty to criticize advertising for having persuaded 87 per cent of American women and 66 per cent of American men to use them. If you don't think people need beer, you are right to criticize advertising for having persuaded 58 per cent of the adult population to drink it. If you disapprove of social mobility, creature comforts, and foreign travel, you are right to blame advertising for encouraging such wickedness. If you dislike affluent society, you are right to blame advertising for inciting the masses to pursue it.
>
> If you are this kind of Puritan, I cannot reason with you. I can only call you a psychic masochist. Like Archbishop Leighton, I pray, "Deliver me, O Lord, from the errors of wise men, yea, and of good men."
>
> Dear old John Burns, the father of the Labor movement in England, used to say that the tragedy of the working class was the poverty of their desires. I make no apology for inciting the working class to desire less Spartan lives.[25]

There is certainly some truth in what Ogilvy says, but at some points he and I must part company. First, he gives the advertisers more credit than may be their due when he asserts that they have persuaded 58 per cent of the adult population to drink beer. It is not at all unlikely that some people would be drinking beer even if it were never advertised. The drinking of beer far antedates the modern advertising industry, and may be traced to causes other than the efforts of copywriters. Secondly, the desires for social mobility, creature comforts, and foreign travel are all exploited by advertisers to sell their products, but advertisers did not invent them or create them. The critics of advertising do not believe that social mobility, creature comforts, and foreign travel are wicked, and to say that they do is to evade the issue. The issue is not the advertiser's *encouragement* of these desires, but his *exploitation* of them. Thirdly, unlike beer, social mobility, and foreign travel, there was never a demand for deodorants until the advertisers created it. They did so, not to create a better society, but to make money. Those who object to the exploitation of normal human desires by persons and corporations intent on making money at a great cost to their customers and by utilizing methods that conceal or distort the facts are not psychic masochists (whatever that may be), nor are they Puritans. They are people who are outraged by what they consider to be the unconscionable methods utilized by some businesses to increase their profits at the expense of people who can often ill afford to be exploited.

Some 2,000 years ago there was a debate between the scholars of two great academies as to whether it was proper to praise the beauty of an ugly bride. According to one faction, the principle that one should refrain from uttering any falsehood required that the honest man refrain from praising the ugly bride. The other group, however, insisted that principles of kindness should prevail and that even if one had to lie, one was obliged to add to the newly-weds' happiness rather than to detract from it. They went on to say that in a matter of far less moment to a man than his marriage, the principle of kindness should take precedence, so that if a person had made a bad bargain at the market, one should not rub it in by telling him so.[26] If they were here to participate in a discussion on the issue presently under consideration, it is not hard to imagine what they might say:

Thousands of men and women are too poor to afford foreign travel, or large and flashy automobiles, or Hathaway shirts, or expensive liquors, or costly cosmetics. What useful purpose is served by dangling these luxuries before their eyes? To some, perhaps, the enticing display of such luxuries may serve as an incentive, spurring them on to greater achievement so that they too may enjoy what their more affluent neighbors take for granted. But to many, and perhaps to most, the display may arouse feelings of frustration, anger, and hurt. "Why," they may ask, "are we unable to have all of these things, when so many others do? Why can we not give our children what those ads show other people giving their children? Why can we not share the happiness that is depicted here?" Before a man is married, it might be appropriate to point out some of his fiancée's faults; but at the wedding, when it's obviously too late, it's unkind to dwell on them. For those who cannot afford the luxuries—and they are luxuries, whatever Ogilvy may say—offered in advertisements that are often directed *specifically at them,* it is cruel to hurt them by offering them what they cannot buy, or to seduce them with false promises of happiness or prestige or success into neglecting their primary obligations in order to seek the fantasy world portrayed in advertisements.

Everyone wants a beautiful bride, I suppose, and it may be good that the working classes no longer desire to live Spartan lives, if they ever did. But some men learn to live very happily with women whose proportions are not even close to those that are currently considered to be the standard of beauty, and it is wrong to jeopardize their happiness by constantly reminding them of that fact; and it would be infinitely worse to parade well-proportioned beauties before them and to urge them to switch. No one is married to a life of poverty. But some people, unable to escape from such a life themselves, have made the adjustment and have found that it is possible to be happy and respectable even on a severely limited income. Is it right to parade the latest fashions in "good living" before their eyes at every opportunity, urging them to buy them *"Now, while our limited supply lasts!"?* Men who have been seduced into discontentment over their wives have been known to commit murder. So have some who have been seduced into dissatisfaction with their style of life. Some of the latter may be partially attributable to advertising.

This is not to say that all advertising is bad; but even when the message is not distorted, those who use the mass media to disseminate it should do so with some sense of social and public responsibility. It is far worse, though, when the message is distorted. And even David Ogilvy, for all his insistence on honesty in advertising, admits that he is "continuously guilty of *suppressio veri* [the suppression of the truth]. Surely it is asking too much to expect the advertiser to describe the shortcomings of his product? One must be forgiven for putting one's best foot forward." [27] So the consumer is *not* to be told all the relevant information; he is *not* to be given all the facts that would be of assistance in making a reasonable decision about a given purchase. In particular, he will *not* be told about the weaknesses of a product, about its shock hazards, for example, if it is an electrical appliance; about the danger it poses to the consumer's health if it is a cleaning fluid; about the danger it poses to his life if it is an automobile tire that is not built to sustain the heavy loads of today's automobile at turnpike speeds; or, if one carries the doctrine to its final conclusion, about the possibly harmful side effects of a new drug that is advertised to the medical profession. Telling the truth combined with *"suppressio veri"* is *not* telling the truth. It is *not* asking too much of the advertiser to reveal such facts when they are known to him, and he should *not* be forgiven for "putting his best foot forward" at his customer's expense. Ogilvy admits, too, that he sometimes tells the truth about the products he advertises in such a way that it seems to the reader that his product is different, in those respects, from similar products, whereas Ogilvy knows that all other products of the same kind possess the same features. All aspirin is the same, for example, whether it is stamped *Bayer* and sells for $1.95 per hundred or whether it is an unadvertised brand of U.S.P. aspirin that sells for 35 cents per hundred. But the advertiser will try to convince you that what is true of Bayer aspirin is not true of the other product. This is unfair to the consumer, whether he is rich or poor; but it is particularly unfair to the poor consumer, who could use the money he spends paying for Bayer's advertising in other ways.

Advertising has an important role to fill in our society. It is not likely to disappear. But it is not always carried on in the most ethical manner. Its supporters tend to exaggerate the benefits that have flowed from it, and they are not at all shy about boasting about its effectiveness in their trade meetings and in their efforts to win new business. But they often shrug off any suggestion that their efforts may have harmful effects upon some segments of society by denying that they are all *that* effective. They cannot have it both ways. If advertising is as effective as its practitioners claim it to be, then it possesses enormous potential for harm as well as for good. Because many, though not all, advertisers are concerned primarily about selling their products and only secondarily, if at all, about telling the truth, it is reasonable to suggest that some government regulation be exercised over this industry; and in particular, that advertisers—both producers and agencies—be held liable for harm or damage that results to consumers from misleading or false claims in advertisements, and that they be required to make good any financial loss that consumers may suffer as a result of reliance upon any misleading advertisement, whether the advertisement was "fraudulent" in the criminal sense or not. If laws were passed, both on the federal level and at the state or provincial level, making agencies and producers responsible for restitution of damages suffered by customers who relied upon their "messages," there would be a great incentive for those concerned to confine their claims to those that could be substantiated and to resort to fewer misleading gimmicks. Though such legislation would not eliminate all abuses, it would go a long way toward assuring the public that the advertising messages to which it was exposed respected the truth.

13

The Search for Truth

DISTORTED NEWS

The problem of distorted news in the mass media is a very serious matter at a time when public emotions are easily inflamed and when important decisions of public policy are profoundly influenced by information transmitted by the press. Most reporters and correspondents are professionals who take their job of reporting the news as it really happens very seriously. But distortions sometimes creep into their work, and many newspapers, magazines, and television broadcasters deliberately edit the news to make it more sensational or to throw it into a light that is in keeping with the biases of the editors or publishers.

Quoting out of context is one of the most serious offenses of poorly trained or sensation-seeking reporters.

CASE 16. THE PROFESSOR'S SPEECH

An article appeared on Page One of a morning newspaper, reporting a talk that had been given by a college professor on the youth scene. The article said, in part:

> At the State College, the professor said, "practically every Jewish student at the college has experimented with marijuana at least once."
>
> Jewish students at the college, he said, turn to marijuana and non-Jewish students, to alcohol.
>
> "The Jewish kids," he explained, "have money for pot and non-Jewish kids can't afford anything more than liquor; it's a lot cheaper."

This was a sensational charge to make against the Jewish students at the college. Now what had the professor actually said? In the text of his address, he introduced the subject in the following way: "The problem of drug use at the university is exceedingly complex. There are all kinds of simplistic notions about it, though. One of my more naive young students was telling me, one day, that in her opinion, practically every Jewish student at the college has experimented with marijuana at least once. She surmised that 'Jewish kids have money for pot. . . .' " He then went on to give his own views on this difficult and complex problem. By omitting the crucial introductory phrases, the reporter completely changed the sense of the statement. What was intended by the speaker to be an example of a naive, simplistic statement with which he clearly disagreed, was converted by the reporter into a statement of the speaker's own position.

When the professor confronted the editor of the newspaper with his prepared text, the editor argued, "But we reported the words you said. You can't deny that you said those words, can you?" Perhaps one must expect an editor to defend his reporter, but one might expect him to have a better sense of reportorial accuracy. By his logic, if the professor had quoted Adolf Hitler as having said that the Jewish people should be exterminated, the newspaper could have run a headline saying "College Prof Advocates Extermination of Jews!" In the present case, the editor finally agreed to run a "correction," but, as one would expect, it did not appear on page 1.[1]

CASE 17. THE PANTHER MURDER STORIES

In 1969 Charles R. Garry, a San Francisco lawyer, told reporters that twenty-eight Black Panthers were "murdered by the police" in that year, adding that "there is a national scheme by various agencies of the government to destroy and commit genocide upon members of the Black Panther party." This statement was widely reported, at first with attribution to Mr. Garry, but later as if it were a well-established fact. Not until 1971 did anyone bother to check the facts. Edward Jay Epstein investigated all the alleged police murders of Black Panthers in 1969 and discovered that Garry could "document" only twenty. Epstein reported that Garry admitted to having given the number twenty-eight because "that seemed to be a safe number." Epstein's own investigation revealed that of the twenty, one was not a Panther. One was killed by a storeowner during a holdup; one by his wife; one in a shootout with an acquaintance; four were killed by members of another black organization; one was killed, after being tortured, by fellow Panthers; and one was killed by an unknown gunman who used a gun not ordinarily issued to policemen.

Of the remaining ten, six were killed by policemen who had been seriously wounded by the victims or their accomplices, two were shot while threatening officers with guns, and one was shot while running from the scene of a gun battle in which three policemen were wounded. This left only one Panther who may have been murdered by a policeman.

Walter Cronkite of CBS News confessed to having been taken in by the bogus figures put out by Garry. The Washington *Star*, in a courageous editorial, admitted that it had "contributed to the climate of uncertainty and fear in a society that was already dangerously divided" by repeating the figures as if they were fact without checking them out. It conceded that its own articles "fed the myth that the Panthers are the targets of a police vendetta—a myth that has, with the passing of time, become a fixed part of American thinking, and that has contributed to a distorted picture of the police in the minds of much of this country's youth, both black and white." [2]

The ancient fallacy of accent is as widely abused in modern news media as it ever was before the invention of the printing press. Tabloid newspapers are guilty of exploiting this device practically every day, when they print, on their front pages, such headlines as:

PRESIDENT DECLARES WAR

followed, in tiny print, by the words . . . *on inflation.* The misplaced emphasis sells papers, but it also contributes to serious misunderstandings on the part of the reading public. Television cameras may be used in much the safe way. By concentrating on a small crowd of demonstrators, by employing appropriate camera angles, and by bringing their microphones in close, they can make a minor demonstration seem to be a major riot. When the film is accompanied by a narrative recited by a near hysterical commentator who uses emotion-laden words to describe the scene, the public may be duped into supposing that the demonstration has national or even international significance. By interviewing seemingly informed people on the spot or in the studio, the drama may be heightened considerably. The charge that television photographers and newsmen *make* news is not entirely unfounded.

Of course, defenders of the networks may reply that whatever they have recorded on film really happened—just as the editor in Case 16 told the professor that the words printed in the article reporting the latter's speech were uttered by him. But from this it does not necessarily follow that the scene was not distorted by the manner in which it was photographed and reported.

Even the best journals are not immune to distortion in their news columns. No newspaper in North America has a finer reputation for objectivity than the *New York Times*, a reputation that it richly deserves. Yet the *Times* is frequently accused by persons who are in a position to know of having distorted the news. An editor of the *Times* has written, in the *Times Magazine:*

No week passes without someone prominent in politics industry, labor, or civic affairs complaining to me, always in virtually identical terms: Whenever

I read a story about something in which I really know what is going on, I'm astonished at how little of what is important gets into the papers—and how often even that little is wrong.

In addition to distortions in the actual reporting of events, which may sometimes be attributed to honest misunderstandings, to reportorial zeal, or to the press of newspaper deadlines, there are distortions by omission, by failure to correct errors once they have been reported to the newspaper. A telling example is the following, which may not be atypical, and is of great concern because it involves one of the most respected newspapers in the United States—again, the *New York Times.*

CASE 18. THE DOOMSDAY STORY

In a front-page story that appeared on September 14, 1970, the *Times* reported that the presidents of nine financially troubled Negro colleges accused the Nixon administration of intensifying racial tensions by failing to support black education. One president was alleged to have said, "It's five minutes before doomsday in this country," and Dr. Vivian Henderson, president of Clark College in Atlanta, was quoted as having said that "the Nixon Administration's utter lack of sensitivity on this point, purposeful or otherwise, is feeding the flames that already roar in the hearts of many black students."

On the following day, Dr. Henderson wrote to the *Times:*

> I am deeply disturbed by the inaccurate reporting of the conference of Presidents of Negro Colleges that appeared in the September 14 issue of the New York *Times.* The following statement is attributed to me: "Instead the Nixon Administration's utter lack of sensitivity on this point, purposeful or otherwise, is feeding the flames that already roar in the hearts of many black students." This is a gross error and misrepresentation of what actually went on at the meeting. To be sure, we were concerned with the limited response of President Nixon to our problems. The fact is, however, that President Nixon has responded. He has not been silent with regard to concerns expressed by the Presidents in the meeting with him last May. Since the meeting with Mr. Nixon, about $27 million additional funds have been made available to black colleges. It would be unfair on our part not to recognize this response, limited though it is.
> I did not make the statement your reporter attributes to me. I do not recall such a statement being made during the course of the conference. . . .

It is distressing to note that though the *Times* devotes a half-page, and sometimes more, to letters to the editor, it did not print this letter. Instead, it continued to elaborate on the original story in various ways for several months. President Henderson's denial was not published,

and, in the minds of those who followed the stories, the impression
was left that the dissatisfaction on the part of the Negro college presidents went much deeper than it did and that they saw fit to use dire
predictions of insurrection (in either veiled or open form) to further
their cause. It is difficult to gauge the effect that such a series of
stories might have had, not only upon the reading public, but upon
the delicate negotiations that these college presidents might have
been engaged in with the executive branch of the federal government.[3]

The instances cited are from respected newspapers. Others, those that
practice "yellow journalism," engage in distortions that make these seem
pale by comparison.

Those who have the power of the press at their disposal have a special
public responsibility, for what they publish can have an enormous impact
upon the common welfare. The power of the press is limited, and must
not be exaggerated. Presidential election campaigns provide dramatic illustrations of the fact that the people are quite capable of deciding for
themselves, regardless of what editorial writers and reporters may say,
and the pollsters have been fooled more than once by the independence
of public opinion. But though the news media are not all-powerful, there
is no denying the impact that they have upon virtually every area of public
concern. In spite of its enormous power, or perhaps even because of it,
the Founding Fathers of the American Union conferred upon it virtually
complete immunity from governmental control. About the only way the
government can enter into a matter concerning the press is if, after the
fact, a damage suit is filed against a newspaper under the laws of libel.
Private citizens can exercise a kind of informal control by refusing to buy
a newspaper that offends them, by subscribing to one that pleases them,
or by placing or withdrawing advertising patronage.

Those who control or write for the published media should be free of
legal restraints, except those included in the laws of libel, but they have
a moral responsibility to print the truth, so far as it is available to them,
and not to distort the facts deliberately. As people become aware of the
fact that their newspapers are not reliable, they tend to rely upon them
less and less; a kind of cynicism sets in, and to the extent that this happens,
communication breaks down. But human communication is important, and
it is important that people be informed about the events that take place
in the world around them. Such information is often vital to their health,
to their economic well-being, and to their political freedom and independence. Anything that throws doubt upon the reliability of the press jeopar-
dizes these vital interests. And when elements of the press betray the trust
placed in them by the public, they are ultimately self-defeating, for they
destroy the very foundation upon which their own usefulness rests.

TRUTH IN EDUCATION

Every society has the right to perpetuate itself by building loyalty to its institutions and its values through the education it provides its youngsters. Tyrannies are often characterized by their use of schools and youth movements to indoctrinate their youth to blind loyalty to the regime, trampling on the truth where necessary, suppressing it when it is expedient for them to do so. Free, democratic societies, however, rest upon the premise that rational persons will choose to be loyal to them if they have access to the truth. The educational system of a liberal democracy, therefore, should be able to develop a commitment to its perpetuation through a course of instruction that develops in its students a spirit of free and unhampered inquiry and a robust respect for critical thinking.

There is some reason to wonder whether the education of North Americans has been free of self-serving propaganda. A number of recent studies of history texts and texts in the social sciences illustrate the point.

A study of American history texts used in California public schools in 1964 concluded that "while the authors of the books must know that there are Negroes in America and have been since 1619, they evidently do not care to mention them too frequently. In one book there is no account of slavery in the colonial period; in a second, there is not a single word about Negroes after the Civil War; in a third (composed of documents and substantive chapters), the narrative does not mention Negroes in any connection." [4]

The study shows how the authors of history texts play down or ignore "the long history of violence between Negroes and whites, suggesting that racial contacts have been characterized by a 'progressive harmony.' In their blandness and amoral optimism, these books implicitly deny the obvious deprivations suffered by Negroes. In several places they go further, implying approval for the repression of Negroes or patronizing them as being unqualified for life in a free society." [5]

Of the books studied, most of them fail to mention any prominent blacks in contemporary society, and of those that do, baseball players and prize fighters are the only blacks mentioned in two of the books. Those that deal with the civil rights movement of the 1950's and 1960's play up the role of the white middle class and tend to ignore the roles played by black men and women and their organizations. In most such treatments the only black leader who is given any credit for whatever progress has been made is Martin Luther King. Other persons who have played an important role are not mentioned at all, or are given virtually no attention. Similarly, some of the organizations that were very significant for a time but have since fallen out of grace with the general public (if they were ever acceptable), such as SNCC, CORE and the Black Muslims, are "purged"—eliminated from the texts as if they had never existed.[6]

The extent of white repression of Negroes is consistently underplayed. The mob violence, the lynchings, the full extent of the discrimination to which the Negroes of the United States have been subjected, the systematic intimidation, all of these are either omitted entirely or played down in such a way as not to offend anyone but those who know and care about the truth.

Periodic reports of purges of certain personalities from Soviet books, including encyclopedias, are dismissed by some people as a disease of totalitarian society, one that would never be permitted to take root here. We have the freedom to publish, distribute, and read books that reflect every point of view, and those who wish to do so may see the ugly as well as the beautiful aspects of American life portrayed in vivid colors, though they are not evident in most textbooks. Countless young people are discovering that the world is not what they thought it was, that their teachers and their textbooks have given them only one side of too many complex questions, and that the facts in many areas have been distorted and slanted as they were presented to them. Many books and curricula are designed to show America in the best possible light, as a nation whose virtues are manifest and whose actions are always, or nearly always, right and just. The American way of life is presented as the best that man has devised, and the American brand of "progress" as the yardstick by which other nations—particularly the "backward" nations of Latin America, Africa, and Asia—ought to be measured. Thus, a recent text on Africa makes no effort whatever to convey any appreciation for the sense of values or the culture of any African group. The Europeans "discovered" Africa, as they "discovered" America (the original inhabitants of both continents were just *there*, like the rest of the native fauna), and proceeded to bring "civilization" to the "Dark Continent." From reading the book one would come away with the impression that the Africans had no culture and no civilization prior to the coming of the benevolent white man, who brought education and "progress" to the primitive and ungoverned tribes who lived there. The book concedes that African handicrafts are nice, but "craftsmen cannot produce the things needed for a modern way of life." It is taken for granted by the authors of the book, and one may assume that most readers will follow them in this, that the "modern way of life" (i.e., the European or American way of life) is vastly superior to the native cultures of the people of the "Dark Continent." Because the modern way of life must come, and ought to come, and because the native craftsmen do not fit into that way of life, the native craftsmen must go. The craftsmen and the culture that they represent are not worth saving, in view of the fact that the "modern way of life" is evidently so vastly superior to the primitive, savage, superstitious culture that is being replaced.[7]

After a three-year survey of textbooks used in high schools in the province of Ontario, Garnet McDiarmid and David Pratt of the Ontario Institute for Studies in Education reported to the Ontario Human Rights Commission that in none of the textbooks was there an adequate presentation of what they described as "one of the atrocious chapters in the whole history of mankind—the Nazi treatment of Jews and other minorities." Nearly half the history and world politics textbooks examined did not mention the topic at all, half were judged to be poor in their treatment of the topic, and only two out of nineteen were adjudged fair. The authors wrote:

> On the whole, the texts mention only Jews among the persecuted groups and are vague about the total number killed. Most of the discussions neglect to mention the philosophical or social roots of anti-Semitism, the Allied failure to assist the Jews, or the Nazis' treatment of political opponents, gypsies, Slavs, and Poles. Above all, there is little or no attempt to indicate to students that the gas chambers and ovens of such concentration camps as Dachau, Auschwitz, and Treblinka are the outcome of discrimination against minorities taken to its extreme conclusion.

They found also that there was considerable stereotyping in the texts that they studied, with Jews, Christians, and "immigrants" being described with such "positive" or "favorable" adjectives as *great, faithful, just, wise,* and *genius,* whereas Moslems, Negroes, and Indians were often described as *fanatical, superstitious, savage,* and the like.

It is noteworthy that attempts to bring changes in the treatment of minority problems into textbooks and classroom discussions often go unheeded. In 1966 the Canadian Jewish Congress brought the treatment (or nontreatment) of the Nazi period in Ontario schools to the attention of school officials. In its brief the Congress noted that in three chapters devoted to World War II, a widely used textbook, *The Modern Age,* contained exactly one sentence on Hitler's racial persecutions. In 1971 the book was still being used in Toronto high schools.[8]

Studies have shown also that contributions of the Jewish people throughout history are ignored, particularly after Biblical times, and persecutions of the Jews before the twentieth century are never mentioned. The reign of Ferdinand and Isabella, for example, can be treated in world history courses without a single mention of their decree to expel all the Jews living within their domain, a decree that caused untold suffering to vast numbers of people and had a profound effect upon later economic and political developments in Spain and Portugal. The Inquisition may be studied with students never having the slightest hint that a substantial part of the Inquisition's activities was directed against Jews who had been forced to convert to Christianity. A fairly typical example is the following excerpt from a widely used college history text:

> The only nagging problem of the monarchs (Ferdinand and Isabella) was the shortage of money. The Church agreeably fed some of its tithes into the royal

treasury, but royal costs, especially to maintain the splendid army and the big diplomatic corps, were like a bottomless pit. To get more money more quickly, the monarchs resorted to unwise fiscal policies which damaged the long-run strength of the economy by inhibiting the development of capitalism and enterprise. Expulsion of the Jews in 1492 was hardly compensated for by the discoveries of Columbus, and New World gold and silver did not begin to flow to Spain regularly until the 1540s. Because wool sold well abroad, the monarchs favored the corporation of sheepherders (the Mesta) with privileges. . . .[9]

The expulsion of the Jews, then, was another incident in the economic history of Spain, like the vesting of privileges in the sheepherders' corporation. It was one of those unwise fiscal policies. How the Jews felt about it is not mentioned.

In the same text, the Nazi concentration camps are discussed in the following paragraph:

A number of detention camps, or concentration camps, were set up all over Germany (and just before and during the war, in annexed and occupied territories). Chief among these camps were Dachau, near Munich; Buchenwald, outside of Weimar; Sachsenhausen, close to Berlin; Mauthausen, near Linz (Austria); and Auschwitz, in occupied Poland. Often the gate to these camps was overarched by the slogan *Arbeit Macht Frei*—"Work Makes Free." But the SS commanders of concentration camps were interested in neither work nor freedom. Their job was to so terrorize the inmates that the very idea of opposition to the regime would die out. In the main they were successful. Many never returned from the camps; their absence was a perpetual reminder to their families and friends of the folly of defiance, or even criticism. Those who did return were often living warnings of what happened to citizens who turned "subversive." [10]

This account is simply incredible, an obscene distortion of the truth! The impression one gets from this sterile and antiseptic account is that these camps were primarily instruments of terror, designed to punish those "citizens" who opposed the regime into acquiescence in its policies. "Many never returned from the camps." Indeed! How many? Why? What happened to them? The commandant of Auschwitz himself confessed that 2 million Jews were exterminated in the gas chambers and ovens of Auschwitz alone! This was no terror campaign to silence critics of the regime, but a brutal racist program of genocide carried out against old and young, men, women, and children. Each of the camps mentioned in this paragraph was designed for slave labor and for systematic extermination of human beings. Those who did not return to their homes did not leave for happier climes, and they did not die of old age. They died of starvation, of beatings, of hanging, of shooting, of attacks by vicious dogs that were kept by the guards, of "experiments" that were carried out on them by German doctors; and those who did not die through these causes were exterminated by mass gassings and burnings and by epidemics that raged through the camps unchecked, though medical supplies were stored within the camp grounds. The job of the SS guards was *not* "to so terrorize the inmates that the very idea of opposition to the regime would die out." The job of the SS guards was to *murder* the inmates because of an insane racist policy that they had accepted and that was the official policy of the regime whose agents they were.

The authors of this history state that it is their "fundamental faith" that history is not an academic discipline, but "requisite for the enlargement of man." They quote Carl Becker's judgment that "the value of history is, indeed, not scientific but moral: by liberalizing the mind, by deepening the sympathies, by fortifying the will, it enables us to control, not society, but ourselves—a much more important thing; it prepares us to live more humanely in the present and to meet rather than to foretell the future." If history's lessons are fundamentally moral, then how can history's most enormous systematic campaign to butcher human beings be totally ignored, passed over as if it never happened, while mentioning the names of the very places where these abominations took place?

Lest it be argued that every historian is limited by space and must make certain choices based upon what he considers to be unimportant, let it be noted that in this same text, five pages are dedicated to an illustrated discussion of the architecture of medieval cathedrals, with detailed explanations of the distinctions between barrel vaults and cross vaults; several pages are devoted to an exposition of St. Thomas Aquinas's "proofs" for the existence of God; more space is dedicated to Baroque church architecture; and a reproduction of a Botticelli painting consumes a half page. No doubt these matters deserve to be treated in a history of Western civilization. But what moral lesson is to be learned from a historian who devotes page after page to church architecture and cannot be troubled to mention history's most gruesome crime—a crime committed against an entire people in our own time—even in passing?

If this were an isolated incident, if this text were one of a few books written by benighted scholars with a perverse sense of values and an aversion to writing about human suffering—especially Jewish or black or Indian suffering, all of which are ignored—it might not be worth mentioning here. But it is a pattern, very nearly universal, that has been documented in study after study.[11] Historians, the very people whose job it is (one would suppose) to present the facts of the past to us, are fully as capable of distorting the truth as the most mendacious advertising man.

The analogy between the historian and the advertising man is not entirely fair. Many historians write texts patterned after the texts that they read themselves when they were students; those texts were written under the influence of theories about history that attempted to justify the relegation of entire peoples to footnotes or to oblivion. According to one widely held theory, all of history has been a movement toward the final flowering of Christian culture, particularly as represented in northern Europe. The Jews and the Moslems, to name only the most prominent peoples who figured in this history, are ancillary factors who have made some contributions, but whose role is tangential at best.[12] This view and others that have profoundly influenced some textbook writers have been repudiated in recent years. But their influence continues to make itself felt.

Even more important, though, is the fact that even now, so little is done to correct the errors and the omissions of the past. Part of this may be a function of the scarcity of good materials on those aspects of history that have been neglected. Because of their neglect, there are not many good materials, and because of the lack of materials, they continue to be neglected. But this excuse has long since ceased to have any persuasive power, for in some areas (notably, in Jewish history), excellent materials have been available for many years. In others, as in black history and the history and culture of Oriental peoples, mountains of materials are now available to the historian who is trained to find them and is sufficiently interested to do the job that is required to "tell it like it is," or, more precisely, "like it was." Because materials are becoming generally available, then, the reasons for the failure of historians to come up with satisfactory texts must be attributed to sloth, to inertia, to lack of interest or lack of motivation, or to outside pressures.

Some textbook writers have complained that they are subjected to powerful pressures by organized groups who influence their publishers to keep certain kinds of material out of their books. It is said, for example, that some Southern school boards have prevailed upon publishers not to introduce "integrated" pictures into textbooks and to keep certain topics that are taboo in their region out of books that deal with those subjects. As a result, the Civil War is treated very gingerly by some houses; recent civil rights cases are either treated not at all or are given very superficial treatment; some biology texts still have no discussion of evolution; and so on. Some publishers have published *two* editions of selected texts, one for the Southern market and the conservative belts of the Midwest and the Far West, and another for the rest of the United States. The power of these "textbook lobbies," if they exist, is likely to be quite significant, for they can control the purchase of tens of thousands of books in their regions.

If textbook writers are bending to the demands of such pressure groups, it would be reasonable to conclude that they, like some merchants and advertisers, are more interested in selling their products than in being truthful with the public. They are prepared to give the public what they think it wants, regardless of the principles of truth, objectivity, and scientific integrity that should be the ultimate standards by which they decide what will and what will not be incorporated into their books. If such intellectual prostitution does take place, and there is evidence that it does, it makes the practices of the advertising community look pale by comparison; for the businessman is honest, at least, in conceding that he is engaged in merchandising and that his primary motive for distorting the truth (if he does distort it) is money. But the professor who writes a distorted textbook pretends that his primary interest is the dissemination of knowledge, and therefore (by definition) of truth, whereas in fact he is prepared to disseminate distortions and half-truths and to doctor up the story to please his buyers if that is necessary to market his product. Plato would probably say that the corrupt advertising man can do no worse than to take our money from us, but the corrupt teacher may corrupt our souls, a crime far worse than mere theft.

But there are no sanctions against corrupt or lazy textbook writers, and there are no policemen to enforce the standards of integrity that every writer of texts should observe. More careful scrutiny of textbooks by interested persons and groups, and more vociferous complaints against books that distort history or treat their subjects with anything less than complete intellectual integrity and candor would be helpful, if there were objective and universal criteria for "integrity" and "candor" and "the distortion of history." Unfortunately, there are not. And even more importantly, books should not be written under the pressure of civil rights advocates any more than they should be written under the pressure of opponents of civil rights. If it is intellectually dishonest to write a book to please one group, it is equally dishonest to write a book to please another, no matter what its physical or political complexion may be. But parents and educators do have the right to demand that certain topics be covered during their children's educational careers; students have the right to demand equal time for points of view that do not have the sanction of tradition and authority; and, as the demand is raised, books will be written to meet the demand. Professional critics abound, and there is some competition in the textbook industry—enough to assure an ample supply of good books to fill the need, once the existence of the need is made known to the industry.

The open market does not guarantee that good books will be available to suit every need, nor does it guarantee that those that are available will not contain distortions or half-truths. But under any other system distortions and half-truths are *bound* to be present in any textbook that treats "sensitive" subjects. The open market and the free press, for all their shortcomings, are still the best assurance we have that the truth will—or at least might—eventually come out.

TRUTH IN THE COURTS

Justice cannot exist where truth is not respected. Courts are designed to provide an orderly procedure for determining guilt and innocence, for meting out punishment to the guilty and protecting the innocent, for protecting rights of citizens, and for resolving grievances that persons have against one another without violence. The courtroom serves as a forum for the resolution of quarrels in a peaceful way, removing the temptation felt by many persons to "take the law into their own hands" by resolving their disputes and settling their grievances by banding together in private committees, posses, vigilante groups, or armies to enforce their own laws. The court system is a giant step away from the law of the jungle. It depends for its existence upon the willingness of those who fall under its jurisdiction to rely upon it to fulfill the functions that they have assigned to it. This in turn depends upon the consistency with which it arrives at fair and just verdicts, and this depends, in turn, upon the reasonableness of the rules under which it operates and the integrity of the officers of the court. It depends also upon the willingness of the people themselves to cooperate with the courts in the fulfillment of their functions, for if a substantial proportion of the population is determined to frustrate the courts, either the administration of justice will break down or the government will have to rely upon coercion to force compliance with the rules of the court. In either case, there is a great temptation to return to the law of self-help, to the principle that might makes right, and to the use of arbitrary methods for arriving at verdicts of guilt and innocence— methods that do not give the accused the protection of an orderly and disciplined inquiry into the facts of the case before the verdict is rendered. The world is only a step removed from the days when disputes were settled by feud rather than by arguments in courtrooms. It would not be difficult to reverse the process and to destroy what has been built up over so many centuries by rendering it ineffective and by frustrating those who rely upon the system to fulfill its promise to them.

It may be useful to review, briefly, the long history that has led to the present system for reaching verdicts in the courts.

TRIAL BY ORDEAL

In ancient Babylonia, in the days of Hammurabi, trial by ordeal was commonplace. Whenever the judge was in doubt about the guilt or innocence of a party who was brought to trial before him, the accused was thrown into the river. If he drowned, he was guilty, but if he did not, he was innocent. Primitive, perhaps, but effective in eliminating a good many suspects and in avoiding logjams in the courts.[13]

In Biblical Israel, if a jealous husband suspected that his wife was committing adultery, he could complain to the court, which would warn the wayward wife that she was not to be alone with any other man. If evidence began to mount up against her, the final trial to determine whether she had committed adultery would consist of the ordeal of the "bitter waters." In a solemn ceremony the priest would have her swear that she had not committed adultery and would then warn her about the ordeal that she was about to undergo. If she persisted in her claim of innocence, a piece of parchment was produced, and on it were written a number of imprecations. This was then immersed in a cup of holy water, the writing was rubbed off into the water, and some of the dust from under the altar was mixed in, as well as some bitter substance. As she drank this water, she was informed that she would die a horrible death if she were guilty; that her womb would become displaced and shrivel up as a sign of her disgrace; and, as a further penalty, that she would become a byword among the women of her community, to be referred to by them whenever they needed an example of a fallen woman.[14]

These were tame, though, by comparison with some of the trials by ordeal that were developed later. In England women suspected of witchcraft were given a water test that surpassed anything devised by the ancients, for the suspect's thumbs were tied to her toes, after her arms were crossed. She was then tossed into the water. If she drowned, her innocence was established and her family could go home, comforted by the thought that she had not been guilty of the dreadful crime. However, if by some miracle she managed to stay afloat, this was a sure sign that she was a witch, so she would be removed from the water and be burnt alive. In the Roman trial by battle, men accused of criminal offenses were sent into the arena to do battle with one another. Those who were slain were considered guilty, whereas those who won were acquitted, unless there was a shortage of prisoners for the next entertainments, in which case their cases would be adjourned until after a later battle. When the public grew weary of gladiatorial combat, the "trial" could be spiced up a bit by introducing a few hungry lions, bears, or other wild animals, who would test the innocence of the suspects by attempting to devour them. The trial of Daniel is an instance of this very common means of determining criminal guilt or innocence.[15]

Elsewhere, guilt or innocence was determined by other forms of ordeal, including ordeal by fire—having the suspect walk on flaming coals or red hot plowshares, his innocence being established if his feet did not blister or burn. Or the boiling water test, in which the victim had to retrieve a stone from a cauldron of boiling water without scalding himself.

TORTURE

The Inquisition perfected the use of torture as a means for getting at the "truth." When a suspect denied a charge that was laid against him, he was tortured until a confession was wrung out of him. There is no need to describe here the ingenious forms of torture that were dreamed up by the holy fathers in their sacred work. Nor is it necessary to elaborate upon other, more elaborate instruments of torture that have been developed since and that have been used in England, Canada, the United States, and other Western nations—devices ranging from the Iron Maiden, which slowly crushes a man to death, to the famous telephone that was allegedly used at the Arkansas State Prison and that has since been utilized in Vietnam, according to some reports, as a means of wringing information from enemy prisoners. The telephone's wires are attached to the interviewee's genitals. When his answers are less than satisfactory his number is dialed.

Such methods can produce answers to the interviewer's questions, but may not go very far toward providing true or reliable answers. One who is subjected to physical or mental torture may ultimately reach a point at which he will give any answer that is demanded of him, whether he believes the answer to be true or not.

Torture was widely accepted and used in Greece and Rome as a means of extracting confessions from those accused of having committed offenses against the criminal law. Although it was condemned by some of the Church fathers, the Church later perfected it as an instrument of propagating the faith, striking terror into the hearts of heretics, and punishing backsliders and sinners. Pope Innocent IV sanctioned the use of torture by the Inquisitorial courts for such purposes. As in Roman law, the accused was not assumed to be innocent until proven guilty; rather, if a credible accusation was laid against a man, he was assumed to be guilty. Torture could then be justified as a form of punishment for him, as well as a means of extracting a confession. Further, since nothing like the immunity guaranteed by the Fifth Amendment to the United States Constitution was recognized, the accused was bound to answer truthfully any question that was put to him, even if his response might be self-incriminating. If, in the judgment of his inquisitors, he was lying or remaining obdurate, he could be tortured in order to punish him for his failure to meet his obligation to respond truthfully, and the torture could continue so long as he did not provide satisfactory answers to the questions that had been put to him.[16]

The individual's immunity against the infliction of violence upon his person was weighed against the state's interest in uprooting crime, heresy, and other evil influences. Those who supported the use of torture maintained that the interests of the state outweighed the rights of the individual in such cases.

Nearly 2,000 years ago Cicero and Seneca argued that the use of torture was futile, for it caused even the innocent to lie. The Roman jurist Ulpian observed[17] that "torture is not to be regarded as wholly deserving or wholly undeserving of confidence. Indeed, it is untrustworthy, perilous, and deceptive, for most men, because of their strong constitutions or the severity of the torture, come so to despise the torture that the truth cannot be elicited from them. Others are so sensitive to pain that they will lie in any direction rather than suffer torture so that their testimony is contradictory, and they incriminate not only themselves, but others as well."

Cesare Beccaria's book *On Crimes and Punishments* is widely acknowledged to have had "more practical effect than any other . . . in the long campaign against barbarism in criminal law and procedure." [18] Beccaria condemns the practice of calling a man guilty before he has been adjudged, and of depriving him of public protection before it has been determined that he has violated the conditions that society has set for having such protection. Nothing but superior force "justifies" a judge's order that a man be tortured, or that he be punished (if it can be called that) before reasonable doubt about his guilt or innocence has been removed.

"It tends to confound all relations," he said, "to require that a man be at the same time accuser and accused, that pain be made the crucible of truth, as if its criterion lay in the muscles and sinews of a miserable wretch." [19] Most people, he observed, are able to tolerate only a certain degree of pain. Once that threshold has been breached, the victim of torture will choose whatever path is the shortest to escape from the pain. The innocent man who is particularly sensitive to pain will confess to being guilty when it appears that he will escape further torment, and the robust scoundrel may be able to hold out long enough to avoid the punishment that is his due. Innocence and guilt become not judgments as to the truth or falsity of an accusation, but the labels affixed to those who pass or fail tests of endurance.

The innocent man, then, is put in a worse situation than the guilty. For if both are tortured, the innocent man either confesses to the crime and is condemned, or is declared innocent and has suffered a punishment he does not deserve. The guilty man, on the other hand, having successfully endured the torture, may be adjudged innocent and thus escape the punishment he deserves. The guilty person, then, may gain from the use of torture, whereas the innocent man inevitably loses.

Even worse, though, if that is possible, is the application of torture to extract the names of accomplices from criminals who have been found guilty. If torture is an unreliable guide to truth, then it is unreliable when used to elicit accusations against other persons, who will themselves be tortured until they confess. And in the meantime, one man is being punished for the supposed or alleged crimes of others.[20]

COURTROOM DIALECTICS AND RHETORIC

In ancient Athens an intellectual form of gladiatorial combat was introduced into the courtroom, the combat of rhetoricians. Here the weapons were words, rather than swords. Plato reserved his most scathing criticism for the abuse of rhetoric in courtrooms after an Athenian jury, swayed by the clever emotional appeals and the fallacious arguments of his accusers, condemned Socrates to death on trumped-up charges. Lawyers still use many of the same tricks, diverting the attention of the jury from the real issues, appealing to emotions, focusing on extraneous matters, twisting logic, introducing evidence that is either irrelevant to the case or misleading. Fastening on an issue that evokes powerful emotions but is not relevant to the issue does not help the cause of justice or truth; it tends instead to confuse the issues. For example, when an attorney argues, on behalf of a client who has been accused of bombing a government office building, that he belongs to a minority group that has been oppressed and exploited for years, he may touch a responsive chord in the hearts of some members of the jury, but he is diverting attention away from *the main point at issue* —whether the accused did or did not bomb that building. Furthermore, he is committing the ancient fallacy of division, which consists of supposing that what is true of a group is true of all members of the group. "The whooping crane is a vanishing species. There's a whooping crane. Therefore, that whooping crane must be vanishing." "Black citizens of the United States have been exploited and oppressed for many years. This defendant is a black citizen of the United States. Consequently, he must have been exploited and oppressed. (And therefore, his bombing of public buildings—if he did it—is excusable.)" Though it may well be true that black Americans have been exploited and oppressed, it may also be true that *this* black American has been neither exploited nor oppressed. Even if it could be proved, it does not follow that such maltreatment constitutes either an excuse or a justification for bombing public buildings. Such fallacious arguments are about as helpful in determining the facts of the case as torture or trial by ordeal would be. The use of rhetoric and the grandstand plays of lawyers contribute immeasurably to the deterioration of public confidence in the judicial system, a system that, for all its imperfections, nevertheless represents a great advance over most earlier ones and is a vital part of a free society.

THE RULES OF EVIDENCE

In earlier times, jurors were often men who already had personal knowledge about the facts of the case and were therefore aligned with one side or the other before the trial ever started. The function of the judge, and sometimes of the jury, was not to decide the facts in the case, but to decide where to place the burden of proof. Once that was decided, the one upon whom the burden was placed had to prove his case as best he could. Around the middle of the seventeenth century, jurors who were informed about the case were replaced by jurors who knew nothing about it. In common-law countries the jury is ideally a passive receptacle that does not take part actively in the inquiry, but merely receives the evidence, digests it, and comes up with a reasoned verdict. This rule of passivity is adhered to quite strongly. If a juror takes the initiative of digging up information about the case for himself—by visiting the scene of the crime, for example—he must be disqualified and there is a mistrial. In civil-law countries, however, the members of the tribunal take an active part in the inquiry, and it is their responsibility to bring out all the facts relevant to the case at issue.

In common-law countries the rules governing the presentation of evidence are designed to increase the likelihood of the truth being discovered during the proceedings

For example, "real evidence"—physical objects such as the weapon used in a murder or an assault, articles of clothing worn by persons at the scene of the crime, and the like—is received with caution and must be identified by someone who can testify of his own knowledge that it is what it is purported to be (e.g., that a particular bullet was the bullet that killed the victim). There are restrictions on the admissibility of real evidence, though. Photographs of a murder victim, for example, may not be admitted into evidence if they are so gruesome as to inflame the passions of the jurors and raise their prejudices.

Some people are excluded from appearance on the witness stand because it is believed that they are incompetent to give reliable testimony. In the past, parties to the action, persons who might have a financial stake in the outcome of the trial, and their close relatives (particularly their spouses) were not permitted to testify, because it was feared that their testimony would be prejudiced. There have also been rules against permitting Jesuits, non-Christians, and Christians who objected to taking an oath to testify. Most of these rules have been abandoned, leaving only the rules on immaturity and mental disability—that is, the rule that small children and people who are adjudged to be mentally incompetent may not testify. But these rules are flexible; if a small child is capable of distinguishing right from wrong and of understanding the questions that are put to him, he may testify.

In order to guarantee that all the evidence will be heard, witnesses can be compelled to appear and to testify, under threat of fine or imprisonment if they fail to do so without adequate excuse. They must respond to questions put to them on matters of which they have direct knowledge, but are not permitted to report conclusions that they may have drawn or opinions that they may have formed. Testimony that the driver of a certain automobile was drunk would be regarded as an opinion, and would be admitted only if the witness could add such details as the manner in which the person walked, or his speech, or his general appearance, or such other features that he observed that led him to conclude that the driver was drunk. Expert witnesses are permitted to deliver opinions on matters about which they have specialized knowledge when the ordinary juror would be unable to make an informed judgment on the question at issue.

Cross examination consists of questions directed to the witness by an attorney other than the one who called the witness to the stand, usually the attorney for the opposing side. It has been called the greatest legal instrument ever invented for the discovery of the truth, for it often elicits facts that would otherwise have been unattainable, and it is a powerful device for casting doubt upon the reliability of a witness's earlier testimony.

By questioning the reliability of the sight or hearing of a witness, by pointing out that statements he made prior to his court appearance are inconsistent with statements that he made on the witness stand, or by showing that he has a bad moral character, an attorney can cast doubt on the reliability or veracity of his testimony.

Circumstantial evidence is generally admissible, but is subject to a number of restrictions. For example, if it would tend to provoke so much prejudice against a party that the probative value of the evidence is outweighed by the prejudice it is liable to arouse, the evidence is inadmissible. Similarly, if the evidence would be confusing to the jurors or raise false or irrelevant issues, or if it would tend to place an unfair burden on the opposing side, because they might not have had sufficient notice to prepare a response to it, it would not be admitted. A defendant's prior criminal record may not be introduced, for even though it has some relevance in establishing whether he might have committed the crime of which he is accused, the risk of raising prejudice in the minds of the jurors is so great that the evidence is excluded.

Hearsay evidence is generally excluded because of the danger that either the witness or the person whose statements are being reported had faulty sense perceptions; that language may have been misused; that one or the other or both persons are insincere or dishonest; that the person testifying is a vicitm of faulty memory; and, most importantly, that the person whose testimony is being recounted is not available for cross examination. There are a number of exceptions to this rule, but they need not be noted here.

Finally, it should be noted that the law grants certain privileges and immunities to people who appear in court, such as the right not to testify against oneself or one's spouse, the right of physicians and clergymen not to reveal confidences that have been entrusted to them in their professional capacity, and others. Here the law has balanced the claim of truth against the claims of other benefits to society and has concluded that justice requires that those benefits outweigh any that might flow from a more rigorous pursuit of truth.

These rules seem well designed to fulfill the aim of discovering the truth in legal cases where the facts are in dispute, but in fact, they often fall far short of doing so. Great reliance is placed upon evidence given by witnesses who are expected to recall events that have occurred at some time in the past. However, even under ideal conditions, people perceive the world about them in rather distorted ways. Lack of attention to details, faulty eyesight or hearing, distracting sights or sounds, preconceived ideas or prejudices can all contribute to considerable differences in perception. In a situation that is fraught with emotion and in which the witness is either startled or frightened, or is tense and bewildered, the chances of faulty perception are increased considerably. Memory is even less reliable than perception. People are asked to recall incidents that may have occurred months or even years before. Persons and objects, spatial relations and temporal sequences, and details that might be crucial to a case all become confused and imprecise in a person's memory over a period of time.

Jurors may be influenced by the clothes a witness wears, or his manner of speaking, or his apparent social background. A witness's apparent sincerity may cause jurors to give his testimony a degree of credibility that it does not in fact deserve, whereas a facial deformity, such as a scar, may unconsciously lead some jurors to conclude that the testimony received is less reliable than it actually is. The skill of the attorneys in presenting their evidence may make a great difference to the final outcome of the case, because evidence that is presented in one sequence may make a great impression, whereas the same evidence presented in some other sequence, or in some other manner, may make very little impression. And after all the evidence has been presented and the arguments are heard, the jury must listen to the judge's instructions and finally retire to the jury room to decide the case. If the case has dragged on for a long time, as some cases do, evidence taken early in the trial may have dimmed in their memories, whereas evidence taken later on may be fresher. Though many jurors seem to be more or less immune to the histrionics and the emotional appeals of lawyers, others may be swayed by them into making decisions that have little justification in fact, in spite of a mountain of evidence contrary to the verdict that is finally rendered.

The atmosphere of the court and the drive of contending attorneys for answers to their questions also have an effect. Witnesses are urged to produce answers, and are discouraged from answering "I don't know" or "I don't remember." And there is the obvious fact that some witnesses deliberately lie, or introduce false records, in spite of the threat of penalties for perjury.

The trial system presently in use, then, is imperfect, though it seems to have served its purpose relatively well. Some authorities have suggested that the inquisitorial process employed in Continental law, where the judge takes an active part in the search for the facts, might well be introduced into our legal system. But this has its own faults, not the least of which is the fact that it gives to the magistrate considerable power that the English system has reserved for the common people. On balance, the English system seems to say, we would prefer to put up with the deficiencies of inexpert and inexperienced jurors drawn from the general population, rather than to confer upon any government official the final and unshared authority to decide the fate of the citizens of our society.

Some of the present system's deficiencies are exacerbated by the exceedingly long delay between the event and the trial. In England it is not unusual for trials to be held within eight or even four weeks of the arrest of a criminal suspect. In the United States the onset of a trial is often delayed a year, two years, or even more after the arrest of the suspect. In addition to the hardships that such long delays work upon those concerned—particularly the suspect and his family, who must live with the uncertainty of a possible conviction, and with a possible lengthy stay in jail pending trial—they increase the likelihood of memories fading and of evidence growing stale, as well as the probability that witnesses may die, or move away, or become otherwise inaccessible. For these reasons and for others it is important that such delays be reduced through better court administration and increased personnel in the courts.

This summary does not even scratch the surface of the rules of evidence or of their weaknesses. I suppose no one is completely satisfied with a system designed to protect the rights of all, but subject so often to error, to mal-administration, and to perversion by those who would use it to further their own interests or their pet causes. But with all their imperfections and with all their mistakes, the courts continue to work for the preservation of justice, of truth, and of civilization and freedom. The temptation to seek justice through other means is great when the quest for justice eludes one's grasp or is long in coming. The courts of the United States particularly, but those of other nations as well, are in dire need of sweeping reforms. When they are used as dumping grounds or retirement havens for old party hacks, or as patronage plums, it is inevitable that some of them will be manned by in-competents and by narrow souls. Those who wield the power to make appointments to the bench must exercise great discretion, and the bar asso-ciations must begin to show a greater sense of responsibility than they have in the past for counseling those who are in a position to make such appoint-ments on the qualifications of potential judges. The legal profession itself must look to its own practices and to its own practitioners. It should re-examine its code of ethics and bring it up to date; and it should enforce its code by applying sanctions against those who violate it. If there is dissatis-faction with the legal profession and with the courts, much of the blame must lie on those who engage in the practice of law.

If the courts are an important and generally reliable instrument for ar-riving at the truth when the facts are in dispute, and if the danger of a return to more inhumane ways of settling disputes is ever-present, as I have suggested, then it is incumbent upon all of those who are concerned with the administration of justice to do what may be necessary to preserve this vital institution and to raise it to the dignified and honored position that it ought to have.

DISRUPTION OF THE COURTS

In recent years a new phenomenon has appeared, one that threatened to destroy or to weaken seriously at least a part of the judicial process if it had been permitted to go on. I am referring to the use of the court as a kind of theater by defendants, spectators, and attorneys who were more interested in spreading their message to the world through the news media than they were in seeing that justice was done in the courtroom. In some of these cases there may have been some justification for the charge that the judges involved were harsh, biased, and injudicious. But in others there is no question that the judges were competent men of the highest integrity, men with a sound reputation for fairness and impartiality. The dramas went on just the same, with planned and spontaneous demonstrations and disruptions, with attacks upon the dignity of the court and upon the judicial process itself.

There is no message so abhorrent to the public that it is not given the freedom of the forum in America. Any man may speak or publish the most unpopular thoughts and ideas. But freedom of speech and freedom of the press do not entail freedom to speak whenever and wherever one pleases. There must be limits, not to what one may say, but to when and where one may say it. An organization convened to discuss mathematics has the right to demand that those who would discuss zoology do so elsewhere, or wait until its meeting is finished. No plea by the zoologist that his subject is at least as important as mathematics is relevant to the question, whether he has a right to harangue mathematicians about the mating habits of the bumblebee if they do not care to hear him, but insist on discussing the properties of the trapezoid, which is on their program. The zoologist who insists upon his right to be heard can quite properly be thrown out of the meeting, for if he had his way, he and other like-minded persons could destroy the mathematics society by making it impossible for its members ever to take care of their business.

Some political activists seem to have assumed that the issues about which they are deeply concerned are of such great moment, and that their opinions about those issues are so vital, that they should have the right to express those opinions anywhere and at any time. But other citizens have the right not to be harangued, even by well-meaning and concerned persons, and they have the right to conduct their business without interference from other people who believe that *their* concerns should take precedence over those of the people whose business they interrupt. The assumptions made by these activists are presumptuous, and though they may be correct in their belief that the issues that they wish to discuss are important, they are *not* right in supposing that they have a right to discuss them wherever and whenever they please, whatever the consequences may be to others. A hospital room, for example, is not the right place for a political speech, no matter what the issue; nor is a house of mourning, unless the mourners have themselves asked to be consoled in that rather unconventional manner; nor is a college class-room, where the professor and his students have the right to carry on the business of learning without interruption by anyone, no matter what his political views and no matter what subject he wishes to discuss. If the Black Panthers have the right to interrupt college classes in order to express their views on racism, so do the Ku Klux Klans, the Communist Party, the American Nazi Party, the John Birch Society, the NAACP, the Anti-Defamation League, and every other organization. To grant every organization that thinks it has a vital opinion to express on a vital subject the right to address college classes at will would undermine the college and destroy its educational function. It would also impinge unconscionably upon the rights of both faculty and students, who should be permitted to do what they came to the classroom to do.

Finally, a courtroom is not the proper place to air such issues, for the court has a specific function to perform—to arbitrate disputes and to settle legal cases that are brought before it. Frustration of the delicate processes that have been developed over many centuries to guarantee, as far as is possible, a fair trial to all the parties concerned can easily lead to the destruction of the entire system. Such demonstrations as have taken place in the recent past could do just that, if they were permitted to continue. Indeed, it has been suggested that that is precisely what some of the participants in those demonstrations intended to do. But others may have been deeply convinced that they had to use the court as a forum to reach the American people, because no other forum, in their opinion, was open to them or would be so effective as that afforded by the court. Even if this latter assumption were true, it would not justify the damage that might be done to the judicial system itself by engaging in such conduct and encouraging others to do the same. But the assumption itself is highly questionable, for there are many legitimate outlets for the expression of opinion, some of them quite effective.

This whole question will be discussed in greater detail in Chapter 15. But the point must be made here that although those who possess the truth, or believe that they possess it, are required, in general, to tell it, there are circumstances in which they are required not to tell it. There are occasions, in fact, when they have the duty to remain silent.

14

Truth and Civil Liberties

THE CASE FOR CENSORSHIP

In some parts of the world censorship has been a normal practice for centuries. In the Iron Curtain countries, in Yugoslavia, in the Union of South Africa, and in many other countries censorship regulations have been enforced for many years. In many parts of the world, including those countries, such as the United States, that have strong safeguards against any interference with the freedom of speech and press, there are thoughtful persons who advocate some degree of censorship. In the Communist world everything from newspaper articles to books on such widely diverse topics as religion, social problems, economic matters, and political thought are subject to censorship, and novels, poetry, and theatrical productions are rigidly controlled. Some of the most respected works of writers in those countries, including those of at least one Nobel Prize winner, have not been published in the Communist countries where they were written, but have been accorded a warm reception in the Western world, where they have been accorded access to the free press.

The reasoning of those who advocate censorship has changed little since Plato first attempted to rationalize it in his *Republic* and again in his later writings. In the *Republic* Plato declared: "If our commonwealth is to be well-ordered, we must fight to the last against any member of it being suffered to speak of the divine, which is good, being responsible for evil. Neither young nor old must listen to such tales, in prose or verse. Such doctrine would be impious, self-contradictory, and disastrous to our commonwealth." [1]

After setting up a system of dogmatic education, he urged his followers to "take the greatest care not to overlook the least infraction of the rule against any innovation upon the established system of education." He even went so far as to advocate legislation against the introduction of new fashions in music, for in his opinion changes in the conventions of music endanger the whole fabric of society. "It is here," in art, music, poetry, and literature, according to Plato, "that lawlessness easily creeps in unobserved . . . in the guise of a pastime, which seems so harmless." But it is not harmless, for "little by little, this lawless spirit gains a lodgement and spreads imperceptibly to manners and pursuits; and from thence with gathering force invades men's dealings with one another, and next goes on to attack the laws and the constitution with wanton recklessness, until it ends by overthrowing the whole structure of public and private life." [2] If innovation is to be curbed, the best place to begin is in the mind, by crushing the inquiring spirit. For the person who asks probing questions, who raises doubts about the system or its values, poses a threat to a rigidly controlled totalitarian regime. Therefore, Plato concluded, "one of the best laws will be the law forbidding any young men to enquire which laws are right or wrong; but with one mouth and one voice they must all agree that the laws are all good, for they came from God; and anyone who says the contrary is not to be listened to." [3]

By this time in his life, Plato was a long way from the views he had espoused early in his career, shortly after the execution of Socrates on charges of corrupting the youth; that is, of "agitating" among the young people of Athens for a rethinking of Athenian values and the Athenian way of life. But he did offer a rationale for censorship that has been appealed to time and time again in subsequent centuries. The argument proceeds under the assumption that the present regime is ordained by God, or at least that it possesses God's sanction and blessing. A further assumption is that only those with special insights or special training are qualified to ordain or even to advocate change in the delicate and highly complex operations of the society. Those who lack such special insights or training, being unqualified, should be discouraged from inquiring too deeply into the structure of the state or its policies and should be forbidden to publish any thoughts they may have on reforms; for such thoughts are subversive, because they are not in accord with the official policies of the state, or the Church, as the case may be. False doctrines—that is, those doctrines that are inconsistent with those that are taught by the state—must be suppressed. For if people are seduced into believing them, they will begin to lose confidence in the state as the final arbiter and purveyor of right and truth. If ordinary citizens may decide for themselves what to believe, they may also attempt to decide for themselves what conduct is right and what conduct is wrong; and this could lead to anarchy, to rebellion, and, as Plato said, to the destruction of the whole structure of public and private life.

Thomas Hobbes put the case for censorship in much the same terms:

> It is annexed to the sovereignty to be judge of what opinions and doctrines are averse and what conducing to peace, and consequently on what occasions, how far, and what men are to be trusted withal in speaking to multitudes of people, and who shall examine the doctrines of all books before they be published. For the actions of men proceed from their opinions, and in the well-

governing of opinions consists the well-governing of men's actions, in order to their peace and concord. And though in matter of doctrine nothing ought to be regarded but the truth, yet this is not repugnant to regulating the same by peace. For doctrine repugnant to peace can no more be true than peace and concord can be against the law of nature.[4]

Censorship rests upon the assumption that the sovereign or some person or committee appointed by him possesses the truth and is the final judge of right and good, and that the ruler is charged with the responsibility of seeing that false or harmful doctrines are not spread abroad. During long periods of history certain propositions have been considered, by virtually all authorities, to be self-evidently true. Anyone who expressed doubts about those propositions was branded a heretic or a madman. Yet those same propositions are now known—or believed, at any rate—to be false. Giordano Bruno was burned at the stake for insisting that the earth was not in the center of the universe, but that it revolved around the sun.

Case 19. The Persecution of Galileo

When Galileo announced that he had discovered four satellites revolving around Jupiter, he concluded that this was a decisive argument in favor of the Copernican (heliocentric) hypothesis. Until this discovery, opponents of the Copernican theory had argued that the earth could not revolve around the sun, for if it were moving along an orbit around the sun, the moon would be left behind. Now he could show that there was a planet moving through an orbit carrying four moons along with it. The objections offered to his book *The Starry Messenger* (*Siderius Nuncius*), in which he announced his discoveries and his conclusions, boiled down to the following: (1) His theory contradicted common sense and everyday experience, for everyone could see the sun rising in the east and setting in the west. (2) The theory of earth moving through space was contrary to the laws of physics. (3) If the earth moved, astronomers on earth should be able to detect parallax in their observations of the stars, but no such observations had ever been recorded. (4) The Copernican theory contradicted Scripture, for Joshua would scarcely have commanded the sun to stand still if it did not move,[5] the Psalmist declared explicitly that God had established the earth on its foundation, not to be moved forever,[6] and Ecclesiastes stated that the sun rises and sets and hastens to the place where it will rise again.[7] Galileo responded by observing that the Bible was not intended to be a source of scientific information and that its authors used ordinary language and figures of speech in order not to confuse their readers. Nevertheless, he conceded that any scientific propositions that were not rigorously demonstrated and that were contrary to Scripture should be considered to be false.

In 1616 eleven theologians were assigned the task of judging Galileo's work. After five days of deliberation, they announced their verdict: The heliocentric theory, they said, "is philosophically foolish and absurd, and formally heretical, inasmuch as it expressly contradicts the doctrines of holy scripture in many places both according to their literal meaning and according to the common exposition and interpretation of the holy fathers and learned theologians." Copernicus's works were put on the Index until they could be purged of any suggestion that the theory presented in them was anything more than a very tentative hypothesis, and all books (including those of Galileo) that attempted to reconcile the Copernican theory with the Bible were condemned.

Nevertheless, in 1632 Galileo managed to publish another important work, *A Dialogue Concerning the Two Chief World-Systems,* with a license from the Holy Office and a dedication to Pope Urban VIII. The Jesuits, after examining the book, concluded that it treated the Copernican system not as a hypothesis but as an established fact, and they denounced it as being more dangerous than all the heresies of Luther and Calvin. The Inquisition forbade all further sales of the book and ordered the confiscation of all outstanding copies. Galileo, sixty-eight years old and very ill, was summoned to the Inquisition to answer the charges of heresy. In its hearings, which dragged on for several months, the Inquisition produced a document that had allegedly been discovered in the files of the 1616 case. In it, Bellarmine, the chief hearing officer, was reported to have ordered Galileo in absolute terms not to hold, teach, or defend the Copernican hypothesis in any way. Galileo, according to the document, expressed his consent to that order. In the new hearings, Galileo denied that any such injunction had been issued, and he denied further that he had ever agreed to comply with such a decree. He insisted throughout his trial that he had no memory of such an injunction. The Inquisition decided that Galileo had obtained the license to publish his book fraudulently, that it had been "extorted" under false pretenses, because he was under orders not to publish his opinions on the Copernican theory. On the strength of the Bellarmine document they were able to prosecute Galileo for "vehement suspicion of heresy," and were successful, at last, in forcing the sick and aged philosopher to recite a formula in which he "abjured, cursed, and detested" his past errors and heresies, swore that he would never again say or assert anything that would give anyone cause to suspect him of harboring heretical thoughts, and promised to denounce any heretic or anyone suspected of heresy to the Holy Office. He was sentenced to life imprisonment and spent the remainder of his life under house arrest in Florence.

There is a general consensus (not universally accepted) among historians, based upon evidence uncovered when the file on Galileo's trial was published in 1877, that the Bellarmine document was a forgery, planted in the 1616 file to give the Holy Office the ammunition it needed to convict Galileo. Without it they had no case, because

Galileo's book had the *imprimatur*. It was necessary to prove that the *imprimatur* had been obtained fraudulently in order to nullify it.

In the course of time, refined instruments enabled astronomers to observe the parallax that was not perceptible with the instruments of Galileo's time, and the laws of physics were revised to account for the phenomena that had been newly discovered. Common sense was shown to be fallible, as were Aristotelian and Biblical doctrines that had been accepted throughout the scholarly world for many centuries.[8]

The persecution of men like Bruno and Galileo illustrates how the disregard of civil liberties and official refusal to allow opinions contrary to established dogmas to be expressed openly and freely can retard the progress of science and the expansion of human knowledge. Countless other men in every field have been subjected to similar persecutions by state churches and totalitarian regimes. They have been deprived of the opportunity to pursue their researches and to publish their findings, and, what is more important, the rest of the world has been deprived of the opportunity to hear what they have had to say and to pass judgment upon their opinions.

THE LIBERTARIAN RESPONSE

More than 100 years ago John Stuart Mill published his essay *On Liberty*, part of which was devoted to establishing the proposition that there should be no restraints on the voicing of opinions, no matter how radical or heretical they might seem to be, no matter how wrong they might be in the light of the "truths" allegedly "known" and "held sacred" by the community.

Mill argued, first of all, that "we can never be sure that the opinion we are endeavouring to stifle is a false opinion." And he argued that even if we were sure that it was false, "stifling it would be an evil still." [9]

No one is infallible, he said. Even the most superficial study of history reveals the grave errors that men have made in the past—men who were invested with great power and authority and were thought by their contemporaries to be very wise—in the conduct of their personal affairs and in their conduct of the affairs of the communities or organizations over which they held sway.

Mill's advocacy of complete freedom from censorship was based upon the principle that the state has no right to legislate on any matter that restricts the citizens' freedoms except in those areas where such restriction is necessary to protect the persons or property of others. Legislation restricting the individual's freedom in order to protect him from harming himself was, in Mill's opinion, insupportable. If censorship was intended to protect people against hurting themselves, it was unjustifiable on the grounds of this basic principle. And if it was intended to protect other persons against harm that might arise because of the spread of false or vicious doctrines or beliefs, then Mill replied that the evil and the harm arising from censorship itself far outweighed any harm that might come from the spread of supposedly evil or false opinions. The harm that resulted from the persecution of Giordano Bruno and Galileo is a case in point. It is impossible to estimate how far the advance of science was set back by the intolerant attitude taken by the Church to the Copernican hypothesis and those who advocated it. As it happened, the Copernican theory eventually won out, in spite of all the effort that went into extirpating it. On the basis of these examples, and others that might be adduced, some people maintain that truth cannot be permanently lost by persecution; rather, they say, if it survives persecution and intolerance, it is established ever the more firmly. Truth, according to this view, may be subjected to trial by ordeal. But such a trial is no more rational when applied to doctrines than it is when applied to persons. Mill noted that persecution is a strange reward to bestow upon those who have endeavored to enlighten mankind. More importantly, there is no guarantee that the truth will survive the persecution and martyrdom of its defenders. Because the losers seldom write the history books, it is impossible to estimate how many people have endured needless suffering because of the suppression of discoveries and theories that might have contributed to human happiness, if they had been given a free forum.

We may flatter ourselves into believing that we no longer persecute heretics or burn those who express unpopular opinions. But we would do well to look at the question more closely. There are among us those who maintain that our society exhibits grave weaknesses, that it is sick unto death, that it ought to be replaced by a new and better social order. These dissidents sometimes express their opinions in a manner that is quite offensive to many of their fellow citizens, who are incensed at any suggestion that their country is not the greatest country in the world or that certain laws and social norms are oppressive and evil. The latter may conclude that those who express such opinions are part of an international conspiracy to take over the world and impose a totalitarian form of government over free people everywhere. When the expression of such unpopular views is accompanied by a life style that is deemed to be undesirable or improper (for example, by living in communes, wearing beards or long hair, wearing garments that are not in keeping with the fashions of the day, engaging in interracial dating or marriage), the members of the community express their intolerance and disapproval by refusing employment to the dissidents, by harassing them legally and in other ways, and in the last resort, by running them out of town.

Mill argued that such official and unofficial intolerance of persons and groups whose views differ from those of the majority is itself a kind of tyranny that ought not to be tolerated, for it tends to stifle discussion, and no one can be so certain that his views are correct that he should prevent those with other opinions, on even the most vital issues, from having their say. Not the greatest evil attendant upon such intolerance is the harm done to those who are not heretics, for their mental development is cramped and their characters are robbed of that healthy skepticism and robust spirit of inquiry that is never welcome where spiritual oppression reigns. They are intimidated by fear of being exposed to public scorn and ridicule if any of their views should turn out to be unacceptable, and their intellects are thus deprived of the stimulation that disagreement and a rich diversity of opinions engenders.

This brings us to another possibility—that the opinions being suppressed are in fact false. Even then, in Mill's opinion, they should be permitted free expression, for they encourage everyone who encounters them to search once again for the roots of his beliefs, for the grounds upon which they are based. Nothing is so destructive to meaningful belief, even in religion, than lack of genuine discussion and blind adherence to orthodox or received opinions. In the course of time unexamined beliefs become empty and meaningless slogans, platitudes and clichés that have no more impact upon those who utter them than do the babblings of a parrot.

More often than not, however, the full truth is found neither in the received opinion nor in that of the dissenters, but in some combination of the two. Only by permitting free expression of both opinions, then, and by encouraging reasoned argument to proceed between opposing factions can the real truth be found.

All of this leads to the conclusion that there should be no restraints on freedom of information, that the community as a whole, and its individual members, benefit from free and open communication and free expression of all opinions.

Those who live in a free society choose to govern themselves, even though self-government entails certain dangers against which the subjects of totalitarian regimes are protected. One of these dangers, if it can be called that, is the danger of slipping into error. Those who live in a free society choose not to be protected against error; they must therefore assume the responsibility of searching for the truth. As another great libertarian, Alexander Meiklejohn, put it:

> We have adopted it [i.e., the search for truth] as our "way of life," our method of doing the work of governing for which, as citizens, we are responsible. Shall we, then, as practitioners of freedom, listen to ideas which, being opposed to our own, might destroy confidence in our form of government? Shall we give a hearing to those who hate and despise freedom, to those who, if they had the power, would destroy our institutions? Certainly, yes! Our action must be guided, not by their principles, but by ours. We listen, not because they desire to speak, but because we need to hear. If there are arguments against our theory of government, our policies in war or in peace, we the citizens, the rulers, must hear and consider them for ourselves. That is the way of public safety. It is the program of self-government.[10]

A self-governing nation is one that is prepared to take the risks that Plato and Hobbes and the other defenders of totalitarianism would concentrate in the hands of a few. It has not yet been shown how the few—whether they be called philosopher–kings, sovereigns, or commissars—are to be chosen in such a way as to avoid error on their own part and assure those who live under their dominion that their best interests will be served if they are kept in ignorance about matters that the few decide may be harmful to them, and if they permit the few to make decisions for them.

THE LIMITS OF LIBERTY

Even the most liberal philosophers have recognized that there must be limits to speech and to the use of the press and that some of those limits may be imposed and enforced by law. In the last chapter, we observed that freedom of speech does not mean that everyone is free to speak on any topic whenever and wherever he pleases. The discussion there centered upon only one respect in which freedom of expression must be restricted and regulated. There are others, even in the most liberal society.

Any society must have rules governing its members' behavior, including their oral behavior. No deliberative body, whether it is a court, a legislature, a professional society, a faculty meeting, or a committee meeting, can grant unlimited rights of free expression to anyone—even its own members—without finding itself reduced to chaos and utter frustration of its efforts to achieve its professed aims. Rules of order have been established because without them, it would be impossible to carry any meeting to a reasonable, effective conclusion. The chairman of a meeting must have some means of controlling the members so that those who wish to be heard may have an opportunity to speak, and so that those who wish to listen to the proceedings may be able to hear what the speakers are saying. During such a meeting, those who have not been recognized by the chair do not have the right to speak, no matter how important they may conceive their statements to be, no matter how urgent they may believe it is that the group hear what they have to say. If they feel that they have the right to disrupt the orderly procedures of the meeting in order to have their way, they must acknowledge the right of those who are conducting the meeting to expel them or to prevent them from gaining access to the hall in order to avoid such disruption. For unless one can demonstrate that the meeting is illegal or so dangerous to the well-being of society that it cannot be permitted to go on, one is on very dangerous ground by claiming to have a right to disrupt it. This stand is particularly dangerous, because undoubtedly there will be others who will harbor similar sentiments about the meetings of one's own groups and organizations. It is very difficult to maintain that I have the right to disrupt your meetings and to deny that you have the right to disrupt mine. It is not easy to demonstrate that I have the right to do my thing without interference from you while at the same time insisting that you do not have the right to do your thing without interference from me.

Of course, there are people who behave in accordance with an ethic similar to this. When Hitler was getting organized, he had groups of bullies stationed at meetings of democratic parties and societies who heckled, shouted, and rioted in an effort (successful, in the end) to destroy them. At his own meetings, though, these same bullies were posted with strict orders to bash in the heads of any who were so bold as to attempt to interfere with the orderly progress of the agenda. Stalinists, Maoists, and fascists of all stripes have had the same double standard wherever they have attempted to assume power. Not by the orderly process of parliamentary debate, not by an attempt to arrive at the truth through the free expression and exchange of ideas and opinions, but by theatrical role playing, by provocative harassment, by violence and by playing on emotions, they have attempted to destroy the workings of democratic deliberative bodies and to impose their own iron-disciplined machines upon those who were unable or unwilling to fend off their attacks.

It is sometimes forgotten that the purpose of a meeting, any meeting, is not unregulated talk, but the conduct of some kind of business. A meeting of any deliberative body is not for the purpose of hearing everyone who wishes to speak say whatever comes to mind, but to hear everything that is worth being said on the subject under discussion so that an informed decision may be reached. Freedom of speech does not mean that speech is totally immune to regulation, but that *no expression of opinion ought to be suppressed because the opinion itself is considered to be false, heretical, harmful, or subversive.* Even the expression of opinions that are generally acknowledged to be true, saintly, beneficial, and patriotic is out of order when the speaker does not have the floor or when his opinions are irrelevant to the goals of the meeting. Opinions as such ought not to be regulated, and there should be public forums for the expression of all opinions, but there are places and occasions when the expression of any opinion, or the expression of opinions on certain subjects, is out of place and may be declared out of order.

Some forms of verbal expression are not expressions of opinion at all and therefore do not come under the protection of the First Amendment or of the liberal theory of freedom of speech and press. Suppose, for example, that someone has concluded that the president of the Chase Manhattan Bank, being a symbol of capitalism and of the military–industrial complex, should be assassinated. Suppose he delivers himself of this opinion before a mob of angry demonstrators in front of the home of that bank official. And suppose that his words tend to inflame the passions of the mob to such a degree that they storm the house and cause serious injury to its occupants. Certainly such speech ought not to be protected.

Suppose that a group of pranksters decides to play a "joke" on the audience assembled in an old theater whose exits are narrow and not easily accessible from the center aisles. During a tense moment in the performance, the pranksters shout "Fire!" and create a panic in the crowd. That single word, uttered in the proper circumstances, can be as damaging as a match lit in an explosive atmosphere. The pain and suffering that might be caused to members of the audience as they rush toward the exits cannot be excused or justified on the ground that free speech is at stake. No legal protection has ever been granted to anyone to use words as weapons to harm others. Just as matches and knives may be used freely and legitimately for certain purposes but not for others, so also may words be used for some purposes but not for others. The use of words as a means of communicating information and opinion is relatively (but not absolutely) unrestricted in free societies; but their use as weapons of destruction and harm to others has always been limited.

Some statements are so damaging to individual citizens that their utterance or publication may subject those who are responsible for them to civil or criminal actions under the laws of defamation of character, slander, or libel. A well-known basketball coach was once accused by a leading national magazine of having accepted bribes to throw important games. Such an accusation, unsubstantiated but widely read, could have destroyed his professional career, and certainly must have caused him and his family months of anguish. A rumor that a certain physician was mentally unbalanced and that he had started to molest his female patients began to circulate in the small town in which he lived. His practice dried up overnight, though there was not a scintilla of truth to the rumor. A high school teacher was accused by a local newspaper of being a communist, though she had never had the slightest interest in politics. In none of these cases could the protection of the right of free speech or freedom of the press be invoked, for they are invasions of the privacy of the individual concerned. The public interest is not served by such statements, and the law provides the opportunity for persons damaged by such false charges to seek compensation through damage suits in the courts. For certain kinds of slander and libel there are criminal penalties as well.

In the common-law countries truth is a defense against a charge of libel or slander. That is, if a person accused of libel can prove that he has published the truth, then no damages can be assessed against him. But in some states truth is not always a defense, for it is believed that some matters should not be afforded the protection of the law when they are widely published, even if they are true. Unless some matter of public welfare is at stake, for example, no one has the right to publish the fact that a particular individual is an alcoholic, that he suffers from severe depressions, or that he has frequent arguments with his wife. Though such reports may be true, no public interest is served by publishing them, and public reports of such facts may cause grievous harm, acute embarrassment, or great anguish to the parties involved. Therefore, on such private matters, laws of slander and libel can be brought to bear to protect persons against their public exposure.

Where private rights, including the right to privacy, come into conflict with the right to speak and to publish freely, the latter may have to give way to the former, particularly when no public interest is served by publication of such material. The courts have held, for example, that exposés of the private lives of public figures are relatively immune to the libel laws, because such exposés may be relevant to public decisions on matters of public policy. Defamatory statements directed against the private conduct of a public official or of a private citizen are not protected by the Constitution of the United States, for purely private defamation has little to do with the political ends of a self-governing society. But where public officials or public matters are concerned, the balance is shifted in favor of freedom of expression rather than against it.[11] Newspapers cannot be required, either, to adhere to a standard that provides that *only* the truth shall be a defense against libel action, particularly where criticism of public officials is at issue; for if critics of public officials and their actions had to guarantee the truth of all their statements under threat of criminal or civil liability, there would be a stifling effect upon them, amounting to a kind of self-censorship. Some libel laws require, therefore, that the person pressing the complaint must demonstrate not only that the report was false, but also that it was made maliciously, with actual knowledge of its falsity, and with reckless disregard of whether it was false or not.[12]

Another area in which the law places restrictions upon the publication of statements, even though they may be true, is in the divulging of the contents of private communications without the permission of the sender or receiver. If a telephone lineman overhears a conversation while repairing a cable, he does not have the right to divulge the contents of that conversation to any other person, and in many states he may be held criminally liable if he does. On the other hand, however, if a telephone employee discovers that the company's lines are being used for unlawful purposes, he may be *required* to furnish such information to the appropriate law enforcement officers or agencies and may be punished if he fails to do so. Thus, there are times when one must remain silent, and there are other times when silence is forbidden. One is not always justified in divulging the truth, nor is one always justified in respecting other persons' privacy.

If truth is not always protected, it is evident that falsehoods should not be. The utterance of some falsehoods is prohibited by criminal law, because they cause so much mischief and are potentially so destructive and so costly that they cannot be justified on the usual grounds reserved for free speech.

A person who initiates or circulates a false report or warning of a fire, explosion, crime, or other emergency under circumstances in which it is likely that public alarm or inconvenience will result cannot plead that he was justified in doing so because of his rights to speak freely. The public inconvenience caused by such false reports is so great that the freedom to make them is not protected by the law, and does not deserve to be protected. On the contrary, legislators are perfectly justified in imposing penalties upon persons who deliberately engage in such public mischief.

Similarly, some kinds of statements may be prohibited, whether they are true or false. The rights of freedom of expression do not extend to the protection of persons who reveal secrets with which they have been entrusted.

Ideas, like material goods, can be stolen or misappropriated. A man working for a chemical company or a pharmaceutical firm might learn the formulas of valuable compounds that had recently been discovered or the methods for producing certain compounds inexpensively. Freedom of speech does not extend to permission for him to reveal these secrets to competing companies which might then use them to take business away from the company for which he had been working. Similarly, attorneys, accountants, and physicians do not have the right to reveal facts about their clients that they have learned in confidential conversations with them, or through their examination of documents relating to their clients' personal lives or businesses. Freedom of the press does not grant a professor the right to publish his students' grades or the contents of letters of recommendation that might have been written to the university at the time of their admission to the institution. To allow such breaches of confidence would undermine the trust that persons put in one another in a number of sensitive areas. For certain kinds of assistance to be given to people, complete trust must prevail. In recognition of this, governments have foregone their customary right to compel people to testify about one another when the relation between them is of such a nature that breach of confidence would not be in the public interest. Thus, lawyers, doctors, ministers, and others are generally immune from the state's power to require that people reveal what they know about one another when called upon to do so in court or in other legitimate governmental inquiries. However, public interest sometimes requires that the right to silence and respect for the confidentiality of the doctor–patient relationship be superseded. Physicians may be *required* to *volunteer* information, even though no official of the state has requested it; and they may be held criminally liable if they fail to make certain reports. If a given patient is discovered to have the plague, for example, it would clearly be in the public interest for the doctor to be compelled to report the fact to the appropriate officials so that the patient might be quarantined, others inoculated, and other steps taken to prevent the spread of the disease. Similarly, if a physician discovers that a child is being beaten, severely maltreated, or neglected in such a way as to endanger its life or its physical or psychological well-being, he may be required by law to report these facts to the proper agencies, so that they may take appropriate action to protect the child against further abuse. The public interest is better served in such cases as these by breaking the trust ordinarily existing between doctor and patient.

There are other areas where the line is not so easily drawn and where there is considerable room for disagreement. One is illustrated by a case that made the headlines in 1971. A physician in England was asked by the minor daughter of a friend of his for a prescription for contraceptives. He reported the request to her father, under the assumption that his duty to look after the welfare of his patient (the young lady) would be best served by informing her father of her sexual activities. Not all of his colleagues in the medical profession agreed, for they considered it to be a gross violation of the doctor–

patient relationship and a breach of professional ethics. Other medical men, however, concluded that it was quite appropriate for him to involve the girl's parents, because they were, after all, her legal guardians and had a responsibility to look after her conduct and her well-being. Whatever one may think of this physician's motives, one must ask what the consequences would be if young people had no assurance that their communications with their doctors would be held in the strictest confidence, particularly where such sensitive problems as contraception, pregnancy, venereal disease, and drug abuse are concerned. There is reason to believe that there would soon cease to be any doctor–patient relationship in such cases, for the young people concerned would stop seeking medical advice from competent physicians. Where there is fear of breach of confidence, many young people have taken their chances on home remedies or black market medicine rather than risk exposure.

These are only some examples of types of speech and publication that are not permitted, even in the most liberal society. The advertiser cannot claim the right to publish what he will about his product, whether it is true or false, under the First Amendment guarantee of freedom of the press, for that guarantee does not apply to commercial advertisements. It applies to expressions of opinion, to the expression of ideas, and to artistic expressions, but publications offering things for sale do not come under the same protection. They *are* protected, though, under the due process clause of the Fifth Amendment, which says that no one "may be deprived of life, liberty, or property without due process of law." The vendor may circulate his advertisements freely, unless he is enjoined against doing so by due process of law. But it is quite clear that his liberty to publish statements about his products is *not* the same as that referred to in the First Amendment's absolute prohibition against restraints upon freedom of the press.

The liberty to speak is not absolute. Nor is the liberty to publish what one pleases completely unrestricted. There are subjects, such as those about which one has been given confidential or secret information, about which one may not be at liberty to speak. And there are facts, such as those whose publication may harm persons who have a right to be protected against such injury, that one ought not to publish, even if they have been verified. There are occasions when one has no right to speak at all, and others when, if one speaks, one must confine oneself to a particular topic. In his own living room, a person may wander from topic to topic at will and hold forth at length on his favorite subject if he so chooses. But he may be restrained from doing this at a meeting or at a rally or in a courtroom where such musings are not on the agenda. A salesman may not (or should not) make false claims for his merchandise, and if he does, there should be sanctions that can be applied against him.

Yet the libertarian claims that freedom of speech and freedom of the press are, or should be, absolute. If it is proper to restrict the freedom of the salesman, to restrain him against disseminating false information whose worst effect may be to deprive his customer of a few dollars, how can it be improper to forbid political, moral, and religious hucksters from spreading false doctrines that may weaken our morals and destroy our society? The libertarian replies by pointing out that the salesman is peddling merchandise, whereas the others are dealing with ideas. There are standard tests for determining whether the claims the salesman makes for his merchandise are true—tests that everyone, including the salesman himself, will acknowledge to be valid. But there are no standard tests for determining whether the clergyman's claims are true; no scales to weigh the capitalist's views against those of the communist; no test to provide an infallible, or even a highly probable, judgment as to whether one economic theory is to be preferred over another.

And finally, the libertarian replies by observing, as Alexander Meiklejohn did, that the free man is prepared to take the risks of living in a society that offers the liberty to speak, to publish, and to think false or incorrect or even harmful thoughts; for the risks of living in a society where those liberties do not exist are so much greater.

Part Four

The Frontiers of Law and Morals

The liberties discussed in the last portion of Part Three are fundamental to a free and democratic society. They have long been recognized as such and were therefore written into the Constitution of the United States and into the bills of rights of other nations. But other liberties have not been accorded such a status, though men of conscience sometimes find it impossible to live without them. As we saw in Part One, the law sometimes intrudes into areas where it has no business, forbidding behavior that ought to be permitted, infringing upon the deeply held beliefs of men and women, limiting their opportunities for free expression and for the development of their own life style. In Part Three we noted that some clearly immoral forms of behavior which cause incalculable harm to ordinary citizens are permitted by the law, and that those who engage in such immoral behavior may even be aided by the law's provisions for the enforcement of contracts, by garnishment acts, and by other legal devices. The law has had settled doctrines on many of these questions for many centuries. Though some changes in detail have been made from time to time, the fact that the law should take a stand on these issues is well established and has a long history. The problem today is more a matter of reforming old and possibly outdated doctrines than the introduction of entirely new ones. But in some areas, the law has no settled doctrines. These areas are not necessarily new, because men have been concerned about them and have been discussing them at least since Plato's day. Such novelty as there is consists in the fact that people are now talking about the institution of laws to deal with these issues.

Civil disobedience is by definition a violation of the law, but it is a

319

violation committed as an act of conscience or as an act of protest against the law itself, and therefore, in the eyes of many people, it constitutes a form of expression that ought to be accorded special privileges, as were freedom of speech and freedom of the press two centuries ago. Here law and morality clash, as it were, on the battlefield of a man's conscience. Consider such a man, whose intention is not to destroy the legal system as such or to harm any person, but merely to change a given law or a particular part of the system so as to make the whole more just and equitable than it is. Should such a person be subjected to the same penalties as those who might have violated the law out of purely selfish motives, or, indeed, should he be punished at all?

In another area—international relations—the law is still in its infancy. It is still quite primitive, lacking many of the powers and the attributes that are sometimes assumed to be essential to the existence of a genuine legal system. As a result, the conduct of men in time of war has been almost completely unregulated, except by their own commanders; but if the latter were vicious, immoral, or indifferent, there has been no limit to what the forces of an invading power could do to those who fell under their domination. The most monstrous crimes could be committed with impunity, because they were crimes only in a manner of speaking—only morally, not legally. Those who perpetrated them could be "punished" only if they were defeated, and even then the punishment would simply be a lawless act of retaliation, without due process, without a hearing, without the possibility of a meaningful defense. Only during the present century has some effort been made to outlaw acts of aggression and, if there is a war, to outlaw the commission of certain atrocities. For the first time men have tried to outlaw such acts, so that they would be considered illegal no matter where they were committed, regardless of the law of the land in which they were perpetrated and regardless of the commands of those who were in authority at the time they were committed. In addition, an attempt has been made to try war criminals and those who have committed crimes against humanity before competent tribunals which could hold them liable for their acts and punish them if they were convicted.

In these areas law and morals meet in a manner that we have not encountered thus far, for in the one case what morality seems to require, the law opposes, whereas in the other what morality requires, the law, until recently—and perhaps even to this day—has totally overlooked.

How, then, can the principles of criminal punishment be squared with the requirements of morality, with the demands of those who want to live in a free society, and with the realities of the law in these frontier areas where law and morals meet, clash, and conflict? And what, if anything, is being done, or ought to be done, to bridge the gap between law and morals in these difficult areas? We turn now to a consideration of these issues.

15

Civil Disobedience

THE DILEMMA OF THE UNJUST LAW

Socrates was convicted of a capital crime, the "crime" of atheism and corrupting the morals of the youth, by the court at Athens. Waiting in his death cell a day or two before his scheduled execution, he was visited by his friend Crito, who had bribed the jailer. Crito explained that he had arranged for Socrates to escape from prison and to be spirited to Thessaly, where he would be safe. But Socrates refused to go, arguing that he had devoted all his life to teaching the importance of doing justice and respecting the laws of the state. It would be rank hypocrisy for him to violate his principles at this time, when the laws had been turned against his private interests.

He constructed an imaginary dialogue between himself and the laws of Athens. As he was preparing for his escape, the laws came to him and said, "By trying to escape, Socrates, what will you effect but the destruction of us, the laws, and the whole state? Do you imagine that a state whose laws are disregarded and subverted by private individuals, and whose court decisions are of no force, can survive?" [1]

Socrates replied that he had been injured by the state, for his case had been judged unjustly. But the laws replied, "Was that our agreement, or was it that you would abide by the state's judgments, whatever they might be?" They went on to explain that they could be compared to Socrates' parents, for his earthly father and mother had brought Socrates into this world with the sanction of the laws, and it was through them and with their protection that he was sheltered, nurtured, and educated. Just as Socrates would not have had the right to retaliate if his father had treated him badly, so did he lack the right to strike back at the laws when he fared badly at their hands.

"If we try to destroy you," they asked, "because we think it just, will you in return do what you can to destroy us, the laws, and your country, and claim that you are acting justly when you do so? . . . Your country is worthier, more to be revered, more sacred, and held in higher honor by both gods and men of understanding than your father and your mother and all your other ancestors. . . . You should therefore respect it, submit to it, and approach it more submissively when it is angry with you than you would your own father. And you should either acquiesce in what it decrees or persuade it to excuse you. And if it sends you to war, where you might be wounded or be killed, or if it decrees that you must endure flogging or imprisonment, then you should obey in silence. That is just." [2]

After giving Socrates all the benefits that they could make available to him, the laws left him free to take his goods and leave for some other place, or to remain. "But if a man remains here, after seeing how we dispense justice and how we govern the state in other matters, he has entered into a tacit agreement that he will do whatever we decree."

Socrates believed, then, that by remaining in the community, he made a kind of tacit agreement to abide by its laws and that that agreement was binding even when it worked to his own disadvantage. For no agreement is meaningful if it can be broken at the whim of one of the parties to it whenever he sees that it is not in his best interests to abide by its provisions. If all men could repudiate their contracts so easily, no one would ever rely upon the solemn undertakings of anyone else and there would soon be no agreements at all. If every man took it upon himself to decide which laws to obey and which to disregard, there would soon be no laws at all—and thus, each man who breaks the law is contributing to the destruction of the entire legal system. Because each man owes a debt of gratitude to the system for all that it has given him and because each man has the duty to be loyal to the state, disobedience is an act of injustice, disloyalty, ingratitude, and impiety. [3]

But only a short time before, at his trial, Socrates had declared that in his teaching, in his conversations with young and old, he was innocent of corrupting the youth and spreading false doctrines about the gods (though that was the charge against him), and he went on to say, "Whether you are persuaded by Anytus [my accuser] or not, whether you acquit me or not, I shall not change my way of life, no, not if I have to die for it many times." [4]

In spite of his deep commitment to the laws, then, even Socrates seems to have felt that there were some things that he would not concede to the law or to the community. He might have to pay a price, and the price demanded might be very heavy (his life!), but he would pay the price rather than give in to a demand that he felt was unjust, or, as he put it, that was contrary to the command that had been given to him by the god.

These two positions taken by Socrates—the one a powerful defense of the view that the law must be obeyed, regardless of the personal consequences to the individual citizen, and the other a resolute refusal to obey an unjust or impious law—represent the two horns of the dilemma upon which many conscientious persons have been impaled when confronted with the vexing and sometimes cruelly painful predicament of being required to act in accordance with a law that they consider to be unjust. The Hebrew midwives who deliberately disobeyed Pharaoh's express command were the earliest civil disobedients on record. They did not put the newborn babies to death, though Pharoah had ordered them to do so, because "they feared God." [5] There was, in their eyes, a law higher than that of Pharaoh—the law of God. The threat of punishment did not deter them from disobeying Pharaoh's law when it came into direct conflict with the law of God. From then until the very latest periods covered by the Hebrew Bible, acts of civil disobedience (such as Mordecai's refusal to prostrate himself before Haman, an act that eventually led to the deposition of a tyrannical ruler, according to the Biblical account) abound, and always they are justified by an appeal to a law higher than that of the state.

Aristotle observed that in order to avoid the destruction of the state, it was vital for its governors to "guard vigilantly against any lawlessness, especially its pettiest forms. For lawlessness in the form of petty crimes creeps in unnoticed, [and ultimately destroys the fabric of the state] just as small expenditures, repeated over and over again, gradually consume an entire fortune." [6] But later thinkers, including John Locke, held that because (in their view) the authority of the state itself ultimately derives from the people, the people have the right to disobey laws that they consider to be unjust. "If I find a law requires me to do what I think it is wrong to do," Locke wrote, "I ought to disobey it." "If the magistrate should enjoin anything by his authority that appears unlawful to the conscience of a private person," he went on, "such a private person is to abstain from the action that he judges unlawful." But he adds that "he is to undergo the punishment which it is not unlawful for him to bear. For the private judgment of any person concerning a law enacted in political matters, for the public good, does not take away the obligation of that law, nor deserve a dispensation." The civil disobedient, then, is not obliged to abide by those laws that go against his conscience, but at the same time he must be prepared to suffer the punishment prescribed by law for his breach of the statute in question. [7]

Thomas Hobbes was a strong opponent of even the slightest violation of the law, for in his view the law is all that stands between civilization and savagery. Without the law, he said, the life of man would be "solitary, poor, nasty, brutish, and short." But even Hobbes conceded that there were occasions when one would be justified in violating the commands of the law, for he maintained that certain rights were inalienable—that is, they could not be transferred to anyone, not even to the sovereign—for it was for the securing of those rights that men entered into civil society in the first place. If those rights are threatened, then the social contract that brought men together into the state is broken, and the original "state of nature," in which every man has a right to all things, returns. These fundamental, inalienable rights are, according to Hobbes, the right to life, the right to liberty, and the right to such things as make life worth living. He would have disagreed, then, with Socrates, in the latter's refusal to escape from his death cell with Crito; for in Hobbes's view, Socrates would have had a perfect right to do everything necessary to preserve his life, even though it might have been forbidden by the law, because his contract with the state came to an end the moment the state threatened to take his life from him.

It appears, then, that philosophers have perennially been disturbed by the dilemma posed by Socrates's seemingly incompatible positions on the day of his trial and in the death cell. How can one justify conscientious disobedience of laws that one considers to be unjust and still maintain a government of laws, in which right is determined not by each individual serving as legislator, judge, and jury in his own case, but by relatively impersonal organs that attempt to distribute justice to everyone alike?

THE HIGHER-LAW APPROACH:
THE DIVINE-LAW VERSION

The midwives and Mordecai had a solution that has appealed to many people in later ages: there is a higher law, God's law, that transcends any merely human command, no matter how exalted the human legislator may be. When man-made law comes into conflict with the eternal law of God, then the law of God must take precedence. So far as ordinary legislation is concerned (i.e., laws dealing with damages, contracts, marriage, the regulation of traffic, commerce, and the like), the "higher-law" advocate can argue that he has no quarrel with any of it and that his disobedience is therefore not directed toward the destruction or overthrow of the state. But when a particular law, such as a law requiring the slaughter of innocent babies or one that violates the deepest religious convictions of a people, is enacted and enforced, he contends that he may rightly refuse to abide by that law's provisions, for its force is nullified by the superior law decreed by God.

For the divine-law theory to work, or to be convincing to skeptics, the latter must have some access to the revelation in which God's laws are set forth. Unfortunately, there is much disagreement, even among believers, over the exact content of the divine revelation; and even those who agree on its contents are frequently at odds over its applicability or its precise meaning. Because no authoritative body exists with the power to render decisions on such matters, it would seem that everyone is left very much to his own devices when it comes to determining the nature of God's law. There are not only divisions among Christians, Jews, Moslems, and adherents of other faiths, but even among the adherents of any given faith there are often sharp divisions on the answers to be given to these questions. And then, of course, there are those who deny that there is any divine law, because they are not convinced that there is a deity, or because the deity whose existence they affirm is not the kind of being who would dictate legal precepts to earthly creatures.

THE HIGHER-LAW APPROACH:
THE NATURAL-LAW VERSION

Partly because of such difficulties as these, another theory, the "natural-law" theory, has developed. Divine revelation may not be accessible to everyone, the natural-law theorists say, but the laws of nature, especially the laws of human nature, are knowable to anyone who will but take the time and make the effort to inquire into them. One of the earliest formulations of the natural-law theory is that of Cicero:

> True law is right reason in agreement with Nature; it is of universal application, unchanging and everlasting; it summons to duty by its commands, and averts from wrong-doing by its prohibitions. And it does not lay its commands or prohibitions upon good men in vain, though neither have an effect on the wicked. It is a sin to try to alter this law, nor is it allowable to attempt to repeal any part of it, and it is impossible to abolish it entirely. We cannot be freed from its obligations by Senate or People, and *we need not look outside ourselves for an expounder or interpreter of it*. And there will not be different laws at Rome and at Athens, or different laws now and in the future, but one eternal and unchangeable law will be valid for all nations and for all times, and there will be one master and one ruler, that is, God, over us all, for He is the author of this law, its promulgator, and its enforcing judge.[8]

The source of the law of nature, then, is God, but it must not be forgotten that for Cicero, the Stoic, God and nature were one and the same. The author and promulgator of the law of nature, then, is nature itself, which is unchanging in its laws. These laws are manifested in each man's own mind, through the exercise of his reason, which is constructed in accordance with the very laws of nature that govern the structure of all the universe. All any man need do, if he is in doubt as to what is required of him by the dictates of the law of nature, is look inside himself, consult his own inner (psychological, rational, moral?) nature, and he will find the answer. Everyone, provided he is endowed with the capacity to reason, is able to perform the necessary operations, for as Cicero put it:

> Those creatures who have received the gift of reason from Nature have also received right reason, and therefore they have also received the gift of Law, which is right reason applied to command and prohibition. And if they have received law, they have received Justice also. Now all men have received reason; therefore, all men have received justice.[9]

In keeping with this tradition, Gratian decreed that natural law is so superior to man-made law that any practice, whether it is merely customary or has actually been committed to writing in the constitution of a state, "if it contradicts natural law, must be considered null and void." [10] And still later, St. Thomas Aquinas wrote:

Rational creatures are subject to divine Providence in a very special way; being themselves made participators in Providence itself, in that they control their own actions and the actions of others. So they have a certain share in the divine reason itself, deriving therefrom a natural inclination to such actions and ends as are fitting. This participation in the Eternal law by rational creatures is called the Natural law. . . . The light of natural reason, by which we discern good from evil, and which is the Natural law, [is] nothing else than the impression of the divine light in us.[11]

And on the question of civil disobedience (or perhaps even outright rebellion), he went on to say:

If a human law is at variance in any particular with the Natural law, it is no longer legal, but rather a corruption of law. . . . Man is bound to obey secular rulers to the extent that the order of justice requires. For this reason if such rulers have no just title to power, but have usurped it, or if they command things to be done which are unjust, their subjects are not obliged to obey them, except perhaps in certain special cases, when it is a matter of avoiding scandal or some particular danger.[12]

Later still, during the great revolutions that changed the entire political climate of the Western world during the last decades of the eighteenth century, similar appeals were voiced by Jefferson and the other authors of the Declaration of Independence, who proclaimed that certain "truths" are "self-evident," namely, "that all men are created equal, that they are endowed by their Creator with certain unalienable Rights, that among these are Life, Liberty and the pursuit of Happiness." Among these self-evident truths were the propositions that governments derive their just powers from the consent of the governed in order to secure those rights, and that when any government "becomes destructive" of those ends, "it is the Right of the People to alter or to abolish it [the government]." Similarly, the French Declaration of the Rights of Man set forth the "natural, inalienable and sacred Rights of Man," which are "simple and indisputable principles"—in phraseology different, but in meaning almost identical to the "self-evident truths" of the American Declaration of Independence.

These sentiments have been used to justify revolutions, but the principles behind acts of civil disobedience should be very similar, if not identical. According to the natural-law theorist, or the one who believes in the doctrine of natural rights, the principles of justice and right are self-evident to any rational person who is exercising his rational faculties. Any law that is inconsistent with these principles is no law at all and is not binding upon anyone, least of all upon anyone who recognizes the fact that it is contrary to the laws of nature or to the natural rights of man.

This is not the place for either a comprehensive history of the natural-law theory or a detailed critique of it. But a few crucial points may be considered:

1. In the last analysis many of the weaknesses of the divine-law theory

have been inherited by the natural-law theory. The epistemological problem is particularly difficult: How is one to know when a given "law" enacted by a human legislature is or is not in conformity with the natural law? One must first know what the natural law is or says or requires. But though the natural-law theorists maintain that its principles are "self-evident" to all "rational" persons, it seems that there is considerable dispute, both about their content and about their application in specific cases. Unless one assumes, for example, that George III was irrational (as he might in fact have been), it is obvious that in the days of the American Revolution there was at least one person to whom the "truths" enunciated in the Declaration of Independence were *not* self-evident; and there were thousands of loyalists, both in other parts of the British Empire and in the American colonies themselves, who were *not* convinced of the propriety of applying those principles (assuming that they accepted them) as the American revolutionaries did.

2. Every natural-law theory seems to recognize the importance of preserving the state and positive or statutory law. No natural-law theory with which I am familiar attempts to justify the destruction of a state unless that state is ruthless and tyrannical, and every such theory hedges the occasions upon which its adherents may engage in civil disobedience very carefully—largely on the ground that (as Aristotle put it) petty crimes multiplied can spell the ruination of a society. When, and under what specific circumstances, is one justified in taking the law into one's own hands? Even supposing that a given law is unjust, is the moral or social gain to be achieved by disobeying it worth the risk of undermining all lawful authority that may be entailed in civil disobedience?

3. Again, can an organized society function, or dispense *even-handed justice*, if its citizens take it upon themselves to decide what laws they will and will not obey? Can a meaningful legal system exist in a place where citizens assume the mantle of righteousness and then do as they please, regardless of the legalities of the matter? If the supporters of school integration can violate those laws that they consider to be unjust in order to further *their* cause, is there any principle that could prevent the Ku Klux Klans or the middle-class racists from acting upon the "truths" that are "self-evident" to *them* and violating other laws that are repugnant to *their* sense of justice? For every Martin Luther King who engages in civil disobedience in support of *his* convictions about justice, there is likely to be a George Wallace who will stand in the schoolhouse door, in defiance of the law, to further *his* version of the just society.

We have seen in this century how thin is the veneer of civilization, how easily it can be stripped away, and how ugly the savage beast that lurks below can be. Where the law of the jungle reigns—that is, where there is no civil law at all—there is likely to be terror, death, and decay. What laws are so unjust, either in their letter or in their application, as to justify the risk of a return to the jungle and the release of the beast that lies in wait in man? The law of nature, if there is one, not only must prescribe which laws are unjust, and therefore need not be obeyed *if considered in isolation, in abstract terms,* but also must provide guidelines for the practical judgment that any man who contemplates an unlawful act must make, as to whether *that particular act, in that particular place and at that particular time,* is one that he ought or ought not to perform. Unfortunately, no theory of natural law, and no book on natural law that has come to my attention, provides such concrete guidelines for real cases.

MARTIN LUTHER KING ON CIVIL DISOBEDIENCE

The most prominent recent advocate of a natural-law theory of civil disobedience was Martin Luther King, Jr. In his "Letter from a Birmingham Jail," Dr. King defended the demonstrations that ultimately led to his conviction—a conviction that was later upheld by the United States Supreme Court—on trespassing charges on the ground that "direct action" is sometimes the only way to get negotiations started. "Non-violent direct action," he wrote, "seeks to create such a crisis and establish such creative tension that a community that has constantly refused to negotiate is forced to confront the issue. It seeks so to dramatize the issue that it can no longer be ignored."

In addition to these utilitarian or political objectives, however, he contended that the laws that he had "violated" were unjust, and that unjust laws are no laws at all. An unjust law, he said, is a man-made rule that is out of harmony with the moral law, the law of God, or the natural law, one that "distorts the soul and damages the personality," and relegates persons to the status of things. Further, laws that are imposed by a majority upon a minority, though they do not apply to the majority itself, are unjust and inconsistent with the divine law or the law of nature. More particularly is this the case when the minority had no part in enacting the law, because it lacked the right to vote.

Such laws, then, according to Dr. King, may be violated, but only after careful determination of the facts, after attempts to negotiate the removal of the injustices, and after "self-purification." In engaging in civil disobedience the violator breaks the unjust law "openly, lovingly," and is prepared to accept the penalty, thus expressing the very highest respect for law. To a large degree these principles follow those laid down by Thoreau in his essay "Civil Disobedience." They have formed the guidelines for much recent discussion of civil disobedience, and may be summarized as follows: *One who engages in civil disobedience violates a law (1) which he believes to be unjust or immoral; (2) in order to bring about a change in the social order; (3) in such a way as to inflict no harm or bodily injury upon any other person (that is, nonviolently); (4) openly and publicly; and (5) with a willingness to pay the penalty, if that should be necessary.*

These conditions distinguish civil disobedience from ordinary lawlessness, for the common criminal typically (1) admits that the laws he breaks are not unjust or immoral; (2) is not interested in changing the social order, but in satisfying his own needs or desires; (3) is often (though not always) unconcerned about any harm that may come to others as a result of his criminal behavior, particularly if they stand in his way; (4) does his deed clandestinely, attempting as far as possible to avoid detection; and (5) is anxious to avoid being caught and to escape punishment.

Though Dr. King's definition may serve as a set of general guidelines for some purposes, its elements are not as clear or as precise as they might be, and they are certainly not the only guidelines or criteria that have been set forth by supporters of one form or another of civil disobedience. Nor has everyone been prepared to accept Dr. King's views as constituting a sufficient justification for disobedient behavior. We shall first go through this list, analyzing some of the implications of each point and noting some other views along the way; then we shall take up certain other suggestions that have been made by students, advocates, and critics of civil disobedience.

CIVIL DISOBEDIENCE AND THE IMMORALITY OF THE LAW

All commentators on civil disobedience agree that every genuine act of civil disobedience *must have broken the law.* But they differ on certain important details regarding the state of mind of the law violator and the ultimate fate of the law itself. Must he be convinced that the law is *unconstitutional,* for example (which is not identical with its being unjust or immoral, unless one is prepared to say the Constitution recognizes only those laws that are both just and moral), or is it sufficient that he is convinced that the law he has violated is unjust or immoral *even though* it may be constitutional? Must the law turn out, in the end, to *be* unconstitutional, or is this *not* a necessary condition for civil disobedience?

The main point is that the law must have been broken: "However vehement, radical, or extraordinary is one's protest," Carl Cohen has written, "if he does not break the law he has not been disobedient. The violation of some law of the body politic is a universal and necessary feature of [civilly disobedient] conduct." [13]

According to a second view, civil disobedience occurs only when the protestor is convinced that the law against which he is protesting will be, or at least has a strong chance of being, nullified by appeal to higher authorities, such as the federal courts or the Supreme Court. "Civil disobedience must take place under an arguable claim of right," one recent commentator has said. He adds that if he can "satisfy the court that higher positive law arguably justifies his conduct or arguably condemns the action his government demands of him, then he is entitled to special treatment as a civil disobedient." [14]

A third opinion holds that the distinction between an act of civil disobedience and merely criminal behavior is finally settled by the courts: If, after all appeals have been exhausted, the defendant's conviction is upheld, then he is a criminal offender and not a true civil disobedient; but if his conviction is reversed, and the law against which he was directing his protest is declared unconstitutional or otherwise nullified, then his act was an act of civil disobedience rather than one of criminal misbehavior. [15]

Civil disobedience may be defined, then, in several different ways, each of which involves a different set of necessary conditions. These may be summarized as follows:

(A) Civil disobedience is behavior that violates a criminal law that the violator believes to be unjust or immoral, though he may believe it to be a valid law within the system of which it is a part.

(B) Civil disobedience is behavior that violates a criminal law that the protestor believes to be invalid.

(C) Civil disobedience is behavior that violates a criminal law that is later declared invalid by the courts.

CIVIL DISOBEDIENCE OF PROTEST AND OF PERSONAL INTEGRITY

The civil disobedient, unlike the revolutionary, generally has considerable respect for government and for law, and is not interested in the overthrow of the entire system, but in the modification of certain of its parts. However, he may not even be particularly concerned about that. He may merely be concerned to avoid doing what the law commands on the ground that obedience to that particular law would be immoral. Aside from self-interest, which is the usual motive of criminal behavior, there are three other motives for the kinds of illegal behavior that presently concern us:

1. Overthrow of the government. (*Revolution.*)
2. Modification or reform of the system. (*Civil disobedience of protest.*)
3. Refusal to participate in immoral activity. (*Civil disobedience of personal integrity.*)

Though the Hebrew midwives may have been dissatisfied with Pharaoh's government, there is no evidence either that they were interested in overthrowing it or in bringing about reforms in its administration or in its laws. The evidence before us justifies the conclusion that they were civil disobedients of personal integrity, that they disobeyed the law because to obey it would have required of them an act that they could not do in good conscience. Many such acts come to the attention of the public from time to time. The Amish who refuse to send their children to public schools are attempting neither to overthrow the government nor to reform the educational systems of the states in which they reside. They merely want to be left free to educate their children in accordance with their own beliefs. Many American draft dodgers, who have fled to Canada or to other hospitable countries in recent years in order to escape from the draft and from criminal prosecution for their refusal to serve in their country's armed forces, have done so in order to avoid fighting in what they considered to be an immoral war or to avoid what they considered immoral in itself—fighting in a war. Some of them, to be sure, wanted their actions to be understood back home as a protest against their government or against the war it was waging in Indochina. But many of them, knowing that their personal actions would have little effect on American foreign policy, fled from their country in order to preserve their personal integrity—to avoid being forced to do what they considered to be immoral.

By contrast, those who engage in civil disobedience of protest do so with the intention of changing the laws or the policies of their government. They choose, therefore, to make their actions as public and dramatic as possible. The illegal sit-ins, lie-ins, and pray-ins that took place at the height of the civil rights drive in the late 1950's and the early 1960's; the illegal marches and parades and demonstrations; the encouragement of public burning of draft cards at mass rallies by people like Dr. Benjamin Spock, who was not himself subject to the draft; the obstruction of traffic in New York, Washington, and other cities as a means of protesting racism or the war; all of these are examples of the disobedience of protest. Their purpose was to change public policy, though they might also have been (in part) designed to encourage or to consist partially of civil disobedience of personal integrity. (Obviously *both* of these forms of civil disobedience may sometimes be present in one and the same action.) An act of *indirect* civil disobedience * is *necessarily* an act of civil disobedience of protest, for it is, strictly, speaking, the violation of a law that the disobedient recognizes to be moral and just, in order to dramatize a protest against some other injustice.

* The distinction between direct and indirect civil disobedience is explained in the next section.

THE CIVIL DISOBEDIENT AND PUNISHMENT

Like Socrates before him, Martin Luther King insisted that one who engages in civil disobedience must be prepared to accept the penalty. But whenever King was convicted of a criminal offense as a result of one of his demonstrations, he carried his appeal to the highest court in the land in an attempt to have the conviction reversed and to have the laws that he violated, or the laws against which he was protesting, overturned. It would seem, then, that in practice his position was not simply that one should be prepared to accept the penalties set by the courts (though that seems to be the implication of his position), but as a willingness to accept punishment *after all legal means of avoiding it have been exhausted*. These two positions may be summarized as follows:

(P₁) The civil disobedient must accept the punishment that the courts mete out to him. (Socrates)

(P₂) The civil disobedient may appeal to the higher courts for elimination of the penalty and nullification of the law that had been violated. (Martin Luther King).

But these are not the only views on this subject. There are still at least two others.

According to some commentators, a violation "committed under a claim of legal right with the intention of seeking redress in the courts . . . can hardly be termed civil disobedience," because "a principle crucial to the philosophy of civil disobedience [is this:] that the violation of pernicious laws is justified by the fact that these laws themselves violate a higher law, which may be called moral law, natural law, or divine law. . . . But if the appeal of the law violator is not simply to moral law, but to positive articulated law such as the Constitution of the United States, it is not civil disobedience we are dealing with, but something else." [16] And Sidney Hook, who is clearly sympathetic to some forms of civil disobedience, wrote:

> An action launched in violation of a local law or ordinance, and undertaken to test it, on the ground that the law itself violates state or federal law, or launched in violation of state law in the sincerely held belief that the state law outrages the Constitution, the supreme law of the land, is not civilly disobedient. . . . [Actions] become civilly disobedient when they are in deliberate violation of laws that have been sustained by the highest legislative and judicial bodies of the nation, e.g., income tax laws, conscription laws, laws forbidding segregation in education, and discrimination in public accommodations and employment. [17]

In short, the advocates of this point of view hold that:

(P_3) The civil disobedient is one who does not appeal to the higher courts and does not rely upon a belief in his ultimate vindication by superior authorities, but appeals only to moral, natural, or divine law for justification of his actions.

Finally, there are those who maintain that if a person believes that the law he has violated is immoral or unjust, he need not acquiesce in any penalty that the courts may impose for such violation. If the law is unjust, they argue, then a penalty for its violation is also unjust; and if one is justified in disobeying unjust laws, one must be equally justified in avoiding punishment for such disobedience. This is the position that Daniel Berrigan finally adopted after his conviction for the destruction of draft records, when he fled from the F.B.I. and spent a number of months eluding the authorities. A fourth position on the question of punishment, therefore is:

(P_4) The civil disobedient may try to avoid punishment altogether, on the ground that punishment for violation of an unjust law is itself unjust (Berrigan)

A careful comparison of the three positions labeled (A), (B) and (C) in the section on Civil Disobedience and the Immorality of the Law with the four positions on punishment, (P_1), (P_2), (P_3), and (P_4), reveals that some of the latter are incompatible with some of the former. Thus, for example, position (P_3)—that the civil disobedient may not appeal to the courts for mitigation of his punishment or for nullification of the law under which he is being punished—is incompatible with both (B) and (C); for (B) permits the civil disobedient to appeal to the courts to invalidate the law against which he is protesting, and (C) makes it *impossible* for a person to be a civil disobedient *unless* the law under which he was convicted is later declared to be invalid by the courts. [Incidentally, position (P_3) may be identical with that of Socrates, position (P_1).]

Position (P_2), on the other hand—that is, Martin Luther King's view that the civil disobedient may appeal to the courts for mitigation of the penalty and invalidation of the objectionable law—is compatible with position (C), but only in the very strangest sort of way. For if (C) were correct, it would follow that one would never know whether a given violation of the law had in fact been an act of civil disobedience until all the appeals had been heard and the final judgment had been rendered. (C), in fact, leaves it to the courts to determine whether a particular law violation was an act of civil disobedience; and if the courts do not decide in favor of the protestor's view that the law against which the protest was directed was invalid, thus upholding his conviction, then it would turn out that his act had not been an act of civil disobedience at all.

Now it is true that there is no law on the books that defines civil disobedience or that provides either special penalties or special considerations for persons who engage in civil disobedience. When a person engages in an act of civil disobedience, he breaks a law that must legally be presumed to be valid at that time. The law itself may be a trespass law, a school-prayer law, a segregation law, a law forbidding indecent exposure, or any of a thousand others. The violation is a violation of one of those laws, not of any specific law forbidding civil disobedience. And for all the violator knows at the time he commits his violation (no matter what he may believe or hope), the law he breaks may well be upheld by the courts. Ordinary usage does not permit us to accept (C) as a definition of "civil disobedience" because in ordinary language, an act is an act of civil disobedience at the time of its performance, and the determination of whether it is or not does not have to wait upon the final determination of the courts. Indeed, Martin Luther King wrote his defense of civil disobedience after his conviction had been upheld by the Supreme Court, and no one was heard to complain that his act was not really civilly disobedient because his conviction was upheld by the highest court in the land and he was forced to serve out his jail sentence. No such complaint was heard because no one made the purely linguistic mistake of supposing that position (C) accurately reflects the ordinary way in which "civil disobedience" is used. Acceptance of (C) would entail that all persons who practiced civil disobedience would be innocent of committing any offense against the law, whereas anyone who attempted to commit an act of civil disobedience and was convicted (and whose conviction was subsequently upheld on appeal) would have committed an offense against the law, but would have failed to commit an act of civil disobedience, though he had every intention of doing so. These conclusions are paradoxical because (C) does not accurately reflect current usage of the term *civil disobedience*.

DIRECT AND INDIRECT CIVIL DISOBEDIENCE

Part of the reason for error that advocates of (C) have made may be a result of a rather elementary confusion between two kinds of civil disobedience. For the sake of simplicity, these may be called *direct* civil disobedience and *indirect* civil disobedience. Direct civil disobedience consists of an act that violates the very law that one is protesting against. Examples would be sit-ins at segregated lunch counters or refusal to register for the draft when one believes that the draft laws are immoral. Indirect civil disobedience consists of an act that violates a law that *may, standing alone, be completely innocuous*, as a means of protesting against *some other law* that one considers to be morally objectionable. Examples of indirect civil disobedience would be Thoreau's refusal to pay taxes as a means of dramatizing his objections to the fugitive slave law and the

Mexican War, sit-ins in government offices (violating the laws of trespass) in order to protest against the Vietnam War or discriminatory practices, and the burning of draft records as a protest against the Vietnam War or the alleged napalming of innocent civilians.[18] Notice the difference between the two kinds of sit-ins. The sit-in that was part of an act of direct civil disobedience was itself forbidden by the law that was being protested against: a law forbidding black citizens to sit at lunch counters. The sit-in that was part of an act of indirect civil disobedience did not itself violate the laws that were being protested (such as the Vietnam War or discriminatory housing regulations), but were merely violative of trespass laws, which even the disobedients would agree are perfectly legitimate.

In view of this distinction, it would seem that (B) will not do either, for (B)—which defines civil disobedience as behavior that violates a criminal law which the protestor believes to be invalid—leaves no room for indirect civil disobedience. We are left, therefore, with (A) as a definition of civil disobedience—not a complete definition, of course, but a statement of one necessary condition of civil disobedience—that every act of civil disobedience must violate some law.

Socrates' views on punishment (P_1), and those of Sidney Hook and others (P_3) demand too much and are clearly not true to modern usage of the term. It is unreasonable to suppose that a person who disobeys a law because it goes against his conscience should passively submit to whatever punishment the state may have set for such violations, without so much as making an effort to defend himself in the courts. In the American scheme of things, there is often no way to test the constitutionality of a law that one finds repugnant to one's conscience without first violating the law, submitting to arrest, and taking the risk of being convicted. Some people have insisted that the true civil disobedient will gladly plead guilty to the charges that are laid against him and meekly rely upon the mercy of the court. Those who say that a man cannot attempt to escape punishment through appeals to the courts are evidently attempting to make a moral point of some kind, but they are certainly not making a logical point; for there is nothing in the meaning of *civil disobedience* that renders the statement "That civil disobedient escaped punishment by appealing to the courts," contradictory or nonsensical, as it would have to do if (P_1) or (P_3) were logically true.

As a moral claim, I suppose there may be something to them, from at least some moral points of view. One may have greater admiration for a man who lays his life or his liberty on the line, as Socrates and Thoreau did, accepting his punishment—not meekly, but courageously. Thoreau's famous statement to Emerson when the latter visited him in prison and asked him why he was there still rings with authenticity and deep conviction. "Why," he asked, "are you *outside?*" Prison is the right place for a man when other men are being imprisoned unjustly, he wrote. A great advocate of nonviolent resistance, Mohandas K. Gandhi, once wrote that he who commits civil disobedience must "cheerfully suffer imprisonment." Not all civil disobedients are interested in martyrdom, and there is some doubt as to whether martyrdom is either necessary or desirable from a tactical point of view. Many acts of civil disobedience are undertaken not only because the conscience of the disobedient is offended by the law that he considers to be unjust, but also because he wants to introduce some *change* into the way things are done in his society. If there is no alternative, circumstances undoubtedly exist in which it is morally right to violate the law, even though one knows full well that the consequence will be loss of liberty or even death itself. But human life and human liberty are far too precious to be given up lightly, particularly when there is a moral alternative. There is nothing morally reprehensible in a person's bending every effort, after he has committed an act of civil disobedience, to have the law that he found morally unacceptable overturned by the courts and thus save himself from the consequences of an unreversed criminal conviction. Far from being morally reprehensible, such a course of action is commendable; for there is another virtue: that of concern for one's fellow men. The civil disobedient who violates the law because he firmly believes that what the law requires of him is unjust or immoral, and then accepts the law's penalties for his illegal behavior, may be behaving morally. But if, though it is possible for him to contest the conviction and possibly to overturn the law, he chooses instead the path of martyrdom, he may be considered righteous, holy and saintly, but there is a clear sense in which what he has done is not moral—or at least not the *most* moral thing that he might have done. For by contesting his conviction *not* in order to save himself from the painful consequences of his illegal behavior, but in order to save *others* from being faced with the awful choice that he had to make, and to save his society from the evil consequences of the bad law that he believes is in its midst, he may not earn the title of martyr, but he will have done his best to bring greater good and greater happiness to his fellow men. This may be what saintliness is all about.

We turn now to the last of the four theories of punishment for civil disobedients, that of Daniel Berrigan, who now maintains that one need not accept the penalty for an act of civil disobedience when the penalty itself is for disobeying an unjust law or is part of an unjust system.

CIVIL DISOBEDIENCE AND REVOLUTION

Daniel Berrigan is not a civil disobedient, but a revolutionary. Revolutionaries also break laws, of course, but their purpose is quite different from that of the civil disobedient. The civil disobedient, though he may violate the provisions of one or a few laws, nevertheless accepts the validity and the authority of the system as a whole. His purpose is *reform* of some parts of the system, not the overthrow of the system itself. As

Martin Luther King put it, the civil disobedient breaks the unjust law "openly and lovingly," and accepts the penalty if he cannot convince the authorities that he should not be punished; he thus expresses his high regard for the law and for the system, and his willingness to suffer personal deprivation if the system itself does not recognize his claim. But Daniel Berrigan, in contrast, has openly stated that his aims went far beyond the mere reform of certain aspects of the system. After his trial, he wrote, "By such action as ours . . . the law itself is being subjected to the scrutiny of revolutionary times. The law is being judged, and the judgment is a harsh one. The law is less and less useful for the living, less and less the servant of men, less and less expressive of that social passion which . . . brought the law into corporate being." And still later, he wrote,

> But suddenly, for all of us, the American scene was no longer a good scene. It was, in fact, an immoral scene. . . . Ours was a scene that moral men could not continue to approve if they were to deserve the name of men. The American scene, in its crucial relationships—the law, the state, the Church, other societies, our own families—*was placed in mortal question.* . . . Catonsville, rightly understood, was a profound "No" aimed not merely at a federal law that protects human hunting licenses. *Our act was aimed,* as our statement tried to make clear, *at every major presumption underlying American life today.* Our act was in the strictest sense a conspiracy; that is to say we had agreed together to attack the working assumptions of American life. Our act was a denial that American institutions were presently functioning in a way that good men would approve or sanction. *We were denying that the law,* medicine, education, and systems of social welfare . . . *were serving the people.* . . . *And in attacking the American assumption, we were beyond any doubt attacking the law and its practitioners.* . . . *We were attacking the assumption that American law, in its present form, can represent us, mediate our sense of justice, judge our actions, punish us.*[19]

These confessions go far beyond those of any civil disobedient, as that term is used here. They are not the words of one who is concerned to preserve the legal and social system while reforming those parts of it that he finds unpalatable. Berrigan's words are those of one who is totally disillusioned with the system, who categorically denies that American law "represents" him, who refuses, both in word and in deed, to accept the law's verdict as to the illegality of his action, and who repudiates "every major assumption underlying American life today." By thus placing himself outside the law, or above it, as some people might want to have it —in spite of the fact that he claims to have moral motivations for doing so—he has gone beyond civil disobedience and entered the ranks of revolutionaries.

Daniel Berrigan aside, however, what may be said for the view that the *civil disobedient* need not acquiesce in his own punishment for violations of laws that he considers to be immoral or unjust? If it is granted that not everyone need be a Socrates, and that considerations of justice and morality do not require of every civil disobedient that he passively accept the verdict of the lowest court on his case, perhaps we may go one step further and concede that some civil disobedients may properly evade punishment altogether.

CRITIQUE OF THE SOCRATIC AND ARISTOTELIAN THEORY

Those who insist, as Socrates and Aristotle did, that every illegal act tends to lead to the destruction of society and the undermining of the law's authority seem to have assumed that every illegal act tends to bring others in its wake. Although this may occur, it need not occur. There does seem to be some tendency for some persons who read about acts of civil disobedience to imitate the illegal behavior that they have read about, or to do their own illegal thing. The massive protests of the 1950's were followed by an escalating and spreading wave of protests in the 1960's that moved from nonviolent demonstrations to violent confrontations and riots. But no cause–effect relationship has been demonstrated to exist between the earlier demonstrations and the later riots. Though it would not be surprising to find that the former contributed, in some measure, to the latter, there is no doubt that other forces were at work, including the Vietnam War, the slow pace of integration, a rising new pride on the part of black citizens in the very qualities that had previously been a source of shame and degradation to them, growing discontent over poverty and slum conditions in a society that was generally affluent, a new awareness on the part of college students of the role that they could play in their own education and a pervasive feeling that they should have more personal autonomy and more influence on local and national policies, and many others. In short, if one person, or a group of persons, violates a given statute out of deep moral convictions, it does not necessarily follow, either logically or from any known social law, that other persons will follow suit, that the particular law against which the protest was directed will fall into general disuse, that all or many citizens will take it upon themselves to disobey other laws not closely related to the one in question, or—in general—that society will disintegrate, that the law will be held in contempt by large numbers of persons, and that there will be a general breakdown of law and order.

Therefore, if some civil disobedients (particularly those who have disobeyed because of personal integrity rather than out of a desire to protest) choose to flee rather than to face the courts, the dire predictions of Socrates and Aristotle about the destruction of the entire legal system will not necessarily come true. It is easy enough to imagine a situation in which a young man, convinced that his participation in what he considers to be an immoral war would be grossly immoral and convinced also that he might spend his time more profitably, for himself and for mankind, in Canada than behind bars at home, might flee from his country with a good conscience and do very little harm, either to the social order of his nation or to any of its citizens. He may feel, for example, that by studying medicine at the University of Toronto he will serve mankind better than he would doing laundry at Leavenworth. I cannot say that such a judgment is morally wrong, though it is clearly a violation of the law.

RESPONSIBILITY OF OTHERS FOR CIVIL DISOBEDIENCE

Every man has a *prima facie* duty to obey the law, and when he chooses to disobey, for whatever reason, the burden of proof is upon him. If he feels that his disobedient act was justifiable, it is up to him to prove that it was. But we must not forget that not only the citizen is involved in an act of disobedience. The law, as well as the citizen, is involved. The fault may not be that of the citizen as much as that of the law that he has disobeyed, or those who administer it. When, in a democracy, the organs of government become so remote from the people that the latter feel that they have no direct means of communicating with those who set the policies that govern their lives, they may be driven, for lack of any other means, to disobey the laws, *merely in order to bring their grievances to the attention of the public at large and of the responsible officials*. Martin Luther King tried to meet with the mayor of Montgomery but was rebuffed, until the bus boycott had achieved so much national publicity that the city's image was badly affected, and business was so seriously hurt that white merchants exercised enough pressure to bring about the changes that were demanded. Albert Bigelow tells how he appeared at the White House gate with petitions bearing 27,000 signatures in hopes of delivering them to the president; even the president's secretary, whose duty it is to handle such matters, refused to see him. After repeated phone calls, he was finally told to leave them with the policeman at the gate. He refused to do so, and later wrote, "It seems terrible to me that Americans can no longer speak to or be seen by their government. Has it become their master, not their servant? Can it not listen to their humble and reasonable pleas?" He concluded, finally, that "the experience has strengthened in me the conviction that we must, at whatever cost, find ways to make our witness and protest heard." That was to be "direct action," for without it, he said, "ordinary citizens lack the power any longer to be seen or heard by their government."[20]

If tens of thousands of young men go into exile, become fugitives from justice, and suffer all the hardships that inevitably accompany such a status rather than serve their country in time of war, then the government ought to take notice and to consider whether its policies are actually on the right course. It is hard to believe that so many of the sons of men who fought bravely at Normandy, at Bataan, at Mindanao, and at the

Ardennes Bulge are either cowards or traitors. Some of them, at least, have not attempted to escape their responsibilities but have done what was in their eyes the most patriotic and responsible thing that they could have done under the circumstances.

When black men and women are given the promise of equal rights and opportunities for themselves and their children and see that such progress as is made barely touches their own children; when they are told to be patient, and watch their own children growing up into a world which seems to them to be little different from the one in which they themselves grew up, so far as meaningful opportunity for advancement is concerned; when they feel that the officers of the law do not treat them fairly or justly and that the laws themselves are often stacked against their interests; and when, finally, the black community is expected to send its sons to another country where they may spill their blood for *its* freedom, while they feel that the extent of their own freedom at home is not all that it should be, it is almost inevitable that some contempt for the law and for legal processes will set in, not only in the black community, but in the white community as well. It is inevitable, too, that some laws will be broken in order to bring the focus of the nation's attention to those of its domestic problems that some of its citizens feel cannot wait any longer.

Some of the responsibility for civil disobedience rests upon the leaders of the government, on leaders of local governments, and on members of the community at large who have failed to exercise their responsibilities to correct the wrongs that have crept into the nation's legal and social structure. There is no penalty for irresponsible, insensitive, or inept political figures, and no stigma attaches to the indifferent citizen who fails to use his voice, his pen, and his vote to change the conditions that finally provoke morally outraged persons into illegal acts. But though the latter bear the brunt of the sanctions of the law, the former must bear their fair share of the moral responsibility for what has happened.

SHOULD THE CIVIL DISOBEDIENT ACCEPT PUNISHMENT?

If law and order is threatened by the civil disobedient, then, it is threatened at least as much by the policies that lead to civil disobedience and by the indifference, callousness, or ineptness of those—including the ordinary voter—who fail to rectify the legal and social wrongs that lead to disrespect for the law. One who has violated such a law, not as protest but because he felt impelled to do so by personal feelings of moral outrage at the thought of obeying it, need not acquiesce passively in any punishment that may be forthcoming. To become an exile if there is a country willing to take him in, or to become a fugitive from justice, subject to arrest and prosecution at any time, is not a particularly cheerful prospect. One would be ill advised to engage in civil disobedience for kicks, as some people have done, for the consequences are very grave indeed.

One who engages in the civil disobedience of protest, however, is in a very different sort of situation, so far as the acceptance of punishment is concerned. His purpose is not merely to avoid doing what he considers to be immoral, but to focus public attention upon the law that forces him and others to make such a choice, and through his action to bring about a change in public attitudes and public policies. Because this is his goal, he must do whatever he can (within moral limits, of course, because by hypothesis he is a person of high moral standards) to further it, and he must avoid doing anything that will interfere with it or that will have the opposite effect.

Ordinarily, one of the things that he must do is to present himself for arrest and abide by the rulings of the courts, for if he makes a fugitive of himself, he loses several points in the battle:

1. He loses the publicity that often attends acts of courageous and open disobedience of the law, of inviting arrest, and of submitting to it when it comes.*
2. He loses the dramatic effect and the publicity of a trial, in which (presumably) the issues with which he is concerned will be brought out.
3. He loses a considerable degree of credibility for himself and his cause, for by "copping out," it begins to appear that he is more concerned for his personal welfare than for justice and morality.
4. He loses his opportunity to test in the courts the validity of the law against which he is directing his protest.

HOW SHOULD THE STATE TREAT THE CIVIL DISOBEDIENT?

So far we have considered the question of punishment only from the side of the disobedient—whether he should submit to being punished or bend his efforts to avoiding punishment. We have seen that persons who engage in the civil disobedience of personal integrity may attempt to avoid punishment, particularly if they feel that their being punished will serve no useful purpose and if they feel that they may do more good outside of jail than inside. Those who ran the underground railroad that was designed to spirit slaves through the northern states and into Canada, where they would be secure against their former masters' attempts to have them returned under the Fugitive Slave Act, would have been foolish if they had submitted to punishment, for then their effort would have been doomed to failure and countless fugitives would have been returned to slavery.[21]

It is time now to consider the problem of punishment from the side of the state. Should the government punish those who have engaged in

---

* There are exceptions to this. The draft dodgers who have gone to Canada and certain persons who have become fugitives have received more publicity than they might have if they had submitted to arrest and prosecution.

acts of civil disobedience, and if it does, should such punishment be heavier or lighter than that which would be imposed upon an offender against the same law who had not engaged in civil disobedience?

The reader will recall the various theories of punishment that were discussed previously—the theories of reform, deterrence, and retribution. So far as retribution is concerned (as that term was used in the chapter on punishment), there is no doubt that the civil disobedient should be punished for his illegal behavior, for his breaking of the rules deserves to be treated like anyone else's, though his motives (namely, to urge the other players to change the rules of the game) differ somewhat from those of the more conventional rule violator.

Reform and deterrence raise special problems that will not be discussed in detail here.[22] A few major points that have been made by others may be noted, however.

Anyone who engages in an act of civil disobedience is guilty of breaking a law deliberately, openly, with complete and admitted knowledge of the nature of his act. It may be argued that such flagrant and open violations of the law should be discouraged, for they set a very bad example for others who may not be aware of the civil disobedient's noble intentions. There is a sense in which the civil disobedient's crime is even worse than a similar act performed by a more conventional criminal, for the disobedient performs his act with the precise intention of violating the law.

On the other hand, there scarcely seems to be any reason to reform the civil disobedient. Reformatory measures are intended, after all, to inculcate in the criminal a respect for law and a feeling of moral and legal propriety that he lacked, in some measure, before. The civil disobedient, however, *is* morally concerned and *is* committed to respect for the law. His offense has come about precisely *because* of his moral concerns and his basic respect for the law, for it is his belief that the law is generally a positive force for good that brings him to contest those provisions that he feels have deleterious effects upon society and to lay his life and his freedom on the line in order to bring about what he considers to be a more just and equitable society.

It should be observed also that civil disobedients seldom harm other persons in the course of their actions. Their offenses are not wrong in themselves, as injuries to persons or property, breaches of official duty, or outrages against public decency and good morals would be if they were done willfully or corruptly. Acts of civil disobedience are usually offenses only because they are defined as such by the law, as, for example, a Negro sitting in at a segregated lunch counter. It may be argued that such offenses, in general, should not be punished as severely as offenses that result in personal injury or injury to property.

Still other reasons for treating civil disobedients with a certain modicum of tolerance are the fact that their behavior is a kind of outlet for what might become violent, revolutionary sentiments if it were suppressed, and the further fact that such behavior enables groups of citizens who had not entered directly into the decision-making processes of the society to play an active role in such processes and to influence the outcome of discussions on major issues in both foreign and domestic affairs. Finally, the civil disobedient often acts out of a sense of social responsibility and moral principle that ought to be encouraged, with the hope that with the passage of time he might "mellow through forbearance." Or, as another commentator has observed, "To assert that the most dangerous man in our society is the one of strong moral conviction and courage is an unhappy admission about the nature of our society. It is one that we should not be in a hurry to make." Although the civil disobedient may be more likely to proselytize others than the common offender, more stubborn and less likely to yield to the threat of mild punishment, it may be wiser to deal leniently with him until the social dangers of his acts become immediate and apparent.

THE COURTS AND CIVIL DISOBEDIENCE

RECENT COURT DECISIONS

As a general principle, the views mentioned in the last paragraph of the preceding section may have some merit, but it is worth noting that in actual practice civil disobedients are *not* being treated particularly leniently in the courts and that the law, as presently constituted, does *not* recognize some of the claims made by civil disobedients for their tactics. A few examples may be helpful.

Some disobedients maintain that the First Amendment to the United States Constitution gives them unlimited rights of free speech and that some actions, which are intended to communicate ideas, constitute a kind of "symbolic speech," which should fall under the protection of the First Amendment. The courts have not upheld either of these contentions, and as a result, many protesters who had expected to be vindicated in their appeals to higher courts have instead been sent to prison for their efforts.

DIRECT ACTION AS A KIND OF SPEECH

A notable example is a case in which a group chose to hold a religious meeting in a public park, in violation of an ordinance requiring a license for such meetings. The group appealed to the Supreme Court, assuming that the Constitutional guarantees of free speech and freedom of religion would protect them from such a restriction on their activities. Speaking for the Court, Justice Reed said:

> The principles of the First Amendment are not to be treated as a promise that everyone with opinions or beliefs to express may gather around him at any public place and at any time a group for discussion or instruction. It is

a *non sequitur* to say that the First Amendment rights may not be regulated because they hold a preferred position in the hierarchy of the constitutional guarantees of the incidents of freedom. This Court . . . has indicated approval of reasonable nondiscriminatory regulation by governmental authority that preserves peace, order, and tranquillity without deprivation of the First Amendment guarantees of free speech, press and exercise of religion.

The valid requirements of license are for the good of the applicants [i.e., the group that held the illegal meeting] and the public. . . . Delay is unfortunate, but the expense and annoyance of litigation is a price citizens must pay for life in an orderly society where the rights of the First Amendment have a real and abiding meaning. . . .[23]

In a later case (1965), Cox, a leader of a peaceful courthouse picket line, exhorted his followers to try to eat in segregated restaurants and lunch counters. He was convicted, and on appeal the Supreme Court reversed the conviction, but with grave reservations:

We emphatically reject the notion urged by appellant [Cox] that the First and Fourteenth Amendments afford the same kind of freedom to those who would communicate ideas by conduct such as patrolling, marching, and picketing on streets and highways, as these amendments afford to those who communicate ideas by pure speech.[24]

Justice Goldberg, who is a liberal and was undoubtedly sympathetic to the aims of the demonstrators, added:

The fact that by their lights appellant and the two thousand students were seeking justice and not its obstruction is as irrelevant as would be the motives of [a] mob. . . . Louisiana . . . has the right to construe its statute to prevent parading and picketing from unduly influencing the administration of justice . . . regardless of whether the motives of the demonstrators are good or bad.

. . . Nothing we have said here . . . is to be interpreted as sanctioning riotous conduct in any form or demonstrations, however peaceful in their conduct or commendable their motives, which conflict with properly drawn statutes and ordinances designed to promote law and order, protect the community against disorder, regulate traffic, safeguard legitimate interests in private and public property, or protect the administration of justice and other essential governmental functions.

Liberty can only be exercised in a system of law which safeguards order. We reaffirm the repeated holdings of this Court that our constitutional command of free speech and assembly is basic and fundamental and encompasses peaceful social protest, so important to the preservation of the freedoms treasured in a democratic society. We also reaffirm the repeated decisions of this Court that there is no place for violence in a democratic society dedicated to liberty under law, and that the right of peaceful protest does not mean that everyone with opinions or beliefs to express may do so at any time and at any place. There is a proper time and place for even the most peaceful protest and a plain duty and responsibility on the part of all citizens to obey all valid laws and regulations.[25]

The following year (1966), a number of persons appealed to the Supreme Court against a conviction for trespass on the grounds of a county jail where they were protesting the arrest of fellow students and segregation. The late Justice Black, who had a well-deserved reputation for being one of the staunchest supporters of the First Amendment's guarantees of freedom of speech and freedom of the press, took a hard line against the defendants in this case and later fell from grace in some liberal circles. Whether his stance in this case and subsequent ones represented a genuine change in his position is dubious, for the question is not one of prior censorship, but of the place and circumstances in which the defendants attempted to exercise their right of free speech. This is what Justice Black wrote on that occasion.

> The First and Fourteenth Amendments, I think, take away from government, state and federal, all power to restrict freedom of speech, press, and assembly *where people have a right to be for such purposes.* This does not mean, however, that these amendments also grant a constitutional right to engage in the conduct of picketing or patrolling, whether on publicly owned streets or on privately owned property. . . . Picketing, though it may be utilized to communicate ideas, is not speech, and therefore is not of itself protected by the First Amendment.

He went on to explain:

> There is no merit to the petitioners' argument that they had a constitutional right to stay on the property . . . because this "area chosen for the peaceful civil rights demonstration was not only 'reasonable' but also particularly appropriate. . . ." Such an argument has as its major unarticulate premise the assumption that people who want to propagandize protests or views have a constitutional right to do so whenever and however and wherever they please. That concept of constitutional law was vigorously and forthrightly rejected in two of the cases petitioners rely on [including the Cox case discussed above]. We reject it again.[26]

It should be noted that Justices Douglas, Warren, Brennan, and Fortas dissented in this case, finding that the jail was a logical place to hold the protest. Justice Black, in another case, observed:

> The crowd moved by noble ideals today can become the mob ruled by hate and passion and greed and violence tomorrow. If we ever doubted that, we know it now. The peaceful songs of love can become as stirring and provocative as the Marseillaise did in the days when a noble revolution gave way to rule by successive mobs until chaos set in.[27]

Nicholas W. Puner has suggested that the hard line taken by the courts in recent years, as opposed to the more lenient interpretations of the laws as applied to civil disobedients at the beginning of the movement for equal rights for Negroes, may be the result of a combination of factors. In the beginning, acts of civil disobedience were localized phenomena, they were relatively harmless (except for the acts of reprisal that they provoked), and great social wrongs were being challenged by them. Now, he says, with the

Black Power movement, a succession of violent summers, considerable progress toward fulfillment of the aims of the original civil rights movement, and
the spread of unlawful protests to the point where they are an everyday occurrence all across the nation, the courts (and others) feel that it is time to
proceed at a more measured and mannerly pace. "To be lenient," Puner says,
"is to help kindle the fire next time." [28]

In 1967 the Court held that the burning of a draft card, though it may have
been intended as a kind of communication, was not a constitutionally protected form of communication, for it could not be construed to be a form of
speech. It held that the law against the mutilation or destruction of draft
cards is constitutional, for the card serves a number of legitimate administrative purposes. [29]

It is evident, then, that the Supreme Court—and along with it, the lower
courts—is taking an increasingly hard line on civil disobedience and that any
person contemplating an act of civil disobedience should be prepared to pay
the price exacted by the law for the particular violation involved. And
though a theoretical case can be made for the view that certain kinds of
action, though they may be nonverbal, are nevertheless forms of communication that may be used to convey ideas in striking and dramatic form, the
courts do not seem disposed at this time to grant to such modes of communication the same immunities as are taken for granted in more formal,
verbal means of imparting ideas and opinions.

THE THEATER OF PROTEST

In recent years dissidents have developed a kind of "theater" approach,
which they have used not only in the streets, but in the courts as well.
Through a variety of dramatic techniques they have attempted to create an
atmosphere in which what they consider to be the absurdity, the injustice,
or the evil qualities of certain institutions will be made manifest. The most
widely reported instance of this technique was the trial of the Chicago Seven
(the so-called Chicago Conspiracy Trial), in which four defendants in particular—David Dellinger, Rennie Davis, Thomas Hayden, and Abbie Hoffman—repeatedly disrupted the court's proceedings by shouts, obscenities,
and a variety of dramatic performances, including the staging of a birthday
party, complete with cake, in the midst of the trial. The judge, who was
much maligned, sentenced these four defendants and two of their attorneys
to lengthy prison terms—subsequently overturned on largely technical
grounds—for contempt of court. The defendants were deliberately attempting to draw public attention to their trial and to *keep* it in the forefront of
the nation's news by their antics. Though some lawyers are noted for their
penchant of playing to the galleries (including not only the juries, but the
audiences in the courtroom and the readers of the daily press), defendants
in criminal trials have never put on such a sustained performance. Never

before, so far as I know, had the civil disobedience of protest been directed against the courts themselves. There is some question whether this can, in fact, be called civil disobedience, or whether it ought rather to be considered a form of revolutionary activity, as defined earlier. For by attacking the courts themselves, the protesters were interfering with the only means society has of dispensing justice, and may, therefore, have been attacking one of the pillars of government and of society itself. Actions that disrupt the operations of the courts or of other agencies of the government, or that attempt to use them to heap scorn, ridicule, and contempt upon the processes of government, are of a very different order from lunch-counter sit-ins, bus boycotts, and even the burning of draft cards. They are directed not at specific laws or practices, but at the very foundations of government itself. The disruption of business at a lunch counter may be hard on those who wish to eat there and on the owner and employees of the business, but disruption of the government's agencies is an attack upon the entire system, and may do great damage to all who live under it.

THE CIVIL DISOBEDIENT AND NONVIOLENCE

Martin Luther King, Mohandas K. Gandhi, Henry David Thoreau, and others have advocated nonviolence both as a tactic and as a guiding principle. They and others have adhered rigorously to the principle of nonviolence. Martin Luther King explained the rationale behind the principle in his speech accepting the Nobel Prize in 1964: "We adopt the means of nonviolence because our end is a community at peace with itself." [30] He recognized the dangers of violence begetting violence. A movement conceived in violence, or furthered by violence, risks the near certainty of retaliatory violence that could reverberate for generations.

Is nonviolence essential to civil disobedience? Is it an ethical principle, a religious principle, or a tactic—a strategy that may be used by some civil disobedients because it works better than violence does?

A great many commentators consider nonviolence to be essential to civil disobedience and refuse to call any violent act one of civil disobedience. They make much of the fact that it is *civil* disobedience—a violation of the law that is *civilized* and restrained. As one has put it, "In order to qualify as an act of civil disobedience, a crime must have been committed without expectation of working undue harm on anyone. . . . No act of violence to the person can ever qualify as civil disobedience." [31] And another, contrasting civil disobedience with "all forms of violence, intentional and otherwise," says that "civil disobedience is disobedience which is 'passive,' 'nonviolent,' 'courteous,' 'not uncivil.' " [32]

But instances of civil disobedience that are violent may exist. Or one can imagine situations in which one would be justified in engaging in an act that would be both violent and civilly disobedient. One may not ordinarily *approve* of violent actions, even when there may be strong justification or excuse for them; and for one who is engaged in the civil disobedience of protest, violence may be counterproductive. But it is impossible without further analysis or question begging to assert categorically that all civil disobedience must (logically) be nonviolent.

For example, suppose a member of the illegal underground railroad (pronounced illegal by the highest court in the land, by the way) is escorting a fugitive slave to the Canadian border. As he approaches a crossing he is met by two men—slave hunters—who have been dispatched to bring fugitive slaves back to their masters. They are armed with court papers giving them the right to carry out their mission. There is no way to escape from them but to fight them. He is faced with the choice of sticking to his nonviolent principles and permitting the fugitive who has been entrusted to his care to be returned to slavery or of using force to overpower the slave hunters, thus ensuring the escape of the slave. A man who chooses, in such circumstances as these, to use force to secure freedom for a man who will otherwise be returned to slavery is a civil disobedient. Though he has not engaged in civil disobedience of protest, he is nevertheless a civil disobedient of personal integrity. He has refused to acquiesce in the process of what he considers an immoral or unjust law; and in order to achieve his aim—what he considers to be a highly moral aim—he finds that he must not only disobey the court order and violate the fugitive slave act, but that he must also assault those who would carry out its provisions. This is not revolutionary, though it is clearly closer to being revolutionary than the mere disregard of the fugitive slave act would be, for the disobedient continues to respect most of the laws of the land and to live as a law-abiding citizen in every respect but this. But where this particular issue is concerned, he finds that mere passive resistance is sometimes not enough. The issues are too fundamental in his eyes to permit even considerations of nonviolence to deter him from fulfilling his mission.

It is not difficult to think of other cases—not cases in Nazi Germany, for under such conditions the rules are very different, but cases that might occur in a democratic but imperfect society. Suppose, for example, that a man has been sent to a mental hospital by some avaricious relatives who intend to use his confinement as a means to take his business interests away from him. Suppose, further, that he is about to be subjected to a form of treatment that will seriously damage his mental capacities and his memory for the rest of his life. Suppose, finally, that because of the way in which the laws of the state have been framed, his confinement is technically legal, and the courts refuse to interfere with the professional practices of physicians. Would one not be justified, under such circumstances, in securing the release of that patient, by force, if necessary, before he was subjected to the treatment that had been prepared for him? And wouldn't such forcible violation of the law be· an instance of the civil disobedience of personal integrity? * Some protesters have gone farther in their tactics than the disciples of nonviolence would have done. They have paraded and picketed in such a way as to make it impossible for persons who wanted to enter or to leave certain buildings to do so—even, on occasion, interposing their bodies so as to constitute a threat of violence or to make violence inevitable if movement into or out of the building was to be effected. They have forcibly interfered with the movements of troop trains and with the operations of construction machinery at sites where racial discrimination was evident. They have thrown rotten vegetables and bags of human excrement at police and at politicians whose views they disapproved. It is difficult to say just when such actions cease to be those of the civil disobedient (the last-named scarcely seem to be civil!) and become those of the hooligan, the anarchist, or the nihilist. Much depends upon the *goals* toward which their actions are aimed and the *total effect* of those actions. The danger that any person who uses force or violence runs—if his aim is to protest against an unjust law or practice—is that he may end up committing a seriously unjust or immoral act himself, in his protest, and that in so doing he will harm the very cause for which he presumably broke the law. As for him who violates the law as a matter of personal integrity, he too runs the risk, once he permits himself to become the judge of when he may use force or violence, of committing an offense far worse than the one that he might have committed had he obeyed the law in the first place.

NONVIOLENCE AS A TACTIC

Nevertheless, it cannot be denied that the most notable civil disobedients have been nonviolent themselves and have counseled their followers to be nonviolent as well. For some (as for Martin Luther King), nonviolence was a religious principle. For others (as for some pacifists) it more closely resembles an ethical principle. But for all—including Gandhi, Martin Luther King, and the other leaders of great protest movements—it is a tactic, one that has proved its worth, in some situations, at least, and its power to effect radical changes in the social order. Martin Luther King drew on history to justify his espousal of the nonviolent tactic. The nonviolence of early Christians, he said, shook the mighty Roman Empire. In his view, the foundation for the freeing of the American colonies was laid in the nonviolent resistance of some of the colonists. And Gandhi, through his nonviolent tactics, was able to liberate his country from the British Empire.

For King nonviolence was not merely an ethical and religious principle, but a valuable technique for winning his battles. To be sure, it was a moral principle. "Moral force," he wrote, "has as much strength and virtue as the

---

* It could be converted into a protest against the state's laws and the hospital's practices as well, but this is not relevant to the purposes of the present discussion.

capacity to return a physical blow. . . . To refrain from hitting back requires more will and bravery than the automatic reflexes of defense." But far more important was its utilitarian justification. Its use enabled the movement to attract thousands of followers from every walk of life who would have been repelled by the use of violence; nonviolence "paralyzed and confused the power structures against which it was directed" and focused the attention of the world upon the events that were taking place; it had enormous psychological impact upon those who participated in the nonviolent direct action movement, raising their self-esteem, giving them dignity, and healing their internal wounds. Louis E. Lomax put the point very well: "Dr. King," he said, "is quite serious about nonviolence; he actually believes that the man who turns the other cheek will win the battle, or if he happens to lose the battle his children will win the war." "As a disciple of nonviolence," he wrote, "Martin Luther King is able to involve thousands of American white people in the Negro's struggle. I have watched white people react to King close up and, without exception, they are caught up by his addiction to nonviolent protest." [33] (Obviously these words were written long ago—in 1962, to be exact—before the great reaction, the "white backlash," had set in.)

It is likely that violence would have brought a reaction that might have set the cause for which he was fighting back by 100 years. (Indeed, there is some reason to believe that the violence of the past several years has had a serious negative effect upon the willingness of Americans to integrate their towns, their schools, and their clubs, and that it has contributed to the development of a new and not altogether flattering stereotype of the black American in the eyes of his white neighbor.) It would have alienated the clergy, the professionals, the intellectuals, and thousands of ordinary citizens who would not have been so ready to sing "Black and White Together" if the movement had been associated with violence. It would have made it impossible for the movement to collect the funds it so desperately needed for bail, for attorneys, for supplies, and for many other necessities—as CORE, SNCC, and other organizations discovered when their leaders began to advocate and participate in violent demonstrations. The credibility of those who claimed that the struggle was a moral one, for a moral cause, by persons of high moral integrity, would have been compromised. And the likelihood of success, against the vastly superior physical force available to those who opposed the movement, was very small indeed.

Nonviolence, then, is not logically necessary for civil disobedience, and it is possible to conceive of circumstances in which violence might be both necessary and justified as an element in civilly disobedient acts.* Nonviolence

* If certain purists insist that such acts are uncivil and are therefore not instances of civil disobedience, I would not make an issue over it; I would merely suggest that there is another class of unlawful acts that *is* accompanied by violence and that can be justified on moral grounds. Let them call it what they will.

may be a moral principle or a religious principle. However that may be, it is a very important element in the tactics of civilly disobedient protest.

SUMMARY AND CONCLUSION

The analysis that has been undertaken in this chapter necessitates the rejection of much of the definition of civil disobedience set forth early on (that of Martin Luther King), at least under certain circumstances. The reader will recall that Dr. King maintained that a civil disobedient was one who violated a law (1) that he believed to be unjust or immoral, (2) in order to bring about a change in the social order, (3) in such a way as to inflict no harm or bodily injury upon any other person, (4) openly and publicly, and (5) with a willingness to pay the penalty. Dr. King was not alone, of course, in adhering to these criteria. Many others have followed him in asserting that all or most of these conditions must be met if any violation of the law is to count as an act of civil disobedience.

Such efforts may be exercises in "persuasive definition," that is, attempts to persuade the general public to adopt a given definition of civil disobedience as the only one that it will recognize as legitimate, thus relegating all other forms of illegal behavior to some other category—lawlessness, perhaps, or defiance of the law. For most people *civil disobedience* has fairly positive connotations. A civil disobedient is generally regarded as a high-minded individual—misguided perhaps, but courageous and principled, idealistic and deeply committed. One who is lawless, however, is thought of as evil, vicious, potentially dangerous, unprincipled, lacking in concern for others, self-serving, a discredit to the community. And one who is deviant refuses to obey the law because he is sick, or because he is immature and irresponsible. He too can be dangerous and a menace to society. If this definition, then, and others like it, is an attempt to persuade people to regard only such unlawful behavior as falls within its scope as morally justified and as the kind of behavior that some people, at least, may engage in with clear consciences—and even *ought* to engage in under certain circumstances—then it is a well-meaning effort, but misguided. For not only does it do violence to the language, but it eliminates from the scope of morally justifiable unlawful acts some that may very well be justifiable, and by doing so, renders the job of some kinds of "civil disobedients" much more difficult, because it makes them seem to be mere lawbreakers.

Of course, the error may be one of insufficient analysis, or of special pleading. However that may be, it should be easier now to distinguish a number of different kinds of unlawful behavior from one another and to discuss each of them with some degree of discrimination.

Civil disobedience certainly always involves the violation of a law, though the law violated may—or may not—later be found to be invalid by the courts. The civil disobedient may himself carry the appeals through the courts to have the offending law overturned.

It is a necessary condition of all civilly disobedient behavior that the violator believe firmly either that it would be morally wrong for him to obey the law in question or that the unlawful act in which he is engaging will tend to promote the cause of justice in his society.

It is necessary, in this connection, to remember the distinction between direct and indirect disobedience, and that between disobedience of protest and disobedience of personal integrity. Though there are a number of permutations and combinations of these various forms of disobedience, civil disobedience of personal integrity must (as I have defined that term) always be an act of direct civil disobedience.

This distinction enables us to draw a number of further conclusions that might otherwise have been tangled in a morass of confusion. Thus, we conclude that one who engages in protest civil disobedience does so in order to bring about a change in the social order; but there are clear cases of civil disobedience of personal integrity where that is not the intention at all. For similar reasons acts of protest will be most effective if they are conducted in the open, but civil disobedience of personal integrity may be carried out in secret and still achieve the desired aim, or even be more advantageous—both to the individual and to society in the long run.

Though nonviolence is an excellent tactic, and though nonviolence is *generally* to be preferred (morally) to violence and the use of force, violence may occasionally be necessary to achieve the desired goals and be justified on moral grounds. Some civilly disobedient acts may be violent. But in civil disobedience of protest, violence almost always backfires and may do more harm to the cause for which the protesters are struggling than good.

In protest civil disobedience, the acceptance of punishment is important for the credibility of the movement. But one who engages in the civil disobedience of personal integrity *need not* (morally) accept punishment for violating what he considers to be an unjust law. However, when he fails to turn himself in, he does his bit to contribute to the undermining of society's legal foundations.

And this brings us back to the dilemma posed at the beginning of this discussion. How can one defy the law—even what one is convinced is an unjust law—and not contribute to the breakdown of one of society's most vital institutions? Obviously, this is not a question that is easily answered. It is not necessary, though, to appeal to such thoroughly questionable theories as the natural-law theory or the divine-law theory to find a justification for disobeying some laws. In spite of what Hobbes has said about the absolute obligation that every man is under to obey the laws at all times and under all conditions (with the exception of those that threaten his three inalienable rights), man may *not always* be duty-bound to obey *any* rule. For the most part, and under most circumstances, one should obey the law, just as one should—for the most part and under most circumstances—tell the truth, keep one's promises, show gratitude to one's benefactors, keep confidences and secrets, and not kill other human beings. But it is not difficult to think of occasions when any of these rules might properly be violated, because there are values other than truth telling, promise keeping, obedience to the law, and the rest. When Daniel Ellsberg turned forty-seven volumes of secret government documents with which he had been entrusted over to the *New York Times,* he violated the law, he betrayed government secrets, he violated the trust that had been placed in him, and he violated the oath that he had taken when he first went to work for the government. But he concluded that all of this was insignificant by comparison with the benefits that might flow from public disclosure of those documents. Those benefits, he felt, far outweighed the harm that might come from his action and justified the strong risk he took of spending a good many years in prison. It is such moral judgments as these that those contemplating civil disobedience must make.

At the time of this writing it does not seem likely that the United States government's entire security apparatus will disintegrate because of Ellsberg's example, or that general lawlessness will ensue, or that any of the dire consequences that Socrates and Aristotle predicted might occur if men engaged in civil disobedience will actually follow. For men who are willing to take the risks inherent in civil disobedience are very rare indeed, and the cost is far higher than most men are prepared to pay.

It is right to be law-abiding. But there may be times when it is not wrong to break the law. There are no easy rules or recipes to guide us in making our choices. Some people, who allow themselves to be governed by expediency and narrow self-interest when they choose to disobey traffic regulations and income tax laws, wax indignant when their neighbors violate laws because their religious and moral convictions do not permit them to do otherwise. Anarchy is a terrible thing. It is all that Hobbes said it was. It is more likely to come from motives like those of the speeder, the drunken driver, and the one who cheats on his income tax, though, than from those of men like Gandhi, King, and Ellsberg.

16

War Crimes and Crimes Against Humanity

DIVINE RIGHT AND SOVEREIGN IMMUNITY

Those who are familiar with the course of events that usually follows a charge of police brutality or the abuse of official powers know how difficult it is to make such a charge stick. Ancient doctrines that can be traced far beyond the medieval theory of the divine right of kings interpose nearly insurmountable obstacles between the citizen who believes that he has been injured (that is, unjustly or illegally harmed) by an officer of the state and the satisfaction of any claim that he may make for reparation of the injury or retribution against the wrongdoer. The officer is surrounded by immunities, for the state does not look kindly upon the suggestion that it has done wrong. The officer, being a part of the state's apparatus, enjoys many of the immunities that the state itself enjoys against its citizens. No one could prosecute the king, for who would hear the case, who would serve as the judge, and who would declare the law? The king was himself the supreme judge and the supreme legislator. How, then, could one ask the king to judge himself? If one complained against one of the king's officers, it was, in a sense, a complaint against the king himself. The king would act upon the complaint only at his pleasure. Officers of the law, then, and judges, governors, presidents, members of Congress and the Senate, and ministers of government enjoy many immunities that ordinary citizens, and even those same persons, in their private capacities, do not have.

If it is difficult to get satisfaction in a claim for damages against an officer of the law, or to convict a public official of a criminal charge with regard to an action that he took in his official capacity, it is *virtually impossible* to get such a judgment against the highest officials of a national state; for, with a few extraordinary exceptions, there is no one to prefer the charges, no one to hear the cases, no one to execute the judgments but these very persons themselves. And even if they are no longer in office, they can claim that when they were, they merely carried out their duties and responsibilities as they saw them and understood them at the time. How can the very state in whose service they performed the acts about which the complaint is being laid now prosecute them and possibly punish them for doing what they did?

Even more difficult, however, is the problem of the aggrieved party who considers himself a victim of unjustified aggression on the part of a foreign state. To whom shall he turn for relief? What court will hear his argument and pass judgment against a sovereign nation? And even if there were such a court, what sovereign nation would submit to its judgment or acquiesce in its demands? If such a hypothetical court rendered judgment against the nation, decreed that it had indeed engaged in a wrongful act of hostility, and ordered it to pay compensation to the aggrieved party, who would enforce the court's order?

Finally, by what rule of law would any court presume to convict him or anyone who had followed his orders? An ancient and respected rule of justice decrees that no one should be convicted or punished for any act that was not forbidden by the law at the time that he committed it. The sovereign may rightly point out that the law under which he performed his allegedly criminal acts was the law of the land at the time. Who would know better than he, after all, for he had signed it himself? He was the sovereign and he made the laws. His subordinates followed the laws, as they and every proper citizen were supposed to do. Therefore, no law was broken by him or any of his subordinates during the time in question. If it be claimed that the law broken was the law of some other state, he can rightly reply that he is not subject to the law of any other state. He is subject only to the law of *his* state. If some foreign state wishes to convict him of a violation of *its* laws, let it do so; but it will be powerless to do more than pronounce words, without laying itself open to a charge of aggression and the strong possibility of reprisals, including the ultimate reprisal of war.

THE JUST-WAR CONCEPT

The concept of the just war extends back through the Middle Ages into late Hellenistic times, and beyond that even into Biblical times. It has been said that the concept of Christian charity is itself one of the foundations of the just-war idea. As Paul Ramsey has put it,

> The justification of warfare and of Christian participation in it was not actually an exception (certainly not an arbitrary one, or a compromise from the purity of Christian ethics), but instead an *expression* of the Christian

understanding of moral and political responsibility. . . . In the ancient theory of just war, Christian conscience took the form of allowing any killing at all of men for whom Christ died only because military personnel were judged to stand, factually and objectively, at the point where, as combatants, resistance to them was judged to be necessary in responsibility to many other neighbors.[1]

He explains that though Jesus advocated turning the other cheek, he did not tell his disciples to raise the head of another oppressed man so that his tormentor could strike him again. For the sake of love itself, he says, Christianity taught that violence could be used, if necessary, to repel invading forces in order to protect the innocent against harm to which they might otherwise have been subjected. Or, to put it another way, it may be a work of charity to resist by force of arms an act of aggression against the forces that enable the citizens of a state or its institutions to carry out their work of healing the sick, educating the young, and feeding the poor.[2]

These principles have their corollaries, of course. If it is meaningful to talk of just wars, then the concept of unjust war must be meaningful as well. Advocates of the just-war theory have, in fact, developed elaborate accounts of the distinctions between just and unjust wars. Grotius, in introducing his discussion of just wars, distinguishes them from the wars of savages, which are fought out of the sheer love of slaughtering and butchering men or facing dangerous situations; and there are also wars of robbers—those who, in the words of Augustine, "from the mere lust of ruling . . . crush peoples who have not troubled [them]." And Philo, too, described those "who have acquired the strength of robbers [and] lay waste whole cities, taking no thought of punishments, because they appear to be stronger than the laws. These are men whose nature is unsuited to civil life, who seek after tyrannies and despotisms, who carry out plundering on a large scale, concealing under the respected names of government and authority what is more correctly called robbery." [3]

Some wars, according to Grotius, merely present an appearance of justice —but the appearance is a false one. Unjust wars are those that are fought for expansionistic purposes or, as the Germans called it, *Lebensraum*. Paternalistic colonialism—the desire to rule others against their will on the pretext that it is for their welfare—is another unjust cause of war. Still another is the war that is fought on the ground that a certain emperor or church has the self-proclaimed right or authority to universal dominion. There are others, but these examples are sufficient.

These principles and guidelines were of great interest to legal and moral scholars and were the occasion for many hours of fascinating discussion. But as one of the great modern authorities in the field of international law has commented, "So long as war was a recognized instrument of national policy, both for giving effect to existing rights and for changing the law, the justice or otherwise of the causes of war was not of legal relevance. The right of war, for whatever purposes, was a prerogative of national sovereignty. Thus conceived, *every war was just."* [4] Until the present century, whatever moralists and writers might have said, war was primarily a means of self-help utilized by nations whenever they felt the need to enforce what they conceived to be their rights under the law. In fact, it mattered little what the law was, for each state decided that issue for itself. States rejected the distinction between just and unjust wars, insisting that international law was itself determined by the actions of states. In the absence of an international legislature, war was one way of changing the law and of "rectifying" or at least altering the rights of states relative to one another. So long as this state of affairs endured, the law of the jungle—might makes right—prevailed, and no war was unjust. As Hobbes wrote in 1651:

> In all times kings and persons of sovereign authority, because of their independency, are in continual jealousies and in the state and posture of gladiators, having their weapons pointing and their eyes fixed on one another—that is, their forts, garrisons, and guns upon the frontiers of their kingdoms, and continual spies upon their neighbors—which is a posture of war. . . . [When there is a state of war—as there is in the relations of one nation to another,] nothing can be unjust. The notions of right and wrong, justice and injustice, have there no place. Where there is no common power, there is no law; where no law, no injustice. [5]

Laws that cannot be enforced are no laws at all. Where there are no enforceable laws, every man is in practice (if not in conscience) free to do what he considers right or what he considers to be in his own interest. Where no enforceable laws exist, nations are in fact governed only by the limits of their own power.

In the relations among the nations of the world, no enforceable laws regarding warfare existed prior to this century, though there were many moral pronouncements as to what nations should do and what they should refrain from doing. Where anarchy reigns, Mao's principle, that right is to be found at the end of a gun, holds true. Therefore, so long as the state of anarchy described so graphically by Hobbes prevailed among the nations of the world, there was no measure of justice and right except that which emerged from the barrels of guns. But in civilized society, justice and right—though they may ultimately have to be enforced by physical power—are not measured in those terms, but are determined, so far as possible, by reasoned responses to the needs, desires, and aspirations of the people. The gun may loom in the background as an ultimate threat, but justice and right are better conceived of as the results of voluntary commitments and concessions made by each man to every other as a means of achieving a degree of mutual security and freedom from the fear of aggression. Similarly, among the nations of the world, law may be regarded, in part, at least, as commitments and concessions made by each nation to the others, one concession being an agreement that each nation sacrifices its prior right to make war against the others in return for a guarantee that they will not make war against it.

FIRST STEPS TOWARD A LAW OF WAR

Writing more than three and a half centuries ago Hugo Grotius, the father of modern international law, said, "Throughout the Christian world I observed a lack of restraint in relation to war, such as even barbarous races should be ashamed of; I observed that men rush to arms for slight causes, or no cause at all, and that when arms have once been taken up there is no longer any respect for law, divine or human; it is as if, in accordance with a general decree, frenzy had openly been let loose for the committing of all crimes." [6] It is not true, he declared, that in war, all laws are in abeyance. "On the contrary, war ought not to be undertaken except for the enforcement of rights; when once undertaken, it should be carried on only within the bounds of law and good faith." [7] The laws of the state may be silent as regards the conduct of war, but certain unwritten laws remain in force, even as regards the conduct of hostile nations. Quoting an ancient author, he declared, "War has its laws no less than peace." The Greeks, the Romans, and others recognized the importance of adhering to just and reasonable policies in war as in peace and often felt that their defeats were due retribution for their failure to settle disputes by arbitration, their hasty decisions to enter into war, their cruel treatment of the enemy or of prisoners, and other wicked deeds. "We try to restrain murders and the killing of individuals," said Seneca. "Why are wars and the crime of slaughtering nations full of glory? Avarice and cruelty know no bounds. In accordance with decrees of the Senate and orders of the people atrocities are committed, and actions forbidden to private citizens are commanded in the name of the state." [8] More than once in ancient times, it was said that those who committed petty crimes were looked upon as villains and scoundrels, whereas those who murdered men by the thousands, plundered great cities, and kidnapped and enslaved whole popualtions were hailed as great heroes and military geniuses. A pirate was once talking about Alexander the Great, conqueror of the world and hero of an entire age. "Alexander," he said, "is a pirate, too, just like me. The difference between the two of us is simply this: I sink only one ship at a time, while he sinks whole fleets of them."

The view that military leaders are all criminals on a grand scale cannot be seriously maintained. To be sure, their profession sometimes requires the killing of other men; the burning of homes, farms, and sometimes entire cities; and the subjugation of whole populations. But not all killing is murder, not all burning is arson, and some instances of the deprivation of civil rights and civil liberties are neither wrong nor unjustified. Charles J. Whitman, an honor student at the University of Texas, was shot to death by the police after he had shot a total of forty-four persons, killing fourteen of them, from a tower on the university campus. He had earlier slain two relatives at home. The police, who clearly had no alternative but to shoot Whitman in order to bring his sniping to an end, could hardly be called murderers. On the contrary, their behavior was courageous and heroic, and was deserving of commendation. The officers and men of the military are often put into a similar situation, but on a far grander scale; for sometimes not only the students, the faculty, and the staff of a university are threatened, but the entire population of a nation. The military are called in, at great risk to themselves, to stave off the aggression and to protect the civilian population. Where there is a clear and immediate danger of overt aggression by one state against another, the threatened state's forces may properly bomb and burn the aggressor's tanks and planes; immobilize his troops; and occupy and subdue areas that are strategically located. If one can see the justification for such acts on the small scale represented by the Whitman case, then it is difficult to see why analogous acts on the larger scale represented by the relationships of nations to one another should not also be justifiable.

But this is not to say that pretense, misrepresentation, the fabrication of evidence or excuses, fraud, or lies would suffice in either case to justify such violent actions. If police fire upon a man or a group of persons on the *pretext* that they or innocent civilians were attacked by them with deadly weapons, then that police action is nothing more nor less than murder, or attempted murder, and a conspiracy to deprive innocent persons of their rights. Similarly, if a nation sends its army onto foreign territory on the *pretext* that the actions that they are to carry out there are necessary for the security of its own people, or through a fraudulent misrepresentation of facts which, if true, would justify such actions under treaties or other binding international agreements, then it would seem that that nation and its leaders are guilty of a crime against the people of the state whose territory they invaded, or whose cities and factories they bombarded, or whose military personnel they wounded, maimed, and killed.

But no behavior is criminal unless it is forbidden by law. No prohibition has anything more than moral or hortatory force unless it is backed up by sanctions, the threat of penalties. Where there is no law, Hobbes once said, all things are permitted to all men. Though men may preach against practices that they consider to be evil, their exhortations ordinarily have no permanent or lasting effect upon human behavior unless they are reinforced by the sanctions of the state. There is no absolute guarantee that men will behave in such a way as to minimize the harm that they do to one another. The law and the sanctions that it brings to bear upon its violators tend, however, to render such harmful behavior less likely than it might be in the absence of such regulation. Law, then, is the handmaiden of morals. It offers some assurance that that which is forbidden by morals—but which moral feelings and beliefs alone are powerless to prevent—will not occur. It is the instrument through which the ideals of justice are realized in this world. In its absence men must look to self-help to right the wrongs inflicted upon them by others, or else they must helplessly suffer them.

The frontier of law and morals in our generation is in the realm of international law. The law of nations is still in a primitive and rudimentary state. Many of its principles remain pious hopes rather than solid achievements. Nowhere is this more evident than in the laws of war, which have been applied to concrete situations for the first time in this half century. Here it is possible, perhaps as nowhere else, to observe a new system of law in the making, the first tentative steps toward the construction of a new international society, the first painful and frustrating efforts of men to reduce their moral ideals and their dreams of a just society to concrete terms that will have a real and noticeable effect upon the lives of the people who inhabit this planet.

War crimes and crimes against humanity are not merely moral problems; they are legal problems as well. But the law governing war crimes and crimes against humanity is not so well developed as that which governs other areas of human concern. In such other areas as torts, contracts, property, and the criminal law of a particular state, the problem is often a matter of conflict of rights and duties, of efforts to reform laws that may have been on the books for many years and that have had a long history. Here the situation is radically different, for it is said by some that there is no law to reform. Even those who concede that there *is* a law agree that it is rudimentary and that nations must learn how to apply it—to make the terms *war crime* and *crime against humanity* as meaningful in the society of nations as *murder* and *larceny* are in a civil society.

The worthy sentiments of Grotius, of Seneca, and of all the learned writers who denounced the lawlessness and the cruelties of men and nations at war had little practical effect upon the actual conduct of states or their citizens, for there was no sanction that could meaningfully be applied against those who violated the so-called unwritten laws of war, even after those laws had been reduced to writing by Grotius and those who came after him. Not until the twentieth century, when tormented mankind suffered through the most barbarous wars ever waged, did the international community finally take its first halting steps toward making the concepts of war crimes and crimes against humanity meaningful and operative in the lives of nations.

No discussion of this subject can be fruitful unless one has some understanding of recent developments in the law. After a survey of the law governing war crimes and crimes against humanity, it will be possible to inquire where we go from here.

THE DEVELOPMENT OF THE LAW ON WAR CRIMES

In the second half of the nineteenth century a number of treaties were signed by a majority of the states of the Western world in which each state agreed to be bound to certain restrictions in its power to wage war. Among these were the abolishment of privateering, a number of provisions to ameliorate the conditions of wounded soldiers in the field, the prohibition of the use of explosive or inflammable bullets, and a codification of the laws of land warfare. These were later replaced or supplemented by treaties and conventions whose general aim was to establish, on humanitarian grounds, that no belligerent should use any kind or degree of violence that was not necessary to overpower his opponent and that every belligerent should respect the human rights of enemy combatants. But again, all of these agreements depended entirely upon the good faith of those who entered into them. There was a gradual approach to the idea that the waging of war and certain kinds of belligerent action constituted international crimes, but that point had not yet been reached. It was still considered more a question of *morals* and of *humanitarianism* but the parties to these arguments were as far from thinking of the possibility of punishment for transgression of these norms as they would have been from the thought of punishing an individual for being uncharitable. In other treaties and conventions of the late nineteenth and early twentieth centuries, nations agreed to appeal to the good offices of friendly powers or to conciliation commissions for mediation and arbitration of disputes before going to war; to respect the neutrality of the citizens of neutral states; not to commence hostilities "without a previous and unequivocal warning, which shall take the form either of a declaration of war, giving reasons, or of an ultimatum with a conditional declaration of war"; not to lay mines that explode automatically on contact unless they are anchored (except that unanchored mines that became harmless after one hour could be used for defensive purposes), and not to lay mines in enemy harbors for the sole purpose of destroying merchant ships; not to subject undefended towns, ports, and other places to naval bombardment, unless they are of a military nature, in which case adequate warning must be given to those who are within them; to take all necessary steps to spare buildings devoted to public worship, art, science, or charitable purposes and historical monuments and hospitals; not to use dum-dum bullets; and to refrain from using missiles that spread poisonous gases.

After World War I a number of new treaties were signed that extended the protections of these treaties and conventions and defined them more closely. These treaties grew out of the atrocities that were committed by Germany and her allies during that war. An adumbration of things to come was a declaration of the governments of France, Great Britain, and Russia in 1915, denouncing the massacre of the Armenian population by the Turks. "In view of these new Turkish *crimes against humanity and civilization*, the allies declare publicly that they will hold all the members of the Ottoman government as well as those of its agents who are found to have been implicated in these massacres *personally responsible*." [9]

After the war, the Preliminary Peace Conference of Paris created a commission whose purpose was to inquire into the responsibilities relating to the war, and it in turn created several subcommissions, of which one was instructed to discover and collect evidence on criminal acts. In its report this subcommission on war crimes compiled a list of crimes, or groups of crimes, that would be breaches of the laws and customs of war. This list included, among others, the following: murders, massacres, systematic terrorism, putting hostages to death, torture or starvation of civilians, rape, enforced prostitution, deportation of civilians, internment of civilians under inhuman conditions, forced labor of civilians in connection with the military operations of the enemy, pillage, confiscation of property, debasement of currency, imposition of collective penalties, wanton devastation and destruction of property, deliberate bombardment of undefended places, wanton destruction of religious, charitable, educational, and historic buildings and monuments, destruction of merchant ships and passenger vessels without warning and without provision for the safety of passengers and crew, breach of various rules relating to the Red Cross, use of poisonous gases, explosive or expanding bullets and other inhuman appliances, ill treatment of wounded and prisoners of war, misuse of flags of truce, and the poisoning of wells.

This list, which is far from exhaustive, was, strictly speaking, a compilation of those cruel and inhuman acts that had been recognized for many years as constituting uncivilized behavior in time of war, with the addition of several special provisions that had become necessary because of the advances in modern technology that made it possible to inflict new, more painful, and more imaginative kinds of injury upon one's opponents.

The commission distinguished broadly between two kinds of offenses: those that were committed in violation of the laws and customs of war (war crimes) and those that were committed by the troops and officers of a state on their own territory and against their own nationals (crimes against humanity). The declaration quoted earlier, threatening punishment of those Turkish officials who were responsible for the massacre of Armenians who lived on Turkish soil, was referring to a crime of the latter sort. This was the first attempt to distinguish these two kinds of offenses and to define *crimes against humanity*.

The American representatives to the commission pointed out, in a "Memorandum of Reservations," that

> war was and is by its very nature inhuman, but acts consistent with the laws and customs of war, although these acts are inhuman, are nevertheless not the object of punishment by a court of justice. A judicial tribunal only deals with existing law and only administers existing law, leaving to another forum infractions of the moral law and actions contrary to the laws and principles of humanity. [One can only assume that that "other forum" is heaven.] A further objection lies in the fact that the laws and principles of humanity are not certain, varying with time, place, and circumstances, and accordingly, it may be, to the conscience of the individual judge. There is no fixed and universal standard of humanity.

Thus, the American representatives emphasized the distinction between an immoral act that might be deserving of condemnation and a criminal one that might be deserving of punishment; and further, they refused to accept the natural-law theory of a universal and eternal standard of humanity.

Still, they contributed to the development of such standards in the law of nations by setting forth a series of principles which should be used in measuring inhuman or atrocious acts during the prosecution of a war:

(1) Slaying and maiming men in accordance with generally accepted rules of war are from their nature cruel and contrary to the modern conception of humanity.

(2) The methods of destruction of life and property in conformity with the accepted rules of war are admitted by civilized nations to be justifiable and no charge of cruelty, inhumanity, or impropriety lies against a party employing such methods.

(3) The principle underlying the accepted rules of war is the necessity of exercising physical force to protect national safety or to maintain national rights.

(4) Reprehensible cruelty is a matter of degree which cannot be justly determined by a fixed line of distinction, but one which fluctuates in accordance with the facts in each case, but the manifest departure from accepted rules and customs of war imposes upon the one so departing the burden of justifying his conduct, as he is *prima facie* guilty of a criminal act.

(5) The test of guilt in the perpetration of an act, which would be inhuman or otherwise reprehensible under normal conditions, is the necessity of that act to the protection of national safety or national rights measured chiefly by actual military advantage.

(6) The assertion by the perpetrator of an act that it is necessary for military reasons does not exonerate him from guilt if the facts and circumstances present reasonably strong grounds for establishing the needlessness of the act or for believing that the assertion is not made in good faith.

(7) While an act may be essentially reprehensible and the perpetrator entirely unwarranted in assuming it to be necessary from a military point of view, he must not be condemned as wilfully violating the *laws and customs of war* or the *principles of humanity* unless it can be shown that the act was wanton and without reasonable excuse.

(8) A wanton act which causes needless suffering (and this includes such causes of suffering as destruction of property, deprivation of necessaries of life, enforced labor, etc.) is cruel and criminal. The full measure of guilt attaches to a party who without adequate reasons perpetrates a needless act of cruelty. Such an act is a *crime against civilisation,* which is without palliation.

(9) It would appear, therefore, in determining the criminality of an act, that there should be considered the wantonness or malice of the perpetrator, the needlessness of the act from a military point of view, the perpetration of a justifiable act in a needlessly harsh or cruel manner, and the improper motive which inspired it.[10]

In a major departure from earlier principles and precedents the commission recommended that "all persons belonging to enemy countries, however high their position may have been, without distinction of rank, including chiefs of States, who have been guilty of offences against the laws and customs of war or the laws of humanity, are liable to criminal prosecution." The privileges and immunities of heads of state apply in municipal law (that is, the law of the state of which a particular person is the head) as a matter of practical expediency. Within a given state there may be good reasons why the head of that state may not be prosecuted for violations of the criminal law. But recognition of the fact that he may not be prosecuted in the criminal courts of the state over which he exercises sovereignty is not the same as granting him immunity from prosecution for crimes committed in the territories of other states, against the nationals of other states, and against the laws of the international community. It would be most unjust, the commission held, to maintain that a man might commit the greatest outrages against the laws of war and the laws of humanity and yet remain immune to punishment.

Again, the American representatives held to a more conservative view. They could not agree that chiefs of states should be liable to criminal prosecution, for there was no precedent for such a doctrine. They held that a sovereign authority cannot be held responsible to the judicial authority of his state, but is responsible only to his political authority. What he does may bind his country and may lead to its condemnation in the community of nations, but he is personally responsible only to the people of his own country. To hold otherwise would be to put him in the strange and awkward position of owing allegiance to the laws of some foreign country or group of countries, when his only allegiance should presumably be to the laws of his own nation.[11]

The Treaty of Versailles provided for the punishment of war criminals by the allies but omitted all mention of crimes against humanity, thus acceding to the American arguments on that point. But the principle that persons who had violated the laws and customs of war could be punished for such violations in the courts of the adversary was set forth, for the first time, in an internationally binding agreement.

Some difficulty ensued in the implementation of these decisions, however, for the Allies acceded to a German request that war criminals be tried by German courts rather than by the courts of other nations or by an international tribunal. The Germans set up a special court to hear war crimes cases, but virtually all of the accused were acquitted, and of the small number who were convicted, only a handful received anything more than a strictly minimal sentence. Even these somehow managed to escape from their prison cells and disappear, obviously with the connivance of the authorities. Thus, the first real attempt to bring the concept of war crimes out of the vague and hazy cloud of moralistic preaching and into the real workings of states was an abject failure.

In the years that followed, more treaties were signed, each of them designed to assure the people of the world that they would never again have to suffer the destruction and the torments of war. The Covenant of the League of Nations stopped short of outlawing war, for, like the Hague Conventions adopted earlier, it merely endeavored to delay the outbreak of wars by insisting on the submission of international disputes to arbitration or some other form of peaceful settlement. One provision of the covenant provided, however, that if the Council of the League could not reach a unanimous decision on a dispute that had been brought before it, "the members of the League reserve to themselves the right to take such action as they may consider necessary for the maintenance of right and justice," thus opening the door for any nation to engage in war against any other with the sanction of legality.

The most important of the postwar treaties is the Kellogg–Briand Treaty, also known as the Pact of Paris (1928) or the International Treaty for the Renunciation of War as an Instrument of National Policy. Its terms were short, simple, and direct:

> *Article 1.* The High Contracting Parties solemnly declare in the names of their respective peoples that they condemn recourse to war for the solution of international controversies, and renounce it as an instrument of national policy in their relations with one another.
> *Article 2.* The High Contracting Parties agree that the settlement or solution of all disputes or conflicts of whatever nature or of whatever origin they may be, which may arise among them, shall never be sought except by pacific means.

This treaty was accepted by a total of forty-four states, including all of the great powers except the Soviet Union. Germany and Japan were among the original signatories.

Important as it was, the Kellogg–Briand Treaty did not completely outlaw war, for it contained a number of important loopholes. War was still lawful (1) when undertaken in self-defense (and the meaning of *self-defense* was construed very broadly—as, for example, by the United States, which informed the other parties to the Pact that the Monroe Doctrine was not overridden by the Pact of Paris), (2) between nations who had signed the Pact and nations who had not, and (3) when undertaken by a signatory to the Pact against another signatory who had broken the Pact by resorting to war in violation of the Pact's provisions. Striking at the very vitals of the Pact was the question of the meaning of *self-defense.* Mr. Kellogg himself wrote to the signatory governments, "That right is inherent in every sovereign state and is implicit in every treaty. Every nation is free at all times and regardless of treaty provisions to defend its territory from attack or invasion and *it alone is competent to decide whether circumstances require recourse to war in self-defence.*" [12] With every state the judge of its own actions, it is clearly impossible to hold any state guilty of violating the Pact's provisions, for every state will claim self-defense if its warlike actions are questioned.

But we should not allow ourselves to be misled by Mr. Kellogg's statement. Nowhere in the Pact itself is it said that a given state accused of aggression against a neighboring state is to be the final arbiter in its own case. In common law the man accused of murder may plead that he acted in self-defense, but it is up to the jury and the judge to determine whether there is any substance to his plea. The nations of the world, in signing the Kellogg–Briand Treaty, were seriously concerned to outlaw aggressive war and could not have intended to make every potential aggressor the judge in his own case or to give him a foolproof way of escaping responsibility for his lawless behavior. It may be difficult, in some cases, to establish the facts and to determine whether there was legitimate cause for warlike activity—whether there was in fact reason for the state accused of aggression to believe that it had to act as it did in self-defense. But such difficulty is not itself sufficient to render the provisions of the Pact of Paris totally useless. A simple example will illustrate my point.

On the thirty-first of August, 1939, a number of German border outposts were attacked by Polish forces. At one, Gleiwitz, a radio transmitter was seized by the Poles and was used to broadcast a message, in Polish, stating that the time had come for the showdown between Germany and Poland and calling on the Poles to unite and to strike down any Germans from whom they met any resistance. German forces were called in and shot members of the invading teams; others escaped across the border. Their bleeding bodies were photographed, and they and their bloodstained uniforms—uniforms of the Polish army—were later displayed before members of the press, who were taken to the sites where the incidents took place. On the following day, Hitler proclaimed, in a radio broadcast:

> The Polish Government, unwilling to establish good neighborly relations as aimed at by me, want to force the issue by war of arms.
> The Germans in Poland are being persecuted by bloody terror and driven from their homes. Several acts of frontier violation, which cannot be tolerated by a great power, show that Poland is no longer prepared to respect the Reich's frontiers. To put an end to these mad acts, I can see no other way but from now onwards to meet force with force.[13]

Germany had entered into an arbitration treaty with Poland at Locarno in 1925, and in 1934 Hitler signed a ten-year nonaggression pact with Poland. In addition both countries were signatories to the Kellogg–Briand Pact. In view of all of this, Poland's aggressive actions against Germany were completely unjustified, and Germany was totally within her rights in replying to the use of force by Poland in the name of self-defense—or was she?

Hitler was in fact planning to invade Poland at least a year before the incidents of August, 1939, that served as her pretext for going to war.

In April, 1939, one of Hitler's top lieutenants issued a directive informing the commanders of the armed forces that the invasion of Poland would take place some time after September 1, 1939. In June, secret plans for a quiet mobilization of German troops and the calling up of reserves were laid. And the "provocations" of August, 1939, were planned by Hitler himself. The Polish "invaders" were actually German troops dressed in Polish uniforms. The broadcast that was aired from the radio transmitter at Gleiwitz was delivered by a Polish-speaking member of the Wehrmacht who read from a script prepared by the supreme command of the German army. And the bodies that were exhibited to newsmen as Hitler's armies prepared to smash into Poland were in fact the bodies of German convicts who were dressed in Polish uniforms and were murdered for the occasion. When the minutes of secret meetings, the orders for the delivery of the "Canned Goods" (i.e., the drugged convicts who were to be shot on location), and the testimony of persons who participated in this ghastly charade were unveiled at the Nuremberg trials, there could be no doubt about the illegitimacy of Hitler's claim to have acted in "self-defense." [14]

In the Nuremberg trials, Kellogg's suggestion that each nation be the ultimate judge of its own acts of "self-defense" was not followed, but the rules of evidence, and an objective appraisal of what actually happened, prevailed. As the International Military Tribunal declared in its judgment rendered in 1946:

> It was . . . argued that Germany alone could decide, in accordance with the reservations made by many of the Signatory Powers at the time of the conclusion of the Kellogg–Briand Pact, whether preventive action was a necessity, and that in making her decision her judgment was conclusive. But whether action taken under the claim of self-defense was, in fact, aggressive or defensive *must ultimately be subject to investigation and adjudication if international law is ever to be enforced.*[15]

The Geneva Conventions of 1949, to which the United States is a signatory and which are a part of American law, because they have been ratified by the United States Senate, represent a significant advance in the law of war. They provide that sick or wounded persons attached to the armed forces of enemy belligerents must be respected, protected, and cared for whenever they fall into the hands of any of the signatories during time of war. The commander in possession of a field of battle is required, after each engagement, to have a search made for the wounded and the dead, and to protect them against pillage and mistreatment. Provision is also made for the protection and free passage of medical personnel and equipment and for the safety of hospitals and other centers for the treatment of the sick and wounded.

A customary law of nations has long required belligerents to respect the dead, and required, in particular, that they not be mutilated and that their bodies be collected and buried or cremated on the battlefield by the victor. The United States Military Government Court at Dachau sentenced a German medical officer, in 1947, for "maltreatment of a dead unknown member" of the American armed forces after it was established that he had cut a dead American airman's head from his body, boiled it, removed the skin and flesh, and kept the skull on his desk. Schmid, the German officer, attempted to justify his behavior on the ground that he had used the skull for instructional purposes.[16]

Other provisions of the Geneva Convention provide for the removal of civilians from battle zones to neutral zones where they should be protected against harm that might come to them were they to remain in their former locations.

In ancient times it was customary to butcher war prisoners, to offer them as sacrifices to the gods, to enslave them, or to put them on public display for the entertainment of spectators, who reveled in watching the captives being torn to pieces by hungry animals. Later the practice of holding them for ransom and of exchanging them for other prisoners developed. Finally, during the eighteenth century, European nations adopted the view that captivity should be used primarily as a means of preventing prisoners from returning to the battle. Still later, the theory that prisoners should be treated as one's own troops were treated (e.g., that they should receive comparable rations, housing, and sanitary facilities) evolved and was embodied in a number of treaties. The Geneva Convention of 1949 provides that persons who take no part in combat, whether they are civilians or members of the armed forces who are sick, wounded, or interned, must "in all circumstances" be treated humanely, regardless of age, sex, race, religion, or any other similar reason. It prohibits "at any time and in any place whatsoever" the following acts:

1. Violence to life and person: in particular, murder of all kinds, mutilation, cruel treatment, and torture.
2. Taking of hostages.
3. Outrages upon personal dignity: in particular, humiliating and degrading treatment.
4. The passing of sentences and the carrying out of executions without previous judgment pronounced by a regularly constituted court affording all the judicial guarantees which are recognized as indispensable by civilized peoples.

The convention further provides that any state that has signed it must abide by its provisions when engaged in a conflict against *any* other state, whether such other state is a party to the convention or not.

The convention provides that no prisoner may be obliged to provide information to his captor other than his name, rank, date of birth, and serial number, and that no physical or mental torture or coercion may be inflicted upon prisoners to compel them to give information.

There are, in addition, numerous provisions to provide for the protection of persons captured at sea, for respect to merchant vessels, for the humane treatment of persons thrown into the sea as a result of shipwreck, and for others of a similar nature.

SOME SPECIAL PROBLEMS ASSOCIATED WITH WAR CRIMES TRIALS

The Nuremberg Tribunal (usually called the International Military Tribunal, or IMT) cleared the first major hurdle to the enforcement of the laws of war by declaring that nations are not completely autonomous but must submit to the judgment of an independent court when there is reason to doubt whether their claim to have initiated or waged a lawful war is justified. But a number of grave issues remained to be settled. These issues are not merely formal legalities, for they bear directly on major moral concerns. The most important of these, of course, is the question of whether there is ever to be a practicable way to prosecute war criminals, so that the scourge of war crimes might at last be alleviated, if not totally eliminated, from mankind. But others had a direct bearing on the conduct of the trials themselves, and on the principles on which the accused were to be judged. Among these were the following:

1. The precise definition of the crimes of which the defendants were accused.
2. The justification for convicting them under laws that were essentially *ex post facto*.
3. The defense of superior orders.
4. The justification for permitting the judges to be drawn from the forces of the enemy, who could not be fair and impartial in trying those against whom they had only lately been fighting, rather than from a panel of neutral persons or persons who come from the defendants' own land.
5. The defense that local law permitted the acts that are now condemned by another system.

DEFINITION OF THE CRIMES
A fundamental principle of justice requires that no man be held liable for the commission of an act that he could not possibly have known to be illegal. Any law that is vaguely worded violates this principle, for it is impossible for a man to know what he is forbidden to do when the law he is expected to obey is vague or obscure.

We have already seen, however, that the covenants entered into by the nations of the world during the years prior to World War II contained lengthy and precise lists of forbidden acts. There is nothing vague about them. In the Charter of the IMT, the various classes of crimes that were to fall within its purview were defined as follows:

(a) *Crimes Against Peace:* namely, planning, preparation, initiation or waging of a war of aggression, or a war in violation of international treaties, agreements or assurances, or participation in a common plan or conspiracy for the accomplishment of any of the foregoing;

(b) *War Crimes:* namely, violations of the laws or customs of war. Such violations shall include, but not be limited to, murder, ill-treatment or deportation to slave labor or for any other purpose of civilian population of or in occupied territory, murder or ill-treatment of prisoners of war or persons on the seas, killing of hostages, plunder of public or private property, wanton destruction of cities, towns, or villages, or devastation not justified by military necessity.

(c) *Crimes Against Humanity:* namely, murder, extermination, enslavement, deportation, and other inhumane acts committed against any civilian population, before or during the war; or persecutions on political, racial or religious grounds in execution of or in connection with any crime within the jurisdiction of the Tribunal, whether or not in violation of domestic law of the country where perpetrated.

Leaders, organizers, instigators, and accomplices participating in the formulation or execution of a common plan or conspiracy to commit any of the foregoing crimes are responsible for all acts performed by any persons in execution of such plan.[17]

There can be little room for doubt as to the meaning of the words in most of these pronouncements, though the legal meaning of some of them is still open to further interpretation. Murder, for example, deportation of civilian populations, the killing of hostages, and enslavement are certainly clear enough, their meaning having been settled over many centuries of active use in the courts as well as in ordinary language. *Aggression,* however, is a word whose meaning is not altogether clear, and there is much room for dispute over what precisely is meant by such terms as *military necessity.*

Consider the seemingly simple problem of the meaning of aggression. Even today its definition is not finally settled. Aggression is, among other things, a moral term, an evaluative term; behavior that is aggressive is (in most uses of the term) behavior that the speaker does not approve of or condemns. Some have branded international aggression as the "greatest crime against mankind."[18] Some modern writers would call every resort to force that is not in self-defense an act of aggression, whereas in an earlier day, it was not unusual to find "aggressive wars" and "offensive wars" used interchangeably, to refer to wars that were fought for just as well as for unjust reasons. If *aggression* implied wrongfulness, though, one would expect the phrase *an act of unjustified aggression* or the phrase *an unjust act of aggression* to be redundant, but it does not seem to be so. Then there are such exotic forms of aggression as indirect aggression, economic aggression, and ideological aggression—thus revealing that although physical force seems somehow to be linked up with the notion of aggression, it need not be. (Soviet lawyers branded the Marshall Plan, which was designed by the American government as a means to provide emergency economic aid to the nations of Western Europe that were left devastated by World War II, as a form of "economic aggression." [19]) Some authorities have suggested that armed aggression should be called *attack,* reserving the term *aggression* for political, economic, and ideological subversion, but this flies in the face of long-accepted usage. If one nation's forces cross its frontiers to attack the forces of another, it does not necessarily follow that that act is an act of aggression, for one can easily conceive of circumstances in which such an attack might more aptly be described as an act of self-defense or as a pre-emptive action designed to ward off an anticipated act of aggression. If the enemy's leaders have been announcing their intention of invading their neighbor's territory, for example, and have mobilized their forces and blockaded their neighbor's waterways, a good case could be made for the view that an attack upon that enemy's forces would not be an act of aggression, but a defensive response to such an act.

In view of all of these difficulties (and here I have merely scratched the surface), it is obvious that this is far more than a verbal or semantic exercise. A more precise definition of the term, in the context of a legal framework—that is, within the framework of international law—is essential if the laws forbidding acts of aggression are to have any effect upon the behavior of national and international leaders. As one author wrote recently,

> The simplicity of the notion of "aggression" in its vulgar version dissolves, as we approach it closely, into a welter of many-faced and multi-dimensional problems of international law and politics. It is seen to raise most of the problems of an inchoate international criminal law and criminology, and of barely formed branches of the international law of torts, and property. The solutions to many of these problems presuppose standards of ethical judgment and of sociological knowledge concerning the nature, destiny and survival of State entities which we have barely begun to explore.[20]

If it is true that an indefinable act cannot be prohibited, it is equally true that operationally, the meanings of some terms whose definitions cannot be exhaustively stated (open-ended terms, as some philosophers have called them) are nevertheless known to many people; that is, people know how to use those terms in *most* cases where they might be applicable, though they may be puzzled about them in borderline or "difficult" cases. It should not be forgotten, either, that in international relations especially, law is not only what has been written down, but what is customary—what people or nations have done over a period of time. The Hague Conventions, discussed earlier, made no pretense of legislating the laws of war. The framers of those conventions made it perfectly clear that they were merely codifying—setting down in written form—what had been accepted by those whom they considered to be the civilized nations of the earth as just and humane practice in the conduct of war. Analogously, then, those who attempted to claim at Nuremberg that they could not have known that what they were doing was aggression failed in their claim, for whatever else aggression might or might not be, what *they* did was clearly aggression. As for the rest, when the evidence was in, there could scarcely be any reliance upon the excuse that they did not know what murder, enslavement, and maltreatment of prisoners of war were, for these terms are clear enough to everyone. What they might claim (and did) was that when they performed these acts, it was not illegal for them to do so, and that the court that was trying them lacked jurisdiction or authority over them.

EX POST FACTO *LAWS*

Because it is morally wrong to hold any man liable for the commission of an act that he could not have known was forbidden by the law, holding men responsible for the violation of laws that are passed after the act has been performed (*ex post facto* laws) is a particularly reprehensible form of injustice. It is for this reason that the Constitution of the United States contains a special provision forbidding Congress (and, since the passage of the Fourteenth Amendment, any other legislative body in the United States) to pass *ex post facto* legislation. The accused war criminals at Nuremberg, and later Adolf Eichmann in Jerusalem, contended that the laws under which they were being tried were passed after the acts that they were accused of having committed had been done. They could not have known that what they were doing was prohibited by law, for the laws did not exist at the time.

The complaint was registered at Nuremberg, and was answered there, as well as in Jerusalem, where the problem was particularly acute, because the state of Israel itself did not exist when Eichmann's crimes were committed.

There are two principal kinds of answer that may be offered to this problem. One is to deny that retroactive (or *ex post facto*) legislation is involved, and the other is to admit that the legislation is retroactive but to insist that some other, overriding principle of justice is served by appeal to such legislation.

The first approach is basically the same as that which was reviewed in the preceding section. The laws existed long before the crimes in question were committed. As one statesman put it during the debate that preceded Eichmann's trial, the law prohibiting murder goes back at least to the time of Moses. The principles violated by the Nazi war criminals are not new. They have been expressed time and again in the laws of every civilized state, in treaties, conventions, and agreements, and they have been regarded for centuries as fundamental precepts of justice and morals. The laws passed by the Allies setting up the IMT merely set up a procedure, for the first time in history, for dealing with war criminals through the judiciary. Section 6 of the Charter was not legislation enunciating for the first time certain crimes for which men might be punished; it set forth, in fairly general terms, the scope of the IMT, and it expressed once again the substance of laws that had been codified many years earlier and that were looked upon by the family of nations as being binding, in some sense, long before they were reduced to writing. The old principles of *nullem crimen sine lega* (there is no crime without a law) and *nulla poena sine lega* (there should be no punishment without a law) are important, but it should not be forgotten that the law is not only what is written in law books; it is the custom and practice of men and of nations as well. The common-law countries recognize this fact explicitly in their everyday legal operations. There is a common law of nations as well, a law that leads "a twilight existence during which it is hardly distinguishable from morality or justice, till at length the *imprimatur* of a court attests its jural quality." [21] The crimes, then, were spelled out in the law— both in the unwritten law of the customs of nations and of the moral principles accepted by all civilized men (even, in a sense, by the defendants themselves, as we shall see), and in the written law of the international treaties and conventions that formed the basis for the enabling legislation of the IMT Charter.

More than 100 years ago, an American judge declared:

> We are not to be told that war is lawful, and slavery lawful, and plunder lawful, and the taking away of life is lawful, and the selling of human beings is lawful. . . . It is not . . . on account of the simple fact that the traffic (in slaves) necessarily involves the enslavement of human beings, that it stands reprehended by the present sense of nations; but that it necessarily carries with it a breach of all the moral duties, of all the maxims of justice, mercy and humanity, and of the admitted rights, which independent Christian nations now hold sacred in their intercourse with each other. [22]

That the Nazis were aware of the laws of war is evident from their own statements and from documents that they wrote during and before the opening of hostilities. The Chief of the High Command, for example, wrote a top-secret document for dispatch to all commanders in April, 1938, in which he declared that "the normal rules of war toward neutrals may be considered to apply on the basis whether operation of rules will create greater advantages or disadvantages for belligerents." Another, from the German Navy staff, states that compliance with international law is desirable, but that "if decisive successes are expected from any measure considered as a war necessity, it must be carried through even if it is not in agreement with International Law." [23] As Justice Robert Jackson, the chief prosecutor at Nuremberg, stated,

> International law, natural law, German law, any law at all was to these men simply a propaganda device to be invoked when it helped and to be ignored when it would condemn what they wanted to do. That men may be protected in relying upon the law at the time they act is the reason we find laws of retrospective operation unjust. But these men cannot bring themselves within the reason of the rule which in some systems of jurisprudence prohibits *ex post facto* laws. They cannot show that they ever relied upon International Law in any state or paid it the slightest regard. [24]

There is solid ground, then, for claiming that the laws existed prior to the commission of the crimes, that the Nazis knew of their existence but chose to ignore them or to use them only when it was to their advantage to do so, and that therefore, the problem of *ex post facto* legislation simply does not arise.

But even if one concedes that, technically speaking, the Nuremberg and Jerusalem laws are retrospective, it is still possible to argue that war criminals may be prosecuted, convicted, and even executed under such laws. Let us assume that, technically, no proper laws regarding their behavior were on the books at the time these men committed their deeds. There is a certain injustice, as we have already remarked, in punishing a man under a retrospective law. But it would also be unjust to allow men who had committed such outrages against international morality as the Nazis had to get away with their crimes and to return to their homes and their businesses as if nothing had ever happened. Men who plunged the entire world into a period of suffering and destruction such as it had never seen before; who ruthlessly slaughtered men, women, and children on the ground that they were Jews, or gypsies, or Slavs; who constructed a machine for the mass extermination of millions of human beings; who extracted their victims' gold teeth before shoving them into the ovens for incineration; who converted the skins of their victims into lampshades and book covers; who forced men and women and small children to work in factories as slaves under inhuman conditions of starvation and brutal physical maltreatment; who terrorized whole populations, and exterminated entire communities—such men as these could not be permitted to escape the rightful retribution that the community of nations wanted to visit upon them on the technical point of a supposedly *ex post facto* law. Or, as Justice Jackson put it,

> If it be thought that the Charter . . . does contain new law I still do not shrink from demanding its strict application by this Tribunal. The rule of law, flouted by the lawlessness incited by these defendants, had to be restored at the cost to my country of over a million casualties, not to mention those of other nations. I cannot subscribe to the perverted reasoning that

society may advance and strengthen the rule of law by the expenditure of morally innocent lives but that progress in the law may never be made at the price of morally guilty lives.[25]

Even if the preceding arguments are rejected, it must not be forgotten that law is made by the practice of nations and by the practice of courts. It is true that there was no judicial precedent for the Nuremberg trials and that the defendants therefore may have had some cause for feeling that there was no law in existence governing their cases or justifying their punishment. But the enforcement of law must begin somewhere. In view of the enormity of their crimes, it was not unreasonable to let the first case—and thus the precedent for all future cases of a similar nature— begin with them. The principles against imposing punishment where there is no clear law forbidding the act whose commission inspires the desire to impose a penalty are important moral principles. But there is another moral principle that may be too easily overlooked: *summum jus summa iniuria* (where there is too much reliance on the letter of the law, there is the greatest injustice).

Law, as we have remarked on more than one occasion, is a necessary condition for the existence of justice. The prohibition against *ex post facto* laws and against the punishment of men for the violation of laws that were passed after the fact is a principle of justice, a principle designed to protect men against the possibility that they might be punished for deeds that they could not have known were wrong at the time they committed them. But the crimes committed by the Nazi war criminals were known by them to be crimes. Those who committed such acts may have thought that they would not be punished for them, either because they believed that they would be on the winning team, because there was no legal precedent for their being punished, or because they were blinded by the circumstances in which they found themselves into believing that what they were doing was right and proper. But none of these conditions or beliefs is relevant to the question of their guilt and of their responsibility for their acts. The injustice of permitting them to get away with their crimes must be weighed against that which might be involved in violating the *ex post facto* principle.

There has always been general agreement that the victors in an armed conflict have the right to execute or otherwise punish those of their vanquished opponents whom they believe to be responsible for harms that have been done to them, to their nation, or to others. The right to dispatch the defendants in the Nuremberg trials *out of hand*, without hearing, and by executive decree or by military command, was accepted by the defendants themselves. In fact, the British, French, and Soviet leaders balked at the idea of holding these trials, and urged summary execution of the principal Nazi leaders. Stalin went further, seriously recommending the execution of 50,000 Nazis immediately after the war, without trial. The

American view prevailed. Though the trials themselves were without precedent, the Americans argued, it was an opportunity to *set* a precedent, to make legal and judicial history. It was an opportunity to set the world on notice that blatant acts of aggression, war crimes, and crimes against humanity would no longer be tolerated, and that those who perpetrated such infamous acts would be held personally liable for them. It was an opportunity, too, to demonstrate that the rule of law *could* be extended to international relations through judicial procedure, and that the laws of war *could* be enforced, not by might alone, but in accordance with rules of evidence and trial procedure. This too could save many lives and avoid much needless suffering in the future, for the threat of punishment *may* serve as a deterrent—in some cases, at least. Now, weighing these considerations against that of retrospective legislation, considering the possibility that many innocent lives might be spared in the future and the possibility that some of the defendants themselves might be found innocent of the crimes they were alleged to have committed (as was in fact the case), the authorities concluded that the balance was heavily on the side of holding the trials and denying the validity of the plea of *ex post facto* laws.

THE DEFENSE OF SUPERIOR ORDERS

We come now to an argument that has been used in every war crimes trial to date, including the trial of Lieutenant William Calley, who was convicted for complicity in the massacre at My Lai. A soldier, it is said, is duty-bound to follow the orders of his superior officers. It is neither fair nor just to pass judgment on a man who has been faced with the necessity of resolving an impossible dilemma: if he obeys his orders, he is courtmartialed for violating the laws of war, and if he disobeys his orders, he is courtmartialed for disobedience. In time of war either charge can carry with it the death penalty. Or, as some of the cries of outrage at Calley's conviction expressed it, how can a man be convicted on a charge that boils down, in essence, to having served his country loyally and faithfully?

There is no easy answer, but answers have been given. One approach (as we have seen in another context) is the higher-law approach. There is a natural law, a divine law, a moral law, or perhaps a law of conscience that has precedence over any order that any man may receive, whether that order comes from a military superior or from a state legislature. As one of Calley's judges put it, "There are some things a man of common understanding and common sense would know are wrong. If you worked for me and I told you to go out and steal a car, would you do it?" [26] It is hard to imagine that the soldiers who committed atrocities during World War II, and those who have committed atrocities during the Vietnam War, did not realize that what they were doing was *at least* immoral, if not illegal. No American soldier can claim that he had no knowledge of policy on treatment of prisoners and civilians, for each man is given a manual in which he is instructed to obey only the lawful orders of his superiors, and each man is given a wallet card on which the following instructions are printed:

> THE ENEMY IN YOUR HANDS. As a member of the U.S. military forces, you will comply with the Geneva Prisoner of War Conventions of 1949 to which your country adheres. Under these Conventions . . . YOU CANNOT AND MUST NOT mistreat your prisoner, humiliate or degrade him, take any of his personal effects which do not have significant military value, refuse him medical treatment if required and available. *ALWAYS TREAT YOUR PRISONER HUMANELY.*[27]

The wallet card at the time of the My Lai massacre said, in part, "All persons in your hands, whether suspects, civilians, or combat captives, must be protected against violence, insults, curiosity, and reprisals of any kind." And the U.S. Army Field Manual on the law of land warfare (27-10) states that the law "requires that belligerents refrain from employing any kind or degree of violence which is not actually necessary for military purposes, and that they conduct hostilities with regard for the principles of humanity and chivalry." A soldier may kill any enemy civilian who seeks to attack him, but he may not deliberately harm any who do not. These rules protect enemy troops, the wounded, parachuting airmen, and other helpless people, in accordance with the Geneva Conventions of 1949. It goes without saying that they apply to civilians as well. It is inconceivable that any officer in the United States Army could have been unfamiliar with these rules, and there is no evidence that Calley was unfamiliar with them. In military law, as in municipal law, ignorance is no excuse. It is every citizen's responsibility to know those laws that apply to him so that he can carry them out, and it is every soldier's duty to know the laws that apply to warfare so that he can comply with them. American soldiers are instructed that they "must disobey an order that a man of ordinary sense and understanding would know to be illegal." Lieutenant Calley contended that he had been ordered to "waste" the village of My Lai, that is, to destroy everything and everyone in it—men, women, and children, regardless of age or infirmity. Professor Telford Taylor of the Columbia University School of Law, and chief counsel to the Prosecution at the Nuremburg War Crimes hearings, has observed that such an order would be so flagrantly in violation of the laws of war, to say nothing of common humanity, that Calley could hardly have taken them seriously, if he were so ordered. One would have expected him at least to have been puzzled and disturbed by such orders, but he was plainly not at all perturbed by them.*

---

* See appendix on the Calley Case at the end of this chapter.

Why don't superior orders excuse the man who carries them out? No society can permit any man to be a law unto himself or to usurp the authority that the law reserves to itself. The army is itself a creature of the law. Its chain of command is sanctioned by the law. And the army is always subordinate to the laws of the state for whose protection it was originally created. It would be inconsistent, then, to suppose that the army could override the laws whenever it saw the need to do so, for this would put into the hands of the army's leaders the power to determine what is and what is not legal, and the law, instead of being protected by the army, would become subordinate to it. No man is above the law, and no man has the legal power to countervene it.*

Every person is presumed to know what those limits are, as part of his duties as a citizen—or, in the case of a soldier, as part of his duties as a member of the armed forces. There are certain other considerations in the law, provisions for what the reasonable man will understand to be permissible and what the reasonable man will understand to be forbidden, which need not be spelled out in explicit detail in the codes.† If evidence were needed that Calley went beyond those limits, it might be provided by those members of his platoon who refused to participate in the slaughter of civilians, even when ordered by Calley to do so.

Though such considerations are the rationale behind the rejection of the plea of superior orders, they are not sufficient in themselves to solve the moral dilemma of the soldier who is confronted by an order emanating from a superior officer when he considers the order to be unlawful. Shall he disobey the order and risk court martial or even summary execution? In one case, the IMT, which rejected the plea of superior orders in general, held that "there is no law which requires that an innocent man must forfeit his life or suffer serious harm in order to avoid committing a crime which he condemns." [28] But the rule that has generally prevailed is that no person is permitted—legally, morally, or otherwise—to avoid suffering or even to save his life at the expense of the life of another person, and even less at the expense of the lives of multitudes of other persons or of suffering on a vast scale. The presence of a clear and definite danger to his own life if he failed to carry out such illegal orders might constitute some reason for mitigation of any penalty that might be imposed upon him, but is not in itself an excuse for committing the act.

---

* That would be a contradiction in terms. The law may provide for suspension of some of its provisions in time of emergency, and men may usurp such power through force or by other means; but such usurpation of power is never legal at the time of its occurrence.

† It is impossible for the codes to specify everything. Some things must be left to the common sense of every citizen. A rule against the operation of motor vehicles in public parks need not specify every conceivable kind of motor vehicle, but may leave such specification to the good sense of those who use the park. Even exceptions not spelled out in the law, such as the operation of motorized wheel chairs, may be left to common sense, unless challenged in the courts.

"The obedience of a soldier," the Nuremberg Tribunal said, "is not the obedience of an automaton. A soldier is a reasoning agent."

On an earlier occasion, the following opinion was published: "No international law of warfare is in existence which provides that a soldier who has committed a mean crime can escape punishment by pleading as his defence that he followed the commands of his superiors. This holds particularly true if those commands are contrary to all human ethics and opposed to the well-established international usage of warfare." It is difficult to disagree with these views in the abstract, but they were written by Hitler's henchman, Goebbels, in defense of the Nazi policy of executing downed Allied airmen, who were accused of committing atrocities in bombing and burning German cities.[29]

Suppose, however, that the defense of superior orders were allowed. It would follow that every soldier, from the foot soldier at the front to the top general at the offices of the Chief of Staff, would be able to escape responsibility for his actions on the ground of such a plea. In a dictatorship, such as that of Nazi Germany, the full responsibility for every atrocity and for every criminal act that took place from the beginning to the last day of the war would fall on one man's shoulders, and on his alone—namely, on those of the dictator himself. In a democracy, particularly in one where the separation of powers is as complete as it is in the United States, it might well be impossible ever to determine where the ultimate responsibility resides. In either case, those who had bloodied their hands would escape retribution, and those who came after them would know that they too would be able to carry out unlawful orders— no matter how brutal they might be—with no fear of reprisal. The world would have lost a powerful deterrent to the commission of war crimes, for the acts themselves are carried out, for the most part, in the field. Of course, the originators of the actions, those who sit in the policy-making councils of the nation, must be held responsible as well. But the plea of superior orders, if successful, invites abuses in the future that could lead once again to enormous and widespread suffering.

IMPARTIALITY OF THE COURT

Those who sat in judgment at Nuremberg were accused of being biased because they were nationals of nations that had only lately been waging war against the state whose leaders were on trial. The court in Jerusalem was attacked by Eichmann's lawyer on the ground that Jews could not be impartial in judging a man who was accused of engineering the mass extermination of more than 6 million Jews and of blotting out nearly the whole of the Jewish community of Europe.

It is said that there was once a gang of thieves whose members were brought to trial. They complained to the judge that the jury was bound to be biased, for it was composed entirely of law-abiding citizens. "A jury of our peers," they said, "as guaranteed to us by the Constitution, would consist of a jury of thieves. Such a jury would be better able to understand our motives and our backgrounds, and would be more likely to sympathize with our behavior than a jury of law-abiding citizens. Being like us, they would be better able to sit in judgment over us."

Such perverse reasoning does have a certain attraction. But it cannot be seriously defended. The victim of a crime must not sit in judgment over one who is accused of having committed the crime. But neither should those who have participated in similar criminal activities themselves, or are close relatives of the criminals who are on trial.

There is some confusion over the proper application of the words *fair* and *impartial* in discussions of fair and impartial juries and judges. Judges are required to be impartial toward the defendants and to weigh the facts of the case as presented in court fairly and without prejudice. But they are not required to be impartial toward crime. Nor does "fairness" require that the judge consider in extenuation of criminal behavior beliefs or attitudes that the criminal believes justify his act. Fairness requires only that the judge apply the law and judge the facts as best he can— *as the law stands and in accordance with the procedures laid down by law and legal custom.* As Gideon Hausner, Eichmann's prosecutor, said, with respect to the argument that Israel's judges could not be impartial and that the trial ought therefore to be held in Germany, "It was a strange argument indeed that a judge could be disqualified because he was a fellow national of a murderer's victims, while his belonging to the nation of the murderer would be regarded as a qualifying feature. If there was a man in the world 'neutral' toward genocide, it was he who should be disqualified as a judge." [30]

As the thief cannot complain if he is tried by a jury of honest citizens, so the international criminal cannot complain if he is tried by a panel made up of citizens of states who may have been victims of their criminal behavior. When a crime is committed against the state of New York, the judge is a New Yorker, the jury is composed of New Yorkers, the prosecutor is a servant of the state of New York, and the law under which he is tried is the law of the state of New York. The propriety of this procedure is manifest. The judge, the jury, and the prosecutor have all been harmed, indirectly, if the defendant has violated the criminal law of their state. But their ability to raise themselves above their rightful distaste for criminal behavior directed against their neighbors and their laws, and to determine impartially, objectively, and in accordance with the law and the rules of evidence, whether the defendant sitting before them is guilty of having committed such a violation, is taken for granted except in the most unusual circumstances. Even in such circumstances, there is no solution but to try the defendant under those conditions or to release him without trial. When crimes as heinous as those with which the Nazi war criminals and Calley were charged are involved, the latter proposal is no solution, for other values, more important in the long run, are at stake. Not the least of these is the deterrent effect that such punishment may have upon others who might be tempted to engage in such behavior in the future, and the moral example that is set by those who uphold the law of nations—an example for their own people as well as for the citizens of other nations.

THE "LOCAL-LAW" DEFENSE

The "local-law" defense is probably the most difficult of all the defenses to be discussed here, for it involves highly complex questions of the conflict of various legal systems. In essence, it boils down to this. Suppose a voting registrar in the state of Mississippi is accused of having discriminated against Negroes in 1963 by administering a registration test that was designed to disqualify virtually every Negro who applied. He might reply:

> This was not discrimination at all—certainly not on my part. I merely did my duty as prescribed by law. The law stipulated that I must administer this test to each person who wanted to vote before permitting him to register. I did precisely what the law required. And I did it scrupulously, honestly, and fairly. I gave the same test to everyone who applied, black or white. I graded them without looking at the names or addresses of those who had taken them, so that any personal bias of mine would not be reflected in the grades I gave the applicants. And I can even show you that some Negroes (not many, but some) passed the test and were duly registered to vote, and some whites (not many, but some) failed the test and were not permitted to vote. How, then, can you accuse me of having done anything that was either immoral or illegal? You might disapprove of the policy, but that's a matter for the government to decide. I'm just a private citizen doing my duty. You might say that I should have resigned, but that would have accomplished nothing, since someone else would have taken over and might have administered the bureau unfairly and unjustly. As long as I was there, at least, the tests were administered and graded fairly and without a trace of discrimination.

Similarly, a Nazi doctor who worked at Auschwitz in the selection process might have argued (and did):

> I did not discriminate against Jews. Not at all. I personally had nothing whatever against the Jews as a race. I merely did my duty as prescribed by law. The law stipulated that I must examine each person who was brought before me to determine his or her fitness to work. Those who were fit were sent to the factories for as long as they remained healthy. Those who were unfit were sent to the gas chambers and the crematorium for disposal. I did precisely what the law required. And I did it scrupulously, honestly and fairly. I looked for the same symptoms and applied the same criteria to every person who passed by me, whether he was Jew or Aryan. I judged them without consulting their records, so that any personal bias of mine would not be reflected in my selections. And I can even show you that some Jews

(not many, but some) passed the examination and were duly permitted to work, and some of them have survived to this day, while some Aryans, and others (not many, but some) failed to pass the examination and were duly exterminated. How, then, can you accuse me of having done anything that was either immoral or illegal? You might disapprove of the policy, but that's a matter for the government to decide. I was merely a private citizen, a physician, doing my duty. You might say that I should have resigned, but that would have accomplished nothing, since someone else would have taken over and might have done the job less meticulously than I did. As long as I was there, at least, the examinations were performed fairly and without a trace of discrimination.

Something is clearly wrong here. On the feeble excuse that resignation will do no good because someone else will do the dirty job anyway, these men seek exoneration for their conduct. If one does not approve of the purposes or the practices of a club, one does not have to join it. If one does not approve of the practices of a government, one does not have to join its service. There is a time to join, in the service of one's country or one's community, and there is a time to resign—with as much noise as possible, if one has the courage to make a lot of noise. No one was forced to be a voter registrar in Mississippi in the days, before the Federal Voting Registration Act was passed, when the tests were rigged to exclude black citizens from the voting rolls. And no German was forced to participate in the selection processes by which some human beings were sent off to slave labor and others were consigned to the flames. Joining the club *and staying in* suggests sympathy with its goals, participation in its projects; in the long run, this may lead to praise or blame for its achievements or its failures or—worst of all—for the harm that it does.

If a man participates in a bank robbery but confines his role to that of getaway driver, he is as responsible for any murder that may be committed by his accomplices as the man who pulls the trigger. He cannot argue later that he obeyed the laws—that he even adhered carefully to all the traffic laws—because he did nothing but drive an automobile, discharge some passengers, pick them up, and take them home again. Those who participated in the giant machines of racial discrimination in the United States were morally guilty of complicity in the wrongs committed by the system of which they were a part. And though no proper comparison can be drawn between the United States and Nazi Germany (every such comparison is obscene!), those who cooperated with the Nazis in their program of racial extermination and world domination, who "did their duty as law-abiding citizens" as the Nazis set the world on fire, are guilty of complicity in those crimes as surely as the driver of the getaway car is guilty of the murder committed by his colleagues.

There is a proper time for civil disobedience and a proper time for rebellion. Some of the Nazi leaders, toward the end of the war, attempted to revolt against Hitler, and nearly succeeded in assassinating him. But their attempt was too late to save them from the moral opprobrium of the nations, for their motive was not to save the world from the madness of National Socialism; they had already done their part to bring National Socialism to the world by force of arms. Their motive was to save themselves and the German nation as it sank under the relentless attacks of the Allies.

The plea that murder of Jews and the inmates of insane asylums was permitted—and even required—by law fails, just as the previous pleas fail, because there comes a point, now becoming fairly firmly established in the law of nations, where one must refuse to abide by the laws of the state and insist instead that the law of nations and the laws of humanity take precedence. When a nation's leaders become a band of international outlaws, it is time to exercise one's prerogatives as a member of the human species, to refuse to collaborate in their atrocities, and to seize any opportunity to overthrow their lawless regime, to replace it by one that respects the rights of man and the laws of mankind.

Respect for law and order is no substitute for respect for human life and dignity.

When the law is converted into an instrument of oppression and slavery, it matters not whether one chooses to say that it ceases to be law, or whether one prefers to say that it is no longer binding upon those who would otherwise be subject to it. The effect is the same. Another rule must be appealed to, whatever it may be called, and whatever its source may be. The exact nature of that rule and its exact content are still in the process of development. The laws of nations are still in their formative stages. Nations are reluctant to give up any of their sovereignty to an independent body that might be empowered to enforce such laws. No international court having the power to bring states charged with violations of the law before it for judgment yet exists, for the nations of the world insist that they will submit to adjudication only when they choose to do so. The first attempts by the United Nations to create an international police force to guard against war and aggression in one of the world's most incendiary trouble spots collapsed in dismal and total failure when the force that had been stationed in the Sinai Peninsula and the Gaza Strip was withdrawn by U Thant, the secretary general, at the behest of Egypt's president, Gamal Abdel Nasser, when the latter decided to enter into battle with Israel. Though the United Nations might have served as a kind of supergovernment, or a genuine world federation of nations, a center for the fashioning and the enforcement of rules of international law, it has instead become a useful forum for the exchange of ideas and, at times, for the promulgation of propaganda. It has been eminently successful in promoting certain kinds of international relief, and it has helped to bring local conflicts under control. It has also served as a center for mediation efforts in both small and large conflicts. But for the most part, and especially where the great powers are concerned, the United Nations cannot act effectively and other means of resolving issues, including the use of force, are being utilized. Even the smaller nations have become more cynical about the usefulness of the United Nations when the chips are down since it proved to be so ineffective when the Soviet Union invaded Hungary and suppressed the "freedom fighters" movement there in 1956, when it proved to be helpless to halt or reverse the invasion of Czechoslovakia by the forces of the Soviet Union and some of its Warsaw Pact allies when they decided to suppress the liberal regime of Alexander Dubcek in 1969, and most especially when its presence in the Middle East withered away so ignobly as the Six Day War erupted in 1967. Nor did its complete inability to assist those who wanted to search for peace in Vietnam add to its prestige.

Though the United Nations has not fulfilled all of the hopes of those who organized it, it has nevertheless fulfilled many useful and important functions and has gone a long way toward securing the recognition of international law in a number of areas. Still, so long as nations are unwilling to give up any significant portion of their sovereignty to some international organization, they seem destined to remain, as Hobbes put it, "in continual jealousies and in the state and posture of gladiators, having their weapons pointing and their eyes fixed on one another—that is, their forts, garrisons, and guns upon the frontiers of their kingdoms, and continual spies upon their neighbors—which is a posture of war." [31] While that condition remains and the danger of war continues to threaten mankind, it is vital that every nation do what it can to strengthen respect for the laws of war, and seek to expand and reinforce those weak and fragile instruments—inadequate as they may be—that presently exist for the application of principles of morality to the international scene.

APPENDIX: THE CALLEY CASE

Lieutenant William Calley was convicted, in April, 1971, of having killed not less than twenty-one civilians at My Lai, Vietnam. There was a remarkable reaction on the part of the public to his conviction and the life sentence that was imposed upon him. Hundreds of thousands of records of a "ballad" dedicated to Calley's heroism were sold within a few days of the verdict, and the president ordered him removed from the stockade and placed under limited house arrest until all appeals had been heard. President Nixon also informed the press that he would personally make the final determination of the disposition of Calley's case. Veterans turned in their medals, and some even turned themselves in to civilian authorities, "confessing" their own violations of the laws of war and demanding that they too be punished. Tens of thousands of protest letters poured in to the White House and Congressional offices, as well as to newspapers and magazines all across the nation, and protests were expressed all over the world, from London and Paris to the battlefields of Vietnam.

Some typical comments made by those who protested the Calley sentence are examined here, because they reveal some of the fallacious reasoning that may be engaged in when such complex and little-understood matters as war crimes are involved.

Edward C. Outlaw, a retired Rear Admiral in the United States Navy, wrote:

> I join the multitude of former military men who say: "I have killed because I was ordered to and because I believed that by so doing I might have shortened the time our country and our men were exposed to danger. I have ordered bombing against targets which unavoidably must have contained citizens; I would do it again if my country so ordered."
> To compare the ridiculous trial of a young lieutenant to the Nuremburg trials is as fallacious as any argument could be. . . . Lieutenant Calley may not have been a hero, but he represents that sort of young man who has always been the salvation of our nation when the chips were down. He should be pardoned from this unjust sentence at once.[32]

Other critics argued that it was wrong to convict Calley alone, in all the chain of command from the White House to the front line. General Westmoreland recommended demotions for the two highest officers of Calley's division, Major General Samuel Koster and Brigadier General George Young, Jr. If the top brass were involved enough to be demoted, it was said, they were involved enough to be prosecuted. And if they were not prosecuted, it was wrong to let Lieutenant Calley bear the entire burden of guilt, serving as scapegoat for the entire military.

Another scapegoat theory went further, contending that Calley was serving as a scapegoat for the guilt of the entire nation. For the entire nation was guilty, not only Calley. The tactics of the army, it was said, were war crimes in themselves, producing death and devastation on a wide scale. Free-fire zones were established, supposedly evacuated of all civilians and then opened to the indiscriminate shooting, bombing, and napalming of anything or anyone that moved. But many civilians refused to be moved, and some returned after forced evacuation. It is doubtful whether such forced evacuation is permissible under the Geneva Conventions; but even if it is, the establishment of such "free-fire zones" has no sanction in international law. Considerable evidence of violations of the laws of war had accumulated. To the extent that the nation was engaged in a massive violation, or series of violations, of those laws, it was said, every citizen of the nation had to bear his share of guilt. One junior officer could hardly be expected to expiate the sins of the entire American people.

As the Very Reverend Francis B. Sayre, Jr., Dean of Washington Cathedral, wrote:

The reason [that America is so distressed] is simply that Calley is all of us. He is every single citizen in our graceless land. This is why everyone is "up so tight" about this conviction. If one young officer is to be singled out for guilt, who among us is guiltless? Who, whether hawk or dove, military or civilian, is exempt from some share, some obedience or lazy acquiescence, in the faceless slaughter not only of human life but of almost all we have been wont to count as precious in this world.

. . . On the right and on the left, no one can relish the harsh sentence of the court, for by any moral canon we are guilty too, no less as individuals than as a nation.

. . . Calley was only part of a system (as who is not?) and therefore only an unwitting victim of an evil machine. Why pick on him?

. . . When is a war clean and when dirty? What hypocrisies have dictated that distinction? Why is bombing from the air to be condoned above shooting on the ground? When it is anonymous? [33]

Sayre's critique carries a further objection to Calley's sentence: That Calley's "crime" was no worse than that which is committed by airmen who drop bombs on centers of civilian population, the suggestion being that if airmen are permitted to kill "anonymous" civilians from the air with impunity, an infantryman should not be punished for killing them face to face on the ground.

The chief arguments against Calley's conviction and sentence, then, were the following:

1. Calley did what any soldier would (or should) have done.
2. Calley was being used as a scapegoat for the whole chain of command or for the entire action.
3. Calley's alleged crime is no worse than those of airmen and others, whose killing of civilians is condoned and even encouraged.

In reply, it should be remembered that there is ample evidence that not every infantryman in Calley's situation would have done as Calley did. Most of Calley's own men seem to have refrained from participating in the massacre.

There is some reason to doubt whether the entire chain of command is guilty of war crimes. Many members of the armed services have served in Vietnam bravely and with distinction, and have not engaged in behavior, as individuals, that is forbidden by the Geneva Conventions or by any other rule of international law. The United States and the Allied Powers recognized, at the end of World War II, that a person's presence in the armed forces of a nation that is guilty of acts of aggression or other war crimes is not sufficient to establish his personal guilt for the commission of such a crime. There is an important difference between personal guilt and collective guilt. Only those who can be shown to have been personally involved in acts that are forbidden in international law can be held personally responsible for the violation of such a law. The German infantryman who participated in the invasion of Poland was not guilty of such a crime. Those who ordered the invasion were guilty. However, the German infantryman who tossed an infant into the air and caught it on his bayonet was guilty of a war crime, whether he was ordered to kill the child or not, because such an action—an individual act, not a collective act—is forbidden by the laws of war. Even if America's involvement in Vietnam is illegal, it does not follow that the entire chain of command is guilty of war crimes. And even if it did follow that everyone from the president down to Calley was guilty of war crimes, that would not detract at all from Calley's guilt. Having done what he did, he is guilty of a war crime and should be punished for it. To argue that because other guilty persons are not being punished, Calley should be exonerated, is the same as arguing that because some murderers get away with their crimes, those who get caught should be released. While deploring the failure of those who are in positions of responsibility to bring other offenders to justice, we ought not to get so carried away as to declare that *no one* should be punished.

The second scapegoat theory reduces to plain absurdities. First, it is alleged that "Calley is all of us, . . . every single citizen in our graceless land," that we are all guilty, both as individuals and as a nation. Such rhetoric may be suitable for sermons, but cannot be taken seriously as an argument against Calley's conviction. What does it mean to say that Calley is all of us, every single citizen? And on what ground is it alleged that everyone among us is guilty? Are those who worked their hearts out to bring the war to an end somehow guilty of the commission of war crimes? By the same logic, it might be said that everyone is guilty of every crime that is ever committed, because we do not do all that we can to make our society so perfect that no one will ever be tempted to break the law. But this is absurd! Those who obey the law must be distinguished from those who break it. Those who work for a better society must be distinguished from those whose actions make society worse than it might otherwise be. Any use of language that permits the guilty and the innocent to be lumped together can only lead to the breakdown of communication about such matters and to muddled thinking. Sloppy use of the word *guilty* results in the word's becoming completely meaningless. If everyone is guilty, no one is guilty and we had better start making the old distinctions in some other way, because the distinctions still exist.

Secondly, the second scapegoat argument won't do because it too assumes that if all guilty parties cannot be punished, no guilty parties should be. But though it would be better for everyone who is guilty to be punished, if they could be, than for only some guilty persons to be punished, it is certainly better to punish some than to punish none, for reasons that will shortly become apparent.

Moral guilt must be distinguished from legal guilt. For many reasons the law does not attempt to right every wrong. Sometimes it refrains from interfering simply because to do so would be too costly. Sometimes it stays out because it is impossible to make objective judgments as to responsibility in most cases of a certain type. Sometimes there are other, more informal ways of settling matters, or it is believed that a given injustice is not so grave as to justify legal remedies. For example, the law provides clear and definite remedies for physical damage that may be done by one person to another. If one man causes another to lose his eyesight through negligence or assault, the injured person has certain remedies if he turns to the law. But the law provides no remedy for hurt feelings. If one person shows lack of gratitude to another, or insults him, or if a lover suddenly leaves his steady date in a cruel and unfeeling way, the pain can be profound—even disabling in extreme cases—and there may be considerable moral guilt, but the law provides no remedy. Similarly, if some citizens are indifferent to political matters, do not inform themselves about their nation's affairs, and refrain from forming independent judgments on matters of great moment, they may be deserving of moral condemnation, but they are guilty of no crime. Perhaps the world would be better if such people would behave differently, but it is not clear that it would be better if their indifference were punishable by law. Their moral guilt, however, if it is that, is not on the same level as that of a man who murders helpless, unarmed civilians, including small infants. For the latter behavior, the law has provided a penalty, in the belief that the harm done is so great as to justify the expense of prosecuting the case. It is fairly evident that the punishment of military men guilty of the massacre of civilians is more likely to make the world a better place than it would be if they were not punished for such crimes, as we shall see. It serves no useful purpose, therefore, to assimilate moral guilt to legal guilt, and by so doing, to exonerate those who are legally guilty.

Consider now the consequences of *not* punishing Lieutenant Calley. Those who opposed his conviction or supported movements to suspend his sentence did. They said that by suspending his sentence or reversing his conviction, the morale of the armed forces would be enormously improved. When translated into ordinary English, this means that those members of the armed forces who had engaged in atrocities would be able to breathe easier, and that they would feel freer to violate the laws of war as they went about their business in the battlefields of Indochina. By not punishing Calley, the government would demonstrate that it is not serious about the Geneva Conventions, and that atrocities are war crimes only when they are committed by our enemies against us, but that there is a different standard of when *our* men kill *them.*

On the other hand, when Calley was convicted and sentenced to life in prison, it was reported that American soldiers in Indochina were "watching a lot closer what they shoot. . . . Everybody's definitely more careful now." [34] If the Geneva Conventions are backed by sanctions, they may be observed more carefully. The punishment of those who violate their provisions may deter others from violating them. And as a result, the lives of many innocent persons may be saved, and many otherwise decent men may be deterred from committing brutal and brutalizing acts. To reduce the legal prohibition against the murder of civilians or the maltreatment of prisoners to a moral commandment is to invite men, in the heat of battle and in the frustration and anger that inevitably grow in every soldier as he wages war against unknown men who present a mortal danger to him at every moment, to avenge themselves and their buddies upon those who fall into their hands in captivity. The fear of punishment may not be enough in all cases, and it may not be the noblest of reasons for refraining from the commission of atrocities; but if it works even in some cases, it is worthwhile.

Finally, it is alleged that as long as airmen are permitted to bomb centers of civilian population with impunity, men like Calley should not be held responsible for the murder of a few people on the ground. And again, without entering into the merits of the case for outlawing aerial bombardment of civilian centers, or places of strategic importance that are known or suspected to have a significant civilian population, I must reiterate that such considerations are not relevant to the question of the guilt of Lieutenant Calley or the propriety of his punishment. The laws governing aerial bombardment are clearly in need of revision and clarification. But these are not the laws under which Calley was convicted.

The rule of law in the relations governing the nations of the world, particularly in warfare, when passions run high, is jeopardized when a great and powerful nation such as the United States fails to apply the rules fairly but firmly to its own nationals. The military tribunal before which Calley was tried performed a valuable service to the cause of international law and morality when it convicted him and sentenced him for the lawless behavior in which he had engaged. The president and others, through their interference with the course of the law in Calley's case, performed a great disservice not only to those abstract principles, but to those men, women, and children—including, perhaps, some American ones—who may some day be in front of the guns of some future Calleys in some future war.

Chapter Notes

Chapter 1. Lord Devlin and the Enforcement of Morals

1. The Wolfenden Report, entitled "Report of the Committee on Homosexual Offences and Prostitution Presented to Parliament by the Secretary of State for the Home Department and the Secretary of State for Scotland by Command of Her Majesty," September 1957 (Cmmd. 247), para. 13.
2. Ibid.
3. Ibid., para. 61.
4. Ibid., para. 247.
5. Ibid., para. 257.
6. Sir Patrick Devlin, *The Enforcement of Morals* (Oxford: Oxford University Press, 1959); reprinted, with later lectures and a new introduction and explanatory notes, in *The Enforcement of Morals* (New York: Oxford University Press, 1965). All citations will be to the latter. Page 6.
7. Ibid., p. 10.
8. Ibid., p. 8.
9. Ibid., p. 15.
10. Ibid., p. 16.
11. Ibid., p. 17.
12. These last qualifications were added by Devlin in the preface to the 1965 edition, cited in note 6, in response to criticisms of this stand by Hart and others in the years following the publication of the Maccabean Lecture. Cf. p. viii.
13. Ibid., p. 17.
14. Ibid., p. 18.
15. Ibid., pp. 20 f.
16. H. L. A. Hart, *Law, Liberty, and Morality* (Stanford, Calif.: Stanford University Press, 1963), Chapter 1.
17. John Stuart Mill, *On Liberty*, Chapter 1. In Library of Liberal Arts edition, p. 13.
18. Ibid.
19. Hart, op. cit., pp. 21 f.
20. Ibid., p. 29.
21. Ibid., p. 32.
22. Ibid., p. 40.
23. Ibid., p. 51.

24. Ibid., p. 52.

25. Ibid.

26. Barbara Wootton, *Crime and the Criminal Law* (London: Stevens and Sons, 1963), p. 43.

27. Ibid., p. 44.

28. Ibid., p. 46.

29. Ibid., p. 55.

30. Cf. Sir Henry Maine, *Ancient Law* (London: Oxford University Press, 1931), Chapter 1, for a number of examples.

31. Wootton, op. cit., p. 56.

32. *Repouille* v. *United States*, 165 F. 2d 152 (1947).

33. Cf. *La. ex. Rel. Francis* v. *Resweber, Sheriff*, 329 U.S. 459 (1947), cited below, and the decision rendered by the United States Supreme Court *In re Kemmler*, 136 U.S. 447, where the Court held that the word *cruel* in the Seventh Amendment "implies . . . something inhuman and barbarous, something more than the mere extinguishing of life."

34. Cf. decision in case cited in note 33 above.

35. *Solesbee* v. *Balkcom*, Warden, 339 U.S. 9 (1949).

36. *Commonwealth* v. *Elliott*, 371 Pa. 70, 89 A 2d 782 (1952). Emphasis added.

37. Cf. Goode and Hatt, *Methods of Social Research*, 1952, p. 173. Cited in R. C. Donnelly, Joseph Goldstein, and Richard D. Schwartz, *Criminal Law* (New York: The Free Press, 1962), p. 36.

38. *U.S.* v. *Rosenberg*, 195 F. 2d 583, 608 (1952).

39. Cf. Alfred C. Kinsey, *Sexual Behavior in the Human Male* and *Sexual Behavior in the Human Female* (Philadelphia: W. B. Saunders Co., 1948 and 1953, respectively).

40. Cf., e.g., *Sexual Behavior in the Human Male*, p. 384, where Kinsey says that "the highest incidences of the homosexual, however, are in the group which most often verbalizes its disapproval of such activity."

41. I am indebted to Louis B. Schwartz's review of the first Kinsey Report in the *University of Pennsylvania Law Review*, Vol. 96 (1946), p. 916, for this example.

42. Cf. the literature cited in the bibliography for some of these critiques.

43. I have not endeavored here to distinguish between scientific, cultural, or sociological relativism, which confines its claim to the fact that moral standards differ from one culture to another, and ethical or normative cultural relativism, which asserts that it is not right to judge the members of one society by the standards of another, and that the facts revealed by anthropological research justify the conclusion that *no* moral judgments have any validity, or any "real" validity, even when they are confined to a given society. For an illuminating discussion of this distinction, see Paul W. Taylor, ed., *Problems of Moral Philosophy: An Introduction to Ethics* (Belmont, Calif.: Dickenson Publishing Co., 1967), pp. 41 ff.

44. Margaret Mead, "The Comparative Study of Culture and the Purposive Cultivation of Democratic Ideals," *Second Symposium, Conference on Science, Philosophy, and Religion* (New York: Harper & Row, 1942), p. 56.

45. W. T. Stace, *The Concept of Morals* (New York: Macmillan, 1937), excerpt in Taylor, op. cit., p. 64.

46. Cf. Plato, *The Republic*, XXXI, 557c ff.

Chapter 2. Homosexuality
1. Leviticus, 18:22, 20:13.
2. Deuteronomy, 23: 18–19.
3. See Louis Ginzberg, *Legends of the Jews* (Philadelphia: Jewish Publication Society, 1911–38), Vol. 1, p. 254, and Vol. V., p. 241, n. 175.
4. Ibid., Vol. V, p. 173, n. 17; p. 178, n. 26; p. 182, n. 39. Cf. also the sources cited there.
5. Ibid., Vol. VI, p. 420, n. 93.
6. Romans 1:26–27.
7. 1 Corinthians 6:9, 10.
8. Confessions, VIII, 1–15.
9. Justinian, *Novellae* (from *Les Novelles de L'Empereur Justinian* (Metz: Lamort, 1811), No. 77.
10. Cf. *The Symposium.*
11. Cf. G. Lowes Dickinson, *The Greek View of Life* (London: Methuen, 1957).
12. See C. S. Ford and F. A. Beach, *Patterns of Sexual Behavior* (New York: Harper & Row, 1951); Ruth Benedict, "Sex in Primitive Society," *American Journal of Orthopsychiatry*, Vol. 9, pp. 570 ff.; Margaret Mead, *Growing Up in New Guinea* (New York: W. Morrow, 1930); D. J. West, *Homosexuality* (Chicago: Aldine, 1967), pp. 17 ff.
13. Cf. M. Hirschfeld, *Sexual Anomalies and Perversions* (London: Francis Aldor, 1944); H. M. Hyde, *The Trials of Oscar Wilde* (London: William Hodge, 1948); West, op. cit., pp. 26 ff.
14. Donald W. Cory, *The Homosexual in America: A Subjective Approach*, Second Edition (New York: Castle Books, 1960), p. 53.
15. These practices are far more widespread than one might suppose, according to the best statistics presently available. Cf. the two Kinsey reports.
16. Cf. the literature cited in the bibliography for this chapter.
17. Cf. Martin Hoffman, *The Gay World* (New York: Harper & Row, 1965), p. 11 et passim; Jens Jersild, *The Normal Homosexual Male Versus the Boy Molester* (Copenhagen: Hyt Nordisk Forlag Arnold Busck, 1967), passim; Kurt Freund, *Die Homosexualität Beim Mann* (Leipzig: Hirzel Verlag, 1963), passim; K. Freund, "On the Problem of Male Homosexuality," *Review of Czechoslovak Medicine*, Vol. 11, pp. 11 ff. Gordon Westwood, surveying a sample of male homosexuals, found only three men, out of a total of 127 interviewed in his study, who evinced a strong preference for boys. The rest either had had no contact with underage boys or (in a total of 7 per cent of the interviews) had had occasional sexual relations with boys fourteen or fifteen years of age. His findings were published in *A Minority* (London: Longmans, 1960). The Kinsey Institute report found that only 9 per cent of all men convicted for homosexual offenses with adults had ever had such a relationship with a child. However, they did find that a third of them had had sexual relationships with sexually mature youths under sixteen. It should be remembered, though, that this study was confined to men convicted of homosexual misbehavior. Whether these figures would hold up for the general run of homosexual society is questionable. Any attempt to use findings in a prison population as a base for drawing inferences about any general population is naturally suspect.
18. Cf., for example, Hoffman, op. cit., Chapter 3.

19. Cory, op. cit., pp. xxi ff.
20. Hoffman, op. cit., p. 166.
21. Ibid., pp. 166 ff.
22. Kinsey, *Sexual Behavior in the Human Female* (Philadelphia: W. B. Saunders Co., 1953), p. 682.
23. L. M. Terman and Catherine C. Miles, *Sex and Personality* (New York: McGraw-Hill, 1936). Cited in West, op. cit., pp. 48 ff.
24. Cf. West, op. cit., p. 50, and the literature cited there.
25. Ibid., pp. 50 ff. and the studies cited there.
26. Sigmund Freud, *Three Essays on the Theory of Sexuality* (New York: Basic Books, 1962), p. 25.
27. Senate Committee on Expenditures in the Executive Departments, "Employment of Homosexuals and Other Sex Perverts in Government," S. Doc. No. 241, 81st Cong. 2nd. Sess. 1, 19 (1950).
28. Karl M. Bowman, "Review of Sex Legislation and Control of Sex Offenders in the United States of America," *California Sexual Deviation Research, Final Report, XX* (1954), p. 31.
29. William Blackstone, *Commentaries on the Laws of England,* Book IV, "Of Public Wrongs." Chapter XV, § 4 (Boston: Brown Press, 1912), pp. 241 ff.
30. *Kelly* v. *U.S.,* 194 F. 2d 150 (D.C. Cir. 1951), Justice Prettyman's decision. Above quotations are cited in this decision.
31. Wolfenden Report, p. 53.
32. See Pope Pius XI, op. cit.
33. Cf. *N.Y. Times Magazine,* October 10, 1971.
34. London *Times,* May 12, 1965; cited in West, op. cit., p. 100.
35. Code 1951, 22-1112 (a), Supp. VIII.
36. *Rittenour* v. *District of Columbia,* 163 A 2d 558 (1960).
37. C. H. Rolph, "The Problem for the Police," *New Statesman* (June 25, 1960), p. 945. Cited in Edwin M. Schur, *Crimes Without Victims* (Englewood Cliffs, N.J.: Prentice-Hall, 1965), p. 80.
38. *Kelly* v. *United States,* 194 F. 2d 150 (D.C. Cir. 1951).
39. *Guarro* v. *U.S.,* 237 F. 2d 578 (D.C. Cir. 1956), quoting *McDermett* v. *U.S.,* D.C. Munic. App. 1953, 98 A. 2d 287, 290.
40. John Hersey, *The Algiers Motel Incident* (New York: Bantam Books), 1968, pp. 75 ff.
41. Cf. James S. Campbell et al., *Law and Order Reconsidered,* Report of the Task Force on Law and Law Enforcement to the National Commission on the Causes and Prevention of Violence (New York: Bantam Books, 1970), Chapter 23, "The Problem of 'Overcriminalization,'" esp. p. 612, and the sources cited there.
42. Report of the British Roman Catholic Advisory Committee on Prostitution and Homosexual Offences and the Existing Law, reprinted in "Homosexuality and the Law: A Catholic Memorandum," *The Dublin Review,* Vol. 230 (Summer, 1956), pp. 60 ff. Reprinted in part in Donnelly et al., *Criminal Law,* pp. 140 ff.
43. Cf. Jersild, op. cit., p. 70.
44. Cited in Stevas, op. cit., p. 229.
45. Cf. the literature cited in Schur, op. cit., pp. 105 ff.

Chapter 3. Contraception and Abortion

1. George N. Shuster, Introduction to *The Problem of Population: Practical Catholic Applications* (Notre Dame, Ind.: University of Notre Dame Press, 1964), pp. x–xi.
2. Excerpted in Leo Pyle (ed.), *Pope & Pill* (Baltimore: Helicon Press, 1969), pp. 86 f.
3. Cf. the excellent discussion of this position by Fr. Thomas B. McDonough, "Distribution of Contraceptives by the Welfare Department: A Catholic Response," in Shuster, op. cit., pp. 94 ff.
4. Cf. *Commonwealth* v. *Gardner*, 15 N.E. 2d, 223 (1938) and *Commonwealth* v. *Corbett*, 29 N.E. 2d, 151 (1940).
5. *Griswold* v. *Connecticut*, 381 U.S. 479 (1965).
6. For a discussion of these figures, and other estimates, see Daniel Callahan, *Abortion: Law, Choice, and Morality* (New York: Macmillan, 1970), pp. 132 ff.
7. Plato, *Republic,* tr. by F. M. Cornford (Oxford: Oxford University Press, 1945), p. 461.
8. Ibid., p. 460.
9. Aristotle, *Politics*, Translation by Ernest Barker in *The Politics of Aristotle* (Oxford: Oxford University Press, 1946), 1265b.
10. Ibid., 1335b.
11. Will Durant, *The Life of Greece* (New York: Simon and Schuster, 1939), p. 81.
12. Ibid., pp. 567 f.
13. See Durant, *Caesar and Christ* (New York: Simon and Schuster, 1944), pp. 221 ff.
14. Ibid., pp. 363 f.
15. Gen. 1.27–28, 9.1; Ex. 23.26; Deut. 7.13–14; cf. Gen. 15.5, 22.17, 26.4, and elsewhere.
16. Luke 20:34–36
17. Matthew 19:12.
18. Ibid., 22:30.
19. 1 Corinthians 7:33–34.
20. John T. Noonan, Jr., *Contraception: A History of Its Treatment by the Catholic Theologians and Canonists* (Cambridge, Mass.: Harvard University Press), pp. 40 ff.
21. 1. Corinthians 7–10.
22. Romans 5:12.
23. Cf. the citations in Noonan, pp. 46 ff.
24. Noonan, op. cit., p. 78, quoting Lactantius. For other quotations, see ibid., pp. 76 f.
25. *Marriage and Concupiscence,* 1:15:17 Cited by Noonan, op. cit., p. 136.
26. Cf. Noonan, op. cit., pp. 162 ff.
27. Cf. e.g., Noonan, op. cit., p. 196.
28. St. Thomas Aquinas, *Summa* 2–2:154:12.
29. Noonan, op. cit., pp. 260 ff.
30. Ibid., p. 400.
31. Ibid., p. 401.

32. Aristotle, *Nicomachean Ethics,* 1175b.
33. Cf. Noonan, op. cit., pp. 292 ff.
34. Ibid., p. 308.
35. Ibid.
36. Ibid., pp. 324 ff.
37. Cf. Noonan, op. cit., pp. 315 ff.; also David M. Feldman, *Birth Control in Jewish Law* (New York: New York University Press, 1968), pp. 83 ff., and Glanville Williams, *The Sanctity of Life and the Criminal Law* (New York: Knopf, 1957), pp. 52 ff.
38. *De Fide,* § 70, cited by Williams, op. cit., p. 194.
39. Canon 747. Cf. *Ethical and Religious Directives for Catholic Hospitals* (St. Louis: 1949), p. 3.
40. *Decisiones Sanctae Sedis,* pp. 19–20. Noonan, op. cit., p. 403.
41. This reasoning, which derived from Ryan, according to Noonan, was embodied in a pastoral letter of the Archbishops and Bishops of the United States, dated September 26, 1919. Cf. Noonan, op. cit., pp. 423 ff.
42. Lambeth Conference, 1930, Resolution 15.
43. *AAS* 22.560.
44. Noonan, op. cit., p. 427.
45. Ibid., p. 428. Cf. also the other opinions cited there.
46. Cf. Noonan, op. cit., last chapters, and Williams, op. cit., Chapters 2, 5, and 6.
47. The encyclical *Humanae Vitae* is now available in many editions. It was published in full in the *New York Times* immediately after its release by the Vatican in September, 1968, and was published in an appendix to Leo Pyle, ed., *Pope & Pill* (Baltimore: Helicon Press, 1969). All references will be to section numbers and subhead titles. The present quotation is from "Conjugal Love," Section 8.
48. "Responsible Parenthood," Section 9. Also "Union and Procreation," Section 12, and "Faithfulness to God's Design," Section 13.
49. "Illicit Ways of Regulating Birth," Section 14. Emphasis added.
50. Ibid.
51. "Illicit Ways of Regulating Birth," Section 14.
52. "Grave Consequences of Methods of Artificial Birth Control," Section 17.
53. Quotation from Archbishop Cowderoy of Southwark, in an encyclical published in Pyle, op. cit., pp. 173 ff. This was one of many that might have been quoted.
54. For an important collection of documents on both sides of the question, both prior to and immediately following *Humanae Vitae,* see Pyle, op. cit.
55. Reprinted in Pyle, op. cit., pp. 118 f.
56. This doctrine goes back to Aristotle's day and is based on some obsolete physiological and psychological theories that we need not pursue here.
57. Cf. Lawrence Lader, *Abortion* (Indianapolis: Bobbs-Merrill, 1966), p. 79, and the letters quoted on p. 185, n. 9.
58. For a review of some of the legislation and court decisions, cf. Lader, op. cit., pp. 85 ff., and Williams, op. cit., pp. 156 ff. An excellent review of the development of the common law and of the law on abortion in Great Britain may be found in Bernard M. Dickens, *Abortion and the Law* (London: MacGibbon and Kee, 1966), pp. 20 ff. The status of British law at the time of the

book's writing is discussed in detail on pp. 29 ff. British law is also discussed, but in less detail, by Williams, op. cit., pp. 152 ff.

59. *Foster* v. *State*, 182 Wis. 298, 196 N.W. 233 (1923), cited in Williams, op. cit., p. 157.

60. For the prayer, cf. Philip Birnbaum, *Daily Prayer Book* (New York: Hebrew Publishing Company, 1949), p. 16, or Chief Rabbi Joseph H. Hertz, *The Authorized Daily Prayer Book*, Rev. Ed. (New York: Bloch Publishing Co., 1948), p. 19. Cf. Hertz's commentary on pp. 18 f.

61. Cf. the excellent discussion in G. F. Moore, *Judaism in the First Centuries of the Christian Era*, Vol. 1 (Cambridge, Mass.: Harvard University Press, 1954), Part III, Chapter 2, esp. pp. 467 ff.

62. Maimonides, *Commentary to Mishnah, Sanhedrin* 7:4.

63. For a thorough discussion of this, see David M. Feldman, *Birth Control in Jewish Law* (New York: New York University Press, 1968), pp. 109 ff., 148 ff.

64. Leviticus 18:16. The Hebrew term *karet*, often translated "cut off," was understood by the Rabbis to refer to heavenly punishment consisting of early death.

65. Cf. Feldman, op. cit., p. 151.

66. Jerusalem Talmud, Yeb. 1:1.

67. *Genesis Rabbah, Bereshit*, 17:2. Cited in C. G. Montefiore and H. Loewe, *A Rabbinic Anthology* (Philadelphia: Jewish Publishing Society, 1960), p. 507.

68. *Ruth Zuta*, ed. Buber, 4:11; in Montefiore and Loewe, op. cit., p. 511.

69. *T'shuvot Rivash*, no. 15, cited in Feldman, op. cit., pp. 41 f. This decision was later incorporated into the codes that were held to be normative from the fifteenth century to the present day.

70. Exodus 21:10 Cf. *Mekilta ad loc.*, Jerusalem Talmud *Ketubot* 5:6.

71. Babylonian Talmud, *Nedarim* 81b, *Ketubot* 61b.

72. Cf. Bailey, *Sexual Relation in Christian Thought* (New York: Harper & Row, 1959), pp. 33 ff.

73. Deuteronomy, 24:5.

74. Maimonides, *Mishneh Torah, H. De'ot*, 3:1.

75. Cf. Gershom Scholem, *Major Trends in Jewish Mysticism*, Third Edition (New York: Schocken, 1954), pp. 106, 235.

76. *Sefer Hasidim*, cited in Scholem, p. 106.

77. Maimonides, *Mishneh Torah, H. Issurei Bi'ah*, 21:9.

78. Translated by Feldman, op. cit., p. 102.

79. The passage is from a *baraita*, and appears a number of times in the Talmud and in the Tosefta. For a full discussion, see Feldman, op. cit., pp. 169 ff.

80. Cf. Tosephta, Yevamot, 8:2.

81. Judah Assad, quoted, among others, in Feldman, op. cit., p. 242.

82. *Resp. Hatam Sofer, E. H.*, no. 20, cited in Feldman, op. cit., p. 242.

83. *Resp. Mahaneh Hayyim*, no. 53, cited in Feldman, op. cit., p. 105.

84. Cf. Feldman, op. cit., p. 248.

85. Exodus 21:12.

86. Babylonian Talmud, *Niddah*, p. 44b.

87. Cf. *Mekilta*, an early legal midrash, ad loc.

88. See *Tosafot* to *Niddah,* pp. 44a-b, s.v. *'ihu,* and the references cited there.

89. Cf. *Mishnah, Oholot,* 7:7; *Bab. Talmud, Sanhedrin* 59a and *Tosafot* s.v. *Leka;* ibid., 72b.

90. For Abulafia, see his commentary, *Yad Ramah,* on *Sanhedrin,* 91b and 72b. Cf. the discussion in Feldman, op. cit., pp. 273 ff.

91. Decided by a rabbi of the early eighteenth century, Yehudah Ayyas. Cf. Feldman, op. cit., p. 287.

92. *Or Dagol,* no. 31. Cited in Feldman, op. cit., p. 287.

93. Ibid., pp. 293 ff.

94. Sherri Finkbine, "The Lesser of Two Evils," in Allan F. Guttmacher, *The Case for Legalized Abortion* (Berkeley, Calif.: Diablo Press, 1967), pp. 15 ff.

95. Lader, op. cit., p. 5.

96. Jerome E. Bates and Edward S. Zawadzki, *Criminal Abortion: A Study in Medical Sociology* (Springfield, Ill.: Charles C Thomas, 1964), p. 41.

97. *Look,* July 11, 1967.

98. See the bibliography for some of the more recent literature on this subject.

99. Richard A. McCormick, S.J., "Abortion," *America,* June 19, 1965, p. 877.

100. Cf. *New York Times,* October 17, 1970, p. 30.

101. McCormick, op. cit., p. 879.

102. Ibid.

103. Cf. ibid., p. 880, and many other articles and books for the same argument in different forms.

104. Ronald M. Green, "Abortion and Promise-Keeping," *Christianity and Crisis,* May 15, 1967, p. 110.

105. The article from which this excerpt came was a defense of liberalization, but its argument is fallacious because of its improper use of *promise.*

106. Cited in Dickens, op. cit., p. 118.

107. See *New York Times,* Oct. 14, 1971, and *Montreal Star,* October 15, 1971.

108. Dr. Henry Morgentaler of Montreal, quoted in *Weekend Magazine,* September 12, 1970.

109. For references on this issue, see Dickens, op. cit., pp. 144 ff.

110. Glanville Williams, *The Sanctity of Life and the Criminal Law* (New York: Knopf, 1957), p. 232.

111. Cf., for example, Edgar R. Chasteen, *The Case for Compulsory Birth Control* (Englewood Cliffs, N.J.: Prentice-Hall, 1971).

Chapter 5. Marijuana

1. See Lester Grinspoon, *Marihuana Reconsidered* (Cambridge, Mass.: Harvard University Press, 1971), pp. 350, 356; John Kaplan, *Marijuana: The New Prohibition* (New York: Pocket Books, 1971), pp. 25, 27.

2. *Interim Report of the Commission of Inquiry into the Non-Medical Use of Drugs* (Ottawa: Department of National Health and Welfare, 1970), p. 142. (Hereafter referred to as *Interim Report.*)

3. Judge G. Joseph Tauro, "Marijuana and Relevant Problems," remarks before the Commonwealth of Massachusetts Drug Dependency Conference, March 12, 1969. Cited in David E. Smith (ed.), *The New Social Drug: Cultural, Medical, and Legal Perspectives on Marijuana* (Englewood Cliffs, N.J.: Prentice-Hall, 1970), pp. 6 f.

4. "Marijuana and Society," statement by Council on Mental Health and Com-

mittee on Alcoholism and Drug Dependence of the American Medical Association, reprinted in *Journal of the American Medical Association*, June 23, 1968, p. 91.

5. Ibid.

6. Testimony before the Senate subcommittee on drug abuse, 1955, cited in Smith, op. cit., p. 112.

7. Cf. the sources cited in James J. Carey, *The College Drug Scene* (Englewood Cliffs, N.J.: Prentice-Hall, 1968), pp. 182 f., as well as in other sources throughout the literature.

8. Cf. Smith, op. cit., p. 115; Carey, op. cit., p. 41; Grinspoon, op. cit., pp. 183 ff.

9. *Time*, November 7, 1969, p. 50.

10. Norman Taylor, *Narcotics: Nature's Dangerous Gifts* (New York: Dell, 1963), p. 2. First published in 1949 as *Flight from Reality*.

11. Andrew T. Weil et al., "Clinical and Psychological Effects of Marijuana in Man," *Science*, Vol. 162 (1968), pp. 1234 ff., reprinted in Smith, op. cit., pp. 23 ff.

12. Reese T. Jones and G. C. Stone, "Psychological Studies of Marijuana and Alcohol in Man," read at 125th Meeting of the American Psychiatric Association, May 1969; cited in John Kaplan, *Marijuana: The New Prohibition* (New York: Pocket Books, 1971), p. 64.

13. Cf. L. D. Clark and E. N. Nakashima, "Experimental Studies of Marijuana," *American Journal of Psychiatry*, Vol. 125 (1968), p. 379, cited in Kaplan, loc. cit.

14. C. J. Schwarz, "Towards a Medical Understanding of Marijuana," paper read at Western Regional Meeting of Canadian Psychiatric Association, Vancouver, B.C., 1969; cited in *Interim Report*, p. 79.

15. T. Clark, "Allen Ginsberg," an interview, in G. Plimpton, ed., *Writers at Work: The Paris Review Interviews, Third Series* (New York: 1967), pp. 291 ff. Cited in Grinspoon, op. cit., p. 104.

16. Cf. Grinspoon, op. cit., p. 148.

17. Ibid., pp. 113 ff.

18. T. H. Mikuriya, "Physical, mental, and moral effects of marijuana: The Indian Hemp Drugs Commission Report," *International Journal of Addiction*, Vol. 3 (1968), pp. 253 ff.

19. From the conclusions of the Commission, cited in *Interim Report*, p. 99.

20. *The Marijuana Problem in the City of New York: Sociological, Medical, Psychological and Pharmacological Studies* (New York: 1944).

21. A. Crancer et al., "Comparison of the Effects of Marijuana and Alcohol on Simulated Driving Performance," *Science*, Vol. 164 (1969), pp. 851 ff.

22. *Task Force Report: Narcotics and Drug Abuse* (Washington, D.C.: Government Printing Office, 1967), p. 13.

23. Ibid., p. 14. Emphasis added.

24. Cf. Roger C. Smith, "U.S. Marijuana Legislation and the Creation of a Social Problem," in Smith, pp. 115 ff., and Richard H. Blum, "Mind-Altering Drugs and Dangerous Behavior: Dangerous Drugs," *Task Force Report*, Appendix A-1, p. 24.

25. J. Mandel, "Who Says Marijuana Leads to Heroin Addiction?" *Journal of Secondary Education*, Vol. 43 (1968), p. 214, cited in Grinspoon, op. cit., p. 243.

26. For an excellent survey of the literature on this subject and a thorough analysis of the arguments and the statistics, cf. Grinspoon, op. cit., Chapter 9.

27. Cf. Blum, op. cit., p. 25.

28. D. D. Schoenfeld, "The Sociological Study," in Mayor's Committee, *The Marijuana Problem* (see n. 20 above), 50, p. 25. Cited in Grinspoon, op. cit., pp. 308 f.

29. Cf. Blum, op. cit., p. 23.

30. Cf. Erich Goode, "Marijuana and the Politics of Reality," in Smith, op. cit., p. 178.

31. *Bulletin of the World Health Organization*, Vol. 32 (1965), pp. 721 f.

32. Cf. John Kaplan, *Marijuana: The New Prohibition* (New York: Pocket Books, 1971), p. 186. (First published by World Publishing Co., 1970.)

33. Plato, *The Republic*, vii, 514a–521b.

34. Cf. Babylonian Talmud, *Hagigah*, p. 14b. Rabbi Akiva was the one who returned unharmed.

35. William James, *The Varieties of Religious Experience*, Lecture 17. (Near end.)

36. *Olmstead* v. *U.S.*, 227 U.S. 438, at 478 (1928).

37. Proceedings of the White House Conference on Narcotic and Drug Abuse, Washington, D.C., September 27–28, 1963, p. 231. Cited in Smith, op. cit., p. 114.

38. Grinspoon, op. cit., p. 350.

39. *World Almanac*, 1971, pp. 68, 78.

40. The harrowing story of Leslie Fiedler is recounted in his book *On Being Busted* (New York: Stein and Day, 1970).

41. *Interim Report*, pp. 242 f.

42. Grinspoon, op. cit., p. 344.

43. "Of Aristocracy," in R. H. M. Elwes, *The Chief Works of Benedict de Spinoza* (London: G. Bell & Sons, 1917), Vol. I, p. 381.

Chapter 6. Obscenity and Pornography

1. Cf. Judge Frank's comments in the Appendix, Part 2, to his opinion in *U.S.* v. *Roth*, 237 F.2d 796, 826 (2d Cir. 1956).

2. *Chicago Tribune*, May 24, 1959, p. 8.

3. Judge Jacobs' opinion in *N.J.* v. *Hudson News Company and Hudson News Dealers Supply Company*, 41 N.J. 247 (1963).

4. Cited by Chief Justice Warren, in his dissent in *Times Film Corp.* v. *Chicago*, 365 U.S. 43 (1961).

5. *Commonwealth* v. *Gordon*, 68 Pa. D. & C. 101 (1949). Among the books that were under attack was *Studs Lonigan*, to name only one.

6. *Ginzburg* v. *United States*, 383 U.S. 463 (1966).

7. *U.S.* v. *One Book Entitled "Ulysses,"* 72 F. 2d 705.

8. American Law Institute, *Model Penal Code*, sec. 251.4.

9. *Roth* v. *U.S.*, 354 U.S. 476 (1957).

10. *Jacobellis* v. *Ohio*, 378 U.S. 197.

11. Harold Gardiner, *Catholic Viewpoint on Censorship* (Garden City, N.Y.: Doubleday, 1961), pp. 62 ff.

12. E. and P. Kronhausen, *Pornography and the Law*, Rev. Ed. (New York: Ballantine Books, 1964), p. 18.

13. George Elliott, "Against Pornography," *Harper's Magazine* Vol. 230 (May 1965), p. 52.
14. Harry M. Clor, *Obscenity and Public Morality: Censorship in a Liberal Society* (Chicago: University of Chicago Press, 1969), Chapter 6.
15. Ibid., p. 244.
16. Ibid., p. 245.
17. *The Report of the Commission on Obscenity and Pornography* (New York: Bantam Books, 1970), p. 32.
18. Ibid., Part IV, pp. 443 ff.
19. *Smith* v. *California,* 361 U.S. 147, and elsewhere.
20. *Davis* v. *Beason,* 133 U.S. 333 (1890).
21. *Trist* v. *Child,* cited in Clor, op. cit., p. 181.
22. Lord Devlin, *The Enforcement of Morals* (New York: Oxford University Press, 1965), p. 94.
23. Clor, op. cit., p. 194.
24. Ibid.
25. *Report* (see n. 17 above), pp. 57 ff.
26. C. P. Magrath, "The Obscenity Cases: The Grapes of Roth," *Supreme Court Review,* 1966, p. 77.
27. Recent developments in American law may be of some interest. In *Stanley* v. *Georgia,* 934 U.S. 557 (1969), the Supreme Court extended the protection of the First Amendment to admittedly obscene material when in the possession of private persons and enjoyed in the privacy of one's own home. *Karalexis* v. *Byrne,* 306 F. Supp. 1363 (D. Mass. 1969), extended this privilege to a public theater which controlled its advertising and admissions so as to confine the display of admittedly obscene materials to consenting adults who were informed of the nature of the material they were about to view. The *Karalexis* decision seems to have been reached on the assumption that a theater is a private place, not a public one; that each person purchasing a ticket of admission is in a sense having a private viewing. *U.S.* v. *Thirty-Seven Photographs,* 30 U.S.L.W. 2440 (D.C. Cal. 1970), upset the prohibition on importation of obscene materials on the ground that such a prohibition interfered with the Constitutional right of individuals to view them in private. Ralph Ginzburg was incarcerated in federal prison in 1972 to begin serving the term imposed upon him and upheld by the Supreme Court in the famous *Ginzburg* case cited above. Some authorities maintain that the difference between the *Ginzburg* cases and others is that Ginzburg engaged in "pandering," which was a major issue in his case, whereas the others have been strictly on the issue of the right to possess, sell, read, distribute, or display allegedly pornographic materials. Others insist that this "pandering" issue was a red herring, and speculate that if Ginzburg's case had been heard a few years later, when far more objectionable materials were being "pandered" at least as openly as his publications were, his case would have been thrown out of court. Ginzburg lost his appeals and went to prison.

Chapter 7. The Concept of Punishment
1. Thomas Hobbes, *Leviathan,* Part I, Chapter 13. Library of Liberal Arts ed., p. 107.
2. Genesis 4:10–11.

3. Numbers 32:33. Cf. also Deuteronomy 21:1–9, *et passim*. Cf. also Shakespeare's portrayal of guilt in such scenes as that in which Lady Macbeth attempts to wash away the blood that she imagines stains her hands.
4. Immanuel Kant, *Philosophy of Law*, tr. by Hastie (Edinburgh: T. & T. Clark, 1887), p. 198.
5. Edmond N. Cahn, *The Sense of Injustice: An Anthropomorphic View of Law* (New York: New York University Press, 1949), p. 12.
6. John Hospers, "Free Will and Psychoanalysis," *Philosophy and Phenomenological Research*, 1950; reprinted in Paul Edwards et al., *A Modern Introduction to Philosophy*, Second Ed. (New York: Free Press, 1965).

Chapter 9. The Death Penalty
1. I am indebted to H. L. A. Hart for this point. See his book *Punishment and Responsibility: Essays in the Philosophy of Law* (New York: Oxford University Press, 1968).
2. Albert Shanker, in his weekly column, published as an advertisement of the United Federation of Teachers in the *New York Times*.

Chapter 10. Juvenile Delinquency
1. Shirley D. McCune and Daniel L. Skolar, "Juvenile Court Judges in the United States—A National Profile," *Crime and Delinquency*, Vol. II (April, 1965), pp. 121 ff.

Chapter 11. The Ethics of Truth Telling
1. Kant, *On a Supposed Right to Tell Lies from Benevolent Motives*, Abbott's tr. (London: Longmans, Green, 1881), p. 361.
2. Ibid., p. 364. For further discussion on this, see Paul Dietrichson, "Kant's Criteria of Universalizability" and Lewis White Beck, "Apodictic Imperatives," in Kant, *Foundations of the Metaphysics of Morals*, ed. by R. P. Wolff (Indianapolis: Bobbs-Merrill, 1969.). Also Paton, "An Alleged Right to Lie," *Kantstudien*, Vol. XLV (1964), pp. 190 ff. and Marcus Singer, "The Categorical Imperative," *Philosophical Review*, Vol. LXIII (1954), pp. 577 ff.
3. *The Metaphysical Principles of Virtue*, tr. by James Ellington (Indianapolis: Bobbs-Merrill, 1964), p. 91.
4. *Lectures on Ethics*, tr. by Louis Infield (New York: Harper & Row, 1963), pp. 227 ff.
5. These lectures on ethics were not written by Kant himself, but were compiled from notes taken by some of his students. How accurately these notes reflected Kant's views is, of course, a matter that remains open to speculation.
6. Cf. *Fundamental Principles of the Metaphysic of Morals*, tr. by T. K. Abbott (Indianapolis: Library of Liberal Arts, 1949), p. 38. I have rephrased the sentence.
7. *Metaphysical Principles of Virtue*, p. 117.
8. Ibid., pp. 121 f.
9. Cf. Dietrichson, op. cit., p. 188.
10. Cf. *Fundamental Principles*, op. cit., p. 46. Again, this is my own translation.
11. For the full story, see Robert McQueen, "Larry: Case History of a Mistake," *Saturday Review*, September 12, 1970.

Chapter 12. **Truth in the Marketplace: Advertising, Salesmen, and Swindlers**

1. Bruce Barton (a founder of Batten, Barton, Durstine and Osborne advertising agency), "Advertising: Its Contribution to the American Way of Life," *Reader's Digest*, Vol. 66, (April 1955), pp. 103 ff.

2. For 1969 figures, see *New York Times Encyclopedic Almanac*, 1971. The figure for 1958, "estimated to be over $10 billion," is from "Questions and Answers about Advertising," a booklet published by the Advertising Federation of America in 1959, quoted in Poyntz Tyler, ed., *Advertising in America* (New York: H. W. Wilson Co., 1959), p. 181.

3. These are not the exact terms used in his dialogues, but they give a more accurate picture of Plato's meaning, in modern terms, than the translations that I have seen thus far. For example, W. C. Helmbold calls gymnastics and medicine *arts*, whereas makeup and cookery are called *knacks. Knack*, in modern English, is very far, in my opinion, from what Plato had in mind. See Helmbold's translation of Plato's *Gorgias* (Indianapolis: Bobbs-Merrill, 1952), pp. 23 ff. Compare other translations of the same passages for similarly inept renderings.

4. These doctrines can be studied best in Plato's dialogue, *The Gorgias*, though they are discussed in many other dialogues in the Platonic corpus. I would recommend particularly *The Republic, The Symposium,* and *The Protagoras,* in that order. Plato's assaults on the Sophists are scattered throughout his writings. His theory of justice received many different expressions, from the early Socratic dialogues (e.g., *The Apology, The Crito,* and *The Euthyphro*) through the lengthy *Republic* to the late dialogues *The Statesman* and *The Laws.*

5. See Robert J. Cole, "New Law Bars Unscrupulous Ruse to Deprive a Debtor of Legal Rights," *New York Times*, August 19, 1971, p. 51.

6. See James G. Burrow, *AMA: Voice of American Medicine* (Baltimore: Johns Hopkins Press, 1963), p. 268, and Arthur J. Cramp, *Nostrums and Quackery and Pseudo-medicine* (Chicago: University of Chicago Press, 1936), Vol. III, pp. 29–31.

7. James H. Young, *The Medical Messiahs* (Princeton, N.J.: Princeton University Press, 1967), pp. 147 f.

8. See David Ogilvy, *Confessions of an Advertising Man* (New York: Atheneum, 1963), p. 86. Also Gerald B. Lambert, "How I Sold Listerine," in *The Amazing Advertising Business,* ed. by the Editors of *Fortune* (New York: Simon & Schuster, 1957), Chapter 5.

9. Young, op. cit., p. 155.

10. *Consumer Reports,* Vol. 36 (September 1971), pp. 525 f.

11. Ibid., p. 561.

12. For the full story of the Hoxsey case, see Young, op. cit., Chapter 17. This is a fully documented account, gleaned from files of the AMA, the FDA, and transcripts of court hearings, as well as from newspapers, journals, and other publications of the period.

13. Mortin Mintz, "Drugs: Deceptive Advertising," in David Sanford (ed.), *Hot War on the Consumer* (New York: Pitman, 1969), pp. 91 ff.

14. CBC, Friday, August 20, 1971.

15. This point, and those below, were made by Dr. Lou Harris of the University of Toronto Medical School on a radio broadcast on the Canadian Broad-

casting Company's Consumer Affairs program. See also Th. H. Van de Velde, *Ideal Marriage*, Revised Edition (New York: Random House, 1965), pp. 28 ff.

16. *Consumer Reports*, Vol. 36 (September 1971), p. 526.
17. For a full discussion of the Holland Furnace fraud, the Aamco Transmission fraud, and many others, see Warren G. Magnuson and Jean Carper, *The Dark Side of the Marketplace* (Englewood Cliffs, N.J.: Prentice-Hall, 1968), Chapters 1 and 2 *et passim*.
18. *Consumer Reports*, Vol. 36 (September 1971), p. 560.
19. For representative figures of financial gains made by persons engaged in fraudulent deals, see Magnuson and Carper, op. cit.; Max A. Geller, *Advertising at the Crossroads* (New York: Ronald Press, 1952); Dexter Masters, *The Intelligent Buyer and the Telltale Seller* (New York: Knopf, 1966); and other works cited in the bibliography for this section.
20. See "The Consumer," an address by Lloyd E. Skinner, president of the Skinner Macaroni Company, in *Vital Speeches of the Day*, Vol. 33 (January 1, 1967), pp. 189 ff., reprinted in Grant S. McClellan, "The Reference Shelf," Vol. 40, No. 3, *The Consuming Public* (New York: H. W. Wilson Company, 1968), pp. 143 ff. He explains that his company produces some nineteen or twenty different kinds of macaroni products, all packaged in the same containers. If his firm were required to standardize by weight, rather than by volume, he would have to invest $86,000 in new machinery over the $300,-000 investment in packaging machinery that he already has, as well as $100,000 in new plant facilities to accommodate the new machines. As opposed to the 90 per cent operating time of the packaging machinery that he had at the time, the new machinery would have been operating only 40 to 50 per cent of the time, according to his estimates. This would have resulted in an increase of 1 to 2 cents per package in the cost of producing macaroni.
21. Cf. *Consumer Reports*, March and August, 1961; follow-up reports, April and August, 1962.
22. The firm is Ogilvy, Benson and Mather.
23. David Ogilvy, *Confessions of an Advertising Man* (New York: Atheneum, 1963), pp. 95 f.
24. Ibid., p. 99.
25. Ibid., p. 159.
26. Babylonian Talmud, *Ketuvot*, p. 17a. The academies were those that went under the names of Shammai and Hillel, respectively. The "debate" was not comparable to the kind of oratory contest that might be staged by college debating teams. It was a serious discussion on matters of legal and moral principle.
27. Ogilvy, op. cit., pp. 158 f.

Chapter 13. The Search for Truth

1. Buffalo *Courier-Express*, February 17, 1969. An interesting contrast may be seen by comparing the story that the Buffalo *Evening News* ran on the same day on the same speech. Anyone reading the two news stories would find it difficult to believe that they were both reporting the same lecture.
2. *Washington Star*, February 21, 1971. Epstein's article appears in the *New*

Yorker magazine, February 13, 1971. Cf. Raymond Heard, "Panthers and the Press," *Montreal Star,* February 26, 1971.

3. For further details on this case and others like it, and for a useful analysis of the entire problem of distorted news coverage, see Daniel P. Moynihan, "The Presidency and the Press," *Commentary,* Vol. 51 (March 1971), pp. 41 ff.

4. See Kenneth Prewitt and Louis L. Knowles, *Institutional Racism in America* (Englewood Cliffs, N.J.: Prentice-Hall, 1970), excerpt quoted in *University of Chicago Alumni Magazine,* Vol. 62, May-June 1970, p. 9.

5. Ibid., p. 10.

6. Ibid.

7. Ibid., pp. 12 f.

8. *IOI,* internal bulletin of the Canadian Jewish Congress, June 1971.

9. John L. Stipp *et al., The Rise and Development of Western Civilization,* One Volume Edition (New York: Wiley, 1969), p. 390.

10. Ibid., pp. 810 f.

11. Cf., e.g., the studies of U.S. high school history texts published by the Anti-Defamation League in 1949 and 1961. The most recent study in this series concludes that not one of the forty-five social studies texts most widely used in American schools provides adequate treatment of minority groups. In a study of fifteen American history texts, fifteen world histories, and fifteen dealing with government or with social problems, it was found that the presentation of facts on Jews, Nazi persecutions, blacks, and American citizens of Oriental, Indian, and Spanish-speaking backgrounds did not measure up in terms of inclusiveness, validity, balance, comprehensiveness, and other criteria. The study found that there had been some improvement during the preceding decade, particularly in the treatment of blacks, but noted that "the contemporary role of other minority groups in our pluralistic society continues, for the most part, to be ignored." Michael B. Kane, *Minorities in Textbooks: A Study of Their Treatment in Social Studies Texts* (Washington, D.C., Anti-Defamation League of B'nai B'rith, 1971).

12. Cf. G. F. Hegel, *History of Philosophy,* tr. E. S. Haldane and F. H. Simon (London: Routledge & Kegan Paul, 1955).

13. Code of Hammurabi, in G. R. Driver and John C. Miles, *The Babylonian Laws* (Oxford: Oxford University Press, 1960).

14. Cf. Numbers 5:11 ff. A full discussion of this practice may be found in the Mishnaic Tractate *Sotah,* in both the Jerusalem Talmud and the Babylonian Talmud in tractates of the same name, and in the various legal codes and commentaries. Cf., for example, Maimonides, *Misneh Torah, Hilchot Sotah.*

15. Cf. Christopher Hibbert, *The Roots of Evil* (Boston: Little, Brown, 1963), pp. 6 f., 29 ff.

16. Cf. St. Thomas Aquinas, *Summa Theologica,* 2a 2a 3, 69.

17. In Justinian's *Digest.*

18. Harry Elmer Barnes and Howard Becker, *Social Thought from Lore to Science* (Washington, D.C.: 1952), Vol. I, pp. 551 f., cited in Henry Paolucci's introduction to his translation of Beccaria's *On Crimes and Punishments* (Indianapolis: Bobbs-Merrill, 1963), p. ix.

19. Beccaria, op. cit., p. 31.

20. Ibid., pp. 32 ff.

Chapter 14. **Truth and Civil Liberties**

1. Plato, *Republic,* tr. by F. M. Cornford (New York: Oxford University Press, 1945), p. 72 (378d).
2. Ibid., p. 115 (424a ff.).
3. Plato, *Laws,* tr. by B. Jowett, 634d.
4. Thomas Hobbes, *Leviathan,* Chapter 18. In Library of Liberal Arts Edition (Indianapolis: Bobbs-Merrill, 1958), p. 147.
5. Joshua 10:12–13.
6. Psalms 103:5.
7. Ecclesiastes 1:5.
8. For an excellent review of the principal facts about this controversy, see the article on Galileo by Giorgia D. de Santillana in the 1967 edition of *Encyclopedia Britannica.* For more details, see Will and Ariel Durant, *The Age of Reason Begins* (Vol. 7 of *The Story of Civilization*) (New York: Simon and Schuster, 1961), Chapter 22. Galileo's own writings are available in a number of translations. See also H. Butterfield, *The Origins of Modern Science* (London: G. Bell, 1957), Lane Cooper, *Aristotle, Galileo, and the Tower of Pisa* (Ithaca, N.Y.: Cornell University Press, 1935), Hermann Kesten, *Copernicus and His World* (New York: Roy, 1945), and D. W. Singer, *Giordano Bruno, His Life and Thought* (New York: Schuman, 1950).
9. John Stuart Mill, *On Liberty,* Chapter 2.
10. Alexander Meiklejohn, *Political Freedom: The Constitutional Powers of the People* (New York: Oxford University Press, 1965), p. 57.
11. See Justice Goldberg's concurring opinions in *New York Times Company* v. *Sullivan* (376 U.S. 255).
12. See Justice Brennan's opinion, for the Court, in the *New York Times* case cited in note 11.

Chapter 15. **Civil Disobedience**

1. *Crito,* 50b (Library of Liberal Arts edition, p. 60).
2. Ibid., 51c (LLA ed., p. 61).
3. Ibid., 54c–d (LLA ed., p. 65).
4. *Apology,* 30b (LLA ed., p. 36).
5. Exodus, I:15ff.
6. Aristotle, *Politics,* V, viii, 1307b.
7. John Locke, *A Letter Concerning Toleration,* 2nd ed. (Indianapolis: Bobbs-Merrill, Library of Liberal Arts), p. 48.
8. *De Republica,* III, xxii, 33. My emphasis.
9. *De Legibus,* I, xii, 33.
10. *Decretalia Gratiani,* I, viii, 2.
11. *Summa Theologica,* la 2ae, quae. 91, art. 2.
12. Ibid., la 2ae, quae. 95 and 104, 6.
13. Carl Cohen, *Civil Disobedience* (New York: Columbia University Press, 1971), p. 4.
14. Craig Colby, "Civil Disobedience: A Case for Separate Treatment"; Bernard G. Segal, and Herbert L. Packer, "Civil Rights and Civil Disobedience to Law," in Hugo Adam Bedau, ed., *Civil Disobedience: Theory and Practice* (New York: Pegasus, 1969), pp. 90 ff.
15. Nicholas W. Puner, "Civil Disobedience: An Analysis and Rationale," *New*

York University Law Review, Vol. 43 (1968), pp. 651 ff. Puner does not hold this view himself, but cites it and criticizes it.

16. William L. Taylor, "Civil Disobedience: Observations on the Strategies of Protest," in Bedau, op. cit., p. 99.

17. Sidney Hook, "Social Protest and Civil Disobedience," *The Humanist*, Vol. 27, 1967, reprinted in Paul Kurtz (ed.), *Moral Problems in Contemporary Society* (Englewood Cliffs, N.J.: Prentice-Hall, 1969), p. 163.

18. I am indebted to Carl Cohen's book *Civil Disobedience* for some of these illustrations.

19. Daniel Berrigan, "Conscience, the Law, and Civil Disobedience," *U.S. Catholic*, June 1969, reprinted in his book *No Bars to Manhood* (New York: Bantam Books, 1970), pp. 40 f. My emphasis throughout.

20. Albert Bigelow, "Why I am Sailing This Boat into the Bomb-Test Area," *Liberation*, February 1956, reprinted in Bedau, op. cit., pp. 146 ff.

21. Again, I am indebted to Carl Cohen for the example.

22. Cf. Cohen, op. cit., Chapter IV, for an excellent treatment of this subject.

23. 345 U.S. 405, 409 (1953).

24. 379 U.S. 536, 555 (1965).

25. 379 U.S. 559, 567, 574 (1965).

26. 379 U.S. 559, 578 (1965).

27. 383 U.S. 168 (1966).

28. Puner, op. cit., p. 697.

29. *U.S.* v. *Miller*, 386 U.S. 911 (1967).

30. *New York Times*, December 12, 1964.

31. Colby, op. cit.

32. Bedau, op. cit., introduction, p. 19.

33. Louis E. Lomax, *The Negro Revolt* (New York: New American Library, 1963), pp. 102 ff.

Chapter 16. War Crimes and Crimes Against Humanity

1. Paul Ramsey, "The Case for Making a 'Just War' Possible," in *The Just War* (New York: Scribner, 1968), p. 150.

2. Paul Ramsey, "Justice in War," in *The Just War*, pp. 142 f. For more on Christian justifications for war, see, for example, Hugo Grotius, *De Jure Belli Ac Pacis, Libri Tres*, tr. by F. W. Kelsey, first published by Carnegie Endowment for International Peace in the "Classics of International Law" series in 1925. Reprinted by Oceana Publications, New York, 1964.

3. Philo Judaeus, *On the Ten Commandments*, § 26. Cf. Grotius, op. cit., Vol. II, Chap. 22, Sec. 4 (p. 548, no. 3). Also cf. Augustine, *City of God*, Vol. IV, Chap. 6, cited in Grotius, p. 548.

4. H. Lauterpacht, *Oppenheim's International Law*, 7th ed. (London: Longmans, 1952), Vol. II, Section 63. My emphasis.

5. Hobbes, *Leviathan*, Library of Liberal Arts edition, p. 108.

6. Grotius, op. cit., Prolegomenon, § 28.

7. Ibid., § 25.

8. Cf. Grotius, op. cit., Vol. II, Chap. 1, § 1.

9. United Nations War Crimes Commission, *History of the United Nations War Crimes Commission and the Development of the Laws of War* (London: 1948), p. 35.

10. "Memorandum on the Principles Which Should Determine Unhuman and Improper Acts of War," in Annex II to Report of Majority of the Commission on Responsibilities of 1919, quoted in U.N. War Crimes Commission Report. (See ibid.)

11. Ibid., p. 40.

12. Julius Stone, *Aggression and World Order* (London: Stevens and Sons, 1958), p. 32, n. 29. Emphasis added.

13. Whitney R. Harris, Tyranny on Trial: *The Evidence at Nuremburg* (Dallas: Southern Methodist University Press, 1954), p. 126.

14. Details on this and other deceptions of a similar nature may be found in Harris, op. cit., or in the transcripts of the Nuremburg trials and the other War Crimes trials of World War II.

15. Cited in Lauterpacht, op. cit., Vol. II, p. 188. Emphasis added.

16. Ibid., p. 362, n. 2.

17. Ibid., p. 578.

18. Cf. Stone, op. cit., p. 15, and especially pp. 15 f., n. 2.

19. Ibid., p. 67, n. 148.

20. Ibid., p. 19.

21. Justice Cardozo, in *N.J.* v. *Del.*, 291 US 383 (1933), cited in Harris, op. cit., 495.

22. *U.S.* v. *La Jeune Eugenie*, 26 Fed. Cas. 832, 846 (Case No. 15, 551) (1822), cited in Harris, op. cit., p. 529.

23. Cited by Justice Robert Jackson, from his opening statement in the Nuremburg trial. Cf. Jackson, *The Nuremburg Case* (New York: Knopf, 1947), p. 81.

24. Ibid., pp. 81 f.

25. Ibid., p. 85.

26. *Newsweek*, April 12, 1971, p. 33.

27. Cf. *Time*, April 12, 1971, p. 23.

28. Lauterpacht, op. cit., p. 571, n. 2.

29. *Deutsche Allgemeine Zeitung*, May 28, 1942, cited in United Nations, op. cit., p. 288.

30. Gideon Hausner, *Justice in Jerusalem* (New York: Harper & Row, 1966).

31. Hobbes, op. cit., p. 108.

32. *New York Times*, April 8, 1971, Op-Ed page.

33. *New York Times*, April 5, 1971, Op-Ed page.

34. *Time*, April 12, 1971, p. 24.

Selected Bibliography

The following list of books is not intended to be complete. It is intended, rather, as a guide for the interested student who may wish to start to delve further into any of the topics discussed here. Many important books and articles have been omitted because of lack of space; but by referring to books listed in this bibliography, the student will be able to trace the literature through footnotes and more specialized bibliographies.

Chapter 1. **Lord Devlin and the Enforcement of Morals**

DEVLIN, SIR PATRICK. *The Enforcement of Morals.* Oxford: Oxford University Press, 1964.

DONNELLY, RICHARD C., et al. *Criminal Law.* New York: The Free Press, 1962.

FLETCHER, JOSEPH F. *Morals and Medicine.* Princeton, N.J.: Princeton University Press, 1954.

FUCHS, JOSEF. *Natural Law,* trans. by Helmut Reckter and John A. Dowling. New York: Sheed and Ward, 1965.

HART, H. L. A. *Law, Liberty, and Morality.* Stanford, Calif.: Stanford University Press, 1963.

MARITAIN, JACQUES. *Man and the State.* Chicago: University of Chicago Press, 1951.

PACKARD, VANCE. *The Sexual Wilderness.* New York: David McKay, 1968.

PACKER, HERBERT L. *The Limits of the Criminal Sanction.* Stanford, Calif.: Stanford University Press, 1968.

PIKE, JAMES A. *You and the New Morality.* New York: Harper & Row, 1967.

ST. JOHN-STEVAS, NORMAN. *Life, Death and the Law.* Bloomington, Ind.: Indiana University Press, 1961.

SCHUR, EDWIN M. *Crimes Without Victims.* Englewood Cliffs, N.J.: Prentice-Hall, 1965.

TAYLOR, PAUL W., ed. *Problems in Moral Philosophy: An Introduction to Ethics.* Belmont, Calif.: Dickenson, 1967.

THIELICKE, HELMUT. *The Ethics of Sex,* trans. John W. Doberstein. New York: Harper & Row, 1964.

WHITELEY, C. H. and W. M. *Sex and Morals.* New York: Basic Books, 1967.

WILLIAMS, GLANVILLE. *The Sanctity of Life and Criminal Law.* New York: Knopf, 1957.

WISDOM, JOHN. *Logic and Sexual Morality.* Baltimore: Penguin, 1965.

WOOTTON, BARBARA. *Crime and the Criminal Law.* London: Stevens and Sons, 1963.

Chapter 2. **Homosexuality**

ALLEN, CLIFFORD. *Textbook of Psychosexual Disorders,* 2nd ed. New York: Oxford University Press, 1969.

BAILEY, D. SHERWIN. *Homosexuality and the Western Christian Tradition.* New York: Longmans, Green, 1955.

BENSON, R. O. D. *In Defense of Homosexuality, Male and Female.* New York: Julian Press, 1965.

BERGLER, E. *Homosexuality: Disease or Way of Life?* New York: Hill and Wang, 1957.

BIEBER, IRVING, et al. *Homosexuality: A Psychoanalytic Study.* New York: Basic Books, 1962.

BRECHER, EDWARD M. *The Sex Researchers.* Boston: Little, Brown, 1969.

BRITISH COUNCIL OF CHURCHES. *Sex and Morality.* London: SCM Press, 1966.

CAPRIO, FRANK S., and DONALD R. BRENNER. *Sexual Behavior: Psycho-Legal Aspects.* New York: Citadel, 1961.

COCHRAN, W. G., et al. *Statistical Problems of the Kinsey Report.* Westport, Conn: Greenwood Press, 1954.

COMMITTEE ON HOMOSEXUAL OFFENSES AND PROSTITUTION. *The Wolfenden Report.* New York: Stein and Day, 1963.

CORY, D. W. *The Homosexual in America,* 2nd. ed. Pasadena, Calif.: Castle Press, 1960.

CORY, D. W., and J. P. LEROY. *The Homosexual and His Society: A View from Within.* New York: Citadel, 1963.

DERIVER, J. PAUL. *Crime and the Sexual Psychopath.* Springfield, Ill.: Charles C Thomas, 1958.

ELLIS, ALBERT. *Homosexuality; Its Causes and Cure.* New York: Lyle Stuart, 1965.

ELLIS, ALBERT, and RALPH BRANCALE. *The Psychology of Sex Offenders.* Springfield, Ill.: Charles C Thomas, 1956.

FLUGEL, J. C. *Man, Morals and Society.* New York: International Universities Press, 1948.

GEBHARD, PAUL H., et al. *Sex Offenders.* New York: Harper & Row, 1965.

GEDDES, D. P., ed. *An Analysis of the Kinsey Reports on Sexual Behaviour in the Human Male and Female.* New York: New American Library, 1962.

GIBBENS, TREVOR C. N., and JOYCE PRINCE. *Child Victims of Sex Offences.* London: ISTD, 1963.

HIRSCHFELD, MAGNUS. *Sexual Anomalies and Perversions.* London: Encyclopaedic Press, 1966.

HOFFMAN, MARTIN. *The Gay World: Male Homosexuality and the Social Creation of Evil.* New York: Basic Books, 1968.

HYDE, H. M. *The Trials of Oscar Wilde.* London: William Hodge, 1948.

JERSILD, JENS. *The Normal Homosexual Male Versus the Boy Molester.* Copenhagen: Nyt Nordisk Forlag Arnold Busck, 1967.

MARMOR, JUDD, ed. *Sexual Inversion: The Multiple Roots of Homosexuality*. New York: Basic Books, 1965.

MASTERS, R. E. L. *The Homosexual Revolution*. New York: Julian Press, 1962.

McCORD, WILLIAM, and JOAN McCORD. *Psychopathy and Delinquency*. New York: Grune and Stratton, 1956.

MOHR, J. W., et al. *Pedophilia and Exhibitionism*. Toronto: Toronto University Press, 1965.

PLUMMER, D. *Queer People*. New York: Citadel, 1965.

RADZINOWICZ, L. *Sexual Offences: A Report of the Cambridge Department of Criminal Science*. London: Macmillan, 1957.

REINHARDT, JAMES M. *Sex Perversions and Sex Crimes*. Springfield, Ill.: Charles C Thomas, 1957.

SCHOFIELD, MICHAEL. *Sociological Aspects of Homosexuality: A Comparative Study of Three Types of Homosexuals*. Boston: Little, Brown, 1966.

SLOVENKO, RALPH, ed. *Sexual Behavior and the Law*. Springfield, Ill.: Charles C Thomas, 1965.

STORR, ANTHONY. *Sexual Deviation*. Baltimore: Penguin, 1964.

WEST, D. J. *The Young Offender*. Baltimore: Penguin, 1967.

WEST, DONALD J. *Homosexuality*. Chicago: Aldine, 1967.

Chapter 3. Contraception and Abortion

ABBOTT, WALTER M. S. J., ed. *The Documents of Vatican II*. New York: Herder and Herder, 1966.

Abortion: An Ethical Discussion. London: Church Assembly Board for Social Responsibility, 1965.

BAILEY, DERRICK SHERWIN. *Sexual Relations in Christian Thought*. New York: Harper & Row, 1959.

BARRETT, DONALD N., ed. *The Problem of Population: Moral and Theological Considerations*. Notre Dame, Ind.: University of Notre Dame Press, 1964.

BATES, JEROME E., and EDWARD S. ZAWADZKI. *Criminal Abortion: A Study in Medical Sociology*. Springfield, Ill.: Charles C Thomas, 1964.

BROMBY, DOROTHY DUNBAR. *Catholics and Birth Control, Contemporary Views on Doctrine*. New York: The Devin-Adair Company, 1965.

BURTON, RICHARD T. *Religious Doctrine and Medical Practice*. Springfield, Ill.: Charles C Thomas, 1958.

CALLAHAN, DANIEL. *Abortion: Law, Choice and Morality*. New York: Macmillan, 1970.

CALLAHAN, DANIEL, ed. *The Catholic Case for Contraception*. New York: Macmillan, 1969.

————. *The American Population Debate*. Garden City, N.Y.: Doubleday-Anchor Books, 1971.

CHASTEEN, EDGAR R. *The Case for Compulsory Birth Control*. Englewood Cliffs, N.J.: Prentice-Hall, Inc., 1971.

CURRAN, CHARLES, ed. *Contraception: Authority and Dissent*. New York: Herder and Herder, 1969.

CURRAN, CHARLES E. *A New Look at Christian Morality*. Notre Dame, Ind.: Fides Publishers, 1968.

DICKENS, BERNARD H. *Abortion and the Law.* Bristol, England: MacGibbon and Kee Ltd., 1966.

DRAPER, ELIZABETH. *Birth Control in the Modern World.* Baltimore: Penguin, 1965.

DUHAMEL, JOSEPH S. *The Catholic Church and Birth Control.* New York: Paulist Press, 1963.

DUPRÉ, LOUIS. *Contraception and Catholics: A New Appraisal.* Baltimore: Helicon, 1964.

EHRLICH, PAUL R. *The Population Bomb.* New York: Ballantine, 1968.

EPSTEIN, LOUIS. *Sex Laws and Customs in Judaism.* New York: Block, 1948.

FELDMAN, DAVID M. *Birth Control in Jewish Law.* New York: New York University Press, 1968.

FREEHOF, SOLOMON. *Recent Reform Responsa.* Cincinnati: Hebrew Union College Press, 1963.

GEBHARD, PAUL H., W. B. POMEROY, C. E. MARTIN, and C. V. CHRISTENSON. *Pregnancy, Birth and Abortion.* New York: Harper & Row, 1958.

GOOD, FREDERICK L., and OTIS F. KELLY. *Marriage, Morals and Medical Ethics.* New York: P. J. Kennedy, 1951.

GORDIS, ROBERT. *Sex and the Family in the Jewish Tradition.* New York: Burning Bush Press, 1967.

GRANFIELD, DAVID. *The Abortion Decision.* Garden City, N.Y.: Doubleday, 1969.

GROUP FOR THE ADVANCEMENT OF PSYCHIATRY: COMMITTEE ON PSYCHIATRY AND LAW. *The Right to Abortion: A Psychiatric View.* New York: Scribner, 1970.

GREEP, ROY O., ed. *Human Fertility and Population Problems.* Cambridge, Mass: Schenkman, 1963.

GUTTMACHER, ALLAN F. *Babies by Choice or by Chance.* New York: Avon, 1961.

GUTTMACHER, ALLAN F., ed. *The Case for Legalized Abortions Now.* Berkeley, Calif.: Diablo Press, 1967.

HALL, ROBERT E. *Abortion in a Changing World,* Vols. I and II. New York: Columbia University Press, 1970.

HIMES, NORMAN. *Medical History of Contraception.* Baltimore: Williams and Wilkins, 1936.

HUSER, ROGER J. *The Crime of Abortion in Common Law,* Canon Law Studies No. 162. Washington, D.C.: Catholic University of American Press, 1942.

JACOBOVITZ, IMMANUEL. *Jewish Medical Ethics.* New York: Philosophical Library, 1959.

JENKINS, ALICE. *Law for the Rich.* London: Victor Gollancz, 1961.

KAHANA, K. *The Concept of Marriage in Jewish Law.* Leiden: E. J. Brill, 1966.

KINSEY, ARTHUR C. et al. *Sexual Behavior in the Human Female.* Philadelphia: W. B. Saunders, 1953.

———. *Sexual Behavior in the Human Male.* Philadelphia: W. B. Saunders, 1948.

LADER, LAURENCE. *Abortion.* Indianapolis: Bobbs-Merrill, 1966.

———. *Margaret Sanger and the Fight for Birth Control.* Garden City, N.Y.: Doubleday, 1955.

LEE, NANCY HOWELL. *The Search for an Abortionist.* Chicago: University of Chicago Press, 1969.

MACE, DAVID. *Hebrew Marriage.* London: Epworth Press, 1953.

MONTAGU, ASHLEY. *Life Before Birth.* New York: New American Library, 1964.

MURRAY, JOHN COURTNEY. *We Hold These Truths.* New York: Sheed and Ward, 1960.

NOONAN, JOHN T. JR. *Contraception.* Cambridge, Mass.: Harvard University Press, 1965.

PADDOCK, WILLIAM, and PAUL PADDOCK. *Famine 1975, America's Decision: Who Will Survive?* Boston: Little, Brown, 1967.

PYLE, LEO, ed. *Pope and Pill.* Baltimore: Helicon Press, 1969.

RAMSEY, PAUL. *Deeds and Rules in Christian Ethics.* New York: Scribner, 1967.

————. *Life or Death: Ethics and Options.* Seattle: University of Washington Press, 1968.

ROCK, JOHN. *The Time Has Come: A Catholic Doctor's Proposal to End the Battle Over Birth Control.* New York: Knopf, 1963.

ROSEN, HAROLD, ed. *Therapeutic Abortion.* New York: Julian Press, 1954.

ST. JOHN-STEVAS, NORMAN. *Birth Control and Public Policy.* Santa Barbara, Calif.: Center for the Study of Democratic Institutions, 1960.

————. *The Right to Life.* New York: Holt, 1964.

SCHULDER, DIANE, and FLORYNCE KENNEDY. *Abortion Rap.* New York: McGraw-Hill, 1971.

SCHUR, EDWIN, ed. *The Family and the Sexual Revolution.* Bloomington: Indiana University Press, 1964.

SHAW, RUSSELL. *Abortion on Trial.* Dayton, Ohio: Pflaum Press, 1968.

SHUSTER, GEORGE N. *The Problem of Population: Practical Catholic Application,* Vol. II. Notre Dame, Ind.: University of Notre Dame Press, 1964.

SMITH, DAVID T., ed. *Abortion and the Law.* Cleveland: Western Reserve University, 1967.

SOCIETY OF FRIENDS, AMERICAN FRIENDS SERVICE COMMITTEE. *Who Shall Live?* New York: Hill and Wang, 1970.

STITSKIN, LEON D. *Studies in Torah Judaism.* New York: Yeshiva University Press, 1969.

SUENENS, LEON JOSEPH CARDINAL. *Love and Control: The Contemporary Problem,* tr. by George J. Robinson. Westminister, Md.: The Newman Press, 1961.

SULLOWAY, ALVAH W. *Birth Control and Catholic Doctrine.* Boston: Beacon Press, 1959.

TORREY, E. FULLER, ed. *Ethical Issues in Medicine. The Role of the Physician in Today's Society.* Boston: Little, Brown, 1968.

TRETZE, CHRISTOPHER, ed. *Bibliography of Fertility Control.* New York: National Committee on Maternal Health, 1965.

Chapter 4. Divorce

AMRAM, DAVID W. *The Jewish Law of Divorce.* New York: Hermon Press, 1968.

BOHANNAN, PAUL, et al. *Divorce and After.* Garden City, N.Y.: Doubleday, 1970.

CALLAHAN, PARNELL J. *Law of Separation and Divorce,* 2nd rev. ed. New York: Oceana, 1966.

CARTER, HUGH, and PAUL C. GLICK. *Marriage and Divorce: A Social and Economic Study.* Cambridge, Mass.: Harvard University Press, 1970.

DeWOLF, ROSE. *The Bonds of Acrimony.* Philadelphia: Lippincott, 1970.

FREID, JACOB L., ed. *Jews and Divorce.* New York: Ktav, 1968.

GOODE, WILLIAM J. *Women in Divorce.* New York: The Free Press, 1965.

GOULD STAFF EDITORS. *Marriage, Divorce and Adoption Laws in the U.S.* Jamaica, N.Y.: Gould Publications, 1971.

McGREGOR, OLIVER R. *Divorce in England.* New York: Fernhill House, 1957.

SHANER, D. W. *A Christian View of Divorce.* Leyden: Brill, 1969.

WALLER, WILLARD. *Old Love and the New: Divorce and Readjustment.* Carbondale, Ill.: Southern Illinois University Press, 1967.

Chapter 5. Marijuana

AARONSON, BERNARD, and HUMPHRY OSMOND, eds. *Psychedelics.* Garden City, N.Y.: Anchor Books, 1970.

ANDREWS, G., and S. VINKEROOG, eds. *The Book of Grass: An Anthology of Indian Hemp.* New York: Grove, 1967.

ANSLINGER, H. J., and W. F. TOMPKINS. *The Traffic in Narcotics.* New York: Funk and Wagnalls, 1953.

BLOOMQUIST, EDWARD R. *Marijuana: The Second Trip.* New York: The Free Press, 1968.

BLUMER, H. et al. *The World of Youthful Drug Use.* Addiction Center Project, Final Report. Berkeley: University of California, 1967.

CANADIAN COMMISSION OF INQUIRY INTO THE NON-MEDICAL USE OF DRUGS. *Cannabis.* Ottawa: Department of National Health and Welfare, 1972.

————. *Interim Report.* Ottawa: Department of National Health and Welfare, 1970.

CAREY, JAMES J. *The College Drug Scene.* Englewood Cliffs, N.J.: Prentice-Hall, 1968.

CHEIN, ISIDOR, et al. *The Road to H: Narcotics, Delinquency, and Social Policy.* New York: Basic Books, 1964.

COMFORT, ALEX. *The Anxiety Makers.* London: Thomas Nelson & Sons, 1967.

DRUG ABUSE PROJECT. *Dealing with Drug Abuse.* New York: Praeger, 1972.

FIEDLER, LESLIE. *On Being Busted.* New York: Stein and Day, 1970.

GELLER, ALLEN, and MAXWELL BOAS. *The Drug Beat.* New York: Cowles, 1969.

GREAT BRITAIN, ADVISORY COMMITTEE ON DRUG DEPENDENCE. *Cannabis: Report of the Committee.* London: Her Majesty's Stationery Office, 1968.

GRINSPOON, LESTER. *Marihuana Reconsidered.* Cambridge, Mass.: Harvard University Press, 1971.

HORMAN, RICHARD E., and ALAN FOX. *Drug Awareness.* New York: Avon, 1970.

KAPLAN, JOHN. *Marijuana: The New Prohibition.* New York: Atherton Press, 1969.

LAURIE, PETER. *Drugs.* Baltimore: Penguin, 1967.

MASTERS, R. E. L., and JEAN HOUSTON. *The Varieties of Psychedelic Experience*. New York: Dell, 1966.

METZNER, R., ed. *The Ecstatic Adventure*. New York: Macmillan, 1968.

NOWLIS, H. H. *Drugs on the College Campus*. Garden City, N.Y.: Doubleday-Anchor, 1969.

O'DONNELL, JOHN A., and JOHN C. BALL, eds. *Narcotic Addiction*. New York: Harper & Row, 1966.

OURSLER, WILL. *Marijuana: The Facts, The Truth*, rev. ed. New York: Paul S. Eriksson, 1970.

POLLARD, J. C., et al. *Drugs and Phantasy: The Effects of LSD, Psilocybin, and Sernyl on College Students*. Boston: Little, Brown, 1965.

SMITH, DAVID E., ed. *The New Social Drug*. Englewood Cliffs, N.J.: Prentice-Hall, 1970.

TAYLOR, NORMAN. *Narcotics: Nature's Dangerous Gifts*, rev. ed. New York: Dell, 1963.

USDIN, E., et al. *Psychotropic Drugs and Selected Compounds*. Washington, D.C.: U.S. Department of Health, Education and Welfare, 1967.

U.S. GOVERNMENT, NATIONAL COMMISSION ON MARIHUANA AND DRUG ABUSE. *Marihuana: A Signal of Misunderstanding*. Washington, D.C.: U.S. Government Printing Office, 1972.

U.S. GOVERNMENT, PRESIDENT'S COMMISSION ON LAW ENFORCEMENT AND ADMINISTRATION OF JUSTICE. *Task Force Report: Narcotics and Drug Abuse*. Washington, D.C.: U.S. Government Printing Office, 1967.

ZAEHNER, R. C. *Mysticism, Sacred and Profane*. New York: Oxford University Press, 1961.

Chapter 6. Obscenity and Pornography

AMERICAN CIVIL LIBERTIES UNION. *Annual Reports*.

BERLIN, ISAIAH. *Four Essays on Liberty*. New York: Oxford University Press, 1970.

BOSMAJIAN, HAIG A. *Principles and Practice of Freedom of Speech*. Boston: Houghton Mifflin, 1971.

BOYER, PAUL S. *Purity in Print*. New York: Scribner, 1968.

CAPALDI, NICHOLAS, ed. *Clear and Present Danger: The Free Speech Controversy*. New York: Pegasus, 1969.

CHAFEE, ZECHARIAH, JR. *Government and Mass Communications*. Hamden, Conn.: Shoe String Press, 1965.

CLOR, HARRY M. *Obscenity and Public Morality: Censorship in a Liberal Society*. Chicago: University of Chicago Press, 1969.

COMMAGER, HENRY S. *Freedom, Loyalty, Dissent*. New York: Oxford University Press, 1954.

COMSTOCK, ANTHONY. *Traps for the Young*. Cambridge, Mass.: Harvard University Press, 1967.

COUNTS, GEORGE S. *Education and the Foundations of Human Freedom*. Pittsburgh: University of Pittsburgh Press, 1963.

EDGERTON, JUDGE HENRY W. *Freedom in the Balance*. Ithaca, N.Y.: Cornell University Press, 1960.

EMERSON, T. I. *The System of Freedom of Expression*. New York: Random House, 1970.

EMERSON, THOMAS I. *Toward a General Theory of the First Amendment.* New York: Random House, 1966.

ERNST, MORRIS L., and ALAN U. SCHWARTZ. *Censorship: The Search for the Obscene.* New York: Macmillan, 1964.

GERBER, ALBERT. *Sex, Pornography, and the Law.* 2nd rev. ed. New York: Ballantine, 1964.

GILMORE, DONALD H. *Sex, Censorship, and Pornography.* San Diego: Greenleaf Classics, 1969.

HACHTEN, WILLIAM. *The Supreme Court on Freedom of The Press: Decisions and Dissents.* Ames, Iowa: Iowa State University Press, 1968.

HAIMAN, FRANKLYN S. *Freedom of Speech.* New York: Random House, 1965.

HANEY, ROBERT W. *Comstockery in America.* Boston: Beacon Press, 1960.

HOOK, SIDNEY. *Paradoxes of Freedom.* Berkeley: University of California Press, 1962.

HOSPERS, JOHN. *Libertarianism: A New Turn in Political Philosophy.* Los Angeles: Nash Publishing Company, 1970.

HOYT, OLGA G., and EDWIN P. HOYT. *Censorship in America.* New York: Seabury Press, 1970.

HUGHES, DOUGLAS A., ed. *Perspectives in Pornography.* New York: St. Martins Press, 1970.

KONVITZ, MILTON R. *Expanding Liberties: Freedom's Gains in Postwar America.* New York: Viking, 1960.

McCLELLAN, GRANT S. *Censorship in the U.S.* New York: H. W. Wilson, 1967.

McCOY, RALPH E. *Freedom of the Press: An Annotated Bibliography.* Carbondale: Southern Illinois University Press, 1968.

MARCUSE, LUDWIG. *Obscene: The History of an Indignation.* New York: Fernhill House, 1965.

MAYER, MILTON, ed. *Tradition of Freedom.* New York: Oceana, 1957.

MEIKLEJOHN, ALEXANDER. *Political Freedom: The Constitutional Powers of the People.* New York: Oxford University Press, 1965.

MEIKLEJOHN, DONALD. *Freedom and the Public: Public and Private Morality in America.* Syracuse: Syracuse University Press, 1965.

NELSON, HAROLD N., ed. *Freedom of the Press from Hamilton to the Warren Court.* Indianapolis: Bobbs-Merrill, 1966.

Obscenity Report. New York: Stein and Day, 1970.

POLANYI, MICHAEL. *Logic of Liberty.* Chicago: University of Chicago Press, 1951.

RANDALL, RICHARD S. *Censorship of the Movies: The Social and Political Control of a Mass Medium.* Madison: University of Wisconsin Press, 1968.

REMBAR, CHARLES. *The End of Obscenity.* New York: Simon and Schuster, 1970.

RUCKER, BRYCE W. *The First Freedom.* Carbondale: Southern Illinois University Press, 1971.

ST. JOHN-STEVAS, NORMAN. *Obscenity and The Law.* London: Secker and Warburg, 1956.

SCHROEDER, THEODORE A. *Free Speech Bibliography.* Philadelphia: B. Franklin, 1969.

————. *Free Speech for Radicals.* Philadelphia: B. Franklin, 1969.

————. *Constitutional Free Speech Defined and Defended.* New York: DaCapo Press, 1970.

SHAPIRO, MARTIN. *Freedom of Speech: The Supreme Court and Judicial Review.* Englewood Cliffs, N.J.: Prentice-Hall, 1966.

SHARP, DONALD B., ed. *Commentaries on Obscenity.* Metuchen, N.J.: Scarecrow Press, 1970.

STRAUSS, LEO. *Persecution and the Art of Writing.* New York: The Free Press, 1952.

WIDMER, ELEANOR, ed. *Freedom and Culture: Literary Censorship in the Seventies.* Belmont, Calif.: Wadsworth Publishers, 1970.

WOETZEL, R. K. *Philosophy of Freedom.* New York: Oceana, 1966.

Chapter 7. **The Concept of Punishment**

ACTON, H. B., ed. *The Philosophy of Punishment.* New York: St. Martin's, 1969.

BARNES, HARRY E. *The Repression of Crime.* Montclair, N.J.: Smith, Patterson, 1969.

BLUMBERG, ABRAHAM S. *Criminal Justice.* Chicago: Quadrangle Books, 1967.

CAHN, EDMOND N. *The Sense of Injustice: An Anthropomorphic View of Law.* New York: New York University Press, 1949.

CAHN, LENORE L., ed. *Confronting Injustice: The Edmond Cahn Reader.* Boston: Little, Brown, 1966.

CRESSEY, DONALD R. *Theft of the Nation: The Structure and Operations of Organized Crime in America.* New York: Harper & Row, 1969.

EAST, SIR W. NORWOOD, ed. *The Roots of Crime.* London: Butterworth, 1954.

FREUND, PAUL A. *On Law and Justice.* Cranbury, N.J.: A. S. Barnes, 1968.

GLUECK, SHELDON. *Law and Psychiatry: Cold War or Entente Cordiale?* Baltimore: Johns Hopkins Press, 1962.

HART, H. L. A. *Punishment and Responsibility: Essays in the Philosophy of Law.* New York: Oxford University Press, 1968.

HIBBERT, CHRISTOPHER. *The Roots of Evil.* Boston: Little, Brown, 1963.

HONDERICH, T., ed. *Punishment: The Supposed Justifications.* New York: Harcourt Brace Jovanovitch, 1970.

McCLINTOCK, FREDERICK H. *Crimes of Violence.* New York: St. Martin's Press, Inc., 1963.

MADDEN, EDWARD H., et al. *Philosophical Perspectives on Punishment.* Springfield, Ill.: Charles C Thomas, 1968.

MENNINGER, KARL. *The Crime of Punishment.* New York: Viking, 1968.

————. *The Vital Balance.* New York: Viking, 1963.

MESSICK, HANS. *The Silent Syndicate.* New York: Macmillan, 1967.

MIDDENDORFF, WOLF. *The Effectiveness of Punishment.* New York: F. B. Rothman, 1968.

MOBERLY, WALTER H. *The Ethics of Punishment.* Hamden, Conn.: Shoe String Press, 1968.

MORRIS, NORVAL. *The Habitual Criminal.* Cambridge, Mass.: Harvard University Press, 1951.

MUELLER, S. O. W. *Crime, Law, and the Scholars.* Seattle: University of Washington Press, 1969.

OSTERMAN, ROBERT. *A Report in Depth on Crime in America*. Silver Springs, Md.: The National Observer, 1966.

PINCOFFS, EDMUND L. *The Rationale of Legal Punishment*. New York: Humanities Press, 1966.

QUINNEY, RICHARD. *The Social Reality of Crime*. Boston: Little, Brown, 1970.

RADZINOWICZ, LEON. *Ideology and Crime*. New York: Columbia University Press, 1966.

RAY, ISAAC. *A Treatise on the Medical Jurisprudence of Insanity*, Winfred Overholser, ed. Cambridge, Mass.: Harvard University Press, 1962.

SALEILLES, RAYMOND C. *The Individualization of Punishment*, trans. by R. S. Jastrow. Montclair, N.J.: Smith, Patterson, 1968.

SAVITZ, LEONARD. *Dilemmas in Criminology*. New York: McGraw-Hill, 1967.

SHAW, GEORGE BERNARD. *The Crime of Punishment*. New York: Citadel Press, 1961.

SUTHERLAND, EDWIN H., and D. R. CRESSEY. *Criminology*, 8th ed. Philadelphia: Lippincott, 1970.

SZASZ, THOMAS. *Psychiatric Justice*. New York: Macmillan, 1965.

TARDE, GABRIEL. *Penal Philosophy*, trans. by R. Howell. Montclair, N.J.: Smith, Patterson, 1968.

TYLER, GUS. *Organized Crime in America*. Ann Arbor: University of Michigan Press, 1962.

WERTHAM, FREDERIC. *A Sign for Cain*. New York: Macmillan, 1966.

WILLIAMS, GLANVILLE L. *The Mental Element in Crime*. London: Oxford University Press, 1965.

WOLFGANG, MARVIN E. *Crime and Race*. New York: Institute of Human Relations Press, 1964.

WOOTTON, BARBARA et al. *Social Science and Social Pathology*. New York: Macmillan, 1959.

WYDEN, PETER. *The Hired Killers*. New York: William Morrow, 1963.

Chapter 8. Imprisonment

CONRAD, JOHN. *Crime and Its Correction*. Berkeley: University of California Press, 1965.

DRESSLER, DAVID. *Practice and Theory of Probation and Parole*. New York: Columbia University Press, 1969.

EDWARDS, GEORGE. *The Police on the Urban Frontier*. New York: Institute of Human Relations Press, 1968.

FISHMAN, JOSEPH F. *Crucibles of Crime: The Shocking Story of the American Jail*. Montclair, N.J.: Smith, Patterson, 1969.

GIALLOMBARIO, ROSE. *Society of Women: A Study of a Women's Prison*. New York: Wiley, 1966.

GLUECK, SHELDON. *Crime and Correction*. Cambridge, Mass.: Kraus Reprint Corporation, 1952.

GOLDFARB, RONALD. *Ransom: A Critique of the American Bail System*. New York: Harper & Row, 1965.

HERSEY, JOHN. *The Algiers Motel Incident*. New York: Knopf, 1968.

JOHNSON, ELMER HUBERT. *Crime, Correction and Society*, rev. edition. Homewood, Ill.: Dorsey, 1968.

KENNEDY, ROBERT F. *The Enemy Within*. New York: Harper & Row, 1960.

KITTRIE, NICHOLAS N. *The Right to be Different: Deviance and Enforced Therapy.* Baltimore: Johns Hopkins University Press, 1972.

KLARE, H. J. *Changing Concepts of Crime and Its Treatment.* New York: Pergamon, 1966.

LEOPOLD, NATHAN F. *Life Plus 99 Years.* Garden City, N.Y.: Doubleday, 1958.

LINDNER, ROBERT M. *Stone Walls and Men.* New York: Odyssey Press, 1946.

MCGRATH, W. T., ed. *Crime and Its Treatment in Canada.* New York: St. Martin's, 1965.

MORRIS, PAULINE. *Prisoners and Their Families.* London: George Allen and Unwin, 1965.

THOMAS, D. A. *Principles of Sentencing.* New York: Heineman, 1970.

WALKER, NIGEL. *Crime and Insanity in England: The Historical Perspective.* Chicago: Aldine, 1968.

————. *Crime and Perspective in Britain.* Chicago: Aldine, 1965.

————. *Sentencing in a Rational Society.* New York: Basic Books, 1970.

WILKINS, LESLIE T. *Evaluation of Penal Measures.* New York: Random House, 1969.

Chapter 9. The Death Penalty

BEDAU, HUGO A. *The Death Penalty in America,* rev. ed. Garden City, N.Y.: Doubleday, 1965.

CHRISTOPH, JAMES B. *Capital Punishment and British Politics.* Chicago: University of Chicago Press, 1962.

GARDINER, GERALD. *Capital Punishment as a Deterrent.* London: Gollancz, 1956.

GOWERS, SIR ERNEST. *A Life for a Life.* London: Chatto and Windus, 1956.

HALE, LESLIE. *Hanged in Error.* Baltimore: Penguin, 1961.

JOYCE, J. A. *Capital Punishment: A World View.* New York: Thomas Nelson & Sons, 1961.

KOESTLER, ARTHUR. *Reflections on Hanging.* New York: Macmillan, 1957.

KOESTLER, ARTHUR, and C. H. RALPH. *Hanged by the Neck.* Baltimore: Penguin, 1961.

POTTER, JOHN D. *The Art of Hanging.* New York: A. S. Barnes, 1969.

The Royal Commission on Capital Punishment 1949–1953 Report. (Cmd. 8932.)

SELLIN, J. T., ed. *Capital Punishment.* New York: Harper & Row, 1967.

SELLIN, THOMAS. *The Death Penalty.* Philadelphia: American Law Institute, 1959.

TUTTLE, ELIZABETH ARMAN. *The Crusade Against Capital Punishment in Great Britain.* Chicago: Quadrangle, 1961.

Chapter 10. Juvenile Delinquency

AMOS, WILLIAM E., RAYMOND MANELLA, and MARILYN A. SOUTHWELL. *Action Programs for Delinquency Prevention.* Springfield, Ill.: Charles C Thomas, 1965.

BLOCK, HERBERT A., and FRANK T. FLYNN. *Delinquency: The Juvenile Offender in America Today.* New York: Random House, 1956.

CANADA, DEPARTMENT OF JUSTICE, COMMITTEE OF JUVENILE DELINQUENCY, *Report*. Ottawa: Queen's Printer, 1965.

CONGER, JOHN J., and WILBUR C. MILLER. *Personality, Social Class and Delinquency*. New York: Wiley, 1966.

CRESSEY, DONALD R., and DAVID A. WARD, eds. *Delinquency, Crime and Social Process*. New York: Harper & Row, 1969.

FERDINAND, THEODORE. *Typologies of Delinquency*. New York: Random House, 1966.

FLEISCHER, BELTON M. *The Economics of Delinquency*. Chicago: Quadrangle, 1966.

FYVEL, T. R. *Trouble-Makers*. New York: Schocken, 1962. (European title: *The Insecure Offenders*. London: Chatto and Windus, 1961.)

GLUECK, SHELDON, ed. *Problem of Delinquency*. Boston: Houghton Mifflin, 1959.

GLUECK, SHELDON, and ELEANOR T. GLUECK. *Delinquents and Nondelinquents in Perspective*. Cambridge, Mass.: Harvard University Press, 1968.

MARTIN, JOHN M., and JOSEPH J. FITZPATRICK. *Delinquent Behavior*. New York: Random House, 1965.

MATZA, DAVID. *Delinquency and Drift*. New York: Wiley, 1965.

NEUMEYER, MARTIN H. *Juvenile Delinquency in Modern Society*. Princeton, N.J.: Van Nostrand, 1949.

QUAY, HERBERT C., ed. *Juvenile Delinquency Research and Theory*. Princeton, N.J.: Van Nostrand, 1965.

REDL, FRETZ, and DAVID WINEMAN. *Children Who Hate*. New York: The Free Press, 1951.

RUBIN, SOL. *Crime and Juvenile Delinquency: A Rational Approach to Penal Problems*, second ed. New York: Oceana, 1961.

SCHWITZEBEL, RALPH. *Street-Corner Research: An Experimental Approach to the Juvenile Delinquent*. Cambridge, Mass.: Harvard University Press, 1964.

SHULMAN, HARRY MANUEL. *Juvenile Delinquency in the American Society*. New York: Harper & Row, 1961.

STERNE, RICHARD S. *Delinquent Conduct and Broken Homes*. New Haven, Conn.: College and University Press, 1964.

TAIT, C. DOWNING, JR., and EMORY F. HODGES, JR. *Delinquents, Their Families and the Community*. Springfield, Ill.: Charles C Thomas, 1962.

VEDDER, CLYDE B. *Juvenile Offenders*. Springfield, Ill.: Charles C Thomas, 1963.

WEST, D. J. *The Young Offender*. Baltimore: Penguin Books, 1967.

Chapter 11. **The Ethics of Truth Telling**

KANT, IMMANUEL. *Foundations of the Metaphysics of Morals*, ed. R. P. Wolff. Indianapolis: Bobbs-Merrill, 1969.

———. *Fundamental Principles of the Metaphysic of Morals*, trans. T. K. Abbott. Indianapolis: Bobbs-Merrill, 1949.

———. *Lectures on Ethics*, trans. L. Infield. New York: Harper & Row, 1963.

———. *The Metaphysical Principles of Virtue*, trans. James Ellington. Indianapolis: Bobbs-Merrill, 1964.

———. "On a Supposed Right to Tell Lies from Benevolent Motives," trans.

T. K. Abbott, in *Kant's Critique of Practical Reason and Other Works on the Theory of Ethics*, 5th rev. ed. New York: Longmans Green, 1898.

McFADDEN, C. J. *Medical Ethics*, 4th ed. Philadelphia: F. A. Davis, 1956.

STANDARD, S., and H. NATHAN, eds. *Should the Patient Know the Truth?* New York: Springer, 1955.

VERWOERDT, ADRIAAN. *Communication with the Fatally Ill.* Springfield, Ill.: Charles C Thomas, 1966.

Chapter 12. Truth in the Marketplace: Advertising, Salesmen, and Swindlers

ALEXANDER, G. J. *Honesty and Competition.* Syracuse, N.Y.: Syracuse University Press, 1967.

BACKMAN, JULES. *Advertising and Competition.* New York: New York University Press, 1967.

BARRIE, GORDON J., and AUBREY L. DEAMOND. *The Consumer, Society and the Law*, rev. ed. London: MacGibbon and Kee, Ltd., 1966.

BAUER, R. A., and S. A. GREYSER. *Advertising in America: The Consumer View.* Boston: Harvard University, Graduate School of Business Administration, 1967.

BERTON, PIERRE. *The Big Sell.* New York: Knopf, 1963.

BURROW, JAMES G. *AMA: Voice of American Medicine.* Baltimore: The Johns Hopkins Press, 1963.

BUZZI, GIANCARLO. *Advertising: Its Cultural and Political Effects*, trans. by B. David Garmize. Minneapolis: University of Minnesota Press, 1968.

CONE, FAIRFAX M. *With All Its Faults: A Candid Account of Forty Years in Advertising.* Boston: Little, Brown, 1969.

COX, EDWARD F. *The Nader Report on the Federal Trade Commission.* New York: Richard W. Baron, 1969.

CRAMP, ARTHUR J. *Nostrums and Quackery and Pseudo-Medicine.* Chicago: University of Chicago Press, 1936.

FREEDOM OF INFORMATION CONFERENCE, UNIVERSITY OF MISSOURI. *Freedom of Information in the Market Place.* Fulton, Mo.: Avid Bell Press, 1967.

GELLER, MAX A. *Advertising at the Crossroads.* New York: Ronald Press, 1952.

GENTRY, CURT. *The Vulnerable Americans.* Garden City, N.Y.: Doubleday, 1966.

GOULD, LESLIE. *The Manipulators.* New York: David McKay, 1966.

HANCOCK, RALPH, and HENRY CHAFETZ. *The Compleat Swindler.* New York: Macmillan, 1968.

HUTCHINSON, R. A. *The Gospel According to Madison Avenue.* New York: Bruce, 1969.

McCLELLAN, GRANT S., ed. *The Consuming Public.* New York: H. W. Wilson, 1968.

MAGNUSON, W. G., and JEAN CARPER. *Dark Side of the Marketplace: The Plight of the American Consumer.* Englewood Cliffs, N.J.: Prentice-Hall, 1968.

MARGOLIUS, SIDNEY. *Innocent Consumer vs. the Exploiters.* New York: Simon and Shuster, 1967.

MARSHALL, M. L., *F.T.C. and Deceptive Advertising.* Freedom of Information Center Report No. 183. Columbia: University of Missouri School of Journalism, 1967.

MASTERS, DEXTER L. *The Intelligent Buyer and the Telltale Seller.* New York: Knopf, 1966.

MINTZ, MORTON. *By Prescription Only,* 2nd ed. Boston: Beacon Press, 1967.

OGILVY, DAVID. *Confessions of an Advertising Man.* New York: Atheneum, 1963.

OPPENHEIM, S. C. *Cases on Federal Anti-Trust Laws.* St. Paul, Minn.: West, 1968.

PACKARD, VANCE. *Hidden Persuaders.* New York: David McKay, 1957.

————. *Status Seekers.* New York: David McKay, 1959.

RIVERS, WILLIAM L., and W. L. SCHRAMM. *Responsibility in Mass Communication,* rev. ed. New York: Harper & Row, 1969.

SANFORD, DAVID, ed. *Hot War on the Consumer.* New York: Pitman, 1969.

SARGENT, W. W. *The Battle for the Mind.* Garden City, N.Y.: Doubleday, 1957.

TYLER, POYNTZ, ed. *Advertising in America.* New York: H. W. Wilson, 1959.

YOUNG, JAMES HARVEY. *The Medical Messiahs: A Social History of Health Quackery in Twentieth Century America.* Princeton, N.J.: Princeton University Press, 1967.

Chapter 13. The Search for Truth

CONFERENCE ON THE SCIENTIFIC SPIRIT AND DEMOCRATIC FAITH. *The Authoritarian Attempt to Capture Education.* Freeport, N.Y.: Books for Libraries, 1945.

CROSS, RUPERT. *Evidence,* 3rd ed. London: Butterworths, 1967.

CRIMINAL LAW REPORTER EDITORIAL STAFF. *Criminal Law Revolution.* Washington, D.C.: Bureau of National Affairs, 1969.

FOOTE, JOSEPH, ed. *Crime and Justice in America.* Washington, D.C.: Congressional Quarterly, 1968.

FRANCK, THOMAS M. *Comparative Constitutional Processes: Cases and Materials: Fundamental Rights in Common Law Nations.* New York: Praeger, 1968.

GROSS, GERALD, ed. *Responsibility of the Press.* New York: Fleet Press, 1971.

INBAU, FRED E., and JOHN E. REID. *Criminal Interrogation and Confessions.* Baltimore: Williams and Wilkins, 1967.

KALVEN, HARRY, JR., and HANS ZEISEL. *The American Jury.* Boston: Little, Brown, 1966.

KANE, MICHAEL B. *Minorities in Textbooks: A Study of Their Treatment in Social Studies Texts.* Washington, D.C.: Anti-Defamation League of B'nai B'rith, 1971.

LYLE, JACK, ed. *The Black American and the Press.* Los Angeles: Ward Ritchie Press, 1968.

MACDOUGALL, CURTIS D. *The Press and Its Problems.* Dubuque, Iowa: William C. Brown, 1965.

MUELLER, GERHARD O., et al. *Comparative Criminal Procedures.* New York: New York University Press, 1969.

PREWITT, KENNETH, and LOUIS L. KNOWLES. *Institutional Racism in America.* Englewood Cliffs, N.J.: Prentice-Hall, 1970.

RINGEL, WILLIAM E. *Arrests, Searches, and Confessions.* Jamaica, N.Y.: Gould Publications, 1966.

ZARR, MELVYN. *The Bill of Rights and the Police.* New York: Oceana, 1970.

ZEISEL, HANS, HARRY KALVEN, JR., and BERNARD BUCHHOLZ. *Delay in Court.* Boston: Little, Brown, 1959.

Chapter 14. Truth and Civil Liberties
See references for Chapter 6.

Chapter 15. Civil Disobedience

AMERICAN ACADEMY OF POLITICAL AND SOCIAL SCIENCE. *Protest in the Sixties.* Philadelphia: American Academy of Political and Social Sciences, 1969.

BEDAU, HUGO A., ed. *Civil Disobedience: Theory and Practice.* New York: Pegasus, 1969.

BELL, INGE P. *CORE and the Strategy of Non-Violence.* New York: Random House, 1968.

COHEN, CARL. *Civil Disobedience.* New York: Columbia University Press, 1971.

BERRIGAN, DANIEL. *No Bars to Manhood.* New York: Bantam, 1970.

COX, ARCHIBALD, et al. *Civil Rights, The Constitution and The Courts.* Cambridge, Mass.: Harvard University Press, 1967.

ERIKSON, ERIK H. *Gandhi's Truth.* New York: Norton, 1969.

FINN, JAMES. *Protest: Pacifism and Politics; Some Passionate Views on War and Nonviolence.* New York: Random House, 1968.

FORTAS, ABE. *Concerning Dissent and Civil Disobedience.* New York: Meridian, 1969.

GANDHI, M. K. *Gandhi on Non-Violence.* New York: New Directions, 1966.

HARE, A. P., and H. H. BLUMBERG, eds. *Non-Violent Direct Action.* New York: World, 1968.

HASKINS, JAMES. *Resistance: Profiles in Nonviolence.* Garden City, N.Y.: Doubleday, 1970.

HEIMLER, EUGENE. *Resistance Against Tyranny.* New York: Praeger, 1967.

HERSHBERGER, GUY F. *War, Peace, and Nonresistance,* 3rd rev. ed. Herald Press, 1959.

KAPLAN, MORTON A. *Dissent and the State in Peace and War.* New York: Dunellen, 1970.

KING, MARTIN LUTHER, JR. *Why We Can't Wait.* New York: New American Library, 1964.

KURTZ, PAUL, ed. *Moral Problems in Contemporary Society.* Englewood Cliffs, N.J.: Prentice-Hall, 1969.

LENS, SIDNEY, ed. *Non-Violence in America.* Indianapolis: Bobbs-Merrill, 1966.

LENS, SIDNEY. *Radicalism in America.* New York: Macmillan, 1969.

LOMAX, LOUIS E. *The Negro Revolt.* New York: New American Library, 1963.

LYND, STAUGHTON, ed. *Nonviolence in America: A Documentary History.* Indianapolis: Bobbs-Merrill, 1966.

MADDEN, EDWARD H. *Civil Disobedience and Moral Law in Nineteenth-Century American Philosophy.* Seattle: University of Washington Press, 1970.

MILLER, W. R. *Nonviolence: A Christian Interpretation.* New York: Schocken, 1966.

MORISON, SAMUEL ELIOT, et al. *Dissent in Three American Wars*. Cambridge, Mass.: Harvard University Press, 1970.

ROBERTS, ADAM, ed. *Civilian Resistance as a National Defence Non-Violent Action Against Aggression*. Baltimore: Penguin Books, 1967.

SIBLEY, M. O., *The Obligation to Disobey*. New York: Council on Religion and International Affairs, 1970.

STEVENS, FRANKLIN. *If This Be Treason*. New York: P. H. Wyden, 1970.

STEVICK, D. B. *Civil Disobedience and the Christian*. New York: Seabury, 1969.

STRINGFELLOW, WILLIAM. *Dissenter in a Great Society: A Christian View of America in Crisis*. Nashville: Abingdon Press, 1967.

————. *My People Is the Enemy: An Autobiographical Polemic*. Garden City, N.Y.: Doubleday, 1966.

THOMAS, NORMAN M. *Great Dissenters*. New York: Norton, 1970.

TOLSTOI, LEO N. *Tolstoy's Writings on Civil Disobedience and Nonviolence*. New York: Bergman Publishers, 1967.

WASKOW, A. *From Race Riot to Sit-in: 1919 and the 1960s*. Garden City, N.Y.: Doubleday, 1966.

U.S. NATIONAL ADVISORY COMMISSION ON CIVIL DISORDERS. *Report*. New York: Bantam, 1968.

U.S. NATIONAL COMMISSION ON THE CAUSES AND PREVENTION OF VIOLENCE. *Rights in Conflict: The Walker Report to The National Commission on the Causes and Prevention of Violence*. New York: Bantam, 1968.

U.S. NATIONAL COMMISSION ON THE CAUSES AND PREVENTION OF VIOLENCE. *To Establish Justice, To Insure Domestic Tranquility: The Final Report of the National Commission on the Causes and Prevention of Violence*. New York: Bantam, 1970.

VEYSEY, LAWRENCE R. *Law and Resistance: American Attitudes Toward Authority*. New York: Harper & Row, 1970.

WALZER, MICHAEL L. *Obligations*. Cambridge, Mass.: Harvard University Press, 1970.

WITTNER, LAWRENCE S. *Rebels Against War*. New York: Columbia University Press, 1969.

ZAHN, G. C. *War, Conscience and Dissent*. New York: Hawthorne, 1967.

ZINN, HOWARD. *Disobedience and Democracy: Nine Fallacies on Law and Order*. New York: Random House, 1968.

Chapter 16. War Crimes and Crimes Against Humanity

APPELMAN, JOHN A. *Military Tribunals and International Crimes*. Indianapolis: Bobbs-Merrill, 1954.

BRIERLY, JAMES LESLIE. *The Basis of Obligation in International Law and Other Papers*. New York: Oxford University Press, 1958.

BROWN, FREDERIC J. *Chemical Warfare: A Study in Restraints*. Princeton, N.J.: Princeton University Press, 1968.

CALDER, NIGEL, ed. *Unless Peace Comes*. New York: Viking, 1968.

CLARKE, ROBIN. *The Silent Weapons*. New York: David McKay, 1968.

DAVIDSON, EUGENE. *The Trial of the Germans: An Account of Twenty-two Defendants before the International Military Tribunal at Nuremberg*. New York: Macmillan, 1966.

FALK, RICHARD A. *Law, Morality and War in the Contemporary World.* New York: Praeger, 1963.

FALK, RICHARD, et al., eds. *Crimes of War: After Songmy.* New York: Random House, 1971.

FROMM, ERICH. *May Man Prevail?* Garden City, N.Y.: Doubleday, 1961.

GLUECK, SHELDON. *The Nuremberg Trials and Aggressive War.* New York: Kraus Reprint, 1946.

————. *War Criminals: Their Prosecution and Punishment.* New York: Knopf, 1944.

HAMMER, RICHARD. *The Court-Martial of Lt. Calley.* New York: Coward McCann, 1971.

HARRIS, WHITNEY R. *Tyranny on Trial: The Evidence at Nuremberg.* Dallas: SMU Press, 1954.

HAUSNER, GIDEON. *Justice in Jerusalem.* New York: Schocken, 1968.

HERSCH, SEYMOUR M. *Chemical and Biological Warfare: America's Hidden Arsenal.* Indianapolis: Bobbs-Merrill, 1968.

HERZ, JOHN H. *International Politics in the Atomic Age.* New York: Columbia University Press, 1959.

KAPLAN, C. A. *Scroll of Agony.* New York: Macmillan, 1965.

KAPLAN, MORTON A., and NICHOLAS KATZENBACH. *The Political Foundations of International Law.* New York: Wiley, 1961.

KEENAN, J. B. *Crimes against International Law.* Washington, D.C.: Public Affairs Press, 1950.

KELSEN, HANS. *Law and Peace in International Relations.* Cambridge, Mass.: Harvard University Press, 1942.

————. *Peace Through Law.* Chapel Hill: University of North Carolina Press, 1944.

KELSEN, HANS, and JULIUS STONE. *Quest for Survival: The Role of Law and Foreign Policy.* Cambridge, Mass.: Harvard University Press, 1961.

KNOLL, ERWIN, et al., eds. *War Crimes and American Conscience.* New York: Holt, 1970.

LACHS, MANFRED. *War Crimes, an Attempt to Define the Issues.* London: Stevens & Sons, 1945.

LESSER, J. *Germany: The Symbol of the Dead.* New York: Yoseloff, 1965.

LONG, EDWARD L. *War and Conscience in America.* Philadelphia: Westminster Press, 1968.

McCARTHY, RICHARD D. *The Ultimate Folly.* New York: Knopf, 1969.

MANVELL, ROGER, and H. FRAENKEL. *The Incomparable Crime.* New York: Putnam, 1967.

NAGLE, WILLIAM J., ed. *Morality and Modern Warfare.* Baltimore: Helicon Press, 1960.

NAUMANN, BERND. *Auschwitz.* New York: Praeger, 1966.

O'BRIEN, WILLIAM V. *Nuclear War: Deterrence and Morality.* Paramus, N.J.: Newman Press, 1967.

————. *War and/or Survival.* Garden City, N.Y.: Doubleday, 1969.

PAPADATOS, PETER A. *The Eichmann Trial.* New York: Praeger, 1964.

POTTER, RALPH B. *War and Moral Discourse.* Richmond, Va.: John Knox Press, 1969.

RAMSEY, PAUL. *The Just War.* New York: Scribner, 1968.

————. *War and the Christian Conscience*. Durham, N.C.: Duke University Press, 1961.

SINGH, N. *Nuclear Weapons and International Law*. New York: Praeger, 1959.

STONE, JULIUS. *Aggression and World Order*. Berkeley: University of California, 1958.

————. *Legal Controls of International Conflict*. New York: Holt, 1954.

TAYLOR, TELFORD. *Nuremberg and Vietnam: An American Tragedy*. Chicago: Quadrangle Books, 1971.

TILLICH, PAUL J. *Love, Power and Justice*. New York: Oxford University Press, 1954.

TUCKER, ROBERT W. *The Just War: A Study in Contemporary American Doctrine*. Baltimore: Johns Hopkins Press, 1960.

UNITED NATIONS. *The Crime of Genocide*. New York: United Nations, 1955.

UNITED NATIONS WAR CRIMES COMMISSION. *History of the United Nations War Crimes Commission and the Development of the Laws of War*. London: 1948.

WALTZ, KENNETH N. *Man, the State and War*. New York: Columbia University Press, 1959.

WASSERSTROM, RICHARD A. *War and Morality*. Belmont, Calif.: Wadsworth, 1970.

WIESENTHAL, SIMON. *The Murderers Among Us*. New York: McGraw-Hill, 1967.

WOETZEL, R. K. *The Nuremberg Trials in International Law*, rev. ed. London: Stevens & Sons, 1962.

Index

Major topics are indicated by being set in SMALL CAPITALS. Within a given topic, pages that contain major discussions of the topic are indicated by being set in **boldface** type. Words and terms that are subjected to analysis are in *italics*. Titles of books and other works are enclosed in quotation marks.

abnormal, equated with *unnatural,* 49f.
abnormal growth, as term to apply to aborted fetus, 100
ABORTION, 11, 14, 25, 31, 48, **69ff.**, 168, 223; and discrimination against the poor and against blacks, 108; and maternal death rates, 108; and quack abortionists, 97; and rape, 94; and rights of fetus, 93; and rights of women, 107; and tacit promise argument, 105; as a form of contraception, 71; compulsory, 106; history of, **74ff.**; if legalized, may lead to promiscuity, 104; illegal abortions (statistics), 73; in ancient Greece and Rome, **74ff.**, in Jewish law, **57ff.**, 93f.; in Scandinavia, 106; mental anguish a justification for, 94; legalized, may lead to governmental abuses, 106; on demand, 94; self-, 98; therapeutic, 84, 93
absolutism, 25ff, 241ff.
abstinence, vows of, 89
Abulafia, Meir, 93
accent, fallacy of, 284
accident, as an excuse, 208
Acton, Lord John Emerich, 186
adultery, 12, 14, 16, 25, 31, 33, 75, 89, 115ff.
adverse reaction, analysis of, 149
ADVERTISING, 5, **252ff.**; and concealment of the truth, 274f.; and the creation of desires, 254, 268ff., 278; and deceptive language, 275; and false claims of need, 268ff.; and health, 255f., 263ff., 267; and illusions, 273f.; and injustice, 257; and misleading contexts, 271ff.; and misleading statements, 271ff.; and rhetoric,

Advertising (*Cont.*)
255ff.; and sophistry, 255ff.; as a kind of swindle, 270; of drugs, 267; of hazardous substances, 267, 270, 280; of vaginal deodorants, 268f.; false and deceptive, 254f., 263ff, 280
Africa, distorted treatment in textbooks, 288
aggression, definition of, 370ff.
alcohol, 157. *See also under* Marijuana
alcoholism, 39, 155
Alexander of Hales, 79
Alexander the Great, 358
Algiers Motel incident, 60n.
ALIMONY, 127ff., 131f., 191; for men, 132
American Advertising Federation, 270
American Cancer Society, 266
American Industrial Bankers Association, 263
American Law Institute, 63f., 108, 174, 178
American Medical Association, 135, 140, 148, 264, 266
American Nazi Party, 303
American Revolution, 327
Amish, 331
amphetamines, 137
amplexus reservatus. See under contraception
"Anatomy of a Murder," 167
Ancyra, Council of, 78
Anglican Church, and contraception, 82
animation, time of, 86, 93, 103
Anslinger, Harry J., 136
Anti-Defamation League, 303
anti-Semitism, 205, 289ff.